MW01251161

Shipping in Inuit Nunangat

Publications on Ocean Development

A SERIES OF STUDIES ON THE INTERNATIONAL, LEGAL,
INSTITUTIONAL AND POLICY ASPECTS OF OCEAN DEVELOPMENT

General Editors

Alex Oude Elferink
Joanna Mossop

VOLUME 101

The titles published in this series are listed at *brill.com/pood*

Shipping in Inuit Nunangat

Governance Challenges and Approaches in Canadian Arctic Waters

Edited by

Kristin Bartenstein and Aldo Chircop

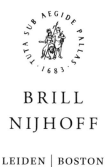

BRILL

NIJHOFF

LEIDEN | BOSTON

Funding for this publication was provided by Social Sciences and Humanities Research Council of Canada (SSHRC), 2017.

The Library of Congress Cataloging-in-Publication Data is available online at https://catalog.loc.gov
LC record available at https://lccn.loc.gov/2023008132

Typeface for the Latin, Greek, and Cyrillic scripts: "Brill". See and download: brill.com/brill-typeface.

ISSN 0924-1922
ISBN 978-90-04-50856-9 (hardback)
ISBN 978-90-04-50857-6 (e-book)

*This book is dedicated to the late Professor Meinhard Doelle,
a dear friend, colleague and contributor to this book, who
tragically left us far too soon, leaving behind him a rich legacy
of teaching and scholarship on climate and environmental law.
Meinhard was admired and loved by all who were fortunate
enough to know him. He will be remembered by all of us.*

∴

Contents

Foreword   XI
Acknowledgements   XIV
List of Figures and Tables   XV
Notes on Contributors   XVII
List of Acronyms   XXIV

1   Introduction   1
    Kristin Bartenstein and Aldo Chircop

PART 1
Understanding the Context of Governance of Shipping in Canadian Arctic Waters

2   "The Sea is Our Mainstay": Shipping and the Inuit Homeland   21
    Monica Ell-Kanayuk and Claudio Aporta

3   Shipping in Arctic Marine Ecosystems under Stress: Recognizing and
    Mitigating the Threats   37
    Warwick F. Vincent, Connie Lovejoy, and Kristin Bartenstein

4   Shipping along the Northwest Passage: A Historical Overview   58
    Adam Lajeunesse and P. Whitney Lackenbauer

5   Comparative Perspectives on the Development of Canadian Arctic
    Shipping: Impacts of Climate Change and Globalization   78
    Frédéric Lasserre

6   Reconsidering Arctic Shipping Governance through a
    Decolonizing Lens   100
    Leah Beveridge

7   Unpacking Canada's Arctic Shipping Safety, Security, and Defence
    Functions   126
    Andrea Charron and David Snider

8   Canadian Icebreaker Operations and Shipbuilding: Challenges and
     Opportunities   157
         Timothy Choi

9   Mitigating the Tyranny of Time and Distance: Community-based
     Organizations and Marine Mass Rescue Operations in Inuit
     Nunangat   182
         Peter Kikkert, Calvin Aivgak Pedersen, and P. Whitney Lackenbauer

     PART 2
*Reimagining the Governance of Shipping in Canadian
Arctic Waters*

10   Canada and the Future of Arctic Coastal State Jurisdiction   213
         Kristin Bartenstein

11   The Modern Case Law on the Powers and Responsibilities of Flag States:
     Navigating Canada's Arctic Waters   243
         Nigel Bankes

12   The Canadian Policy, Legal and Institutional Framework for the
     Governance of Arctic Shipping   265
         Aldo Chircop

13   Goal-based Standards, Meta-Regulation and Tripartism in Arctic
     Shipping: What Prospects in Canadian Waters?   297
         Phillip A. Buhler

14   Modernizing the Governance of Passenger Vessel Operations in the
     Canadian Arctic   323
         Meagan Greentree

15   Governing Canadian Arctic Shipping through Low-impact Shipping
     Corridors   351
         Jackie Dawson and Gloria Song

16   The New Federal *Impact Assessment Act* and Arctic Shipping:
     Opportunities for Improved Governance   375
         Meinhard Doelle, David V. Wright, A. John Sinclair, and Simon Dueck

17   Indigenous Self-determination and the Regulation of Navigation and
      Shipping in Canadian Arctic Waters   407
          Suzanne Lalonde and Nigel Bankes

18   Conclusion   440
          Aldo Chircop and Kristin Bartenstein

      Index   456

Foreword

For a considerable period of time in the post-World War II era, writings by international lawyers and international relations scholars in Canada concerned with the Arctic focused on 'Arctic sovereignty.' The passage of the USS *Manhattan* through the Northwest Passage in 1969 and the enactment of the *Arctic Waters Pollution Prevention Act* in 1970 gave the issue an environmental focus. But it was still fundamentally for Canada a sovereignty issue. And behind that, but integrally related, were the ever-present security concerns. The regulation of Arctic shipping was about Canadian jurisdiction, Canadian security and Canadian sovereignty.

While much of that is still true, much has changed. The Arctic is now more readily understood as the homeland of Indigenous peoples whose livelihoods, interests and aspirations have to be seen as core to any consideration of the Arctic. Climate change is wreaking a fundamental change in the Arctic. The raising of temperatures and the receding of the sea ice have enormous consequences for shipping in the Arctic, for living and non-living resources exploration and exploitation, for marine pollution and other harmful environmental effects, and for the lives and well-being, and indeed the survival, of Indigenous peoples.

Arctic States have increasingly responded to what is occurring in the Arctic. Greater recognition of the claims, aspirations and rights of Indigenous Arctic peoples, the formation of the Arctic Council in which Indigenous peoples play a key role, and the increased regional cooperation amongst Arctic States are all critical developments in the Arctic in recent years. Indeed, many of the issues concerning shipping and the uses of Arctic waters have been highlighted through the research and monitoring activities sponsored by the Arctic Council.

Concerns about shipping in the Arctic have moved from the reality of coastal movement between communities and the mirage of large-scale transit of the Northwest Passage, to a new reality of increased traffic, cruise ships, and the transit of the Arctic Ocean. The development by Russia of the Northern Sea Route in the Northeast Arctic is sometimes seen as a model that could be emulated in the Northwest Passage. More generally, greater recognition of the Inuit identity in the Arctic, and climatic and sea use changes all call for a rethinking and re-evaluation of governance in the Arctic and, in particular, Canada's approach to regulation and governance of shipping in Arctic areas.

This volume, *Shipping in Inuit Nunangat: Governance Challenges and Approaches in Canadian Arctic Waters*, responds to that need. It is a book that reflects the fundamental changes in respect of the Arctic, and it focuses on what today are the critical issues. The very title of the book, *Shipping in Inuit Nunangat*, shifts the description of the area from its historical, colonial designation to an identification of the area as where Inuit live—the Inuit homeland. This focus in a sense brackets the whole book, starting with the sea as the mainstay of the Inuit based on a discussion with Inuit leader Monica Ell-Kanayuk (Ell-Kanayuk and Aporta, Chapter 2) and ending with Indigenous self-determination and its implications for the regulation of shipping (Lalonde and Bankes, Chapter 17). Inuit concerns appear throughout the book, including looking at Arctic governance through a 'decolonizing lens,' particularly through the work of the Inuit in the Arctic Council (Beveridge, Chapter 6), or considering the development of low-impact shipping corridors for maritime navigation (Dawson and Song, Chapter 15). The centrality of Inuit concerns is also emphasized in both the Introduction and the Conclusion.

The book sets out the context for the consideration of Arctic shipping today and then turns attention to how the governance of shipping in Canadian Arctic waters might be reimagined. While the book offers a new and contemporary approach to the governance of Arctic shipping, the past is not neglected. There is an historical overview of shipping in the Northwest Passage (Lajeunesse and Lackenbauer, Chapter 4) and the traditional 'sovereignty' debate is both traversed and rethought in the light of contemporary developments (Bartenstein, Chapter 10). Throughout the book broad themes emerge, relating to the operation of shipping in the particular environment of the Arctic, safety at sea in the ever-harsh environmental conditions in Arctic waters and responding to marine emergencies, the consequences of increased economic activity in the Arctic, long-standing defence and security concerns, and the developing legal framework for governance and future needs. At heart there is the fundamental concern of protecting the unique Arctic ecosystem in the light of the wide-scale changes that have been occurring.

The editors and contributors to this volume are to be congratulated in bringing to the fore, in comprehensive and readily accessible analyses, the challenges facing Canada in respect of shipping in Arctic waters and the governance imperatives to which these give rise. And they have done so in a sensitive manner that places the interests of the inhabitants of Inuit Nunangat front and centre. They have also sounded the call for approaching the issue of Arctic shipping in the context of the imperatives of climate change—a call for action in light of one of the most vital issues affecting not just the Arctic but humankind more generally.

There is a sense of urgency in addressing the governance issues relating to Arctic shipping in this book. Not only are the climatic effects calling for increased attention, but there is also increased interest from States outside the Arctic region in Arctic shipping as well as in resource development and exploitation. Claims to treat the Arctic as a form of international commons have been heard. In these circumstances, it is critical for Canada, not only to continue asserting the leadership role it took in 1970, which it then enhanced through regional cooperation and in international fora, but also to be an example to other countries in the governance measures it takes to regulate shipping in Arctic waters.

Donald McRae
Ottawa, Ontario, Canada
September 2022

Acknowledgements

In the preparation of this volume, the editors received invaluable assistance and support from a number of people and institutions.

The editors acknowledge the Insight Grant from the Social Sciences and Humanities Research Council of Canada (SSHRC) received by Professor Kristin Bartenstein and her team to develop interdisciplinary scholarship under the project titled *Navigating Canadian Arctic Waters: Uniformity and Unilateralism in Law-making in the Era of the International Polar Code*. Further support was provided by the SSHRC-funded Canada Research Chair (Tier I) grant held by Professor Aldo Chircop.

For the second authors' workshop, held in hybrid mode for online participation and in-person participation in Halifax, the editors were assisted by Lisa Sillito, administrative assistant of Professor Chircop, Sarah Davis, IT specialist of the Law IT Services at the Schulich School of Law, and Geordie Lounsbury, instructional media specialist at the Schulich School of Law. Their dedication and professionalism ensured a smooth working of the workshop and enabled fruitful exchanges between participants. The editors gratefully acknowledge the support provided by the Schulich School of Law in hosting the workshop and the support provided by the Faculty of Law of the Université Laval in administering the SSHRC grant.

On behalf of the entire team of authors, the editors wish to express their gratitude to Monica Ell-Kanayuk, then president of the Inuit Circumpolar Council (ICC) Canada, for graciously accepting to give a keynote presentation at the authors' workshop and exchange with the participants. They also thank Lisa Smith and Stephanie Meakin of ICC Canada, for enabling Monica Ell-Kanayuk's presentation.

Last but not least, the editors owe special thanks to Susan Rolston of Seawinds Consulting Services. Her competent management of many logistic aspects of this project was of great assistance to the editors. Thanks to her efficient and skillful copy editing of the entire book, it now reads as an integrated piece of work.

Kristin Bartenstein
Aldo Chircop

Figures and Tables

Figures

1.1 Geographic scope of application of the AWPPA, NORDREG and the
Polar Code 7

1.2 Inuit Nunangat 8

1.3 Canadian Arctic coastal communities 9

2.1 Selected place names between the communities of Arctic Bay and Pond Inlet,
Nunavut, with a view from the north towards the south 24

2.2 Traditional Inuit trails around Killiniq, at the crossroads of Nunavut, Nunavik
and Nunatsiavut 25

5.1 Extension of Arctic sea ice at its summer minimum, 2010, 2016, 2018
and 2021 80

14.1 Condensed outline of passenger vessel permit process 333

15.1 Map of marine regions in Arctic Canada 353

15.2 Total annual voyage counts and unique ship counts in the Canadian Arctic
between 1990 and 2019 (left) and total number of ship voyages for vessels with
different levels of ice strengthening (right) 356

15.3 Low-impact shipping corridors in Arctic Canada 361

15.4 ACNV community mapping workshop 365

15.5 Culturally significant marine areas 367

15.6 Culturally significant marine areas (CSMAs) and ecologically and biologically
significant areas (EBSAs) locations (left) and CSMAs and EBSAs inside
identified low-impact shipping corridors (right) 367

16.1 Overview of IAA process for designated projects 383

16.2 Map identifying the boundaries of the Inuvialuit Settlement Region 391

Tables

5.1 Vessel movements in the Canadian Arctic, number of voyages, NORDREG
zone 81

5.2 Vessel movements in Northern Sea Route waters, number of voyages 83

5.3 Transit traffic along the Northwest Passage, 2006–2021 87

5.4 Transit traffic along the Northern Sea Route, 2006–2021 88

5.5 Share of voyages performed by commercial vessels operated by foreign
companies in Russian Arctic waters 91

5.6   Share of voyages performed by commercial vessels operated by foreign
       companies in Canadian Arctic waters   92
7.1   Examples of issues along the conflict continuum   130
7.2   Total number of SAR cases north of 55 degrees   132
14.1   Comparison of Canada, Russia and Svalbard passenger vessel permitting   339
15.1   Main vessel types (ASMA class) found in the NORDREG zone   355
15.2   Summary of identified strengths and weaknesses of the low-impact shipping
       corridors framework   368

Notes on Contributors

Claudio Aporta
is Professor and Canadian Chair, Marine Environmental Protection, at the World Maritime University, in Malmö, Sweden. He was also Professor (2012–2022, on leave) in the Marine Affairs Program, Dalhousie University, Halifax, Canada, and in the Department of Sociology and Anthropology at Carleton University (2005–2012), Ottawa, Canada. He received his PhD in Cultural Anthropology from the University of Alberta, Edmonton, Canada. His research has focused on documentation and mapping of Inuit and Indigenous environmental knowledge in Canada.
ORCID 0000-0002-7883-7885

Nigel Bankes
is Emeritus Professor of Law, University of Calgary, Canada.
ORCID 0000-0002-2115-7395

Kristin Bartenstein
is Professor at the Faculty of Law, Université Laval, Quebec, Canada. She holds law degrees from Ludwig-Maximilians-Universität, Munich, Germany, and Université Paris II Panthéon Assas, Paris, France and an LLD from Université Laval. Her research and teaching focus on the international law of the sea, international environmental law, general public international law and legal theory. She has written extensively on Arctic legal issues, including as a contributor to the *UNCLOS Commentary*. Currently, she is the lead investigator of the research project *Navigating Canadian Arctic Waters: Uniformity and Unilateralism in Law-making in the Era of the International Polar Code*, which is funded by the Social Sciences and Humanities Research Council of Canada and gave rise to this volume.
ORCID 0000-0003-0089-027X

Leah Beveridge
is a doctorate candidate in the Interdisciplinary PhD Program at Dalhousie University, Halifax, Canada. She received her Master of Marine Management from Dalhousie in 2013, after which she began studying Arctic shipping broadly. Her research is now focused on the process of decolonizing marine safety and shipping in Canada.
ORCID 0000-0001-9935-8480

Phillip A. Buhler

has practiced maritime law for over thirty years and is a Partner at Moseley, Prichard, Parrish, Knight & Jones (Florida). He is a Dozent (lecturer) in international and US civil procedure at the Universität zu Köln, Germany, and has been a Dozent in maritime law and intermodal transportation at the Universität Hamburg. He serves on the Polar Shipping International Working Group and its Antarctic Shipping Sub-Committee of the Comité Maritime International. He is a PhD candidate at the Schulich School of Law, Dalhousie University, Halifax, Canada, with a research focus on the application of non-prescriptive regulatory options to commercial shipping in the polar regions.
ORCID 0000-0001-5212-7677

Andrea Charron

is Director of the Centre for Defence and Security Studies, and Associate Professor, Political Studies, University of Manitoba, Winnipeg, Canada. She holds a PhD from the Royal Military College of Canada (Department of War Studies). Dr. Charron worked for various federal departments including the Canadian Privy Council Office in the Security and Intelligence Secretariat before beginning her academic career. She writes extensively on Arctic security, NATO, NORAD and Canadian defence policy. She is co-author of *NORAD: In Perpetuity and Beyond* (McGill-Queen's University Press, 2022) and several other books on sanctions.
ORCID 0000-0002-1847-9342

Aldo Chircop

JSD, is Professor of Law and former Canada Research Chair in Maritime Law and Policy (Tier I). Based at the Marine and Environmental Law Institute, Schulich School of Law, Dalhousie University, Halifax, Canada, his fields of research and teaching are Canadian maritime law, international maritime law, and the law of the sea. He is currently working on the regulation of Arctic shipping, decarbonization, autonomous ships, and area-based management in shipping. He is the current chair of the CMI International Working Group on Polar Shipping. Professor Chircop has advised several governments, international organizations, law firms, non-governmental organizations, and community organizations. He has published extensively and is co-editor of the *Ocean Yearbook* (Brill). Professor Chircop is a member of the Nova Scotia Barristers Society and the Canadian Maritime Law Association.
ORCID 0000-0003-4238-034X

Timothy Choi

holds a PhD from the University of Calgary's Centre for Military, Security and Strategic Studies. His dissertation asked how Danish, Norwegian, and Canadian naval forces developed in response to the adoption of the 200 nautical mile exclusive economic zone. This has seen him sailing with Danish and Norwegian patrol vessels. He is a former Predoctoral Fellow at Yale University and is a Fellow with the Canadian Global Affairs Institute. He serves on the editorial board of and is the photo editor at the *Canadian Naval Review*, and consults on naval affairs at the British American Security Information Council.

ORCID 0000-0001-7407-7914

Jackie Dawson

is Professor and Canada Research Chair (Tier 1) in Human and Policy Dimensions of Climate Change, Department of Geography, Environment, and Geomatics at the University of Ottawa, Canada. She is also the Scientific Director of the Network of Centres of Excellence, ArcticNet. She is an applied scientist working on the human and policy dimensions of environmental change in ocean and coastal regions and is considered an expert in Arctic shipping, Arctic tourism, and Arctic Ocean governance. She has served on two Canadian Council of Academies' Expert Panels, is an elected member of the College of the Royal Society of Canada and is a Fellow of the Royal Canadian Geographic Society. She led the drafting of the 2018 G7 science statement focused on the Arctic Ocean and resilient communities, is a lead author on the IPCC AR6, and recently won the prestigious 2020 SSHRC Impact Connection Award and 2021 Governor General's Innovation Award.

ORCID 0000-0002-3532-2742

Meinhard Doelle

was Professor of Law, Schulich School of Law, and Associate Dean, Graduate Studies, Dalhousie University, Halifax, Canada. He was the Canadian Chair at the World Maritime University from 2019–2021, and previously served as Associate Dean, Research, and as an Associate Director and Director of the Marine & Environmental Law Institute (MELAW). He wrote on a variety of environmental law topics, including climate change, energy, environmental assessments, and public participation in environmental decision-making. His most recent books deal with loss and damage from climate change, and with the new federal *Impact Assessment Act* in Canada, both published in 2021.

ORCID 0000-0002-7650-0330

Simon Dueck

studied natural resource management at the Natural Resources Institute at the University of Manitoba, Winnipeg, Canada. His Master's thesis was titled "The Role of Project-based Impact Assessment in Considering the Impacts of Resource Development Related Arctic Shipping," and addressed the impact assessment of numerous mineral developments in Nunavut with shipping implications.

ORCID 0000-0002-4004-3588

Monica Ell-Kanayuk

is the past president of the Inuit Circumpolar Council Canada. She was an MLA in Nunavut (2011–2013), and she served as Director of Programming for the Inuit Broadcasting Corporation. She is a former Director of Economic and Business Development at Nunavut Tunngavik Incorporated. She has also served as President of the Nunavut Economic Forum, President of the Baffin Chamber of Commerce, Vice-President of the Atuqtuarvik Corporation and Vice-President of Pauktuutit.

Meagan Greentree

is a Strategy and Planning Analyst for Manitoba Transportation and Infrastructure. As a public policy and planning practitioner, she is broadly interested in transportation, logistics and security challenges in the Canadian Arctic. Meagan is a former Research Fellow for the North American Arctic Defence and Security Network (NAADSN). Her previous public sector employers include Transport Canada and the Department of National Defence. In 2021, Meagan graduated with a Master of Public Administration (MPA) degree from the University of Manitoba, Winnipeg, Canada; her contribution to this volume was adapted from her Graduate Capstone Project.

Peter Kikkert

is Irving Shipbuilding Chair in Arctic Policy and Assistant Professor of Public Policy and Governance in the Brian Mulroney Institute of Government at St. Francis Xavier University, Antigonish, Nova Scotia, Canada.

ORCID 0000-0003-1338-3648

P. Whitney Lackenbauer

PhD, is Canada Research Chair in the Study of the Canadian North and Professor in the School for the Study of Canada at Trent University, Ontario, Canada. He is network lead of the North American and Arctic Defence and Security Network (NAADSN). He has (co-)written or (co-)edited more than fifty books and more than one hundred academic articles and book chapters, many of which explore Arctic history, policy, sovereignty, and security issues. His recent books include *The Joint Arctic Weather Stations: Science and Sovereignty in the High Arctic, 1946–72* (co-authored, 2022); *Lines in the Snow: Thoughts on the Past and Future of Northern Canadian Policy Issues* (co-edited, 2022); *On Thin Ice? Perspectives on Arctic Security* (co-edited, 2021); and *Breaking Through? Understanding Sovereignty and Security in the Circumpolar Arctic* (co-edited, 2021).

ORCID 0000-0002-2240-5338

Adam Lajeunesse

PhD, is Associate Professor in the Public Policy and Governance Program at St. Francis Xavier University, Antigonish, Canada. He is the author of the award-winning book *Lock, Stock, and Icebergs* (2016), a political history of the Northwest Passage, as well as co-author of the 2017 monograph *China's Arctic Ambitions and What They Mean for Canada*, and co-editor of *Canadian Arctic Operations, 1941–2015: Lessons Learned, Lost, and Relearned* (2017). He works on questions of Arctic sovereignty and security policy and has written extensively on Canadian Armed Forces Arctic operations, maritime security, Canadian-American cooperation in the North, and Canadian Arctic history.

ORCID 0000-0002-7074-932X

Suzanne Lalonde

is Professor of Public International Law and the Law of the Sea at the Law Faculty of the Université de Montréal, Canada. She holds a PhD in Public International Law from the University of Cambridge. Her research and publications focus on core international legal principles, in particular those pertaining to sovereignty and the determination of boundaries on land and at sea, with an emphasis on the Arctic. She was a member of the ILA Committee that reported on "Baselines under the Law of the Sea" (2018) and co-editor of *Ocean Development and International Law* from 2017 to 2019. She is a member of the Canadian Arctic Security Working Group chaired by Joint Task Force North, the North American Arctic Defence and Security Network and is a co-author in the PAME project on the Central Arctic Ocean.

ORCID 0000-0002-0682-7725

Frédéric Lasserre

is Professor in the Department of Geography, Université Laval, Quebec, Canada. He acted as Project Director with the ArcticNet research network. He also chairs the Conseil québécois d'Études géopolitiques (Quebec Council for Geopolitical Studies, CQEG) at Laval University. He holds a Master of Commerce (ESC Lyon, 1990), an MBA (York U., Toronto, 1991), a DEA in Geopolitics (U. Paris VIII, 1992) and a PhD in Geography (U. Saint-Étienne, France, 1996). He has conducted extensive research in the field of Arctic geopolitics, water management and transport geopolitics.

ORCID 0000-0001-5220-9787

Connie Lovejoy

is Professor and an Arctic oceanographer in the Département de Biologie, Institut de Biologie Intégrative et des Systèmes (IBIS) and Takuvik International Laboratory, Université Laval, Quebec, Canada and a member of Québec-Océan consortium at Université Laval. She is also Director of the Quebec interuniversity PhD program in oceanography.

ORCID 0000-0001-8027-2281

Calvin Aivgak Pedersen

is a search and rescue volunteer, a former member of the Nunavut legislative assembly, and has served as a Canadian Ranger for 22 years. He is from Kugluktuk, Nunavut.

A. John Sinclair

is Professor and Director at the Natural Resources Institute, University of Manitoba, Winnipeg, Canada. His main research interest focuses on governance and learning as they relate to resource and environmental decision-making. His most recent book deals with the new federal *Impact Assessment Act* in Canada, published in 2021.

ORCID 0000-0002-5865-0036

Captain David (Duke) Snider

is the CEO and Principal Consultant of Martech Polar Consulting Ltd, providing global ice navigation services and support for polar shipping, ice navigation, polar research, expedition logistics support and ice-related consulting. He is a Master Mariner and with 40 years at sea and is author of the book *Polar Ship Operations*, as well as many other papers on ice navigation. He was awarded the Queen's Diamond Jubilee medal in 2011. He also holds the Canadian Coast Guard Exemplary Service Medal, and the United States Coast Guard Antarctic Service Medal. In 2020 he was awarded the Maritime Museum of British Columbia's Beaver Medal for his championing of best practice and safety in ice-related shipping.

Gloria Song

is a PhD Candidate in the Faculty of Law, University of Ottawa, Canada, with doctoral research focus on access to justice and housing in Nunavut. She

formerly practiced as a civil litigation lawyer for the Legal Services Board of Nunavut while based in Cambridge Bay, Nunavut, at the Kitikmeot Law Centre, and as a policy analyst for Polar Knowledge Canada. She currently serves as an access to justice representative and project coordinator at the Law Society of Nunavut. She is part of Dr. Jackie Dawson's Environment, Society and Policy Group and a member of the University of Ottawa's Human Rights Research and Education Centre. She has a LLM from University of Ottawa, a JD from Osgoode Hall Law School, and BA in communication with a concentration in political science from University of Ottawa.
ORCID 0000-0003-3246-3686

Warwick F. Vincent
is Professor and holder of the Canada Research Chair in Aquatic Ecosystem Studies in the Département de Biologie, Institut de Biologie Intégrative et des Systèmes (IBIS) and Takuvik International Laboratory, Université Laval, Quebec, Canada. He is a member and former Director of the Centre for Northern Studies (CEN) at Université Laval.
ORCID 0000-0001-9055-1938

David V. Wright
is Associate Professor in the Faculty of Law, University of Calgary, Canada, where he is a member of the Natural Resources, Energy and Environmental Law Research group. Prior to his faculty appointment, David held positions with Canada's Commissioner of the Environment and Sustainable Development, the United Nations Development Programme, the Government of Nunavut, the law firm of Stewart McKelvey, and the Marine and Environmental Law Institute at Dalhousie University. David was also General Counsel for the Gwich'in Tribal Council in Canada's Western Arctic region, where he regularly advised on duty to consult, Indigenous governance, and regulatory matters. He holds an MA and JD from Dalhousie University and an LLM from Stanford University. David's research focuses on natural resources and environmental law with a particular emphasis on climate change, impact assessment and the rights of Indigenous peoples.

Acronyms

ACGF	Arctic Coast Guard Forum
ACNV	Arctic Corridors and Northern Voices project
AECO	Association of Arctic Expedition Cruise Operators
AIRSS	Arctic Ice Regime Shipping System
AIS	automatic identification system
AMSA	*Arctic Marine Shipping Assessment*
ANPF	Arctic and Northern Policy Framework
AOPS	Arctic and offshore patrol ship
ASD	alternative service delivery
ASSPPR	*Arctic Shipping Safety and Pollution Prevention Regulations*
ASWG	Arctic Security Working Group (Canada)
AWPPA	*Arctic Waters Pollution Prevention Act*
CAF	Canadian Armed Forces
CASARA	Civil Air Search and Rescue Association (Canada)
CBO	community-based organization
CBSA	Canadian Border Services Agency
CCG	Canadian Coast Guard
CCGA	Canadian Coast Guard Auxiliary
CDEM	construction, design, equipment and crewing
CDSS	Centre for Defence and Security Studies (Canada)
CEAA 2012	*Canadian Environmental Assessment Act, 2012*
CHNL	Center for High North Logistics (Russia)
CHS	Canadian Hydrographic Service
CIRNAC	Crown-Indigenous Relations and Northern Affairs Canada
CIS	Canadian Ice Service
CITES	Convention on International Trade in Endangered Species of Wild Fauna and Flora
CMAC	Canadian Marine Advisory Council
COLREGS	Convention on the International Regulations for Preventing Collisions at Sea
CPR	command and control regulation
CPSO	community public safety office
CSA 2001	*Canada Shipping Act, 2001*
CSMA	culturally significant marine area
CTA	*Canada Transportation Act*
DEW Line	Distant Early Warning Line

DFO	Department of Fisheries and Oceans (Canada)
DND	Department of National Defence (Canada)
EBSA	ecologically and biologically significant area
ECCC	Environment and Climate Change Canada
EEZ	exclusive economic zone
FPIC	free, prior and informed consent
FSA	formal safety assessment
GAIRS	generally accepted international rules and standards
GHG	greenhouse gases
GSAR	ground search and rescue
HFO	heavy fuel oil
HRC	Human Rights Committee (ICCPR)
IAA	*Impact Assessment Act*
IACS	International Association of Classification Societies
ICC	Inuit Circumpolar Council
ICCPR	International Covenant on Civil and Political Rights
ICESCR	International Covenant on Economic, Social and Cultural Rights
ICJ	International Court of Justice
ICPC	Inuit-Crown Partnership Committee
IFA	Inuvialuit Final Agreement
IIBA	Inuit Impact and Benefit Agreement
ILO	International Labour Organization
IMA	Inuit Management Authority
IMMP	Inuit Marine Monitoring Program
IMO	International Maritime Organization
IPCC	Intergovernmental Panel on Climate Change
ISR	intelligence, surveillance and reconnaissance
ITK	Inuit Tapiriit Kanatami
ITLOS	International Tribunal for the Law of the Sea
IUU	illegal, unreported and unregulated fishing
JRCC	Joint Rescue Coordination Centre
JSS	joint support ship
LISC	low-impact shipping corridor
LOSC	United Nations Convention on the Law of the Sea
M	nautical mile
MAJAID	Major Air Disaster
MARPOL	International Convention for the Prevention of Pollution from Ships
MCTS	Marine Communications and Traffic Services
MDA	maritime domain awareness

MEPC	Marine Environment Protection Committee (IMO)
MMIWG	National Inquiry into Missing and Murdered Indigenous Women and Girls
MPA	marine protected area
MRO	mass rescue operation
MSC	Maritime Safety Committee (IMO)
MSOC	Marine Security Operations Centre
MTSA	*Marine Transportation Security Act*
NAFO	Northwest Atlantic Fisheries Organization
NATO	North Atlantic Treaty Organization
NAVWARNS	Navigational Warnings
NEAFC	North East Atlantic Fisheries Commission
NEB	National Energy Board
NGO	non-governmental organization
NIRB	Nunavut Impact Review Board
NMC	Nunavut Marine Council
NMCA	National Marine Conservation Area
NORAD	North American Aerospace Defense Command
NORDREG	*Northern Canada Vessel Traffic Services Zone Regulations*
NOTMAR	Notice to Mariners
NOTSHIP	Notice to Shipping
NPC	Nunavut Planning Commission
NSA	Nunavut Settlement Area
NSR	Northern Sea Route
NSRA	Northern Sea Route Administration
NSS	National Shipbuilding Strategy (Canada)
NuPPAA	*Nunavut Planning and Project Assessment Act*
NWP	Northwest Passage
NWT	Northwest Territories
OFSV	offshore fisheries science vessel
OOSV	offshore oceanographic science vessel
OPP	Oceans Protection Plan
PAME	Protection of the Arctic Marine Environment Working Group (Arctic Council)
PBM	Permanent Bilateral Mechanism
PHAC	Public Health Agency of Canada
POLARIS	Polar Operational Limit Assessment Risk Indexing System
PVM	Proactive Vessel Management
PVRC	Private Vessel Remote Clearance project
PWOM	Polar Waters Operations Manual

RCAF	Royal Canadian Air Force
RCAP	Royal Commission on Aboriginal Peoples
RCMP	Royal Canadian Mounted Police
RCN	Royal Canadian Navy
RJOC	Regional Joint Operation Centre
SAR	search and rescue
SOLAS	International Convention for the Safety of Life at Sea
SOPF	Ship-source Oil Pollution Fund
SSCZ	Shipping Safety Control Zone
STCW	International Convention on Standards of Training, Certification and Watchkeeping for Seafarers
TC	Transport Canada
TRC	Truth and Reconciliation Commission of Canada
TSB	Transportation Safety Board of Canada
TTX	tabletop exercise
UNCLOS	United Nations Conference on the Law of the Sea
UNDRIPA	*United Nations Declaration on the Rights of Indigenous Peoples Act*
UNDRIP	United Nations Declaration on the Rights of Indigenous Peoples
USCG	United States Coast Guard
VCLT	Vienna Convention on the Law of Treaties
VOI	vessels of interest
WAHVA	*Wrecked, Abandoned or Hazardous Vessels Act*
YESAA	*Yukon Environmental and Socio-economic Assessment Act*

CHAPTER 1

Introduction

Kristin Bartenstein and Aldo Chircop

Abstract

This chapter introduces *Shipping in Inuit Nunangat: Governance Challenges and Approaches in Canadian Arctic Waters*. The volume intends to offer timely reflection on governance issues related to shipping in Canadian Arctic waters at a time of tremendous physical and ecological changes due to warming temperatures, a shifting legal environment prompted among others by the Polar Code, and a new sense of agency that motivates Inuit to play an active part in shaping the future of their homeland, Inuit Nunangat. The Introduction describes the geographical focus of the book before turning to the main governance concerns that emerge from the following chapters. Prominent among them is the challenge for Canadian policy-makers to plot a path out of Canada's colonial past, which still undermines relationships between Inuit and the Crown, including with respect to shipping regulations. Another key concern is related to the fragile Arctic ecosystem and the need to make efficient protection against vessel-source disturbances a priority to minimize additional stressors as much as possible. These concerns need further to be squared with considerations related to the region's economic development and issues of sovereignty, safety, security and military defence. The last part of the Introduction provides an overview of the chapters that follow.

Keywords

Arctic waters – Arctic shipping regulations – Canada – Inuit Nunangat

1 Context and Purpose

As sea ice is decreasing at a concerning pace, the Arctic region is experiencing profound physical transformations that threaten ecosystems and Indigenous ancestral ways of life and livelihoods, including in Inuit Nunangat, the homeland of Inuit ('the people') in Canada.[1] At the same time, these rapid physical changes also provide unprecedented opportunities for economic development, which reverberate throughout the Arctic and beyond. Essential to many human activities in the Canadian Arctic, shipping activities have been on the rise and are expected to further increase in the years to come. Against the background of an extending navigation season, shipping is likely to be driven by growing demands for community resupply and support of mining operations, marine scientific research, and a developing tourism sector. Despite decreasing ice cover and improving technologies, navigation in Arctic waters will, however, remain a hazardous and potentially harmful activity.

Since the 2000s, this acknowledgment has accelerated the pace of regulatory action undertaken by States and intergovernmental organizations and by the industry sector itself. A prominent example of the latter are the Unified Requirements for Polar Class Ships first adopted in 2006 by the International Association of Classification Societies (IACS),[2] in coordination with the effort deployed by the International Maritime Organization (IMO) to provide guidance for navigation in ice-covered waters.[3] In 2010, Canada reinforced its coastal State regulations notably by converting the ship reporting system in its Arctic waters, known as NORDREG, into a mandatory scheme.[4] At the international level, significant momentum was created by the 2017 entry into force of the IMO's mandatory International Code for Ships Operating in Polar Waters, the so-called Polar Code.[5] Flag States, including the five Arctic coastal States, were prompted to make this first international set of tailor-made rules and standards for polar navigation applicable to their polar-going vessels,

---

1   This is the alarming core message of a special report of the Intergovernmental Panel on Climate Change (IPPC) on the matter, see in particular chapter 3, Michael Meredith *et al.*, "Polar Regions," in *IPCC Special Report on the Ocean and Cryosphere in a Changing Climate*, eds., H.-O. Pörtner *et al.* (Cambridge, UK and New York, NY: Cambridge University Press, 2019), 203–320, https://www.ipcc.ch/site/assets/uploads/sites/3/2019/11/07_SROCC_Ch03_FINAL.pdf.

2   International Association of Classification Societies (IACS), *Unified Requirements for Polar Class Ships*, 22 August 2006, IACS Req. 2006 (UR I1, I2 and I3) (as amended), https://iacs.org .uk/download/1803.

3   Guidelines for Ships Operating in Arctic Ice-Covered Waters, IMO Doc MSC/Circ.1056, MEPC/ Circ.399 (23 December 2002). These were later updated and expanded, IMO Resolution A.1024(26) (2 December 2009), Guidelines for Ships Operating in Polar Waters.

4   *Northern Canada Vessel Traffic Services Zone Regulations*, SOR 2010–127.

5   IMO Resolution MSC.385(94) (21 November 2014, effective 1 January 2017); Amendments to the International Convention for the Safety of Life at Sea 1974, IMO Resolution MSC.386(94) (21 November 2014, effective 1 January 2017); Amendments to MARPOL Annexes I, II, IV and V, IMO Resolution MEPC.265(68) (15 May 2015, effective 1 January 2017).

while the Arctic coastal States also extended them to vessels navigating in their Arctic waters.[6]

Given its particular situation as an Arctic coastal State with its own pre-existing regulations applicable to shipping in its Arctic waters, Canada was prompted to overhaul its regulatory regime with the aim to implement the Polar Code for Canadian vessels navigating polar waters and to make adjustments to its coastal State regulations, mostly aligning them with the Polar Code.[7] While the entry into force of the Polar Code was a major milestone, setting off a frenzy of domestic regulatory action, it did not spell the end of regulatory developments, neither at the international nor national level.

In this context of shifting physical and legal environments, it is more urgent than ever for Canada to develop a coherent policy and legal approach and to strengthen its institutions with the objective to craft a decisive, effective and equitable response to the changes underway. As the contents of this book will demonstrate, the governance of shipping in Canadian Arctic waters is fragmented and needs new directions. This entails finding a balance between the economic and technological constraints of shipping on the one hand and the imperative of minimizing impacts detrimental to the vulnerable Arctic ecology on the other. In the contemporary context, the balancing act, however, also entails honouring Canada's commitment to work towards socioeconomic and cultural equity and support Inuit self-determination in accordance with the United Nations Declaration on the Rights of Indigenous Peoples (UNDRIP) and as expressed in the 2022 Inuit Nunangat Policy.[8]

This volume aims to offer a timely discussion of contemporary issues of governance related to shipping in Canadian Arctic waters, which form part of Inuit Nunangat. Arctic shipping has attracted interest from a broad range of academic disciplines for years and has been the focus of intense scholarly

---

6 Aldo Chircop and Miriam Czarski, "Polar Code Implementation in the Arctic Five: Has Harmonisation of National Legislation Recommended by AMSA been Achieved?," *The Polar Journal* 10:2 (2020): 303–321, https://doi.org/10.1080/2154896X.2020.1799614.

7 *Arctic Shipping Safety and Pollution Prevention Regulations*, SOR/2017–286. For a discussion, see Kristin Bartenstein, "Between the *Polar Code* and Article 234: The Balance in Canada's *Arctic Shipping Safety and Pollution Prevention Regulations*," *Ocean Development and International Law* 50:4 (2019): 335–362.

8 Inuit Nunanganut Atuagaq (Inuit Nunangat Policy), Prime Minister of Canada (21 April 2022), https://pm.gc.ca/en/news/news-releases/2022/04/21/inuit-crown-partnership-committee-endorses-historic-inuit-nunangat.

investigation.[9] This specific scrutiny of Arctic shipping has taken place against the background of a much broader interest in the Arctic region and a great many related governance issues.[10] While the topic of Arctic shipping is neither new nor novel, *Shipping in Inuit Nunangat: Governance Challenges and Approaches in Canadian Arctic Waters* aims to make an original contribution to the existing literature by focusing its attention on shipping in Canadian Arctic waters and on the specific governance challenges faced by Canada.

By taking stock of past, current and prospective developments, the chapters of the volume set out to provide a comprehensive understanding of the challenges and opportunities that will shape Canadian governance of Arctic shipping. With the objective of guiding future policy and legal decisions, the contributing authors propose insights from various disciplines and angles to help address the many concerns that come with the rapid and drastic changes affecting the Arctic. To this end, the book calls upon the complementary expertise of a group of Canadian or Canada-based authors composed of established

---

9   This is attested by the following, necessarily incomplete, list of recent book publications: Igor Ilin, Tessaleno C. Devezas, Carlos Jahn, eds., *Arctic Maritime Logistics: The Potentials and Challenges of the Northern Sea Route* (Cham: Springer, 2022); Aldo Chircop, Floris Goerlandt, Claudio Aporta and Ronald Pelot, eds., *Governance of Arctic Shipping: Rethinking Risk, Human Impacts and Regulation* (Cham: Springer, 2020); Frédéric Lasserre and Olivier Faury, eds., *Arctic Shipping: Climate Change, Commercial Traffic and Port Development* (New York: Routledge, 2020); Lawrence P. Hildebrand, Lawson W. Brigham and Tafsir Johansson, eds., *Sustainable Shipping in a Changing Arctic* (Cham: Springer, 2018); Robert C. Beckman *et al.*, eds., *Governance of Arctic Shipping: Balancing Rights and Interests of Arctic States and User States* (Leiden: Brill Nijhoff, 2017); Willy Østreng *et al.*, *Shipping in Arctic Waters: A Comparison of the Northeast, Northwest and Trans Polar Passages* (Berlin: Springer, 2013); Tafsir Johansson and Patrick Donner, eds., *The Shipping Industry, Ocean Governance and Environmental Law in the Paradigm Shift: In Search of a Pragmatic Balance for the Arctic* (Cham: Springer, 2015).

10   See, for example, Eva Pongrácz, Victor Pavlov and Niko Hänninen, eds., *Arctic Marine Sustainability: Arctic Maritime Businesses and the Resilience of the Marine Environment* (Cham: Springer, 2020); Gunhild Hoogensen Gjørv, Marc Lanteigne and Horatio Sam-Aggrey, eds., *Routledge Handbook of Arctic Security* (New York: Routledge, 2020); Mary Durfee and Rachael Lorna Johnstone, *Arctic Governance in a Changing World* (Lanham: Rowman & Littlefield, 2019); Klaus Dodds and Mark Nuttall, *The Arctic: What Everyone Needs to Know* (New York: Oxford University Press, 2019); Svein Vigeland Rottem and Ida Folkestad Soltvedt, *Arctic Governance* (3 volumes) (New York: I.B. Tauris, 2017–2020); Timo Koivurova, *Arctic Law and Governance: The Role of China, Finland, and the EU* (Portland: Hart Publishing, 2017); Lassi Heininen, *Future Security of the Global Arctic: State Policy, Economic Security and Climate* (New York: Palgrave Macmillan, 2016); Ingvild Ulrikke Jakobsen, *Marine Protected Areas in International Law: An Arctic Perspective* (Boston: Brill Nijhoff, 2016); Lilly Weidemann, *International Governance of the Arctic Marine Environment: With Particular Emphasis on High Seas Fisheries* (Cham: Springer, 2014); Jessica Michelle Shadian, *The Politics of Arctic Sovereignty: Oil, Ice and Inuit Governance* (London: Routledge, 2014).

and emerging scholars from a broad range of disciplines, including anthropology, biology, history, political science, geography, geopolitics and the law.

The book is the main outcome of the research project titled *Navigating Canadian Arctic Waters: Uniformity and Unilateralism in Law-making in the Era of the International Polar Code* and supported by a research grant of the Canadian Social Sciences and Humanities Research Council. The initial interdisciplinary project team of seven was expanded to benefit from a broad spectrum of complementary expertise. The authors were first brought together by the editors for a virtual workshop in January 2021 to discuss the scope, content and coordination of the book. Results of the research and writing period that ensued were then submitted for collegial peer feedback and coordination in a second workshop convened in Halifax in May 2022.

2 Geographical Focus

The decision to train the spotlight on shipping in Arctic waters under Canadian jurisdiction entails concentrating mainly on governance challenges and approaches Canada faces as a coastal State. This warrants a few observations on the geographical areas concerned. First of all, Canada's maritime zones are defined in the *Oceans Act*[11] in line with the United Nations Convention on the Law of the Sea (LOSC).[12] Within this framework, Canada has defined the area to which its domestic coastal State regulations on Arctic shipping apply (Figure 1.1). For the purposes of vessel-source pollution prevention, "arctic waters" are defined in the *Arctic Waters Pollution Prevention Act* (AWPPA) as

> the internal waters of Canada and the waters of the territorial sea of Canada and the exclusive economic zone of Canada, within the area enclosed by the 60th parallel of north latitude, the 141st meridian of west longitude and the outer limit of the exclusive economic zone [except where the presence of the international boundary between Canada and Greenland requires a lesser extent].[13]

With the outer-most limit of Canadian Arctic waters at 200 nautical miles (M) measured from the Canadian Arctic shoreline, Canada takes full advantage of the

11 SC 1996, c 31.
12 United Nations Convention on the Law of the Sea, 10 December 1982 (in force 16 November 1994), 1833 *UNTS* 396.
13 *Arctic Waters Pollution Prevention Act*, RSC 1985, c A-12, s 2.

jurisdictional extent afforded to the coastal State by the international law of the sea.[14] The 60th parallel of north latitude, which marks the southern boundary of Canada's Arctic waters, also marks the southern limit of Canada's three Arctic territories, that is, the Yukon, the Northwest Territories and Nunavut, making it a coherent choice. However, the 60th parallel cuts right across Hudson Bay and Ungava Bay, both of which experience Arctic shipping conditions to some extent throughout their entire expanse. With regard to safety of navigation, the geographical scope of NORDREG therefore also spans waters south of the 60th parallel, thus including the areas off the coast of northern Manitoba, northern Ontario and Nunavik, the Quebec region north of the 55th parallel of north latitude (Figure 1.1).

Another, much broader definition of Arctic waters is used for the purposes of the Polar Code (Figure 1.1), according to identical definitions provided in the SOLAS and MARPOL conventions respectively.[15] Designed for the application of international shipping regulations throughout the entire Arctic Ocean, this definition encompasses Canada's Arctic waters as defined in the AWPPA, but necessarily extends well beyond. On the Pacific side, "arctic waters" are located north of a line following the 60th parallel north, thus including waters of the Bering Sea. On the Atlantic side, that line dips south to 58 degree north to circumvent Greenland, before it then passes north of the 60th parallel between Greenland and Iceland to join the south cap of Jan Mayen (Norway) slightly north of 70 degrees, then a point near Bjørnøya (Svalbard/Norway) slightly north of 73 degrees, and finally Cap Kanin Nos (Russia) slightly north of 68 degrees. The area thus excluded from the definition of Arctic waters, located north of the 60th parallel between Greenland and the European continent, where the Atlantic Ocean and Arctic Ocean connect, does not experience ice cover that would warrant application of Polar Code regulations.

The fact that Canada's Arctic sea area forms an integral part of the Inuit homeland and has been used from time immemorial by Inuit has increasingly come to the fore in governance circles, adding a new dimension to the understanding of the region. The acknowledgement that the Arctic is indeed a homeland has recently translated into the use of 'Inuit Nunangat' to refer to the region,

14   According to the AWPPA initial version, adopted in 1970, the waters defined as Canada's "arctic waters" extended only 100 nautical miles (M) seaward, see SC 1969–1970, c 47, s 3(1).

15   See International Convention for the Safety of Life at Sea Convention, 1 November 1974 (in force 25 May 1980), 1184 UNTS 278 [SOLAS], Chapter XIV, Regulation 1.3; International Convention for the Prevention of Pollution from Ships, 2 November 1973, 1340 UNTS 184, as amended by the Protocol of 1978 Relating to the International Convention for the Prevention of Pollution from Ships, 17 February 1978 (both in force 2 October 1983), 1340 UNTS 61 [MARPOL], Annex I, Regulations 1.11.7 and 46.2; Annex II, Regulations 13.8.1 and 21.2; Annex IV, Regulations 17.2 and 17.3; and Annex V, Regulations 1.14.7 and 13.2, as reproduced in IMO Resolution MSC.385(94) (n 5).

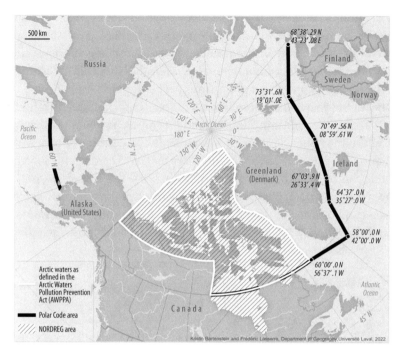

FIGURE 1.1   Geographical scope of application of the AWPPA, NORDREG and the
              Polar Code

including in official government language.[16] The term is derived from the Greenlandic Inuktitut term 'Inuit Nunaat,' which refers to the homeland of the Inuit,
that is, the area that "stretches from Greenland to Canada, Alaska and the coastal
regions of Chukotka, Russia."[17] The Canadian Inuktitut term 'Inuit Nunangat,' for
its part, designates the homeland of Inuit in Canada, extending over four distinct
Inuit regions of Canada, which all benefit from land claims agreements: the Inuvialuit Settlement Region (Northwest Territories), Nunavut, Nunavik in northern
Quebec and Nunatsiavut in Newfoundland and Labrador (Figure 1.2).

The term 'Nunangat' has a broader meaning than 'Nunaat' in that it refers not
only to the land, but explicitly also to the water and ice of the Inuit homeland.
Precisely for that reason, it was adopted by Inuit Tapiriit Kanatami, the organization representing the interests of Inuit in Canada, as the official term to refer

---

16   See notably Inuit Nunangat Policy (n 8).

17   Inuit Circumpolar Council, *A Circumpolar Inuit Declaration on Sovereignty in the Arctic*,
      April 2009, Article 2.1, https://www.itk.ca/wp-content/uploads/2016/07/Declaration_
      12x18_Vice-Chairs_Signed.pdf. Note that Greenland is referred to in Greenlandic Inuktitut
      as Kalallit Nunaat, meaning the homeland of the Greenlandic Inuit.

to the Canadian Inuit homeland.[18] While there is significant overlap between Canada's Arctic maritime areas and Inuit Nunangat maritime areas, the latter do not extend to the entirety of the former. Most notably, large parts of the Hudson Bay are not part of the Inuit homeland, while the Nunatsiavut territory is outside the scope of application of Canada's Arctic shipping regulations.

According to the 2021 census numbers, more than 48,500 Inuit live in Inuit Nunangat,[19] almost two thirds in Nunavut and roughly 25 percent in Nunavik, 4 percent in the Inuvialuit Settlement Region and 6 percent in Nunatsiavut. The population is scattered across the vast territory in communities mostly located along the coast of the Canadian mainland and the Canadian Arctic Archipelago (Figure 1.3). Not part of Inuit Nunangat, but still considered significant coastal communities of the Canadian Arctic, are Fort Severn (Ontario) and Churchill (Manitoba). The coastal communities of Nunatsiavut, including

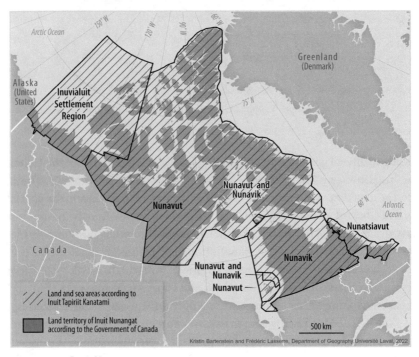

FIGURE 1.2   Inuit Nunangat

18   See "About Canadian Inuit," Inuit Tapiriit Kanatami, https://www.itk.ca/about-canadian
        -inuit/.
19   See overview at Statistics Canada, "First Nations people, Métis and Inuit in Canada,"
        last modified 21 September 2022, https://www150.statcan.gc.ca/n1/pub/11-627-m/11-627
        -m2022057-eng.htm.

FIGURE I.3   Canadian Arctic coastal communities

Hopedale, Nain and Rigolet are part of Inuit Nunangat, but because of their location south of the 60th parallel north do not fall within the geographical scope of Arctic shipping regulations.

3   Key Concerns

The chapters of this book are bound together by a number of crosscutting themes. Two of these certainly stand out as key concerns that seem central to a contemporary understanding of governance in the Arctic and expectations regarding decision-making. The first such theme is related to Canada's colonial history and its current commitment to the truth and reconciliation process.[20]

---

20   Among others, the Truth and Reconciliation Commission (TRC) of Canada, established under the Indian Residential Schools Settlement Agreement, has done important work, compiled in numerous reports, to help Canada come to terms with the dark chapters of its colonial past. See in particular Truth and Reconciliation Commission of Canada, *Honouring the Truth, Reconciling for the Future: Summary of the Final Report of the Truth and Reconciliation Commission of Canada*, 2015, https://ehprnh2mwo3.exactdn.com /wp-content/uploads/2021/01/Executive_Summary_English_Web.pdf. This report has been accepted by the Government of Canada with the promise to "fully implement the Calls to Action of the Truth and Reconciliation Commission" (Statement by Prime

Well into the recent past, much of Canada's dealings with the Arctic was tainted by colonial attitudes, if not driven by downright colonial objectives. This past, which has destroyed much of the basis on which mutual trust can be built, has created an uneasy relationship between the Crown and Inuit communities, including with regard to activities that take place in Inuit Nunangat, such as shipping. In preliminary exchanges between the authors of this volume, it became clear that this is a major and—for its complexity—a most difficult governance issue. This volume seeks to provide perspectives on how to address the practical difficulty of transforming the awareness of Canada's colonial past and the still reverberating effects into concrete and meaningful policy and regulatory action.

The second theme that runs through many chapters is the urgency of drastically stepping up the protection of the Arctic marine environment. With the warming climate being the worst threat to Arctic ecosystems, significant reduction of global greenhouse gas emissions is—despite its delayed effect—among the most effective measures.[21] It is also among the most elusive as it requires international consensus and willingness to act. While as a middle power State Canada's influence on the international response to the unfolding climate catastrophe may be limited, it has a moral duty to do its part. Given the dire situation of its Arctic expanse and consequences for Inuit, Canada has every interest in playing a leadership role. A systemic change in approach seems indispensable. First, decisions made in and for the South need to become more relevant for the North, but at the very least, it is critical to avoid making them at the expense of the North. This requires a shift towards decompartmentalized decision-making. Second, with the objective of achieving the United Nations Sustainable Development Goals,[22] principles of sustainable development, such as the preventative and precautionary approaches, need to guide governance decisions.[23] With respect to the issue of shipping, Canada has room to adopt such approaches, alone or as part of the international community, and to minimize the consequences that are harmful

---

Minister on release of the Final Report of the Truth and Reconciliation Commission, 15 December 2015, https://pm.gc.ca/en/news/statements/2015/12/15/statement-prime-minister-release-final-report-truth-and-reconciliation).

21   *IPCC Special Report on the Ocean and Cryosphere in a Changing Climate* (n 1), Summary for Policymakers, in particular B.1.7.

22   See the 17 Sustainable Development Goals declared in 2015. United Nations General Assembly, *Transforming Our World: The 2030 Agenda for Sustainable Development*, UN Doc A/RES/70/1 (21 October 2015).

23   For these principles, see United Nations Conference on Environment and Development, *Rio Declaration on Environment and Development*, UN Doc A/CONF.151/26 (vol. I) (14 June 1992).

to Arctic ecosystems and habitats. The chapters in this volume offer guidance as Canada needs to thoroughly scope out these challenges and carefully use the domestic and international leverage it has.

The integration of Inuit voices in future governance decisions and the protection of the Arctic environment as a top priority intersect when it comes to the economic future of the region. Both wanted and dreaded within the region and beyond, economic development of the Arctic region rests very much on shipping, as does the region's wellbeing. Shipping indeed enables community supply and development, mining operations and tourism, to name just a few. Yet, it also increases the strain on marine ecosystems that are already under stress, threatening not only Arctic habitats, but also the way of life and livelihoods of Arctic communities. Boon and bane in equal measure, shipping and its consequences therefore need to be actively considered in any development decision. Several chapters of this volume give context and guidance on how to tackle the difficult task of finding the right balance.

Further issues raised by shipping in the Canadian Arctic are addressed in this book. Among them are concerns related to safety of navigation and safety of life at sea. Although first and foremost centred on the ship, crew, cargo and operations, these concerns are interwoven with others, such as the impact of shipping on the environment, community well-being and emergency preparedness and response. Moreover, in any discussion on shipping in Canadian Arctic waters, the issues of Canada's sovereignty over these waters and control of the Northwest Passage loom in the background. While matters of sovereignty are inevitably related to regulatory authority, they occasionally also extend to military and strategic concerns. This volume seeks to provide perspectives on these issues as well.

4   Structure

This book has 16 chapters divided into two parts. Part I, *Understanding the Context of Governance of Shipping in Canadian Arctic Waters*, sets the stage for in-depth analysis of governance issues by examining shipping in the Canadian Arctic, from both a historical and a contemporary perspective, with chapters focusing on social, environmental and economic aspects of shipping as well as on safety, security and defence issues and related strategies. Under the heading *Reimagining the Governance of Shipping in Canadian Arctic Waters*, Part II then takes a closer look at specific policy and legal issues raised by the governance of shipping in the Canadian Arctic. Scrutiny ranges from the contemporary state of the international legal framework to various issues raised by the practical operationalization of an appropriate Canadian policy and legal framework. The conclusion builds on insights and governance directions drawn from each of the chapters to map out future governance approaches and imperatives.

Part 1 comprises five chapters addressing aspects that are or need to be considered key to conceptualizing the future governance of shipping in the Canadian Arctic. It starts with chapter 2 titled "'The Sea Is Our Mainstay': Shipping and the Inuit Homeland," a conversation between anthropologist Claudio Aporta and Monica Ell-Kanayuk, president of the Inuit Circumpolar Council (ICC) Canada from 2018 to 2022. Through Ell-Kanayuk's eyes, the reader gets a sense of the particularly close relationship Inuit have with their marine environment, a defining feature of their homeland, and their perception of shipping in the region. The conversation also explores the importance ICC attaches to the provisional consultative status it was recently granted with the IMO. Inspired by his exchange with Ell-Kanayuk, Aporta then reflects on the challenges and opportunities that Arctic shipping and its governance hold for Inuit and stresses the critical importance that Inuit attribute to increasing agency over their lives and homelands with regard to shipping activities.

Chapter 3 on "Shipping in Arctic Marine Ecosystems under Stress: Recognizing and Mitigating the Threats" is co-authored by Warwick Vincent, Connie Lovejoy and Kristin Bartenstein. It provides a broad overview of the many unique ecological features of the Arctic Ocean and explains how climate change and other global stressors wreak havoc on the fragile balance, causing the ocean's current precarious state. The authors zoom in on the additional perturbations increasing ship traffic threatens to provoke, including through chemical, physical and biological stressors that come with shipping. Against the background of the particular vulnerability of the Arctic marine environment, they advise on how regulation of shipping could contribute to hold these risks in check.

In chapter 4 on "Shipping along the Northwest Passage: A Historical Overview," Adam Lajeunesse and P. Whitney Lackenbauer focus on shipping that moves into and out of the Arctic using the waterways of the Northwest Passage. They provide a historical overview of the activity that starts in the nineteenth century, but then concentrate mainly on the twentieth century. They show that steady shipping for community resupply and government operations is overlaid by repeating boom-and-bust cycles, fueled by successive defence and economic crises and opportunities, such as the Second World War, the Cold War and the prospects of resource extraction in the 1970s and 1980s. They caution that Canada's current interest in the Arctic region due to melting ice and increased maritime accessibility may decline as resource extraction cycles continue to oscillate, the marine transportation sector makes its own profitability calculations, and Inuit and Northern Canadians gain agency over the future of their homeland.

This is followed by chapter 5 on "Comparative Perspectives on the Development of Canadian Arctic Shipping: Impacts of Climate Change and Globalization," in which Frédéric Lasserre looks at the factors that shape shipping in the Canadian Arctic, contrasting the Canadian with the Russian situation. While reduction of ice facilitates navigation, Lasserre emphasizes that development of shipping volumes is driven mainly by community resupply, resource extraction, transit shipping and tourism. Perceptions of how well the Arctic fits into the global market are a notable factor as well, in particular with regard to resource extraction, shipping and commercial transit shipping. Lasserre further opines that the emerging business model based on transshipment hubs and high-ice class shuttle vessels may hold limited promise for the Canadian Arctic, and that Canada's low-impact shipping corridors—a hands-off approach compared to Russia's active development of the Northern Sea Route—may still require investment in infrastructure to manage and control increased traffic.

Leah Beveridge's chapter 6 titled "Reconsidering Arctic Shipping Governance through a Decolonizing Lens" seeks to offer a new perspective on discussion of the future of Arctic shipping governance. Beveridge begins by charting the role ships played in facilitating the mistreatment of Inuit and attempts at assimilation, drawing on first-hand accounts collected through the work of the Royal Commission on Aboriginal Peoples and the Truth and Reconciliation Commission. She then turns to the gradual recognition of the rights of Indigenous peoples, which became more pronounced following the 1982 constitutional reform, notably yielding five Inuit land claims and self-government agreements, and reached a new stage in 2021 with the promulgation of the *United Nations Declaration on the Rights of Indigenous Peoples Act*. Beveridge finally explores how the Crown-Inuit relationship with regard to governance of Arctic shipping may evolve under the 2022 Inuit Nunangat Policy, given this relationship's troubled past.

The subsequent three chapters address issues concerning the safety, security and defence continuum. In chapter 7, "Unpacking Canada's Arctic Shipping Safety, Security, and Defence Functions", Andrea Charron and David Snider detail these three functions with regard to shipping in Canadian Arctic waters and explain how dedicated organizations mandated to execute these functions are prone to compartmentalized action. Drawing on concrete examples, they then explore how cooperation between government agencies, territorial governments and local Indigenous communities may lead to more integrated and ultimately better responses to the many safety, security and defences challenges related to shipping in the Canadian Arctic.

In chapter 8, "Canadian Icebreaker Operations and Shipbuilding: Challenges and Opportunities," Timothy Choi discusses icebreakers as instrumental in the provision of federal government services such as route assistance, ice routing and information services, harbour breakouts, Northern resupply and tasks related to ensuring Canada's 'Arctic sovereignty.' Given the real—but in circumpolar comparison common—problem of the aging Canadian Coast Guard (CCG) fleet of icebreakers, the chapter centres on Canada's National Shipbuilding Strategy. Choi explains the difficulties of replacement strategies to deliver icebreakers through domestic construction and examines alternative strategies to fill some of the gaps in the fleet's availability. He discusses the possibility for Canada to follow the Danish example of drawing upon vessels that have icebreaking capabilities without being designated icebreakers—in Canada's case the new *Harry DeWolf*-class Arctic and offshore patrol vessels built for the Royal Canadian Navy and the CCG—to fulfill some of the tasks usually performed exclusively by CCG icebreakers.

Peter Kikkert, Calvin Pedersen and P. Whitney Lackenbauer share experience gained on mass rescue operations (MRO) in chapter 9 titled "Mitigating the Tyranny of Time and Distance: Community-Based Organizations and Marine Mass Rescue Operations in Inuit Nunangat." In the vast and remote Canadian Arctic, such operations face serious challenges that are exacerbated by austere environmental conditions, limited support infrastructure, inadequate local medical capacity and likely few vessels of opportunity able to provide assistance. Based on a tabletop exercise held in Nunavut and follow-up work, the authors argue that community-based organizations (CBOs) may be valuable force multipliers, at sea and shoreside, during a marine MRO. Highlighting the limitations faced by CBOs, they also discuss how community responders may be best prepared to take on these roles and how their capabilities may be reflected in relevant mass rescue and emergency plans.

Part 2 of the book is devoted to reimagining the governance of shipping in Canadian Arctic waters. It opens with three chapters taking a broad view by considering overarching issues, such as coastal State and flag State jurisdiction, and Canada's policy, legal and institutional framework and their significance for governance of shipping in the Canadian Arctic. Chapter 10, authored by Kristin Bartenstein, starts with a look at "Canada and the Future of Arctic Coastal State Jurisdiction." Against the background of changes in the physical and ecological environment of the marine Arctic due to climate change and in the legal environment brought about by the Polar Code that call for a fresh look at Arctic coastal State jurisdiction, Bartenstein explores how Canada may use the exceptional jurisdiction provided under Article 234 of the LOSC. She starts by tracing Canada's history of regulating shipping in its Arctic waters, which still informs Canada's governance decisions. With a view to highlighting lessons for future regulatory action, she then examines the geographical and material scope of jurisdiction under Article 234 and discusses Canada's strategy to subject navigation in its Arctic waters to a single set of rules.

In chapter 11, "The Modern Case Law on the Powers and Responsibilities of Flag States: Navigating Canada's Arctic Waters," Nigel Bankes looks at recent jurisprudence to assess the powers and responsibilities of flag States. He finds that while the plenary and exclusive nature of flag State jurisdiction is confirmed by recent international cases, the due diligence obligation of flag States to enforce relevant laws and standards, notably on safety of navigation and protection of the environment, is emphasized as well. He then examines the implications of this case law for flag State powers and responsibilities within an Arctic context, especially in light of the adoption of the Polar Code, which includes rules of reference encompassed by the due diligence obligation.

Aldo Chircop then portrays "The Canadian Policy, Legal and Institutional Framework for the Governance of Arctic Shipping" in chapter 12. He provides a broad account of the myriad policy and regulatory instruments and the numerous departments and agencies relevant to the governance of shipping in general and Arctic shipping in particular, underlining their unwieldiness, complexity and fragmentation. In his discussion, he questions the traditional model of a centralized maritime administration, and while recognizing the importance of uniform rules and standards for shipping, he argues for high governance standards that ensure environment protection and Indigenous engagement and participation in decision-making.

The final five chapters focus on specific issues relevant to the future governance of shipping in the Canadian Arctic. Under the title "Goal-Based Standards, Meta-Regulation and Tripartism in Arctic Shipping: What Prospects in Canadian Waters?," chapter 13 by Phillip Buhler examines regulatory models. He investigates alternative approaches to prescriptive regulation as a way to avoid problems such as lack of flexibility, lack of financial and technical resources of the regulator, economic inefficiencies, and imbalance of expertise between regulator and regulatee. His discussion of prospects for Canada focuses in particular on meta-regulation, that is, regulator-monitored self-regulation, which includes industry-developed technical rules to support goal-based standards such as those developed by the IMO and used within the Polar Code. He further highlights the opportunity for regulatory tripartism, which would allow Inuit participation in regulatory processes.

In chapter 14, Meagan Greentree addresses the issue of "Modernizing the Governance of Passenger Vessel Operations in the Canadian Arctic." Based on the finding that the loosely coordinated governance of passenger vessel

operation in the Canadian Arctic has produced a complex and inefficient permitting system, she explores approaches to streamlining the various permitting
processes and concludes that systemic reform is required. She recommends
that permitting of passenger vessels should ideally be conducted by a single
entity established within Transport Canada.

In chapter 15, titled "Governing Canadian Arctic Shipping through Low-
impact Shipping Corridors," Jackie Dawson and Gloria Song shed light on the
concept of low-impact shipping corridors (LISC) that has been developed by
the Government of Canada since the early 2000s to support shipping in the
Canadian Arctic by prioritizing scarce infrastructure and service investments
to dedicated shipping corridors. After tracing the temporal and spatial development of shipping activities in Arctic Canada, they describe the strategies used
to determine the location of corridors that enables safe navigation, but also
protection of ecologically and culturally significant marine areas. They discuss
strengths and weaknesses of the LISC concept and its effectiveness in supporting sustainable ocean governance that allows for self-determination of Inuit.

In chapter 16, under the title "The New Federal *Impact Assessment Act* and
Arctic Shipping: Opportunities for Improved Governance", Meinhard Doelle,
David V. Wright, A. John Sinclair and Simon Dueck explore opportunities to
improve the governance of shipping and related activities in Canadian Arctic
waters. They explore the application of the federal *Impact Assessment Act*
(IAA) to shipping operations related notably to supply for northern communities and industries, transportation of resources extracted in the Canadian
Arctic, and transit shipping. The authors next analyze the four distinct IAA
assessment processes that are relevant to the governance of shipping and their
potential role. They finally consider how the IAA's processes may interact with
other existing assessment processes, such as those conducted at territorial and
Indigenous levels of government.

Many of the issues discussed in the preceding chapters converge in
chapter 17, where Suzanne Lalonde and Nigel Bankes examine "Indigenous
Self-Determination and the Regulation of Navigation and Shipping in Canadian Arctic Waters." Their exploration is prompted by the observation that
increased shipping traffic in the Canadian Arctic, encouraged by decreasing
sea ice and favourable socio-economic factors, is not only testing Canada's
marine safety and security regime, but also creating significant challenges for
northern Indigenous communities that rely on the marine environment for
their food, transport, culture and way of life. The authors assess the legal and
policy opportunities available to Inuit communities in the Canadian Arctic,
under both international and domestic law, to achieve self-determination with
respect to navigation and shipping activities in their homeland.

In the concluding chapter 18, co-editors Aldo Chircop and Kristin Barten-stein reflect and draw upon the insights and policy directions offered by the preceding chapters to share cumulative and integrative thoughts on the complexity and prospects of governing shipping in the Canadian Arctic waters and future directions. They call for a thorough governance reform to overcome the vertical and fragmented approach that has characterized much of the policy, legislative, management and institutional action so far. To address the challenges posed by warming temperatures, decreasing ice, increasing ship traffic and new expectations towards policy- and decision-makers, future policy and legal developments need to be guided by principles of integration, reconciliation and precaution.

5   Concluding Remark

While the field of governance of shipping in the Canadian Arctic is extensive and evolving and therefore difficult to capture in all its subtleties and nuances, this volume offers an overview of and insights into the key issues that Canada needs to address in the coming years. Its findings are intended to complement the existing literature and to spark new research and scholarship. They are also intended to inform policy-makers around the globe on Canadian perspectives on issues of Arctic shipping in Canadian waters and to assist Canadian decision-makers, stakeholders and rights holders in the development of future law and policy meant to govern shipping in Inuit Nunangat.

Acknowledgements

The maps in this chapter were prepared by Professor Frédéric Lasserre and Louise Marcoux of the Department of Geography at Université Laval. Their assistance is gratefully acknowledged.

PART 1

Understanding the Context of Governance of Shipping in Canadian Arctic Waters

∵

"The Sea is Our Mainstay": Shipping and the Inuit Homeland

Monica Ell-Kanayuk and Claudio Aporta

Abstract

This chapter is based on a conversation between Claudio Aporta (an anthropologist who has done research with Inuit communities for over 20 years) and Monica Ell-Kanayuk, the president of the Inuit Circumpolar Council (ICC) Canada. It explores Ell-Kanayuk's perspectives on the impacts and possibilities created by the present and projected increase of shipping traffic on the waters of Inuit Nunangat. It describes and analyzes the significance of the relationship of Inuit with their marine environments, and it discusses the recently given provisional consultative status of ICC in the International Maritime Organization. The significance of such designation for Indigenous peoples is discussed and analyzed. The chapter concludes with an analysis of Ell- Kanayuk's reflections.

Keywords

Inuit – Inuit Circumpolar Council – International Maritime Organization – Arctic shipping – Indigenous rights

1 Introduction

In November 2021, a press release by the Inuit Circumpolar Council (ICC) informed that, during the 34th Extraordinary Meeting of the International Maritime Organization (IMO), ICC had become the first Indigenous organization to receive IMO provisional consultative status.[1] Then Chair of ICC, Dalee Sambo Dorough, remarked that

---

1 See "IMO Council, Extraordinary Session (CES 34), 8–12/22 November 2021," IMO Media Centre, https://www.imo.org/en/MediaCentre/MeetingSummaries/Pages/Council,-Extraordinary -Session-(CES-34).aspx.

> [t]his is a significant accomplishment for the ICC, especially given our relationship with and reliance upon the coastal seas and Arctic Ocean by Inuit communities throughout Inuit Nunaat. Our marine environment is affected by the decisions, guidelines, and policies set by the IMO. This status is crucial for us. It will be used by the ICC to represent ourselves, to advance our status, rights and role autonomously from those whose interests are not always neatly aligned with our perspectives as Indigenous peoples.[2]

This milestone could potentially make headways in terms of effectively implementing the provisions of the United Nations Declaration on the Rights of Indigenous Peoples (UNDRIP) in the international maritime context. Other maritime Indigenous peoples around the world are expectant as to how this will play out, particularly as this recognition could have an impact on shared concerns, such as food security, cultural protection, and economic sustainable growth of coastal communities. Most important, the inclusion of ICC could be the first step in giving Indigenous peoples a voice in matters that affect them, but where they are not usually consulted.

For Inuit, the event is timely, as climatic changes are opening Arctic waters to an increasing number of ships, and as Inuit in Canada have been called to participate in the development of the Northern Low-Impact Shipping Corridors Initiative, a federal government initiative co-lead by the Canadian Coast Guard, Transport Canada and the Canadian Hydrographic Service, which seeks "to minimize potential effects of shipping on wildlife, respect culturally and ecologically sensitive areas, enhance marine navigation safety, and guide investments in the North."[3]

Inuit communities and organizations are looking at the increase in Arctic shipping with mixed feelings, both as an opportunity of economic and social development and as the potential source of environmental, social and cultural threats. Detailed views of Inuit communities can be found in the excellent reports of the Arctic Corridors, a large research initiative led by Jackie Dawson at the University of Ottawa, that involves numerous researchers from

---

2   Inuit Circumpolar Council (ICC), "Inuit Voices to be Heard at IMO on Critical Shipping Issues," Press Release, 9 November 2021, https://www.inuitcircumpolar.com/news/inuit-voices-to-be-heard-at-imo-on-critical-shipping-issues/.

3   Fisheries and Oceans Canada, "Northern Low-Impact Shipping Corridors," Government of Canada, last modified 9 February 2022, https://www.dfo-mpo.gc.ca/about-notre-sujet/engagement/2021/shipping-corridors-navigation-eng.html.

communities, academia, and non-governmental organizations (NGOs).[4] The engagement of Inuit in marine and maritime governance seems to be at a critical point, signaling some efforts from the Government of Canada to advance on issues of reconciliation, Indigenous engagement and Indigenous rights,[5] and as environmental assessments become more comprehensive, including social and cultural factors.[6]

The connection of Inuit to the marine environment is well documented,[7] but the implications of considering those marine areas as homelands are not sufficiently (if at all) considered in shipping debates and policies. Inuit connections to the sea are manifested at different levels, from local to regional and circumpolar. Studies of Inuit uses of the sea ice show how intimately the marine environment is known, and how it is used seasonally throughout the year. Inuit traditional trails (both sled and boat routes) illustrate interconnections among communities and intricate links between land and sea, to the point that landfast ice extends the land for several months of the year and allows for sled access to critical open water resources, mainly at the floe edge. Across the totality of the Inuit homeland, from Russia to Greenland, Inuit place names along the coasts reveal the depth of connection between humans and animals in the marine environment, as can be seen in Figure 2.1.

The Figure 2.1 map shows well-established trails documented by Aporta in Arctic Bay, and place names documented by the Aporta and by Inuit Heritage Trust. The place names are reflective of Inuit communities' close relationship with the environment: Salirraq is an old camping site, and refers to the straight shape of the shore; Sigguat is a camping place known for polar bear and walrus hunting; Aqiarurnak is a camping place known as a good spot for seal hunting, while Aqiarurnaup Tiriqqua ('the corner of Aqiarurngnak') is good for caribou hunting; Qakuqtaqtujut is a good camping place with white rocks; the

---

4 Jackie Dawson *et al.*, "Infusing Inuit and Local Knowledge into the Low Impact Shipping Corridors: An Adaptation to Increased Shipping Activity and Climate Change in Arctic Canada," *Environmental Science & Policy* 105 (2020): 19–36; Nicolien Van Luijk *et al.*, "Community-identified Risks to Hunting, Fishing, and Gathering (Harvesting) Activities from Increased Marine Shipping Activity in Inuit Nunangat, Canada," *Regional Environmental Change* 22:1 (2022), https://doi.org/10.1007/s10113-022-01894-3.

5 See Beveridge in this volume.

6 See Doelle *et al.* in this volume.

7 See, for example, Emma J. Stewart *et al.*, "Characterising Polar Mobilities to Understand the Role of Weather, Water, Ice and Climate (WWIC) Information," *Polar Geography* 43:2–3 (2020): 95–119, https://doi.org/10.1080/1088937X.2019.1707319; Igor Krupnik *et al.* (eds.), *SIKU: Knowing Our Ice, Documenting Inuit Sea-Ice Knowledge and Use* (Dordrecht: Springer, 2010); Claudio Aporta, D.R. Fraser Taylor and Gita J. Laidler (eds.), "Special Issue: Geographies of Inuit Sea Ice Use," *The Canadian Geographer* 55:1 (2011): 1–142.

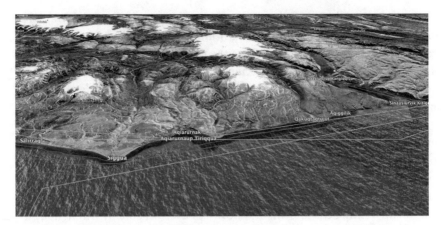

FIGURE 2.1   Selected place names between the communities of Arctic Bay and Pond Inlet,
                       Nunavut, with a view from the north towards the south

camping site Aqiggilik is known as a good place for ptarmigans; Sinaasiurviup
Kangiqqlua is a place where the ice is safe for travel, and good for narwhal
hunting; at Sinaasiurvik Kitiqqliq the floe edge forms across the inlet in the
spring, where seal and narwhal can be hunted.

    For Inuit communities, who have established important relations with ship-
ping since the beginning of European contact, the threats posed by an increase
of shipping traffic are several, including oil spills, underwater sound, seasonal
disturbances of marine life and sea ice, social impact of cruise tourism, and
lack of infrastructure in case of a disaster. The potential benefits are fewer but
relevant, and they all depend on a well-managed and participatory system of
governance, regulations that prevent ships from damaging environmentally
and culturally sensitive areas, implementation of clean shipping technologies,
and the prospects of economic benefits for communities. The engagement of
Inuit in arenas that rule maritime affairs has never been more important. Inuit
organizations seem to be having a pragmatic approach: the increase in Arctic
shipping seems inevitable, and the focus for Inuit is to preserve the sense of
homeland while having a critical say on how shipping develops and on how it
is governed and regulated.[8]

    I, Claudio Aporta, contacted Monica Ell-Kanayuk, then President of ICC
Canada, after I was invited to contribute a chapter to this volume, with the
understanding that it would be co-written with an Inuit author. After discussing
the contribution with her, I suggested that her views would be better expressed

---

8   ICC Canada, *The Sea Ice is Our Highway* (Ottawa: ICC, 2008); ICC Canada, *Circumpolar Inuit
      Response to Arctic Shipping Workshop Proceedings* (Ottawa: ICC, 2013).

in the form of an interview, in order to leave Monica's narrative unfiltered, and separate from my own perspectives as an Arctic researcher. This approach to documenting and portraying narratives in context has been extensively used in Indigenous knowledge research and Indigenous-led projects,[9] and it is in line with methodological frameworks aiming at decolonizing research.[10]

The importance of the sea to Inuit is rooted in deep senses of local connection that include individual and collective memories, as well as current and ongoing marine related activities. The political positions of Inuit organizations about shipping, whether at the international, national, regional or local levels, are rooted in concrete community stories and memories.[11] The interview with Monica explores both personal and political connections with the marine environment, as well as the implications of shipping, and the impact of the new ICC status in IMO.

Monica has had an impactful political career representing communities and fighting for the rights and wellbeing of Inuit in several capacities. She was

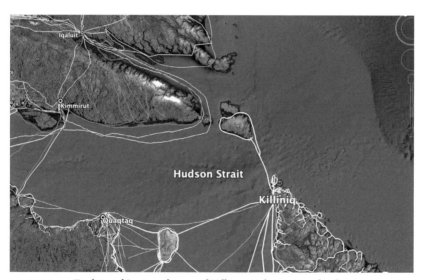

FIGURE 2.2   Traditional Inuit trails around Killiniq, at the crossroads of Nunavut, Nunavik and Nunatsiavut

9   Julie Cruikshank, *Life Lived Like a Story: Life Stories of Three Yukon Native Elders* (Vancouver: University of British Columbia, 1990); Milton M.R. Freeman, "Looking Back-and Looking Ahead-35 Years after the Inuit Land Use and Occupancy Project," *The Canadian Geographer* 55:1 (2011): 20–31.

10   Linda Tuhiwai Smith, *Decolonizing Methodologies : Research and Indigenous Peoples* , 2nd ed. (London ; NewYork: Zed/ Palgrave Macmillan, 2012).

11   Claudio Aporta and Charlie Watt, "Arctic waters as Inuit homeland," in Timo Koivurova *et al.* (eds.), *Routledge Handbook of Indigenous Peoples in the Arctic*, 1st ed. (Routledge, 2020).

an MLA [Member of the Legislative Assembly] in Nunavut (2011–2013), and she served as Director of Programming for the Inuit Broadcasting Corporation. She is a former Director of Economic and Business Development at Nunavut Tunngavik Incorporated, the institution that ensures that the federal and territorial governments fulfill their obligations as established in the Nunavut Agreement. She has also served as President of the Nunavut Economic Forum, President of the Baffin Chamber of Commerce, Vice-President of the Atuqtu-arvik Corporation and Vice-President of Pauktuutit, the national organization representing Inuit women.

Monica speaks from a place of genuine love for the Arctic, and from a place of knowledge that goes beyond personal experience with the land. What follows is not an official ICC position, but her views on the significance of the marine environment for Inuit, and of the challenges and opportunities that increasing shipping poses for Inuit.

The conversation was done virtually, with Monica in Iqaluit and myself in Halifax, in December 2021. As a starting point of the conversation, we discussed the maps of Inuit trails I have developed with Inuit communities over many years of research (Figure 2.2),[12] and which I shared on the screen as we talked. The trails interconnect communities across the Inuit homeland, making the different scales of Inuit identity (local, regional, pan-Arctic) clear. In Monica's narrative, her memories of travel and childhood lead to the significance of marine areas and to a multidimensional articulation of Inuit positions on shipping.

2   The Conversation

Claudio: I didn't do any mapping in Iqaluit ... that is something I think we should do because these trails that you see there ... they were probably mapped by people from other communities that know the trail.

Monica: Well, it's the same with all of these communities, none of these communities existed 50–60 years ago.

Claudio: Where were you born?

Monica: I'm from a small island called Coral Harbour [Salliq].

Claudio: I'm sure you remember, Monica, when you were a child, maybe you would go out to the country.

---

12   Id.

Monica: I don't remember that area much at all, I left when I was one or so. I've gone back a few times.

Claudio: Where did you move to?

Monica: Oh gosh. I think we went to Iqaluit first, in Apex.[13] I remember being in a tent. Housing was not developed. I don't have a picture unfortunately. Then we were moved to a building before the winter. It was a lot of fun; it was an experience. We were used to living like that, going all over the place. Apex is where I grew up.

Claudio: You told me you're not 'a land person,' but you interact with a lot of people that travel the land and harvest on a regular basis, including your husband.

Monica: He's been travelling quite a lot. My dad too. He was a fisherman, carving stone miner, and yeah. Lots of people still in the summertime go by boat. That I know of. My dad went to Newfoundland a couple of times, all the way up the Labrador coast. I went on one of his trips. That was interesting. He picked up a Peter Head boat. He used to go from Iqaluit in the summertime to just past Cape Dorset, to quarry soapstone. After all that, he'd go down to the point to do an annual walrus hunt. Then, he'd provide the community with the walrus.

Claudio: Do you know if they would go to the Nunavik side?

Monica: From what I remember he would do transport delivery to what used to be Port Burwill (Killiniq, Figure 2.2), it's not in existence now .... It used to be a small community, Killiniq. Way back when I worked as an administrator for economic development. Somehow, they got me to go there to translate to the people being moved from there to wherever they wanted to go. Most of the people wanted to go to some communities in northern Quebec, but there's so much stuff there that they were leaving behind. Lots of seals, frozen into the snow near the houses. The ships wouldn't want to go there, my father knew the area very well. He would know how to navigate through there. And provide the sea lift. But the thing is, because the government couldn't provide the proper sea lift, they ended up closing it down.

Claudio: So, those trips were mostly for the Hudson Bay trading post in Killiniq?

Monica: I don't know really; I was very young. It was just a community; there were people there. By the time I was there most had already gone, there were a few remaining.

---

13   Apex (Niaqunngut in Inuktitut) is a small community about 5 km from the present town of Iqaluit, Nunavut. Most Inuit lived in Apex before the present settlement developed.

Claudio: You know, when you tell those stories, and then you look at the map—you can tell that the marine environment is very important for the Inuit, right?

Monica: Yes, it is very important for the Inuit. It's our livelihood. It's not just the marine, but the land and the sea, everything. We are nomadic people. That's where we've been for millennia. It's important.

Claudio: So, both the land and the marine areas are extremely important. I guess the sea ice also plays a role, right? Important for Inuit people to hunt and travel on the sea ice.

Monica: Of course. We had dog teams before the snowmobiles came. People travelled by dog team on sea ice. That's where we get our food, our seals, walrus. Even some of the birds stay here. We're very dependent on the sea. At times, we are called 'the people of the sea.' The sea is our mainstay. That's how we exist. It's part of our culture, our way of life. We're a maritime people. It's central to our culture, and it's the way we live. I don't know whether we have more ties to the marine environment than others. It's our highway, in a way.

Claudio: Have you heard of people talking about the sea ice changing, and making it more difficult to hunt and travel?

Monica: I can only talk from my own experience. One summer we had patches of ice for the entire summer. It made it very difficult to go out on a boat, it became dangerous. That's a change in itself. This year, it's still open. People are still going out. A ship has just arrived. Maybe the last one. It's starting to frost now finally. If you've heard the news, October was very mild. The weather is changing. Last spring, there were some near disasters with thin ice. One of our staff posted a picture of her family stuck up somewhere. Here in Iqaluit, the ice is changing for sure. Sometimes it's not as thick or thickening as it should be. Some hunters say it's hard to predict the weather now. They can be experts of the sky and clouds, but apparently the movement and the appearance of the clouds ... it is more difficult to predict what the weather will be like.

Claudio: I've heard those stories all over the Arctic.

Monica: It's becoming not as clear how the weather will turn out sometimes. Of course, we have the forecast, but it can be more accurate using our experience and the land around us. But that is starting to change.

Claudio: The environmental clues are changing; people can't predict the weather as well. In some areas there is less ice, and that means there is easier access to minerals and other resources, as well as more shipping. Are people worried about the increase in shipping? Or do they see it as an opportunity?

Monica: Overall, Inuit are more concerned with increased shipping in the Arctic. Some may see an opportunity. I'll give you an example of an opportunity of the ship that passed through the Arctic, what was the name of that big cruise ship? The one that passed through the Northwest Passage.[14] People in other areas where the ship would pass were concerned about the movement of the marine mammals—specifically the walruses and the seals. So, they got together with the hunters' organizations and other community members that were concerned, and they clarified which route the ship would take. So that it wouldn't go through any areas where there might be calving being produced. That was a big concern. At one point they were taking pictures of polar bears being very close to their boats. On their website they showed the pictures and people were upset. The owners were forced to make a payment because they broke some of the rules when they were passing through. The other thing too is that you think with more tourists there's going to be an opportunity for income to the communities ... for their crafts. But because a lot of the people on the ships are from the United States, they're not buying things made of seal or ivory. The communities needed to be taught what sorts of crafts they could provide for them to be able to make income. The experience to the community was more, in the end, needing further protection of their livelihood connected to marine and land animals.

Claudio: So, communities are worried about some of the impacts of shipping. I suppose they're worried about potential events in case of an emergency?

Monica: All of those things. The fuel. The potential for fuel spill. Lack of infrastructure to help clean any spills that might happen. The length of time that it would take to get help. All of the communities were supposed to have spill response equipment, but I have heard of some not having access to it. Very unorganized for an emergency response. It would be a disaster for a spill to happen up North. Like the one that happened in Alaska.[15]

Claudio: Would Inuit be more supportive of shipping if the ships were more sustainable and if safety was a priority?

Monica: I mean, Inuit right now depend on shipping in the summer for goods and services. We can't have everything coming in by cargo. So every community has a ship or two every summer, or more often. We've been talking about having the cargo ships to become more fuel efficient. We also don't want to increase the cost of shipping to Nunavut. So they've been given some time to think about how they're going to switch from heavy fuel oil to a more energy efficient oil. We're hoping maybe they can get funding to be able to do that. We don't want the cost to deliver goods to our communities to get increased. If there is no funding provided, they will pass on the costs of shipping to our

---

14   This is a reference to the luxury cruise liner *Crystal Serenity*, which in 2016 spent 36 days navigating the Northwest Passage, carrying more than 1,000 people on board.

15   A reference to the Exxon Valdez oil spill in Prince William Sound, Alaska (24 March 1989).

communities. Things are already at a very high cost to live up here. That is one aspect.

The other aspect is that the fisheries are starting to happen. More and more activities. It's a good thing. It can create economic opportunities for people in the Arctic. But we also don't want to see overfishing, or any kind of spill.

It's all a balance in nature and in our way of life. Right now, the Qikiqtaaluk Corporation is putting a new ship out, named after one of their board members who has seen an opportunity for Nunavut to have economic opportunities from their oceans and land.[16] So, it's a research ship that will go to communities to identify opportunities, such as snails, shrimps. We have lots of clams. I think it's great for the future, but we also don't want to damage our way of life. It's a concern.

The cruise ships are a different story. Some communities are not as receptive to cruise ships. They still don't see the opportunity for their community. Tourism is trying to work hard, but people don't understand or don't see the benefit of tourists coming into their communities. That's a long-term strategy with Tourism Nunavut to help the people of the North to understand the economic viable opportunities for tourism. It will increase production of arts and crafts. The problem is, again, not just the need to educate the people in Nunavut, but also to educate the tourists arriving. They also need to know that the hotels and other things are not 5-star rated in our communities. And you might have to share a bathroom or two when you get to a community. Tourists need to understand, so they're not disappointed. We want people respected in the communities as well. It's a twofold thing that needs to be worked on.

Claudio: The one thing we haven't mentioned is the shipping related to mining or other extractive industries. For instance, people seem to be concerned with the extension of the shipping season in the Mary River project.[17] They seem to be worried about ice breaking in spring and fall.

Monica: Of course, we're worried about pollution. That Mary River project, it has potential for damage to our waters, but they're trying their best to convince Nunavut that they're trying to do it in an environmentally friendly way that doesn't affect our wildlife's behaviour too much. I haven't followed this too closely, but they are concerned. I have seen pictures of the iron dust, and I

---

16 A reference to the research vessel *Ludy Pudluk*, which made its maiden voyage from St. John's, Newfoundland, to Nunavut on 25 July 2021.

17 The Mary River Mine is owned by Baffinland Iron Mines Corporation, and is located in northern Baffin Island, Nunavut (in the Inuit region of Qikiqtaaluk). According to the company's website (https://baffinland.com/), the site has one of the richest iron ore deposits ever discovered, consisting of nine-plus high-grade iron ore deposits.

wouldn't want to have water from there either. Pollution from ships comes in many forms: black carbon, burning of heavy fuel oil, and inability of communities to clean it up. The invasive species in their bilge water is a big concern to many people across the Arctic. We haven't seen recent reports from Mary River, on their wastewater, garbage, plastics, or even paint from the bottom of ships. The underwater noise is the most concerning to the people up there. Increased shipping of their cargo will definitely increase underwater noise and may harm marine mammals. Even the sound of ice breaking is of concern for the marine environment. We're very much a marine people. They need to have safe shipping corridors.

Of course, we're worried about increased shipping, but we also want to see people employed, because there are not that many opportunities in Nunavut. If they can do it safely and not harm our land or destroy our marine environment. I think they're trying to be inclusive of all of that, but it's a concern.

Claudio: Beyond the Mary River, when you look at how the Canadian government is engaging Inuit in these conversations, over the future of the Arctic, shipping, the low-impact shipping corridors .... Are things going in the right direction? What are your thoughts?

Monica: I don't really have an answer for that because it's the federal government in the end that will make the decision for increased traffic to improve Mary River. But I can talk about the regulations that come on the domestic areas, such as the *Arctic Waters Pollution Prevention Act* and the global regulations through the United Nations Convention on the Law of the Sea. And the Polar Code. The regulations are in place to keep the Arctic safe, but there is so little monitoring or enforcement of them. So pollution from shipping can come in many forms, and that's a worry. If the federal government does not have an effective way of cleaning should some disaster happen.

Claudio: So, do you think that Inuit should have more room for engagement or more to say in issues of shipping management?

Monica: Yes. I think Inuit have an inherent right to self-determination of Inuit Nunangat. We believe we have sovereignty over these lands, and the Inuit must be at all levels of the decision- making. Right from the communities, we've heard of comments where they are not allowed to speak ... our MP [Member of Parliament] was not allowed into the hearings of Mary River. That's terrible. We need to make sure that all levels of decision making are from the communities to regional to national to circumpolar to global. Because the oceans are connected. We must work with Transport Canada, Fisheries and Oceans (DFO), Coast Guard, DND [Department of National Defence], in our country, and other national organizations in Greenland, United States, Russia, and with international organizations like IMO.

Claudio: Is that why ICC applied for consultative status at IMO?

Monica: Yes. IMO is an important avenue where we can voice our opinions, and to let people know that Inuit need to be at the table when decisions are being made. As we said in the last ICC General Assembly: *If it's about us, it should be with us.*

Claudio: What about industry? Are there proper means of communication with industry? Shipping in the Arctic is a multi-dimensional activity, but the shipping industry is quite critical, of course. Is there any engagement or communication with the shipping industry?

Monica: It all depends on what industry you're talking about. Shipping, fishing, cargo, tourism, mining, resupply, local hunters. If it's resupply, Inuit are very involved with the shipping industry of resupply to the Arctic. However, if it's tourism shipping, Inuit are trying to have regulations in place but it's a bit of a struggle and a learning curve right now. If it's fisheries, Inuit are involved; again, they're trying to work through regulations with being involved with DFO when they're not getting the proper quota they deserve. If it's regulations with the federal government, the organizations that I mentioned, Inuit need to be having discussions on what regulations are needing improvement. And Inuit need to be at the table with them.

With the resupply, the government must work with the industry to subsidize transportation costs to transition to cheaper fuel. But Inuit organizations have been growing every year. They're amazing, actually. They're able to be more consultative, just in their ability to work with the federal government. I think they're increasing their way to do that. They have access to experts that they've never had before. They're maturing.

Claudio: That's good to know. You mentioned that Inuit requested to be part of the IMO, what does it mean for ICC to be granted provisional consultative status in IMO?

Monica: The provisional status means that ICC will provide a report to IMO after two years to illustrate our contribution to IMO, and what we bring from Inuit across our four membership countries that is important to the international shipping body. That status is crucial to us, and it will be used by ICC to represent ourselves: no one else is going to represent us now at IMO. It will advance our status, our rights, our role, autonomously from those who may have interests that are not always aligned with our perspectives as Indigenous people. There are many foreign actors in this space, shipping companies, investors, resource companies ... and this is Inuit Nunangat ... this is our homeland, we see our sovereignty over these waters. We need to be part of the decisions both in the Arctic and elsewhere. Our voices must be heard, and this is one avenue to have our voices heard.

ICC is not just Canada, it's Alaska, Greenland, Russia. We're the four countries that form the ICC. The history of ICC is that Inuit wanted to have a common space to discuss our commonalities. Of course, shipping and marine environment is one of those things that we're all impacted by, all Inuit in the four regions. We are all marine people; we are all land people; we are all ice people. The Arctic is our homeland.

Claudio: When you look at the traditional trails across the Inuit Arctic, you see how interconnected the Inuit regions are, including across marine areas. The marine environment is a homeland for Inuit, but a place of transit for ships ...

Monica: Yes. It's lots of open water. With the ice melting, it's a concern to have increased shipping, but all of our lives we've been tradespeople. So we have an ability to adapt to situations. Our only concern is that we're not affected by any major disaster or disruption to our way of life. That is our main concern. We don't shy away from having economic opportunities, but we are very much a land, sea, ice people. Our life is dependent on the food we bring in from those areas. That is our utmost priority, our food as it's our mainstay.

3   Concluding Discussion

What follows is not an interpretation of the conversation with Monica Ell-Kanayuk, but some reflections on the challenges and opportunities ahead regarding Arctic shipping activities and governance, inspired by her narrative.

From the conversation, as well as from several documents and public statements by ICC, Inuit Tapiriit Kanatami, and other Inuit organizations, it is evident that there is a strong voice from Inuit to make clear that the marine areas of the Canadian Arctic, including the shipping corridors, must be considered as part of the Inuit homeland. As Monica puts it: "There are many foreign actors in this space, shipping companies, investors, resource companies ... and this is Inuit Nunangat ... this is our homeland, we see our sovereignty over these waters."

As such, Inuit are seeking to be engaged in decision-making and policies that affect or regulate shipping activities at different scales, from the local to the international.

The environmental concerns triggered by ongoing and projected increases in shipping traffic are well known, and they are not limited to the Arctic. But Arctic ecosystems are particularly sensitive to environmental damage, and Arctic communities (both for their geographic isolation and the lack of capacity to respond) are particularly vulnerable to shipping-related incidents.

Monica also makes clear a position that has been also brought up by other Inuit organizations and leaders: that Inuit are not against economic development, including shipping. The problem is in the balance between creating and promoting economic opportunities that are badly needed for communities, and the protection of the marine environment and resources that are essential for Inuit livelihoods and cultural identity. Industrial activity is welcomed, when it does not create undue pressures on the environment and the people (as in the extension of the shipping season through ice breaking in sensitive areas). The message is clear: fishing without overfishing; resource extraction without significant impacts on the ecosystem; tourism, as long as communities find a way to benefit from it. The complexity of making accurate risk assessments for projected activities makes local support regarding expansion or intensifying of industrial activities challenging.

In this sense, closer links of Inuit with shipping technology developers, research, and shipping industries in general can be key to envisioning a future of better economic prospects without increasing the risk of damage to the environment and communities.

The engagement of Inuit in matters that pertain to shipping in the Arctic is progressing, but the effectiveness of the engagement remains to be seen. Participation can mean different things to different people, and power differences can hinder participatory processes.[18] In order to strengthen communities' adaptive capacity and resilience in times of change, a process of social learning that is dynamic, fair and multifaceted is essential in governance, and the learning should include all actors involved.[19]

As Beveridge points out in this volume, there are clear and concreate ways through which the Government of Canada is engaging Inuit in marine and shipping matters. These processes are taking place in (and have been triggered by) several broad policy and legal milestones, such as the implementation of the Oceans Protection Plan,[20] the legal obligations resulting from land claims agreements, the follow-up policy directions resulting from the Truth and Reconciliation Commission's Final Report,[21] and, finally, the implications of Canada's adoption of UNDRIP.

---

18   Sherry R. Arnstein, "A Ladder of Citizen Participation," *Journal of the American Planning Association* 85:1 (2019): 24–34.

19   Kevin Collins and Ray Ison, "Jumping Off Arnstein's Ladder: Social Learning as a New Policy Paradigm for Climate Change Adaptation," *Environmental Policy and Governance* 19:6 (2009): 358–373.

20   Office of the Prime Minister, Canada's Oceans Protection Plan (Ottawa: Office of the Prime Minister, 2016).

21   Truth and Reconciliation Commission of Canada, *Calls to Action* (Winnipeg: 2015).

However, as Monica points out, "I can talk about the regulations that come on the domestic areas, such as the *Arctic Water Pollution Prevention Act*, and the global regulations through the United Nations Convention on the Law of the Sea. And the Polar Code. The regulations are in place to keep the Arctic safe, but there is so little monitoring or enforcement of them." These challenges can only be significantly addressed if Inuit organizations and communities are involved from pre-implementation stages of governance and management.

The ICC's recent inclusion in IMO is also encouraging, even when the status involves no direct decision-making power. As Monica says, "having our voices heard" is of crucial importance.

The challenges that remain are significant. To participate in national and international conversations, fora, etc., Indigenous organizations are given opportunities that are also heavy burdens. These include: (1) having to adapt their knowledge to the frameworks, language, ontologies and tools that are prevailing in Western governance and management; (2) having limited resources and people to undertake research and participate meaningfully in discussions and decision-making; (3) having to constantly prove the value of their knowledge and skills to others; and (4) limited capacity to deal with different dimensions of governance/management initiatives (research, legal, technical, etc.).

Links with academia can produce opportunities to tackle those challenges. Dawson and Song (this volume) describe how partnerships between Indigenous communities and organizations, universities, and NGOs can produce significant results. But even when efforts are placed in capacity-building, Indigenous organizations remain quite dependent on external actors and funding, and it remains a fact that communities are generally skeptic of researchers (a result of historical injustices perpetrated in the name of science, as Beveridge describes in this volume). Furthermore, there is often a challenge in synching the rhythm and time frame of a research project with the concrete, time-sensitive and ongoing needs of Indigenous organizations and communities, who often need to rely on external consultants. From Dawson's project (as well as others), it seems crucial that good partnerships are based on trust, include bottom-up design and governance structures, and are carried out by interdisciplinary teams to tackle the interconnectedness of issues involved in real life situations.

As mentioned above, one area that remains underdeveloped and unexplored is the strengthening of links between Indigenous groups and engineering, technology developers, and industry. One of the reasons for this could perhaps be the misconception that Inuit are naturally opposed to economic development initiatives. In the case of shipping, a key area of intersection between the shipping industry, regulators, technology developers and communities is the mandate to develop cleaner fuels, engines and ships to reduce greenhouse emissions in support of the United Nations Sustainable Development Goal 13.[22]

There are examples in the Canadian Arctic of technological developments that took into account the input of those that would be most affected by their operations, and the results of such collaborations are often remarkable.[23]

Finally, one of the most important takeaways from Monica's narrative is the idea that the ultimate goal for Inuit is to increase agency over their lives and homelands. Sovereignty may have different meanings, levels, and dimensions, but it ultimately is linked to the right to exercise power over events and decisions that affect one's life and territories. 'To be heard' is by no means an end in itself, but a means towards a much deeper and longer goal. Tangible improvements are connected to an increase of power for those who do not have it, and ultimately to an increase of local and organizational capacity. In other words, intensification of shipping (and of other industrial activities) may be welcomed in the Arctic, if the risks are minimized and if they result in effective improvements of living conditions and opportunities. If those goals are not clearly established and if clear paths for their achievement are not laid out, new developments will likely be resisted by Inuit. Participatory governance approaches that involve Inuit from the start (from the planning phase) are critical for defining sustainable and empowering projects.

With the advances of UNDRIP, the Oceans Protection Plan and the process of reconciliation in Canada, the opportunities for positive changes are real, but clear partnerships where Inuit voices are really taken into account are key for the outcome of future developments. As Monica sums up: "It's all a balance in nature and in our way of life."

---

22   IMO Initial Strategy for the Reduction of Greenhouse Emissions from Ships, IMO Resolution MEPC.304/72, annexed in the *Report of the MEPC on its 72nd Session*, IMO Doc MEPC 72/17/Add.1 (18 May 2018).

23   Katherine Wilson *et al.*, "The Mittimatalik Siku Asijjipallianinga (Sea Ice Climate Atlas): How Inuit Knowledge, Earth Observations, and Sea Ice Charts Can Fill IPCC Climate Knowledge Gaps," *Frontiers in Climate* 3 (2021), https://doi.org/10.3389/fclim.2021.715105; Shari Gearheard *et al.*, "The Igliniit Project: Inuit Hunters Document Life on the Trail to Map and Monitor Arctic Change," *The Canadian Geographer* 55:1 (2011): 42–55.

CHAPTER 3

Shipping in Arctic Marine Ecosystems under Stress: Recognizing and Mitigating the Threats

Warwick F. Vincent, Connie Lovejoy, and Kristin Bartenstein

Abstract

The Arctic Ocean and its adjacent seas have many unique ecological features, including species and food webs that are highly adapted to the cold polar environment. These ecosystems are now under intense pressure from climate change, which is proceeding rapidly at high northern latitudes and acting in concert with other global stressors. The Arctic Ocean ecosystem is therefore in a precarious ecological state and is vulnerable to additional perturbations. Arctic shipping has entered a phase of rapid expansion, and is imposing new threats to the survival and health of Arctic marine life. These threats include potential chemical impacts through discharges and emissions; physical impacts through noise pollution, icebreaking and ship collisions with animals; and biological impacts through the dispersal of invasive species living on ship hulls or in ballast waters. The cold water ecosystems of the Arctic are especially vulnerable to oil pollution that would result from collisions or grounding. There are ways to reduce the risk of catastrophic and cumulative impacts of shipping in the region, building on the Polar Code and with further attention to marine protected areas. Given the precarious state of the Arctic Ocean, all current and future shipping activities need to be closely scrutinized, monitored and regulated.

Keywords

Arctic Ocean – climate change – icebreaker impacts – invasive species – marine pollution – noise pollution – oil pollution – sea ice ecosystems – shipping

1   Introduction

Global climate change is imposing severe stresses on ecosystems throughout the world, and nowhere more so than in Arctic seas and their surrounding lands. Climate warming is amplified at these high northern latitudes and is resulting in rapid changes in the ice regimes that polar marine life depends upon. These changes are also impacting the Indigenous communities that have lived in the region for millennia, and whose traditional cultures are closely linked to the ice and ecosystem health of the Arctic Ocean. Warming temperatures and loss of ice habitats, combined with ocean acidification and contaminant inputs, have moved Arctic marine ecosystems towards a precarious state that is vulnerable to additional stresses.

The ongoing loss of Arctic sea ice has opened up opportunities for new shipping operations in the region, and much greater maritime traffic is projected for the future. Cargo shipping through the Northern Sea Route increased by nearly fourfold since between 2013 and 2018,[1] and is also increasing across the Canadian Arctic.[2] Global warming above 2°C is projected to allow navigability through the Northwest Passage for all vessel types during the ice-free season, and to increase the season length for shipping in the Beaufort Sea region to 100–200 days, rising to 200–300 days at 4°C.[3] Given the uncertainties of the Arctic ice regime, ongoing changes in Arctic ship traffic[4] will be tempered by operational and commercial risks,[5] but further large increases could occur if operators are prepared to risk marginally unsafe conditions.[6]

Although shipping brings socioeconomic benefits including employment opportunities and the transport of people, resources and vital supplies, it also has potentially negative effects on marine ecosystems and the adjacent coastal land-based ecosystems. These include physical impacts, such as noise pollution, icebreaking and collisions with animals, chemical impacts, such as oil pollution, aerosol release and wastewater discharge, and biological impacts, such as the transport of invasive species and disruption of seasonal bird and mammal migrations. In the polar regions, these impacts are amplified by many features that are characteristic of high latitudes, such as persistent cold

1   Malte Humpert, "Russia's Northern Sea Route Sees Record Cargo Volume in 2018," *High North News*, 20 February 2019, https://www.arctictoday.com/russias-northern-sea-route-sees-record -cargo-volume-in-2018/.

2   Jackie Dawson *et al.*, "Temporal and Spatial Patterns of Ship Traffic in the Canadian Arctic from 1990 to 2015," *Arctic* 71 (2018): 15–26, https://doi.org/10.14430/arctic4698. See also Lasserre in this volume.

3   Lawrence R. Mudryk *et al.*, "Impact of 1, 2 and 4° C of Global Warming on Ship Navigation in the Canadian Arctic," *Nature Climate Change* 11 (2021): 673–679, https://doi.org/10.1038 /s41558-021-01087-6.

4   See also Lasserre in this volume.

5   Frédéric Lasserre, "Arctic Shipping: A Contrasted Expansion of a Largely Destinational Market," in *The GlobalArctic Handbook*, eds., Matthias Finger and Lassi Heininen (Berlin: Springer, 2018), 83–100, https://doi.org/10.1007/978-3-319-91995-9_6.

6   Mudryk *et al.* (n 3).

temperatures that limit the break-down of pollutants, the short summer season for peak biological activities, and the reduced species diversity that lessens the resilience to perturbations.

Our aim in this chapter is to review the current state of Arctic Ocean ecosystems and their vulnerability to increased shipping traffic. We first introduce the key features of these ecosystems, including ecological values that make the region of special interest and concern for long-term conservation. We summarize recent observations of rapid change, the projections of future change, and evidence of increasing multiple stresses across the Arctic Ocean and its coastal lands. We then summarize the potential negative effects of shipping, with attention to the particularities of Arctic marine ecosystems, and conclude by identifying mitigation strategies that may allow future shipping developments to proceed carefully, and with reduced risk of catastrophic impacts.

2   Arctic Marine Ecosystems

The Arctic Ocean differs from the rest of the world ocean in many respects, and its unique features deserve special consideration for setting conservation objectives and policies. It is a semi-enclosed ocean surrounded by continental lands, in sharp contrast to the Southern Ocean that surrounds the ice-covered landmass of Antarctica. This means that the Arctic Ocean is strongly influenced by its terrestrial environment, and is sensitive to changes on land as well as to those offshore. This semi-isolated nature has also allowed the basin to develop its own unique ecosystems, with many species that are found only within the Arctic Ocean. These organisms are highly adapted to the conditions of persistent ice, cold temperatures and strong seasonal fluctuations, from continuous light in summer to continuous darkness in winter. Recent molecular studies have shown that even at the microscopic level, the Arctic Ocean contains many unique planktonic species[7] organized into networks of biological interactions that are distinct from elsewhere in the world ocean.[8] As a result of this unique ecology, perturbations of species or biological communities in

7   Connie Lovejoy *et al.*, "Plankton," in *State of the Arctic Marine Biodiversity Report*, CAFF (Akureyri: Conservation of Arctic Flora and Fauna (CAFF) International Secretariat, 2017), 63–83, https://oaarchive.arctic-council.org/bitstream/handle/11374/1945/SAMBR_Scientific _report_2017_FINAL_LR.pdf?sequence=1.
8   Samuel Chaffron *et al.*, "Environmental Vulnerability of the Global Ocean Epipelagic Plankton Community Interactome," *Science Advances* 7 (2021): eabg1921, https://doi.org/10.1126/sciadv .abg1921.

the Arctic Ocean may cause irreplaceable losses from the biosphere, and any such impacts must be considered a threat to global as well as local biodiversity.

Arctic seas are not completely isolated from the world ocean, but are connected to the Pacific Ocean via Bering Strait and to the Atlantic Ocean via the eastern Fram Strait and the Barents Sea. These inflow gateways allow the transport of heat, nutrients and southern species into the Arctic, and provide conduits for animal migration and access points for shipping. Ice and water are circulated within the Arctic Ocean via large-scale transport processes, notably the Beaufort Gyre and the Transpolar Drift.[9] This means that pollution resulting from a discharge or accident will not remain localized, but can be rapidly transferred from one region to another, including across national boundaries.

Sea ice is an important feature of both the north and south polar oceans, and in the Arctic Ocean can be seasonal first year ice or persist throughout the year as multiyear and mobile pack ice. This contrasts with the Southern Ocean, where ice forms over winter and then melts out almost completely each summer. This Antarctic annual sea ice is on average thinner than the Arctic multiyear sea ice. Unlike the South Polar Region, Arctic ice-covered seas extend all the way to the pole, and experience longer periods of continuous light and continuous darkness at these higher latitudes. In both oceans, the seawater remains at near-zero temperatures throughout the year, although there may be localized surface warming in coastal regions of the Arctic influenced by freshwater inflows over the shallow continental shelves.

The numerous riverine inputs to the Arctic Ocean, including the large Arctic rivers of Russia and the Mackenzie River in Canada, are another feature that distinguishes this marine environment from not only Antarctica, but also from all other oceans. Arctic seas account for only 1 percent of the total volume of the world ocean, yet they receive 10 percent of the total runoff of the world.[10] This results in an unusually strong density layering of the ocean that shifts much of the biological production to lower, more nutrient-rich depths, below the freshwater-influenced surface layer. The sea ice itself contains communities of microscopic algae that live in the salt-water (brine) channels of the ice. This is a rich food source for animals that live in the surface waters of the ocean, as well as for benthic (bottom-dwelling) animals such as scallops and

9   Mary-Louise Timmermans and John Marshall, "Understanding Arctic Ocean Circulation: A Review of Ocean Dynamics in a Changing Climate," *Journal of Geophysical Research: Oceans* 125 (2020): 1031–1032, https://doi.org/10.1029/2018JC014378.

10   Richard B. Lammers *et al.*, "Assessment of Contemporary Arctic River Runoff Based on Observational Discharge Records," *Journal of Geophysical Research: Atmospheres* 106 (2001): 3321–3334, https://doi.org/10.1029/2000JD900444.

sea urchins that feed on the algae (especially diatoms) that are released from the melting ice and sink to the seafloor.

Shallow benthic environments are especially important in the Arctic Ocean because of its vast areas of coastal shelves with depths less than a few hundred metres,[11] and these are habitats for many species. The region also contains a myriad of islands, including the Canadian Arctic Archipelago, and the total coastline of the Arctic is exceptionally long. Animals living along the coast, therefore play a major role in Arctic marine ecology, and provide food for Indigenous communities, such as Inuit, who have lived in this coastal environment for millennia. The rivers transport nutrients for plankton living in the Arctic Ocean, and although coastal erosion can bring in additional nutrients, the resultant higher sediment inputs can affect marine life adversely. All of these features draw attention to the distinct nature of the Arctic Ocean ecosystem, and the close association of biological communities, sea ice and persistent cold water temperatures.

Another unique feature of the Arctic Ocean is its soundscape.[12] The waters are isolated from surface wind and wave effects by the persistent layer of sea ice, and Arctic marine animals have evolved in an exceptionally quiet environment relative to elsewhere in the world ocean. Ambient noise levels beneath the ice are low during most of the year, but with periods of loud sounds during sea ice fracturing and break-up.[13] Additionally, the cold, lower salinity surface waters of the Arctic Ocean act as an acoustic duct or channel, bounded by the sea ice at the top and denser seawater below, and sound can travel unusual distances of tens to hundreds of kilometres through this channel. Arctic marine animals such as whales, seals and fish that use sound for navigation, reproductive behaviour and prey detection are adapted to low background noise levels, and a reliance on biological sound cues that are all the more important in the continuous darkness of winter and beneath the thick, light-shading snow and ice in other seasons.

3   Global Stressors

Multiple stressors that are global in origin are now acting on all ecosystems throughout the Arctic. The most severe of these is climate change because of its greater magnitude at high northern latitudes, and its wide range of impacts

---

11   Martin Jakobsson, "Hypsometry and Volume of the Arctic Ocean and its Constituent Seas," *Geochemistry, Geophysics, Geosystems* 3 (2002), https://doi.org/10.1029/2001GC000302.

12   William D. Halliday, Matthew K. Pine and Stephen J. Insley, "Underwater Noise and Arctic Marine Mammals: Review and Policy Recommendations," *Environmental Reviews* 28:4 (2020): 438–448, https://doi.org/10.1139/er-2019-0033.

13   Id., 439.

on ice-dependent ecosystems. Arctic amplification of warming is caused by a number of feedback effects,[14] and these will continue to result in much greater temperature increases in the North than at lower latitudes. Climate models indicate that a 2°C rise in mean annual global temperatures by 2100 at a global scale would result in a 4 to 7°C rise in Arctic temperatures (with large differences among different locations), while a global increase of 3°C would translate to 7 to 11°C in the Arctic (mean night-time temperatures).[15] Snow and ice are important features of the Arctic, and small increases in temperature can result in thawing and melting, thereby causing large-scale physical changes in the environment, with wide-ranging impacts on northern ecosystems and the Indigenous communities that depend upon them.[16] In addition to this ongoing climate perturbation, Arctic Ocean ecosystems are experiencing large increases in ambient ultraviolet (UV) radiation, chemical effects of acidification, and a continuing influx of pollutants, including from world ocean currents and long-range atmospheric transport.

Climate warming imposes a stress on Arctic marine ecosystems in five different but interrelated ways: loss of ice habitats, increased variability of ice conditions, changes in water temperature and salinity, changes in inflows and currents, and facilitation of new species invasions and replacement. Ice loss is the most conspicuous of these changes, and in some locations is resulting in rapid contraction or even complete loss of certain habitat types. These changes have been strikingly apparent in the coastal margin along northern Ellesmere Island and Greenland, which contains the thickest, oldest sea ice of the Arctic Ocean. This wide marginal zone has been dubbed the Last Ice Area and is considered an ultimate refuge for marine ice-dependent species.[17] However, the Arctic ice shelves, ancient floating ice sheets up to 100-m thick and attached to land, have undergone rapid collapse over the last few decades, with associated loss of some ecosystem types.[18] Other thick ice features have also contracted

14   Marika M. Holland and Cecilia M. Bitz, "Polar Amplification of Climate Change in Coupled Models," *Climate Dynamics* 21 (2003): 221–232, doi: 10.1007/s00382-003-0332-6.

15   IPCC, *Special Report on Global Warming of 1.5°C* (SR15) (Geneva: Intergovernmental Panel on Climate Change (IPCC), World Meteorological Organization, 2018), retrieved from https://www.ipcc.ch/sr15/.

16   Warwick F. Vincent, "Arctic climate Change: Local Impacts, Global Consequences, and Policy Implications," in *The Palgrave Handbook of Arctic Policy and Politics*, eds., Ken S. Coates and Carin Holroyd (UK: Palgrave Macmillan, 2020), 507–526, doi:10.1007/978-3-030-20557-7_31.

17   Robert Newton, Stephanie Pfirman, L. Bruno Tremblay and Patricia DeRepentigny, "Defining the 'Ice Shed' of the Arctic Ocean's Last Ice Area and Its Future Evolution," *Earth's Future* 9 (2021): e2021EF001988, https://doi.org/10.1029/2021EF001988.

18   Warwick F. Vincent and Derek Mueller, "Witnessing Ice Habitat Collapse in the Arctic," *Science* 370 (2020): 1031–1032, https://doi.org/10.1126/science.abe4491.

rapidly in this area, including 90 percent loss of multiyear land-fast sea ice, some of it over 50 years old,[19] and 85 percent loss of floating glacier tongues.[20] For the Arctic Ocean as a whole, the ice pack has greatly contracted in area and become much thinner, with much of the multiyear ice replaced by annual sea ice. For late summer (September) over the period 1979 to 2020, this has resulted in 48 percent reduction in sea ice area and 77 percent reduction in sea ice volume.[21] Ongoing contraction is expected over the course of this century, however, renewed sea ice growth would occur rapidly in response to greenhouse gas reductions.[22]

Arctic sea ice is the habitat for a variety of highly adapted species, from microbes to zooplankton, fish and mammals.[23] The ongoing attrition of this habitat is likely to impose unusual stresses on the biota at all levels in the food chain, and will impair many ecosystem services.[24] An ecological risk analysis of the eleven marine mammals that occur in Arctic seas has shown that three species are especially vulnerable to sea ice change: hooded seals, narwhals and polar bears.[25] Polar bears in particular have high metabolic rates and high energetic costs for survival and reproduction, and therefore depend on an energy-rich diet. They may die by starvation if they are forced to swim over large distances rather than walking on sea ice to find their preferred diet of seals, or if they shift to coastal land-based foods, which are of much lower energy content.[26] The low genetic diversity of polar bears may also limit their ability to adapt to change.[27]

---

19   Sierra Pope, Luke Copland and Derek Mueller, "Loss of Multiyear Landfast Sea Ice from Yelverton Bay, Ellesmere Island, Nunavut, Canada," *Arctic, Antarctic, and Alpine Research* 44 (2012): 210–221, https://doi.org/10.1657/1938-4246-44.2.210.

20   Adrienne White and Luke Copland, "Area Change of Glaciers across Northern Ellesmere Island, Nunavut, between ~1999 and ~2015," *Journal of Glaciology* 64 (2018): 609–623, doi: 10.1017/jog.2018.49.

21   David Docquier and Torben Koenigk, "A Review of Interactions between Ocean Heat Transport and Arctic Sea Ice," *Environmental Research Letters* 16 (2021): 123002, https://doi.org/10.1088/1748-9326/ac30be.

22   Newton, Pfirman, Tremblay and DeRepentigny. (n 17).

23   David N. Thomas (ed.), *Sea Ice*, 3rd ed. (Chichester: John Wiley & Sons Ltd, 2017).

24   Nadja S. Steiner *et al.*, "Climate Change Impacts on Sea-Ice Ecosystems and Associated Ecosystem Services," *Elementa Science of the Anthropocene* 9 (2021): 00007, https://doi.org/10.1525/elementa.2021.00007.

25   Kristin L. Laidre *et al.*, "Quantifying the Sensitivity of Arctic Marine Mammals to Climate-induced Habitat Change," *Ecological Applications* 18 (2008): S97–S125, https://doi.org/10.1890/06-0546.1.

26   Anthony M. Pagano and Terrie M. Williams, "Physiological Consequences of Arctic Sea Ice Loss on Large Marine Carnivores: Unique Responses by Polar Bears and Narwhals," *Journal of Experimental Biology* 224 (2021): jeb228049, https://doi.org/10.1242/jeb.228049.

27   Id.

In the recent past, thick multiyear sea ice buffered the natural variations in climate and maintained a continuity of ice cover, even in the warmest years. With the shift to annual ice that is quicker to melt and reform, the extent of open water is now much more variable from year-to-year, and this variability is increasing, along with the average duration of open water.[28] In addition, and as a further result of global change, the Arctic climate is becoming more variable, with episodes of extreme warming becoming more frequent. In winter this warming can result in added snow fall, which limits light penetration through first year ice, affecting both sea ice algae and animals dependent upon early spring production. This unpredictability from year-to-year may impair the synchronization between marine food web levels such as ice-associated algae and the zooplankton reproduction cycle.[29] Other movements of animals are tightly coupled at the edge of the sea ice, in the marginal ice zone. More variable conditions can create stress for marine mammals, such as narwhals that become trapped in open water, with new ice blocking their exit.[30]

In most parts of the Arctic Ocean, the sea water remains cold throughout the year, and Arctic marine biota are therefore adapted to optimal growth and reproduction at low temperatures. For example, the most abundant photosynthetic cells in the Arctic Ocean plankton, minute green algae, grow rapidly at near-zero temperatures and have impaired growth above 6°C.[31] Warming of Arctic seas may impose a stress on these organisms at the base of the food web, and favour invading species from the south. Modelling of Arctic cod based on its physiological temperature limits indicated that there could be a 17 percent decrease in Arctic cod populations in the western Canadian Arctic over the course of this century caused by thermal stress effects.[32] Experimental studies on the endemic Arctic seaweed (kelp) *Laminaria solidungula* indicate

---

28   Mathieu Ardyna and Kevin Robert Arrigo, "Phytoplankton Dynamics in a Changing Arctic Ocean," *Nature Climate Change* 10 (2020): 892–903, https://doi.org/10.1038/s41558-020 -0905-y.

29   Thibaud Dezutter *et al.*, "Mismatch between Microalgae and Herbivorous Copepods Due to the Record Sea Ice Minimum Extent of 2012 and the Late Sea Ice Break-up of 2013 in the Beaufort Sea," *Progress in Oceanography* 173 (2019): 66–77, https://doi.org/10.1016/j .pocean.2019.02.008.

30   Pagano and Williams (n 26).

31   Connie Lovejoy, Ramon Massana and Carlos Pedrós-Alió, "Diversity and Distribution of Marine Microbial Eukaryotes in the Arctic Ocean and Adjacent Seas," *Applied and Environmental Microbiology* 72 (2006): 3085–3095, https://doi.org/10.1128/AEM.72.5.3085 -3095.2006.

32   Nadja S. Steiner *et al.*, "Impacts of the Changing Ocean-Sea Ice System on the Key Forage Fish Arctic Cod (*Boreogadus saida*) and Subsistence Fisheries in the Western Canadian Arctic—Evaluating Linked Climate, Ecosystem and Economic (CEE) Models," *Frontiers in Marine Science* 6 (2019): 179, https://doi.org/10.3389/fmars.2019.00179.

that this important species is physiologically stressed by rising temperature and decreasing salinity, and that this combination of stresses could drive it to local extinction in the future.[33] Other Arctic species may be more resilient to such changes, and may even become more abundant with increasing light and warming, for example, crustose coralline algae in subtidal seas.[34]

The inflows and circulation regimes of the Arctic Ocean are changing through several factors driven by global climate change. Precipitation is increasing and this is resulting in more freshwater runoff into the Arctic Ocean, with large ongoing changes expected in the near future.[35] Through increasing river flow and sea ice melt, the Arctic Ocean is freshening faster than other parts of the ocean. Changes in salinity also affect the vertical structure of the water column, favouring a shift to smaller size phytoplankton that thrive at lower nutrient levels.[36] This change from more diatom-dominated communities to smaller algae alters food web dynamics, as large Arctic copepods are dependent on the larger algal species. The loss of these large lipid-rich Arctic copepods (*Calanus glacialis*) would impair Arctic cod (*Boreogadus saida*), which are the primary food source for seals.[37] It may be noteworthy that decreasing salinity results in lower density waters that directly affect ship buoyancy; this raises the issue of the need for specific Arctic load lines to ensure safe freeboard.[38]

Thinner sea ice means that it is more mobile and that ice transport rates are accelerating. In addition, there is evidence pointing to recent increases in the influx of Atlantic water, bringing in more heat as well as new biota. This 'Atlantification' of the Arctic Ocean may be to the benefit of more southern species, including zooplankton. A small, boreal copepod species (*Calanus finmarchicus*) is found in Atlantic waters, but appears to be gaining prominence further

33   Nora Diehl, Ulf Karsten and Kai Bischof, "Impacts of Combined Temperature and Salinity Stress on the Endemic Arctic Brown Seaweed *Laminaria solidungula* J. Agardh," *Polar Biology* 43 (2020): 647–656, https://doi.org/10.1007/s00300-020-02668-5.

34   Branwen Williams *et al.*, "Arctic Crustose Coralline Alga Resilient to Recent Environmental Change," *Limnology and Oceanography* 66 (2021): S246–S258. https://doi.org/10.1002/lno.11640.

35   Michelle R. McCrystall *et al.*, "New Climate Models Reveal Faster and Larger Increases in Arctic Precipitation than Previously Projected," *Nature Communications* 12 (2021): 6765, https://doi.org/10.1038/s41467-021-27031-y.

36   William K.W. Li, Fiona A. McLaughlin, Connie Lovejoy and Eddy C. Carmack, "Smallest Algae Thrive as the Arctic Ocean Freshens," *Science* 326 (2009): 539–539, https://doi.org/10.1126/science.1179798.

37   Caroline Bouchard and Louis Fortier, "The Importance of *Calanus glacialis* for the Feeding Success of Young Polar Cod: A Circumpolar Synthesis," *Polar Biology* 43 (2020): 1095–1107, https://doi.org/10.1007/s00300-020-02643-0.

38   Aldo Chircop *et al.*, "Polar Load Lines for Maritime Safety: A Neglected Issue in the International Regulation of Navigation and Shipping in Arctic Waters?," *CMI Yearbook* (2014): 345–356.

northwards, close to the ice edge in Fram Strait[39] and potentially competing with the key species *C. glacialis*, to the detriment of the extant Arctic Ocean food web. *C. finmarchicus* is but one of several marine species that may profit from global climate change and the increased opportunities for invasion and establishment in the Arctic basin. For example, there has been a rise in killer whale sightings in the region, which may reflect the longer open water conditions, among other factors. Population increases of this top predator are likely to continue in the future, which would add further pressure on narwhal populations.[40] Killer whales can also attack the young of bowhead whales, which are in greater danger of coming into contact with this predator as their ice refuge shrinks.[41]

UV radiation is another potential stress on marine food webs because of its many effects on biological processes, ranging from cellular mutagenesis to physiological and life cycle impacts. The banning of chlorofluorocarbons, brought about by the 1985 Vienna Convention for the Protection of the Ozone Layer and its 1987 Montreal Protocol on Substances that Deplete the Ozone Layer,[42] has slowed the loss of stratospheric ozone that acts as a UV shield for Earth; however, Arctic ozone depletion events are still recorded, including record losses in spring of 2020.[43] In addition, the loss of sea ice is resulting in a sudden increase in UV exposure to underwater communities that have been shaded in the past.

Many contaminants are concentrated at high latitudes because of long-range transport and condensation processes. The global use of persistent organic pollutants (POPs) is now reduced as a result of international agreements, including the 1979 Convention on Long-range Transboundary Air Pollution and its 1998 Protocol to the 1979 Convention on Long-Range Transboundary Air Pollution on Persistent Organic Pollutants and the 2001 Stockholm Convention on

39   Geraint A. Tarling *et al.*, "Can a Key Boreal *Calanus* Copepod Species Now Complete Its Life-cycle in the Arctic? Evidence and Implications for Arctic Food-webs," *Ambio* 51 (2022): 333–344, https://doi.org/10.1007/s13280-021-01667-y.

40   Kyle John Lefort *et al.*, "A Review of Canadian Arctic Killer Whale (*Orcinus orca*) Ecology," *Canadian Journal of Zoology* 98 (2020): 245–253, https://doi.org/10.1139/cjz-2019-0207.

41   Cory J.D. Matthews, Greg A. Breed, Bernard LeBlanc and Steven H. Ferguson, "Killer Whale Presence Drives Bowhead Whale Selection for Sea Ice in Arctic Seascapes of Fear," *Proceedings of the National Academy of Sciences of the United States of America* 117 (2020): 6590–6598, https://doi.org/10.1073/pnas.1911761117.

42   Vienna Convention for the Protection of the Ozone Layer, 22 March 1985 (in force 22 September 1988), 1513 *UNTS* 293; Montreal Protocol on Substances that Deplete the Ozone Layer, 16 September 1987 (in force 1 January 1989), 1522 *UNTS* 3 (as amended).

43   Boyan Petkov *et al.*, "The 2020 Arctic Ozone Depletion and Signs of Its Effect on the Ozone Column at Lower Latitudes," *Bulletin of Atmospheric Science and Technology* 2 (2021): 8, https://doi.org/10.1007/s42865-021-00040-x.

Persistent Organic Pollutants.[44] However, POPs are still in evidence in the Arctic, including in apex predators, such as polar bears.[45] Emerging contaminants are rapidly transported to the Arctic; for example, perfluorinated chemicals have been detected in the anadromous fish species *Salvelinus alpinus* (Arctic char), even in the northernmost lakes of the Canadian High Arctic that connect to the sea.[46] Other contaminants are continuing to rise, including mercury. This is in part due to the mobilization of heavy metals from thawing permafrost landscapes[47] and transport by rivers into the Arctic Ocean, which also transport pollutants over long distances from human activities in the South. Plastic litter is now appearing in the Arctic Ocean in large quantities, and is an indicator of more general pollution. The area has become a global accumulation site for plastic particles, which are brought in by ocean circulation pathways.[48] For example, there are large influxes of polyester fibres, a major component of microplastics pollution, into the Arctic basin via inflowing currents from the Atlantic Ocean.[49] Ingested plastics have now been detected in Arctic marine organisms at almost all levels of the food web.[50]

Arctic seas are also increasingly subject to the rapidly increasing stress of acidification, and more so than anywhere else in the world ocean. Ocean acidification refers to the decrease in pH of seawater as it absorbs more carbon dioxide because of the rising concentrations in the atmosphere. This process is of particular concern for marine biota that precipitate calcium carbonates to form part of

---

44 Convention on Long-range Transboundary Air Pollution, 13 November 1979 (in force 16 March 1983), 1302 *UNTS* 217; Protocol to the 1979 Convention on Long-Range Transboundary Air Pollution on Persistent Organic Pollutants, 24 June 1998 (in force 23 October 2003), 2230 *UNTS* 79 (as amended); Stockholm Convention on Persistent Organic Pollutants, 22 May 2001 (in force 17 May 2004), 2256 *UNTS* 119 (as amended).

45 Heli Routti *et al.*, "State of Knowledge on Current Exposure, Fate and Potential Health Effects of Contaminants in Polar Bears from the Circumpolar Arctic," *Science of the Total Environment* 664 (2019): 1063–1083, https://doi.org/10.1016/j.scitotenv.2019.02.030.

46 Julie Veillette *et al.*, "Perfluorinated Chemicals in Meromictic Lakes on the Northern Coast of Ellesmere Island, High Arctic Canada," *Arctic* 65 (2012): 245–256, https://journalhosting .ucalgary.ca/index.php/arctic/article/view/67260/51170.

47 Kimberley Miner *et al.*, "Emergent Biogeochemical Risks from Arctic Permafrost Degradation," *Nature Climate Change* 11 (2021): 809–819, https://doi.org/10.1038/s41558-021-01162-y.

48 Andrés Cózar *et al.*, "The Arctic Ocean as a Dead End for Floating Plastics in the North Atlantic Branch of the Thermohaline Circulation," *Science Advances* 3 (2017): e1600582, https://doi.org/10.1126/sciadv.1600582.

49 Peter S. Ross *et al.*, "Pervasive Distribution of Polyester Fibres in the Arctic Ocean is Driven by Atlantic Inputs," *Nature Communications* 12 (2021): 106, https://doi.org/10.1038/s41467 -020-20347-1.

50 France Collard and Amalie Ask, "Plastic Ingestion by Arctic Fauna: A Review," *Science of the Total Environment* 786 (2021): 147462, https://doi.org/10.1016/j.scitotenv.2021.147462.

their biological structure, notably shellfish, pteropods ('sea butterflies') and certain corals. Increased acidification causes these structures to not form properly or to even dissolve, impairing survival, growth and reproduction. The Arctic Ocean is especially prone to acidification because its dissolved carbonate is naturally low, due to its cold temperature and dilution by the large river inflows. Furthermore, the solubility of gases such as carbon dioxide increases with decreasing temperature; consequently, the cold polar oceans have the greatest absorption capacity for this greenhouse gas. The alarming potential for major changes in pH was first signaled more than a decade ago,[51] and current models show that under a business as usual scenario, both mineral forms of calcium carbonate (aragonite and the more stable calcite) would be soluble by the end of this century,[52] posing an environmental threat for some Arctic species.

Climate change, sea ice loss, contaminants and food web perturbation are all of vital concern to the Indigenous communities that live at the Arctic coast in close association with the marine environment.[53] In their assessment of Arctic shipping in the context of these global changes, the Inuit Circumpolar Council identified a wide range of issues, especially those relating to the health of marine ecosystems that Inuit depend upon for traditional food supplies, culture and general well-being.[54]

4   Ecological Consequences of Arctic Shipping

The impacts of shipping on marine life occur at multiple levels, from effects on individuals and populations, to perturbation of biological communities, food webs and ecosystems. In Canada, the federal Department of Fisheries and Oceans has developed a detailed framework to assess these impacts by way of 'Pathway of Effects' (PoE) conceptual models.[55] These involve identifying

51   Marco Steinacher *et al.*, "Imminent Ocean Acidification in the Arctic Projected with the NCAR Global Coupled Carbon Cycle-Climate Model," *Biogeosciences* 6 (2009): 515–533, https://doi.org/10.5194/bg-6-515-2009.

52   Jens Terhaar, Olivier Torres, Thimothée Bourgeois and Lester Kwiatkowski, "Arctic Ocean Acidification Over the 21st Century Co-driven by Anthropogenic Carbon Increases and Freshening in the CMIP6 Model Ensemble," *Biogeosciences* 18 (2021): 2221–2240, https://doi.org/10.5194/bg-18-2221-2021.

53   See chapters by Ell-Kanayuk and Aporta, and Beveridge in this volume.

54   Inuit Circumpolar Council (ICC), *The Sea Ice Never Stops: Circumpolar Inuit Reflections on Sea Ice Use and Shipping in Inuit Nunaat* (Ottawa: Inuit Circumpolar Council, 2014), https://oaarchive.arctic-council.org/handle/11374/410.

55   Department of Fisheries and Oceans, *Science Advice for Pathways of Effects for Marine Shipping in Canada: Biological and Ecological Effects*, Canadian Science Advisory Secretariat,

the known linkages between shipping activities, stressors and effects, and then assessing the ecological risk associated with these specific pathways relative to the conservation goals within a particular area. Stressors that would be relevant to such an assessment, can be separated into three categories: chemical, physical and biological.

4.1   *Chemical Pollution*

The most devastating effects of shipping on Arctic Ocean ecosystems would be through oil pollution, resulting, for example, from vessel collisions or grounding. These have the potential to cause serious impacts anywhere in the world, but the consequences for northern marine environments are worsened by several factors that are specific to the Arctic and to cold polar seas. The remoteness of the Arctic Ocean and the sparse distribution of land-based infrastructure mean that clean-up operations would be slow to mobilize and difficult to ramp up, with activities further constrained by the severe weather conditions at high latitudes. Microbes that degrade hydrocarbons do occur naturally in the polar oceans, but incubation experiments with Arctic seawater show that their degradation rates are extremely slow at the cold ambient temperatures.[56] Similarly, evaporation rates are slow in the cold, and the ocean currents and increasingly mobile sea ice would likely disperse the oil spills over large areas and extensive tracts of coastline. Finally, the specialized food webs of the Arctic Ocean, already under stress, have limited resilience to chemical pollution and would likely collapse in the face of this type of catastrophic event.

The impacts of oil pollution can persist well into the future. When the oil tanker TV *Exxon Valdez* ran aground in subarctic Prince William Sound, Alaska, in 1989, the resultant oil pollution caused the death of 250,000 seabirds, thousands of marine mammals and millions of fish eggs. In addition to these acute impacts, there were chronic effects on the coastal ecosystem. A pod of killer whales that were heavily impacted will likely never recover, and 27 years later, patches of oil were still found on the beaches and are likely to persist for decades longer.[57] To assess the socioeconomic impacts of a potential oil

---

National Capital Region, Science Advisory Report 2020/030 (2020), https://waves-vagues .dfo-mpo.gc.ca/Library/4090278x.pdf.

56   Ana Gomes *et al.*, "Biodegradation of Water-accommodated Aromatic Oil Compounds in Arctic Seawater at 0°C," *Chemosphere* 286 (2022): 131751, https://doi.org/10.1016/j .chemosphere.2021.131751.

57   Mace G. Barron, Deborah N. Vivian, Ron A. Heintz and Un Hyuk Yim, "Long-term Ecological Impacts from Oil Spills: Comparison of *Exxon Valdez*, *Hebei Spirit*, and *Deepwater Horizon*," *Environmental Science & Technology* 54 (2020): 6456–6467, https:// doi.org/10.1021/acs.est.9b05020.

spill on a community in the Canadian Arctic, a recent study simulated the conditions of an *Exxon Valdez* spill in the Rankin Inlet region and asked a broad range of respondents with different backgrounds and expertise to evaluate this scenario.[58] The simulation indicated that social as well as financial costs would increase through time over several years associated with the impacts on hunting, the local economy, culture and social activities, with lasting psychological effects and legal costs.

In regular shipping operations, chemical pollution can occur from multiple types of discharges from underway or anchored vessels, including antifouling substances, ballast water, black water, grey water, tank cleaning, cooling water, scrubber water, bilge water, propeller shaft lubricants, solid waste and atmospheric pollution.[59] Atmospheric releases from ships include black carbon (soot) and other particles that absorb light and accelerate the melting of snow and ice that they settle upon, along with sulphur and nitrogen oxides that are biologically and chemically active. A study in a remote Svalbard fjord showed that the presence of tourist ships increased fine particle concentrations in the local atmosphere by up to 81 percent, and the observations implied that large areas of the Svalbard archipelago already experience some chemical influence from shipping.[60] A model analysis for the Canadian Arctic indicated that the effects of shipping are currently low, but that further shipping expansion up to the year 2030 could increase total deposition of pollutants by 20 percent for sulphur, 50 percent for nitrogen and up to 30 percent for black carbon.[61] The deposition of ship-derived acidic sulphur and nitrogen oxides may also influence Arctic freshwater and terrestrial ecosystems. In a chemical study of more than 1,000 Arctic Canadian lakes, a high percentage were found to be sensitive to acid deposition, which would impair their habitat quality for Arctic char.[62]

58   Mawuli Afenyo, Adolf K.Y. Ng and Changmin Jiang, "A Multiperiod Model for Assessing the Socioeconomic Impacts of Oil Spills during Arctic Shipping," *Risk Analysis* 42:3 (2022), https://doi.org/10.1111/risa.13773.

59   See Figure 2 in Jana Moldanová *et al.*, "Framework for the Environmental Impact Assessment of Operational Shipping," *Ambio* 51 (2022): 754–769, https://doi.org/10.1007/s13280 -021-01597-9.

60   Sabine Eckhardt *et al.*, "The Influence of Cruise Ship Emissions on Air Pollution in Svalbard–A Harbinger of a More Polluted Arctic?," *Atmospheric Chemistry and Physics* 13 (2013): 8401–8409, https://doi.org/10.5194/acp-13-8401-2013.

61   Wanmin Gong *et al.*, "Assessing the Impact of Shipping Emissions on Air Pollution in the Canadian Arctic and Northern Regions: Current and Future Modelled Scenarios," *Atmospheric Chemistry and Physics* 18 (2018): 16653–16687, https://doi.org/10.5194/acp-18 -16653-2018.

62   Tanner Liang and Julian Aherne, "Critical Loads of Acidity and Exceedances for 1138 Lakes and Ponds in the Canadian Arctic," *Science of the Total Environment* 652 (2019): 1424–1434, https://doi.org/10.1016/j.scitotenv.2018.10.330.

4.2   *Physical Stressors*

Noise pollution by ships has become an ecological threat of increasing concern throughout the world ocean,[63] and although much of the Arctic Ocean is acoustically quiet, ship noise represents a new intrusion. Arctic marine animals are known to be sensitive to noise, and ship noise pollution is already rising to levels that may be causing stress. Narwhals are especially sensitive, with reactions up to 40 km distant from a ship and cessation of foraging at distances of 7–8 km.[64] A recent analysis has identified noise risk hotspots at the eastern end of the Northwest Passage where there is a combination of elevated shipping noise and high population densities of narwhals and seabirds.[65]

Ice integrity is critical for certain ecosystem processes in the Arctic, and the timing and magnitude of icebreaker shipping activities are therefore of concern. For example, terrestrial animal migration in the Canadian Arctic Archipelago is important for genetic exchange and for access to seasonal food resources.[66] The rupture of ice bridges, used by migrating animals and already weakened by climate warming, could have lasting impacts on animal populations. Surveys in the south central part of the Archipelago over the period 1977–1980 identified 73 crossing sites on sea ice for caribou. The study concluded that ship tracks through the ice would severely impede migration, and that the "the ice shelf and the ice-block rubble pushed-up along the edges of the track could be a death-trap" for caribou on the ice.[67] In the Last Ice Area at the top of Canada, the ice is retained by an ice arch that forms between Ellesmere Island and Greenland. This arch appears to be weakening as a consequence of climate change,[68] and extensive icebreaker activities in this area could threaten the integrity of this important conservation area.

---

63   Carlos M. Duarte *et al.*, "The Soundscape of the Anthropocene Ocean," *Science* 371 (2021): eaba4658, https://doi.org/10.1126/science.aba4658.

64   Outi M. Tervo *et al.*, "Narwhals React to Ship Noise and Airgun Pulses Embedded in Background Noise," *Biology Letters* 17 (2021): 20210220, https://doi.org/10.1098/rsbl.2021.0220.

65   William D. Halliday *et al.*, "Vessel Risks to Marine Wildlife in the Tallurutiup Imanga National Marine Conservation Area and the Eastern Entrance to the Northwest Passage," *Environmental Science & Policy* 127 (2022): 181–195, https://doi.org/10.1016/j.envsci.2021.10.026.

66   For Inuit, ice is connecting people, animals, land and sea, and as such is critical to their way of life and culture; see Claudio Aporta, Stephanie C. Kane and Aldo Chircop, "Shipping Corridors Through the Inuit Homeland," *Limn* 10 (Chokepoints) (2018), https://limn.it/articles/shipping-corridors-through-the-inuit-homeland/.

67   Frank L. Miller, Samuel J. Barry and Wendy A. Calvert, "Sea-ice Crossings by Caribou in the South-central Canadian Arctic Archipelago and Their Ecological Importance," *Rangifer* 16 (2005): 77–88, https://doi.org/10.7557/2.25.4.1773.

68   G.W. Kent Moore *et al.*, "Anomalous Collapses of Nares Strait Ice Arches Leads to Enhanced Export of Arctic Sea Ice," *Nature Communications* 12 (2021): 1, https://doi.org/10.1038/s41467-020-20314-w.

Finally, collisions with marine animals are unlikely events, but the probability increases with increasing ship traffic, and incidents have been reported for dozens of species throughout the world.[69] Some Arctic animals may be especially susceptible. In an analysis of bowhead whales harvested in Alaska from the Bering-Chukchi-Beaufort Seas population, about 1 percent showed scars from ship collisions[70] and even sublethal strikes increase the stress on animals that are contending with multiple other pressures. In a vulnerability assessment of 80 subpopulations of seven Arctic marine mammals in the Northern Sea Route and the Northwest Passage, more than half were exposed to open water vessel routes, with narwhals the most vulnerable given their high sensitivity and exposure.[71]

4.3   *Biological Effects*

Ships are well known vectors for the transfer of new species into marine ecosystems, often with severe ecological and economic consequences. In the Arctic, of 54 known species invasions, 39 percent could be attributed to ships, via either ballast water or by fouling of the ship hull.[72] Under the 2004 International Convention for the Control and Management of Ship's Ballast Water and Sediments, ships are required to exchange their ballast waters at sea to avoid biological contamination of ports and coastal areas,[73] but modelling of ballast

69   Renée P. Schoeman, Claire Patterson-Abrolat and Stephanie Plön, "A Global Review of Vessel Collisions with Marine Animals," *Frontiers in Marine Science* 7 (2020): 292, https://doi.org/10.3389/fmars.2020.00292.

70   John C. George *et al.*, "Frequency of Killer Whale (*Orcinus orca*) Attacks and Ship Collisions Based on Scarring on Bowhead Whales (*Balaena mysticetus*) of the Bering-Chukchi -Beaufort Seas Stock," *Arctic* 47 (1994): 247–255, https://cdm.ucalgary.ca/index.php/arctic /article/download/64350/48285.

71   Donna D.W. Hauser, Kristin L. Laidre and Harry L. Stern, "Vulnerability of Arctic Marine Mammals to Vessel Traffic in the Increasingly Ice-free Northwest Passage and Northern Sea Route," *Proceedings of the National Academy of Science of the United States of America* 115 (2018): 7617–7622, https://doi.org/10.1073/pnas.1803543115.

72   Farrah T. Chan *et al.*, "Climate Change Opens New Frontiers for Marine Species in the Arctic: Current Trends and Future Invasion Risks," *Global Change Biology* 25 (2019): 25–38, https://doi.org/10.1111/gcb.14469.

73   Adopted 13 February 2004 (in force 8 September 2017), 3282 *UNTS*, authentic text at https://treaties.un.org/doc/Publication/UNTS/No%20Volume/55544/Part/I-55544 -080000028053b465.pdf, in particular Annex, Regulation B-4. In addition, according to Part II-A, 4.1 of the International Code for Ships Operating in Polar Waters (Polar Code), the Guidelines for ballast water exchange in the Antarctic treaty area (International Maritime Organization (IMO) resolution MEPC.163(56)) should also be taken into consideration. Polar Code, IMO Resolution MSC.385(94) (21 November 2014, effective 1 January 2017); Amendments to the International Convention for the Safety of Life at Sea

water discharges in the Arctic indicate that currents may then transport such waters to localized coastal areas where invasive species may accumulate and perhaps establish.[74] Climate change is likely to accelerate the habitat expansion of some invasive species. For example, the European brown shrimp (*Crangon crangon*) is thought to have entered Icelandic coastal waters via ship ballast in the early 2000s. It is now well established there, and has become an important predator of plaice (*Pleuronectes platessa*), a commercially valuable fish species.[75] Along with several other invasive species, the northward expansion of brown shrimp is likely, and may be favoured by climate warming.[76] Potential biological effects by ship discharges under the International Convention for the Prevention of Pollution from Ships (MARPOL) have not been evaluated in the Arctic, but local pelagic as well as bottom-dwelling communities could be impacted by discharge of pathogens and invasive species.

5   Policy Directions to Minimize Shipping Impacts

As a consequence of climate change and other global processes, the Arctic Ocean is experiencing large-scale perturbations that are likely to worsen over the course of this century. Plans to extend shipping routes and increase traffic must therefore be evaluated with the knowledge that not only do Arctic marine ecosystems have unique ecological features requiring special care and protection, but they also have uniquely limited resilience to environmental change, which is already pushing these biological systems to their limits. Shipping now imposes a new set of pressures on Arctic ecosystems and their increasingly stressed biota and food chains. Efforts to avoid catastrophic impacts are required at multiple levels, from global mitigation of carbon emissions to

---

1974, IMO Resolution MSC.386(94) (21 November 2014, effective 1 January 2017); Amendments to MARPOL Annexes I, II, IV and V, IMO Resolution MEPC.265(68) (15 May 2015, effective 1 January 2017); Amendments to the International Convention on Standards of Training, Certification and Watchkeeping for Seafarers (STCW) 1978, as amended, Resolution MSC.416(97) (25 November 2016, effective 1 July 2018); Amendments to Part A of the Seafarers' Training, Certification and Watchkeeping (STCW) Code, Resolution MSC.417(97) (25 November 2016, effective 1 July 2018).

74   Ingrid L. Rosenhaim *et al.*, "Simulated Ballast Water Accumulation along Arctic Shipping Routes," *Marine Policy* 103 (2019): 9–18, https://doi.org/10.1016/j.marpol.2019.02.013.

75   Björn Gunnarsson, Þór Ásgeirsson and Agnar Ingólfsson, "The Rapid Colonization by *Crangon crangon* (Linnaeus, 1758) (Eucarida, Caridea, Crangonidae) of Icelandic Coastal Waters," *Crustaceana* 80 (2007): 747–753, https://www.jstor.org/stable/20107859.

76   Chris Ware *et al.*, "Biological Introduction Risks from Shipping in a Warming Arctic," *Journal of Applied Ecology* 53 (2016): 340–349, https://doi.org/10.1111/1365-2664.12566.

protect and restore Arctic sea ice, to the strengthening of pollution prevention, safety and emergency standards and protocols, the establishment and
expansion of marine protected areas, and further scrutiny and regulation of
maritime practices in north polar waters.

The risk of invasive marine species from the south via ship hulls and ballast
water, as well as the risk of accidental and operational discharge of pollutants, such as oil, noxious liquid substances and sewage, in frigid Arctic waters
that have little capacity for microbial breakdown of pollutants require stringent measures of prevention and response. Recognition of the risks related to
discharge has prompted the negotiation of the International Code for Ships
Operating in Polar Waters (Polar Code).[77] This landmark instrument contains
both guidelines and regulations. The latter have become mandatory through
amendments to the International Convention for the Safety of Life at Sea
(SOLAS)[78] and MARPOL,[79] and both parts of this instrument are relevant to
protecting Arctic marine ecosystems. There is a need for continued efforts to
broaden the scope of these provisions in the light of new ecological information about the Arctic Ocean and its biota, and more stringent regulations are
required. Revisions to the Polar Code should be based on the precautionary
approach, with restrictions on substances and activities, even if the exact
extent of their harmfulness is not yet scientifically determined.

Efforts to further strengthen existing rules and standards also need to continue beyond the framework of the Polar Code. Regarding the use of heavy fuel
oil (HFO) and ship emissions, such as sulphur and black carbon, restrictions
greatly lessen the extent of atmospheric pollution. Modeling analysis of the
Canadian Arctic showed that emission controls, such as those applied to
the current North American Emission Control Area created under MARPOL
in 2011,[80] would substantially reduce the impact of shipping on atmospheric

---

77   Polar Code (n 73).
78   Adopted 1 November 1974 (in force 25 May 1980), 1184 *UNTS* 278 (SOLAS), as amended by
     IMO Resolution MSC.386(94) (21 November 2014), in IMO, *Report of the Maritime Safety
     Committee on its Ninety-Fourth Session*, Annex 7, IMO Doc MSC 94/21/Add.1 (27 November
     2014).
79   International Convention for the Prevention of Pollution from Ships, 2 November 1973,
     1340 *UNTS* 184, as amended by Protocol of 1978 Relating to the International Convention
     for the Prevention of Pollution from Ships of 1973, 17 February 1978 (both in force 2 October
     1983), 1340 *UNTS* 61 (MARPOL), as amended by IMO Resolution MEPC.265(68) (15 May
     2015), in IMO, *Report of the Marine Environment Protection Committee on its Sixty-eighth
     Session*, IMO Doc MEPC 68/21/Add.1 (5 June 2015), Annex 11.
80   Amendments to the Annex of the Protocol of 1997 to Amend the International
     Convention for the Prevention of Pollution from Ships, 1973, as Modified by the Protocol

pollutants in this region.[81] Combustion of HFO results in the highest marine fuel emissions of black carbon, sulphur and other pollutants; additionally, release of this fuel type into the water would be especially dangerous for Arctic marine ecosystems given its high viscosity, slow degradation and likelihood of being trapped and transported by the sea ice. Although a ban on the carriage and use of HFOs by ships in Arctic waters will take effect on 1 July 2024, exemptions and waivers will remain applicable until 1 July 2029.[82] Furthermore, the sulphur content in fuel oil used by ships worldwide, including in the Arctic, has been limited to a maximum amount of 0.5 percent m/m (mass by mass) since 1 January 2020.[83] However, uncertainties remain about the behaviour of lower sulphur marine fuels in the Arctic, including the question of whether they may in some cases generate higher black carbon emissions.[84] Between 2015 and 2019, black carbon emissions grew by 72 percent for ships using HFO in the Arctic and by 85 percent overall for all ships operating in the Arctic.[85] International Maritime Organization discussions on how best to protect the Arctic from black carbon emissions of ships are underway,[86] but for the time being, States and ship operators are simply invited "to voluntarily use distillate or other cleaner alternative fuels or methods of propulsion."[87]

The high sensitivity of Arctic marine animals to noise is now supported by recent scientific analyses (described above), yet only general, non-binding Guidelines for the Reduction of Underwater Noise from Commercial Shipping

---

of 1978 Relating Thereto (North American Emission Control Area), IMO Resolution MEPC.190(60), 26 March 2010, IMO Doc MEPC 60/22 (17 June 2010), Annex 11.

81   Gong *et al.* (n 61).

82   Amendments to MARPOL Annex I (Prohibition on the Use and Carriage for Use as Fuel of Heavy Fuel Oil by Ships in Arctic Waters), IMO Resolution MEPC.329(76), 17 June 2021, IMO Doc MEPC 76/15/Add.2 (12 July 2021), Annex 2.

83   Amendments to MARPOL Annex VI (Prohibition on the Carriage of Non-Compliant Fuel Oil for Combustion Purposes for Propulsion or Operation on Board a Ship), IMO Resolution MEPC.305(73), 26 October 2018, IMO Doc MEPC 73/19/Add.1 (26 October 2018), Annex 1.

84   Franciso Malta, "Why New VLSFO 0.5% Sulphur Fuels Emit Higher Black Carbon Emissions," Safety4Sea, 10 July 2020, https://safety4sea.com/why-new-vlsfo-0-5-sulphur -fuels-emit-higher-black-carbon-emissions/.

85   Bryan Comer, Liudmila Osipova, Elise Georgeff, and Xiaoli Mao, *The International Maritime Organization's Proposed Arctic Heavy Fuel Oil Ban: Likely Impacts and Opportunities for Improvement* (International Council on Clean Transportation, September 2020), available online https://theicct.org/wp-content/uploads/2021/06/Arctic-HFO-ban-sept2020.pdf.

86   Protecting the Arctic from Shipping Black Carbon Emissions, IMO Resolution MEPC.342(77), 26 November 2021, IMO Doc MEPC 77/16/Add.1 (16 December 2021), Annex 3.

87   Id.

to Address Adverse Impacts on Marine Life exist at present.[88] As these 2014 Guidelines are currently undergoing revision,[89] there may be a window of opportunity to specifically address noise caused by shipping in polar waters and to work towards binding regulations.

Marine protected areas (MPAs), defined broadly as "clearly defined geographical spaces recognized, dedicated, and managed, through legal or other effective means, to achieve the long-term conservation of nature with associated ecosystem services and cultural values,"[90] offer an approach to reduce the overall stress on ecosystems by providing wildlife refugia in which local environmental pressures are removed or at least reduced. There are international efforts to link MPAs across the Arctic, and to maximize the conservation value of these regions for further expansion and protection at a basin-wide scale.[91] The establishment of such conservation zones, however, has not always been entirely successful in limiting ship traffic, or even designed to do so. For example, in the provisional MPA Tuvaijuittuq, north of Ellesmere Island, created with the aim of protecting the Last Ice Area of the Arctic, tourist ships and research vessels could be visitors in the longer term provided they have the capacity to break the very ice that the MPA is intended to protect. The largest increases in Canadian Arctic shipping have ironically been in a marine conservation area, the Tallurutiup Imanga at the eastern end of the Northwest Passage, where shipping length per year increased twofold between 2009 and 2018. These increases were driven mostly by the development of the large-scale Mary River iron ore mine, and much greater shipping activity is expected in the near future if current plans for expansion of the mine go ahead.[92] Such industrial developments should be subject to rigorous environmental impact assessments that extend to the shipping activities they generate, given the global pressures on the Arctic Ocean ecosystem, the need to minimize additional stressors in the face of these pressures, and the exceptional importance of Arctic marine refuges like the Tallurutiup Imanga. The legal framework of such impact assessments is analyzed in detail by Doelle *et al.* in this volume.

---

88   Guidelines for the Reduction of Underwater Noise from Commercial Shipping to Address Adverse Impacts on Marine Life, IMO MEPC.1/Circ.833 (7 April 2014).

89   Secretariat, *Outcome of MEPC 76 on the Review of MEPC.1/Circ.833*, IMO Doc SDC 8/14 (1 October 2021).

90   PAME, *Framework for a Pan-Arctic Network of Marine Protected Areas*, (Akureyri: PAME International Secretariat, 2015), 11, https://pame.is/images/03_Projects/MPA/MPA_Report.pdf. See also Lalonde and Bankes in this volume.

91   PAME (n 90).

92   Halliday *et al.* (n 65).

A selective and focused approach may help reconcile the contradictory needs for shipping activities and environmental protection. Certain areas would benefit from seasonal protection of ice integrity, essential for example in the Northwest Passage during the season of caribou migration over the sea ice, critical phases of marine mammal activity and periods when Indigenous hunters are on the ice. Localized measures may be another valuable approach. Among those, routeing measures, which may be adopted under SOLAS Chapter V,[93] are an effective tool to reduce noise disturbance and ship strikes. Routeing measures may establish areas-to-be-avoided, including seasonal exclusions from shipping during marine animal migration periods.[94] Mandated reductions in ship speed and noise could also prove to be significant mitigation measures.[95] Ongoing improvements in the automated monitoring of animal migrations and noise signatures of individual ships may eventually allow real-time decisions to be made for ecologically safe speeds and routeing. These regulatory schemes, including their technological support for an even more targeted effect, should be an integral part of the initiative of low-impact corridors for shipping in the Canadian Arctic Archipelago, currently developed under the leadership of the Canadian Coast Guard, the Canadian Hydrographic Service and Transport Canada, and portrayed in more detail by Dawson and Song in this volume.

Acknowledgements

Our research on Arctic environmental issues is supported by NSERC, SSHRC, FRQNT, ArcticNet (NCE), Sentinel North (CFREF) and the Canada Research Chair program. We thank Vincent Bonin-Palardy for assistance with manuscript preparation, and Aldo Chircop for insightful review comments. This is a contribution to the IASC project Terrestrial Multidisciplinary distributed Observatories for the Study of Arctic Connections (T-MOSAIC).

---

93 See SOLAS (n 78), Regulation V/10; see also General Provisions on Ships' Routeing, IMO Resolution A.572(14), 20 November 1985, as amended.

94 An example of such a seasonal area to be avoided (ATBA) is the Roseway Basin ATBA, south of Nova Scotia, Canada, which aims to reduce the risk of ship strikes to right whales and is effective for the period from 1 June to 31 December. See IMO Doc MSC 83/28/Add.3 (2 November 2007), Annex 25.

95 Paul B. Conn and Gregory K. Silber, "Vessel Speed Restrictions Reduce Risk of Collision-related Mortality for North Atlantic Right Whales," *Ecosphere* 4 (2013): 43, https://doi.org/10.1890/ES13-00004.1.

CHAPTER 4

Shipping along the Northwest Passage: A Historical Overview

Adam Lajeunesse and P. Whitney Lackenbauer

Abstract

This chapter furnishes an overview history of booms and busts in Arctic shipping, with a focus on the bubbles created by successive defence and economic crises and opportunities in the twentieth century. The first significant non-Indigenous maritime activity centered on furs and whale oil. The Second World War and early Cold War saw fleets of American naval, coast guard and merchant marine vessels move into the region to construct installations. In the 1970s, resource extraction attracted the attention of southern companies, and the North seemed to be the next great development frontier. By the 1980s, surging oil and gas prices raised hopes for a bonanza, with government estimates forecasting hundreds of Arctic transits by resource carriers as early as the 1990s. Instead, fleets of icebreaking tankers remained on the drawing board at century's end—where they remain today. In between these booms, Arctic shipping did not disappear, with community resupply and government operations continuing on a predictable basis.

Keywords

Arctic shipping – Northwest Passage – marine transportation history – Canadian Arctic – Second World War – Cold War – oil and gas development

1 Introduction

In 1921, Canadian Arctic explorer Vilhjalmur Stefansson published *The Friendly Arctic*, an account of his time in the North and his views on the region's future. Stefansson made the dramatic prediction that the Arctic would soon become a region of great strategic and commercial importance. Crisscrossed by international air and sea traffic, the polar basin was to be the Mediterranean of the modern age.[1] It was a bold prediction and one that fit into the pattern of Arctic shipping: a pioneering spirit imbued with optimism. That optimism has proven fleeting over the past century, however, as Arctic shipping has followed a boom-and-bust pattern. Each boom was driven by a strategic or economic catalyst, only to end with changing circumstances. The first significant European maritime activity centered on furs and whale oil, surging and then declining in line with those industries. The Second World War and early Cold War saw fleets of American naval, coast guard, and merchant marine vessels move into the region to construct weather and radar stations as part of a larger system of continental defence. When those sites were completed and strategic circumstances changed, that activity declined. In the 1970s, resource extraction attracted the attention of southern companies and the North seemed to be the next great development frontier. By the 1980s, surging oil and gas prices raised hopes for a bonanza, with government estimates forecasting hundreds of Arctic transits by resource carriers as early as the 1990s.[2] Instead, commodity prices put paid to these visions. The hundreds of millions of dollars invested in oil and gas returned few rewards, and the fleets of icebreaking tankers remained on the drawing board at century's end—where they remain today.

This chapter furnishes an overview history of these booms and busts in Arctic shipping, with a focus on the bubbles created by successive defence and economic crises and opportunities. In between these booms, Arctic shipping did not disappear, with community resupply and government operations continuing on a regular and predictable basis (often below the radar of anyone outside the Arctic).[3] Our focus is on shipping into and out of the region and excludes local small-craft maritime activity. The routes that make up what is commonly called the Northwest Passage have served as highways for Inuit since time immemorial, and this maritime activity lies at the heart of Canada's claim to sovereignty over these waters.[4] This important facet is covered in the chapters by Claudio Aporta and Leah Beveridge in this volume.

---

1   Vilhjalmur Stefansson, *The Friendly Arctic: The Story of Five Years in Polar Regions* (MacMillan, 1921).

2   Memorandum for Cabinet, "Status of Arctic Archipelagic Waters," 1 June 1982, Library and Archives Canada (LAC), RG 12, vol. 5561, file 8100-15-4-2(s), pt. 4.

3   For statistics on marine transportation in the Canadian Arctic, see Christopher Wright's comprehensive study *Arctic Cargo: A History of Marine Transportation in Canada's North* (self-published, 2016).

4   See for instance External Affairs Minister Joe Clark's statement during the *Polar Sea* crisis: Canada, House of Commons, *Debates*, 10 September 1985, 33rd Parliament, 1st session, p. 6463.

2   Whalers and Traders

Early exploration in the North American Arctic by the Norse and then English using rudimentary navigation instruments yielded important 'discoveries' for Europe but had limited impact on the Arctic itself. Furthermore, the coveted northern maritime route to the riches of Asia proved elusive—and commercially unfeasible. Instead, until the middle of the eighteenth century, the fur trade provided the basis for the Canadian economy and shipping in Arctic waters. For a century, the Hudson's Bay Company built its empire around a business model exploiting a chain of posts at the mouths of rivers flowing into Hudson Bay. Each year, three to four sailing ships would carry trade goods through Hudson Strait and into the bay, and then return to England with furs. Competition with the Northwest Company after the conquest of New France stimulated an increased focus on terrestrial and riverine networks until the two companies merged in 1821, but explorers continued to search for a Northwest Passage by sea and land. The fur trade would persist as a significant economic force in the Arctic well into the twentieth century, with posts established along the Arctic Ocean coast where they were resupplied by sea.[5]

The whaling industry dramatically increased the scale of shipping activity in the Canadian Arctic. Dutch, German, English, and Scottish whalers plied their trade along the eastern (Greenland) side of Davis Strait in the seventeenth century. After British explorers John Ross and W. Edward Parry crossed Baffin Bay and proved the route into Lancaster Sound in 1818 and 1819, these activities extended into the Canadian archipelago. Dominated by British whalers, this activity in what is now the eastern Canadian Arctic peaked from 1820–1840, when nearly one hundred ships operated in and around Davis Strait area (typically from April to October). In 1840, Scottish whaling Captain William Penny and his assistant Eenoolooapik explored Cumberland Sound and it soon became one of the most important whaling grounds in the eastern Canadian Arctic. With the advent of intentional overwintering on Baffin Island in the 1850s, interactions between the whalers and Inuit intensified, with the latter supplying crews with food, clothing, and labour. This contact also led to the emergence of permanent shore stations at Kekerton and Blacklead Island,

---

5   Harold Innis, *The Fur Trade in Canada* (Toronto: University of Toronto Press, 1930); E.E. Rich, *The Hudson's Bay Company 1670–1870* (Winnipeg: Hudson's Bay Record Society, 1958); Daniel Francis and Toby Morantz, *Partners in Furs: A History of the Fur Trade in Eastern James Bay, 1600–1870* (Montreal & Kingston: McGill-Queen's University Press, 1983); Arthur J. Ray, *The Canadian Fur Trade in the Industrial Age* (Toronto: University of Toronto Press, 1990).

with the in-migration of Inuit making them the largest settlements in the Sound until the end of the whaling era in 1915.[6]

While the British dominated the whaling industry in the east, Americans dominated in Hudson Bay and the west. American ships opened the fishery in the northwest corner of Hudson Bay in 1860, and the Pacific whaling fleet pushed eastward past Point Barrow in the Beaufort Sea in 1889. Although the whaling era in the Beaufort Sea and Amundsen Gulf spanned a relatively limited period of time (1889 until about 1914), several hundred American seamen overwintered in the region, and this presence had transformative effects on local populations. During voyages that typically spanned two or three years, whalers congregated in sheltered harbours such as Pauline Harbour on Herschel Island, where Inuit and First Nations worked as pilots, hunters, dog drivers, and seamstresses in exchange for European trade goods and liquor. Whaling crews introduced measles, typhus, scarlet fever, tuberculosis, and sexually transmitted infections that swept through Indigenous populations, with epidemics decimating the Mackenzie Delta Inuit population and the Sadlermiut of Southampton Island in Hudson Bay.[7]

Foreign whaling activities in Canadian waters ultimately spurred the Canadian government to assert its sovereignty over the Arctic Archipelago. Canada had acquired whatever rights Britain had in the area in 1880, but Ottawa had done little to act upon them. After all, Sir John Franklin's ill-fated 1845 expedition and the search parties that had followed in its wake had proven the existence of an Arctic maritime route while also demonstrating its lack of utility. After Confederation in 1867, southern Canadians invested their resources and energies into establishing east-west linkages to consolidate the Dominion of Canada; securing its northern limits seemed a distant, future consideration.[8] Accordingly, the absence of Canadian official presence in the Arctic left foreign whalers to operate without any regulation. At the turn of the century, rumours

6   See, for example, W. Gillies Ross, ed., *Arctic Whalers, Icy Seas: Narratives of the Davis Strait Whale Fishery* (Toronto: Irwin, 1985); Daniel Francis, *Arctic Chase : A History of Whaling in Canada's North* (St. John's: Breakwater, 1984); Anne Keenleyside, "Euro-American Whaling in the Canadian Arctic: Its Effects on Eskimo Health," *Arctic Anthropology* 27:1 (1990): 1–19; Dorothy Eber, *When the Whalers Were Up North: Inuit Memories from the Eastern Arctic* (Montreal & Kingston: McGill-Queen's University Press, 1996).

7   W. Gillies Ross, *Whaling and Eskimos: Hudson Bay 1860–1915* (Ottawa: National Museum of Man, 1975); W. Gilles Ross, ed., *An Arctic Whaling Diary: The Journal of Captain George Comer in Hudson Bay, 1903–1905* (Toronto: University of Toronto Press, 1984); Francis (n 6); Keenleyside (n 6).

8   For a sweeping overview, see Shelagh Grant, *Polar Imperative: A History of Arctic Sovereignty in North America* (Vancouver: Douglas & McIntyre, 2011).

circulated that the United States might use the activities of American whalers as a pretext to annex parts of the Canada's Arctic. Thus, sovereignty concerns prompted Ottawa to act. In 1903, the North-West Mounted Police established detachments at Herschel Island, off the north coast of the Yukon, and at Cape Fullerton, in the northwest corner of Hudson Bay, to collect customs, regulate the liquor traffic, impose whaling licences, and maintain order.[9]

Official Government of Canada expeditions into the Northwest Passage, matched by flag planting and asserting a Canadian 'sector claim' up to the North Pole, sought to assert authority in and over Arctic lands and waters.[10] Between 1904 and 1911, Captain Joseph-Elzéar Bernier led several voyages to the eastern Arctic on the government ship *Arctic*, culminating in the placement of a cairn and plaque on Melville Island claiming the entire Arctic Archipelago for Canada. To give practical weight to this claim, the federal government established more Mounted Police posts along the Arctic coast and on the Arctic islands, eventually extending to Craig Harbour (1922) and Bache Peninsula (1926) on Ellesmere Island. Resupply of these remote outposts was conducted by the annual Eastern Arctic Patrol, inaugurated in 1922. Led by a civil servant, the maritime patrol transported doctors, scientists, court officials and police to visit coastal camps and later settlements across the Eastern Arctic. After a short hiatus following the sinking of HMCS *Nascopie* in 1947, the patrol resumed in 1950 with a particular focus on testing Inuit for tuberculosis, many of whom were evacuated to southern hospitals—a practice that continued until 1968 and is also discussed in Leah Beveridge's chapter in this volume.[11]

3   The Second World War

The Second World War brought the Canadian Northwest into new strategic focus, imprinting the novel idea that the region also constituted a military frontier. Although the dramatic highway, pipeline, and airfield projects in the Canadian Northwest did not have an ocean shipping component, other

---

9   William R. Morrison, *Showing the Flag: The Mounted Police and Canadian Sovereignty in the North, 1894–1925* (Vancouver: UBC Press, 1985).

10   On sovereignty in the Canadian Arctic before the Second World War, see Gordon W. Smith, *A Historical and Legal Study of Sovereignty in the Canadian North: Terrestrial Sovereignty, 1870–1939*, ed., P.W. Lackenbauer (Calgary: University of Calgary Press, 2014) and Janice Cavell and Jeff Noakes, *Acts of Occupation: Canada and Arctic Sovereignty, 1918–25* (Vancouver: UBC Press, 2011).

11   See C.S. Mackinnon, "Canada's Eastern Arctic Patrol 1922–68," *Polar Record*, 27:161 (1991): 93–101.

activities in the Eastern Canadian Arctic did. The Crimson Staging Route, a series of airfields and depots that the United States established (with Canadian approval) to facilitate the transfer of planes and other material from North America to Europe, established footprints in Fort Chimo (Kuujjuaq), Frobisher Bay (Iqaluit), and Padloping Island. By 1943, Goose Bay, Labrador (then part of the separate colony of Newfoundland) boasted the largest airfield in the Western Hemisphere. As the region's first large-scale development project, the military base changed life in Labrador. Radio sites were also established throughout the Canadian North, greatly facilitating communications over vast distances. In the words of Malcolm MacDonald, the British High Commissioner to Canada, the Americans "treated ... with indifference the obstacles which Nature—whose sovereignty in the Arctic is even more supreme than that of the Canadian Government—put in their way."[12]

Establishing these sites required surveys and supplies. For example, trawler convoys carried north five separate construction crews, weather station personnel, food, and building materials in late September 1941. As a result, the three 'Crystal' weather and radio stations were completed by mid-November.[13] The following summer, a convoy of cargo ships and trawlers carrying men, equipment and supplies set out for Fort Chimo, Frobisher Bay, and Southampton Island. Lieutenant Command Alexander Forbes and veteran Arctic explorer Captain Bob Bartlett were sent on ahead to chart the waters of Frobisher Bay and to pilot the supply ships safely to the base site. Near Resolution Island aboard *Effie M. Morrissey*, Forbes recounted:

> Entering the ice floes we dodged the larger pans and steered a more tor-turous course as the pack ice became thicker. It was an old story to this seasoned crew. The man in the barrel at the foremast head picked the lanes through the ice and directed the man at the wheel, and as he yelled "Port" or "Starboard," the schooner zigzagged dizzily. When feasible, he followed leads of open water; when these didn't serve, the schooner simply rammed the pans with a jarring crunch ..., leaving a streak of red bottom paint on the ice as it floated away on the quarter. These men knew what the ship could take and they let her take it.[14]

12   Quoted in Shelagh Grant, *Sovereignty or Security? Government Policy in the Canadian North, 1936–1950* (Vancouver: UBC Press, 1988), 275.
13   Shelagh Grant, "American Defence of the Arctic, 1939–1960," paper presented to the Canadian Historical Association (1990), copy in possession of P. Whitney Lackenbauer.
14   Alexander Forbes, *Quest for a Northern Air Route* (Cambridge: Harvard University Press, 1953), 57. See also William S. Carlson, *Lifelines through the Arctic* (New York: Duell, Sloan and Pearce, 1962).

They succeeded in transferring the men and equipment to the permanent location near the mouth of the Sylvia Grennell River. Although the supply fleet was delayed when a German U-boat sunk one of the cargo ships off the coast of Labrador, it arrived in August with 350 men, building materials, and heavy construction equipment. It was increasingly clear that shipping was a critical enabler for air operations—and, by extension, continental defence.

4   The Cold War

The onset of the Cold War renewed pressures on Canada to balance sovereignty concerns with continental security imperatives. Polar projection maps revealed how Canada's strategic situation had changed when the United States and the Soviet Union became rivals. When the United States pushed for access to Canada's Far North to build airfields and weather stations beginning in 1946, Canadian officials proved apprehensive in authorizing new installations, and journalists began to talk about a looming sovereignty crisis.[15] Some scholars argue that Canadian apathy in the face of American security interests threatened our sovereignty in the late 1940s,[16] while others paint a more benign portrait of bilateral cooperation, with Canadian policy-makers preserving and extending Canadian sovereignty through quiet diplomacy and careful negotiations that extended into the 1950s and beyond.[17] Whatever the verdict,

---

15   For example, Grant 1988 (n 12).

16   See, for example, Grant 1988 (n 12); Adam Lajeunesse, "Lock, Stock, and Icebergs? Defining Canadian Sovereignty from Mackenzie King to Stephen Harper," CMSS Occasional Paper No. 1 (Calgary: Centre for Military and Strategic Studies, 2007); J.L. Granatstein, "The North to 1968," in *The Arctic in Question*, ed., Edgar Dosman (Toronto: Oxford University Press, 1976), 13–33.

17   See, for example, David Bercuson, "Continental Defense and Arctic Security, 1945–50," in *The Cold War and Defense*, eds., Keith Neilson and Ronald G. Haycock (New York: Praeger, 1990), 153–170; P. Whitney Lackenbauer, "Right and Honourable: Mackenzie King, Canadian-American Bilateral Relations, and Canadian Sovereignty in the Northwest, 1943–1948," in *Mackenzie King: Citizenship and Community*, eds., John English, Kenneth McLaughlin, and P. Whitney Lackenbauer (Toronto: Robin Brass Studio, 2002), 151–168; P. Whitney Lackenbauer and Peter Kikkert, "Sovereignty and Security: The Department of External Affairs, the United States, and Arctic Sovereignty, 1945–68," in *In the National Interest: Canadian Foreign Policy and the Department of Foreign Affairs and International Trade, 1909–2009*, eds., Greg Donaghy and Michael Carroll (Calgary: University of Calgary Press, 2011), 101–120; P. Whitney Lackenbauer and Peter Kikkert, "The Dog in the Manger – and Letting Sleeping Dogs Lie: The United States, Canada and the Sector Principle, 1924–1955,'" *International Law and Politics of the Arctic Ocean: Essays in Honour of Donat Pharand*, eds., Suzanne Lalonde and Ted L. McDorman (Leiden: Brill, 2014), 216–239; Daniel Heidt and

the notion that there were "no boundaries upstairs" when it came to North American air defence[18] had entered the military imagination and could no longer be simply ignored, thus initiating a process of military modernization in the region.[19]

In the 1950s, the Americans decided to build extensive air defence systems in the Arctic to secure advance warning to protect the US Air Force's nuclear deterrent and the industrial heartland of North America.[20] The most northern of the radar networks was the Distant Early Warning or DEW Line, a mega-project staggering in both its scale and the speed with which it was constructed. "Stretching for 2,500 miles across the Arctic, it required the biggest task-force of ships since the invasion of Europe and the largest air operation since the Berlin airlift to take in the supplies," Department of Northern Affairs and National Resources official Charles Marshall described in *Geographical Magazine.* "More than 7,000 men laboured through two short Arctic construction seasons to complete the work on schedule. Small wonder that many consider the project one of the most dramatic engineering achievements of our time and a milestone in the development of the Arctic."[21]

Between the end of the Second World War and the completion of the DEW Line, the US Navy and Coast Guard sent hundreds of icebreakers and cargo ships to the waters of the Canadian Arctic Archipelago. Over time, the size and scope of Arctic convoys grew, requiring innovative planning, elaborate preparations, and complex joint (Canada-United States) interdepartmental and interagency coordination that applied lessons learned from previous missions.[22] The scale of activity in Canada's Arctic waters was unprecedented. During the construction phase from 1955–1957, the US Military Sea Transportation Service (MSTS), moved over 460,000 tons of equipment and supplies into the Canadian Arctic, including enough gravel to build two copies of the Great

P. Whitney Lackenbauer, *The Joint Arctic Weather Stations: Science and Sovereignty in the High Arctic, 1946–1972* (Calgary: University of Calgary Press, 2022).

18   See Joseph Jockel, *No Boundaries Upstairs: Canada, the United States, and the Origins of North American Air Defence, 1945–1958* (Vancouver: UBC Press, 1987). For a recent reflection on this important book, see Daniel Heidt, "Revisiting Joseph Jockel's No Boundaries Upstairs," *International Journal* 70:2 (2015): 339–349.

19   On this theme, see Matthew Farish and P. Whitney Lackenbauer, "High Modernism in the Arctic: Planning Frobisher Bay and Inuvik," *Journal of Historical Geography* 35:3 (2009): 517–544.

20   The essential study on this process remains Jockel, *No Boundaries Upstairs* (n 18).

21   C.J. Marshall, "North America's Distant Early Warning Line," *Geographical Magazine* 29: 12 (1957): 616.

22   See Peter Kikkert and P. Whitney Lackenbauer, "Setting an Arctic Course: Task Force 80 and Canadian Control in the Arctic, 1948," *Northern Mariner* 21:4 (2011): 327–358.

Pyramid of Giza.[23] Nevertheless, the maritime task forces that operated in the region faced age-old environmental challenges associated with unpredictable ice conditions, weather, and extreme isolation. Shepherding and then landing enormous loads of construction equipment and material by landing craft over Arctic beaches, after first charting and clearing the approaches, posed enormous challenges. "The work was not glamorous or adventurous," Captain Owen Robertson explained about the Royal Canadian Navy (RCN) icebreaker HMCS *Labrador*'s Arctic voyages. "Most of it was just plain hard work, long-hours, bad weather and monotony; but we did know that what we were doing was important to Canada—that was our reward."[24] The RCN's Arctic foray was brief, however, and the Navy opted out of its Arctic role when it transferred the *Labrador* to the Canadian Coast Guard in 1957.[25]

Nevertheless, the DEW Line and previous military development projects reshaped the socio-economic and cultural geographies of Arctic Canada. Although planners had intended to protect Inuit so that military activities did not disrupt their lives, this proved impossible once airplanes and ships began shipping southern materiel into the Arctic. "Every place a box landed became a beach-head for industrialized society," documentary filmmaker Kevin McMahon later observed. "The boxes soon became the foundation for the Canadian government, which the military had given cause to worry about its sovereignty. Boxes were added, and more of our society—with its various virtues and vices, machines and organizations, ideals, morals, values and goals—were shipped north."[26] On the other hand, opening the North brought benefits from a national development standpoint. "Canada fell heir

---

23   Western Electric, *The t Line Story* (c.1960).

24   O.C.S. Robertson, "Foreword" to T.A. Irvine, *The Ice Was All Between* (Toronto: Longmans Green, 1959), XXII.

25   On *Labrador*, see also J.M. Leeming, "HMCS *Labrador* and the Canadian Arctic," in *RCN in Retrospect, 1910–1968*, ed., James Boutilier (Vancouver: UBC Press, 1982), 286–307; Naval Historical Section, Royal Canadian Naval Headquarters, *HMCS* Labrador: *An Operational History*, eds., P. Whitney Lackenbauer, Adam Lajeunesse, and Lieutenant(N) Jason Delaney (Antigonish: Mulroney Institute on Government, Arctic Operational History Series 1, 2017).

26   Kevin McMahon, *Arctic Twilight* (Toronto: Lorimer, 1987). On this theme, see also P. Whitney Lackenbauer and Ryan Shackleton, "Inuit-Air Force Relations in the Qikiqtani Region during the Early Cold War," in *De-Icing Required: The Canadian Air Force's Experience in the Arctic*, eds., P. Whitney Lackenbauer and W.A. March (Trenton: Canadian Forces Air Warfare Centre, *Sic Itur Ad Astra:* Canadian Aerospace Power Studies Series 4, 2012), 73–94; P. Whitney Lackenbauer, "At the Crossroads of Militarism and Modernization: Inuit-Military Relations in the Cold War Arctic," in *Roots of Entanglement: Essays in Native-Newcomer Relations*, eds., Myra Rutherdale, P. Whitney Lackenbauer, and Kerry Abel (Toronto: University of Toronto Press, 2018), 116–158.

to the by-products of the DEW Line construction," Eyre notes. "Airfields were built, beach landing sites were developed, charts and maps were improved, aids to navigation were installed. These developments significantly improved access to what had hitherto been a virtually inaccessible area. There was some initial anticipation that a flood of mineral exploration would follow in their wake. This notion proved to be as chimerical as Frobisher's search for gold."[27]

5   The Arctic Oil And Gas Frontier: Dreams of a Bonanza

As shipping activity from defence construction was winding down in the late 1950s, a new driving force for northern activity was beginning to emerge. Resource development in the North had historically been limited by the region's inaccessibility, as poor charting and harsh ice conditions had always made large-scale commercial operations a daunting proposition. Some of that perception of impenetrability was stripped away by the successful continental defence operations of the preceding decade, with military infrastructure facilitating a surge of survey work and resource exploration.

Over the course of the 1950s, the Geological Survey of Canada undertook large-scale aerial surveys which outlined promising geological conditions and, by the end of that decade, published estimates defining a wide variety of minerals and hydrocarbon reserves spread across the Arctic Islands.[28] By 1960, the government had issued over 40 million acres of exploration permits to both Canadian and international companies.[29] Small survey teams were flown into all parts of the Arctic Islands, often using defence infrastructure to facilitate the initial work confirming the economic viability of so many reserves. While the geology was promising, the question of transportation remained unsettled and the need for effective and reliable shipping quickly became clear. In a spirit of optimism, Cam Sproule (the chief executive officer of J.C. Sproule and Associates and a pioneer in early Arctic resource exploration) wrote in a 1962 edition of *Oilweek* that "it should not take science long to devise icebreakers that could move more or less at will through the Arctic Islands for at least the greater part of the year."[30] Where only a decade earlier American crews

---

27   Kenneth C. Eyre, "Forty Years of Military Activity in the Canadian North, 1947–87," *Arctic* 40:4 (1987): 292–299, at 294–295.

28   Gordon H. Jones, "Economic Development – Oil and Gas," in *A Century of Canada's Arctic Islands, 1880–1980*, ed., Morris Zaslow (Ottawa: Royal Society of Canada, 1981), 222.

29   Penelope E. Grey and Laura K. Krowchuk, *Spirit of Success: The Sproule Story* (Calgary: Sproule Associates Ltd., 1997), 223.

30   Id., 62.

were still learning how to work in the polar waters, Sproule now was telling the industry world that large-scale submarine freight traffic was "so far advanced as to be practically assured within the next five to eight years."[31] More than an ambitious outlier, this enthusiasm represented the energy and optimism of the early resource pioneers and their determination to open the Northwest Passage to Canadian shipping.

Building reliable shipping routes was essential to these development plans, but surveys soon found that transportation costs constituted half of their entire budget. Air freight was frequently relied upon to reach inaccessible areas, but the use of aircraft was five times more expensive that maritime transport.[32] One of the first efforts to distribute costs and develop those shipping routes came in the form of a pooling of resources. Panarctic Oils was a consolidation of 75 corporate and individual land holdings with major support from the Government of Canada, which had a vested interest in the development of the North and the establishment of improved sea lanes.

Launched in 1968, Panarctic was intended to provide affordability through scale. In its first year, the organization sea-lifted 5,000 tons of drilling supplies and 500,000 gallons of fuel to its northern bases.[33] This large-scale shipping effort was central to supporting industry's aggressive plans, which saw over CDN$700 million worth of exploration work undertaken across the Archipelago in 1969 and 1970. Despite the initial industry enthusiasm, the difficulties of supplying Arctic projects became evident very quickly. The high costs of moving supplies, coupled with the lack of any return on those early investments called into question the long-term viability of the many Arctic projects and, by 1970, Panarctic investors were becoming nervous.[34]

Circumstances conspired to give Canadian shipping and resource exploration efforts fresh life. In 1968, Atlantic Richfield and Humble Oil made a major oil discovery at Prudhoe Bay on Alaska's North Slope. The *Anchorage Times* headline read "Arctic Oil Find is Huge" and conservative estimates put the reserve at between five and ten billion barrels of oil, making it by far the largest on the continent.[35] As was the case in the Arctic Islands, the question of transportation was central. From the North Slope, oil had to travel roughly 3,200

---

31   Id.

32   Richard Rohmer, *The Arctic Imperative* (Toronto: McClelland Stewart Ltd, 1973), 176.

33   Chas R. Hetherington, "A Story of Arctic Exploration," *UBC Business Review* (1971).

34   Jennifer Lewington, "Lessons of the Arctic Pilot Project," in *Politics of the Northwest Passage*, ed., Franklyn Griffiths (Kingston: McGill-Queens University Press, 1987), 167.

35   Ross Cohen, *Breaking Ice for Arctic Oil* (Fairbanks: University of Alaska Press, 2012), 24. In 2009 Prudhoe Bay's reserves were placed at 15.7 billion barrels produced with an additional 35–36 billion in proved reserves remaining (including nearby fields subsequently discovered); National Energy Technology Laboratory (NETL), *Alaska North Slope Oil and*

km to refineries in Washington State or 8,000 to the East Coast (through the Northwest Passage). At the time, the widespread assumption was that tanker transportation would be both easier and cheaper. Calculations varied but some estimates put tanker costs at up to 50 percent less than the pipeline alternative, with projected savings of up to USD$1.2 million per day.[36] Still, this was all speculation and guess work, since no company had ever attempted to run a tanker through the harsh ice-covered waters of the Arctic. Nor had any shipyard built anything like the necessary ice-strengthened vessels capable of year-round operations. What experience existed in Arctic navigation was largely confined to purpose-built icebreakers or seasonally employed cargo ships incapable of handling thick multiyear ice. If tankers were to be considered, a major test would be required, both to ensure that a passage could be made safely and to gather much of the technical data needed to build future fleets.

Rapid progress ensued. Only three months after the Prudhoe Bay discovery, Imperial Oil began working with the Canadian Department of Transport to arrange an Arctic tanker experiment. Requests were naturally made for Canadian icebreaker support and any ice data that the government could provide.[37] The ship which the Americans would send through Canadian waters was the 150,000-ton SS *Manhattan*, a retrofitted tanker and one of the most ice-capable vessels in the world at the time. If these tests proved successful, plans called for the construction of 26 to 30 massive 1,200 feet long icebreaking ultra large crude carriers of 350,000 tons, capable of carrying 1 million barrels of oil each.[38] By the end of August 1969, *Manhattan* was ready to sail.[39]

Overall, *Manhattan's* voyage was a success. The supertanker reached Prudhoe Bay in September 1969 and returned to the Eastern Seaboard the following month. While McClure Strait had proven impenetrable, the more southerly route through Amundsen Gulf was accessible, and transited without incident. While the ship withstood the Arctic ice very well, plans for future fleets were sunk in the Texas boardrooms by spreadsheets and evolving cost calculations. On 21 October 1970, Humble Oil suspended its icebreaker project in a shift

---

Gas: A Promising Future or an Area in Decline? Addendum Report DOE/NETL-2009/1385 (April 2009).

36   A.H.G. Storrs and T.C. Pullen, "S.S. Manhattan in Arctic Waters," *Canadian Geographic Journal* 80:5 (1970): 167; Cohen (n 35), p. 29.

37   A.H.G. Storrs to Dr. Claude Isbister, 5 March 1969, LAC, RG 12, vol. 5561, file 8100-15-4-2, pt. 1.

38   Minutes of the 73rd meeting of the Advisory Committee on Northern Development, 19 December 1968, LAC, RG 112, vol. 29803, file 170–80/A6, pt. 7.

39   For the most detailed account of the *Manhattan's* voyage and the economics and corporate strategy surrounding it see Cohen (n 35) and Whitney Lackenbauer and Adam Lajeunesse, eds., *In Manhattan's Wake*, Arctic Operational Histories (Antigonish: Mulroney Institute of Government, 2019).

towards pipelines. Initial cost estimates, which had given tankers the edge had
changed during *Manhattan*'s transit and, by March 1970, were twice what they
had been the previous year. By autumn 1970, Humble was assuming costs of
US$1.1 billion for new Arctic port facilities, with much of the expense com-
ing from significant dredging needed to deepen sea lanes and build loading
facilities in the shallow waters of Prudhoe Bay. American physicist Edward
Teller even suggested excavating with H-bombs. The 30 icebreaking tankers
would have cost an additional US$2.2 billion.[40] Against the estimated US$1
billion for a pipeline across Alaska to Valdez, the Northwest Passage seemed
uneconomical.[41]

While the tanker route to Alaska never materialized, Canadian resource
companies were still energized by the North Slope discoveries. The effects of
the Arab oil embargo of 1973–74, which quadrupled oil prices from US$3.00
to US$12.00 in less than a year, compounded that interest. By the summer of
1972, exploration activity and shipping in the Arctic islands was surging. In July
alone, 17 ships carried 10 million gallons of petroleum, oil, and other lubricants
and 100,000 tons of general cargo. Most of this was heading to Panarctic's base
of operations at Rae Point on Melville Island, as well as forward stations on
Ellef Ringnes, Ellesmere, Axel Heiberg, and Cornwallis islands.[42]

By the end of 1972, Panarctic had drilled 26 wells and discovered eight
trillion cubic feet of recoverable gas,[43] with the largest discovery at Drake Point
on the southern shore of Melville Island. There, the company's grand plan was
to bring 250 million cubic feet of Drake Point gas per day to a liquefaction
plant on the south shore. The scheme was ambitious, involving two year-round
icebreaking LNG tankers, each longer than three football fields and able to
move continuously through up to seven feet of ice, making 32 trips per year to
facilities in Eastern Canada. The project was expected to cost CDN$1.5 billion
for the ships and infrastructure, with a start date of 1983.[44]

To get the program started, four Canadian and American shipping companies (later reduced to three Canadian companies) formed Melville Shipping.
In the words of Michael Bell, the senior Montreal shipping executive
assembling the project, "everything depends on the shipping element. He who
controls the transportation system controls the Arctic."[45] Control over that

---

40   Cohen (n 35), p. 135.
41   It should be noted that the Trans-Alaska Pipeline System, completed in 1977, also came in
        above budget, about US$7 billion over; Cohen (n 35), p. 163.
42   Richard Rohmer, *The Arctic Imperative* (Toronto: McClelland Stewart Ltd, 1973), 174.
43   Grey and Krowchuk (n 29), p. 116.
44   Lewington (n 34), p. 168.
45   Id., 166.

future shipping remained an open question, and by the early 1980s it seemed that Dome Petroleum—one of the largest commercial actors in the Arctic off-shore—would come to dominate. Financed by debt and government support, Dome operated a significant fleet of icebreaking support and drill ships, managed principally by its drilling subsidiary Canadian Marine (Canmar). Some of these ships represented significant advancements over what industry had at its disposal when the boom began a decade earlier. The 2,000-ton *Canmar Kigoriak*, for instance, was an Arctic Class 3 vessel built in 1979 in less than a year. It spent a decade protecting drill ships in the Beaufort and many of its engineering innovations were incorporated into later icebreaker designs.[46]

Just to the east of the Drake field lay another important hydrocarbon asset. The Bent Horn oil field on Cameron Island was discovered in 1974 and brought online in 1986. Producing roughly 500 barrels of oil per day for Panarctic, it exported its product aboard MV *Arctic* after that ship's conversion into an Arctic tanker. The first cargo, sent to Montreal, totalled 100,000 barrels, with production increasing to 821 barrels per day in 1988.[47] Oil flowed from Bent Horn out through the Northwest Passage for ten years without incident and closed in 1996 after producing 2.6 million barrels of oil. This was Canada's most significant High Arctic hydrocarbon project, and the shipping that surrounded it was seen as both essential to its viability and a symbol of Canadian sovereignty and capability in its Far North. Those political considerations were ever-present for the Canadian government, which subsidized Canadian companies to ensure that this shipping would be done by Canadian vessels.[48]

While that optimism centred on oil and gas, mineral resource exploration and development surged ahead as well. The Nanisivik mine started shipping zinc and lead concentrate in 1977 and the Polaris mine came online in 1982. Resupply and cargo shipping often linked the two mines together, with ice strengthened cargo vessels MV *Arctic*, *Gothic Wasa*, and *Baltic Wasa* doing the lion's share of the shipping.[49] In the heady times that were the early 1980s, new zinc, iron, lead, cadmium, silver, copper, nickel, and other vital minerals were also expected to come from new and expanded mines at Strathcona Sound, Bathurst Inlet, Little Cornwallis Island, and Deception Bay.

---

46 "New Powerful Icebreaker Under Construction at Gotaverken Arendal," *Maritime Reporter and Engineering News* (August 1988), 37.

47 Peter McKenzie-Brown, Gordon Jaremko, and David Fitch, *The Great Oil Age: The Petroleum Industry in Canada* (Calgary: Detselig Enterprises Ltd., 1993), 90.

48 Memorandum to Cabinet, "Arctic Shipping Policy and PanArctic's Bent Horn Project," 16 October 1984, LAC.

49 Wright (n 3), p. 183.

While the Arctic Islands saw the most mineral and gas production and ship-ping activity, the real opportunities seemed to lie further west in the Beaufort Sea. In the early 1970s, a fleet of drilling vessels hunted for more oil and gas, looking to recreate the North Slope successes in the Canadian offshore. New ship designs and technology allowed industry to push into the deeper offshore areas and extend the shipping and drilling season to up to four months. In 1972, Imperial Oil began building artificial islands from gravel dredged from the ocean floor and, over the course of the 1970s and early 1980s, major innovations in icebreaker design enabled a significant seasonal presence in those waters.[50]

This activity seemed to have positioned the Northwest Passage to become a major sea route. Estimates of hydrocarbon reserves across the Canadian North were increasing and oil was trading for 11 times more in 1980 than it had ten years earlier. In 1982, the Canadian Department of External Affairs provided Cabinet with a 15-year estimate of Arctic shipping which anticipated 390 annual full or partial transits of the Northwest Passage by 1987, increasing to 894 full or par-tial one-way trips by 1995.[51] Corporate forecasts were equally ambitious. In 1980, Dome anticipated commercial production of petroleum to start as early as 1986 and reach up to 1.5 million barrels per day by 2000.[52] To put these figures into per-spective, when the government first opened offshore drilling in 1976, the country's oil production amounted to only 479,397 barrels per day.[53] If Dome's estimates were correct, national output would have seen a 300 percent plus increase.

Government tax incentives propelled this boom. The most significant was the Frontier Exploration Allowance, more commonly referred to as "super depletion" or the "Gallagher Amendment."[54] This 1977 amendment meant that 200 percent of expenditures over CDN$5 million per well could be written off against resource income elsewhere, putting companies' net cost below zero for those with marginal income tax rates above 50 percent. This policy was clearly aimed at the Arctic, given that nowhere else did a well cost CDN$5 million to drill. In 1979, the *Calgary Herald* calculated that, of the CDN$150 million spent in the Beaufort Sea in 1978 alone, Canadian taxpayers had covered between CDN$130 and 140 million in deferred taxes.[55]

---

50   Id., 208.

51   Memorandum to Cabinet, "Status of Arctic Archipelagic Waters," 1 June 1982, LAC, RG 12, vol. 5561, file 8100-15-4-2 (s), pt. 4.

52   Dome Petroleum, *Beaufort Sea/Mackenzie Delta Development Plan*, Arctic Institute of North America Library, University of Calgary.

53   Statistics Canada, *Historical Statistics of Canada,* Table Q19–25, online: http://www.statcan .gc.ca.

54   So named after Jack Gallagher, the CEO of Dome Petroleum and the man most responsi-ble for the lobbying which resulted in the system.

55   Jim Lyon, *Dome Petroleum: The Inside Story of its Rise and Fall* (New York: Buffalo Books, 1983).

The possibility of major international traffic along the route was a cause for celebration within the Canadian government, which had long hoped to spark economic growth in the region. Paradoxically, it also rekindled old concerns of sovereignty and control. In direct response to the voyages of *Manhattan*, Pierre Trudeau's Liberal Government instituted sweeping new environmental protection legislation to preserve the fragile Arctic marine ecosystem. Politically, the *Arctic Waters Pollution Prevention Act* (AWPPA) also served to solidify Canadian regulatory power over the region in the face of any potential American challenge to Canada's sovereignty.[56] At the same time, Canada expanded its territorial sea from three to 12 nautical miles to close parts of the Northwest Passage as territorial sea.

Further government efforts throughout the decade sought to strengthen and codify Canadian jurisdiction. In 1976, Cabinet informed the relevant government departments that they should begin applying Canadian law and regulations to the northern waters. How this was to be executed prompted discussion and debate, since existing legislation might render enforcement difficult. Canada's right to apply its customs duties or criminal law to ships or drilling installations outside of the 12-mile territorial limit remained uncertain. The *Customs Act* and the Criminal Code only applied within waters that were officially declared Canadian—thus excluding much of the water in the Arctic Archipelago.[57] Formally claiming sovereignty over these waters was politically sensitive given the ongoing resistance to such claims by the United States.[58] As such, Canada continued to control and regulate Arctic activity outside any explicit claim to sovereignty over what it considered internal waters. In 1977, the *Northern Canada Vessel Traffic Services Zone Regulations* (NORDREG) were established to facilitate vessel reporting and track ship positions for vessels over 300 tons. In short, Canada followed a functional and pragmatic course.

Enforcing Canadian jurisdiction and supporting Arctic development was also a practical consideration. As such, the federal icebreaker fleet expanded. The icebreaker *John A. Macdonald* was completed in 1960, and *Norman McLeod Rogers* and *Louis S. St. Laurent* both launched nine years later. *Louis S. St. Laurent* was the first Canadian icebreaker built primarily for Arctic work and remains the government's largest and most powerful icebreaker. In the late 1970s and early 1980s three medium icebreakers were also completed. CCGS

---

56 On the AWPPA see Christopher Kirkey, "The Arctic Waters Pollution Prevention Initiatives: Canada's Response to an American Challenge," *International Journal of Canadian Studies* 13 (Spring 1996): 41–59.

57 Memorandum to Cabinet, "Status of Arctic Archipelagic Waters," 1 June 1982, LAC, RG 12, vol. 5561, file 8100-15-4-2 (s), pt. 4.

58 On this dispute see Adam Lajeunesse, *Lock, Stock, and Icebergs: The Evolution of Canada's Arctic Maritime Sovereignty* (Vancouver: University of British Columbia Press, 2016).

Pierre Radisson entered service in 1978, *Sir John Franklin* the following year, and *Des Groseilliers* in 1982, replacing *N.B. McLean* and *d'Iberville* (which were retired in the early 1980s). Displacing 6,600 tonnes, these new ships belonged to the Coast Guard's 1200-class and, while they spent some time in the Arctic, they were not principally intended for polar operations. The Canadian Coast Guard also received several light icebreakers capable of Arctic operations— but which were primarily intended for more southerly waters. CCGS *Griffon* was completed in 1970 and, in 1971, the government started to order its fleet of 3,800 tonne, type 1100 light icebreakers, with deliveries starting in 1985.

Canadian icebreakers supported offshore development by facilitating shipping while also contributing to the ongoing industry experiments into ice dynamics and ship design. Most of their work, however, was in support of local shipping and community activity. While dramatic voyages like that of *Manhattan* dominated the headlines, most Arctic shipping was routine community sealift. From the 1960s to the 1970s, somewhere between 90,000 and 110,000 short tons of supply traveled by sealift.[59] By the 1970s, the Hudson's Bay Company had left the business and this work shifted to private shippers, normally contracted by the Government of Canada. As was the case with industry, community shipping costs were high, ranging from CDN$125–200 per ton,[60] with most of these goods carried by a small number of companies with specialized craft: Fednav, Resolute Shipping, Chimo Shipping, Logistec Nav, and CA Crosbie.[61] By the early 1980s, Fednav emerged as the dominant shipping company in the Canadian Arctic. Primarily a dry cargo carrier, it operated two tankers, MV *Arctic* and *Axel Heiberg*, which supported the DEW Line sites, several mines, and all essential community resupply.

As shipping developed during the 1970s and 1980s, the optimism surrounding it was often tempered by persistent fears of its environmental impacts. The AWPPA had its roots in political concerns surrounding sovereignty and jurisdiction, but was also a genuine effort to stave off a potentially devastating spill. Several major oil spills from the time highlighted the dangers of moving that cargo through the North. The wrecks of the Liberian tankers *Torrey Canyon* in 1967 and *Arrow* in 1970 captured international attention and intensified fears about pollution in icy and often dangerous Arctic waters. Naturally, an exponential increase of large vessels carrying hydrocarbons or minerals across ice-infested, poorly charted passages raised the possibility of catastrophic disaster. After all, during its maiden Arctic voyage, *Manhattan*'s hull was torn

59   Wright (n 3), p. 291.
60   Price corrected to inflation in 1974 dollars.
61   See full table in Wright (n 3), p. 310.

open by the thick ice in McClure Strait—though without serious consequence to the ship or the environment.[62]

The response was a massive research and development program and, over the course of the 1970s and 1980s, Canadian resource and shipping companies developed new icebreaking designs and safety systems that proved highly effective. There were no major oil spills and little real damage to the growing fleet of Arctic capable vessels. The only major loss during the period was the *Finn Polaris*, a cargo vessel that ran into ice and sank in Baffin Bay in 1991.[63]

Engineering work done in the 1980s by industry groups reflected a great deal of confidence that regular Arctic shipping could be done safely. Companies like Dome Petroleum spent significant time and effort in designing new ships and calculating risks, ultimately concluding that the Arctic ships then on the drawing boards would be much safer than a conventional tanker operating in warmer waters, and as much as one hundred times less likely to have an accident.[64]

Maritime safety and environmental preservation were natural concerns for the residents of the Arctic as well. Canada's Inuit communities use Arctic waterways in their homeland for travel, hunting, and fishing. Indeed, the Inuit rely on these waters for their physical and cultural survival. In submissions to the Macdonald Royal Commission on economic development, Inuit spokespersons insisted that government policy recognize not only the value of shipping through the Arctic, but also "the importance of the Arctic seas to the economy of Inuit."[65] The Inuit Circumpolar Council (Canada) made the point even more succinctly in a 2008 publication entitled "the sea ice is our highway."[66]

As some of the major oil and gas projects progressed, Inuit Tapirisat of Canada (now Inuit Tapiriit Kanatami), which represented the 25,000 Inuit in communities across the Canadian North, offered criticism in the 1980s. Many Inuit feared marine pollution or disruption to their hunting grounds by tankers cutting through the ice or scaring away marine mammals. These concerns led to some of the first large-scale scientific studies of icebreaker impacts on

62   See P. Whitney Lackenbauer and Elizabeth Elliot-Meisel, *"One of the Great Polar Navigators": Captain T.C. Pullen's Personal Records of Arctic Voyages, Volume 1: Official Roles,* Documents on Canadian Arctic Sovereignty and Security (DCASS) No. 12 (Calgary: Arctic Institute of North America, 2018).

63   Wright (n 3), p. 183.

64   Ray Lemberg, "Hydrocarbon Transport and Risk Assessment," in *The Challenge of Arctic Shipping,* eds., David L. Vanderzwaag and Cynthia Lamson (Montreal: McGill-Queen's University Press, 1990), 198.

65   Peter Jull, "Inuit Politics and the Arctic Seas," in Griffiths, ed. (n 34), p. 56.

66   Inuit Circumpolar Council, *The Sea Ice is Our Highway: An Inuit Perspective on Transportation in the Arctic* (March 2008).

mammals and Inuit mobility. Inuit also voiced concerns through the Inuit Circumpolar Council (ICC).[67]

In addition to the practical considerations of pollution prevention, the prospect of large-scale shipping and development generated new impetus amongst Canadian Inuit to see a political settlement over their Arctic lands claims before any resource projects moved forward. In the Western Arctic, Justice Thomas Berger conducted the Mackenzie Valley Pipeline Inquiry to investigate the social and economic impact of moving Beaufort Sea gas south via the Mackenzie Valley. In 1976, the Berger inquiry recommended a ten-year moratorium on pipelines to resolve critical Aboriginal land claims issues.[68] In the east, the Canadian government and Inuit began the Nunavut land claim negotiations in 1975. The prospect of Arctic shipping catalysed discussions of Inuit self-government and influenced political discussions that ultimately produced new northern governing structures in the Canadian Arctic.

These political impacts outlived the shipping boom itself. In the early 1980s, Canadian oil and gas companies continued to design massive tankers, bring pilot projects online, expand their acreages, and even buy up shipyards[69] to help fulfill ambitious shipping and development plans. By the mid-1980s, however, industry confronted a new reality: low global prices. Arctic operations had always been premised on high global resource prices and generous government support, and both slipped away. Crude prices began to dip in 1981 and then fell precipitously in 1985. Drilling activity in the North quickly dried up and several of the largest companies folded. Dome Petroleum—the country's leader in Arctic offshore operations—was the most dramatic example, collapsing completely in 1987. Low oil and metal prices effectively scuttled the dreams of an Arctic bonanza so that, by the late 1980s, the oil, gas, and mining industries had largely evacuated the region. What the Canadian government and industry had expected to evolve into a major shipping route quickly reverted to a region of regular sealift and light tourist activity. Arctic scholar Oran Young's portending of an "age of the Arctic" in the mid-1980s proved premature.[70]

---

67   Lewington (n 34), p. 174. The ICC is a multinational non-governmental organization representing Inuit across the circumpolar North.

68   Sarah Bonesteel, *Canada's Relationship with the Inuit: A History of Policy and Program Development* (Ottawa: Indian and Northern Affairs Canada, 2006), 55.

69   Dome Petroleum alone operated a fleet of three drill-ships, seven ice-reinforced supply ships and a cargo/base vessel through its subsidiary Canadian Marine Drilling; Dome Petroleum, *Beaufort Sea/Mackenzie Delta Development Plan* (November, 1980).

70   Oran Young, "The Age of the Arctic," *Foreign Policy* 61 (Winter, 1985–1986): 160–179.

6   Conclusion

As the chapters in this volume demonstrate, shipping and related issues in Canada's Arctic waters have returned to the forefront of academic, practitioner, and political discussion and debate in the early twenty-first century. Growing awareness about the effects of climate change on the cryosphere has stimulated both excitement and concern about the prospect of more accessible Arctic waters.[71] New patterns of maritime activity have emerged alongside a heightened tempo of longstanding ones. Nevertheless, one hundred years after Stefansson proclaimed the Arctic to be the 'new Mediterranean,' applying such a descriptor to Canadian Arctic waters remains more hyperbole than reality.[72]

Will Canada retain its resurgent interest in the region, or will it once again follow the boom-and-bust pattern of the last century? Will increased maritime accessibility, owing to reduced sea ice extent and thickness, exacerbate risks related to ship operations? Will new forms of Inuit-Crown partnership represent a break from the Ottawa-centric, colonial decision-making patterns of the twentieth century? Will efforts to designate low-impact shipping corridors, designed in coordination with the local Inuit communities to address concerns about the effects of expanded traffic on marine mammals and ecosystems, bear fruit? While the following chapters discuss these issues, enduring realities remain. Despite melting sea ice, challenges and dangers associated with maritime operations in the Canadian Arctic will persist. So too will the need to temper boosterism around newly 'accessible' sea routes with the sobering realities of oscillating cycles of resource extraction, a fickle and generally risk-averse marine transportation sector, and increasingly confident assertion by Inuit and other Northern Canadians about their desired futures for their homeland.

---

71   See, for example, Lawrence R. Mudryk *et al.*, "Impact of 1, 2 and 4°C of Global Warming on Ship Navigation in the Canadian Arctic," *Nature Climate Change* 11:8 (2021): 673–679.

72   See, for example, Frédéric Lasserre and Sébastien Pelletier, "Polar Super Seaways? Maritime Transport in the Arctic: An Analysis of Shipowners' Intentions," *Journal of Transport Geography* 19:6 (2011): 1465–1473; Lasserre, "Arctic Shipping: A Contrasted Expansion of a Largely Destinational Market," in *The GlobalArctic Handbook*, ed., Lassi Heininen (Cham: Springer, 2019), 83–100; Jackie Dawson, Alison Cook, Jean Holloway, and Luke Copland, "Analysis of Changing Levels of Ice Strengthening (Ice Class) among Vessels Operating in the Canadian Arctic over the Past 30 Years," *Arctic* 75:4 (December 2022): 2–17.

CHAPTER 5

Comparative Perspectives on the Development of Canadian Arctic Shipping: Impacts of Climate Change and Globalization

Frédéric Lasserre

Abstract

Climate change does impact sea ice, with a significant reduction of its extent and thickness. Climate change thus facilitates navigation, without making it easier, and indeed has contributed to the expansion of traffic in the Canadian Arctic, with a five-fold increase since 2000. However, there is a discrepancy between expectations that the melting of sea ice triggered and actual levels of shipping, especially regarding transit volumes. This can be accounted for by the fact that drivers of shipping in the Arctic, especially in Russian waters, are linked to the development of natural resources extraction and the perception that Arctic shipping markets may not readily fit into global strategies adopted by shipping companies. Potential economic drivers of Arctic shipping, extraction and transit, are related to the insertion of the region into globalized markets. With regard to climate change, conditions for the development of shipping in the Canadian and Russian Arctic are increasingly shaped by market, political and legal developments from outside the region, giving credence to the idea that the Arctic is increasingly inserted into the global economy. This chapter analyzes the evolution of Canadian Arctic shipping in the face of these developments.

Keywords

climate change – Arctic shipping – natural resources – Russia – Canada – ports – transit – destinational shipping – globalization

1 Introduction

Climate change does impact sea ice, with a significant reduction of its extent and thickness. Climate change thus facilitates navigation, without making it easier, and indeed has contributed to the expansion of traffic in the Canadian

Arctic,[1] with a fivefold increase since 2000. However, there is a discrepancy between expectations that the melting of sea ice triggered and actual levels of shipping, especially regarding transit volumes. This can be accounted for by the fact that drivers of shipping in the Arctic, especially in Russian waters, are linked to the development of natural resources extraction and the perception that Arctic shipping markets may not readily fit into global strategies adopted by shipping companies. Besides transit and resource extraction, a third engine of growth, community resupply, is indeed expanding, but so far companies have increased vessel size rather than the number of voyages. In other words, potential economic drivers of Arctic shipping, extraction and transit, are related to the insertion of the region into globalized markets. With regards to climate change, conditions for the development of shipping in the Canadian and Russian Arctic are increasingly shaped by market, political and legal developments from outside the region, giving credence to the idea that the Arctic is increasingly inserted into the global economy.[2] In this chapter, the evolution of Canadian Arctic shipping is compared with trends in the Russian Arctic.

2   Impacts of Climate Change: Navigability

Since 1979, the yearly minimum extent of sea ice in the Arctic has decreased by about 55 percent, from 7.2 million km² to 3.41 million km² in 2012, 3.74 million km² in 2020 and 4.72 million km² in 2021.[3] Several conclusions can

---

1   The literature abounds with diverse definitions of the Arctic. In this chapter, largely relying on traffic figures provided under the *Northern Canada Vessel Traffic Services Zone Regulations* (NORDREG) (SOR/2010-127), it is NORDREG's definition of Canadian Arctic waters that was adopted: north of 60°N in the Labrador Sea and Baffin Bay on the Canadian side of the maritime border with Greenland; the whole of Ungava and Hudson bays; then landward to the Arctic Circle but encompassing the entire Canadian Archipelago up to 200 nautical miles. The *Arctic Waters Pollution Prevention Act* (RSC 1985, c A-12) definition comprises waters north of 60°N, thus excluding Ungava and Hudson bays. With regard to the figures provided by NORDREG for Canadian marine traffic, it must be mentioned that vessels 300 gross tons and less are not required to report. Several, for security reasons, do report as they have automatic identification system (AIS) equipment on board, but it may be that some small vessels do not appear in official figures.
2   Matthias Finger and Lassi Heininen (eds), *The GlobalArctic Handbook* (Cham: Springer, 2019); Frédéric Lasserre, "L'essor des Activités Économiques en Arctique : Impact des Changements Climatiques et de la Mondialisation," *Belgéo, Revue Belge de Géographie* 1 (2021), https://doi .org/10.4000/belgeo.44181.
3   National Snow & Ice Data Center (NSIDC), "Arctic Sea Ice at Highest Minimum Since 2014," *Arctic Sea Ice News & Analysis*, 22 September 2021, https://nsidc.org/arcticseaicenews /2021/09/arctic-sea-ice-at-highest-minimum-since-2014/, accessed 3 October 2021.

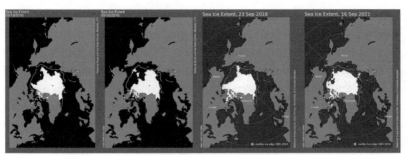

FIGURE 5.1   Extension of Arctic sea ice at its summer minimum, 2010, 2016, 2018 and
2021
ADAPTED BY THE AUTHOR FROM NSIDC, "ARCTIC SEA ICE AT
HIGHEST MINIMUM SINCE 2014," *ARCTIC SEA ICE NEWS & ANALYSIS*
(22 SEPTEMBER 2021) WITH PERMISSION

be inferred from the non-linear evolution of the September minimal sea
ice extent. First, the extent of Arctic sea ice at its minimum is decreasing,
and this trend is accelerating since the slope of the regression lines is more
pronounced for recent periods until 2020. Second, a significant year-to-year
variation is apparent: despite the general declining trend, there are years
with more ice than the previous years, which make the year-on-year change
unpredictable.

The spatial distribution of the September minimal sea ice (Figure 5.1) is
revealing of two facts: first, the Siberian coast is much more ice-free than the
Canadian archipelago; and second, despite the general trend towards a shrinking sea ice cover, significant inter-annual variability in sea ice distribution
remains, with some areas being open waters some years, but not others.

Variability of navigability in Canadian Arctic Achipelago channels, especially the Northwest Passage (NWP), is typically more pronounced than in
the Northern Sea Route (NSR).[4] This makes long-term planning more difficult
despite the long-term reduced sea ice trend.[5]

---

4   Penelope M. Wagner *et al.*, "Sea-Ice Information and Forecast Needs for Industry Maritime
Stakeholders," *Polar Geography* 43(2–3) (2020): 160–187.
5   Nadine Blacquière, Assistant Director Operations, Desgagnés Transarctik, personal
communication, Montreal, 17 February 2018; Alexis Dorais, Assistant Manager, Arctic Operations and Ice Services, Fednav, personal communication, Montreal, 10 March 2021; Suzanne
Paquin, President and Chief Executive Officer, NEAS, personal communication, Montreal,
23 January 2018; Rym Msadek *et al.*, "Prévoir les variations saisonnières de la glace de mer
arctique et leurs impacts sur le climat," *La Météorologie* 111 (2020): 24–33.

3   Contrasted Evolution of Traffic

Given this foreseeable future for sea ice in the Arctic, which presents contrasted trends and evolution depending on the region, what can be said about the evolution of Arctic shipping? Traffic volume has grown significantly in the Arctic, both in general[6] and along the Northwest Passage and in the Canadian Arctic.[7] In the Arctic as a whole, the number of single vessels entering the area increased by 25 percent between 2013 and 2019.[8]

3.1   *Arctic Traffic Expansion due to Natural Resources Extraction*
As seen in Tables 5.1 and 5.2, vessel voyages[9] are definitely increasing in the Arctic. From 2009 to 2021, traffic multiplied by 1.97 in the Canadian Arctic, and by 1.7 between 2016 and 2020 in the waters of the Northern Sea Route.[10]

TABLE 5.1   Vessel movements in the Canadian Arctic, number of voyages, NORDREG zone[11]

	2009	2011	2013	2014	2015	2016	2017	2018	2019	2020	2021
Ship tonnage, million tons (dwt)	–	1.28	1.39	1.43	1.8	2.79	3.54	4.38	5.16	7.6	14.6
Voyages	225	319	348	302	315	347	416	408	431	345	444
Of which:											
Fishing boats	65	136	137	119	129	131	138	139	137	132	134
Cargo or barges	109	126	127	108	120	147	188	197	223	183	289

6   Protection of the Arctic Marine Environment Working Group (PAME), *The Increase In Arctic Shipping 2013–2019. Arctic Shipping Status Report (ASSR) #1* (Akureyri: Arctic Council, 2020), https://www.pame.is/document-library/pame-reports-new/pame-ministerial -deliverables/2021-12th-arctic-council-ministerial-meeting-reykjavik-iceland/793-assr -1-the-increase-in-arctic-shipping-2013-2019/file.

7   PAME, *Shipping in the Northwest Passage: Comparing 2013 with 2019. Arctic Shipping Status Report (ASSR) #3* (Akureyri: Arctic Council, 2021), https://oaarchive.arctic-council.org /bitstream/handle/11374/2734/ASSR%20Report%203_.pdf?sequence=1&isAllowed=y.

8   PAME (n 6).

9   A voyage is the movement of a vessel in the NORDREG zone, between its entry point and its exit point.

10   The Northern Sea Route comprises Russian Arctic waters between the Kara Gate and the Bering Strait. Thus, traffic in the Barents Sea is not included in NSR figures, nor is traffic in Russia's Arctic Pacific waters.

11   The author would like to express gratitude to NORDREG and XST Xpert Solutions Technologiques Inc. for their cooperation in the framing of this research.

TABLE 5.1   Vessel movements in the Canadian Arctic, number of voyages, NORDREG zone
(*cont.*)

	2009	2011	2013	2014	2015	2016	2017	2018	2019	2020	2021
Of which:											
General cargo	23	38	35	32	34	36	50	48	59	41	55
Tanker	23	30	28	25	27	23	24	29	28	31	36
Dry bulk	27	23	27	33	36	53	72	89	106	91	167
Tugs and barges	36	33	36	18	23	35	42	31	30	20	31
Pleasure craft	12	15	32	30	23	22	32	17	19	2	1
Cruise/ passenger	11	11	17	11	18	20	19	21	24	0	0
Government vessels (icebreakers, navy)	21	20	17	23	16	20	22	18	20	21	11
Research vessels	7	11	20	10	9	6	13	13	8	4	3
Others	–	–	–	–	3	3	6	3	–	3	6

SOURCE: FIGURES COMPILED BY THE AUTHOR FROM DATA SUBMITTED BY NORDREG,
IQALUIT, AND BY XST XPERT SOLUTIONS TECHNOLOGIQUES INC.

The years 2020 and 2021 were unusual because of the impact of the COVID-19 pandemic, which either affected mining[12] or triggered a ban on cruise shipping in Canada, for instance. In the Canadian Arctic, 2020 is marked by a decrease in traffic (20 percent), largely attributable to the drop in traffic of pleasure craft and cruise ships, which were banned from entry due to the pandemic. The number of merchant ships has decreased, but the total tonnage has increased, an indication of the arrival of larger ships to serve operating mining sites like Mary River on Baffin Island or Raglan and Jilin Jien in northern Quebec. For 2021, the ban on tourism-related traffic (cruising and yachting) was still enforced,[13] but fishing traffic recovered while commercial traffic exploded, increasing 43.5 percent from 2020 and 19.7 percent above 2019 figures.

12   Magali Vullierme, "Arctic Mines Facing COVID-19: Global Pandemic, Specific Strategies," *Regards Géopolitiques* 7(1) (2021): 18–25, https://cqegheiulaval.com/2021/03/30/arctic-mines-facing-covid-19-global-pandemic-specific-strategies/.
13   The only pleasure craft voyaging in the Canadian Arctic in 2021 was a Chinese craft, *Zhai Mo 1*, which was not authorized to enter Canadian waters. Similarly, in 2020 the

TABLE 5.2   Vessel movements in NSR waters, number of voyages

	2016	2017	2018	2019	2020	2021
Volume transported, million metric tons	7.265	10.713	20.18	31.53	32.97	34.85
Voyages in NSR waters	1,705	1,908	2,022	2,694	2,905	3,227
Of which:						
Tanker	477	653	686	799	750	705
LNG tanker	–	13	225	507	510	528
General cargo	nd	nd	nd	nd	49	800
Bulk	519	515	422	546	710	94
Container	169	156	150	171	171	177
Icebreaker	58	101	232	231	220	354
Supply	–	57	104	169	264	156
Research	91	87	85	93	114	138

SOURCE: ADAPTED FROM CHNL

Despite the general and substantial increase in vessel traffic observed in the two areas, contrasting trends can be observed from these figures. In the Canadian Arctic, in terms of number of voyages, fishing vessels experienced a steady expansion between 2009 and 2011, going from 65 to 136 voyages, but fishing traffic has since stalled. The increase in traffic was due to cargo ships activity (+145 percent from 2009 to 2021), of which dry bulk experienced the largest expansion (+518.5 percent), driven by mining activities, and general cargo (+139.1 percent), driven by community resupply. Part of community resupply is also performed by barges pushed by tugs, from Hay River on the Great Slave Lake and then down the Mackenzie River, or from the port of Moosonee to northern Ontario communities. Significant growth in tonnage is largely due to the expansion of bulk cargo traffic, growing from 1.28 million dwt in 2011 to 14.6 million dwt in 2021 (+1,040.6 percent).

Bulk traffic has benefited from the exploitation of Arctic and Subarctic mines, such as Voisey's Bay (Labrador), Raglan and Canadian Royalties/Jilin Jien (Quebec), and Mary River (Baffin Island, Nunavut). This expanding traffic volume has largely compensated for the dwindling traffic to and from Churchill since the port closed down in 2016 before reopening in 2019 (there were only 4 voyages of grain-carrying bulk vessels in 2019 and 3 in 2020); modernization

---

New Zealand *Kiwi Roa* pleasure craft entered the NORDREG zone without clearance and transited the NWP (NORDREG database).

of the rail tracks led the port to close down in 2021 until 2023.[14] For instance, Baffinland Iron Mines shipped 920,000 tons of ore from its mine in Mary River through its port of Milne Inlet in the first year of activity in 2015, then 4.1 million tons in 2017,[15] 5.1 million tons in 2018[16] and 5.5 million tons in 2020.[17] The company intends to eventually reach an annual volume of 12 million tons in the next few years, and eventually 30 million tons.[18] Other active gold mines north of Rankin Inlet also generate traffic related to the logistics of mining operations. In the Canadian Archipelago, Fednav operates ice-strengthened Polar Class 4 vessels (*Arctic, Umiak, Nunavik, Arvik*) capable of navigating in winter, servicing the two Deception Bay mines in northern Quebec. The company may develop a business model in partnership with mining companies for year-round shipping to Deception Bay and Milne Inlet (operational) as well as Steensby Inlet (projected). The logistics of mining activities are dominant in terms of tonnage in the Canadian Arctic: in 2020, the capacity of bulk carriers servicing mines (measured in cumulated vessel dwt), at 6.1 Mt, accounted for 77.3 percent of the tonnage capacity of traffic (measured in dwt); in 2021, at 12,32 Mt, it accounted for 84.4 percent. Large, powerful dry bulk carriers transport ore from the maritime terminal built to service the mines: the construction of deep-water docks is required for base-metal mines that ship large quantities of ore, as is the case at Milne Inlet (Mary River) and Deception Bay (Raglan and Jilin Jien).

In Russia, tanker traffic increased 147.8 percent between 2016 and 2021. LNG tanker traffic went from nil to 528 voyages, and icebreaker voyages increased 510 percent. Tanker traffic experienced a sustained growth due to the oil and gas developments in the Kara Sea (Prirazlomoye and Varandey oil terminals)[19]

14 Glen Hallick, "Port of Churchill will close for two years", Western Investor, 12 November 2021, https://www.westerninvestor.com/british-columbia/port-of-churchill-will-close-for-two-years-4751102.
15 "Baffinland Iron Mines Ships Record Tonnage in 2017," *Maritime Magazine* 87 (2018): 98–99.
16 Christopher Debicki, "Rapid Expansion of Mary River Mine Could Undermine Inuit Economic Benefit," Oceans North, 1 March 2019, https://oceansnorth.org/en/blog/2019/03/rapid-expansion-of-mary-river-mine-could-undermine-inuit-economic-benefits/.
17 Baffinland, "Baffinland Iron Mines 2020 Annual Report to the Nunavut Impact Review Board," 6 May 2021, https://www.baffinland.com/_resources/2020-NIRB-Annual-Report.pdf.
18 Id.; David Venn, "Baffinland Still Plans to Move Forward with Steensby Inlet Route," *Nunatsiaq News*, 1 November 2021, https://nunatsiaq.com/stories/article/baffinland-still-plans-to-move-forward-with-steensby-inlet-route/.
19 S Agarcov, S Kozmenko and A Teslya, "Organizing an Oil Transportation System in the Arctic," *IOP Conference Series: Earth and Environmental Science* 434 (2020): 012011, https://iopscience.iop.org/article/10.1088/1755-1315/434/1/012011/pdf.

and on the Yamal peninsula and Ob Bay, with Sabetta and Novy Port the main terminals and the impending opening of an Arctic LNG 2 terminal.[20] The scheduled opening of new oil fields (Vankor in particular) in the Taymyr peninsula, east of the Yenisei delta, should contribute to the expansion of traffic: the Vankor field alone should produce 30 million tons from 2024. With the programmed opening of coal, lead and zinc mines, and more ore shipments from the port of Murmansk, bulk traffic should grow fast in the Russian Arctic as well.[21] Fishing, concentrated in the Barents and Bering Seas, as well as passenger traffic, do not appear in these statistics (25 voyages for fishing in 2021 and 1 voyage for passenger vessels).

It is apparent that the main driver for the expansion of shipping in both the NWP and the NSR is natural resources exploitation, including mining, oil and gas, and fishing. Resource extraction, in particular, accounts for the expansion of traffic: more and bigger ships account for a rapid increase in transported tonnage, especially along the NSR where resource extraction is more active than in Arctic Canada.[22] Presently there is more activity in the oil and gas sector along the NSR, whereas mining is the leading extractive sector in the Canadian Arctic. Community resupply in Canadian waters also experienced a sustained growth, with a temporary dip in 2020 due to the COVID-19 pandemic.

3.2 *Transit Traffic Remains Weak along Arctic Passages*

Contrary to popular belief and widespread expectations, however, transit traffic remains very limited along Arctic passages in Canada and Russia. Despite the ongoing melting of sea ice, transit traffic remains rather limited along the Northwest Passage and the Northern Sea Route, here again for different reasons.[23]

---

20   Atle Staalesen, "Big Oil Comes to Icy Arctic Bay," *The Barents Observer*, 17 December 2018, https://thebarentsobserver.com/en/industry-and-energy/2018/12/big-oil-comes-icy-arctic -bay; E Katysheva, "The Role of the Russian Arctic Gas Industry in the Northern Sea Route Development," *IOP Conference Series: Earth and Environmental Science* 539 (2020): 012075, https://iopscience.iop.org/article/10.1088/1755-1315/539/1/012075/pdf.

21   Nickel ore is shipped in containers from the port of Dudinka, thus the apparently high container traffic in fact reflects shipments of mineral and metallurgical semi-transformed products, in addition to limited reefer shipments of fish from Kamchatka to Arkhangelsk and St. Petersburg.

22   Frédéric Lasserre and Pauline Pic, "Exploitation des ressources naturelles dans l'Arctique. Une évolution contrastée dans les soubresauts du marché mondial," *Études du CQEG* 3, 2021, https://cqegeseiulaval.files.wordpress.com/2021/01/etudes-cqeg-rn-arctique-jan-2021.pdf.

23   A methodological note is necessary here. The term transit is interpreted differently by the various administrations that collect and publish figures describing transit along Arctic passages. In Canada, figures are collected by the Canadian Coast Guard section responsible for the enforcement of NORDREG. The definition used by NORDREG for transit is a movement between Baffin Bay to the Beaufort Sea. Robert Headland and his team at

In both cases, there is a definite trend towards expansion, but with differentiated histories and composition (Tables 5.3 and 5.4). Transit numbers across the Northwest Passage were higher at the beginning of the period, experienced growth until 2012, witnessed a moderate decline, expanded again until 2017, then collapsed in 2018, only to recover in 2019 and then collapse because of the ban on cruise and pleasure craft transits. Transit in the NWP was largely composed of pleasure boats as opposed to between zero and two commercial vessels. This may be about to change: 3 transits were made by cargo vessels in 2019, 5 in 2020 and 3 in 2021. Vessels from the Dutch shipping company Royal Wagenborg accounted for 2 of the transits in 2019, all 5 in 2020 and all 3 in 2021. The company openly advertises the voyages, hinting it may attempt to develop this market in the future.[24] As far as cargo vessels are concerned, tankers and bulkers were prevalent among the few transits before 2017; now general cargo vessels dominate. It is interesting to note that the expansion of mining in the Canadian Arctic does not support transit expansion, despite the fact ore is at times delivered to China. In 2014, a Fednav vessel transited the NWP to deliver nickel ore to China from the Raglan mine; however, in 2018 (two transits), in 2019 (one transit) and again in 2021 (one transit), shipments of iron ore from

------

the Scott Polar Research Institute (SPRI) use a definition whereby transits are counted between the Labrador Sea and Bering Strait. This difference does impact figures since a vessel servicing the community of Inuvik from Montreal will be counted as a transit by NORDREG, but not by the Scott Polar Research Institute. This is why the SPRI counts 32 transits in 2017 (33 for NORDREG), and 3 in 2018 (5 for NORDREG) for instance. In Russia, figures are collected by the Northern Sea Route Administration (NSRA), then formatted and published by the Center for High North Logistics (CHNL), a private association and therefore not an official Russian administration. CHNL bases its figures on the NSRA definition of transit, which is a voyage between the Bering Strait and the Kara Gate. Thus, a ship from Kamchatka to Murmansk will be counted a transit by CHNL despite the fact the ship is still in Russian Arctic waters. Other voyages, like those carried out in 2009 by heavy lift vessels *Beluga Foresight* and *Beluga Fraternity* from South Korea are counted as transits by CHNL despite the fact they unloaded their cargo at Yamburg before proceeding to Germany, thus making their voyages destinational. On these methodological issues, see Frédéric Lasserre and Olga Alexeeva, "Analysis of Maritime Transit Trends in the Arctic Passages," in *International Law and Politics of the Arctic Ocean: Essays in Honour of Donat Pharand*, eds., Suzanne Lalonde and Ted L McDorman (Leiden: Brill Academic, 2015), 180–193; Frédéric Lasserre *et al.*, "Compared Transit Traffic Analysis Along the NSR and the NWP," in *Arctic Shipping. Climate Change, Commercial Traffic and Port Development*, eds., Frédéric Lasserre and Olivier Faury (London: Routledge, 2019), 71–93. This chapter uses the official NORDREG figures and semi-official CHNL figures.

24   "Wagenborg is Increasingly Knocking on the Door of the North Pole," Wagenborg, 2019. https://www.wagenborg.com/cases/wagenborg-is-increasingly-knocking-on-the-door-of-the-north-pole; "Polar Season 2020 Closed Successfully after Five North West Passages," Wagenborg, 9 November 2020, https://www.wagenborg.com/news/polar-season-2020-closed-successfully-after-five-north-west-passages.

the Mary River mine to China transited across the NSR.[25] In 2013, the Baffinland CEO made it clear that the company would not use the NWP for transit to
Asia;[26] the company somewhat softened its stance in 2019, but apparently has
yet to use what it considers an "alternative shipping route."[27]

TABLE 5.3   Transit traffic along the Northwest Passage, 2006–2021

Vessel type	2006	2010	2011	2012	2013	2014	2016	2017	2018	2019	2020	2021
Icebreaker	2	2	2	2	2	4	3	2	2	1	1	1
Cruise	2	4	2	2	4	2	3	3	0	5	0	–
Pleasure boat	–	12	13	22	14	10	15	22	2	13	1	–
Tug	1	1	–	2	–	–	–	3	1	1	–	–
Cargo ship	0	0	1	1	1	1	1	2	0	3	5	3
Of which:												
Bulk	–	–	–	–	1	1	–	–	–	–	1	–
Tanker	–	–	1	1	–	–	–	1	–	–	–	–
General cargo	–	–	–	–	–	–	1	1	–	3	4	3
Research	1	–	1	1	1	–	–	1	–	–		–
Other	–	–	–	–	–	–	1	4	–	–	–	1
Total	6	19	18	30	22	17	23	33	5	23	7	5

SOURCE: FIGURES COMPILED BY THE AUTHOR FROM DATA SUBMITTED BY NORDREG,
    IQALUIT AND BY XST XPERT SOLUTIONS TECHNOLOGIQUES INC.

25   Leo Ryan, "Record Iron Ore Shipments from Canadian Arctic to Europe-Asia," *AJoT*, 28
      November 2018, https://tinyurl.com/AJoT-Iron-Ore-NSR; Atle Staalesen, "As Ice Shrinks
      to Year's Low, a Powerful Fleet of Tankers Sail Arctic Route to Asia," *The Barents Observer*,
      3 October 2019, https://thebarentsobserver.com/en/arctic/2019/10/ice-shrinks-years-low
      -powerful-fleet-tankers-sail-arctic-route-asia; Atle Staalesen, "Brand New Bulk Carrier
      Brings North Canadian Ore to China Via Arctic Route," *The Barents Observer*, 25 October 2021,
      https://thebarentsobserver.com/en/arctic/2021/10/brand-new-bulk-carrier-brings-north
      -canadian-ore-china-arctic-route.
26   Paul Waldie, "Baffinland CEO Says No to Shipping Ore through Northwest Passage," *The
      Globe & Mail*, 17 October 2013, https://www.theglobeandmail.com/report-on-business
      /industry-news/energy-and-resources/baffinland-ceo-says-no-to-shipping-ore-through
      -northwest-passage/article14915542/.
27   Elaine Anselmi, "Baffinland Clarifies Northwest Passage Shipping Plans," *Nunatsiaq News*,
      26 September 2019, https://nunatsiaq.com/stories/article/baffinland-clarifies-northwest
      -passage-shipping-plans/.

TABLE 5.4   Transit traffic along the NSR, 2006–2021

	2008	2010	2011	2012	2013	2014	2015	2016	2017	2018	2019	2020	2021
Icebreaker	–	–	2	3	2	2	1	2	–	1	–	2	–
Government ship	–	–	1	0	1	1	3	1	–	–	–	–	–
Cruise	–	1	1	0	1	3	1	1	–	–	–	1	1
Tug, supply vessel	1	4	4	5	1	1	4	4	1	2	–	5	–
Cargo ship	2	6	31	38	64	24	15	11	24	23	32	51	84
Of which :													
Bulk	2	–	5	10	16	1	–	–	–	2	3	16	28
Tanker	–	3	17	27	33	14	2	–	5	3	9	7	8
General cargo	–	–	2	–	14	8	4	9	11	12	14	26	36
Container	–	–	1	–	–	–	–	–	–	1	1	2	1
Reefer		–	6	1	1	–	4	2	3	2	5	–	3
Heavy lift		2	–	–	–	1	1	–	5	3	–	–	8
Research		2	2	0	2	0	0	–	–	–	2	–	
Fishing		–	–	–	–	1	–	–	2	1	3	5	
Total official transit	3	13	41	46	71	31	18	19	27	27	37	64	85
Volume transported, million metric tons		0.11	0.82	1.26	1.18	0.27	0.04	0.21	0.19	0.490	0.697	1.281	2.027
Total volume handled in the NSR, million metric tons	2.219	2.085	3.225	3.75	3.914	3.982	5.432	7.265	10.73	20.18	31.53	32.97	34.85

SOURCE: CHNL DATA COMPILED AND ADAPTED BY AUTHOR, HTTPS://ARCTIC-LIO.COM/

Figures show that both in terms of voyages and tonnage, transit represents a small share of total traffic along the NSR, despite the recent increase in transit voyages and tonnage since 2018, with transit tonnage increasing to 1.2 Mt in 2020 and 2 Mt in 2021. In transit traffic along the NSR, cargo vessels are more diversified than in the NWP; between 2010 and 2014, tankers dominated transits, with general cargo vessels dominating since 2015. Bulkers were a significant share of vessels in 2012, 2013 and again in 2020 and 2021. As far as tonnage is concerned, bulkers represented the largest component of transit in 2020, with 1.004 Mt of iron ore shipped from Murmansk (78.4 percent) being largely responsible for the rapid expansion of transit that year. In 2019, crude oil represented 43.3 percent of transiting cargo and iron ore 21.5 percent. It is noteworthy that these shipments of iron ore from Murmansk represent transit from an Arctic port and thus can be considered as Arctic destinational traffic,[28] a methodological point discussed above.

Transit traffic along the NSR was initially very modest. It expanded to a high of 71 voyages in 2012, collapsed to 18 in 2014, and recovered gradually to 37 in 2019 and 74 in 2021. It may be that the increase will be an ongoing process, but that does not hide the fact that transit traffic remains modest, especially when compared to destinational traffic along the NSR, and when compared to transit traffic along major straits or canals like Malacca, Suez or Panama.[29] This transit level is clearly out of step with media forecasts announcing the advent of heavy traffic along Arctic routes.[30]

The composition of this traffic also differs by region. Commercial cargo ships represent the largest share of transit traffic along the NSR, whereas transit along the NWP is largely composed of pleasure boats, with commercial vessels comprising between zero and two units (except for five in 2019). One element that explains this weak interest in transit traffic along the NWP is a higher ice concentration in summer,[31] the absence of promotion of the NWP as opposed to a very proactive stance in Russia, and a higher level of equipment and infrastructure along the NSR, including ports that could harbor a damaged ship.[32] Icebreaker support also varies greatly, with Canada having only nine

---

28 Destinational traffic, as opposed to transit traffic where ships are merely transiting and not stopping, represents vessels that go to an Arctic destination, stop over to load or unload or perform an economic activity, then leave to another destination. By stopping over they place themselves under the State of the port legislation.

29 Frédéric Lasserre and Pierre-Louis Têtu, "The Geopolitics of Transportation in the Melting Arctic," in *A Research Agenda for Environmental Geopolitics*, ed., Shannon O'Lear (Northampton, MA: Edward Elgar, 2020), 105–120.

30 Frédéric Lasserre *et al.*, "Polar Seaways? Maritime Transport in the Arctic: An Analysis of Shipowners' Intentions II," *Journal of Transport Geography* 57(2016):105–114; Jean-François Doyon *et al.*, "Perceptions et stratégies de l'industrie maritime de vrac relativement à l'ouverture des passages arctiques," *Géotransports* 8 (2017): 5–22.

31 NSIDC (n 3); National Aeronautics and Space Administration (NASA), "Ice Persists in the Northwest Passage," Earth Observatory, 22 August 2021, https://earthobservatory.nasa.gov/images/148802/ice-persists-in-the-northwest-passage.

32 Lasserre *et al.* 2016 (n 30); Doyon *et al.* (n 30).

Arctic-capable icebreakers as opposed to Russia's five nuclear and 37 diesel icebreakers.[33]

This comparison between total and transit traffic underlines the fact that destinational traffic (ships going to the Arctic, stopping there to perform an economic task and then sailing back) remains the driving force in Arctic shipping along the NSR, but all the more so in the NWP where commercial transit was until recently very low and still is limited. This destinational traffic is fueled by the servicing of local communities. However, traffic is growing significantly due to the expanding exploration for and exploitation of natural resources, including mining, oil and gas, and fishing. Natural resources extraction is by far the strongest driver in Arctic shipping, whether in the Russian Arctic, or the Canadian Arctic with mining,[34] but less so in Greenlandic waters since oil and gas companies have lost interest in exploiting Greenland's natural resources.[35]

While some natural resource discoveries are promising in Alaska, Canada and Russia, the large-scale development and operation of these projects remains uncertain in North America, whereas Siberian projects are benefiting from the Russian government's willingness to push for the rapid expansion of extraction of resources. These ventures remain risky, since operating costs are high, but also because the industry remains very sensitive to world prices.[36] The high volatility that marked 2020, between the pandemic and price wars, has had a definite impact on current projects, and it remains to be seen what the impact will be in the long term. Nevertheless, the moderate but ongoing expansion of cargo transit traffic and the strong expansion of destinational traffic fueled by resource extraction attest to the influence of the ongoing globalization of the Arctic, and Arctic economic expansion that is largely fueled by markets from outside the region. From that perspective, it will be interesting to observe to what extent the war in the Ukraine will impact NSR shipping.

4   Expansion of Foreign Shipping?

An examination of the share of vessels operated by foreign shipping companies gives useful information regarding the internationalization of traffic in Canadian and Russian Arctic waters.

---

33   See chapter by Choi in this volume.
34   Oil exploration is halted in Canada because of the moratorium decided in 2016.
35   Lasserre and Pic (n 22).
36   Lasserre 2021 (n 2).

In a 2018 legislative move that appeared to contradict Moscow's desire to promote Arctic shipping, a Russian regulation banned foreign-flagged oil and gas carriers from the NSR. A new decree in 2019 allowed foreign-owned carriers like Teekay, Mitsui, China Shipping or Dynagas to keep operating oil or LNG carriers registered until the end of 2021.[37] Observers wondered to what extent the move would damage Russian efforts to promote foreign use of the NSR, despite the reported rising interest of foreign shipping companies, in particular Asian companies. It turns out that the share of voyages operated by foreign shipping companies appears to be moderately growing, with a significant share of 27.92 percent (Table 5.5). As far as transits are concerned, the recent expansion described above seems to be due to foreign shipping companies, whose share went from 37.84 percent in 2019 to 87.84 percent in 2021, while the share of Asian companies did expand, but more moderately, from 21.62 to 25.68 percent.[38]

In the Canadian archipelago, all commercial transits were performed by European foreign shipping companies in 2019, 2020 and 2021. Given the prevalence of pleasure craft in transit traffic in Canadian waters up to 2020, it is not very useful to compare foreign or domestic pleasure craft with foreign commercial vessels. What is interesting, however, is the rising share of foreign companies in total traffic in Canadian Arctic waters (Table 5.6).

TABLE 5.5   Share of voyages performed by commercial vessels operated by foreign companies in Russian Arctic waters

	NSR, transit traffic (%)			NSR, total traffic (%)	
	2019	2020	2021	2019	2020
Foreign companies	37.84	65.63	87.84	23.53	27.92
Asian companies	21.62	37.5	25.68	7.83	9.6

SOURCE: CALCULATED BY AUTHOR FROM CHNL DATA

---

37   Malte Humpert, "Novatek Allowed to Operate Foreign LNG Carriers on Northern Sea Route," *High North News*, 21 March 21 2019, https://www.highnorthnews.com/en/natural -gas-company-novatek-was-granted-exemption-new-law-banning-foreign-flagged-oil -and-gas.

38   In these statistics, joint ventures like Teekay/China Shipping are counted as Asian shipping companies despite the other partner being North American.

TABLE 5.6   Share of voyages performed by commercial vessels operated by foreign companies
            in Canadian Arctic waters

	2018	2019	2020	2021
Foreign companies	18.14	22.74	26.67	39.41
Asian companies	1.2	6.03	7	10.36

SOURCE: CALCULATED BY AUTHOR FROM NORDREG AND XST DATA

It appears that, contrary to the picture that prevailed a few years ago, traffic in the Canadian Arctic is gradually becoming globalized as foreign shipping companies are increasing their share of voyages, particularly in the mining market segment. Most of these vessels are bunkers coming to the Canadian Arctic to service mining operations. The share of foreign companies in total voyages grew from 18.14 to 39.41 percent from 2018 to 2021, and the share of Asian companies from 1.2 to 10.36 percent. This attests to the developing internationalization of shipping in the Canadian archipelago, a feature that will probably keep developing over the next few years with the ongoing development of new mining sites serviced by sea transportation.[39]

4.1   Potentially Counterproductive Promotion of the NSR by Russia

There are contrasted approaches between Canada and Russia as to how to adapt or take advantage of this insertion of the Arctic into the global economy. Canadian authorities have taken a low-profile approach regarding the would-be advantages of transit shipping along the NWP: Transport Canada has never publicly advertised the Passage among shipping companies, especially as ice has remained present in the Northwest Passage in recent years.[40] This low-profile approach is in contrast with the Russian approach of highlighting the benefits of transiting through the NSR as opposed to using the Suez Canal, especially after a container ship, the *Ever Given*, blocked the canal in March 2021. Russia's state nuclear energy corporation, responsible since 2018 for the management of operations along the NSR, "made big fun of the trouble for global shipping caused by the wedged cargo ship in the Suez Canal" with a view

39 Frédéric Lasserre, "Canadian Arctic Marine Transportation Issues, Opportunities and Challenges," *The School of Public Policy Publications* (University of Calgary) 15:6 (February 2022).

40 NASA (n 31); Frédéric Lasserre, "Shipping in the Arctic: Is Climate Change a Game Changer?," in *Towards a Sustainable Arctic: International Security, Climate Change and Green Shipping*, eds., Michael Goodsite and Niklas Swanström (Singapore: World Scientific Publishing, 2022 forthcoming).

to depicting transit of the NSR as a profitable alternative.[41] This public relations push was met with skepticism by the shipping industry,[42] all the more so after more than 20 cargo ships were stuck in early winter ice for weeks in November 2021 in the eastern part of the NSR with Rosatomflot unable to free them quickly.[43] This severely damaged the corporation's credibility and the reliability of being able to navigate the NSR late in the season.[44] This episode should remind shipping companies that, despite the long-term trend towards a melting sea ice cover, significant inter-annual variability remains regarding the extent and rhythm of the melt and refreeze.

4.2 *A New Business Model: The Advent of Transshipment Hubs?*

Russian officials are well aware of the reluctance of shipping companies to develop transit traffic along the NSR, let alone the NWP. Shorter routes are proving to be a poor incentive when considering the difficulties of Arctic shipping. Thus, a new business model is gradually emerging based on regular shipping routes and classic vessels with Arctic transshipment hubs and high-ice class shuttle vessels that could offer year-round service. The advantage of this business model rests in the possibility for shipping companies to benefit from year around service and thus regular service permitting (in theory) just-in-time delivery without having to invest in costly high-ice class ships. This model implies the construction of sets of port hubs, one at each entrance of the Arctic routes, and relies on the advantage of shorter routes outweighing the need for two transshipments.

Arctic transshipment hub projects have blossomed in recent year across the Arctic, with proposed sites in Iceland (Finnafjord), Norway (Kirkenes), Russia (Murmansk, Arkhangelsk, and Indiga on the Atlantic and Vladivostok,

41   Thomas Nilsen, "Making Fun of Suez Traffic Jam, Rosatom Promotes Russia's Arctic route as an Alternative," *The Barents Observer*, 25 March 25 2021, https://thebarentsobserver .com/en/industry-and-energy/2021/03/making-fun-suez-traffic-jam-rosatom-promotes -northern-sea-route.

42   Polina Leganger Bronder, "Russia's Northern Sea Route Push is Met with Scepticism," *The Barents Observer*, 5 April 2021, https://thebarentsobserver.com/en/arctic/2021/04/russias -northern-sea-route-push-met-scepticism.

43   Atle Staalesen, "Two Icebreakers Are on the Way to Rescue Ice-Locked Ships on Northern Sea Route," *The Barents Observer*, 10 November 2021, https://thebarentsobserver.com /en/arctic/2021/11/two-icebreakers-are-way-rescue-ice-locked-ships-northern-sea-route; Atle Staalesen, "Ice-Locked Arctic Towns Might Not Get Needed Supplies," *The Barents Observer*, 24 November 2021, https://tinyurl.com/Ships-stuck-in-ice.

44   Malte Humpert, "Early Winter Freeze Traps Ships in Arctic Ice, Highlighting Weak Safety Regime," *High North News*, 26 November 2021, https://www.highnorthnews.com/en/early -winter-freeze-traps-ships-arctic-ice-highlighting-weak-safety-regime.

Zarubino and Petropavlovsk on the Pacific), Japan (Tomakomai), South Korea (Busan), Alaska (Nome), Maine (Portland), Greenland (Nuuk), France (St-Pierre, south of Newfoundland), and Canada (Halifax, St Anthony, Churchill, Iqaluit, Nanisivik and Qikiqtarjuaq).[45] It is unlikely, given the required investments in port infrastructure and shuttle vessels, that all these projected Arctic hubs will ever be built. Some projects definitely appear to be ahead in the developing competition between all these projects, with the support of local and national authorities. Other projects have had setbacks, like Kirkenes, which suffered a major blow when the projected railway between Kirkenes and Rovaniemi that would have connected the port with the European railway network was blocked by the Lapland Regional Council.[46] Several other projects have not even received the formal approval of regional authorities.

In this struggle to establish Arctic transshipment hubs, Russia definitely appears to have the lead. It has already experimented with transshipment of oil and gas in Murmansk.[47] The Russian government seems willing to set up and subsidize a dedicated container shuttle company between Murmansk and Kamchatka, very likely Petropavlovsk or Vladivostok. It may even subsidize directly foreign shipping companies that opt to use this new shuttle service[48] along a planned Northern Sea Transport Corridor.[49] Further, construction for the expansion of the port of Murmansk in under way with the Lavna terminal being dedicated to the planned expansion of coal exports as well as containers.[50] With Arctic ports already in place facing the Atlantic and the Pacific, and with Moscow's willingness to set up the shuttle company, there may be little room for hub projects along the NWP, which already suffers from a higher

45   Alexandra Cyr, *Les projets de hubs de transbordement arctiques*, *Études* du CQEG n°5 (Conseil québécois d'études géoplitiques, 2021), https://cqegeseiulaval.files.wordpress .com/2021/08/etudescqeg-hubs-arctiques-acyr-final.pdf.

46   Thomas Nilsen, "Lapland Regional Council Rejects Arctic Railway," *The Barents Observer*, 17 May 2021, https://thebarentsobserver.com/en/industry-and-energy/2021/05/lapland -regional-council-rejects-arctic-railway.

47   Lasserre and Têtu (n 29).

48   Malte Humpert, "Proposed Russian State-Owned Shipping Operator to Subsidize Container Shipping in Arctic," *High North News*, 23 October 2019, https://www.highnorthnews .com/en/proposed-russian-state-owned-shipping-operator-subsidize-container-shipping -arctic; Atle Staalesen, "Moscow Mulls Subsidies for shippers sailing Northern Sea Route," *The Barents Observer*, 3 September 2021, https://thebarentsobserver.com/en/arc tic/2021/09/moscow-mulls-subsidies-shippers-sailing-northern-sea-route.

49   Atle Staalesen, "Russian Arctic Shipping Could Follow This New Route," *The Barents Observer*, 19 May 2020, https://thebarentsobserver.com/en/arctic/2020/05/russian-arctic -shipping-could-follow-new-route.

50   Thomas Nilsen, "Construction Resumes at Murmansk Transport Hub," *The Barents Observer*, 20 September 2021, https://thebarentsobserver.com/en/industry-and-energy /2021/09/construction-resumes-murmansk-transport-hub.

ice concentration. The port of Iqaluit, which is about to be finished, is merely a wharf with little equipment.[51] The idea of building a port in Qikiqtarjuaq stemmed from the desire to support the fishing industry,[52] but also from the vision of developing a "little Singapore of the Arctic" with the help of "Chinese investors"[53] whose identity remains elusive.[54] This project is reportedly stalled, especially as Chinese investors may not be welcome now in the context of tense Sino-Canadian relations. Senator Patterson recently included the Qikiqtarjuaq port in his budget recommendations for Nunavut's development,[55] but the government does not seem to have followed suit.[56] Halifax may be better positioned as it boasts functioning infrastructure and a solid reputation, but the Arctic hub project seems preliminary, as is the case for St Anthony in Newfoundland.[57]

5 Environmental Pressures

There appears to be momentum to adopt tighter environmental measures regarding Arctic commercial shipping, although there are differences in the way Canadian and Russian authorities enforce environmental regulations. A general framework has been adopted internationally with the entry into force of the Polar Code in 2017.[58] With a view to limiting pollution and black carbon emission that accelerate the melting of sea ice, in June 2021 the International Maritime Organization (IMO) banned the use and carriage for use of heavy fuel oil (HFO) in Arctic waters after 2024. However, Arctic States were authorized to waive the ban for ships flying their own flag while traveling in their

---

51 Lasserre 2022 (n 39).

52 "Qikiqtaaluk Deep Sea Port," Qikiqtaaluk Corporation, https://www.qcorp.ca/qc-services /qikiqtarjuaq-deep-sea-port/.

53 Sima Sahar Zerehi, "Nunavut Hamlet Seeks Chinese Investors to Build Dream Port," CBC News, 30 August 2016, https://www.cbc.ca/news/canada/north/nunavut-port-chinese -investors-qikiqtarjuaq-1.3740470.

54 Nadine Blacquière, Assistant Director Operations, Desgagnés Transarctik, personal communication, Montreal, 24 February 2021.

55 Mélanie Ritchot, "Nunavut Economy Should Depend Less on Southern Labour, Says Patterson," Nunatsiaq News, 8 February 2021, https://tinyurl.com/Qik-deepseaport.

56 Lasserre 2022 (n 39).

57 Cyr (n 45).

58 International Code of Safety for Ships Operating in Polar Waters (Polar Code), IMO Res MSC.385(94) (21 November 2014) and IMO Res MEPC.264 (15 May 2015) (both in force 1 January 2017); Amendments to the International Convention on the Safety of Life at Sea, 1974, IMO Res MSC.386(94) (21 November 2014, in force 1 January 2017); Amendments to MARPOL Annexes I, II, IV and V, IMO Res MEPC.265(68) (15 May 2014, in force 1 January 2017).

domestic waters until 1 July 2029, a crucial concession to secure Russia's support.[59] The Canadian shipping company NEAS criticized the then projected HFO ban arguing that it would have a limited impact on emissions given the low traffic in the Canadian Arctic, but a high impact on operational costs and thus on communities.[60] However, the Canadian government indicated that it would nevertheless support the ban and would introduce in 2021 a proposal to address the cost impacts on northern communities.[61] This proposal remains to be made public.

When it comes to enforcement of shipping regulations, both Canada and Russia appear willing to adopt more stringent national regulations than the Polar Code provisions,[62] a position that has attracted little criticism from the shipping industry.[63] However, with a view to promoting the development of commercial shipping, Russian authorities unveiled their intention to soften national regulations and allow lower ice-class vessels to navigate along the NSR.[64] This latter move was criticized as underlining Moscow's desire to give priority to commercial considerations over safety,[65] especially in light of several

59   Malte Humpert, "IMO Moves Forward with Ban of Arctic HFO but Exempts Some Vessels Until 2029," *High North News*, 24 February 2020, https://www.highnorthnews.com/en /imo-moves-forward-ban-arctic-hfo-exempts-some-vessels-until-2029; Reuters, "UN Adopts Ban on Heavy Fuel Oil Use by Ships in Arctic," *Reuters*, 17 June 2021, https: //www.reuters.com/business/energy/un-adopts-ban-heavy-fuel-oil-use-by-ships-arctic -2021-06-17/.

60   Paquin (n 5); Leo Ryan, "Phase-In Ban on Heavy Fuel Oil in Arctic Shipping," *Maritime Magazine* 96 (2020): 7–12.

61   "2020 to 2021 Integrated Plan for Regulatory Framework and Oversight," Transport Canada, last modified 2 March 2021, https://tc.canada.ca/en/corporate-services/transparency /open-tc/2020-2021-integrated-plan-regulatory-framework-oversight; Jim Bell, "HFO Ban Could Lead to Big Arctic Price Increases, Transport Canada Says," *Nunatsiaq News*, 4 February 2020, https://nunatsiaq.com/stories/article/hfo-ban-could-lead-to-big-arctic -price-increases-transport-canada-says/.

62   Pauline Pic, Julie Babin, Frédéric Lasserre, Linyan Huang and Kristin Bartenstein, "The Polar Code and Canada's Regulations on Arctic Navigation: Shipping Companies' Perceptions of the New Legal Environment," *The Polar Journal* 11(1) (2021): 95–117, https: //doi.org/10.1080/2154896X.2021.1889838; Andrey Todorov, "Russia's Implementation of the Polar Code on the Northern Sea Route," *The Polar Journal* 11(1) (2021): 30–42, doi: 10.1080/2154896X.2021.1911044.

63   Pic *et al.* (n 62).

64   "RS Sets New Ice Class Standards," *The Naval Architect* (November 2019): 26–29, https: //rs-class.org/upload/iblock/d7c/d7ce2d0fbfe5fe7950cb3a3028781e5a.pdf; Aker Arctic, "New Regime and Regulations on Northern Sea Route" *Arctic Passion News* 19 (2020): 4–7, https://akerarctic.fi/app/uploads/2020/03/new_regime_and_regulations-1.pdf.

65   Malte Humpert, "Kremlin Prioritizes Commercial Considerations in Arctic Safety Dispute," *High North News*, 4 May 2018, https://www.highnorthnews.com/en/kremlin

safety incidents.[66] The new rules were made public in 2020.[67] Safety violations and a debatable enforcement of rules points to the larger issue of a rivalry for regulatory control over the NSR between Rosatom and the Ministry of Transportation within the framework of the Kremlin's push for a fast increase in cargo traffic.[68] Canadian authorities appear to be going the opposite direction with no traffic objectives, no promotion of shipping along the NWP, and the gradual definition and implementation of northern low-impact shipping corridors that would not be mandatory but would be used as preferred shipping routes and as a framework to guide future investments to support marine navigation safety.[69] Russian authorities have designated vessel traffic systems only in the Kara Strait and the Bering Strait in cooperation with the United States.[70]

Citing environmental concerns due to climate change and the disturbance to ecosystems as a result of the melting of sea ice, non-governmental organizations (NGOs) are pressuring shipping companies and manufacturers to rule out the option of Arctic shipping. Notably, Ocean Conservancy initiated the Arctic Shipping Corporate Pledge whereby companies formally promise

---

-prioritizes-commercial-considerations-arctic-safety-dispute; Atle Staalesen, "Russia Slackens Ice-Class Demands for Arctic Shipping," *The Barents Observer*, 6 November 2018, https://thebarentsobserver.com/en/industry-and-energy/2018/11/russia-slackens-ice -class-demands-arctic-shipping.

66 Malte Humpert, "Dozens of Vessels Violate Safety Rules on Northern Sea Route," *High North News*, 19 October 2017, https://www.highnorthnews.com/en/dozens-vessels-violate -safety-rules-northern-sea-route; Malte Humpert, "Yamal LNG Carrier *Boris Vilkitsky* in Gross Violation of Safety Rules on NSR," *High North News*, 19 April 2018), https://www .highnorthnews.com/en/yamal-lng-carrier-boris-vilkitsky-gross-violation-safety-rules -nsr; Malte Humpert, "Arctic Cargo Ship Violates Safety Rules Prompting Month-long Rescue Operation", *High North News*, 14 January 2021, https://tinyurl.com/HighNorthNews.

67 Government of Russia, "Правила плавания в акватории Северного морского пути [Rules of Navigation in the Water Area of the Northern Sea Route]," Presidential Office, Decree No. 1487 of 18 September 2020, http://www.nsra.ru/files/fileslist/137-ru893-2020.pdf.

68 Humpert 2021 (n 66); Frédéric Lasserre, "La navigation Arctique en 2021", *L'année arctique 2021. Revue annuelle* n°3 (2021): 21–31, Observatoire de la politique et la sécurité de l'Arctique (OPSA), https://cirricq.org/wp-content/uploads/2021/12/Navigation.pdf.

69 Jackie Dawson *et al.*, "Infusing Inuit and Local Knowledge into the Low Impact Shipping Corridors: An Adaptation to Increased Shipping Activity and Climate Change in Arctic Canada," *Environmental Science & Policy* 105 (2020): 19–36; PAME, *Overview of Low Impact Shipping Corridors & Other Shipping Management Schemes* (Akureyri: Arctic Council, 2021), https://www.pame.is/projects-new/arctic-shipping/pame-shipping-highlights/454 -low-impact-shipping-corridors-in-the-arctic. See also the chapter by Dawson and Song in this volume.

70 PAME 2021 (n 69).

never to use Arctic sealanes for transport of their products. Launched in 2019,[71] the pledge has been signed by well-known clothes manufacturers like Nike, Columbia Sportswear, Ralph Lauren, Puma, Gap, H&M, Allbirds; logistics operators and forwarders like EV Cargo, Hillebrand, Li & Fung and Kuehne & Nagel, and five shipping companies, CMA-CGM, MSC, Hapag Lloyd, Evergreen and Hudson Shipping.[72] No further shipping company has signed since 2019 and all but Hudson are container shipping companies that are known not to consider the Arctic as a credible sealane.[73] The momentum Ocean Conservancy hoped to garner is thus limited, despite MSC publicly renewing its pledge in 2021,[74] inasmuch there have been no further signatories and those who are signatories really have not surrendered anything they could hope to benefit from.

6   Conclusion

The shipping market in the Arctic has been long dominated by community resupply and modest fishing activity. With increasing impacts from climate change and renewed interest in natural resources extraction, actively supported by the federal state in Russia or pulled by market forces in Norway, Greenland and in the North American Arctic, the picture of shipping is transforming in the Arctic. Similarities, but also major differences, have emerged between the Canadian and the Russian situations.

In Canada, pleasure craft and cruise ships dominated the gradually expanding transit traffic before being halted by public health measures put in place due to the COVID-19 pandemic. Increased commercial transit traffic could be in the making with the initiatives of the Dutch shipping company Wagenborg.

---

71   "Nike et Ocean Conservancy s'associent pour protéger l'Arctique," *La Dépêche*, 28 October 2019, https://www.ladepeche.fr/2019/10/28/nike-et-ocean-conservancy-sassocient-pour-proteger-larctique,8509829.php; Malte Humpert, "Nike and Ocean Conservancy Call On Companies to Join Pledge Against Arctic Shipping," *High North News*, 31 October 2019, https://www.highnorthnews.com/en/nike-and-ocean-conservancy-call-companies-join-pledge-against-arctic-shipping.

72   "Take the Arctic Corporate Shipping Pledge," Ocean Conservancy, 2021, https://oceanconservancy.org/protecting-the-arctic/take-the-pledge/.

73   Frédéric Lasserre and **Sébastien** Pelletier, "Polar Super Seaways? Maritime Transport in the Arctic: An Analysis of Shipowners' Intentions," *Journal of Transport Geography* 19(6) (2011): 1465–1473; Lasserre *et al.* 2016 (n 30).

74   Hwee Hwee Tan, "MSC Reaffirms Northern Sea Route Rejection as Russia Ramps Up Arctic Rhetoric," *Lloyd's Loading List*, 6 April 2021, https://www.lloydsloadinglist.com/freight-directory/news/MSC-reaffirms-northern-sea-route-rejection-as-Russia-ramps-up-Arctic-rhetoric/78809.htm#.Ybun9GjMKUk.

In Russia, transit voyages, pushed by the Russian government, represent modest but expanding commercial activity where foreign shipping companies are active, contrary to past transit traffic that was largely composed of Russian vessels to or from Murmansk.

General traffic is expanding in both the Canadian and the Russian Arctic, albeit with more in the Russian Arctic. Both regions are witnessing the expansion of traffic generated by natural resources extraction and increased participation of foreign shipping companies, attesting to the accelerating globalization of economic activity in the Arctic.

There are major differences between the Canadian and the Russian shipping portraits. Both States welcomed and adopted the Polar Code in 2017, and both have been pressured by NGOs and the IMO to adopt tighter environmental regulations, notably through the gradual ban of HFO. However, there seems to be the temptation in Russia to ease regulations with a view to facilitating the development of commercial traffic, whereas Canada tries to frame shipping activities through the definition of low-impact shipping corridors. This is consistent with the efforts in Russia to promote and advertise shipping in the Russian Arctic, notably through the development of an alternate business model of transshipment hubs. This model is also discussed in Canada, but it remains at very preliminary stages when compared to Russia, Iceland or Norway.

Shipping is developing in the Canadian Arctic, driven by external market forces and partly shaped by international political forces. However, it remains much more modest than in the Russian Arctic. There is a political choice to be made: is the Canadian government satisfied with the status quo, which will probably witness a gradual expansion of traffic driven by resource exploitation and international shipping markets, or, subject to agreement with Inuit communities, does it want to promote traffic, whether through communications, improved services to shipping, or construction of harbors for transshipment and provision of havens for crippled vessels? In all cases, the upward pressure of traffic imposes the need to develop the capacity to manage and control traffic in Arctic waters.

CHAPTER 6

Reconsidering Arctic Shipping Governance through a Decolonizing Lens

Leah Beveridge

Abstract

Inuit are increasingly being considered within Arctic shipping governance, most often regarding how the industry impacts the marine environment and their subsistence diet, and how their traditional knowledge can inform governance. Such questions are typically viewed through the lens of environmental, economic and operational frameworks, but less addressed is the context of the relationship between Inuit and the Crown. This chapter begins by presenting important moments within this relationship that targeted the colonization of Inuit and that relied in part or in entirety on shipping. These moments and the path towards recognizing the rights of Indigenous peoples are then positioned alongside the development of the Arctic shipping governance regime, and inconsistencies between the recognition of rights narrative and the consideration and involvement of Inuit in the development of the regime are highlighted. The final portion of the chapter presents evidence that, under the narrative of a renewed relationship between Indigenous peoples and the Crown, change may be underway. However, this change must continue in three key areas if it is to be meaningful and long-lasting: in legislation, guided by the *United Nations Declaration on the Rights of Indigenous Peoples Act*; in policy and programs, guided by the Inuit Nunangat Policy; and in society writ large, guided by Inuit themselves.

Keywords

decolonization – reconciliation – Arctic shipping – Inuit – Indigenous rights – United Nations Declaration on the Rights of Indigenous Peoples

1 Introduction

Inuit are increasingly being considered within the realm of Arctic shipping governance. How the industry impacts the marine environment and subsequently their subsistence diet, and how their traditional knowledge can inform governance are often key pieces of these conversations. But Inuit are more than simply a stakeholder in the context of Arctic shipping; they are Indigenous rights-holders and their relationship with the bodies that govern the shipping industry today are plagued with a history of colonization. The need for reconciliation within the broader Inuit-Crown relationship is sometimes cited, but rarely further discussed in this context. In this chapter, the intent is to centre reconciliation, and more specifically, decolonization:

> 'Decolonizing' is a social and political process aimed at resisting and undoing the multi-faceted impacts of colonization and re-establishing strong contemporary Indigenous Peoples, Nations, and institutions based on traditional values, philosophies, and knowledge systems.

> A decolonizing mindset requires people to consciously and critically question the legitimacy of the colonizer and reflect on the ways we have been influenced by colonialism. According to expert in Indigenous research methodologies Margaret Kovach, the purpose of decolonization is to create space in everyday life, research, academia, and society for an Indigenous perspective without its being neglected, shunted aside, mocked, or dismissed.[1]

The Royal Commission on Aboriginal Peoples (RCAP), the Truth and Reconciliation Commission of Canada (TRC), and the National Inquiry into Missing and Murdered Indigenous Women and Girls (the National Inquiry) all emphasize 'relationships' as a central piece of moving forward together in a positive way. The latter, in particular, emphasizes the need to look at not only the structural and institutional relationships between Indigenous peoples and the Crown, but the way those play out in the lives of individuals through what the National Inquiry refers to as 'encounters.'[2] Relationship-building requires human interactions, or encounters, which means there must be compassion for the multigenerational experiences and intergenerational traumas of Indigenous peoples. Such compassion is not possible unless there is an understanding of the true histories and realities of Inuit and the Inuit-Crown

---

1   National Inquiry into Missing and Murdered Indigenous Women and Girls, *Reclaiming Power and Place: The Final Report of the National Inquiry into Missing and Murdered Indigenous Women and Girls volume 1a* (Ottawa, 2019) [MMIWG], 78, citing Margaret Kovach, *Indigenous Methodologies: Characteristics, Conversations, and Contexts* (Toronto: University of Toronto Press, 2009).

2   Id.

relationship.[3] Therefore, this chapter begins by drawing attention to some of the ways that ships were involved in key events over the course of the history of the Inuit-Crown relationship before moving into a description of how Inuit have (or have not) participated in the governance of shipping in their waters over this same period of time. In the spirit of moving forward in a better way together, this chapter closes with a discussion of some of the ways that the Inuit-Crown relationship appears to be shifting, and identifies key areas of focus for further decolonizing shipping governance in Canada and the Inuit-Crown and Inuit-settler relationship more broadly.

2   The Role of Ships in Facilitating the Mistreatment and Attempts to Assimilate Inuit

There is no shortage of stories and publications on the history of shipping in the Canadian Arctic and the roles ships played in the 'development' and 'defence' of the region,[4] most of which are written by, for, and from the viewpoint of the colonizers themselves. Here, though, the intent is to highlight the role that ships played in some of the assimilative initiatives undertaken by the federal government that are often less talked about in the context of the history and governance of shipping: residential schools, the High Arctic Relocation, and the tuberculosis epidemic. In alignment with the decolonizing focus of this chapter, the findings of the RCAP, TRC and the National Inquiry will be centred. The author does not attempt to speak in any depth to the experiences of Inuit or Indigenous peoples out of respect for those who lived the events described herein and/or who continue to be impacted today.

2.1   *Mission Schools, Residential Schools, Boarding Schools, Day Schools and Hostels*
The federal residential school system commenced its policies and programs aimed at assimilating Indigenous peoples in southern Canada in the 1800s, but in the North, the 'school' system was run by Anglican and Catholic missionaries. Similar to the southern federal system, though, the intent was to change Inuit, in

---

3   Call to Action #57 of the Truth and Reconciliation Commission of Canada (TRC) also calls for education on the "history and legacy of residential schools," Indigenous rights and law, and Indigenous-Crown relations (TRC, *Calls to Action* (Winnipeg, 2015)).

4   See Lajeunesse and Lackenbauer in this volume.

this case, to convert them to Christianity,[5] and involved removing children from their homes, oftentimes facilitated by ship. The schools "were often great distances, sometimes hundreds or even thousands of kilometres" away from children's families.[6] Anthony Thrasher, in his testimony to the TRC, "remember[s] waving to [his father] from the railing as *The Immaculata* pulled out into the bay and headed south towards Aklavik. [He] was crying."[7] Anthony was six years old when the mission schooner took him away. Polar navigation, even more so than today, "was difficult and often dangerous," and as a result, children were not often returned home, "often [going] years without seeing their parents."[8]

Ships also brought the goods and materials necessary for some of the mission-run schools to operate, including food. Given the challenges in transportation at the time, food was often scarce, and sometimes the schools would rely on local food sources gathered through hunting and trapping, sometimes even by the parents of the children attending the school. The fish caught would have to be preserved, but, as Bill Erasmus explained to the TRC when speaking of his father's experience, this was not always done properly. The result was that the fish would rot, "but they would still feed them to the kids, and they were forced to eat that."[9] Not surprisingly, "disease and death [were] common in the northern mission schools."[10]

Some students recalled positive moments of their time at the schools. Masak, for example, attended the Anglican All Saints Residential School in Aklavik in 1937 and told the TRC of traveling by the school barge to berry-pick along the Mackenzie River.[11] These moments would not discount the unpleasant memories and long-lasting traumas, though. In her same testimony, Masak spoke of becoming ashamed of her language and divided from her family because she could not speak to them or participate in their way of life.[12]

It would not be until the 1940s that the Government of Canada would begin to turn its attention North. Throughout the Second World War there was a strong American military presence in the Canadian North, and American officers and civilians publicly questioned Canada about the poverty and lack

---

5   Willem Rasing, *Too Many People: Contact, Disorder, Change in an Inuit Society, 1822–2015,* 2nd ed. (Iqaluit: Nunavut Arctic College Media, 2017).

6   TRC, *The Final Report of the Truth and Reconciliation Commission of Canada Volume 2, Canada's Residential Schools: The Inuit and Northern Experience* (Winnipeg: 2015).

7   Id., 39.

8   Id., 17.

9   Id., 33.

10   Id., 27.

11   Id., 38.

12   Id.

of care given to the Indigenous peoples, leading to "diplomatic embarrass-ment."[13] Between this embarrassment, the growing interest in military activity and natural resource extraction in the region, and the social movements that emerged over the course of World War II, Canada's interest in the North grew, including with regards to the education system. In 1954, a federal report came to the conclusion that "the residential school [was] perhaps the most effective way of giving children from primitive environments, experience in education along the lines of civilization leading to vocational training to fit them for occupations in the white man's economy."[14] There were other stud-ies that, at the same time, documented that the residential school system was not appropriate and in the south, the federal government was closing the res-idential schools, but the decision was still made to proceed with establishing residential schools in the North. Nine federal schools opened in the Northwest Territories and northern Quebec between 1948 and 1954;[15] in 1949 there were just over 100 full-time Inuit students and by 1959 this number had increased more than ten-fold.[16]

Even though the federal government 'took over' the educational aspects of the schools, the Anglicans and Catholics continued to be responsible for boarding the students, creating a hostel-day school system as opposed to the residential school system known to the south.[17] "The classroom learning [was to] provide the theoretical lessons about modernity and life in Canada, and the hostel would make these lessons concrete."[18] For some, the experiences in the classroom, "although extremely strict", were positive;[19] the education was "top notch" and "the classroom was a safe haven" from the physical and sexual abuse that took place in the hostels after school hours.[20] "The overall assessment, however, was that their time at the school had alienated them from [their] communities, broken their links to their culture, and diminished their capacity to serve as effective parents."[21]

This system operated until the end of the 1960s, after which time the Governments of the Northwest Territories and Yukon took over responsibility. This means that there are many people in communities today who had to

---

13   Id., 51.
14   Id., 54.
15   Id., 52.
16   Id., 82.
17   Id., 83.
18   Id., 87.
19   Id., 88.
20   Id., 99.
21   Id.

watch their children get taken away, who went to the schools and hostels themselves, and who are children of survivors. The perseverance of Inuit to maintain their culture and their community through the Government of Canada's attempt to assimilate them is a testament to the strength of individuals, families, communities, and Inuit as a people. Even in the face of constant reminders of the past—such as the schooner *Our Lady of Lourdes*, which took children away from their families and now sits in the centre of Tuktoyaktuk in the Inuvialuit Settlement Region—Inuit continue to have a strength and unity that is truly humbling.

2.2   *The High Arctic Relocations*

In 1934, in the name of sovereignty through occupation, the federal government sanctioned the relocation of Inuit to the High Arctic for the first time. The Hudson Bay Company, with authorization from the federal government, sought to establish a trading post at Dundas Harbour on Devon Island. By this point, whalers and traders had already been relocating Inuit for years, with reports dating back to the early 1900s,[22] but this would be the first time such an act was undertaken with the express permission of the Government of Canada. As part of the agreement, the Hudson's Bay Company was fully and solely responsible for the welfare of any individual it transferred from Cape Dorset. The press release of the relocation experiment at the time highlighted the importance of occupying the Arctic to ensure other States did not try to claim territory.[23]

Less than two decades later, the Government of Canada executed another plan to relocate Inuit to the High Arctic, this time from Inukjuak (Nunavik) and Pond Inlet (Nunavut) to Craig Harbour and Resolute Bay. In July 1953, the *C.D. Howe* left Inukjuak with seven families, stopping in Pond Inlet late August to pick up an additional three families. The *C.D. Howe* first stopped in Craig Harbour where it split the groups into two: one group would remain in Craig Harbour while the other would continue onboard the *d'Iberville* with the intent of continuing on to Cape Herschel and Resolute Bay. Inuit were not aware upon departing Inukjuak that they would be separated, and "were suddenly forced to make decisions on how to split into two groups" while aboard the *C.D. Howe*.[24] The vessel was unable to reach Cape Herschel due to ice conditions,

---

22   Royal Commission on Aboriginal Peoples (RCAP), *The High Arctic Relocation: A Reporting on the 1953–55 Relocation* (Ottawa: Royal Commission on Aboriginal Peoples, 1996), 43.

23   Id., 42.

24   Inuit Tapirisat of Canada (ITC), *Submission of the Inuit Tapirisat of Canada to the Royal Commission on Aboriginal Peoples* (Ottawa: Inuit Tapiriiksat Kanatami, 1994), 96.

so returned the families intended for Cape Herschel to Craig Harbour before proceeding to Resolute Bay with the remaining families in September.[25] In the end, there were three families from Inukjuak and one from Pond Inlet in Resolute Bay, and four families from Inukjuak and two from Pond Inlet in Craig Harbour. In 1955, another family from Inukjuak was relocated to Craig Harbour, and three families from Inukjuak and two from Pond Inlet were relocated to Resolute.

Over the years there have been debates about the reasoning behind the federal plan, but the findings of the RCAP are that this was another case of the federal government experimenting with Inuit, this time through a rehabilitation program intended to restore Inuit to a lifestyle that relied on the land as opposed to federal handouts.[26] At the time, many Inuit around Inukjuak had become part of the fur trade and accustomed to the lifestyle that came with monetary income and the amenities of living near the settlement itself. By the 1950s, the community had a Hudson's Bay Company post, a police post, church missions, a school, a nursing station, a Department of Transport weather station and radio facility, and a port facility.[27] However, with the collapse of the fur trade, the income was scarce, the result being "substantial continuing reliance [of Inuit] on government income support in the form of family allowance, old age security and relief."[28] The federal government's solution to this 'economic and social' problem was to try to return Inuit to their traditional lifestyle, which did not depend on the federal government, with the added strategic benefit of asserting Canadian sovereignty in the High Arctic.[29] The experiment was to determine whether the land around Craig Harbour or Resolute Bay could support Inuit,[30] and whether Inuit from Inukjuak could adapt to these new lands thousands of miles from their homes and families.[31] The latter is the reasoning for relocating Inuit from Pond Inlet; as existing residents of the High Arctic, they were brought to help the Inuit of Inukjuak adapt to the resources of the area and teach them to survive the extreme cold and months-long darkness.

25   RCAP (n 22).
26   Id.
27   Id., 75.
28   Id., 52.
29   Id., 53, 133.
30   "The government did not conduct extensive or systematic surveys of game resources in the area" prior to actioning this plan, and soon after the relocation "government officials were beginning to express concern that perhaps the game in the area would not support more people." (Id., 110).
31   Id., 96.

As described by RCAP, federal proposals in the 1950s had the prevailing attitude of paternalism; "the just, strict Victorian father who knows best what is good for his charges, despite sometimes painful consequences."[32] Inuit from Inukjuak came from a place with vegetation and berries, trees that could be used for fires, and completely different game and fish. While learning how to survive on the tundra in the dark, harvesting marine mammals from the sea and sourcing freshwater from icebergs,[33] there were many accounts of extreme hunger and starvation.[34] Inuit testimonials speak to "the lack of adequate shelter, food, clothing and equipment in the early years, and the resulting hunger, cold, pain and suffering experienced by them."[35] As Anna Nungaq told the RCAP, "they just left us there and we saw the ship sailing away and we were just dumped in a place where there was absolutely nothing."[36] The supply stores in Resolute Bay and Craig Harbour were only stocked enough to supplement what Inuit were meant to harvest from the land and there was no budget to support the potential scenario that this experiment failed, that is, that the land could not support Inuit or that Inuit could not adapt fast enough to this new way of living before perishing. The limited supplies that were available were controlled by the Royal Canadian Mounted Police (RCMP) on behalf of the federal government, and were given out in limited amounts to ensure the 'necessary encouragement' was provided to Inuit to return to their traditional state of self-sufficiency.[37] Inuit testified to the RCAP "about living in tents the first winter and resorting to the garbage dump of the Airforce base for food and other essential items."[38] The RCMP were also instructed "to enforce conservation measures to ensure that the Inuit did not take [harvest] more than they actually needed and, in particular, to ensure that resources were not depleted."[39]

In addition to the physical suffering of trying to live without enough food, clothing or shelter, Inuit also suffered the psychological hardships of being separated from family, community and home. The federal government was fully aware of the cultural connections between Inuit and the land and the potential impacts of removing them from their homes and families.[40] But the best interests or wellbeing of Inuit were never the priority. Although the

---

32   Id., 36–37.
33   Id., 95.
34   Id., 27.
35   ITC (n 24), p. 96.
36   RCAP (n 22), p. 25.
37   Id., 74.
38   ITC (n 24), p. 96.
39   RCAP (n 22), p. 89.
40   Id.

federal government has at times claimed the relocation was with the consent of the Inuit families who left Inukjuak, this is far from true. The known power imbalance and cultural differences between Inuit and non-Inuit at the time were exploited and Inuit were coerced into going; "There was material non-disclosure, and there were material misrepresentations" with respect to what Inuit from Inukjuak were agreeing to.[41]

> Those [Inuit] testifying [to the RCAP] said that the RCMP were persistent and insistent that the people should go; that many people did not under-stand that they had the right to refuse to go; that the agreement to go was given reluctantly and was induced by misrepresentations and promises such as the promise to return [after two years]; and that some people went because members of their immediate or extended families were going and they did not wish to be separated from their relatives.[42]

Responsibility for the 'relocation project' and all Inuit affairs at the time fell to the Department of Resources and Development. Although the project was never discussed by Cabinet, the Department did not execute the project alone. The RCMP was responsible for supervising Inuit in the new communities and the Department of Transport operated the annual ship supply. These two orga-nizations, along with the Hudson's Bay Company, were engaged early to gain their support and co-operation to 'rehabilitate' Inuit.[43] In the end, these other organizations supported the Department of Resources and Development and participated in a project that ultimately "exceeded the government's legal authority ... was inhumane in its design and its effects,"[44] and was based on "the fundamental denial of individual freedom, human equality, and personal dignity."[45]

2.3   *Tuberculosis Epidemic*
While the High Arctic Relocation project and the residential school system were more direct efforts to colonize Inuit, the provision of health care by the federal government to Inuit is also considered an element of colonization by the National Inquiry.[46] As part of the social movement that followed World

---

41   Id., 150.
42   Id., 16.
43   Id., 69.
44   Id., 160.
45   Id., 151.
46   MMIWG (n 1), p. 307.

War II, the *C.D. Howe* began patrolling communities to offer medical services.[47] When the ship arrived in a community, Inuit were brought on board and "treated like cattle as they moved through the various stages of examination, only to be marked with a serial number on their hand that indicated which tests they had undergone."[48] The *C.D. Howe* thus earned the name *Matavik* by Inuit, meaning "where you strip."[49]

Of all the diseases brought to Inuit Nunangat (the Inuit homeland in Canada), tuberculosis in particular wreaked havoc on Inuit. At the time that *Matavik* was patrolling the Arctic shores, it was anticipated that one-third of Inuit were infected with tuberculosis, and by 1956, over 1,500 were being treated for the disease.[50] The federal approach to providing this treatment was "especially notorious" for causing social harm to Inuit, in addition to the obvious impacts of the disease itself.[51] If the onboard medical exam revealed tuberculosis, the individual was marked with 'TB' on their hand and immediately transported to a sanatorium south of Inuit Nunangat. Their age did not matter, and most often there was not an opportunity to collect belongings, to say goodbye, or to make any arrangements to ensure families were cared for.[52] Annie B., for example, told the National Inquiry about being removed from Pangnirtung, Nunavut at the age of four or five and transported, by herself, to a treatment facility in Toronto.[53]

The forced and immediate removal of Inuit from communities and families had major implications both for those removed and for those left behind.[54] Elder Elisapi Davidee Aningmiuq, for example, spoke to the National Inquiry about "how the forced separation of children from their families resulted in emotional trauma for Inuit and alienation from their families because of the length and distance of separation."[55] As with the experience of children in residential schools, those who were removed often did not return for years, in part because of the short shipping season.

---

47 Id., 271.
48 Id., 307.
49 Id.
50 TRC (n 6), p. 74. Inuit, today, continue to consistently experience higher rates of tuberculosis than any other group in Canada; in 2016, "the rate of TB among Inuit was almost 300 times higher than the rate in the Canadian-born, non-Indigenous population" (Canada's Chief Public Health Officer (CPHO), *The Time Is Now: Chief Public Health Officer Spotlight on Eliminating Tuberculosis in Canada* (Ottawa: Public Health Agency of Canada, 2018), 8).
51 MMIWG (n 1), p. 307.
52 Inuit Tapiriit Kanatami (ITK), *Inuit Tuberculosis Elimination Framework* (Ottawa, 2018), 8.
53 MMIWG (n 1), p. 475.
54 ITK (n 53), p. 8; CPHO (n 50), p. 7.
55 MMIWG (n 1), p. 475.

In many cases, families left at home were not aware of where their loved ones had been taken, whether they were alive, and if or when they would return. Some died at the sanatoria and were buried near the treatment facility while others, such as young Annie B., were taken to residential school instead of being returned to their community and faced abuses there; Annie's whereabouts were never communicated to her family, who assumed she was no longer alive. "Those who did return, particularly the children, faced new challenges including reduced physical capacities related to their illness or its treatment (e.g., removal of diseased portions of the lungs), and the loss of language and other aspects of Inuit culture."[56] As with the residential schools and the High Arctic Relocation, the federal government was aware of the impacts of removing Inuit from their surroundings and had been advised against it.[57] But "in the face of the cost-effectiveness of using existing hospitals and expertise and the difficulty of persuading medical experts to go north," the federal government chose to go against this advice yet again.[58]

3   Recognizing the Rights of Inuit and Indigenous Peoples

The rights of Indigenous peoples in Canada would not be formally acknowledged until 1982 when the Canadian Constitution was amended to recognize and affirm "the existing aboriginal and treaty rights of the aboriginal peoples of Canada"[59] and to provide a guarantee that the Canadian Charter of Rights and Freedoms would "not be construed so as to abrogate or derogate from any aboriginal, treaty or other rights or freedoms that pertain to the aboriginal peoples of Canada including" those "recognized by the Royal Proclamation" and "that now exist by way of land claims agreements or may be so acquired."[60] Today, there are five Inuit land claims and self-government agreements in place: the Inuvialuit Final Agreement (1984); the Nunavut Land Claims Agreement (1993); the James Bay and Northern Quebec Agreement (1975) and the Nunavik Inuit Land Claims Agreement (2006); and the Labrador Inuit Land Claims Agreement (2005). Collectively, these four settlement areas (the Inuvialuit Settlement Region, Nunavut, Nunavik and Nunatsiavut) comprise Inuit Nunangat, the homeland of Inuit in Canada. This space includes marine waters

---

56   ITK (n 52), p. 8.
57   RCAP (n 22), p. 39.
58   Id.
59   *Constitution Act, 1982*, being Schedule B to the *Canada Act 1982* (UK) 1982, c 11, s 35.
60   Id., s 25.

out to the boundary of the territorial sea east of Nunavut and Nunatsiavut and west to include the exclusive economic zone in the Inuvialuit Settlement Region. Lalonde and Bankes in this volume explore how these agreements could be leveraged with regards to shipping governance in the waters of Inuit Nunangat, and therefore they are not discussed here. Indigenous rights, as per section 35 of the Canadian Constitution, are to be understood as a 'full box of rights,'[61] though only some are articulated within the land claims agreements. The United Nations Declaration on the Rights of Indigenous Peoples[62] (UNDRIP) is important to consider in this regard.

In 1982, the same year amendments to the Canadian Constitution were introduced to recognize Indigenous rights, the United Nations established a Working Group on Indigenous Populations (WGIP) under the Economic and Social Council's Sub-Commission for Prevention of Discrimination and Protection of Minorities. The WGIP was instructed, among other items, to analyze information on the promotion and protection of the human rights and fundamental freedoms of Indigenous peoples and to give "special attention to the evolution of standards concerning the rights of Indigenous populations."[63] Indigenous peoples' representatives, including the Inuit Circumpolar Council (ICC), which represents Inuit internationally, participated directly in the discussions of the WGIP,[64] and it was from this Working Group that the vision of an international declaration concerning the rights of Indigenous peoples emerged.[65] In 2007, the vision materialized with the adoption of UNDRIP at the United Nations with an "overwhelming majority."[66] UNDRIP itself is not a legally binding document, but is considered to reflect the state of customary law with regards to the rights of Indigenous peoples, and thus is an important

---

61   Department of Justice, *Principles Respecting the Government of Canada's Relationship with Indigenous Peoples* (Ottawa: Department of Justice Canada, 2018), 3.
62   United Nations Declaration on the Rights of Indigenous Peoples, UN Doc A/RES/61/295 (13 September 2007) [UNDRIP].
63   Study of the Problem of Discrimination Against Indigenous Populations, ECOSOC Resolution 1982/34, UN Doc E/RES/1982/34 (1982), para 2.
64   Asbjørne Eide, "The Indigenous Peoples, the Working Group on Indigenous Populations and the Adoption of the UN Declaration on the Rights of Indigenous Peoples," in *Making the Declaration Work: The United Nations Declaration on the Rights of Indigenous Peoples,* eds., Claire Charters and Rodolfo Stavenhagen (Copenhagen: International Work Group for Indigenous Affairs, 2009), 32.
65   Erica-Irene A Daes, "The Contribution of the Working Group on Indigenous Populations to the Genesis and Evolution of the UN Declaration on the Rights of Indigenous Peoples," in eds., Charters and Stavenhagen (n 64), 48.
66   United Nations Permanent Forum on Indigenous Issues (UNPFII), *Partnering with Indigenous Peoples: Experiences and Practices* (no date), 6.

formal articulation of the "minimum standards for the survival, dignity and well-being of the indigenous peoples of the world."[67] It contains 46 articles of "interrelated, interdependent, indivisible and interconnected" rights,[68] but at the apex lies the right to self-determination,[69] "without which indigenous peoples' human rights, both collective and individual, cannot be fully enjoyed."[70]

At the time UNDRIP was adopted, Canada was one of only four States (alongside the United States, New Zealand and Australia) to withhold their support for UNDRIP due to the perceived veto power of the right to free, prior and informed consent. Canada changed its position on UNDRIP in 2010 to one of support, though with qualification; it was interpreted by Canada as "a non-legally binding document that [did] not reflect customary international law nor change Canadian laws."[71] In 2016, however, the Government of Canada changed its position again, this time to one of full support and with a commitment to implement UNDRIP in Canada,[72] and on 21 June 2021, the *United Nations Declaration on the Rights of Indigenous Peoples Act*[73] (UNDRIPA) received Royal Assent. The UNDRIPA acknowledges UNDRIP as the framework for reconciliation[74] and affirms Canada's commitment to taking effective legislative, policy and administrative measures at both the national and international levels to achieve its objectives.[75]

---

67   UNDRIP (n 62), Article 43.
68   United Nations Economic and Social Council (ECOSOC), *Report of the UNPFII on its 10th Session*, UN Doc E/2011/43-E/C.19/2011/14 (2011), para 25.
69   United Nations General Assembly (UNGA), *Progress Report on the Study of Indigenous Peoples and the Right to Participate in Decision-making*, UN Doc A/HRC/EMRIP/2010/2 (2010), para 34; UNGA, *Final Report of the Study on Indigenous Peoples and the Right to Participate in Decision-making*, UN Doc A/HRC/18/42 (2011), para 20; James Anaya, "The Rights of Indigenous Peoples to Self-Determination in the Post-Declaration Era," in eds., Charters and Stavenhagen (n 64), 184.
70   UNGA, *Report of the Special Rapporteur on the Situation of Human Rights and Fundamental Freedoms of Indigenous Peoples by James Anaya*, UN Doc A/HRC/12/34 (2009), para 41.
71   "Canada's Statement of Support on the United Nations Declaration on the Rights of Indigenous Peoples" (12 November 2010) archived at Indian and Northern Affairs Canada, https://www.rcaanc-cirnac.gc.ca/eng/1309374239861/1621701138904.
72   Carolyn Bennett, *Announcement of Canada's Support for the United Nations Declaration on the Rights of Indigenous Peoples*, Speaking Notes for the Honourable Carolyn Bennett, Minister of Indigenous and Northern Affairs for the UNPFII (New York: United Nations Permanent Forum on Indigenous Issues, 2016); Governor General of Canada, *A Stronger and More Resilient Canada*, Speech from the Throne to Open the Second Session of the Forty-third Parliament of Canada (Ottawa, 2020).
73   SC 2021, c 14.
74   Id., Preamble, para 1.
75   Id., Preamble, para 13.

4   Inuit and the Governance of Arctic Shipping

Over the course of the decades (and centuries) that Canada was implementing various assimilative efforts towards Indigenous peoples, now understood as acts of cultural genocide,[76] the international shipping regime was taking shape, including through the establishment of the International Maritime Organization (IMO)[77] and the foundational international marine safety and environmental protection conventions that remain in place today.[78] Canada's domestic regime was also being developed, and, in the 1970s, Canada brought into force the first polar-specific maritime legislation: the *Arctic Waters Pollution Prevention Act*[79] (AWPPA). In 2009, the international shipping community also decided to pursue mandatory requirements to address the unique risks of operating ships in polar waters; up until the adoption of the Polar Code in 2014–2015, the IMO only had guidelines for ships operating in Arctic ice-covered,[80] polar,[81] and remote waters.[82] Rather than develop a new convention, the IMO decided to build on the existing framework to add aspects specific to polar navigation.

That same year, the Protection of the Arctic Marine Environment Working Group of the Arctic Council[83] released the widely known and referenced *Arctic*

---

76   MMIWG (n 1).

77   The International Maritime Organization was originally called the Inter-Governmental Maritime Consultative Organization (IMCO). It was established by the Convention on the Intergovernmental Maritime Consultative Organization, 6 March 1948, 289 *UNTS* 3 and 1520 *UNTS* 297 which entered into force on 17 March 1958. The Convention was amended to the Convention on the International Maritime Organization, 9 November 1977, 1276 *UNTS* 468, and the name of IMCO was changed to the International Maritime Organization in 1982.

78   For example: International Convention for the Safety of Life at Sea, 1 November 1974 (in force 25 May 1980), 1184 *UNTS* 2, as amended [SOLAS]; International Convention for the Prevention of Pollution from Ships, 2 November 1973, 1340 *UNTS* 184, as amended by the Protocol of 1978 Relating to the International Convention for the Prevention of Pollution from Ships, 17 February 1978 (both in force 2 October 1983), 1340 *UNTS* 61 [MARPOL].

79   RSC 1985, c A-12 [AWPPA].

80   Guidelines for Ships Operating in Arctic Ice-covered Waters, IMO Doc MSC/Circ.1056, MEPC/Circ.399 (23 December 2002).

81   Guidelines for Ships Operating in Polar Waters, IMO Resolution Doc A.1024 (26) (2 December 2009).

82   Guidelines on Voyage Planning for Passenger Ships Operating in Remote Areas, IMO Resolution A.999(25) (29 November 2007) [Guidelines on Passenger Ships in Remote Areas].

83   The Arctic Council was established in 1996 as an intergovernmental and political forum where Arctic States (the United States, Canada, Denmark, Iceland, Norway, Finland, Sweden, and Russia) and Indigenous peoples (Aleut International Association, Arctic Athabaskan Council, Gwich'in Council International, Inuit Circumpolar Council, Russian

Marine Shipping Assessment (AMSA).[84] The AMSA report was considered to be "the most comprehensive assessment of shipping risks in the Arctic to date and provides a policy road map for decision-makers to enhance safety, security and environmental protection of Arctic waters"[85] through its 17 recommendations, including to develop stronger measures for ship safety and pollution prevention. The AMSA report recommends that States have "mechanisms to engage and coordinate with the shipping industry, relevant economic activities and Arctic communities (in particular during the planning phase of a new marine activity) to increase benefits and help reduce impacts from shipping,"[86] which is somewhat reflective of the right to free, prior and informed consent. However, the only place in the entire document where reference to the rights of Indigenous peoples can be inferred is in mention of the World Wildlife Fund's Principles and Codes for Arctic Tourism, which "encourage[s] tourism development that ... respects the rights and cultures of Arctic residents and increases the share of tourism revenues that go to northern communities."[87] The interests and concerns of Indigenous peoples are discussed throughout the report, but the lack of reference to Indigenous rights is curious given UNDRIP was adopted two years before AMSA was released, and given the engagement of Arctic Indigenous peoples in the development of AMSA and in the Arctic Council itself. Six international Indigenous organizations, including the ICC which participated in the development of UNDRIP, participate at the Arctic Council as Permanent Participants, all of whom are consulted on negotiations and decisions that take place within the Council but do not hold voting power like the Arctic States.[88]

The IMO's efforts to add polar-specific provisions to the existing framework evolved into a significantly more comprehensive regulatory overhaul and development, which was strongly supported by the Arctic Council Member States.[89] The result was a new Chapter XIV in the International Convention for the

Association of Indigenous Peoples of the North, and the Saami Council) promote and practice cooperation and coordination on common Arctic issues, particularly those surrounding sustainable development and environmental protection.

84   Arctic Council, *Arctic Marine Shipping Assessment 2009 Report* (April 2009).
85   Louie Porta *et al.*, "Shipping corridors as a framework for advancing marine law and policy in the Canadian Arctic," *Ocean and Coastal Law Journal* 22 (2017): 63, at 81.
86   Arctic Council (n 84), p. 6.
87   Id., 100.
88   See note 85.
89   Aldo Chircop, "Jurisdiction over Ice-Covered Areas and the Polar Code: An Emerging Symbiotic Relationship?" *Journal of International Maritime Law* 22 (2016): 275, at 286.

Safety of Life at Sea[90] (SOLAS) on Safety Measures for Ships Operating in Polar Waters, and substantial amendments to four annexes in the International Convention for the Prevention of Pollution from Ships[91] (MARPOL). These were, for the most part consolidated in the International Code for Ships Operating in Polar Waters[92] (the Polar Code), which entered into force 1 January 2017. The Polar Code also includes recommendations and guidance pertaining to safety and pollution prevention measures, and additional requirements for training, certification and watchkeeping,[93] which entered into force 1 January 2018.

Throughout the work to negotiate and develop the Polar Code, the potential concerns of Indigenous peoples with respect to polar navigation were only considered briefly in the context of environmental protection provisions. Individual Inuit were brought to the IMO by environmental non-governmental organizations (ENGOs) to speak during the lunch hour of a Marine Environment Protection Committee (MEPC) session on the Polar Code about their concerns, but were not given any formal platform upon which to present their perspectives; they did not participate in negotiations, nor did they prepare submissions to the Committees or Sub-Committees working on the Polar Code. Some of their interests were presented by ENGOs within these negotiations and submissions,[94] which included, as articulated in the submissions, concerns

---

90 SOLAS (n 78).

91 MARPOL (n 78).

92 International Code for Ships Operating in Polar Waters (Polar Code), IMO Resolution MSC.385(94) (21 November 2014, effective 1 January 2017); Amendments to the International Convention for the Safety of Life at Sea 1974, IMO Resolution MSC.386(94) (21 November 2014, effective 1 January 2017); Amendments to MARPOL Annexes I, II, IV and V, IMO Resolution MEPC.265(68) (15 May 2015, effective 1 January 2017).

93 Introduced through amendments to the International Convention on Standards of Training, Certification and Watchkeeping, 7 July 1978 (in force 28 April 1984), 1361 *UNTS* 2 (in force 28 April 1984), as amended) [STCW Convention] and the Seafarers' Training Certification and Watchkeeping Code (STCW Convention, Annex, as amended).

94 WWF, *Work Programme of the Committee and Subsidiary Bodies: Mandatory requirements for polar shipping*, IMO Doc MEPC 59/20/7 (2009); FOEI *et al.*, *Proposed Mandatory Code for Ships Operating in Polar Waters: Shipping management issues to be addressed*, IMO Doc DE 53/18/3 (2009); FOEI *et al.*, *Development of a Mandatory Code for Ships Operating in Polar Waters: Additional MARPOL provisions for the Polar Code*, IMO Doc DE 54/13/8 (2010); FOEI *et al.*, *Proposed Mandatory Code for Ships Operating in Polar Waters: Wider environmental provisions for the Polar Code*, IMO Doc DE 54/13/9 (2010); WWF *et al.*, *Reports of Sub-Committees: Outcome of DE 55: Arctic shipping and cetaceans, Recommendations regarding mitigation measures and the development of the mandatory Polar Code*, IMO Doc MEPC 62/11/6 (2011); FOEI *et al.*, *Development of a Mandatory Code for Ships Operating in Polar Waters: Heavy fuel oil use in Arctic waters*, IMO Doc DE 56/10/10 (2011); FOEI *et al.*, *Development of a Mandatory Code for Ships Operating in Polar Waters: Developing a Strong Polar Code*, IMO Doc DE 56/INF.14 (2011).

regarding the protection of their subsistence livelihood, be it through risk mitigation measures for pollution,[95] namely from oil spills,[96] and the use of heavy fuel oils (HFO),[97] or the full array of potential impacts on marine mammals.[98] However, in the views of Dalee Sambo Dorough, the elected International Chair of the ICC, many of these ENGOs were "attempt[ing] to capitalize on the concerns and agenda of Indigenous peoples in the context of marine environmental protection," as opposed to truly representing their interests and concerns.[99]

Although "Canada played an instrumental role in the development of the Polar Code" at the IMO,[100] it was generally silent with respect to formally representing its Inuit treaty partners during this time. There are only three Canadian authored or co-authored submissions to IMO sessions during the development of the Polar Code that acknowledge 'Arctic communities,'[101] none of which reflect a recognition of the rights or potential roles of Indigenous peoples in the region. "This begs the question as to how the delegations of these Arctic rim countries were, if at all, advancing the interests, concerns or perspectives of Inuit specifically or Arctic Indigenous peoples generally."[102]

It is important to note that Article 42 of UNDRIP calls upon specialized agencies of the United Nations to "promote respect for and full application

---

95   DE 53/18/3 (n 94), para 6.
96   DE 56/INF.14 (n 94), Annex, p. 21.
97   DE 56/10/10 (n 94), para 11; FOEI, WWF and Pacific Environment, *Any Other Business: Arctic indigenous food security and shipping*, IMO Doc MEPC 70/17/10 (2016), para 3.
98   MEPC 62/11/6 (n 94), para 14.
99   Dalee Sambo Dorough, "The Rights, Interests and Role of the Arctic Council Permanent Participants" in *Governance of Arctic Shipping: Balancing Rights and Interests of Arctic States and User States*, eds., Robert C Beckman, Tore Henriksen, Kristine Dalaker Kraabel, Erik J Molenaar, and J Ashley Roach (Leiden: Brill, 2017), 68, at 99.
100   Drummond Fraser, "A Change in the Ice Regime: Polar Code Implementation in Canada," in *Governance of Arctic Shipping*, eds., Aldo Chircop, Floris Goerlandt, Claudio Aporta, and Ronald Pelot (Springer Polar Sciences, 2020), 285, at 285.
101   One submission in 2009 mentions subsistence hunting in the context of the impacts of air emissions on the environment (United States and Canada, *Interpretations of, and Amendments to, MARPOL and Related Instruments: Proposal to Designate an Emission Control Area for Nitrogen Oxides, Sulphur Oxides and Particulate Matter*, IMO Doc MEPC 59/6/5 (2009)) and two in 2014 regarding the need to ensure that the Polar Code did not have the effect of reducing supply to Arctic communities by introducing an administrative burden so great that companies either no longer consider charters for Arctic voyages and/or cannot meet deadlines (Canada, Liberia, and Marshall Islands, *Mandatory Code for Ships Operating in Polar Waters: Reduction of Administrative Burden*, IMO Doc MEPC 67/9/11 (2014)), or because they are unable to source a crew that meets training requirements (Canada, *Consideration and Adoption of Amendments to Mandatory Instruments: Draft International Code for Ships Operating in Polar Waters (Polar Code) – Clarification of Certification and Consideration of Administrative Burden*, IMO Doc MSC 94/3/11 (2014)).
102   Dorough (n 99), p. 100.

of the provisions of [the] Declaration" and to "facilitate indigenous peoples' participation in their processes" given the right to participate in making decisions that may affect them. Arguably this article applies to the IMO as a specialized agency of the United Nations. In 2011, the United Nations Permanent Forum on Indigenous Issues explicitly called upon the IMO "to promote respect for and full application" of UNDRIP as per Article 42.[103] However, the final version of the Polar Code does not mention Indigenous peoples or subsistence activities. The only evidence that such aspects were considered is found in paragraph four of the Preamble, which "acknowledges that coastal communities in the Arctic could be, and that polar ecosystems are, vulnerable to human activities, such as ship operation";[104] and paragraph 12 of Part I-B, which provides guidance for voyage planning, suggesting that "[i]n developing and executing a voyage plan ships should consider ... planning to minimize the impact of the ship's voyage where ships are trafficking near areas of cultural heritage and cultural significance."[105] Although only a recommendation, the latter statement is something new for the IMO; consideration of culturally important areas or anything similar are not present in the IMO's Guidelines for Voyage Planning[106] or for Voyage Planning in Remote Areas.[107]

Even though Inuit were not permitted a direct voice at the Polar Code development tables, nor were they a part of Canada's delegations to the IMO, they were still vocal with respect to their concerns and interests for Arctic shipping on the international stage, namely through the ICC and its Canadian branch. For example, in 2008, ICC Canada released a report in contribution to the AMSA project that provides Inuit perspectives on transportation in the Arctic, highlighting the linkages and connectivity between the lives and culture of Inuit.[108] After the release of AMSA, ICC convened a workshop to understand and develop an Inuit response to the report, and to document Inuit sea ice use across Inuit Nunaat (the circumpolar Inuit homeland).[109] They also prepared a second report on Inuit perspectives with respect to their use of the

---

103   ECOSOC (n 68), para 31; noted in Annexes 17–37 in IMO, *Report of the MEPC on its 62nd Session*, IMO Doc MEPC 62/24/Add.1 (2011), Annex 20, 3.
104   This wording first arose in IMO, *Report of the MSC on its 93rd Session*, IMO Doc MSC 93/22/Add.3 (2014).
105   This wording first arose in IMO, *Development of a Mandatory Code for Ships Operating in Polar Waters*, IMO Doc SDC 1/3 (2013), Annex, 49.
106   Guidelines for Voyage Planning, 25 November 1999, IMO Resolution A.893(21), IMO Doc A 2/Res.893 (4 February 2000).
107   Guidelines on Passenger Ships in Remote Areas (n 82).
108   ICC Canada, *The Sea Ice is Our Highway* (Ottawa: Inuit Circumpolar Council, 2008).
109   ICC Canada, *Circumpolar Inuit Response to Arctic Shipping Workshop Proceedings* (Ottawa: Inuit Circumpolar Council, 2013).

sea ice and interactions with shipping in 2014, with the Arctic Council as
its intended audience.[110] The message of these reports has been consistent:
the Inuit way of life is intrinsically linked to the marine environment, be it
through fishing, whale harvesting, or traveling on the open water or frozen
sea; shipping has the potential to greatly impact this way of life in numerous
ways and Inuit must have a voice in managing the activities of the industry in
their waters.[111] Further, still, in 2016, ICC established the Pikialasorsuaq Commission to consult with those communities in Nunavut and Greenland that
are closely connected to Pikialasorsuaq[112] to develop a vision for the future
use and management of the region.[113] They released their final report in 2017
with recommendations, including that there should be an Inuit-led management authority for the Pikialasorsuaq region which, among other items, would
establish a framework for regulating shipping. Concurrently, ICC was exploring and pursuing a more formal role at the IMO and, in November 2021, successfully secured provisional consultative status for two years, making them
the first Indigenous organization to do so.[114]

Canada also seemed to be shifting how it considered and treated Inuit with
regards to international shipping matters around this time; in a 2016 submission to MEPC co-authored with the United States, the Government of Canada
portrayed its relationship with Indigenous peoples at the IMO in a different
way.[115] The item under discussion was the potential ban by the IMO for the
use or carriage for use of HFO in the Arctic. A group of ENGOs had submitted
a paper that outlined the risks of oil spills and subsequent impacts on ecosystems, wildlife, and the food security of Indigenous peoples, and argued for
the need to safeguard coastal communities and Indigenous peoples.[116] Canada
and the United States agreed that remote Indigenous populations needed to be
considered, but now articulated that both States intended to identify issues and
possible options to address them through work with stakeholders, including

110   ICC Canada, *The Sea Ice Never Stops* (Ottawa: Inuit Circumpolar Council, 2014).
111   See Ell-Kanayuk and Aporta in this volume.
112   The Pikialasorsuaq is the North Water Polynya that lies north of Baffin Bay between
      Nunavut and Greenland. A polynya is a body of year-round open water, and as such, is
      often highly important ecologically.
113   ICC, "Inuit led Pikialasorsuaq Commission to Study the Important Northwater Polyna",
      ICC Press Release (19 January 2016).
114   Relations with non-governmental organizations, IMO Resolution A.1169(32) annexed
      in the *Report on External Relations with Non-governmental Organizations*, IMO Doc A
      32/20(c) (15 November 2021). For more, see Ell-Kanayuk and Aporta in this volume.
115   Canada and United States, *Any Other Business; Comments on document MEPC 70/17/4 –
      Heavy fuel oil use by vessels in Arctic waters*, IMO Doc MEPC 70/17/11 (2016).
116   Id.

local and Indigenous communities. In doing so, Canada and the United States not only recognized that Indigenous peoples have a stake (though not yet a right) in the matter, but they stated internationally that they would work with them in the process of identifying issues and solutions.

5 Towards a Renewed Inuit-Crown Relationship

The difference in Canada's presentation of its relationship with Indigenous peoples at the IMO occurred at the same time as many other changes regarding the consideration of Indigenous peoples, their interests, and their rights that align with the election of the Liberal Government led by Justin Trudeau in October 2015, including the aforementioned change to fully adopt and implement UNDRIP. One of the consistent elements of this Liberal Government's platform has been a renewal of the relationship between Indigenous peoples and Canada within the mandates of all federal ministers, officials, and other employees. One of the ways a renewed relationship is being fostered is through the creation of the Permanent Bilateral Mechanisms (PBM) with each of First Nations, Métis, and Inuit. In February 2017, the Inuit-Crown Partnership Committee (ICPC), the Inuit-specific PBM, was established[117] to serve as a forum for Inuit and the Government of Canada to work together 'to collaboratively identify and take action on shared priorities' towards greater socioeconomic and cultural equity between Inuit and other Canadians. As the name would imply, the ICPC represents a partnership that is based on the recognition of the rights of Inuit as Indigenous peoples. Over the course of its first five years, the ICPC has made much progress towards its goals,[118] the most recent of which is the co-development of the Inuit Nunangat Policy.[119]

On 21 April 2022, the Inuit Nunangat Policy was endorsed at the ICPC Leader's Meeting and announced by the Prime Minister and the President of Inuit

---

117 The ICPC was established with the signing of the Inuit Nunangat Declaration on Inuit-Crown Partnership (Office of the Prime Minister, *Inuit Nunangat Declaration on Inuit-Crown Partnership* (Ottawa: Office of the Prime Minister, 2017)) by the Prime Minister of Canada, the President of Inuit Tapiriit Kanatami, and the leaders of the four Inuit land claims organizations in Canada: Inuvialuit Regional Corporation, Nunavut Tunngavik Incorporated, Makivik Corporation, and the Nunatsiavut Government.

118 For details, please see "New permanent bilateral mechanisms," Government of Canada, last modified 21 April 2022, https://www.rcaanc-cirnac.gc.ca/eng/1499711968320/15291054 36687?wbdisable=true.

119 Crown-Indigenous Relations and Northern Affairs Canada, *Inuit Nunangat Policy* (2022), https://www.rcaanc-cirnac.gc.ca/eng/1650556354784/1650556491509.

Tapiriit Kanatami.[120] In alignment with the intent of the ICPC itself, the Policy aims to improve socioeconomic and cultural equity for Inuit and support their self-determination by providing guidance to federal public servants. The Policy applies to all federal departments and agencies in the design, development and delivery of new and renewed policies, programs, services and initiatives that apply in Inuit Nunangat or benefit Inuit, including programs of general application. The direction of the Policy is simple: when the interests, rights, people, or lands (including waters and ice) of Inuit Nunangat are implicated in a policy, program, service or initiative, Inuit should be engaged, regardless of whether such engagement is required by one of the land claims agreements or the duty to consult. "Inuit are the most knowledgeable about the issues affecting their communities, regions, and society and must, therefore, maintain an integral role and progressive responsibility in decision-making over matters that apply to Inuit and/or in Inuit Nunangat."[121]

5.1   A Renewed Relationship in the Context of Shipping Governance?

The cornerstone of the Government of Canada's efforts to change its relationship with Indigenous peoples and coastal communities in the maritime context has been the Oceans Protection Plan (OPP). Launched shortly after the 2015 election, this CDN$1.5 billion investment aimed at four pillars of work: (1) developing a world-leading marine safety system through prevention and response; (2) preserving and restoring marine ecosystems; (3) establishing a strong evidence base to improve decision-making; and (4) strengthening Indigenous partnerships.[122] In order to enable the engagements necessary to start to build relationships and perhaps even partnerships, both the federal government and Indigenous peoples were supported to participate. Transport Canada was particularly well-resourced, with funding to create six engagement hubs: one in Ottawa and each of its five regions (Pacific, Arctic, Ontario, Quebec, Atlantic). Public servants working within these hubs were supported with healthy budgets to travel to communities, and Indigenous peoples were supported to participate in engagements through the Indigenous and Local

---

120   Office of the Prime Minister, *Inuit-Crown Partnership Committee Endorses Historic Inuit Nunangat Policy to Better Support Inuit Self-determination* (Ottawa: Office of the Prime Minister, 2022).

121   Inuit Nunangat Policy (n 119), para 3.1.4.

122   Office of the Prime Minister, *Canada's Oceans Protection Plan* (Ottawa: Office of the Prime Minister, 2016).

Communities Engagement and Partnership Program and the Community Participation Funding Program.[123]

The Arctic Engagement Hub was co-chaired by Transport Canada and the Canadian Coast Guard and had dedicated staff to support engagements and the relationship-building process, namely with Inuit. For its first year, this group traveled across Inuit Nunangat meeting with Inuit leaders to introduce themselves and to understand the interests of Inuit in the OPP and how they would like to be engaged over the program's lifetime. The Arctic Engagement Hub also supported initiatives of the OPP in Transport Canada and the Canadian Coast Guard, including through internal workshops, liaising with Inuit partners to support the initiation and planning of events, accompanying initiatives to workshops and presentations to support the conversations and relationship-building process across the departments, and the internal dissemination of 'What We Heard' reports following engagements.[124]

All those working under the OPP that were to be engaging with Indigenous peoples, including those in the Arctic Engagement Hub, were given the opportunity to participate in a unique training opportunity over three, two-day sessions led by an Elder in a healing lodge. Instead of providing participants a step-by-step checklist for engaging Indigenous peoples, participants were asked to engage with the Indigenous ceremony of Circle and with concepts including Creator, the Ancestors, and the Universe. The training was personal and required participants to look inwards and reflect on feelings of judgement, leadership, and forgiveness, among others. "Bringing the personal into the professional learning space had a profound impact on many of the individuals that participated," and subsequently on their own interactions with Indigenous peoples; it changed reconciliation from a federal agenda item to a personal obligation and responsibility.[125]

The outcomes of many of the OPP initiatives suggest a culture change may be underway within Canada's maritime administration. One such initiative is Proactive Vessel Management (PVM), which aims to explore mechanisms "to reduce conflicts, improve safety, and provide environmental and cultural protection in local waters" with affected stakeholders, including Indigenous peoples.[126] The initiative was launched in September 2017, and was advanced

123   Leah Beveridge, *Demystifying Shipping Governance in Canada: Engagement of Indigenous Peoples* (Clear Seas Centre for Responsible Marine Shipping, 2021).
124   Robert Brooks, former co-chair of the Arctic Engagement Hub, Canadian Coast Guard, interview with author, Ottawa, 21 September 2021.
125   Beveridge (n 123).
126   Transport Canada, *Draft National Framework: Proactive Vessel Management* (2019) online, p. 5.

through pilot projects, one of which was based in Nunavut. The specific pilot site—Cambridge Bay—was chosen in partnership between Transport Canada, the Canadian Coast Guard and Nunavut Tunngavik Incorporated; the pilot project itself was carried out in partnership between Transport Canada and the Ekaluktutliak[127] Hunters and Trappers Organization, with participation from other federal departments and key stakeholders.[128] Through the PVM process of collaboration and dialogue, the PVM team published a Notice to Mariners (NOTMAR) in 2021 to address concerns regarding potential interactions between icebreakers and Inuit hunters and/or the Dolphin and Union Caribou; both Inuit and the caribou travel across the sea ice that forms a bridge between mainland Nunavut and Victoria Island, which can be broken by icebreakers putting Inuit and caribou at risk of being stranded.[129] Although not mandatory, the NOTMAR outlines a protection zone and defines voluntary avoidance and slowdown measures that all vessels should employ within this zone.[130]

Canada's consideration of Inuit also changed in the context of its international work. As committed to in 2016,[131] Inuit were engaged as part of the process to evaluate the potential positive and negative impacts of a ban on the use and carriage for use of HFO in Arctic waters.[132] Inuit are considered throughout the assessment, which notes the downstream implications of environmental impacts for Inuit, and the potential consequences of increasing costs for industry on their own lives. This is a stark contrast from the lack of reference at all in Canadian submissions prior to the change in government in 2015. Under the OPP, Canada also invited a member of the Inuvialuit Game Council to participate as an observer to Canada's delegation to the IMO for the 7th session of the Sub-Committee on Pollution Prevention and Response where the potential ban of HFO was being discussed.[133]

127   Cambridge Bay.
128   Beveridge (n 123).
129   Canadian Coast Guard, *Vessels Intending to Navigate in Kitikmeot Region in Canada's Northern Waters*, Notices to Mariners 1 to 46, s A3 Notice 7C (Montreal: Fisheries and Oceans Canada, 2021).
130   Beveridge (n 123).
131   MEPC 70/17/11 (n 115).
132   Canada, *Development of Measures to Reduce Risks of Use and Carriage of Heavy Fuel Oil as Fuel by Ships in Arctic Waters: Assessment of the benefits and impacts associated with a ban on the use and carriage of heavy fuel oil as fuel by ships operating in the Arctic*, IMO Doc PPR 7/INF.16 (2019), para 9.
133   IMO, *List of Participants at PPR for its 7th Session*, IMO Doc PPR 7/INF.1 (2020).

Although the majority of the OPP initiatives were policy or program based, there were also legislative initiatives, including amendments to the *Canada Shipping Act, 2001*[134] (CSA 2001) and the finalization of the *Wrecked, Abandoned or Hazardous Vessels Act*[135] (WAHVA). There was substantial engagement on both initiatives, which resulted in a significant development in Canadian maritime law for Indigenous peoples: The CSA 2001 and WAHVA now have provisions that enable the relevant ministers to enter into agreements or arrangements with Indigenous governments, councils, or representative entities to authorize them to exercise powers and perform duties and functions under the two Acts.[136] Prior to these legislative initiatives, the only maritime legislation to reference Indigenous peoples was the *Arctic Waters Pollution Prevention Act*, but it is only in the preamble and in the prevailing tone of the 1960s and 1970s: that Inuit are a group whose welfare was the responsibility of the federal government,[137] not as a people with inherent Indigenous rights. Nowhere else in the AWPPA or any of its pursuant regulations is there a reference to Inuit or any Indigenous peoples.

The domestic Arctic shipping regime has recently been amended to replace the *Arctic Shipping Pollution Prevention Regulations*[138] with the *Arctic Shipping Safety and Pollution Prevention Regulations*[139] (ASPPR) to implement the Polar Code in Canada. However, for various reasons, including a limited timeframe, the scope of the review was solely focused on Polar Code implementation.[140] Therefore, outside the Polar Code amendments, the Arctic-specific regime in Canada continues to exist within the same framework as when it was developed, with Inuit portrayed as wards of the State as opposed to a people who could enter into agreements or arrangements with ministers with respect to the implementation of maritime legislation.[141] As described by Fraser (Transport Canada), there is an acknowledgement by Transport Canada that the ASPPR do not address all the environmental concerns of shipping in Canadian Arctic

---

134   SC 2001, c 26 [CSA 2001].

135   SC 2019, c 1 [WAHVA].

136   CSA 2001 (n 134), ss 10(1)(c); id., s 6(1). The only exception is section 11 of WAHVA, which pertains to the exclusion of vessels and wrecks from the provisions of WAHVA by means of an order.

137   AWPPA (n 79), Preamble, para 2.

138   CRC c 535 (repealed).

139   SOR/2017-286.

140   Fraser (n 100).

141   The CSA 2001 (n 134) and WAHVA (n 135) apply in arctic waters, and therefore Inuit are able to enter into agreements with the Ministers with respect to exercising powers or performing duties under these two Acts.

waters.[142] The Transport Canada website indicates that Canada is considering updating the AWPPA, but does not include Inuit or Indigenous rights or reconciliation as one of the 'modern-day concerns' that would drive such an undertaking.[143] With the coming into force of the UNDRIPA and the pursuant requirement to review all Canadian laws and policies to ensure alignment with UNDRIP, though, it would seem appropriate to include an assessment of how the AWPPA could support the rights of Inuit. Given the AWPPA's direct reference to its role in regard to the 'welfare' of Inuit and the precedent set by WHAVA and the amendments to the CSA 2001, the concept that Inuit may have a role in decision-making and be empowered to exercise the powers or perform the duties and functions under the AWPPA does not seem unreasonable to consider.

6   Conclusion

Since colonization began, Inuit have been victims of State-led human rights violations. Federal organizations such as Transport Canada were directly involved in the assimilative programs of the federal government, including by removing children from their homes and delivering them to residential schools, relocating families to the High Arctic on false pretenses, and removing Inuit from their families to isolate them in tuberculosis sanatoria for undetermined amounts of time, sometimes until their far too early death. Inuit have tirelessly advocated for their rights to their culture, way of life and land at the national and international levels. They continue to advocate for their participation in domestic and international forums that affect their interests, including with regards to shipping throughout Inuit Nunaat. While Inuit have been faced with many barriers along this path, they have also achieved many successes, most recently being the granting of provisional consultative status at the IMO and the endorsement of the Inuit Nunangat Policy. This should serve as testament to the strength and perseverance of Inuit and to their ability to advance their interests and rights even in the face of adversity over generations.

There is evidence that the Government of Canada is endeavouring to shift its consideration of Inuit in the context of shipping governance in Arctic waters. The Oceans Protection Plan was an important investment in this regard, but the coming years will reveal whether there will be long-lasting change towards

---

142   Fraser (n 100).

143   "Debate and Direction of Arctic Shipping Policy", Transport Canada, accessed 9 June 2022, https://tc.canada.ca/en/marine-transportation/arctic-shipping/debate-direction-arctic -shipping-policy.

decolonization. There are three areas where this change must occur: within legislation, within policies and programs, and within society itself. Legislative change must be driven by the UNDRIPA, and in the context of Arctic shipping, a key place to begin is with the review of the AWPPA to ensure that Inuit self-determination within the scope of the Act is supported. Policy and program change, however, should be guided by the Inuit Nunangat Policy, which calls upon all federal departments and agencies to engage with Inuit and support their self-determination when a non-legislative undertaking applies to Inuit or their homeland. Ultimately, though, these legislative, policy and programmatic changes will not likely occur in a way that truly transforms the institution of maritime governance and the Inuit-Crown relationship if there are not concurrent changes within society itself. In this regard, the words of Qajaq Robinson, Commissioner of the National Inquiry on Missing and Murdered Indigenous Women and Girls should serve as a reminder of the responsibilities of all in Canada:

> We must be active participants in decolonizing Canada. We must challenge all institutions, governments and agencies to consciously and critically challenge the ideologies that govern them. We must critically examine our systems of laws and governance to identify how they exclude and oppress Indigenous Peoples. We must challenge and call on all leaders to protect and uphold the humanity and dignity of Indigenous ... peoples. And when they fail to do so, we must hold them accountable.[144]

---

144   MMIWG (n 1), p. 10.

CHAPTER 7

Unpacking Canada's Arctic Shipping Safety, Security, and Defence Functions

Andrea Charron and David Snider

Abstract

Ensuring safe, efficient shipping is the purview of civilian safety and security agencies, such as Transport Canada, Canada Ice Service, the Canadian Coast Guard and the Royal Canadian Mounted Police. Defending Canadian national interests, of which one includes unimpeded shipping, is the purview of the Canadian Armed Forces. The safety, security and defence functions consist of allocated mandates which could create stovepiped responses. However, Canada has several fora, exercises and a new Arctic-capable ship platform that promote and encourage a common understanding of Canadian Arctic shipping activity and provide opportunities for whole-of-government responses. This chapter outlines the three functions, safety, security and defence, to enable successful shipping in Canada's Arctic waters, followed by a discussion of the challenges for each. The chapter concludes with examples of how government agencies, territorial governments and local Indigenous populations are working together in more integrated ways all to the benefit of Canadian Arctic shipping.

Keywords

safety – security – defence – Canadian Arctic – integration

1   Introduction

In Canada's system of governance, government agencies and departments are all allocated set mandates which limit their powers and jurisdiction. When it comes to ensuring safe, secure and defended shipping in the Canadian Arctic, many agencies, as well as territorial governments, organizations and local communities, play important roles. With compartmentalized mandates rooted in national law comes the tendency to stovepipe processes and interactions to ensure mandates are respected. Risks, hazards and threats, however, have no set 'mandates' or 'jurisdictions' and certainly bad actors can exploit the seams between jurisdictions to disrupt and threaten the State.

In today's global age of great power competition, there is an assumption that the Canadian Armed Forces (CAF) should assume the 'lead' in the Arctic because of overstated concerns about the possibility of armed conflict in the Arctic.[1] Despite considerable tensions around the world and even egregious State aggression by Russia against Ukraine, the Arctic States still maintain that the Arctic is unlikely to be the source or theatre of conflict.[2] What is anticipated are accidents, incidents and miscalculations given the higher tension generally that could lead to an unintentional escalation. Nevertheless, this does not mean that the CAF takes over other mandates or changes its core mission from protecting the State to becoming a police force. Rather, when it comes to safe shipping in the Arctic, it is in a support role to deal with the effects of climate change, disasters and consequence management.

This chapter seeks to outline the three functions required to ensure safe shipping in Canada's Arctic; namely, safety, security and defence. Departments and their personnel ensure safe shipping via information, education and aids to navigation (safety function), enforcement of shipping laws (the constabulary or security function) and providing credible deterrence and defence against threats (the defence mandate). Thus, when it comes to safe shipping in Canada's Arctic, Transport Canada, Canadian Ice Service (CIS), Canadian Hydrographic Service (CHS) and the Canadian Coast Guard (CCG) as well as others, ship operators, and Indigenous governments, organizations, local communities and territorial governments, work to ensure that shipping in Canada's Arctic is safe. Other agencies, including the CAF, contribute to safety to be sure, but the main agencies of note are mainly civilian and local agencies. The Royal Canadian Mounted Police (RCMP), Transport Canada, the Department of Fisheries and Oceans (DFO), the Canadian Border Services Agency (CBSA) and others ensure Canadian laws are respected. To deter and

---

1   David Bercuson, "Should Canada Boost Its Military Presence in the Arctic?," *Legion Magazine*, 16 September 2021, https://legionmagazine.com/en/2021/09/should-canada-boost-its-mili tary-presence-in-the-arctic/; Jeffrey Collins, "On the Arctic Watch: Why We Need to Protect Canada's Sovereignty and Security in the Far North: Jeff Collins for Inside Policy," Macdonald Laurier Institute, 17 January 2022, https://macdonaldlaurier.ca/what-we-need-vs-what-we -have-assessing-canadas-defence-capabilities-in-the-arctic-jeff-collins-for-inside-policy/; Marcus Kolga, "Winter is Coming to Canada's North. Vladimir Putin Will Make Sure of It," *Maclean's Magazine*, 26 May 2021, https://www.macleans.ca/opinion/winter-is-coming-to -canadas-north-vladimir-putin-will-make-sure-of-it/.
2   Elizabeth Buchanan, "The Ukraine War and the Future of the Arctic," RUSI, 18 March 2022, https://rusi.org/explore-our-research/publications/commentary/ukraine-war-and-future-arctic.

prosecute armed conflict, the CAF, especially the Royal Canadian Navy (RCN), seek to deter, deny and defeat State and non-State-based threats, such as a sea-launched missile, and monitor the movement of other military vessels.

We begin by outlining the roles and mandates of the three functions and then turn to a discussion of the challenges for each of these functions. We finish with a discussion of several Canadian initiatives that help to promote an integrated whole-of-government approach between federal agencies. They include greater maritime domain awareness via the Marine Security Operations Centre (MSOC East) in Halifax, the new Arctic and Offshore Patrol Ships (AOPS), a series of four Arctic exercises under the umbrella name NANOOK, and the Canadian Arctic Security Working Group (ASWG). Of course, these are not the only examples of both formal and informal integration efforts, but they are the highest profile, yet often misunderstood. First, however, it is important to understand the scale of shipping in Canada's historic, internal Arctic waters.

2   Shipping Trends in the Canadian Arctic

The Northwest Passage (NWP) is not yet the hotbed of commercial vessel traffic many media reports suggest.[3] The Arctic Council's Protection of the Arctic Marine Environment (PAME) working group issued a report on vessel traffic in Canada's Arctic waters comparing data from 2013 and 2019.[4] Canadian-flagged ships are the majority in both years, which is consubstantial with the types of vessels transiting the Arctic waters—they are mainly government or commercial resupply vessels to Arctic hamlets. Few transit the entire NWP; rather, their traffic is destinational.[5] The other classes of vessels not captured, because of their smaller size and therefore not subject to certain (especially) international regulations, are local fishing vessels, small crafts and adventurers. Increasingly, these are the ships of concern in terms of need of search and rescue. In a report on shipping for Inuit Tapiriit Kanatami (ITK) between 2015 and 2019, fishing vessels travelled more than 2,048,611 km while government and research vessels travelled 1,088,318 km and cargo resupply vessels travelled 1,319, 537 km in

---

3   See Dawson and Song in this volume.
4   PAME, "Shipping in the NWP: Comparing 2013 with 2019," Arctic Shipping Status Report #3, Arctic Council, April 2021, https://www.pame.is/document-library/pame-reports-new /pame-ministerial-deliverables/2021-12th-arctic-council-ministerial-meeting-reykjavik -iceland/795-assr-3-shipping-in-the-northwest-passage-comparing-2013-to-2019/file.
5   See further chapters by Lasserre, and Dawson and Song in this volume.

Arctic waters.[6] There are 51 Inuit communities that are highly dependent on the marine and coastal environment.[7] If shipping is to be safe and secure, these represent key classes of vessels that need to be targeted because automatic identification systems (AIS) for smaller vessels are not mandatory, although there are discussions to extend the Polar Code to non-SOLAS (International Convention for the Safety of Life at Sea) vessels.[8]

3   The Safety, Security and Defence Functions

3.1   *Safety*

The number of Canadian agencies, departments and local community volunteers involved in ensuring safe, efficient shipping in the Arctic is staggering. In fact, there are roughly a dozen federal departments/agencies that are responsible for the governance of maritime activities in Canada. According to Meagan Greentree and Aldo Chircop, however, Canada is an outlier.[9] Whereas many States have one agency responsible for maritime administration,[10] Canada has multiple actors. This means, for example, that to obtain a permit as a passenger vessel to navigate Canada's Arctic waters, ship operators must seek permission from representatives of the federal government, territorial governments and rights holders (Indigenous peoples).[11]

If we focus on safety issues only, the referent of concern is the protection of human lives and secondarily, environment and wildlife (Table 7.1). The activities within the safety column include waterways maintenance, search

6   Nicolien van Luijk, Jean Holloway, Natalie A Carter, Jackie Dawson, and Andrew Orawiec, *Gap Analysis: Shipping and Coastal Management in the Inuit Nunagat* (Ottawa: University of Ottawa, Environment, Society and Policy Group, 2021), 17. The statistics need to be used in context. For example, fishing vessels often circle in search of target fish, thus increasing their miles steamed as recorded from AIS and other remote data collection sources.
7   Id., 7.
8   International Maritime Organization (IMO), "International Code for Ships Operating in Polar Waters (Polar Code), Polar Code (second phase)," https://www.imo.org/en/Our Work/Safety/Pages/polar-code.aspx.
9   See chapters by Greentree and Chircop in this volume. See also Meagan Greentree, *Modernizing the Governance of Passenger Vessel Operations in the Canadian Arctic* (MPA Capstone thesis, University of Manitoba and University of Winnipeg, 2020), 8.
10   Maritime administrations refers to the bureaucratic body(ies) responsible for the administration of a State's seafaring commercial activity (e.g., the use of ships to transports goods and passengers).
11   Transport Canada, *Guidelines for Passenger Vessels Operating in the Canadian Arctic*, TP-13670 (Ottawa: Government of Canada, 2018), https://tc.canada.ca/en/marine-transpor tation/marine-safety/guidelines-passenger-vessels-operating-canadian-arctic-tp-13670.

TABLE 7.1   Examples of issues along the conflict continuum

Safety issues (protecting people and wildlife)	Policing/security issues (enforcing laws)	Defence issues (protecting the State)
Land and maritime search and rescue	Illegal, unreported and unregulated fishing	Detect, deter and defeat (sovereignty and presence)
Oil spill and other cleanup	Smuggling and trafficking of people or goods	Intelligence, surveillance and reconnaissance
Charting	Violation of pollution or other maritime laws	Collective defence (NATO and Article 5), joint defence of North America via NORAD and many bilateral arrangements
Ice management/ icebreaking	Surveillance	Acts of aggression
Crew and passenger safety	Espionage	Support and assistance to requests from civilian authorities
Consequence management	Regulatory mandate and risk mitigation	Aeronautical and maritime search and rescue
Waterway management (aids to navigation)	Marine patrols	Chemical, biological, radiological and nuclear defence and response
Education, outreach and certification (e.g., safe boating, pleasure craft operator license)	Education and outreach and registration of vessels (especially if commercial or above certain tonnage)	Support to safety and security agencies

and rescue (SAR), oil spill cleanup, charting activities, ice management services, assistance to communities and vessels in time of natural or other disasters, and education, outreach and certification. The immediate concern of
safety is consequence management. If there was fault, criminal activity or even
malfeasance, investigations, prosecutions and seizures are secondary to survival and often the domain of other agencies. Consequently, the organizations
charged with safety generally do not have officer powers that allow for the
enforcement of laws and regulations. Rather, their primary focus is on saving
lives and protecting the environment. We anchor our analysis on the protection of crews and passengers especially.

Some of the safety agencies include CIS (for ice condition reports), Transport Canada (for regulations), CHS (for continued charting of the NWP), the CCG (for maritime search and rescue, aids to navigation, Marine Communications and Traffic Services (MCTS), icebreaking services, as well as primary responsibility for oil spill cleanup in the Arctic when the polluter is not known, unwilling or unable to assist). The most likely responders to provide community and small vessel safety services in the Arctic, however, are local community groups via the CCG Auxiliary and Inshore Rescue Boat student program. As well, the Indigenous Guardians program will begin training soon, and the Inuit Marine Monitoring Program (IMMP) assists by establishing land-based AIS. Surprisingly, the majority of small fishing vessel SAR and community-based disaster assistance support is provided by local volunteers, not paid professionals.[12] Larger vessels, especially cruise ships, or those carrying dangerous materials, require rescue by the CCG, often with assistance from the CAF and very occasionally, vessels of opportunity.

The volunteer auxiliary arm of the CCG is a case in point.[13] It provides maritime SAR from local Arctic hamlets. The CCG has observed areas of higher SAR cases in western Hudson Bay, Gjoa Haven, the Labrador coast, Iqaluit and the Beaufort Sea. Rankin Inlet has a CCG Inshore Rescue Boat Station operated during the summer months by Indigenous post-secondary students under the supervision of an experienced CCG officer. In 2020, the CCG Auxiliary responded to 32 incidents, the Inshore Rescue Boat Station responded to 6 SAR cases, and the CCG icebreakers (the professionals) to 12.[14] Since 2017, the CCG has provided vessels under the Oceans Protection Plan to hamlets across the Arctic in recognition of the increased number of SAR incidents, and to support their participation in the Auxiliary.[15] These statistics, however, need to be put into context because of 'station generated statistics.' When a station is opened, their new station statistics increase dramatically because they are there, not because the incidents suddenly increased. Local SAR cases, however,

---

12   See Kikkert *et al.* in this volume.

13   It is essential to understand that the Canadian Coast Guard (CCG) operates as a civilian federal safety agency only, unlike the United States Coast Guard (USCG), which can fall under the Department of Homeland Defense and fulfill safety and security missions, or under the US military to fulfill defence duties.

14   Daniella Koroma, Nicholas Glesby, Denys Kovtun and Andrea Charron, "Virtual JABAS - Joint Agile Basing Airpower Seminar 18 February 2021: Arctic SAR/PR, Part II" (Winnipeg: Centre for Defence and Security Studies (CDSS), 2021), 3, https://umanitoba.ca/arts/sites/arts/files/2022-07/JABAS-Feb-2021-part2.pdf.

15   Id.

are less likely to be reported to the federal system unless there is an auxiliary unit in place.

The top ten Arctic Canada cruise vessel destinations in terms of passenger/crew member movements accounted for 50.1 percent of the movements into/out of hamlets in 2019. They include Pond Inlet, Beechey Island, Dundas Harbour, Croker Bay, Cambridge Bay, Demarcation Point, Ulukhaktuk, Gjoa Haven, Iqaluit, and Queen's Harbour which is equivalent to 38,552 tourists and crew members.[16] (Recall, the population of the Canadian Arctic is approximately 135,000.) Cruise vessel transits were banned for the 2020 and 2021 summer shipping seasons because of the COVID-19 pandemic. The CCG has found that there are approximately five times more SAR incidents than are reported to the federal SAR system (Table 7.2).[17] At the same time, areas of historical elevated risk are subject to Joint Rescue Coordination Centre (JRCC) notification. The CCG is targeting these areas for additional CCG auxiliary units (i.e., trained volunteers).

The CCG is finding success by assigning the same CCG contacts to the same community year-after-year. Further, the CCG is working to reduce the administrative burden and provide administrative training to volunteers compiling claims and compensation reports.

TABLE 7.2   Total number of SAR cases north of 55 degrees

Case classification	2019	5-year average (2015–2019)
Aeronautical	25	29
Maritime	34	36
Humanitarian	34	30
Unknown/false alarm	132	111
Outside Canadian area of responsibility	169	182
Total	394	388

SOURCE: CENTRE FOR DEFENCE AND SECURITY STUDIES, "VIRTUAL JABAS - JOINT AGILE BASING AIRPOWER SEMINAR, 18 FEBRUARY 2021, ARCTIC SAR/PR, PART II" (18 FEBRUARY 2021), 4, HTTPS://UMANITOBA.CA/ARTS/SITES/ARTS/FILES/2022-07/JABAS-FEB-2021-PART2.PDF

16   Id.
17   Id.

The Indigenous Guardians program is a federal government-funded pilot project to empower Indigenous peoples to monitor and steward resources.[18] While some of the projects are land-based, many are marine-based given the importance of the marine environment to the cultural and economic well-being of Arctic residents. Via data collection on species, as well as tracking fishing and hunting activities, the local communities are often the first to learn of and respond to accidents and disasters. For example, when the MS *Clipper Adventurer* ran aground in 2010 near Kugluktuk, Nunavut, the passengers were evacuated to the community, where they were fed and sheltered.[19]

The IMMP takes an innovative approach to vessel monitoring in Nunavut that couples Inuit marine monitors with real-time vessel tracking technology, using AIS, especially for smaller fishing vessels. IMMP was developed because there has been a recent increase in shipping around Nunavut. With this increase, the communities have many concerns, such as potential accidents, increased pollution and oil spills, wildlife disturbance, and interference with hunting and traditional practices. The monitoring program helps Nunavut communities implement policy guidelines for the NWP. The program also provides Inuit with a greater role in shipping management and monitoring. The IMMP collects information of ships travelling through the Arctic, including:

– ship characteristics such as the vessel type, colour, and flag;
– wildlife, noise, and pollution concerns;
– location, speed, and heading of vessels;
– behaviour, activity and timing of ships;
– any suspicious vessels in the area; and
– concerns identified by the community.[20]

While approximately 14.8 percent of Canadian Arctic waters have been surveyed to either modern or adequate standards, most of the surveyed area is found along the low-impact shipping corridors where the Government of Canada wishes vessels to transit to minimize potential effects of shipping on wildlife and respect culturally and ecologically sensitive areas.[21] That means,

---

18   "Indigenous Guardians Pilot Map," Government of Canada, last modified 7 September 2022, https://www.canada.ca/en/environment-climate-change/services/environmental-funding /indigenous-guardians-pilot/map.html.

19   Id., 4.

20   Daniel Kiesman and Andrea Charron, "Virtual Arctic Air Power Seminar," CDSS, 27 May 2021, https://umanitoba.ca/arts/sites/arts/files/2022-07/Arctic-Air-Power-Seminar-May -2021-part3.pdf. See comments by Mr. Daniel Taukie at p. 10.

21   See "Arctic Charting," Government of Canada, last modified 3 August 2022, https: //www.charts.gc.ca/arctic-arctique/index-eng.html. Note, however, that the Auditor General of Canada stated : "The CHS estimates that about one percent of Canadian Arctic

outside of the corridors, there is a high likelihood that there will be insufficient bathymetric and other navigational data. There have been only three groundings, outside well-charted corridors, of passenger vessels and one chartered yacht in the Canadian Arctic since 1996 with no lives lost,[22] because most ships navigate only along charted paths. The *Hanseatic* ran aground in Simpson Strait in 1996,[23] the *Clipper Adventurer* ran aground in 2010 near Kugluktuk, and the *Akademik Ioffe* ran aground in 2018 off the Gulf of Boothia, Nunavut. All of these vessels ventured outside of chartered waters, failed to take additional precautions and made assumptions about the navigability of the narrows. Safety concerns associated with groundings, therefore, are associated with vessels that ignore the warnings and information provided by the Government of Canada and pursue routes outside of tested transit ways. However, it might also be a case of sheer luck that there have been so few disasters. The potential for complicated and dangerous SAR scenarios increases as vessel traffic increases and because professional rescue services are often very far away.

Efforts to augment CHS surveys have been focused primarily on the main shipping corridors, especially those used to resupply Arctic hamlets, with no timeline for completion in other areas of the Arctic.[24] The need for multiple, verifiable and government documented soundings, coupled with the limited shipping season compared to the size and scope of the area, means that the NWP likely will never be fully charted. However, experienced, professional

---

waters are surveyed to modern standards." The jump from 1 percent to 14.8 percent in fewer than ten years is a result of concentrating surveying efforts along the corridors. Office of the Auditor General of Canada, *2014 Fall Report of the Commissioner of the Environment and Sustainable Development*, Chapter 3: Marine Navigation in the Canadian Arctic, section 3.18: Nautical charts.https://www.oag-bvg.gc.ca/internet/English/parl_cesd _201410_03_e_39850.html#hd4a.

22   Transportation Safety Board of Canada (TSB), "Backgrounder: Safety Communications related to TSB Investigation M18C0225 – August 2018 Grounding of Passenger Vessel *Akademik Ioffe* in Nunavut," http://bst-tsb.gc.ca/eng/medias-media/fiches-facts/m18c0225 /m18c0225-20210521-02.html.

23   TSB, *Marine Investigation Report M96H0016: Grounding – Passenger Vessel Hanseatic, Simpson Strait, Northwest Territories, 29 August 1996*, https://www.tsb.gc.ca/eng/rapports -reports/marine/1996/m96h0016/m96h0016.html.

24   As noted above, approximately 14.8 percent of Canadian Arctic waters have been surveyed to either modern or adequate standards, but approximately 40.4 percent of the combined draft primary and secondary low-impact shipping corridors in the Arctic have been surveyed to either modern or adequate standards. See "Arctic Charting" (n 21). Inuit and local expertise should also be acquired to better understand the corridors, specifically information about safe areas of refuge that are not obvious on a map/chart. This has been recently done in Labrador with the Nunatsiavut Government.

mariners are expected to stay within chartered waters. The most likely sources of future groundings and disasters are with irresponsible seafarers who may succumb to providing 'never seen before views' and fishers searching for new fishing grounds.

Of course, in most safety incidents the shipping operators themselves are the first to take action to mitigate damage and loss of life. The Polar Code, as implemented by regulations under the *Canada Shipping Act, 2001*, and the *Arctic Waters Pollution Prevention Act* (AWPPA) provide standards for navigational and other safety equipment that must be onboard ships.[25] They are critical to avoiding accidents in the first place. Even the smallest commercial fishing vessels must comply with Transport Canada regulations, including being equipped with specific navigational, life saving and fire-fighting equipment and the hope is that the 2012 Cape Town Agreement, which is designed for fishing vessels, will come into force soon.[26] The Cape Town Agreement is an internationally-binding instrument that includes mandatory international requirements for stability and associated seaworthiness, machinery and electrical installations, life-saving equipment, communications capabilities and fire protection, as well as fishing vessel construction. Whether or not it is sufficient for polar conditions, however, is unclear.

In addition to regulations, shore-based and floating navigational aids are in place to support small vessels. Several CCG navigational aids have been changed to be operational all year so that users can take advantage of them during winter snowmobile operations. With more unpredictable ice movement, vessel and snowmobile operators can find themselves in trouble with no cellphone coverage and hundreds of kilometres away from rescue services.

Some of the key safety responsibilities of ship operators are to ensure that they have the latest ice conditions information, up-to-date charts, including the CCG's Notice to Mariners or NOTMAR (for archival information), Navigational Warnings (NAVWARNS)[27] and Notice to Shipping (NOTSHIP), which provide

---

25   See Chircop in this volume.

26   International Maritime Organization (IMO), *Report of the Maritime Safety Committee on its Ninety-Second Session*, IMO Doc MSC 92/26/Add.2 (30 June 2013), Annex 25, International Regulations for the Safety of Fishing Vessels (2012 Cape Town Agreement). See "2012 Cape Town Agreement to Enhance Fishing Safety," IMO, https://www.imo.org/en/MediaCentre/HotTopics/Pages/CapeTownAgreementForFishing.aspx.

27   The CCG's Navigational Warnings (NAVWARNS) take an all-hazard approach to announcing to the maritime community by listing military exercises, drifting hazards, obstructions, offshore works, waterway information and so forth.

necessary information to update all charts and nautical publications, advise of new initiatives, services and important announcements concerning the maritime community. Ships entering Arctic waters are expected to have all of this information on hand prior to their voyage. If they are not fully equipped, including with all documents, they are deemed to be unseaworthy, which has consequences for marine insurance cover. Circumstances en route can change, however, and if new information is needed while in the Arctic, difficulties can arise. Satellite linkups are often necessary to access government information, which not all vessels have, especially smaller ones.

The other safety responsibility of ship operators is to have sufficiently trained officers and crew to operate in ice-infested waters. This can take decades of practice. Ice navigation and ice piloting require weeks of training, months of in-ice ship operation and certification. The International Convention on Standards of Training, Certification and Watchkeeping for Seafarers (STCW) and STCW Code[28] require specific bridge officers on certain ships to possess certificates of proficiency in either polar waters basic or advanced training, and experience navigating in polar waters is required before the advanced certificate can be issued. However, these requirements do not specifically ensure competence in operating in ice-covered waters. The only internationally recognized certification in ice navigation is provided by the Nautical Institute Ice Navigator Certificates. Applicants must possess the International Maritime Organization's (IMO) STCW other recognized mariner bridge watchkeeping officer qualification and have completed both a Level 1 and Level 2 course and accumulated sufficient and acceptable watchkeeping time in ice-covered waters.[29]

Transport Canada delegates Marine Safety Inspectors to provide oversight on regulated vessels within the Canadian Arctic using statutory inspections, risk-based compliance inspections, port State control inspections of foreign vessels and by providing oversight to vessels transiting through ice using the Arctic Ice Regime Shipping System (AIRSS) or equivalent risk indexing systems. When a non-compliance or violation is identified, Transport Canada Marine Safety

---

28   International Convention on Standards of Training, Certification and Watchkeeping for Seafarers, 7 July 1978 (in force 28 April 1984), 1361 *UNTS* 2; the STWC Code was adopted as an annex to the STCW Convention. See "International Convention on Standards of Training, Certification and Watchkeeping for Seafarers, 1978," IMO, https://www.imo.org/en/OurWork/HumanElement/Pages/STCW-Conv-LINK.aspx, for more information.

29   International Union of Marine Insurance, "Nautical Institute launches Ice Navigator Accreditation Standard," *Insurance Marine News*, 26 July 2017, https://iumi.com/news/news/nautical-institute-launches-ice-navigator-accreditation-standard; "Ice Navigation," The Nautical Institute, https://www.nialexisplatform.org/certification/ice-navigation/.

Inspectors use a scaled approach to choose the right enforcement instrument and penalty amount. They may issue a verbal warning, written warning, assurance of compliance or administrative monetary penalty (AMP). In certain cases, where appropriate based on the violation or non-compliance, Transport Canada may pursue penalties based on a summary conviction in a court of law. It should be noted that AMPs are not an enforcement tool under the AWPPA or *Arctic Shipping Safety and Pollution Prevention Regulations* (ASSPPR) as those violations are not listed in the *Administrative Monetary Penalties and Notices (CSA 2001) Regulations.*[30]

3.2   *Security*

Security issues are often related to a violation of Canadian laws, damage to property and infrastructure, or hybrid tactics, such as illegal surveillance while posing as a research vessel or smuggling goods or people. The agencies assigned to the security portfolio generally have officer powers, meaning they can enforce Canadian laws and seize a vessel and/or arrest and/or prosecute individuals and entities. Agencies connected to security and constabulary functions include the RCMP, Transport Canada, and fishery officers from DFO. Sometimes members of the CAF, RCMP and Transport Canada are given temporary fisheries' officer powers. Additionally, as of 2019, the CCG has enforcement powers to address damaged or hazardous vessels. A hazardous vessel is defined as one that could cause harm to infrastructure, the environment, economic interests of the public, a vessel significantly degraded, dismantled or *incapable of being used for safe navigation*—the latter being in the purview of the CCG.[31] Under the *Wrecked, Abandoned, or Hazardous Vessels Act* (WAHVA), CCG has powers to address hazardous vessels[32] by providing risk-based assessments and enforcing directions to shipowners or take appropriate actions on hazardous vessels (e.g., fix, move, or remove and dispose of vessel).

---

30   *Arctic Waters Pollution Prevention Act*, RSC 1985, c A-12 [AWPPA]; *Arctic Shipping Safety and Pollution Prevention Regulations*, SOR/2017-286 [ASSPPR]; *Administrative Monetary Penalties and Notices (CSA 2001) Regulations*, SOR/2008-97. Transport Canada is proposing amendments to the *Administrative Monetary Penalties and Notices (CSA 2001) Regulations* that will include the ASSPPR. See Transport Canada, "Discussion Paper: Updating Administrative Monetary Penalties under the Canada Shipping Act, 2001," Government of Canada, last modified 4 May 2022, https://tc.canada.ca/en/corporate-services/consultations/discussion-paper-updating-administrative-monetary-penalties-under-canada-shipping-act-2001.

31   *Wrecked, Abandoned or Hazardous Vessels Act*, SC 2019, c 1, ss 4 and especially 27.

32   Id., s 6(1).

Canada has more than fifty regulations under the *Canada Shipping Act, 2001* (CSA 2001) alone.[33] The main legislation of concern include the CSA 2001, *Coasting Trade Act, Marine Liability Act,* and *Marine Transportation Security Act,* and four Arctic-specific legislation; namely, the AWPPA, *Northern Canada Vessel Traffic Services Zone Regulations* (NORDREG), *Shipping Safety Control Zone Order* and the ASSPPR.[34]

As a coastal State, Canada regulates navigation of domestic and foreign vessels within Canada's territorial waters, including the coastal waters surrounding the Canadian Arctic Archipelago. As a flag State, Canada subjects Canadian flagged ships to Canadian safety, pollution prevention and security rules and standards wherever they are. Transport Canada and the DFO and its special operating agency, the CCG, combined have the regulatory mandate to implement various risk mitigation measures to reduce the likelihood and consequences of a vessel running aground in Arctic waters, stop IUU fishing and pollution.[35] As noted in the safety section above, regulations do not ensure that accidents and dangerous navigation and/or perilous conditions disappear, however. There are of course additional regulations of goods and people which fall to the CBSA, Immigration, Refugee and Citizenship Canada and the RCMP.

Transport Canada conducts port State control inspections of foreign vessels in accordance with Paris and Tokyo MOUs and inspects domestic vessels under the flag State control program. Transport Canada also carries out a risk-based inspection when required, under the CSA 2001 and the AWPPA. Vessels entering the Canadian Arctic are subject to reporting requirements and are monitored throughout their passage. Transport Canada maintains 24/7 duty officers monitoring the shipping traffic in close conjunction with the CCG and other government agencies. Prior to entry into Canadian waters, operators are required to report to Transport Canada advising that the vessel meets requirements such as being in possession of a Polar Ship Certificate (which indicates the vessel meets Polar Code requirements) and bridge watchkeeping officers meet minimum Polar Code training requirements for the vessel and ice conditions expected.[36] Any deficiencies are required to be reported, but this of course depends upon the truthfulness and understanding of the operator.

---

33   For a listing of Canadian statutes and regulations, see the annexes in Aldo Chircop *et al.* (eds), *Canadian Maritime Law* 2d (Toronto: Irwin Law, 2016).

34   See chapters by Bartenstein and Chircop in this volume for details.

35   See Bankes in this volume.

36   Other requirements include ballast water reports and a pre-arrival report at least 96 hours before arriving in the Canadian waters and vessels are required to report to Marine Communication Traffic Services (MCTS), Iqaluit (information provided by Transport Canada).

Operators new to polar operations may be simply ignorant of some of the fine details of regulatory requirements. Without a physical inspection, intentional or unintentional non-compliance may not be caught in the reporting process. Nevertheless, regulations like NORDREG,[37] which require ships to provide important identifying information prior to entering the Arctic, coupled with AIS and the other statutes listed above, allow security organizations to identify potential vessels of interest. Vessels of interest (VOI) are vessels of potential police, intelligence or counter-intelligence value because of a vessel's registry, cargo, route, behaviour or activities.[38] Screening and risk assessment of all vessels allows security agencies to direct their surveillance and enforcement efforts more efficiently toward those constituting a threat.

Cruise ship operators, for example, are eager for early detection and early processing of international passenger lists. When the *Crystal Serenity* made its voyages through the NWP in 2016 and 2017, carrying nearly 1,800 passengers and crew from around the world, the challenge became screening everyone by CBSA personnel in the Arctic. With no permanent CBSA offices in the Arctic and unable to pre-screen from Alaska, the decision was made for CBSA officers to board the *Crystal Serenity* in Ulukhaktok, NWT on the west coast of Victoria Island to process everyone. This meant that the *Crystal Serenity* was already deep into Canadian territory. For companies like Crystal Cruises, which are rule abiding, and because passengers had also been processed by United States' officials in Alaska, this was an acceptable risk. For nefarious companies and actors, this is a potential loophole. For non-commercial vessels carrying fewer than 50 passengers and crew, the CBSA has developed a Private Vessel Remote Clearance (PVRC) project to address the challenges of reporting in remote areas of the Arctic region.[39] The PVRC pilot project is intended to simplify and expedite the clearance process for non-commercial pleasure craft looking to enter Canadian waters in the Baffin Island and Northwest Passage region of Nunavut. Of course, the PVRC project is dependent on the compliance of scrupulous operators to pass along the correct and authentic papers for processing.

As there are numerous national, territorial and regional regulations that are essential for passenger vessels operating in the Arctic, Transport Canada

---

37   CCG manages the transactional elements of NORDREG via MCTS Iqaluit on behalf of Transport Canada.

38   "Termium Plus: Vessel Interest," Government of Canada, accessed 10 June 2022, https:// www.btb.termiumplus.gc.ca/tpv2alpha/alpha-eng.html?lang=eng&i=1&srchtxt=VESSEL +INTEREST&index=alt&codom2nd_wet=1#resultrecs.

39   "Private Vessel Remote Clearance Project," Canada Border Services Agency, last modified 30 April 2019, https://www.cbsa-asfc.gc.ca/travel-voyage/pv-vp-eng.html.

created the Guidelines for Passenger Vessels Operating in the Canadian Arctic to highlight the myriad regulations and considerations.[40] For example, the Guidelines outline some basic rules for cruise ships that offer helicopter rides for passengers for sightseeing. They bring together the requirements of seventeen different agencies and responsibility centre requirements. Thirty-eight separate acts, or regulations are listed, and many apply to vessels other than those of the passenger/cruise/expedition sector operating in the Arctic.

Finally, fishing vessels engaging in illegal, unreported and unregulated (IUU) fishing can be prosecuted thanks to aerial surveillance patrols conducted by DFO and Transport Canada's National Aeronautical Surveillance Program (which is a more flexible instrument for monitoring and supporting prosecution of violations in many domains regulated by the Government of Canada). In April 2022, for example, a Nunavut Court of Justice sentenced a man under the *Fisheries Act* for fishing illegally.[41] Prosecuting violators of safety, environment and navigation violations in small vessels, however, can be challenging given their size and the fact that many are not required to have AIS. Education, outreach and training are important tools used in local communities to make operators aware of the regulations.

3.3   *Defence*

The defence portfolio of issues is seemingly bottomless. The CAF has the remit to defend the State of Canada with deadly force if necessary.[42] Most of the time, especially in the Arctic, it serves in a support capacity for other government agencies. Nevertheless, the calls for more CAF presence in the Arctic are growing from both external and internal sources. Externally, as members of the North American Aerospace Defense Command (NORAD) and the North Atlantic Treaty Organization (NATO) and as a close ally of the United States, increased attention by these alliances and/or the United States to the Arctic

---

40   Transport Canada (n 11).

41   Government of Canada, "Arctic Aerial Surveillance Leads to Significant Penalties of $35,000 for Captain of a Nunavut Fishing Vessel," Fisheries and Oceans Canada News Release, 16 May 2022, https://www.canada.ca/en/fisheries-oceans/news/2022/05/arctic-aerial-surveillance-leads-to-significant-penalties-of-35000-for-captain-of-a-nunavut-fishing-vessel.html.

42   Other government agencies can use deadly force as well. CCG enables other agencies, such as the Royal Canadian Mounted Police (RCMP) or the Department of Fisheries and Oceans Canada's (DFO) Conservation and Protection branch to use deadly force proportional to external stimuli, by using CCG as a support platform during armed boardings (e.g., during the Turbot War, an international fishing dispute between Spain and Canada).

maritime domain requires Canada to follow in kind or at least satisfy important allies that it is not a weak link in the partnership.

Given the rise in strategic competition between the United States, Russia and China, "command of the commons"[43] (or domination of the world ocean) becomes vital to ensure deterrence, global reach and, for the United States, continued hegemony. Given the proximity of Russia to the United States via the Arctic, North America is an avenue of approach for any air or marine-based attacks. While a 'hot' conflict in or about the Arctic Ocean is unlikely and all eight Arctic States and observer States readily point to various international agreements to ensure that the Arctic remains rules-based, all domain awareness is the goal of all States to deter potential State and non-State adversaries.

The CAF is instrumental in providing intelligence, surveillance and reconnaissance (ISR) information (coordinated acquisition and processing of data and intelligence) to support command and alliance decision-making. Via its ships, satellites, radars, and intelligence, the CAF and its various capabilities are an important tool of deterrence. The CAF also depends heavily on the information from civilian agencies and other allied partners. Not only does the CAF need to have a common operating picture of the Arctic and all activities within the (especially Canadian) Arctic, but it needs to be able to defeat any threats if detection, deterrence and denial tactics fail. As the United States has pivoted its attention to the Arctic (as evidenced by every US service issuing an Arctic strategy),[44] Canada can expect pressure to ensure ISR and defeat capabilities are sufficient to protect Canada and its allies. RCN frigates, coastal defence vessels, and submarines are not capable of operating in ice-infested waters. They are open-water platforms that are not suited for warfighting in an Arctic context. It is also unclear if the RCN's future platforms (the surface combatants and *Protecteur* class joint support ship) will be suitable in ice-infested waters either. The latter two, however, are on the 'pointy end' of Canada's deterrence and defeat capabilities and will be used to enhance Canada's support to NORAD and NATO operations.

Internal Canadian agency and government requests account for most of the increased calls for more CAF presence in the Arctic. Municipal, territorial governments and other federal agencies can turn to the CAF for assistance. The

---

43 Barry Posen, "Command of the Commons: The Military Foundation of U.S. Hegemony," *International Security* 28 (1): 5–46.

44 US Office of the Under Secretary of Defense for Policy, *Department of Defense Arctic Strategy* (2019); USCG, *Arctic Strategic Outlook* (April 2019); US Department of the Air Force, *Arctic Strategy* (July 2020); US Department of the Navy, *A Blue Arctic: A Strategic Blueprint for the Arctic* (January 2021); and United States Army, *Regaining Arctic Dominance* (January 2021).

CAF is meant to be the last resort. The reasons for the national calls for assistance from the CAF are two-fold. First, the CAF is the only agency in Canada with the air-lift capacity (for goods and personnel) and until very recently, limited maritime capacity, to reach the Arctic. Second and related, CAF personnel are the only public servants with unlimited liability—they can be sent into dangerous situations that may result in death.[45] While police, fire and search and rescue personnel do put their lives on the line every day, legally they cannot be forced to act when they know it will result in death. Given the vast distances and lack of infrastructure and rescue capabilities in the Arctic, it is this latter expectation that is the most worrying regarding the expanded scope of operations in the Arctic. While the unlimited liability has never been resorted to, CAF members accept and understand that they are subject to being lawfully ordered into harm's way under conditions that could lead to the loss of their lives.

The CAF (and particularly the Royal Canadian Air Force) has the primary responsibility of providing aeronautical SAR services (searching for a downed aircraft for example) and the CCG is responsible for maritime SAR services. (RCMP, Parks Canada officials and local volunteers are responsible for land SAR operations.) SAR responses are always jointly coordinated by RCAF and CCG personnel at JRCCs and they employ whatever assets—military, civilian, commercial, auxiliary, vessels or aircraft of opportunity—that are available to assist in saving lives.

4   Challenges

The Canadian government has long been in an uncomfortable position when it comes to the safety/constabulary/defence functions in the Arctic.[46] Neither Canadians nor its allies think that the Government of Canada has adequate capabilities in any of the portfolio of functions anywhere in Canada, but especially in the Arctic. This is a perennial problem for Western democracies; there will always be calls for more government presence. As soon as there is a rescue that fails, a crime that goes unpunished, a perception of

---

45   Canada, Department of National Defence, "Professional Expectations: 2. Accepting Unlimited Liability," in *Canadian Armed Forces Ethos: Trusted to Serve* (Ottawa: Queen's Publishers, 2022), 34.

46   Mathieu Landriault, "Public Opinion on Canadian Arctic Sovereignty and Security," *Arctic* 69:2 (June 2016): 160–168; Marian Corera, "Regions in Review: Is Canada Taking Arctic Security Seriously?," NATO Association of Canada, 7 December 2018, https://natoassociation .ca/regions-in-review-is-canada-taking-arctic-security-seriously/.

State sovereignty challenged, the public wants more government presence. Conversely, there is always too much enforcement and too many defence forces in authoritarian or repressive regimes; there is no shortage of police crackdowns and heavy-handed military presence. This is one of the major differences between the two State-types. There will always be calls for more CCG, RCMP and RCN presence, but does that mean that it is required or that it will result in more safety, enforcement and defence, especially in Canada's Arctic?

4.1   Safety First

Let's begin with the safety portfolio. Search and rescue in the Arctic continues to be a mainly voluntary and civilian-led affair. With fewer than 135,000 people living in 40 percent of Canada's land mass that contributes to the largest coastline in the world, without spending eye-watering amounts of money, there is no way to achieve southern levels of emergency service in Canada's Arctic. Instead, as has been the trend, volunteers, with access to more equipment and surveillance and navigational aids to assist with small vessel responses, have been the pragmatic and practical solution. There are, however, restrictions as to what they can do, and the training is limited. Transport Canada, the CCG and CHS are working on a low-impact shipping corridors project that will provide preferred navigation routes through the NWP.[47] The routes, when deemed 'completed,' will be supported by navigational aids and adequately charted to modern standards, with SAR resources and services prepositioned. The voluntary compliance of use of these corridors is of particular concern to those living in the Arctic. And, of course, some vessels may choose to venture into unchartered waters for which there are much greater risks.

Assuming the Canadian government will never spend billions to preposition professional safety services within minutes of reaching any accident or disaster in the Arctic what is the solution? Partnerships and self-rescue.

At the international level, the CCG represents Canada on the Arctic Coast Guard Forum (ACGF) which, until Russia's attack on Ukraine on 24 February 2022, brought together all eight Arctic States to share best practices related to search and rescue, oil spill cleanup procedures and to promote safe, secure and environmentally responsible shipping in the Arctic.[48] The ACGF was created via a recommendation of the Arctic Council's Emergency Prevention,

---

47   See Dawson and Song in this volume.
48   See the Arctic Coast Guard Forum website, https://www.arcticcoastguardforum.com/. The ACGF terms of reference state that everything within the mandate of individual coast guard members is within the purview of the ACGF.

Preparedness and Response working group. The ACGF is chaired by the State which also chairs the Arctic Council (on hiatus since 3 March 2022). The ACGF met twice annually to share best practices and conduct a few tabletop exercises. Some State members of the ACGF have security and even defence organizations as their representatives, which is reflective of how they organize SAR activity nationally. All members agree, however, that defence issues are not discussed in this forum.

The 2011 Agreement on Cooperation on Aeronautical and Maritime Search and Rescue[49] and the 2013 Agreement on Cooperation on Marine Oil Pollution Preparedness and Response in the Arctic[50] bring together the eight Arctic States to work on SAR and oil spill cleanup missions. The United States and Denmark (Greenland) are particularly important partners for Canada given the locations of entrance/exit of the NWP.

Of course, the closest rescuers are likely to be volunteers in hamlets along the NWP and vessels of opportunity in the area. The CCG has been working closely with many communities to provide training, establish auxiliaries and ease the administrative burden that inevitably comes with partnering with government agencies. Organizations, like the volunteer Civil Air Search and Rescue Association (CASARA), have been vital to SAR efforts everywhere in Canada, including the Arctic, but they are dedicated to land surveillance, not maritime surveillance. There are technical and capability limits as to what volunteers can provide, especially for large vessels and/or dangerous cargo.

The challenge, especially in the Canadian Arctic, is too few people in the hamlets, who are also often CAF Rangers (a reserve arm of the Army that contributes vital Indigenous and local knowledge to CAF exercises and operations), volunteer firefighters and emergency coordinators. In a crisis, the same people are often wearing multiple hats which means they can be overstretched very quickly. However, communities are organizing and receiving more training. For example, Kikkert *et al.* in this volume discuss training operations in the Kitikmeot region of Nunavut.

It is clear that ship operators are key to professional, secure and legal navigation in Canada's Arctic. Vessel operators in the Arctic must prepare well in advance to ensure that their ship and crew are up to not only the regulatory requirements, but the geographic and meteorological conditions inherent in Arctic shipping. The Polar Code requires operational assessments to be

49   Agreement on Cooperation on Aeronautical and Maritime Search and Rescue in the Arctic, 12 May 2011, Arctic Council, https://oaarchive.arctic-council.org/handle/11374/531.

50   Agreement on Cooperation on Marine Oil Pollution Preparedness and Response in the Arctic, 15 May 2013, Arctic Council, http://hdl.handle.net/11374/529.

completed, covering region and season of operation relative to specific ship capability prior to developing a Polar Waters Operations Manual (PWOM) to guide crew in risk mitigation and operations in polar waters.[51] The PWOM is required to provide specific guidance on self-reliance in polar waters, keeping in mind the lack of infrastructure and potentially greater incident response time for SAR and environmental emergencies. Mitigation measures can include increased onboard capability (increased fuel capacity, survival equipment, voyage 'duration' ability, such as carriage of greater food stores) and the significant work the CCG does with cruise operators to ensure they are prepared. This includes tabletop and live exercises. Other mitigation measures, such as tandem operation of cruise/expedition vessels, which is common in the Antarctic, or as seen with the two voyages of the *Crystal Serenity*, or charter of an accompanying support ship, are best practices for Canada's Arctic.

4.2 *Complying with Regulations*

As shipping numbers increase, more maritime enforcement will be expected to ensure that international and Canadian laws are respected. The promise of States to follow internationally negotiated treaties and respect the national jurisdiction of States, is said to be 'challenged' with a rise in new powers seeking to interpret differently or even rewrite some of the rules and/or non-State actors who benefit from operating illegally.[52] Leaving aside the fuzziness of what the rules based international order is, which specific rules are included or the debate about its state of crisis,[53] we begin with the assumption that maritime and shipping laws in an Arctic context are desirable given the dangerous navigational conditions of Canadian Arctic waters that can create safety problems.

---

51 The manual creates a checklist of requirements outlined in the Polar Code. See International Chamber of Shipping (ICS) and Oil Companies International Marine Forum (OCIMF), *Guidelines for the Development of a Polar Waters Operations Manual* (London: ICS and OCIMF, 2019), https://www.pame.is/images/03_Projects/Forum/Web-Portal /Submissions/Guidelines_for_the_Development_of_a_Polar_Water_Operational_Manual .pdf.

52 Crown-Indigenous Relations and Northern Affairs Canada, "Arctic and Northern Policy Framework: International Chapter," Government of Canada, last modified 22 October 2019, https://www.rcaanc-cirnac.gc.ca/eng/1562867415721/1562867459588.

53 For an interesting discussion of the nebulous nature of the rules based international order, see Stéphanie Martel, *Unpacking the "Crisis" of the "Rules Based International Order": Competing Hero Narratives and Indo-Pacific Alternatives*, Working Paper (Waterloo: Defence and Security Foresight Group, July 2020), https://uwaterloo.ca/defence-security -foresight-group/publications-0/2019-2020-publications.

The other issue is that should Canadian laws become systematically violated (which is not the case currently), particularly if by State-sponsored actors, incidents can escalate to become a de facto challenge to Canadian sovereignty which could require a diplomatic, constabulary or, and as a very last option, a defence response. To date, there have been relatively few blatant violations of Canada's Arctic specific maritime statutes and regulations. This is partly a function of the low number of commercial ships that navigate Canada's Arctic waters and the general respect mariners have for the shipping laws in place. Despite certain States decrying the legality of Canada's NORDREG vessel traffic system when first made mandatory[54] and the grumblings around the cost of compliance with the IMO's now mandatory Polar Code, shipping in compliance with international standards is more cost effective than illegal shipping. However, that does not mean that this eliminates certain economic or political gains to be had by violating regulations.

Another issue is that many of the regulations are intended for large, commercial vessels. In some areas of regulation, small private, recreational and fishing vessels lack similar robust regulatory guidance beyond safety requirements and fishing quotas.

Canada's *Marine Personnel Regulations* are currently under revision to incorporate new polar waters training and certification requirements.[55] Until the coming into force of the amended Marine Personnel Regulations, the following interim measures have been put in place: Since 1 July 2018, basic and advanced certificate of proficiency for personnel on ships operating in polar waters has been required for deck officers at the operational and at the management level.[56] These are regulatory measures implementing the amended STCW

---

54 James Kraska, "Canadian Arctic Shipping Regulations and the Law of the Sea," in *Governing the North American Arctic*, eds., Dawn A Berry, Nigel Bowles and Halbert Jones (London: Palgrave Macmillan, 2016), 51–73, https://doi.org/10.1057/9781137493910_3.

55 SOR/2007-115. See "Marine Safety and Security Initiatives planned for April 2022–April 2024: Marine Personnel Regulations, 2023," Transport Canada, last modified 3 April 2022, https://tc.canada.ca/en/corporate-services/acts-regulations/forward-regulatory-plan/marine-initiatives-planned#marine-personnel-reg.

56 See "How to Meet STCW Requirements for Masters, Deck Officers and Other Crew Members of Certain Canadian Ships Operating in Polar Waters - SSB No.: 01/2018," Transport Canada, 28 February 2015, https://tc.canada.ca/en/marine-transportation/marine-safety/ship-safety-bulletins/how-meet-stcw-requirements-masters-deck-officers-other-crew-members-certain-canadian-ships-operating-polar-waters-ssb-no-01-2018.

Convention and the accompanying STCW Code to address polar seafaring.[57] It will be mandatory for all personnel on ships operating in polar waters to be familiar with the procedures and equipment contained or referenced.[58] These STCW requirements, however, do not adequately address the necessity to have acceptable competence operating ships in ice-covered waters.

The issue of compliance with regulations is multifaceted. For the flag State, compliance starts with ship registration and continues with regular ship surveys. For the port State, compliance is based on inspections to ensure observance of the key safety and security regulations. Substandard ships may be detained in port. The real weakness likely lies with the coastal State, that is, Canada in the Arctic. Canada relies on NORDREG reporting, but the requested information is minimal. Under the AWPPA and CSA 2001, the Minister is empowered to direct the movements of any ship, for example, to a port for inspection, but there are no ports in the Arctic.[59] Instead, what are needed are more inspections before ships enter Canadian Arctic waters, especially in the non-Arctic 'staging' ports (e.g., Halifax, St. John's, and Quebec City).

Monitoring vessel movement via AIS is not sufficient to ensure regulatory compliance. Non-SOLAS vessels are not necessarily required to have AIS on board. And AIS can be switched off during transit by vessels that do not want to be monitored. AIS can provide awareness of vessel location and transit information, but it is not the entire answer. AIS only tells government officials where the vessels that are transmitting are physically located. It does not reveal anything about how well trained their crews are, or how compliant the ship is. Finally, an AIS signal is not infallible (a tug was recently reported as noncompliant because the AIS signal indicated it was running in excess of a local speed limit, which it was, to get to a ship dragging anchor and prevent an

57   Amendments to the International Convention on Standards of Training, Certification and Watchkeeping for Seafarers (STCW) 1978, as amended, Resolution MSC.416(97) (25 November 2016, effective 1 July 2018); Amendments to Part A of the Seafarers' Training, Certification and Watchkeeping (STCW) Code, Resolution MSC.417(97) (25 November 2016, effective 1 July 2018). See STCW Code s B-V/g: "Guidance regarding training of masters and officers for ships operating in polar waters."

58   STCW Code s A-V/4: Polar Code (November 2016 Amendment), created mandatory minimum requirements for the training and qualifications of masters and deck officers on ships operating in polar waters. See "STCW V/4 - STCW Polar Code for Seafarers in Polar Waters," EduMaritime, last updated 11 August 2021, https://www.edumaritime.net/stcw-code/stcw-v-4-polar-waters.

59   Transport Canada, *Enforcement of the Canada Shipping Act, 2001 and the Arctic Waters Pollution Prevention Act* TP 13585 E (2018), para 2.4, https://tc.canada.ca/en/marine-transportation/marine-safety/enforcement-canada-shipping-act-2001-arctic-waters-pollution-prevention-act.

environmental catastrophe).[60] Separating the false positives from true crises often requires additional, direct information. However, volunteer 'monitoring' from communities is not without its issues, mainly due to a lack of response capabilities.

4.3   Avoiding Geopolitical Mishaps, Accidents and Incidents

The Department of Defence and CAF have one of the largest budgets of any of the federal agencies and have 64+ years of experience defending the Arctic aerospace approaches to North America with the United States via NORAD. Given current geopolitical tensions, when 'more' needs to be done in the Arctic, the Canadian public seems to turn to its military forgetting that many of the civilian agencies and local communities are key providers of vital security responses. Nevertheless, many of the legacy gravel runways and NORAD radar systems, which benefit civilian operations as well, were initially constructed mainly by the United States during World War II and the Cold War. Canada has a very modest military footprint in the Arctic centred around its Joint Task Force North Headquarters in Yellowknife and the Rangers—part of the Reserves of the Canadian Army—who help to patrol remote areas of Canada, including in the Arctic, and support the CAF on deployments in the Arctic.[61]

The RCN has only recently returned to operating in the Arctic outside of Arctic military exercises, such as the Operation NANOOK series.[62] The RCN has never had a purpose-built Arctic ship[63] until now with the *Harry DeWolf*-class offshore patrol ships, but it is only suitable for first year ice up to 1–1.2 metres in thickness (Polar Class rating of 5). But the type of ship is only part of the equation. Mariners must have the skills to operate in polar waters, skills that take years to develop. The current rotation schedule of CAF members means they are unlikely to spend decades in the same role, which is required to gain such expertise.

The United States has made quite a dramatic and recent pivot to the Arctic as noted by the release of an Arctic strategy for every military service.[64] The

---

60   Personal knowledge of David Snider.

61   "About the Canadian Rangers," Government of Canada, last modified 11 January 2022, https://www.canada.ca/en/ombudsman-national-defence-forces/education-information/caf-members/career/canadian-rangers.html.

62   Adam Lajeunesse, *The RCN in the Arctic: A Brief History*, Naval Association of Canada, Niobe Paper 2 (Naval Association of Canada, 2019), 2.

63   The HMCS *Labrador* was a *Wind*-class icebreaker that operated under the RCN from 1954 to 1957 before transfer to Transport Canada as CGS *Labrador* (and eventually CCGS *Labrador* when the CCG was formed).

64   See note 44.

policies concentrate more on the Bering Strait and the north Atlantic, not Canada's Arctic. The United States does not currently have any ships, other than the two USCG icebreakers (the *Healy* and *Polar Star*), which are designed for polar conditions. The pivot to the Arctic, therefore, is mostly driven by concerns about Russian and Chinese intentions in the world, not specifically about the Arctic.[65]

Two regional Arctic-specific military fora have been affected by Russia's aggression in Ukraine. The annual Arctic Chiefs of Defence Staff discussions (involving the heads of the militaries of the eight Arctic States) have been on hiatus since 2014 until 2022 (without Russia), while the Arctic Security Forces Roundtable (ASFR) (which included military representation from the eight Arctic States and the United Kingdom, France, Germany and the Netherlands) continues to meet, but without Russian participation. ASFR is hosted by the US military's European Combatant Command Commander and aims to discuss the Arctic region's security dynamics and architecture, as well as the full range of military capabilities and cooperation. While Russia has expressed interest in rejoining these fora, there is no appetite by Western allies to 'reward' Russia's egregious behaviour. Instead, academics have called for a code of unplanned encounters at sea[66] (similar to one that exists for the South and East China Sea) to apply in the Arctic to limit the escalation of tensions during an accident, incident or mishap.

However, recent Chinese military activity in the Bering Strait, coupled with a focus on homeland defence writ large for the United States,[67] may put added pressure on the RCN to assist with more patrols in the Arctic. In the late summer of 2021, the US Coast Guard (USCG) encountered Chinese warships

65   Congressional Research Services, *Changes in the Arctic: Background Issues for Congress*, updated 24 March 2022, https://sgp.fas.org/crs/misc/R41153.pdf. See especially p. 19: "While there continues to be significant international cooperation on Arctic issues, the emergence of great power competition (also called strategic competition) between the United States, Russia, and China, combined with the increase in human activities in the Arctic resulting from the diminishment of Arctic ice, has introduced elements of competition and tension into the Arctic's geopolitical environment, and the Arctic is viewed by some observers as an arena for geopolitical competition among the three countries."
66   Andrea Charron, "Arctic Security," in *Turning the Tide: How to Rescue TransAtlantic Relations*, Simone Soare, ed. (European Union Institute for Security Studies, 2020), 137–153; Duncan Depledge, Mathieu Boulègue, Andrew Foxall and Dmitriy Tulupov, "Why We Need to Talk About Military Activity in the Arctic: Towards an Arctic Military Code of Conduct," *Arctic Yearbook* (2019), https://arcticyearbook.com/images/yearbook/2019/Briefing-Notes/4_AY2019_BN_Depledge.pdf.
67   North American Aerospace Defense Command (NORAD) and USNORTHCOM Public Affairs, "COMMANDER NORAD and USNORTHCOM Releases Strategic Vision," NORAD News, 15 March 2021, https://www.norad.mil/Newsroom/Article/2537173/commander-norad-and-usnorthcom-releases-strategic-vision/.

near Alaska's Aleutian Islands unexpectedly.[68] While the warships were not breaking any international laws, in geopolitically-contested times, unplanned encounters between great powers can lead to unintentional incidents and possible escalation. If the United States Navy and USCG engage in more patrols in the Bering Sea and the approaches to North America, the RCN may be expected to backfill to provide coverage pulling focus from the RCN's support to other government agencies in the NWP.

The other area of concern is an approach outside of Canada's Arctic, but a strategic maritime liability for NATO. The Greenland, Iceland UK-Norway Gap (GIUK-Norway Gap), which connects the North Atlantic and Arctic Ocean has returned as an area of concern because of increased Russian activity, and also NATO's disappearance of a former position that ensured surveillance of the Gap. This absence was only recently reimagined with the reformation of the US 2nd Fleet (in 2018, fully operational at the end of 2019) and NATO's new Joint Force Command Norfolk (established in 2019 and fully operational in 2021). These commands, headed by the same commander, patrol the North Atlantic (including GIUK-Norway Gap) and the Arctic. Canada has personnel embedded in both and a Canadian has been the Vice-Commander of the 2nd Fleet since 2018.

For now, the assessment of the CAF is that there is unlikely to be a military-related threat in Canada's Arctic, but that could change. A ship carrying dangerous goods may require CAF crisis management expertise and geopolitical conditions can change unexpectedly as the conflict in Ukraine demonstrated strikingly. The challenge for the CAF generally is that current recruitment and retention levels means that there is 10,000+ deficit in numbers of trained professionals.[69] For the RCN specifically, the *Halifax*-class vessels' inability to operate in the Arctic for most of the year was an impediment to acquiring Arctic operating skills. Now that the first of the *Harry DeWolf*-class vessels is deployed there will be an improvement, although the RCN is still limited in its ability to project power and influence in the Arctic due to its fleet composition.

---

68   Melody Schreiber, "US Coast Guard Patrol Unexpectedly Encountered Chinese Warships near Alaska's Aleutian Islands," ArcticToday, 16 September 2021, https://www.arctictoday.com/a-us-coast-guard-patrol-unexpectedly-encountered-chinese-warships-near-alaskas-aleutian-islands/.

69   The Canadian Press, "Military Dealing with More Than 10,000 Unfilled Positions Amid Growing Pressures," *National Post*, 18 January 2022, https://nationalpost.com/pmn/news-pmn/canada-news-pmn/military-dealing-with-more-than-10000-unfilled-positions-amid-growing-pressures.

5   Greater Integration

5.1   *Maritime Domain Awareness and the MSOC East*

The 'separation' of jurisdictions is important for legal, operational and capability reasons. CAF members, for example, cannot arrest civilians nor does the CCG have the capabilities and resources to conduct anti-submarine warfare. In the Arctic, given the vastness of the maritime territory, whole-of-government and society responses are vital, which means creating fora, exercises and common platforms for responders to come together, share information and important lessons learned. Maritime domain awareness (MDA) is the essential starting point for all of the safety, security and defence functions; if you do not know what activity is taking place and the nature of the vessels operating in a region, then safety, enforcement and defence actions cannot be planned and conducted.

Canada's MDA definition is "the effective understanding of anything in the maritime environment that could adversely affect Canadian security, safety, economy or environment."[70] Some of the MDA priorities include: 1) preventing terrorist attacks and criminal, harmful or hostile acts across the maritime domain by State and non-State actors; 2) protecting population centres and critical infrastructure; and 3) minimizing damage to, and expedite recovery of, the maritime transportation system and related infrastructure in the wake of human-made or natural disasters.

Prompted by the 11 September 2001 (9/11) attacks in the United States, recommendations of a binational planning group chaired by the Deputy NORAD Commander (to date always a Royal Canadian Air Force Lieutenant General) resulted in the creation of new organizations and bilateral enforcement programs. The concern was that if North America could be attacked from its own airspace, better surveillance of maritime, cyber and land activity was needed. Recognizing the limited resources versus the enormous maritime security territory to surveil, the main safety and security agencies, along with the CAF, created multi-organizational intelligence fusion teams to improve common domain awareness among the various agencies. In 2004, the Canadian federal government, through its National Security Policy,[71] established three Maritime Security Operation Centres (MSOCs); two under the administrative

---

70   Binational Planning Group, *Final Report on Canada-United States (CANUS) Enhanced Military Cooperation* (13 March 2006), 36.

71   Government of Canada, *Securing an Open Society: Canada's National Security Policy* (Ottawa: Queen's Printers, April 2004).

coordination of the Department of National Defence and co-located respectively on the West Coast with Regional Joint Operation Centre (RJOC) Pacific and on the East Coast with RJOC Atlantic. The third, the Great Lakes and St. Lawrence Seaway MSOC, is located on the Great Lakes at Niagara, and is under the administrative coordination of the RCMP as a function of its focus on transnational crime in the Great Lakes. MSOC East is responsible for the Arctic as well as the east coast.

The MSOCs, despite the name, are neither 'operation' centres nor 'security' centres. MSOCs are more rightly called maritime intelligence analytical fusion centres. The impetus for their creation was to facilitate the sharing of intelligence[72] among the six federal government agencies concerned with marine-based threats that could negatively affect safety or security. The CAF, CCG, Transport Canada, CBSA, RCMP, and the Conservation and Protection arm of DFO are represented at the MSOCs.[73]

There is a daily situation update to share intelligence from the various agencies that is focused on a fulsome maritime picture in Canada's area of operations at the MSOCs. It includes vessels that are deemed to be of interest to one or more partners, as well as information related to surveillance flights, radar satellite passes, weather and ice updates, and potential protests or similar activities. MSOC East was the driving force behind the creation of a weekly Arctic MDA teleconference hosted by DND during the Arctic shipping season. Plans are afoot to replace the teleconference by another avenue through which to communicate important Arctic information with national and international stakeholders in the future.[74]

---

72   CCG is not listed under the *Security of Canada Information Disclosure Act* (SCIDA) (SC 2015, c 20, s 2) which means that it cannot freely receive security information, unless there is a need to know. This is the same for the DFO: they are not listed under the SCIDA. The amount of information that gets shared with CCG varies from one MSOC to another. The SCIDA provides a clear, express authority for all federal government institutions to disclose information to a designated group of 17 departments and agencies with recognized national security mandates and/or responsibilities. It empowers these institutions to receive and share information quickly, effectively and responsibly with each other in order to identify, prevent and respond to national security threats when there are no other authorities enabling them to do so.

73   For a full report on Canada's maritime domain awareness and NORAD warning function, see Andrea Charron *et al.*, *Left of Bang: NORAD's Maritime Warning Mission and Domain Awareness* (Winnipeg: CDSS, 2015), https://umanitoba.ca/arts/sites/arts/files/2022-07/NORAD-2015-Maritime-Warning-Mission-and-North-American-Domain-Awareness.pdf; LCmdr Greg Adamthwaite, *Northern Exposure: Canada's Marine Security Framework: The Security Challenge in the Canadian Maritime Realm* (MDS thesis, Canadian Forces College, 2011), https://www.cfc.forces.gc.ca/259/290/297/286/Adamthwaite.pdf.

74   Invitees are to include MSOC East partners, especially the CCG and RCMP, a number of US and Canadian military partners, especially NORAD's maritime warning mission

Knowing what is happening in the Arctic is vital to being able to share information to enforce Canadian laws, share air surveillance time, and preposition the right people to enforce laws for which they are mandated. Satellite information and AIS are vital to creating a maritime picture of vessels of interest. Increasingly, Canada is sharing and using information from allies to help with risk mitigation measures and identify early potential problems.

What is missing is regular and formalized information from local Arctic communities other than via federal agencies in situ who can report activity and/or ad hoc community level reports. Likewise, while the domain awareness 'picture' for the Arctic is shared with federal and international law enforcement and military allies, it is not shared with local Arctic communities. Therefore, for example, if a VOI (perhaps carrying dangerous materials) is operating in the Arctic, local communities will not be told via MSOC East. While the safety and security of the information must be protected, there may be a way for local communities to have access to some of the information in the future, especially given that they are often the first responders on scene for disasters and/or will be essential to house victims until they can be relocated south.

5.2   *AOPS and Exercises*

The other important tool of integration of the various maritime partners is the AOPS (*Harry DeWolf*-class vessel). While currently a CAF capability, the AOPS' most important feature is as a platform from which to bring other government departments (including health experts or any service provider) directly to communities and one which the CCG will adopt in the future. The first vessel only just finished operational trials in 2019 and made the first circumnavigation of North America in the summer of 2021. While not exclusive to the Arctic, it will be used mainly in a support capacity. The AOPS have the following capabilities:

- **Conducting armed presence and surveillance operations throughout Canada's waters, including in the Arctic;**
- **Supporting the CAF in sovereignty operations;**
- Participating in a wide variety of international operations, such as anti-smuggling, anti-piracy, and international security and stability;
- Contributing to humanitarian assistance, emergency response and disaster relief domestically and internationally;

---

personnel and JRCCs. Local input, however, is still missing. The authors are grateful to the *Canadian Naval Review* for permission to reuse information on the MSOCs from its blog. See Andrea Charron, "Ode to Canada's Maritime Security Operations Centres," Canadian Naval Review Broadsides Discussion Forum, 10 February 2020, https://www.navalreview .ca/2020/02/ode-to-canadas-maritime-security-operation-centres/.

- Conducting SAR and providing communications relay to other units, as required;
- Supporting CAF core missions, including capacity building in support of other nations;
- Supporting other government departments in their ability to enforce their respective mandates by providing government situational awareness of activities and events in regions of operation; and
- Conducting a diverse range of missions worldwide.[75]

The first two bullets on the list (bolded) are the only capabilities that fall exclusively in the defence portfolio (i.e., protecting the State). They require unpacking. First, all RCN vessels are limited to operating in the ice-free summer months. (Recall, the *Harry DeWolf*-class vessels are limited to a Polar Class 5 rating.) Next, the AOPS have limited fire power. Its Mark 38 25mm machine gun system and M242 autocannon were designed to support domestic law enforcement actions, not State-on-State armed aggression or anti-missile capabilities. Indeed, the AOPS have the potential to be the quintessential whole-of-government tool. The AOPS, for example, can produce potable water for communities. It has a helicopter pad and can accommodate a small utility aircraft up to the new CH-148 maritime helicopter. The stern of the ship can accommodate multiple payload options, such as shipping containers, underwater survey equipment, or landing craft. The ship is also equipped with a 20-tonne crane, providing self-load and unload capability. It has multi-role rescue boats that can reach speeds of 35+ knots (~65 km/h) and are 8.5 metres long. They can be used in support of rescue operations, personnel transfers and boarding operations.[76]

The NANOOK series of Arctic exercises (of late, four different foci named Tuugaalik, Tatigiit, Nunkaput, and Nunalivut) are held year-round. It began as one, yearly fall exercise beginning in 2007. With the creation of four exercises held at different times of the year, multiple scenarios, capabilities and partners are included. Some of the exercises focus on interoperability with other allied partners, such as the United States, Denmark, and Norway, while others involve whole-of-government partners and have a particular maritime focus, such as a series of presence activities along the Northwest Passage or a maritime domain defence and security exercise or disaster response focus.

75   "Arctic and Offshore Patrol Ships," Government of Canada, accessed 21 May 2021, https://www.tpsgc-pwgsc.gc.ca/app-acq/amd-dp/mer-sea/sncn-nss/npea-aops-eng.html.

76   "Harry DeWolf-class Arctic/Offshore Patrol Ship t" National Defence and Royal Canadian Navy, https://www.tpsgc-pwgsc.gc.ca/app-acq/amd-dp/mer-sea/sncn-nss/npea-aops-eng.html.

For example, OP NANOOK-TATIGIIT 2021 addressed the Government of Nunavut's drive for a whole-of-government response to a cruise ship incident that delivers many passengers to a small community on a few hours' notice. At sea there was a concurrent mass rescue operation rehearsal, separate from the onshore portion. OP NANOOK-NUNAKPUT 2021 integrated Northern partners in a series of presence activities along the NWP supported by the Canadian Army, the RCN, the Royal Canadian Air Force, the CCG, Transport Canada and Indigenous government agencies to develop domain awareness, foster greater interoperability and increase overall readiness. OP NANOOK-TUUGALIK 2021 integrated multinational partners in a combined joint maritime domain operation in northern Labrador, Nunavut and Greenland and was designed to foster greater combined and joint interoperability. The RCN was joined by the Royal Danish Navy, the French Navy, and the United States Navy.[77]

5.3   *Arctic Security Working Group*
Finally, the Arctic Security Working Group (ASWG), hosted by the CAF's Joint Task Force North in Yellowknife, brings together all federal and territorial agencies and departments with a safety or security nexus. It is hoped that, in the future, ASWG will include the land claim areas of Nunatsiavut and Nunavik to ensure a full, Canadian Arctic perspective. It meets biannually, often with academic observers, and rotates among the territorial governments to co-lead the discussions. Participation by local Indigenous groups has helped the ASWG to focus on the immediate concerns and work on realistic and local solutions to challenges in the maritime and land domains. For example, attention to critical infrastructure (especially heating and water supplies) has been an important topic of late. Community evacuations are a last resort and therefore, in situ problem solving is paramount.[78]

6   Conclusion

There are three functions that Canada must provide: safety, security and defence. Many federal agencies play lead roles, but increasingly, safe shipping

---

77   LCol Steve Burke, "Joint Task Force North Op Nanook: Meeting Northern Challenges with Regional Collaboration," presentation to RUSI, 18 November 2020, https://rusi-ns.ca/wp-content/uploads/2020/11/JTFN_201118.pdf.

78   Government of Yukon, "Statement from Premier Silver on Keynote Address to the Arctic Security Working Group," News, 31 May 2022, https://yukon.ca/en/news/statement-premier-silver-keynote-address-arctic-security-working-group.

in Canada's Arctic requires the assistance of local communities, volunteers and integrated responses with international, federal, regional, industry and local actors. The functions exist over a continuum from safety at sea, to enforcement of Canadian laws to deterrence of adversaries with allies. Given the size of Canada's Arctic and the number of jurisdictions and regulations, Canada has no choice but to involve many agencies and partners.

Canada's whole-of-government approach to the Arctic has encouraged a shared understanding of shipping activity in Canada's Arctic and a chance to practice operating together. The MSOC East Arctic teleconference, the AOPS' platform, OP NANOOK and the ASWG are all undervalued boons to safe shipping and conditions in the Arctic generally. Canada has some best practices to share with other Arctic States about bringing Arctic rights holders and stakeholders together to discuss issues of concern. Nevertheless, improvements can still be made, including finding a way to share more information with local communities and vice versa with the MSOC East.

Given changing climate conditions, the Arctic security community is expecting more calls for search and rescue and emergency assistance. There is only so much the local hamlets can provide by way of emergency management and concerns are that an overtaxed Canadian Armed Forces dealing with crisis management across Canada will stretch resources too finely. More will be expected of the shipping industry to ensure mariners in the Arctic are trained, have adequate ice navigation experience and that ships are compliant with the latest (Polar Code-based) Canadian regulations. Most importantly, Canada will continue to encourage and incentivize ships to use low risk corridors to protect lives, the environment, marine wildlife and Indigenous cultural practices. To date, the majority of professional mariners comply fully. The concerns remain with small vessels that lack mandatory AIS requirements and unscrupulous ship operators that insist on transiting in uncharted waters.

Acknowledgements

The authors are grateful to the editors and anonymous reviewers for their helpful comments. Representatives of the Canadian Coast Guard, Canadian Armed Forces and Inuit Tapiriit Kanatami provided invaluable guidance in drafts of this paper. All errors and omissions remain those of the authors.

CHAPTER 8

Canadian Icebreaker Operations and Shipbuilding: Challenges and Opportunities

Timothy Choi

Abstract

This chapter surveys the tasks of icebreakers in the Canadian context to answer what challenges and opportunities the Canadian Coast Guard (CCG) may face as a function of Canada's ongoing icebreaker recapitalization attempt under the National Shipbuilding Strategy (NSS). It will examine the NSS's icebreaker component, which initially aimed to replace the CCG's current fleet of aging Arctic icebreakers through domestic construction. Despite early goals aimed at timely delivery of replacements while strengthening Canadian shipbuilding industry, not a single icebreaker construction contract had been signed ten years after the strategy's promulgation. Instead, the Liberal Government has procured foreign second-hand icebreakers to fill gaps in the fleet's availability. Meanwhile, the Royal Canadian Navy and the CCG are receiving eight new Arctic and Offshore Patrol Vessels. Despite not being designed as dedicated icebreakers, their ability to sail through substantial amounts of first year ice may well result in their fulfilling a narrow range of roles formerly exclusively conducted by CCG icebreakers. The utility of such (para)military vessels in civilian icebreaking roles will be explored with reference to the Danish Navy's experience in Greenland, where their patrol ships engage in icebreaking tasks in the absence of icebreakers.

Keywords

icebreakers – shipbuilding – Royal Canadian Navy – Canadian Coast Guard – National Shipbuilding Strategy – Arctic and Offshore Patrol Ships – Greenland – Denmark – offshore patrol vessels

1   Introduction

Within the global discourse concerning the so-called 'race for the Arctic,' one major element that is often held as a metric of competition in the region is the

© TIMOTHY CHOI, 2023 | DOI:10.1163/9789004508576_009

number of modern icebreakers possessed by each Arctic State.[1] An oft-touted point of concern amongst Western observers is that there is an 'icebreaker gap' between the Russian Federation's fleet and that possessed by the other four Arctic Ocean States.[2] This concern is especially prevalent in the United States, where popular and policy discussions often highlight how Russia has over forty icebreakers operating in their Arctic while the United States only possesses two aging vessels, albeit with six new ships on the way.[3] For Canada, the disparity is somewhat less extreme as the Canadian Coast Guard (CCG) operates a fleet of sixteen icebreakers (as of March 2022) of varying capabilities, though the same 'gap' discourse is prevalent as well with an emphasis on age rather than numbers.[4]

---

1   For examples, see the following: Charlie Gao, "Icebreaker Technology: Is America Losing the Race for the Arctic?," *The National Interest*, 23 December 2021, https://nationalinterest.org /blog/reboot/icebreaker-technology-america-losing-race-arctic-198230; AFP, "Russia Races to Build Giant Ice-breakers for Arctic Dominance," *France24*, 15 July 2021, https://www.france24 .com/en/live-news/20210715-russia-races-to-build-giant-ice-breakers-for-arctic-dominance; Rebecca Kheel, "GOP Rep to Trump: Russian Activity in Arctic a 'Tremendous Concern'," *The Hill*, 21 February 2017, https://thehill.com/policy/defense/320475-gop-rep-to-trump-russian -activity-in-arctic-should-be-tremendous-concern/.

2   For examples and critiques of the "icebreaker gap" discourse, see Charlie Gao, "The 'Icebreaker Gap': How Russia is Planning to Build more Icebreakers to Project Power in the Arctic," *The National Interest*, 19 August 2018, https://nationalinterest.org/blog/buzz/icebreaker -gap-how-russia-planning-build-more-icebreakers-project-power-arctic-29102; Jen Judson, "The Icebreaker Gap," *Politico*, 1 September 2015, https://www.politico.com/agenda/story /2015/09/the-icebreaker-gap-000213/; Keith Johnson and Dan De Luce, "U.S. Falls Behind in Arctic Great Game," *Foreign Policy*, 24 May 2016, https://foreignpolicy.com/2016/05/24/u-s -falls-behind-in-arctic-great-game/.

3   Milosz Reterski, "Breaking the Ice: Why the United States Needs Nuclear-Powered Ice-breakers," *Foreign Affairs*, 11 December 2014, https://www.foreignaffairs.com/articles/united -states/2014-12-11/breaking-ice; Gregory Noddin Poulin, "America Must Build More Ice-breakers or We'll Lose the Battle for the Arctic," *Wired*, 5 January 2016, https://www.wired .com/2016/01/america-must-build-more-icebreakers-or-well-lose-the-battle-for-the-arctic/; Ragnhild Grønning, "Expert: No Icebreaker Race with Russia in the Arctic," *High North News*, 2 November 2018, https://www.highnorthnews.com/en/expert-no-icebreaker-race-russia-arctic; Lin A. Mortensgaard and Kristian Søby Kristensen, "The 'Icebreaker-Gap' – How US Ice-breakers are Assigned New, Symbolic Roles as Part of an Escalating Military Competition in the Arctic," *Safe Seas*, 5 January 2021, http://www.safeseas.net/the-icebreaker-gap-how -us-icebreakers-are-assigned-new-symbolic-roles-as-part-of-an-escalating-military-competition -in-the-arctic/; Paul C. Avey, "The Icebreaker Gap Doesn't Mean America is Losing in the Arc-tic," *War on the Rocks*, 28 November 2019, https://warontherocks.com/2019/11/the-icebreaker-gap -doesnt-mean-america-is-losing-in-the-arctic/; Craig H. Allen Sr., "Closing the US Strategic Gap in Icebreaker Capacity," *Pacific Maritime* (November 2017): 36–39; United States Congressional Research Service, *Coast Guard Polar Security Cutter (Polar Icebreaker) Program: Background and Issues for Congress: Updated April 1, 2022*, by Ronald O'Rourke, RL34391 (1 April 2011), 5.

4   Canadian Coast Guard (CCG), "Icebreaking Fleet of the Canadian Coast Guard," Government of Canada, last modified 12 May 2021, https://www.ccg-gcc.gc.ca/icebreaking-deglacage

Such 'gap' discussions ignore each Arctic Ocean state's unique requirements for surface vessels capable of operating in Arctic sea ice. Icebreakers serve different functions either on their own or in support of other users of the seas. They do not operate in a vacuum where their existence only serves to balance their counterparts in the neighbouring State as though they were bumper boats on a fairground.[5] This chapter thus surveys the tasks and purposes of icebreakers in the Canadian context. It also seeks to answer what challenges and opportunities Canadian maritime activities in the Arctic may face as a function of Canada's ongoing attempt at acquiring new icebreakers.

This chapter will examine the history of Canada's 2010 National Shipbuilding Strategy (NSS, originally known as the National Shipbuilding Procurement Strategy) from the perspective of its icebreaking component, which initially aimed to replace the CCG's current fleet of aging icebreaking vessels through new domestic construction.[6] Despite early goals that aimed to balance timely delivery of replacements with establishing an enduring Canadian shipbuilding industry, no new icebreakers have begun to be built ten years after the Strategy's promulgation. This has resulted in some disruption within the Canadian shipbuilding sector as shipyards that did not succeed in the initial NSS bids have been able to convince both the government and industry partners to incorporate them into the NSS over the past three years.[7] Meanwhile, the

---

/fleet-flotte-eng.html; CCG, "Canadian Coast Guard's Latest Icebreakers," Government of Canada, last modified 9 February 2022, https://www.ccg-gcc.gc.ca/fleet-flotte/icebreaker -brise-glace-eng.html; K. Joseph Spears, "The Arctic Icebreaker 'Gap,'" *FrontLine Safety and Security* 10:3 (Fall 2015): 29; Megan Drewniak, Dimitrios Dalaklis, Anastasia Christodoulou, and Rebecca Sheehan, "Ice-Breaking Fleets of the United States and Canada: Assessing the Current State of Affairs and Future Plans," *Sustainability* 13:2 (2021): 716; Stewart Webb, "Mackenzie Institute Report: Returning to Port: A Needed Course Correction to Keep the National Shipbuilding Strategy off the Rocks," *DefenceReport*, 9 May 2017, https://defencereport .com/mackenzie-report-returning-to-port/; Ron R. Wallace, "Canada and Russia in an Evolving Circumpolar Arctic," in *The Palgrave Handbook of Arctic Policy and Politics*, eds., Ken S. Coates and Carin Holroyd (Palgrave Macmillan, 2020), 363.

5   Robert David English and Morgan Grant Gardner, "Phantom Peril in the Arctic: Russia Doesn't Threaten the United States in the Far North – But Climate Change Does," *Foreign Affairs*, 29 September 2020, https://www.foreignaffairs.com/articles/united-states/2020-09-29/phantom -peril-arctic.

6   Public Works and Government Services Canada, "Government of Canada announces National Shipbuilding Procurement Strategy," Government of Canada, News Release, 3 June 2010, https://www.canada.ca/en/news/archive/2010/06/government-canada-announces-national -shipbuilding-procurement-strategy.html.

7   Seaway Marine & Industrial Inc. was one of the original bidders for the NSPS, though its Port Weller/St. Catharines drydocks at 340 Lakeshore Road has been taken over by Heddle Shipyards since 2017 and it is this company that has teamed up with Seaspan Vancouver Shipyards to build their polar icebreaker; Davie Shipyards in Quebec, meanwhile, is in the midst of government negotiations to become the third NSS construction yard to build the

Liberal Government has procured second-hand icebreakers from abroad to fill gaps in the fleet's operational availability.[8] In some instances, however, the unique mission requirements of the Canadian icebreaking fleet may not be met by the very limited market supply, throwing into question the limits of such approaches. At the same time, the Royal Canadian Navy and the CCG are slated to receive eight new Arctic and offshore patrol ships (AOPSS).[9] Despite not being designed for icebreaking duties, their ability to sail through substantial amounts of first year ice in an era of decreasing Arctic multiyear ice may well result in their fulfilling a narrow range of roles formerly exclusively conducted by Coast Guard icebreakers. The utility of such ice-capable (para) military vessels in civilian icebreaking roles will be explored with reference to the Danish Navy's experience in Greenland, where their patrol ships often engage in icebreaking tasks in the absence of dedicated icebreakers.

2   Icebreaker Missions in Canada: Challenges and Requirements

The CCG is the sole federal operator of dedicated icebreakers as well as the sole government agency in charge of the Government of Canada's civilian vessels. Its icebreaking areas of operations include not just the Arctic (defined as north of the northern tip of Labrador), but Atlantic Canada, the St. Lawrence Seaway,

second polar icebreaker and six medium icebreakers. Tom Ring, "The National Shipbuilding Procurement Strategy: How Did We Get to Where We Are Now," Policy Update, *Canadian Global Affairs Institute*, March 2016, https://www.cgai.ca/the_national_shipbuilding_pro curement_strategy; "Seaway Marine Gets Big Contract," *Niagara This Week – St. Catharines*, 6 February 2012, https://www.niagarathisweek.com/news-story/3263517-seaway-marine -gets-big-contract/; "The Port Weller Dry Docks has a Bright Future," *Heddle Shipyards*, 29 January 2020, https://heddleshipyards.com/news/the-port-weller-dry-docks-has-a-bright -future/; Seaspan Shipyards, "Seaspan Shipyards and Heddle Shipyards Join Forces in Bid to Deliver to the Polar Icebreaker to the Canadian Coast Guard," Seaspan, 9 June 2020, https: //www.seaspan.com/press-release/seaspan-shipyards-and-heddle-shipyards-join-forces-in -bid-to-deliver-the-polar-icebreaker-to-the-canadian-coast-guard/; Public Services and Pro curement Canada, "Government of Canada Receives Chantier Davie's Supporting Materials to Become Third Shipyard Under National Shipbuilding Strategy," Government of Canada, 14 July 2021, https://www.tpsgc-pwgsc.gc.ca/comm/vedette-features/2021-07-14-00-eng.html.

8   CCG, "Canadian Coast Guard's Latest Icebreakers" (n 4).

9   Public Services and Procurement Canada, "Arctic and Offshore Patrol Ships-Canadian Coast Guard," Government of Canada, last modified 28 April 2021, https://www.tpsgc-pwgsc.gc.ca/app -acq/amd-dp/mer-sea/sncn-nss/arctique-coastgd-eng.html; Public Services and Procurement Canada, "Large Vessel Shipbuilding Projects," Government of Canada, last modified 7 May 2021, https://www.tpsgc-pwgsc.gc.ca/app-acq/amd-dp/mer-sea/sncn-nss/grandnav-largeves-eng.html.

and the Great Lakes.[10] The scope of this chapter will be limited to ships which are employed in Arctic waters, though they do operate in southern waters during winter as well. For the CCG, 'icebreaker' refers specifically to "a ship specially designed and constructed for the purpose of assisting the passage of other ships through ice."[11] Therefore, a ship that is designed simply to sail through ice but not having the responsibility to assist other vessels in doing the same is not considered an icebreaker even though it will be breaking ice.

In the Arctic, then, the Canadian Coast Guard employs its fleet of icebreakers for the following services: route assistance; ice routing and information services; harbour breakouts; Northern resupply; and Arctic sovereignty.[12] Scientific and hydrographic surveys are also included, albeit subsumed under Arctic sovereignty.[13] The term 'icebreaking' refers specifically to the organized program whose objectives are to employ ice-capable ships to carry out these four major sets of services in the Arctic. The icebreaking program includes additional services that apply to the southern parts of Canada, such as flood prevention in the St. Lawrence River, but those will not be discussed here.

The service of route assistance is probably the one that is most commonly associated with the popular conception of what icebreakers do. It includes "freeing vessels beset in ice, maintaining shipping routes, escorting ships through ice-covered waters, [and] organizing convoys (escorts of 2 or more ships) to maximize services in favourable conditions."[14] In Arctic waters, these services are provided only during the summer months in order to support other users of the seas and science missions.[15] The act of 'escort' in this context refers to the literal breaking of sea ice by the escorting icebreaker as it sails closely in front of other ships that are not capable of independent sailing through and maneuvering within that ice. An alternative to this approach would be what is often done in southern Canada, where icebreakers maintain a relatively clear

10   CCG, "Icebreaking Operations Directive: 1. Provision of Icebreaking Services and Harbour Breakouts," Government of Canada, last modified 26 July 2019, https://www.ccg-gcc.gc.ca /publications/icebreaking-deglacage/icebreaking-operations-directives/provision -services-eng.html.

11   Id.

12   CCG, "Icebreaking in Canada," Government of Canada, last modified 31 March 2022, https://www.ccg-gcc.gc.ca/icebreaking-deglacage/program-programme-eng.html; George Da Pont, *Canadian Coast Guard: Levels of Service: May 2010 (Update)* (Ottawa: Fisheries and Oceans Canada, 2010), 18.

13   CCG, "Icebreaking in Canada" (n 12).

14   Id.

15   CCG, "Icebreaking Requirements 2017–2022: 3. Icebreaking Services," Government of Canada, last modified 18 November 2019, https://www.ccg-gcc.gc.ca/publications/icebreaking -deglacage/requirements-besoins/icebreaking-services-eng.html.

path through shore-fast ice that allows commercial and civilian traffic to pass through without close escort. The more dynamic nature of sea ice in Arctic waters and the much less frequent traffic likely precludes such an approach for the Arctic. Not all ships traversing Canada's ice-covered waters require close escort by an icebreaker due to their own ice-strengthened hulls, but in the event that they become trapped ('beset') in ice beyond their own capabilities, CCG icebreakers can be requested to assist with freeing them from the ice.

While there had been an increasing number of maritime transits through and to the Canadian Arctic, the COVID-19 pandemic drastically curtailed the number of such voyages due to restrictions on non-essential users. For example, the 2020 summer saw only eight vessels, which included cargo and CCG icebreakers, making complete transits of the Northwest Passage (NWP) in comparison to 27 such transits in 2019.[16] A similar phenomenon occurred for the number of ice escort missions, though with a much lower disparity: 45 escorts occurred in 2020, 51 in 2019, an unusual 93 in 2018, and around 50 in 2017.[17] These figures suggest that the vast majority of CCG escort missions in the Arctic are for escorting commercial resupply vessels, which are vital to Arctic communities and which must continue regardless of the pandemic situation. Indeed, a list of all NWP transits by Cambridge University's Scott Polar Research Institute shows most vessels simply passing through NWP do so without CCG escort.[18] The spike in activity in 2018 illustrates a busy season for CCG icebreakers, which would also result in local users of sea lanes to seek an alternative solution to CCG icebreaking services.

---

16   CCG, "Canadian Coast Guard Finishes Unique 2020 Arctic Operations Season," Government of Canada, News Release, 11 December 2020, https://www.canada.ca/en /canadian-coast-guard/news/2020/12/canadian-coast-guardfinishes-unique-2020-arctic -operations-season.html.

17   Id.; CCG, "2019 Arctic Operations for the Canadian Coast Guard Complete," Government of Canada, News Release, 2 December 2019, https://www.canada.ca/en/canadian -coast-guard/news/2019/12/2019-arctic-operations-for-the-canadian-coast-guard-complete .html; CCG, "Canadian Coast Guard 2018 Arctic Operations Coming to an End," Government of Canada, News Release, 19 November 2018, https://www.canada.ca/en/canadian -coast-guard/news/2018/11/canadian-coast-guard-2018-arctic-operations-coming-to-an -end.html; Fisheries and Oceans Central & Arctic Region, "Arctic Season Winding Down but Coast Guard Continues to Support Industry and Programs in the North," *Cision*, 12 October 2017, https://www.newswire.ca/news-releases/arctic-season-winding-down-but -coast-guard-continues-to-support-industry-and-programs-in-the-north-650602733.html.

18   R.K. Headland *et al.*, "Transits of the Northwest Passage to End of the 2021 Navigation Season," Scott Polar Research Institute, 12 November 2021, https://www.spri.cam.ac.uk /resources/infosheets/northwestpassage.pdf.

Illustrating the limited availability of CCG icebreakers for escort tasks, the Bafflinland Mary Rivers iron mine has contracted the Estonian icebreaker *Botnica* to service their shipping needs for the summer periods of at least 2018–2022.[19] With the CCG warning Arctic stakeholders that the 2018 ice season would be especially severe and limit the availabilities of its icebreakers, Baffinland decided to acquire the services of its own icebreaker.[20] This decision also speaks clearly to the issue of purpose-built icebreakers versus ships that are only 'ice-strengthened.' The hiring of foreign ships requires a coasting trade license, which can only be granted by the Canadian Transportation Agency if no Canadian-registered ship is available under the *Coasting Trade Act*.[21] Baffinland's hiring of a foreign vessel met with objections by the Canadian firms Canship Innu Marine and Amarok Enterprises in 2021, which put forth their own Canadian-registered ships as alternatives. Amarok withdrew their objection for undisclosed reasons, while Canship Innu continued with the Newfoundland-based cargo-ferry MV *Northern Ranger* that they acquired in 2020.[22] These objections were overturned by the Canadian Transportation Agency, which accepted Bafflinland's argument and evidence that the *Botnica* had dedicated icebreaking capability which the *Northern Ranger* lacked as a mere 'ice-strengthened' ferry. Such capability included sufficient width to clear a path for wide ore carriers in a single pass, engine power, and crew expertise. Baffinland argued these were necessary to ensure ore carriers could enter and leave the mine's port at the beginning and end of the shipping season when the ice conditions would approach the limits of those carriers' ability to deal with ice.[23] Using a non-icebreaker like *Northern Ranger* would require multiple passes to clear sufficient ice for the PANAMAX-sized carriers to proceed and, in a worst-case scenario of heavy ice, require CCG icebreaking assistance which defeats the purpose of having a contracted icebreaker. Given that it was

---

19   The Baltic Times Staff, "Estonian Icebreaker Botnica Embarks on Journey to Canadian Arctic," *The Baltic Times*, 28 June 2021, https://www.baltictimes.com/estonian_icebreaker _botnica_embarks_on_journey_to_canadian_arctic/.

20   Tom Hoefer, "Logistics in the Northern Minerals Industry," NWT & Nunavut Chamber of Mines, presentation to the Arctic Security Working Group, 28 November 2018, 43, https://www.miningnorth.com/_rsc/site-content/library/Infrastructure/2018-11-28 _ChamberMines-for-Arctic-Security-WG.pdf.

21   J. Mark MacKeigan, "Decision No. 23-W-2021," Canadian Transportation Agency, 12 April 2021, https://otc-cta.gc.ca/node/570013.

22   Amarok had proposed their *Polar Prince, Arctic Wolf,* and *Thorbjorn.* MacKeigan (n 21); Tyler Mugford, "Northern Ranger to Sail Again on Labrador Coast," *CBC News*, 3 January 2020, https://www.cbc.ca/news/canada/newfoundland-labrador/mushuau-innu-first-nation -buys-northern-ranger-1.5413360.

23   MacKeigan (n 21).

the lack of availability of CCG icebreakers that drove the decision to resort to contracted private icebreakers in the first place, it became clear to the CTA that Baffinlands was justified in retaining the services of the *Botnica*.[24]

While close escort of shipping is one of the CCG icebreakers' core purposes, the limited number of icebreakers means other vessels are best served by taking routes that do not require icebreakers. This is enabled through the provision of ice routing and information services by the CCG in close coordination with the Canadian Ice Service.[25] The information for this is provided by a combination of icebreakers, aerial assets, satellites, and other sources that are processed and made available via land-based CCG centres. Some of this information is disseminated by the CCG as it deems necessary while maritime users in the Arctic can request more specific information tailored to their needs. The information collected by the CCG's various sources range from the tactical to the strategic, which describes the level of fidelity regarding the state of the ice in relation to the user's position and objectives.[26] Users who are entering ice-infested waters will be prioritized for this information while those who are still in the voyage planning stages will be deprioritized.[27]

Harbour breakouts refer to breaking ice that is preventing vessels from both accessing port infrastructure and leaving their ports for open water. This applies to both commercial and fishing harbours, though the latter are a "low priority compared to the other icebreaking services."[28] Indeed, it is not offered for the CCG's Arctic region, though it is offered for the Labrador and Newfoundland coasts.[29] The response times for icebreaker assistance for fishing harbour breakouts are also the longest out of all icebreaking services regardless of region, with a target response time of twenty-four hours instead of eight to twelve for more highly prioritized services in both Arctic and southern Canada.[30] Commercial harbour breakouts do occur in the CCG's Arctic area of operations, though it is not common. In the 2018 and 2020 seasons, for example, there was only one instance.[31]

---

24   Id.

25   CCG, *Ice Navigation in Canadian Waters* (Ottawa: Fisheries and Oceans Canada, 2012), 8.

26   CCG, *Icebreaking Operations: Levels of Service* (Fisheries and Oceans Canada, 2001), 17.

27   Id., 18.

28   CCG, "Icebreaking Operations Directive: 1" (n 10).

29   Glen Whiffen, "Spring Ice-break on Hold," *The Northern Pen*, 11 April 2018, https://www .pressreader.com/canada/northern-pen/20180411/281835759277729.

30   Da Pont (n 12), p. 18.

31   CCG, "Canadian Coast Guard Finishes Unique 2020 Arctic Operations Season" (n 16); CCG, "Canadian Coast Guard 2018 Arctic Operations Nearing Mid-season," Government of

Northern resupply is another notable service provided by the CCG's icebreakers in the Arctic. This involves icebreakers carrying and directly delivering vital goods to remote Arctic civilian and military communities which could not access commercial resupply services. This appears to be due to especially severe ice conditions that prevent commercial cargo ships from entering these communities' waters.[32] CCG icebreakers carry dry goods and fuel that can be transported to these communities via barges and helicopters.[33] Still, the vast majority of communities receive their resupplies from private commercial carriers: by 2014, the only Nunavut communities still receiving annual CCG resupply were Kugaaruk (formerly Pelly Bay) and Eureka weather/science station.[34] This situation has been around since at least 2000.[35] It is worth noting that Kugaaruk's and Eureka's supplies were delivered first to the deep water station of Nanisivik by private shipping companies, from where they were picked up for final delivery to Kugaaruk or Eureka by the CCG's icebreakers.[36]

In rare instances, attempts to conduct resupply fail due to excessive ice, such as 2014's efforts to supply Kugaaruk, which resulted in the temporary storage of goods in Churchill, Manitoba.[37] This incident helps illustrate the need for powerful icebreakers even as the Arctic undergoes rapid warming. Kugaaruk no longer depends on CCG resupply, with arrangements made after the 2014 failure of its CCG deliveries to receive direct commercial resupply via Nunavut Sealink and Supply Incorporated's vessels, which can deliver the increasing volume of

---

Canada, News Release 30 August 2018, https://www.canada.ca/en/canadian-coast-guard /news/2018/08/canadian-coast-guard-2018-arctic-operations-nearing-mid-season.html.

32   Sarah Rogers, "Western Nunavut Community Gets Rare, Direct Sealift Delivery," *Nunat-siaq News*, 8 September 2015, https://nunatsiaq.com/stories/article/65674kugaaruk_gets _direct_sealift_delivery/.

33   CCG, "Icebreaking Operations Directive: 1" (n 10); Lisa Gregoire, "Multi-year Ice-pack Blocks Sealift Delivery to Nunavut Hamlet," *Nunatsiaq News*, 7 October 2014, https://nunatsiaq .com/stories/article/65674ice_pack_ends_sealift_re-supply_to_nunavut_hamlet/.

34   Gregoire (n 33).

35   CCG, *Icebreaking Operations: Levels of Service* (n 26), p. 30; "Government Welcomes Canadian Coast Guard Ships Home After Successful Trip to the Arctic," Government of Canada, News Release, last modified 8 November 2012, https://www.canada.ca/en/news /archive/2012/11/government-welcomes-canadian-coast-guard-ships-home-after-successful -trip-arctic.html.

36   Gregoire (n 33); Sarah Rogers, "GN to Ship Portable Classrooms to Fire-damaged Kugaaruk this Summer," *Nunatsiaq News*, 8 March 2017, https://nunatsiaq.com/stories/article /65674gn_to_ship_six_portable_classrooms_to_kugaaruk_this_summer/; Public Works and Government Services Canada, "Runway Rehabilitation, Eureka, NU: Addendum No. 1," Government of Canada, 9 January 2015, https://buyandsell.gc.ca/cds/public/2015/01/09 /d8a6c97ff73476d7b1a712724fe47b40/ABES.PROD.PW_PWZ.B014.E9286.ATTA005.PDF.

37   Gregoire (n 33).

goods in a single trip.[38] This was followed by a Government of Nunavut contract with Nunavut Eastern Arctic Shipping Inc., which now supplies Kugaaruk and 17 other Nunavut communities directly without going through the CCG.[39] This is especially important because the much smaller cargo volume of CCG icebreakers requires multiple trips over a greater period of time, which can result in a higher risk of incomplete cargo deliveries due to sea ice accumulation in excess of CCG icebreaking capabilities such as what happened in 2014. By 2019–2021, the only northern resupply missions carried by the CCG appear to be Eureka Station and Killiniq radio transmitter, and even these trips were limited to refuelling rather than dry goods.[40] It is important to note that this section only discusses the direct resupply of communities by CCG icebreakers. It does not cover the use of icebreakers as escorts for commercial resupply vessels, which falls under the 'route assistance' role of the icebreakers.[41] It also does not include deliveries such as bicycle donations to local communities under the Polar Bike Project.[42]

Finally, the 'Arctic sovereignty' mission includes several core CCG responsibilities that are also conducted in southern Canada: search and rescue, environmental response, and Marine Communications and Traffic Services (MCTS).[43] These efforts, made possible in part by the physical presence of CCG icebreakers, "elicits recognition of Canadian sovereignty, through requests for, dependence on, efficient government support to authorized foreign ship transits. Historic occupancy and the ability to monitor and manage activity in an area are sovereignty characteristics exercised by CCG icebreaking operations."[44] While physical challenges to Canadian sovereignty over its Arctic waters have

---

38   Rogers 2017 (n 36); Rogers 2015 (n 32).

39   Jane George, "NEAS Sails Off with Big Nunavut Sealift Contract," *Nunatsiaq News*, 26 April 2019, https://nunatsiaq.com/stories/article/neas-sails-off-with-big-nunavut-sealift-contract/.

40   CCG, "Canadian Coast Guard Begins 2021 Arctic Season," Government of Canada, News Release, 22 June 2021, https://www.canada.ca/en/canadian-coast-guard/news/2021/06/canadian-coast-guard-begins-2021-arctic-season.html; CCG, "Canadian Coast Guard 2021 Arctic Season," Government of Canada, News Release, 9 June 2020, https://www.canada.ca/en/canadian-coast-guard/news/2020/06/canadian-coast-guard-2020-arctic-season.html; CCG, "Canadian Coast Guard 2019 Arctic Season Underway," Government of Canada, News Release, 19 June 2019, https://www.canada.ca/en/canadian-coast-guard/news/2019/06/canadian-coast-guard-2019-arctic-season-underway.html.

41   For more discussion of northern resupply by commercial vessels, see Lasserre in this volume.

42   CCG, "Canadian Coast Guard Arctic Operations Nearing Mid-season," Government of Canada, News Release, 28 August 2017, https://www.canada.ca/en/canadian-coast-guard/news/2017/08/canadian_coast_guardarcticoperationsnearingmid-season.html.

43   CCG, "Icebreaking in Canada" (n 12).

44   CCG, *Icebreaking Operations: Levels of Service* (n 26), p. 33.

been limited in recent years, there have been instances where CCG icebreakers played their part in asserting Canadian jurisdiction and sovereign responsibility in Arctic waters. The most dramatic of these in recent years was the 2018 grounding of the Russian-owned cruise/expedition vessel *Akademik Ioffe* around 78 nautical miles north-northwest of Kugaaruk, which saw both the CCG medium icebreakers *Amundsen* and *Pierre Radisson* coming to its assistance.[45] Otherwise, the Arctic sovereignty element of the CCG's icebreaking program relies on its ability to routinely and reliably carry out its other main services listed in this section, rather than any explicit dedicated duty aimed at challenging foreign assertions.

The number of occurrences of each of these five services helps to illustrate the limited, though regionally vital, demand for the CCG icebreaking fleet. Unlike Russia's maritime Arctic, Canada's Arctic has relatively little in the way of frequent maritime trade that requires the massive number of ships in Russia's fleet.[46] This being said, the gradual reduction in the number CCG Arctic icebreakers since the 1990s has led to increased strain on the remaining fleet, especially as they increase in age and require more time in maintenance or refits.[47] This has led to the CCG's decision to lease five icebreakers between 2018 and 2038 to help meet demand as the older vessels undergo life extensions.[48] This relationship between supply of and demand for CCG icebreaking services is reflected in the CCG's documents and plans, most notably in the *Icebreaker Requirements*, which has been updated every five years since 2009.[49] The latest version covers the years 2017–2022, and thus one can expect an updated version by the time this volume has been published.

---

45 "Marine Transportation Safety Investigation M18C0225," Transportation Safety Board of Canada, 21 May 2021, https://www.tsb.gc.ca/eng/enquetes-investigations/marine/2018/m18c0225/m18c0225.html.

46 For detailed comparison between Russia and Canada on their respective traffic levels and users, see Lasserre in this volume.

47 CCG, "Icebreaker Requirements 2017–2022: 6. Planned Icebreaker Deployment," Government of Canada, last modified 18 November 2019, https://www.ccg-gcc.gc.ca/publications/icebreaking-deglacage/requirements-besoins/icebreaker-deployment-eng.html.

48 Fabian Manning and Marc Gold, *When Every Second Counts: Maritime Search and Rescue* (Ottawa: Senate of Canada, 2018), 12.

49 CCG, "Icebreaker Requirements 2017–2022: 2. Background," Government of Canada, last modified 18 November 2019, https://www.ccg-gcc.gc.ca/publications/icebreaking-deglacage/requirements-besoins/background-eng.html.

3   **Current Arctic Icebreaking Fleet**

To provide the services above, the CCG's icebreaker fleet of mid-2022 includes two heavy icebreakers, six medium icebreakers, and nine multi-purpose vessels/light icebreakers.[50] Two air-cushioned vehicles (hovercrafts) are also employed for icebreaking duties in southern Canada, while an additional second-hand medium icebreaker and light icebreaker are currently undergoing conversion for CCG service after their purchases from previous commercial owners. With the exception of the hovercrafts and the second-hand light icebreaker, the remaining ships are expected to contribute to Arctic icebreaker services during the summer navigable season in accordance with their respective capabilities.[51] This includes the light icebreakers, which have operated in the Arctic though not regularly or frequently.[52] The navigable season changes year by year depending on ice conditions, but it can be expected to last between July and October, inclusive.[53]

Many of these icebreakers are approaching or are past thirty years of age and require increasing numbers of refits and maintenance that prevent them from being in service.[54] This may not be such a major problem if the CCG operated only in the Arctic, as that would allow them ample months during the winter to conduct such maintenance when Arctic traffic is absent.[55] However, both heavy and medium icebreakers, alongside their light cousins, are also needed during the winter for icebreaking in southern Canadian waters.[56] While there are more icebreakers in the fleet than the five that industry and the CCG deem the minimum necessary for the Arctic, the fact that winters also require one heavy and all medium icebreakers dramatically limits the opportunities

---

50   CCG, "Icebreaker Requirements 2017–2022: Appendices," Government of Canada, last modified 18 November 2019, https://www.ccg-gcc.gc.ca/publications/icebreaking-deglacage /requirements-besoins/appendices-eng.html. The heavy icebreakers were formerly known as Type 1300 and the mediums as Type 1200. The light icebreakers are also known as high/medium endurance multi-tasked vessels, with the high endurance ships known as Type 1100 while the medium endurance ships are known as Type 1050.
51   CCG, *Icebreaking Operations: Levels of Service* (n 26), p. 34.
52   "Maiden Voyage to Arctic for Coast Guard Ship," *Welland Tribune*, 16 July 2018, https: //www.wellandtribune.ca/news/niagara-region/2018/07/16/maiden-voyage-to-arctic-for -coast-guard-ship.html.
53   CCG, *Icebreaking Operations: Levels of Service* (n 26), p. 34.
54   CCG, "Icebreaker Requirements 2017–2022: Appendices" (n 50).
55   CCG, "Vessels Ten Year Maintenance Calendar," Government of Canada, last modified 30 April 2021, https://www.ccg-gcc.gc.ca/fleet-flotte/vessel-maint-navire-2021-22-eng.html.
56   CCG, "Icebreaker Requirements 2017–2022: Appendices" (n 50).

available for both regular maintenance and lengthy life extensions.[57] Further-more, of the six medium icebreakers, one of them, the *Amundsen*, is dedicated to science missions when operating in the Arctic and is therefore not included in the icebreaking program except in emergency situations, such as the afore-mentioned grounding of the *Akademik Ioffe*.[58]

Much has been noted about the icebreaker fleet's age and the urgency of its replacement. This is certainly accurate for some of the most well-known members of the fleet, though others are younger than the average age of the much-touted Russian fleet, which Russian media has pegged at 39 years old by 2022.[59] For instance, while the *Louis St. Laurent*, the largest and most capable of Canadian icebreakers, was built in 1969 and is the focus of most discussions regarding the CCG's aging fleet, its fellow heavy icebreaker *Terry Fox* was built much later in 1983. The four mediums built for CCG service were constructed between 1978 and 1987. Rounding this out, the light icebreak-ers of the high-endurance multitask vessels were built in 1986–1987.[60] More recently, the interim medium icebreakers (*Captain Molly Kool, Jean Goodwill*, and *Vincent Massey*) purchased from private European owners in 2018 were built in Norway in 2000–2001.[61] Compared to the Russian figure of 39 years, Canada comes out slightly ahead at 37.5 years old for the average age of its icebreakers. There are limits to these figures, as it is unknown how the start date of each ship's 'life' is determined: is it the day they were launched, the day they underwent sea trials, the day they had their naming ceremonies, the day they were delivered to their owners, or the day they were commissioned? This could make several years of difference in the final figures. Regardless of the exact age of the Russian or Canadian ships, it becomes clear that their average ages are not as far apart as the 'icebreaker gap' discourse suggests. While some may critique the inclusion of light icebreakers into the calculations, lim-iting the list to only the medium and heavy icebreakers that provide the bulk

---

57   Id.
58   Id.
59   "Russia's Fleet to Receive Ten New Icebreakers by 2030," TASS *Russian News Agency*, 3
       November 2020, https://tass.com/defense/1219675.
60   CCG, "Icebreaker Requirements 2017–2022: Appendices" (n 50).
61   CCG, "CCG Fleet: Vessel Details: CCGS CAPTAIN MOLLY KOOL," *Government of Canada*,
       n.d., https://inter-j01.dfo-mpo.gc.ca/fdat/vessels/2243; CCG, "CCG Fleet: Vessel Details:
       CCGS JEAN GOODWILL," Government of Canada, n.d., https://inter-j01.dfo-mpo.gc.ca
       /fdat/vessels/2424; Davie Shipbuilding, "Canadian Coast Guard Icebreaker CCGS
       Vincent Massey Leaves Davie Drydock," *Cision*, 25 March 2022, https://www.newswire.ca
       /news-releases/canadian-coast-guard-icebreaker-ccgs-vincent-massey-leaves-davie
       -drydock-862316207.html. *Vincent Massey*'s conversion had not been completed at the
       time of writing and is expected to be completed in Fall 2022.

of Arctic icebreaking services would actually improve the average fleet age to 32 years old thanks to the relative youth of the interim second-hand medium icebreakers. None of this is to say Canada's icebreaking fleet is young or that the processes behind their replacements do not need to be well underway, only that the Russian fleet does not have the overwhelming age advantage suggested in the discourse.

Ultimately, the age metric should not be used at the expense of other key characteristics of the icebreakers themselves and the contexts in which they serve. There are qualitative issues at play, for instance, most notably that six of Russia's icebreakers in 2022 are nuclear-powered with much greater endurance and icebreaking capability.[62] At the same time, it has been noted above in this chapter and elsewhere in this volume that commercial traffic in the Canadian Arctic is relatively limited and a capability like Russia's fleet of nuclear icebreakers remains far in excess of need (see further Lasserre in this volume). The continual but unpredictable accumulation of loose multiyear ice in the western Canadian Arctic due to the Beaufort Gyre and other circulation regimes is expected to continue into the mid-century with its attendant suppression of commercial traffic through the region.[63] In this context, the future of the CCG icebreaking fleet needs to mainly focus on its replacement rather than numerical expansion, which the following section will address.

4   The National Shipbuilding Strategy and the Future Coast Guard Icebreaking Fleet

Despite the favourable average age of Canada's icebreaking fleet compared to Russia's, the fact that the most powerful Canadian ship, the *Louis St. Laurent*, is over 50 years old means that Canada's ability to reliably carry out heavy ice-breaking is much more curtailed than the overall fleet age suggests. At the same time, the lengthy decade-long timeframe required to procure and construct large complex vessels like icebreakers means even the younger vessels needed to have their replacements planned by the late 2010s. This replacement effort has been subsumed under the National Shipbuilding Strategy (NSS), formerly

62   Thomas Nilsen, "Second Giant Nuclear Icebreaker Handed Over to Rosatomflot," *The Barents Observer*, 25 December 2021, https://thebarentsobserver.com/en/arctic/2021/12/second-giant-nuclear-icebreaker-handed-over-rosatomflot.
63   D.G. Barber *et al.*, "Climate Change and Ice Hazards in the Beaufort Sea," *Elementa: Science of the Anthropocene* 2: (2014): 10, https://doi.org/10.12952/journal.elementa.000025.

known as the National Shipbuilding Procurement Strategy (NSPS). Announced by the Conservative Government of Stephen Harper on 3 June 2010, the NSS sought to replace the Royal Canadian Navy and CCG's major vessels through domestic construction.[64] The construction would occur in two shipyards, one for non-combat vessels and the other for combat vessels. One and a half years later on 12 January 2012, Harper announced that Irving Shipbuilding in Halifax had won the competition to build the latter, while Seaspan Vancouver Shipyards would build the former with its predominantly CCG ships.

Davie Shipyard in Quebec was also in the running for one of the NSS shipyards, which was a status they employed to attract one or more potential purchasers to resolve their debts.[65] The lengthy attempts at canvasing the global market for potential buyers took up much of the time allotted to potential shipyards to prepare their bids. One of the failed negotiations was Italy's Fincantieri shipyards, while Davie Shipyards was eventually sold to a consortium of Upper Lakes Group, SNC-Lavelin, and South Korea's Daewoo Shipbuilding and Marine Engineering just shortly before submissions were due for the NSS shipyard bid.[66] Davie itself attributes its failure to become one of the two major NSS partners to "its poor financial position at the time," during which 1,600 workers had been laid off and the yard was shuttered. It was eventually rescued on a more permanent basis when British firm Zafiro Marine bought Davie's yard in November 2011.[67] Zafiro would eventually become part of Inocea Group, which is now the parent company behind Davie.[68] As will be seen below, Davie would make a come-back at the end of the decade as the

---

64   Martin Shadwick, "The National Shipbuilding Procurement Strategy (NSPS) and the Royal Canadian Navy (RCN)," *Canadian Military Journal* 12:2 (2012): 77.

65   Osler, Hoskin & Harcourt LLP, "No.: 200-11-019127-102, Province of Québec, Canada. Motion for Authorization to sell substantially all of the assets of the debtor and for the issuance of a vesting order and to extend the stay of proceedings," Montréal, 19 July 2011, 5, https://www.insolvencies.deloitte.ca/Documents/ca_en_insolv_Davie_MotionAuthSellAllAsset_VestingOrderExt_071911.pdf.

66   Allison Martell, "UPDATE 3-Canada's Davie Yards Sold Ahead of Federal Contract," *Reuters*, 21 July 2011, https://www.reuters.com/article/canada-shipbuilding-idUSN1E76K20P20110721.

67   Chantier Davie Canada Inc., *The Davie Strategic Journey: Generation 2040* (Inocea Group, 2020), 16, http://www.davie.ca/wordpress/wp-content/uploads/2021/02/Davie-Shipbuilding-SJ_Final_EG_web1.pdf; Mark Cardwell, "Ahoy Davie! British Shipbuilders, American Investors Team Up to Refloat Canada's Oldest and Biggest Shipyard," *Canadian Sailings*, 16 December 2013, https://canadiansailings.ca/ahoy-davie-british-shipbuilders-american-investors-team-up-to-refloat-canadas-oldest-and-biggest-shipyard/; Matt Powell, "Davie Shipyard Relaunched," *Plant: Advancing Canadian Manufacturing* 72:8 (November/December 2013): 12–13, https://www.plant.ca/wp-content/uploads/2013/11/PLNT_NovDec2013DE.pdf.

68   Cardwell (n 67).

Government of Canada realized the two winning NSS yards would be insufficient to replace all CCG vessels.

One of the top priority builds for Seaspan was the polar icebreaker, dubbed
the CCGS *John G. Diefenbaker* as early as 2010.[69] It is expected to replace the
Louis St. Laurent, which was already recognized as reaching the limits of its
service life. However, a number of factors have led to the *Diefenbaker* remaining just a set of digital drawings by 2022. Firstly, even though Seaspan was
selected in January 2012 to build its package of ships, the yard required massive
modernization to make it suitable for building modern large vessels, which
was compounded by the need for special machinery to work with the heavy
steel plates of a polar icebreaker.[70] This CDN$170 million modernization was
completed nearly three years later in October 2014, funded by Seaspan itself.[71]
Secondly, the polar icebreaker would not be built until the completion of three
offshore fisheries science vessels (OFSVs) and one offshore oceanographic
science vessel (OOSV), while uncertainty concerned whether the *Diefenbaker*
or the Navy's two joint support ships (JSS) would come first.[72] Consequently,
this meant the construction of the *Diefenbaker* could not begin at the shipyard
until nearly a decade after the yard finished its modernization due to the limited capacity to build multiple ships at once. The order of construction within
this non-combat package had been a subject of some debate, though many
noted the need to ensure the yard gained sufficient experience building the
relatively simple OFSVs before tackling something as complex as the *Diefenbaker*. By 2022, Seaspan had delivered the three OFSVs, and the first JSS is well
underway, having been decided as the greater priority.[73] The OOSV has been
rescheduled to fit in between the first and second JSS.[74] The *Diefenbaker* itself,

69   "Shipbuilding for the Canadian Coast Guard," Government of Canada, News Release,
      4 July 2010, https://www.canada.ca/en/news/archive/2010/06/shipbuilding-canadian
      -coast-guard.html.
70   Author's tour of Seaspan Vancouver Shipyards, 2014.
71   R. Bruce Striegler, "Seaspan's Vancouver Shipyards Yard Modernization Complete:
      First Blocks for Coast Guard's Offshore Fisheries Science Vessels under Construction,"
      Canadian Sailings, 29 December 2014, https://canadiansailings.ca/seaspans-vancouver
      -shipyards-yard-modernization-complete-first-blocks-for-coast-guards-offshore-fisheries
      -science-vessels-under-construction/.
72   Id.; Shadwick (n 64), p. 79.
73   Anita Anand, *Canada's National Shipbuilding Strategy: 2020 Annual Report* (Ottawa:
      Government of Canada, 2021), 4; Seaspan, "Photo Gallery," *Seaspan*, 2022, https://www
      .seaspan.com/photo-gallery/?_image_gallery=vancouver-shipyards; Manning and Gold
      (n 48), p. 12.
74   Jane Seyd, "Seaspan to Cut Steel on Offshore Science Ship This Month," *North Shore News*,
      9 March 2021, https://www.nsnews.com/local-news/seaspan-to-cut-steel-on-offshore

on the other hand, remains some years into the future and far from the original 2017 service date optimistically envisioned by the Harper government.[75]

Citing these delays and the importance of having a polar icebreaker in a timely manner, the Liberal Government in June 2019 announced that they would remove the *Diefenbaker* from Seaspan's order books, replacing it instead with sixteen multipurpose vessels (MPVs) similar to the existing light icebreakers while looking to build the *Diefenbaker* elsewhere.[76] Seaspan argued the MPVs were already promised by the Harper government, though records only indicate five such vessels and five offshore patrol vessels.[77] But less than two years after the removal of the *Diefenbaker* from Seaspan, Trudeau's Liberal Government made an abrupt about-face. In May 2021, it announced that not only would the *Diefenbaker* return to Seaspan, but that it would be accompanied by a sistership, bringing the total number of heavy Arctic icebreakers to two.[78] This second ship would go to a third yard that is in the process of being added to the National Shipbuilding Strategy's main partners: Davie Shipbuilding. The yard that had failed to win either of the NSS packages a decade

---

-science-ship-this-month-3526538; Public Services and Procurement Canada, "Government of Canada Takes Next Step Toward Construction of Offshore Oceanographic Science Vessel for Canadian Coast Guard," Government of Canada, 18 February 2021, https://www.canada.ca/en/public-services-procurement/news/2021/02/government -of-canada-takes-next-step-toward-construction-of-offshore-oceanographic-science -vessel-for-canadian-coast-guard.html.

75   Lee Berthiaume, "Vancouver Shipyard Renews Fight to Build Coast Guard's New Polar Icebreaker," *CBC News*, 21 September 2020, https://www.cbc.ca/news/canada/british -columbia/seaspan-canadian-coast-guard-new-ship-1.5732309.

76   Paul Withers, "Trudeau Government Moves Heavy-icebreaker Job Out of Vancouver," *CBC News*, 12 June 2019, https://www.cbc.ca/news/canada/nova-scotia/icebreaker-vancouver -seaspan-national-shipbuilding-strategy-1.5173027.

77   Seaspan ULC, "Seaspan to Build 10 More Canadian Coast Guard Ships," *Professional Mariner: Journal of the Maritime Industry*, 8 October 2013, https://professionalmariner. com/seaspan-to-build-10-more-canadian-coast-guard-ships/; Public Works and Government Services Canada, "Vancouver Shipyards to Build Medium Endurance Multi-Tasked Vessels and Offshore Patrol Vessels for the Canadian Coast Guard," Government of Canada, News Release, 7 October 2013, https://www.seaspan.com/wp-content/uploads /Federal-New-Release-10072013.pdf.

78   Lee Berthiaume, "Vancouver, Quebec Shipyards to Each Get New Heavy Icebreaker; Cost Remains a Mystery," *The Globe and Mail*, 6 May 2021, https://www.theglobeandmail.com /politics/article-ottawa-to-reveal-plans-for-building-long-overdue-heavy-icebreaker-for/; CCG, "Government of Canada Announces Polar Icebreakers to Enhance Canada's Arctic Presence and Provide Critical Services to Canadians," Government of Canada, News Release, 6 May 2021, https://www.canada.ca/en/canadian-coast-guard/news/2021/05 /government-of-canada-announces-polar-icebreakers-to-enhance-canadas-arctic -presence-and-provide-critical-services-to-canadians.html.

ago had finally succeeded in acquiring what has become a multi-billion-dollar contract, pending its official approval as a formal NSS shipyard.

The original NSS plans only included the polar icebreaker and the light ice-breakers, leaving the workhorse mediums untouched. In August 2019, this was addressed when Trudeau's Liberal Government authorized six 'program ice-breakers' to replace the *Terry Fox* heavy icebreaker and the four Cold War-era medium icebreakers.[79] These are planned to be built at Davie Shipbuilding as well, and indeed were planned to be Davie's bread and butter for much of the 2020s and 2030s. It remains to be seen how the program icebreakers and the newly-added second heavy icebreaker will be prioritized in Davie's shipyard, which requires its own modernization akin to that carried out by Seaspan a decade ago.[80] Although Davie has styled itself as an icebreaker specialist with multiple refits and conversions of existing icebreakers under its belt, it has not built an icebreaker from scratch since 1969, and the last vessels it built were a pair of large ferries in 2018.[81]

Ultimately, the CCG's icebreaking fleet is at or nearing ages that require their replacement. At present, all of them are covered by existing government plans to build new ships in Canada to replace them. At the same time, the delays, pri-oritization of other construction, and limited capacity of Canadian shipyards have led to several temporary 'interim' measures to cover for the periods when the original fleets need to be taken out of service for their modernizations and refits. These consist of the three medium icebreakers converted from commer-cial vessels, as well as the ongoing process to convert a light icebreaker acquired in 2021. This latter project is perhaps indicative of the Canadian shipbuilding industry's perceived capacity limitations. Despite its small size and presum-ably quicker pace of construction compared to medium and heavy icebreak-ers, the Canadian Coast Guard and Public Services and Procurement Canada were not willing to publicly discuss the possibility of a new build, whether in

79   CCG, "Canadian Coast Guard's New Icebreakers," Government of Canada, Backgrounder, 2 August 2019, https://www.canada.ca/en/canadian-coast-guard/news/2019/08/canadian-coast-guards-new-icebreakers.html.

80   Public Services and Procurement Canada, "Government of Canada Receives Chantier Davie's Supporting Materials" (n 7); Public Services and Procurement Canada, "Canada's National Shipbuilding Strategy Process to Add a Third Shipyard," Government of Canada, Backgrounder, 2 August 2019, https://www.canada.ca/en/public-services-procurement/news/2019/08/canadas-national-shipbuilding-strategy-process-to-add-a-third-shipyard.html.

81   Berthiaume 2020 (n 75); Tim Colton, "Davie Shipbuilding," *Shipbuilding History*, 7 May 2021, http://shipbuildinghistory.com/canadayards/davie.htm; Chantier Davie Canada Inc. (n 67).

a Canadian or foreign shipyard.[82] On the part of Canadian shipbuilders, there was certainly no lack of interest as evidenced by both NSS and non-NSS yards being present at the 'Industry Day' presentation by the Government of Canada on the proposed light icebreaker.[83]

Yet, the unique size and draft requirements of Canada's Great Lakes canal locks meant there were very few international options that existed in a surplus State. Nonetheless, one was found from an unlikely source: Turkmenistan.[84] Originally acquired for use in supporting the country's oil and gas projects in the Caspian Sea, the recent oil price collapse likely led to a reduced need for the twelve-year-old *Mangystau-2*, providing an opportunity for Canada to acquire it as a rapid solution to the reduced availability of its light icebreaking fleet as they enter their vessel life extensions.[85] While this appears to have little direct relevance for Canada's Arctic, it must be remembered that even light icebreakers occasionally visit the Arctic, which limits the number of vessels available for duties in the south either due to lack of available hulls or refit cycles. Having an interim vessel can help fill gaps resulting from such operational and maintenance demands. Indeed, one of the question-and-answer documents for the initial 18 February 2019 request for information regarding the prospective interim light icebreaker explicitly mentioned that the new vessel would "supplement the operational capabilities of multiple ships, not just

82   Murray Brewster, "Shipbuilding Industry Pushes Back as Federal Government Shops for Used Icebreaker," *CBC News*, 6 October 2020, https://www.cbc.ca/news/politics/ship building-icebreaker-coast-guard-great-lakes-1.5751143.

83   Public Works and Government Services Canada, "Brise-glace léger, Solicitation No. F7013-180034/A, Amendment No. 004," Government of Canada, March 29, 2019, Signing Sheets, https://buyandsell.gc.ca/cds/public/2019/03/29/2d6e7f310e26637275fcd7fadf45f749 /ABES.PROD.PW__MB.B003.E27203.EBSU004.PDF.

84   CCG, "Canadian Coast Guard Announces an Addition to the Southern Icebreaking Fleet with the Purchase of Light Icebreaker from Atlantic Towing Limited," *Cision*, 10 November 2021, https://www.newswire.ca/news-releases/canadian-coast-guard-announces-an-addition -to-the-southern-icebreaking-fleet-with-the-purchase-of-light-icebreaker-from-atlantic -towing-limited-831919031.html.

85   "Canadian Coast Guard Buys Light Icebreaker for Great Lakes; Vessel Currently in Turkmenistan," *Welland Tribune*, 14 November 2021, https://www.wellandtribune.ca/news /niagara-region/2021/11/14/canadian-coast-guard-buys-light-icebreaker-for-great-lakes -vessel-currently-in-turkmenistan.html; "Caspian Offshore Construction (COC)," Offshore Technology, 2022, https://www.offshore-technology.com/contractors/vessels/cas pian-offshore-construction/; Bruce Pannier, "Plunge in Oil Prices Deals Another Blow to Kazakhstan, Turkmenistan," *RadioFreeEurope/RadioLiberty*, 23 April 2020, https://www .rferl.org/a/qishloq-ovozi-plunging-oil-prices-kazakhstan-turkmenistan-economic -problems/30572905.html; Public Works and Government Services Canada, "Solicitation No. F7013-180034/A, Amendment No. 004" (n 83).

CCGS Griffon and Samuel Risley."[86] It is noteworthy that the latter has escorted resupply vessels to the US Air Force base in Thule, Greenland, making even the interim light icebreaker a potential candidate for Arctic operations.[87]

5   Making Use of Presence: Lessons from Danish Naval Ships in
         Greenland for RCN AOPS Vessels

Clearly, the CCG's icebreaking capacity is at a critical juncture where it is meeting its mission requirements in the Arctic but is at risk of no longer being able to do so due to a series of delayed procurement projects aimed at renewing its aging ships. Several interim measures have been implemented to alleviate such concerns, but construction contracts have yet to be signed for the replacement vessels that will each require approximately a half-decade to build. As the CCG fleet ages and the replacements await their time in the water, there will likely be increasing stress on the existing fleet's availability and reliability, requiring alternative solutions.

One possible path for alleviating this strain would be to order from foreign shipyards with greater experience and capacity that can provide quicker replacements than Canadian yards. Proposals for such an approach have been put forth for the combat portion of the NSS but less so for the CCG's icebreakers.[88] However, this approach ignores the complex engineering work that is required to convert a ship's design into instructions and materials that a foreign shipyard can work with, as well as the limited number of available yards.[89] In the last decade, there have only been two icebreakers built in Western shipyards that approach the capabilities of the CCGS *Louis St. Laurent*, the one most urgently in need of replacement. Australia's heavy research icebreaker RSV *Nuyina* was built in Damen's shipyards in Romania, which took approximately five years to enter service.[90] The United Kingdom's RRS *Sir David Attenborough*,

86   Public Works and Government Services Canada, "Solicitation No. F7013-180034/A,
       Amendment No. 004" (n 83), p. 5.
87   *Welland Tribune* 2018 (n 52).
88   Eric Lerhe, *Fleet-Replacement and the 'Build at Home' Premium: Is It Too Expensive to Build
       Warships in Canada?* (Ottawa: Conference of Defence Associations Institute, 2016), 3.
89   Timothy Choi and Jeffrey F. Collins, "If Only Warships Grew on Trees: The Complexities of
       Off-the-Shelf Defence Procurement," Policy Perspective (Calgary: Canadian Global Affairs
       Institute, March 2022), https://www.cgai.ca/if_only_warships_grew_on_trees.
90   Australian Antarctica Division, "New Icebreaker RSV Nuyina Heads South," Australian
       Government, 23 December 2021, https://www.antarctica.gov.au/nuyina/stories/2021
       /new-icebreaker-rsv-nuyina-heads-south/; Australian Antarctica Division, "Australia's

somewhat smaller than *Nuyina*, took over four years to be built in Cammell Laird's yard in England, and a further year before its maiden voyage.[91] Even if such construction timelines were notably faster than the start-to-finish process of an equivalent vessel in a Canadian yard, the time required to solicit and select a suitable foreign shipyard and then change the ship's design so that it can be built in that yard using materials from the local supply chains would extend the timeline to something similar to the current plan of building under the National Shipbuilding Strategy using Canadian yards.[92] Looking abroad is not, therefore, likely to result in significantly reduced timelines and will not solve the coming strain on the CCG's icebreaking fleet as they require more and more maintenance.

One near-term solution may be to leverage the *Harry DeWolf*-class Arctic and offshore patrol vessels, six of which are currently being built under the combat portion of the NSS in Halifax for the Royal Canadian Navy with two more on the order books for the CCG after suitable modifications.[93] These ships have not been designed as icebreakers. They were not built with the width or power to carve routes in heavy ice while escorting large civilian and commercial vessels. Nonetheless, the first two ships that have conducted their ice trials have demonstrated a respectable ability to operate in the Canadian Arctic in February–March when no other vessels are in the region. During these trials, they have shown an ability to exceed their designed ice capability of 1.2 m of first-year ice with multiyear inclusions, with HMCS *Margaret Brooke* encountering limited amounts of 2 m first-year ice.[94]

This performance by the 6,700 t AOPS is important. It exceeds the empirical performance of the Royal Danish Navy's 3,500 t *Thetis* and 2,000 t *Knud Rasmussen*-class patrol ships operating in and around Greenland, which have considerably lower ice ratings of 80 cm of ice with occasional encounters

New Icebreaker – RSV Nuyina," Australian Government, 24 September 2020, https://www .antarctica.gov.au/antarctic-operations/travel-and-logistics/ships/icebreaker/.

91   Jonathan Amos, "Ceremony Marks Start of Attenborough Polar Ship Construction," BBC *News*, 17 October 2016, https://www.bbc.com/news/science-environment-37648915; British Antarctic Survey, "RRS *Sir David Attenborough*," Natural Environment Research Council, n.d., https://www.bas.ac.uk/polar-operations/sites-and-facilities/facility/rrs-sir -david-attenborough/.

92   Choi and Collins (n 89).

93   Public Services and Procurement Canada, "Large Vessel Shipbuilding Projects" (n 9).

94   Irving Shipbuilding, "ICYMI … From Halifax Harbour to Canada's North," (@IrvingShip-build, 24 March 2022), https://twitter.com/IrvingShipbuild/status/1507068233781706752; technical briefing provided by high level personnel involved with *Margaret Brooke*'s ice trials and the Arctic and Offshore Patrol Ships project, 30 March 2022.

exceeding that.[95] Absent dedicated icebreakers, Denmark employs these
patrol ships for many of the icebreaking duties for which CCG icebreakers
are responsible on the Canadian side of the Davis Strait. This includes route
assistance, harbour breakouts, and freeing small vessels beset in sea ice. The
Thetis-class vessel HDMS *Triton* helped lead cargo ships resupply settlements
in Greenland in summer 2020 by breaking ice;[96] in 2015, *Triton* also escorted
the supply ship *Arina Arctica* to resupply the towns along Disko Bay on the
west side of Greenland, during which it freed both *Arina Arctica* and a smaller
cargo ship when they were stuck in the ice.[97] That same season in late March,
Triton conducted harbour breakouts in Sisimiut to allow local fishers to reach
open waters.[98] Although individuals often request breakout assistance, they
are only carried out at the request of the local municipalities, such as when
Triton responded to the Avanaata Kommunia's request for its services to open
up the seaways to the settlements of Ikerasak and Saattut in June 2022.[99] Later
that month, the smaller *Knud Rasmussen*-class vessel HDMS *Lauge Koch* broke
ice at Nuussuaq south of Kullorsuaq in order to allow supply ships carrying
vital fuel to replenish local settlements.[100]

    With eight AOPSs to enter service by 2027, Canadian authorities would be
prudent to explore the use of these new assets to help support the CCG's icebreaking service in similar ways to their Danish counterparts. It should be kept
in mind, however, that the sea ice conditions in western Greenland are much
different from that in different parts of the Canadian Arctic, which limit the
utility of the Danish comparison. Still, while the AOPSs were not designed as
icebreakers and the RCN is unlikely to make their ships available to the CCG
as regular 'on call' assets for the icebreaking service, they may nonetheless

95   Timothy Choi, "Maritime Militarization in the Arctic: Identifying Civil-Military Depen-
      dencies," in *Arctic Yearbook 2020*, eds., Lassi Heininen, Heather Exner-Pirot, and Justin
      Barnes (Akureyri, Iceland: Arctic Portal), 71.

96   I. Eskadre, "5. Besætning på inspektionsskibet TRITON," Facebook, 15 July 2020, https:
      //www.facebook.com/permalink.php?story_fbid=3087079501375849&id=776180525799103.

97   Marinestaben, "Inspektionsskibet TRITON Brød Isen for Forsyningsskib," Værnsfælles Fors-
      varskommando, 8 April 2015, http://forsvaret.dk/MST/Nyt%20og%20Presse/nationalt
      /Pages/InspektionsskibetTRITONbroedisenforforsyningsskib.aspx, archived at https://
      web.archive.org/web/20150429101207/http://forsvaret.dk/MST/Nyt%20og%20Presse
      /nationalt/Pages/InspektionsskibetTRITONbroedisenforforsyningsskib.aspx.

98   Jonas-Løvschall-Wedel, "Triton Hejælper Fiskere," *Kalaallit Nunaata Radioa*, 29 March
      2015, https://knr.gl/da/nyheder/triton-hj%C3%A6lper-fiskere.

99   Arktisk Kommando – Joint Arctic Command, "Isbrydning Ved Uummannaq," Facebook, 2
      June 2022, https://www.facebook.com/watch/?v=589198116113038.

100   Arctic Command (@arktiskkommando), "Lauge Koch Breaks Ice at Nuussuaq," Instagram
      reel, 8 June 2022, https://www.instagram.com/reel/Cei6b3Qjgwl/.

prove useful as emergency vessels in situations with lower ice requirements. As noted in the first section of this chapter, not all CCG Arctic icebreaking tasks involve escorting large commercial vessels through heavy ice. Harbour breakouts and freeing beset vessels and community resupply are additional missions that require CCG resources even though demand for such missions have somewhat reduced in recent years. The potentially less onerous ice requirements for some of these mission (as always, dependent on the location and that year's specific conditions) may allow the lighter icebreaking capabilities of the AOPSs to help reduce the operational load on the CCG's remaining aging icebreakers. Given the relatively smaller dimensions of the AOPSs compared to the CCG's heavy and medium icebreakers, they may actually be preferable when operating along some of the northern low-impact shipping corridors currently being planned as they may be less disruptive to sea ice.[101] Their contribution to regional on-water presence can also reduce the need for CCG icebreakers to transit at high speeds during emergencies, thereby reducing engine and noise pollution that may negatively wildlife in the Arctic broadly and in these corridors.

While the AOPSs will not be able to replace the CCG icebreakers in their core task of escorting large commercial vessels through ice, they will likely be able to take some of the burden in situations where less ice capability is required. In some emergency search and rescue (SAR) scenarios, for example, there is a high likelihood that most Arctic traffic will stay in waters relatively clear of ice anyway, making the AOPSs more than adequate for coming to a vessel in need of assistance (assuming no heavy ice is along the way). While Joint Rescue Coordination Centres already utilize all public and private elements to carry out such SAR activities, new levels of coordination between the RCN and CCG will be required for other tasks requiring icebreaking and pollution control capabilities. This may be accomplished under a memorandum of understanding and/or the embarkation of CCG subject matter experts who specialize in those areas. The latter can help reduce the challenges caused by the 'up and out' nature of naval promotion, which sees the departure of personnel from their ships as they are promoted higher in rank soon after they have acquired the specific skills necessary for specific tasks. Regardless, the presence of eight new ships capable of significant operations in sea ice provides an opportunity that cannot be ignored while long-term replacements for the CCG icebreakers are being built. Much as navies often employ a mixed fleet of high-end and low-end combatants each suitable for an array of tasks, the

101   For more on low-impact shipping corridors, see Dawson and Song in this volume.

same logic may apply to icebreaking requirements in the Arctic. Not all situations require the power of a dedicated medium or heavy icebreaker, and the relatively large numbers of AOPS s can help fill the lower end of the icebreaking spectrum's requirements.

6   Conclusion

The future of shipping in the Canadian Arctic remains somewhat uncertain. While popular media observers expect dramatic increases in the coming years, the past several years have shown a fairly steady level of activity that remains just barely capable of being met by the CCG's Arctic icebreakers. At the same time, the future remains uncertain especially after the COVID-19 pandemic. While non-essential voyages (i.e., anything other than community resupply) slowed down dramatically during the pandemic, the post-pandemic period is already seeing a limited resurgence of commercial and leisure activities in Canada's Arctic, and several cruise operators have already been booking tickets for the 2022 summer season.[102] In this context, there is a need to ensure Canada has the ability to maximize its assets capable of providing icebreaking service in the Arctic. With the limited number of CCG icebreakers at present and reduced availability as they further age, there is a need to look elsewhere for additional solutions. The new AOPS s may provide such a solution for very limited situations, which can help free up the medium and heavy CCG icebreakers for tasks that require their unique capabilities. As an indicator of the

---

102   Trine Jonassen, "Canada Prepares Increased Cruise Traffic Due to Climate Change," *High North News*, 21 April 2022, https://www.highnorthnews.com/en/canada-prepares-increased-cruise-traffic-due-climate-change; Karli Zschogner, "Inuvik, N.W.T., Braces for Surge in Tourism," *CBC News*, 6 April 2022, https://www.cbc.ca/news/canada/north/inuvik-tourism-boom-1.6409630; Joanne Stassen, "Tour Operators in Thaidene Nëné Indigenous Protected Area Poised for Post-pandemic Boom," *CBC News*, 30 January 2022, https://www.cbc.ca/news/canada/north/thaidene-nene-lutselk-e-tourism-1.6332375; CBC News, "'A Light at the End of the Tunnel': As Flights Return to the N.W.T., Tourism Operators Prepare for Guests," *CBC News*, 9 March 2022, https://www.cbc.ca/news/canada/north/flights-return-to-nwt-tourism-1.6377958; "As Arctic Marine Tourism Increases, How Can We Ensure It's Sustainable?," Arctic Council, May 10, 2021, https://arctic-council.org/news/as-arctic-marine-tourism-increases-how-can-we-ensure-its-sustainable/; "Canadian Arctic Cruises," Ponant, 2022, https://en.ponant.com/destinations/canadian-arctic; "View All Departures," Quark Expeditions, 2022, https://www.quarkexpeditions.com/ca/departures?f%5B0%5D=departure_destination%3Acanada; "Itinerary and Pricing: Heart of the Arctic," Adventure Canada, 2022, https://www.adventurecanada.com/expedition-cruise/heart-of-the-arctic/heart-of-the-arctic-2022.

likelihood of such a future, Marc Mes, Director General of Canadian Coast Guard Fleet and Maritime Services, had indicated in May 2022 that the CCG is actively exploring how the RCN's AOPSs can contribute to the CCG's missions in the Arctic. In his words, the AOPSs have the potential to serve as effective 'force multipliers' for the CCG's icebreakers.[103] With two AOPSs expected to carry out Arctic patrols in summer 2022 despite only three of the six having been built, it is clear that the AOPSs will have a high degree of presence during the busiest season in the Arctic and will provide much of the federal government's on-water response capabilities into the future.[104]

---

103   Marc Mes, Canadian Coast Guard Director General Fleet and Services, interview with author and public remarks, Westin Ottawa, Canadian Global Affairs Institute, Defending the Continent: A Pan-Domain and Pan-Canada Approach, 19 May 2022.

104   Sheldon Gillis, "The @RoyalCanNavy ships @HMCS_NCSM_HDW, #MARGARETBROOKE and #GOOSEBAY will sail with our Danish allies in #HDMSTRITON this summer for CA's #OPNANOOK22" (@HighSeasSkipper, 13 June 2022), https://twitter.com/HighSeasSkipper/status/1536511677470068741.

Mitigating the Tyranny of Time and Distance: Community-based Organizations and Marine Mass Rescue Operations in Inuit Nunangat

Peter Kikkert, Calvin Aivgak Pedersen, and P. Whitney Lackenbauer

Abstract

In Inuit Nunangat, increased vessel traffic, uncharted seabed, the presence of ice hazards, extreme weather, and inexperienced operators increase the risk of marine transportation accidents and concomitant mass rescue operations (MRO). Marine MROs are low-probability, high-consequence scenarios that are complex and challenging wherever they occur. In Inuit Nunangat, challenges are exacerbated by austere environmental conditions, limited support infrastructure, inadequate local medical capacity, and fewer vessels of opportunity that can be called upon for assistance. Perhaps the most serious challenges are those posed by the tyranny of time and distance. Given the vast distances involved and the position of Canada's primary search and rescue assets in the southern parts of the country, the arrival of SAR resources on-scene can take significant time. In this chapter, we argue that community-based organizations (CBOs) would act as valuable force multipliers both at sea and shoreside during a marine MRO. We use the results of a mass rescue tabletop exercise involving community responders from Nunavut, follow-up interviews, and additional scenario-based discussions to develop the functions that CBOs could perform. We also provide a roadmap for how to best prepare community responders to take on these roles and to ensure that their capabilities are reflected in relevant mass rescue and emergency plans.

Keywords

major marine disaster – mass rescue operation – search and rescue – community-based organizations – Canadian Arctic

© PETER KIKKERT ET AL., 2023 | DOI:10.1163/9789004508576_010

1   **Introduction**

On 27 August 2010 at 1832 Mountain Daylight Time (MDT), the expedition cruise ship *Clipper Adventurer*, with 128 passengers and 69 crew on board, ran aground on a known shoal in Coronation Gulf, approximately 55 nautical miles east of the community of Kugluktuk, Nunavut. With the vessel listing 5° to portside the crew carried out emergency procedures, sounded the tanks, and lowered the lifeboats. The accident caused "extensive damage" to the hull and holed thirteen double–bottom tanks and compartments, including four full diesel oil tanks.[1] Over the next few hours, passengers carried on with their regular routine while the crew made two unsuccessful attempts to back off the shoal and refloat the ship. The situation could have escalated quickly and dramatically during this critical period. After its investigation into the incident, Canada's Transportation Safety Board found that the vessel's master did not have "sufficient damage stability information to assess whether or not the vessel would be stable once off the shoal" and concluded that without a complete seaworthiness assessment and on-scene search and rescue resources, the refloat attempts could have placed the passengers and crew at great risk.[2]

At 1915 MDT on 27 August, Marine Communications and Traffic Services (MCTS) Inuvik advised Joint Rescue Coordination Centre (JRCC) Trenton of the grounding, which immediately issued an Enhanced Group Calling (EGC) SafetyNet broadcast with distress priority at a 200-mile radius around the stricken vessel to alert possible vessels of opportunity. At 1932 MDT, JRCC Trenton tasked the Canadian Coast Guard (CCG) icebreaker *Amundsen* to respond to the incident, while preparing a Hercules aircraft with air-droppable search and rescue kits on board to proceed to the scene with an estimated time of arrival (ETA) of 3 hours. The SAR coordinator stood the aircraft down, however, when *Clipper Adventurer*'s captain advised that the vessel was not taking on water and was in no immediate danger. *Amundsen* arrived on scene at 1000 MDT on 29 August after transiting 270 nautical miles and conducting hydrographic surveys on the way to ensure its own safety. While all 69 crew members remained on board the cruise ship, *Amundsen* took off the passengers and safely disembarked them in Kugluktuk shortly after midnight on 30 August.[3]

---

1   Transportation Safety Board of Canada (TSB), *Marine Transportation Safety Investigation Report M10H006* (Gatineau: Transportation Safety Board, 2012), https://www.bst-tsb.gc.ca /eng/rapports-reports/marine/2010/m10h0006/m10h0006.html. See also E.J. Stewart and J. Dawson, "A Matter of Good Fortune? The Grounding of the Clipper Adventurer in the Northwest Passage, Arctic Canada," *Arctic* 64:2 (2011): 263–267, https://doi.org/10.14430/arctic4113.

2   TSB 2012 (n 1).

3   Id.

Throughout the two-day incident, the Coast Guard and JRCC provided community leaders and responders in Kugluktuk with minimal information. The community's well organized and effective marine and ground search and rescue (SAR) responders were not mobilized, nor was its Canadian Ranger patrol or other first responders, such as the volunteer fire department. Only a couple of hours before the passengers were offloaded did the Coast Guard inform Kugluktuk's hamlet office that they were in bound. Unfortunately, no one in the office knew where to locate the community's emergency plan, let alone put it into operation.[4] Hamlet officials quickly called Nunavut Emergency Management asking for instruction, particularly on how to handle the sudden influx of passengers given the limited resources available in the community.[5] When the Coast Guard started to barge in the passengers, hastily organized community volunteers used their truck lights to illuminate the landing site, while groups were loaded onto Kugluktuk's commercial bus and taken to the recreational complex. Meanwhile, hamlet officials scrambled to gather blankets and pillows for the passengers and asked the owner of the local Northern store to open to provide food. Fortunately for Kugluktuk's supplies and essential services, the evacuees did not remain in the community for long—that morning a Canadian North charter arrived to take them south.[6]

Looking back on the incident, Kugluktuk's SAR volunteers, Rangers, and other first responders wonder what would have happened if *Clipper Adventurer* had required immediate assistance. What if the weather or sea state had been less than pristine? What if the passengers had been evacuated into zodiacs or lifeboats? What if they had to establish a temporary camp on the land? What if Kugluktuk had to house, feed, and provide medical aid to passengers and crew for an extended period? What would their impact have been on the community's limited fuel, food, and sanitation resources?[7] "[The *Clipper Adventurer*] was kind of a wake-up call, you know. I mean, if things had worked out differently, those people may have needed a lot of help from us, they weren't that far from the community," explained one community responder. "We started

4   Jane George, "Nunavut Communities Fear Disasters from Air and Sea," *Nunatsiaq News*, 26 August 2011.

5   Liane Benoit, *Perspectives on Emergency Response in the Canadian Arctic: Sinking of the MS Arctic Sun in Cumberland Sound, Nunavut. Part C: Findings of the Hypothetical Scenario* (Toronto: Munk-Gordon Arctic Security Program, 2014), 14, http://gordonfoundation.ca /resource/perspectives-on-emergency-response-in-the-canadian-arctic-part-b.

6   TSB 2012 (n 1); Jane George, "Stranded Passengers Find Warmth in Kugluktuk," *Nunatsiaq News*, 30 August 2010.

7   Kugluktuk Coast Guard Auxiliary, Ranger Patrol, and GSAR team, interview with Peter Kikkert, October 2019, Kugluktuk, Nunavut.

talking about it more, what we could do, what the community could do, what it would be like."[8]

Subsequent years have brought additional accidents and more vessel traffic to the waters of Inuit Nunangat—the Inuit homeland in Canada. Several tanker, resupply, and fishing vessels have run aground, hit ice, or experienced mechanical problems. In 2018, the research vessel *Akademik Ioffe* grounded on a rocky shoal in the Gulf of Boothia about 78 nautical miles north-northwest of Kugaaruk. While passengers were evacuated and transferred to *Ioffe*'s sister passenger vessel *Akademik Sergey Vavilov*, it had been a close call.[9] In its aftermath, residents of Kugaaruk asked the same questions as their counterparts in Kugluktuk, while lamenting the quality of information and communication provided to the community over the course of the incident.[10] These accidents occurred against the backdrop of increased vessel traffic in Inuit Nunangat, which grew 37 percent from 2015 and 2019—a trend that is expected to continue as sea ice conditions improve.[11] Uncharted seabed, the presence of ice hazards, extreme weather, inexperienced operators, and the tendency of expedition cruise vessels to leave well-known shipping routes, all increase the accident risk. While more marine traffic means more vessels of opportunity that could respond during such an event, any mass rescue operation (MRO) in the region would still be incredibly challenging. "I'm not too worried about supply ships that come up every year, even though they could run into trouble," noted one community responder. "The cruise ships though … Obviously, we haven't had them up here the last couple of years because of COVID. But they'll come back and they might not know what they are doing, or have some bad luck, or go somewhere they shouldn't. We have to keep on getting ready."[12]

In this chapter, we argue that community-based Canadian Coast Guard Auxiliary (CCGA) units, Marine SAR Societies, ground search and rescue (GSAR)

---

8   Community responder from Kugluktuk, interview with by Peter Kikkert, January 2022.

9   TSB, *Marine Transportation Safety Investigation Report M18C0225* (Gatineau: TSB, 2021), https://www.tsb.gc.ca/eng/rapports-reports/marine/2018/m18c0225/m18c0225.html.

10   Kugaaruk Ground Search and Rescue team members and Canadian Ranger Patrol, interview with Peter Kikkert, January 2020, Cambridge Bay, Nunavut.

11   N. van Luijk, J. Holloway, N. Carter, J. Dawson, and A. Orawiec, *Gap Analysis: Shipping and Coastal Management in Inuit Nunangat. A Report Prepared for Inuit Tapiriit Kanatami* (Ottawa: ITK, 2021); Jackie Dawson, L. Pizzolato, S.E.L. Howell, L. Copeland, and M.E. Johnston, "Temporal and Spatial Patterns of Ship Traffic in the Canadian Arctic from 1990 to 2015," *Arctic* 71:1 (2018):15–26; Jackie Dawson, L. Copeland, O. Mussells, and N. Carter, *Shipping Trends in Nunavut 1990–2015: A Report Prepared for the Nunavut General Monitoring Program* (Ottawa, Canada and Iqaluit, Nunavut, 2017).

12   Kugluktuk Ground Search and Rescue Team and Marine Rescue, interview with Peter Kikkert, January 2022.

teams, Canadian Ranger patrols, Inuit Guardians and Marine Monitors, Civil Air Search and Rescue Association members, volunteer fire departments, and other community-based first responders would act as valuable force multipliers both at sea and shoreside during a marine mass rescue operation. Currently, federal and territorial agencies have done little to determine the specific roles and responsibilities these groups could take on. We use the results of a mass rescue tabletop exercise involving community responders from the Kitikmeot Region of Nunavut and their government partners, follow-up interviews, and additional scenario-based discussions to develop the functions that community-based organizations could perform during a major marine disaster and mass rescue operation in Inuit Nunangat/Canadian Arctic. We also provide a roadmap for how to best prepare community responders to take on these roles and to ensure that their capabilities are reflected in relevant mass rescue and emergency plans.

2   Background: Mass Rescue Operations, the Capability Gap, and the Arctic

The International Maritime Organization (IMO) defines an MRO as "an immediate response to a large number of persons in distress so that the capabilities normally available for search and rescue authorities are inadequate."[13] MROs are low-probability, high-consequence scenarios that are complex and challenging wherever they occur, requiring well planned and coordinated responses from multiple organizations and governance levels, shared situational awareness, comprehensive evacuation protocols, sustained accountability of passengers, the transportation of large numbers of survivors, and, potentially, a large-scale medical response. The condition of the vessel, distance from shore, and severity of the environment make a difference during an MRO, as does the adequacy of equipment and procedures aboard the distressed vessel.[14]

---

13   International Maritime Organization (IMO), *Guidance for Mass Rescue Operations* (London: IMO, 2003), http://imo.udhb.gov.tr/dosyam/EKLER/201381214504COMSAR1Circ31Guidance ForMassRescueOperations.Pdf; IMO, *International Aeronautical and Maritime Search and Rescue IAMSAR Manual* (London: IMO, 2016).
14   See, for instance, Richard Button and Thomas Gorgol, "Understanding the Challenge: Mass Rescue Operations at Sea," in *Cooperation and Engagement in the Asia-Pacific Region*, eds., Myron H. Nordquist, John Norton Moore, and Ronán Long (Leiden: Brill Nijhoff, 2020), 356–390; United States Coast Guard Research and Development Center, *Mass Rescue Operations Scoping Study, Final Report* (April 2007); International Maritime Rescue Federation (IMRF), *The International Maritime Rescue Federation Mass Rescue*

In the North American Arctic, these challenges are exacerbated by austere environmental conditions, cold temperatures, poor charting, limited support infrastructure, distant rescue forces, inadequate local medical capacity, communications difficulties, and fewer vessels of opportunity that can be called upon for assistance.[15] While a mass rescue could involve a tanker or resupply vessel, generally with 30 crew members or less on board, more worrisome is the volume of passengers that may have to be evacuated from a cruise ship. A

Operations Project. The Challenge: Acknowledging the Problem, and Mass Rescue Incident Types (IMRF, 2019), https://www.international-maritime-rescue.org/Handlers/Download.ashx?IDMF=d592a796-9d30-4bec-ab67-305294odab4d.

15   See, for instance, Arctic Domain Awareness Center (ADAC), *Rapporteur's Report Arctic-Related Incidents of National Significance Workshop on Maritime Mass Rescue Operations*, ADAC, 21–22 June 2016, https://arcticdomainawarenesscenter.org/Downloads /PDF/Arctic%20IoNS/ADAC_Arctic%20IoNS%202016_Report_160906.pdf; Rasmus Dahlberg, Morten Thanning Vendelø, Birgitte Refslund Sørensen and Kristian Cedervall Lauta, "Offshore is Onshore: Scalability, Synchronization, and Speed of Decision in Arctic SAR," *Scandinavian Journal of Military Studies* 3:1 (2020): 157–168, https://doi.org/10.31374/sjms; Rasmus Dahlberg, "Who is in the Center? A Case Study of a Social Network in an Emergency Management Organization," *International Journal of Emergency Services* 6:1 (2017): 52–66; James D. Ford and Dylan G. Clark, "Preparing for the Impacts of Climate Change Along Canada's Arctic Coast: The Importance of Search and Rescue," *Marine Policy* 108 (2019): 1–4, https://doi.org/10.1016/j.marpol.2019.103662; Floris Goerlandt and Ronald Pelot, "An Exploratory Application of the International Risk Governance Council Risk Governance Framework to Shipping Risks in the Canadian Arctic," in *Governance of Arctic Shipping: Rethinking Risk, Human Impacts and Regulation*, eds., Aldo Chircop, Floris Goerlandt, Claudio Aporta and Ronald Pelot (Cham: Springer, 2020), 15–41; Peter Kikkert and P. Whitney Lackenbauer, "Search and Rescue, Climate Change, and the Expansion of the Coast Guard Auxiliary in Inuit Nunangat / the Canadian Arctic," *Canadian Journal of Emergency Management* 1:2 (July 2021): 26–62; Kristian C. Lauta, Morten Thanning Vendelø, Bbirgitte Refslund Sørensen and Rasmus Dahlberg, "Conceptualizing Cold Disasters: Disaster Risk Governance at the Arctic edge," *International Journal of Disaster Risk Reduction* 31 (2018): 1276–1282, https://doi.org/10.1016/j.ijdrr.2017.12.011; Rebecca Pincus, "Large-scale Disaster Response in the Arctic: Are We Ready? Lessons from the Literature on Wicked Policy Problems," in *Arctic Yearbook 2015*, eds., Lassi Heininen, Heather Exner-Pirot, and Joël Plouffe, 1–13; Johannes Schmied *et al.*, "Maritime Operations and Emergency Preparedness in the Arctic: Competence Standards for Search and Rescue Operations Contingencies in Polar Waters," in *The Interconnected Arctic—UArctic Congress 2016*, eds., Kirsi Latola and Hannele Savela (Cham: Springer, 2017), 245–255; Timothy William James Smith, *Search and Rescue in the Arctic: Is the U.S. Prepared* (Santa Monica: RAND Corporation, 2017); United States Coast Guard, *Mass Rescue in Polar Waters: Case Study*, Office of Search and Rescue CG-534 (2010). See also Natalia Andreassen, Odd Jarl Borch, Svetlana Kuznetsova, and Sergey Markov, "Emergency Management in Maritime Mass Rescue Operations: The Case of the High Arctic," in *Sustainable Shipping in a Changing Arctic*, eds., Lawrence P. Hildebrand, Lawson W. Brigham and Tafsir M. Johansson (Cham: Springer International Publishing, 2018).

mass rescue operation involving hundreds of crew members and passengers would seriously strain Canada's SAR system, while the sudden influx of hundreds of evacuees would pose a significant challenge to the infrastructure and essential services of most communities in Inuit Nunangat.

Perhaps the most serious challenges are those posed by the tyranny of time and distance. Given the vast distances involved and the position of Canada's primary SAR assets in the southern parts of the country, the arrival of search and rescue resources on-scene can take significant time. *Amundsen*, for instance, took almost 40 hours to arrive on-scene during the *Clipper Adventurer* incident. The timelines for the aerial and marine response to the *Akademik Ioffe* incident are even more illustrative. In this incident, the vessel ran aground at 1113 MDT and issued a distress call an hour later, which reached JRCC Trenton at 1219 MDT, allowing it to initiate a response four minutes later. It tasked CCG icebreakers *Pierre Radisson* and *Amundsen* to deploy to the scene, with ETAs of 36 and 24 hours respectively, as well as *Ioffe*'s sister ship, *Akademik Sergey Vavilov*, with an ETA of 14 hours. At 1255 it also tasked two CC-130H Hercules aircraft from Trenton, Ontario, and Winnipeg, Manitoba, to respond, followed by another from Greenwood, Nova Scotia, and two CH-149 Cormorant helicopters from Greenwood and Gander, Newfoundland and Labrador.[16] The first Hercules was tasked at 1255 and took off from Trenton at 1359. With a maximum range of 7,222 km, it was able to fly directly to the scene, arriving at 2021 MDT, 6 hours and 22 minutes after having departed its airbase and 9 hours after *Ioffe*'s initial distress call. The first Cormorant was tasked at 1345, departed Gander at 1520, and with a maximum range of 1,018 km, required multiple fuel stops at Goose Bay, Newfoundland and Labrador, and Kuujjuaq, Quebec, before landing in Iqaluit at 0143 on 25 August, where, with its services no longer required, it remained.[17] Given how long it can take icebreakers and aircraft to arrive to an incident, if one occurs within the range of community responders, they have a good chance of being the first on-scene, possibly by several hours.

The literature on mass rescue operations has highlighted the value of local first responders and spontaneous volunteers, particularly on the shoreside

---

16   TSB 2021 (n 9). The TSB report states: "Two hours following the initiation of its SAR response, as JRCC staff became concerned that the *Akademik Ioffe* was attempting to refloat itself and might have to be abandoned by its complement, the MAJAID contingency plan was activated. The MAJMAR contingency plan was activated 37 minutes later. Because all aeronautical SAR assets were stationed at their respective airbases in Winnipeg, Trenton, Gander, and Greenwood, multi-hour flights were forecasted and extra relief flight crews and SAR specialists were paged from their homes."

17   Id. *Amundsen* deployed its Bell 429 helicopter at 0741 to oversee the evacuation of *Ioffe*'s passengers to *Vavilov* and the icebreaker arrived on scene at 0758.

component of a response.[18] The definition of an MRO is based on the idea of a capability gap: that 'capabilities normally available to the SAR authorities are inadequate'—both in terms of SAR assets and shoreside emergency response resources. Mass rescues require SAR planners and coordinators to 'think outside the box' and identify additional capabilities to help close this gap.[19] While vessels of opportunity and other government resources fall into this category, so to do local responders from an array of emergency services and spontaneous volunteers who may possess a wide range of skills and equipment.

Recent workshops and studies on mass rescue operations in the Arctic have also emphasized the potential value of local responders and volunteers, particularly if an incident were to occur near a community. Past maritime mass rescue tabletops and workshops in Alaska have explored how local communities could best be partnered with to improve shared situational awareness by leveraging local knowledge and by providing shoreside support.[20] In the Canadian context, the 2014 case study completed by Liane Benoit for the Munk-Gordon Arctic Security Program, which involved the hypothetical sinking of a cruise ship in Cumberland Sound near Pangnirtung, Nunavut, highlighted the ability and willingness of local officials and community members to be involved in a rescue. More negatively, Benoit's study indicated that a lack of planning and preparation, jurisdictional issues, and general confusion over mandates and approaches could undermine these efforts.[21] Thus, while previous studies have

---

18   See, for instance, Joshua Gilbert, *The United States Coast Guard and Spontaneous Volunteers: Collaboration or Chaos During Disaster Response* (MA Thesis, Naval Postgraduate School, 2021); Button and Gorgol (n 14); and the various chapters in IMRF, *The International Maritime Rescue Federation Mass Rescue Operations Project* (IMRF, 2019), https://www.international-maritime-rescue.org/Pages/Site/mass-rescue-operations/Category/mro-library.

19   IMRF, *The Challenge* (n 13); IMRF, *The International Maritime Rescue Federation Mass Rescue Operations Project: Mass Rescue Operations: The Capability Gap* (IMRF, 2019), https://www.international-maritime-rescue.org/Handlers/Download.ashx?IDMF=3a282858-673e-43c0-be77-f83f0188a446.

20   Alaska Mass Rescue Operation (MRO) Exercise 2009, 15 July 2009, https://www.international-maritime-rescue.org/Handlers/Download.ashx?IDMF=6574f86a-6780-48dd-92b5-bba4c1275c91; Arctic Domain Awareness Center, *Rapporteur's Report Arctic-Related Incidents of National Significance Workshop on Maritime Mass Rescue Operations*, 21–22 June 2016, Anchorage, Alaska, https://web-oup.s3-fips-us-gov-west-1.amazonaws.com/default/assets/File/Final%20Arctic%20related%20IoNS%20Report%206%20Sep%202016.pdf.

21   Liane Benoit, *Perspectives on Emergency Response in the Canadian Arctic: Sinking of the MSArctic Sun in Cumberland Sound, Nunavut. Parts A, B, C* (Toronto: Munk-Gordon Arctic Security Program, 2014), http://gordonfoundation.ca/resource/perspectives-on-emergency-response-in-the-canadian-arctic/.

suggested the potential value of community responders to an MRO in the Arctic context, they have done little to flesh out the specific functions these actors could fulfill that are reflective of their mandates, training, and capabilities.

3   Methodology: The Kitikmeot SAR Project

Exploring the roles of community-based organizations in mass rescue operations was a primary objective of the ongoing Kitikmeot Search and Rescue Project. Launched in 2019, the project focuses on identifying strengths, challenges of, and new approaches to community-based SAR operations in Nunavut's Kitikmeot region, which encompasses the communities of Kugluktuk, Cambridge Bay (Ikaluktutiak), Gjoa Haven, Taloyoak, and Kugaaruk. Data gathering for the project started with interviews and focus groups with SAR responders in each community to assess local capabilities.[22] This data was then used to facilitate capability-based planning exercises, which determined whether a community has the right mix of assets it requires to respond to the wide array of SAR missions it might face. During this phase of the project, community responders flagged major marine disasters and mass rescue operations as a growing concern.[23]

During the capacity-mapping and capability-based planning workshops in October 2019, community participants highlighted the need to elevate discussions to the regional level, where participants could share their knowledge with and learn from practitioners in other communities and discuss capacity

22   The Kitikmeot SAR Project was based on a community-collaborative approach that emphasizes the co-creation of knowledge between community responders, government practitioners, and a diverse and interdisciplinary team of researchers. With the Kitikmeot SAR groups' support, the Nunavut Research Institute (license 04 009 20R-M) and the St. Francis Xavier University Research Ethics Board (Certification: 23923) approved the project. This project was guided by Inuit Tapiriit Kanatami's *Inuit Research Strategy*, particularly its core emphasis on respectful and beneficial research for all Inuit, on building Inuit research capacity, and on ensuring that funding aligns with Inuit research priorities. Inuit leadership shaped and drove the development and execution of every aspect of the project. See Inuit Tapiriit Kanatami (ITK), *National Inuit Strategy on Research* (Ottawa: ITK, 2018). The research project also followed the principles of ownership, control, access, and possession (OCAP), and was carried out in accordance with Chapter 9 of the *TCPS2 Tri-Council Policy Statement: Ethical Conduct for Research Involving Humans: Research Involving First Nations, Inuit, and Métis Peoples of Canada*, https://ethics.gc.ca/eng/tcps2-eptc2_chapter9-chapitre9.html#toc09-1.
23   See Peter Kikkert and P. Whitney Lackenbauer, "'A Great Investment in Our Communities': Strengthening Nunavut's Whole of Society Search and Rescue Capabilities," *Arctic* 74:3 (September 2021): 258–275, https://doi.org/10.14430/arctic73099.

issues with federal and territorial partners. They pointed out that a roundtable would serve as both a research opportunity and a resilience-building measure. In January 2020, we held the Kitikmeot Roundtable on SAR at the Canadian High Arctic Research Station in Cambridge Bay. It brought together fifty-five community responders from the five Kitikmeot communities, academics, and representatives of federal and territorial departments and agencies to discuss best practices, lessons learned, and future requirements for search and rescue.[24] Given ongoing community concerns about the roles they might have to play in a marine mass rescue, community responders also asked that the roundtable be used to conduct an MRO tabletop exercise (TTX).

Guided by a facilitator, tabletop exercises are discussion-based sessions where responders meet in informal, classroom-like settings to discuss emergency roles and to work through a particular emergency situation. In this case, roundtable participants worked through a scenario involving the grounding of an expedition cruise ship off Unahitak Island near Cambridge Bay. Chris Bianco and Jay Collins, members of the CCG Arctic Region's Training and Exercising Industry Program, which works to improve interoperability and preparedness among key stakeholders in the event of an incident in the Canadian Arctic, facilitated the exercise. They set the scene and then moved through a series of scenario injects that gradually increased the complexity and difficulty of the rescue operation. Broken into small groups, participants worked through the basic scenario to determine responses and to work through challenges. The facilitators also encouraged participants from the other Kitikmeot communities to apply the scenario to their specific local contexts to discuss how the responses and challenges might differ. Following each scenario inject, the facilitators brought the entire group back together for a debrief.

The exercise involved representatives from the major community, territorial, and federal organizations that would be involved in a mass rescue operation in the Kitikmeot (for further discussion of these entities see Charron and Snider in this volume). Participants included members from the CCGA units in Cambridge Bay, Kugluktuk, and Gjoa Haven. CCGA units are made up of trained local volunteers who use their own vessels or a community vessel (such as those provided under the Indigenous Community Boat Volunteer Pilot Program) to respond to emergencies. CCGA members receive specialized training, insurance coverage, and reimbursement for certain operational costs, but they

---

24   Peter Kikkert, Angulalik Pedersen and P. Whitney Lackenbauer, *Kitikmeot Roundtable on Search and Rescue: Summary Report / Qitiqmiuni Katimatjutauyuq Qiniqhiayinit Annaktinillu – Naunaitkutat*, Kitikmeot SAR Project, 2020, https://kitikmeotca.files.wordpress.com/2020/08/kitikmeot-roundtable-on-sar-summary-report.pdf.

also fundraise to purchase additional equipment. Cambridge Bay and Kugluk-tuk have long-established Auxiliary units, while Gjoa Haven's stood-up in 2017 as part of the federal government's Oceans Protection Plan (OPP) which seeks to expand the CCGA throughout the Arctic. Members of Arctic Auxiliary units strengthen SAR operations by improving response times, serving as SAR detectives, contributing to marine safety, and, most importantly, by integrating their local and traditional knowledge and skills into the broader search and rescue system.[25] In 2022, the CCGA counted 32 units in the Coast Guard's new Arctic Region, with 451 members and 46 vessels and plans for future expansion.[26]

Members of each community's all-volunteer ground search and rescue teams and SAR Committees also engaged in the TTX. While GSAR members volunteer their time and typically use their personal equipment, Nunavut Emergency Management (NEM) provides funding to cover expenses such as training, fuel, lubricants, emergency supplies, food, and equipment repair.[27] In northern communities that lack a Coast Guard Auxiliary unit, marine search and rescue is often conducted by SAR Committees and GSAR team members, as is the case in Taloyoak and Kugaaruk.

Representatives from the Canadian Ranger patrols in each Kitikmeot community also shared their insights during the TTX. Canadian Rangers are part-time, non-commissioned Canadian Armed Forces (CAF) Reservists who serve as the "eyes, ears, and voice" of the Canadian Armed Forces in remote parts of the country "which cannot conveniently or economically be covered by other elements of the CAF."[28] They are not intended to act as combat forces and receive no tactical military training. Instead, their regular tasks include surveillance and presence patrols, collecting local data for the CAF, reporting unusual sightings, participation in community events, and assisting with domestic military operations. By virtue of their capabilities and presence, Rangers also regularly support other government agencies in preventing, preparing for, responding to, and recovering from the broad spectrum of emergency and

---

25   See Kikkert and Lackenbauer (n 15).
26   Christian Bertelsen, Regional Director, Arctic Programs, Arctic Region, Canadian Coast Guard, Presentation to Advancing Collaboration in Canada-U.S. Arctic Regional Security III (ACCUSARS III) Virtual Conference: The Eastern North American Arctic Regions, 24–25 March 2022.
27   See Kikkert and Lackenbauer (n 23).
28   Defence Administrative Orders and Directives (DAOD) 2020–2, "Canadian Rangers," Department of National Defence, 21 May 2015, https://www.canada.ca/en/department-national-defence/corporate/policies-standards/defence-administrative-orders-directives/2000-series/2020/2020-2-canadian-rangers.html.

disaster scenarios facing isolated communities.[29] Further, they often serve as search and rescue volunteers who know how to work effectively as a group. When searches go on for extended periods, the search area is too vast to be covered by all-volunteer SAR teams, and/or there are insufficient community volunteers, Rangers can be formally activated by the CAF and are then considered on an official military tasking for which they are paid. The CAF provides Canadian Rangers with flexible training that is tailored to local terrain and environmental conditions but generally involves several elements directly related to SAR and emergency response capabilities: first aid, wilderness first aid, GSAR, constructing emergency airstrips on land and ice, and communications.[30]

Importantly for the purposes of marine mass rescue operations, Rangers have an established maritime role. The official Ranger tasking list includes coastal and inland water surveillance. Ranger patrols often employ their boats to support their monitoring of vessel traffic in the Northwest Passage during Operation NANOOK-NUNAKPUT, and during training exercises Rangers often use boats to travel between destinations. In carrying out these tasks, Rangers employ their own marine vessels, for which they receive reimbursement according to an established equipment usage rate.[31]

Rounding out the community-based SAR organizations at the TXX were several Civil Air Search and Rescue Association (CASARA) volunteers from Cambridge Bay and Gjoa Haven. With funding and support from the military, CASARA supports the CAF's SAR mission by making available private aircraft, trained volunteer crews, and spotters for military aircraft during search missions. The CASARA members from Gjoa Haven and Cambridge Bay have received training as aerial spotters aboard military aircraft.[32]

---

29   See, for example, P. Whitney Lackenbauer, *The Canadian Rangers: A Living History* (Vancouver: UBC Press, 2012); P. Whitney Lackenbauer and Peter Kikkert, *Measuring the Success of the Canadian Rangers* (Report to the 1st Canadian Ranger Patrol Group, released October 2020) (Peterborough: North American and Arctic Defence and Security Network, 2020), https://www.naadsn.ca/wp-content/uploads/2020/10/Rangers-Success -Metrics-Lackenbauer-Kikkert-high-res.pdf; P. Whitney Lackenbauer, *The Canadian Armed Forces' Eyes, Ears, and Voice in Remote Regions: Selected Writings on the Canadian Rangers* (Peterborough: North American and Arctic Defence and Security Network, 2022).

30   Peter Kikkert and P. Whitney Lackenbauer, "The Canadian Rangers: Strengthening Community Disaster Resilience in Canada's Remote and Isolated Communities," *The Northern Review* 51 (2021): 1–33, https://doi.org/10.22584/nr51.2021.003.

31   See Peter Kikkert and P. Whitney Lackenbauer, "Bolstering Community-Based Marine Capabilities in the Canadian Arctic," *Canadian Naval Review* 15:2 (2019): 11–16.

32   Civil Air Search and Rescue Association, "What We Do," CASARA, n.d., https://www .casara.ca/en/casara.

Representatives from the Cambridge Bay hamlet office, the community's Royal Canadian Mounted Police (RCMP) detachment, and its volunteer fire department and ambulance services also attended. In case of a mass rescue operation, hamlet officials, in particular, the senior administrative official and assistant senior administrative official, would be heavily involved in coordinating emergency plans and mobilizing resources. RCMP, fire, and ambulance personnel would also provide valuable human power during a mass rescue, particularly shoreside and in the community.

In some communities, Inuit Guardians and Marine Monitors constitute other local resources that could be used to respond to a mass rescue operation, though they were not represented at the Roundtable. In the Kitikmeot Region, a team of Inuit Guardians from Gjoa Haven have protected and monitored the Wrecks of HMS *Erebus* and HMS *Terror* National Historic Site and offer an emergency response capability to any accidents or SAR activities that occur in the surrounding area.[33] In the Eastern Arctic, the Qikiqtani Inuit Association, with the support of Parks Canada and the Government of Nunavut, has established a Guardians program to monitor and manage the Tallurutiup Imanga National Marine Conservation Area (Lancaster Sound).[34] The Nunavut Inuit Marine Monitoring Program (IMMP) is an Inuit-led initiative that aims to collect information on shipping activities in the region that is relevant and useful to communities. The IMMP employs Inuit Marine Monitors during the shipping season to observe vessel activity and report on environmental conditions and wildlife.[35] During the TTX, responders were asked to consider what members of these groups could contribute, particularly in terms of improving on-scene situational awareness.

Finally, representatives from the Coast Guard, the Canadian Armed Forces, and Nunavut Emergency Management—all of which would be heavily involved in an Arctic marine disaster and mass rescue operation—also participated in the TTX. In the Kitikmeot, a marine mass rescue operation would be managed by JRCC Trenton (a CAF unit, staffed by personnel of the Royal Canadian Air

---

33   Kikkert and Lackenbauer (n 31).

34   Eilis Quinn, "Inuit Association Gets $900,000 to Monitor Marine Protected Area in Arctic Canada," *Eye on the Arctic*, 19 July 2018, https://www.rcinet.ca/eye-on-the-arctic/2018 /07/19/inuit-association-gets-900000-to-monitor-marine-protected-area-in-arctic -canada/.

35   Erin Abou-Abssi, "A New Way to Track Arctic Vessels, Oceans North," Oceans North, 11 January 2018, https://www.oceansnorth.org/en/blog/2018/01/nti-monitoring-program/; Fisheries and Oceans Canada, *Departmental Plan 2019–20* (Government of Canada, 2019), http://www.dfo-mpo.gc.ca/rpp/2019-20/dp-eng.html.

Force and the Canadian Coast Guard).[36] The CAF bears overall responsibility for the effective operation of the federal coordinated maritime and aeronautical search and rescue system.[37] During major marine and air disasters, the CAF is called upon to provide initial care and survival support, medical evacuation, and the deployment of its Major Air Disaster (MAJAID) Kits.[38] The CAF was represented at the TTX by the Staff Officer Search and Rescue Readiness, 1 Canadian Air Division Headquarters and by personnel from Joint Task Force North. The participation of CCG personnel in the TTX was key as the service is responsible for maritime SAR and actively engages in planning and preparing for marine disasters in the Arctic on an ongoing basis, particularly through its exercising program and crafting of the Major Maritime Disaster Contingency Plan. Lastly, Nunavut Emergency Management, which is based in Iqaluit, but would be heavily engaged in coordinating the establishment of shore facilities and casualty reception points and in mobilizing local resources, was represented at the TTX by its primary SAR trainer.[39]

The tabletop exercise was completed over the course of four hours. A post exercise debriefing attempted to summarize some of the key lessons learned during the exercise. Many community responders, however, indicated that they wanted more time to think through the situation and offer more concrete examples of how their organization might be able to respond. As a result, in

---

36   Royal Canadian Air Force, "An Overview of Our Search and Rescue Aircraft," Government of Canada, National Defence, Backgrounder, last modified 17 January 2022, https://www .canada.ca/en/department-national-defence/maple-leaf/rcaf/2020/09/an-overview-of -our-search-and-rescue-aircraft.html. The RCAF's primary SAR squadrons are: 442 (Transport and Rescue) Squadron/19 Wing Comox, BC; 435 (Transport and Rescue) Squadron/17 Wing Winnipeg, MB; 424 (Transport and Rescue) Squadron/8 Wing Trenton, ON; 413 (Transport and Rescue) Squadron/14 Wing Greenwood, NS; 103 (Rescue) Squadron/9 Wing Gander, NF.

37   Royal Canadian Air Force, "Search and Rescue," Government of Canada, last modified 20 January 2022, https://www.canada.ca/en/air-force/programs/search-rescue.html.

38   The RCAF has 4 MAJAID Kits and one training kit. Each can be air dropped and contain tents, sleeping bags, clothing, medical supplies, heaters, generators, water, and rations to support 80 people for up to 24 hours (so this response could support 400 people for 24 hrs, or 80 people for upwards of 5 days). See Department of National Defence, "Operation NANOOK," Government of Canada, last modified 14 July 2022, https://www.canada.ca /en/department-national-defence/services/operations/military-operations/current -operations/operation-nanook.html; Richard Lawrence, "OPERATION NANOOK - EXERCISE SOTERIA (MAJOR AIR DISASTER - MAJAID)," *Esprit de Corps*, 11 October 2018, http: //espritdecorps.ca/richard-lawrence/operation-nanook-exercise-soteria-major-air-disaster -majaid.

39   JRCC Trenton, *Trenton Search and Rescue Region: Major Maritime Disaster Contingency Plan* (Trenton: JRCC, 2011).

the months after the exercise, we also conducted follow-up interviews with participants, and, in the longer term, engaged in scenario-based discussions, in which the research team inserted new injects into the basic scenario (e.g., different environmental conditions, smaller and larger vessel complements, different locations) to elicit more responses. Discussions about mass rescue operations continued during community workshops and responder interviews in 2021 and 2022. We have integrated these responses and insights into the following narrative—an attempt to prioritize *unikkaaqatigiinniq* (the Inuit philosophy of story-telling) to relay meaning.

4   Scenario Case Study: The Sinking of MS *Arctic Explorer*

In late July 2023, MS *Arctic Explorer* is in the middle of a first-time eastbound transit of the Northwest Passage. Sailing through Coronation Gulf, the vessel has enjoyed excellent weather and favourable ice conditions and is on schedule to arrive in the community of Cambridge Bay on the morning of 28 July. Even though new to the waters of the Canadian Arctic, the expedition's organizers have foregone the common 'buddy system' which sees cruise ships pair up for mutual support. The vessel has 310 people on board, 110 crew members and 200 passengers, who range in age from 15–85.

The good fortune *Arctic Explorer* has enjoyed so far in terms of ice conditions ends abruptly when the presence of hard, multi-year ice forces the vessel to alter its pre-established route while transiting towards Cambridge Bay. Due to its lack of familiarity with the region, at 0833 MDT, *Arctic Explorer* ran aground on the southeastern point of Unahitak Island, just over 23 nautical miles from the community. The temperature is 3°C, there is a steady, cold drizzle, and a moderate wind, resulting in light chop. The ship's captain follows the proper protocols and informs Marine Communications and Traffic Services Iqaluit, which then alerts JRCC Trenton.

Eager to get eyes on scene to verify the severity of the incident, the SAR Mission Coordinator at the JRCC in turn contacts the Cambridge Bay Coast Guard Auxiliary and tasks the unit to respond. The coordinator then tasks two Hercules aircraft from Trenton and Winnipeg to respond, with the first to arrive on scene in just over 5 hours, as well as the closest Coast Guard icebreaker, which is 20 hours away. The JRCC also notifies the Bell 212 helicopter that is often stationed in Cambridge Bay to service the North Warning System and asks it to be on standby to assist, while asking CASARA Nunavut to task two local spotters to the helicopter. Given that it is the summer months, many members of the Coast Guard Auxiliary unit are in the community rather than on the land in case their services are required. The CCGA unit leader is able to quickly gather twelve members and depart for the stricken vessel on their 28-foot, Silver Dolphin craft—obtained through the Indigenous Community Boat Volunteer Pilot Program—and their 17-foot Boston whaler. They arrive on scene at 1000 MDT, approximately an hour and a half after *Arctic Explorer* ran aground, and immediately make contact with the vessel's captain, while reporting vital information on the status of the ship and environmental conditions back to JRCC Trenton. The SAR Mission Coordinator designates the Auxiliary unit leader the on-scene coordinator, responsible for coordinating search and rescue operations on scene.

Meanwhile, the commanding officer of 1st Canadian Ranger Patrol Group activates the Cambridge Bay Ranger Patrol, tasking them to load up the six canvas Fort McPherson tents, Coleman stoves and lanterns, camping gear, satellite phones, first aid kits, and rations provided to the unit and as much fresh water as they can carry, before heading to the incident in their personal boats. Fourteen Rangers are able to gather on short notice and depart for the scene on five boats by 1000. At the same time, the Ranger patrol in Kugluktuk is placed on standby and its leaders are able to gather 15 members on short notice. The Rangers are told to stay in the community and await further instruction. If their services are required in Cambridge Bay, they can jump on the regularly scheduled Canadian North flight between the two communities and be there in hours.

On board *Arctic Explorer* the crew has sounded the tanks and determined that the vessel is taking on water. Bilge pumps have been activated, but are struggling to keep up with the ingress. At 1030 MDT, two hours after running aground, the ship's captain decides to temporarily evacuate the passengers into the ship's zodiacs. Like most adventure cruise ships, *Arctic Explorer* has zodiacs on board, and crew and passengers are far more familiar with their use than the vessel's lifeboats. The choppy waters, however, make the long zodiac ride to Cambridge Bay untenable. After the on-scene coordinator discusses the situation with the captain, members of the Cambridge Bay Auxiliary unit confer and identify a potential landing site on Unahitak Island, with a beach sloping down seaward to make the disembarking process safer, easier, and faster. Soon after, the Auxiliary vessels start to shepherd the zodiacs to the landing site.

As the first zodiacs are guided to the beach, the Canadian Rangers arrive and are briefed by the Auxiliary unit. They head to shore with the first zodiacs and, as crew members disembark passengers, the Rangers proceed to set up their MacPherson tents, use their stoves and lanterns to provide heat, and start brewing tea. The sight of the well-organized Ranger patrol wearing their bright red hoodies and quickly putting up tents and offering shelter, warmth, and hot drinks has a calming effect on the first passengers to arrive on the island. As more passengers land, they take turns warming themselves in the Ranger tents, and additional shelters are eventually provided by expedition staff from the ship. Many Rangers have first aid training, as do members of the Auxiliary, and can provide basic care to injured passengers and watch for signs of deterioration due to the environmental conditions. Through it all, the on-scene coordinator feeds information back to the JRCC, while the Rangers provide consistent situation reports to Joint Task Force North, keeping it apprised of the situation on the ground.

Since the first reports of the grounding reached them shortly after JRCC Trenton initiated its response, Nunavut Emergency Management personnel in Iqaluit have been in contact with the Senior Administrative Officer, the RCMP, and other hamlet officials in Cambridge Bay. Together they activate the community's emergency plan, establish an emergency operations centre, and mobilize the community's health centre, GSAR team, volunteer fire department, and ambulance services—at least those individuals not already out with the Rangers and Auxiliary. They then inform the community's hotels and restaurants, the Co-op and Northern Store, the Canadian High Arctic Research Station, and schools of the situation and of the possible influx of hundreds of passengers and crew. Previous capacity mapping has shown that, as a regional hub, Cambridge Bay has the capacity to safely accommodate, feed, and support up to 1,700 evacuees for 72 hours, although potential challenges would arise around the availability of cots and bedding, hygiene and sanitation services.[40] This knowledge makes the community's leadership far more confident about their ability to sustain evacuees from the cruise ship.

At 1330 MDT, with the wind and chop dying down, the captain makes the decision to evacuate all passengers and most of the crew to Cambridge Bay. The Rangers on Unahitak Island and the Coast Guard Auxiliary members, who have remained in their boats in case the crew remaining on the ship require assistance, confer and suggest that they could cut the distance in half by disembarking at Long Point, which is only 15 km from town and has road access. This would reduce the water distance and allow the boats to shuttle people more quickly to shore. The JRCC confirms the plan and asks the North Warning System helicopter to carry any injured or infirm from Unahitak to Long Point. While some Rangers remain on the island to assist in warming passengers, the rest of the patrol takes to their boats and starts working with the zodiacs to carry evacuees to Long Point, helping to expedite the process. At this point, several community members have also ventured to the scene in their private

40   Task Force Nunavut, *Hamlet of Cambridge Bay: Capacity Analysis*, Department of National Defence, Operation NUNALIVUT 2018.

craft and the on-scene commander is able to direct them to assist with carrying passengers to Long Point. The CCGA boats shepherd the watercraft, while the on-scene coordinator manages the operation with the cruise ship's captain.

Meanwhile, informed of the decision, the hamlet's emergency operations centre mobilizes the community's seven buses and shuttles and sends them, with RCMP escort, to the gravel pit just off the beach at Long Point. To provide extra assistance, they ask the community's GSAR team and ambulance services to drive out to the landing site as well. They then make a plan to send the passengers directly to the Canadian High Arctic Research Station. This will be the major muster and reception point in the community. Several desks are quickly set up at the entrance to the station and run by members of the volunteer fire department, who are told how to account for the passengers and what essential information to gather as they check them in—for instance, if any immediately require prescription medications that they were forced to leave on the ship. Hamlet officials have also been in touch with the expedition company that has chartered *Arctic Explorer* and, with their direction and funds, have organized for warm food and beverages to be brought to the research station. While some of the 44 beds in the station are being used by researchers, many are open, and plans are made for elderly and infirm passengers to be taken to these accommodation units as soon as they are fed.

As the Ranger boats and zodiacs bring the first wave of passengers to Long Point, the community GSAR team and ambulance staff help to disembark them and quickly guide them to the awaiting buses and shuttles. Informed that buses would be waiting for them, expedition staff have already devised a plan to account for passengers at the bus doors, which they can then compare with the check-ins done by the community volunteers at the research station. As the first passengers make the short ride to Cambridge Bay, the first Hercules flies over the scene. The Rangers and zodiacs head back to Unahitak for the next wave of passengers.

As the passengers are dropped off at the research station, they are registered by the community volunteers, enjoy a hot meal, and are allowed to explore the large facility. To avoid swamping the station as more passengers arrive, hamlet officials and other community volunteers take small groups to the community hall and the school gyms to await their flight home, which, if weather prevails, should come in early the next morning.

When the final group of passengers is registered at the research station, one of the first evacuees informs an expedition staff member that she cannot find an elderly friend she had met on the voyage. They had been separated when he went back to his cabin to retrieve medication during the initial zodiac evacuation from *Arctic Explorer*. A quick check of the lists of passengers registered at Long Point and at the research station show the passenger to be missing, while the crew that have remained on board the cruise ship also cannot locate him. This information is communicated to the Auxiliary unit, which quickly works with the Hercules overhead to begin a marine search, while the Rangers begin a search on Unahitak Island, and the GSAR team begins a shoreline search at Long Point. The missing passenger's information is also provided to the community radio, which issues an alert to Cambridge Bay residents—if he made it into town, he will be recognized before too long. It is the Rangers who find the man, however. One of the last people to be brought from the ship to Unahitak Island, he had decided to go for a quick walk along the shore, only to badly hurt his ankle. The Rangers quickly stabilize him and transport him back to Cambridge Bay in one of their boats, in time to be flown south with the rest of the passengers.

5 Assessment and Analysis: Community Responders and Mass Rescue Operations

The Kitikmeot SAR Project's mass rescue TTX and discussions with community responders highlight the sophistication of their understandings of and plans for MROs and their willingness to provide assistance. If an incident occurred close enough to their communities, not only would they respond, but they would likely be the first responders. One member of the Cambridge Bay Ranger Patrol explained that, "If a major emergency happened ... people would come from the community to help. That's just the way it is up here."[41] In discussing a potential marine disaster off the shores of their community, another TTX participant noted that, "We may not be happy that you've brought this trouble, but we will try our best to help you out of it."[42] A community responder offered an explanation for this willingness to help, the sentiment of which was shared by many: "We have a responsibility for what happens on the Northwest Passage. These are our waters. We will protect them. We will help the people using them. It's simple."[43]

In terms of specific roles and responsibilities that community-based groups could play in a mass rescue, the first is information sharing. The local

---

41   Cambridge Bay Canadian Ranger, interview with Peter Kikkert, Cambridge Bay, Nunavut, April 2019.

42   Community participant, Kitikmeot Roundtable on Search and Rescue 2020, Cambridge Bay, Nunavut, January 2020.

43   Kugluktuk Ground Search and Rescue and Marine Rescue, interview with Peter Kikkert, February 2022.

knowledge and information that community-based groups could provide on geography, environmental conditions, and community resources would be absolutely vital and could save lives. During the TTX, Cambridge Bay participants provided information on the geography of Unahitak Island, environmental and sea conditions, the safest evacuation routes, where passengers could be safely disembarked, and local resources that could be mobilized on the shoreside. They used their local knowledge to draw up a plan to move passengers from Unahitak to Long Point, rather than directly to Cambridge Bay, which would have involved more time on the water and a longer evacuation process. In a subsequent scenario-based discussion that focused on a cruise ship running aground beyond the range of community boats, community responders were able to identify a sheltered cove close to the incident site with a number of hunting cabins—a place of safety in which crew members and expedition staff could easily establish a temporary camp to await rescue.[44] "We know the local weather," explained one participant in the TTX. "We know the conditions. We know the water and ice, the rocks. We know how the ice works. We know the best routes to take, the fastest, the safest routes to take. We know things that you can't get from a GPS or a weather report. We know how the tides work ... You have to listen."[45]

The information-sharing function of community responders is closely related to another important role: their ability to improve situational awareness. During the TTX, the Coast Guard Auxiliary unit was able to provide JRCC Trenton with a comprehensive visual assessment and ongoing appraisal of the situation: the condition of the ship, the conduct of its crew and captain, the weather and sea state, and on-scene SAR actions. During an actual mass rescue operation, this kind of sustained situational awareness would be vital to a SAR Mission Coordinator. One Ranger noted that a mass rescue operation would require patrol members to fulfill their primary function: acting as the 'eyes and ears' for the Canadian Armed Forces. Another Ranger noted that the protection of their communities is one of their most important responsibilities, so they would want to get eyes on the incident to assess whether there had been an oil or fuel spill, which they could then report to the proper authorities. In a mass rescue situation in which it might take hours for federal assets to arrive to an incident, the on-scene situational awareness provided by community responders would be invaluable.

---

44   Kugluktuk Canadian Ranger Patrol and Marine Rescue members, interview with Peter Kikkert, February 2021.

45   Community participant, Kitikmeot Roundtable on Search and Rescue 2020, Cambridge Bay, Nunavut, January 2020.

During the TTX, the leader of the Coast Guard Auxiliary unit also took on the essential role of on-scene coordinator. Usually this is the person in charge of the first rescue vessel to arrive on the scene, until relieved by a more capable vessel or unit. This individual will coordinate the scene, maintain communications with the JRCC and enact its instructions, share on-scene search actions, resources, and recommendations, relay the status of survivors, and generally support the commander of the vessel in distress. This individual or someone designated by them (e.g., a small-craft marshal), would also be in charge of directing spontaneous volunteers—for instance, additional community boats that might arrive on scene looking to assist.[46] The ability of spontaneous volunteers to provide assistance during a disaster event relies on the "capacity of agencies and authorities to integrate them quickly and effectively into a coordinated strategy."[47] Given their familiarity with their fellow community members, a local on-scene coordinator would be able to effectively coordinate their activities. Even in cases where a community responder is not the on-scene coordinator, directing community volunteers may still be best executed by any Auxiliary members present. "Other community members know who we are and what we do. They'd be willing to follow our lead, our instructions. Directing them would be an important role for us," concluded one Auxiliarist.[48]

Over the course of the TTX and subsequent discussions, community responders elaborated on several other key on-scene tasks they could undertake. They could retrieve people from the water, shepherd lifeboats or zodiacs to safe havens or to the community, help in offloading and tracking passengers, search for missing passengers, establish a camp to provide warmth and shelter, give first aid, provide predator control, and have a positive influence on morale by reassuring evacuees that the situation is under control. Further, if there are injured or at-risk passengers, community boats could be used to rapidly bring them to the community for medical treatment and evacuation. Even when Coast Guard icebreakers or other vessels of opportunity are on scene, small community watercraft could still play important SAR roles. One common MRO coordination practice is to establish a 'cordon' to avoid vessels entering areas in which they would be of minimal assistance or do harm. The cordon is generally a circle of ships centred on the vessel in distress. If there

46   IMRF, *The International Maritime Rescue Federation Mass Rescue Operations Project: The On Scene Coordinator* (IMRF, 2019), https://www.international-maritime-rescue.org/Han dlers/Download.ashx?IDMF=6f3fba63-da98-41f9-b7fb-7233947824b7.

47   International Federation of Red Cross and Red Crescent Societies cited in Gilbert (n 18).

48   Cambridge Bay Coast Guard Auxiliary Unit member, interview with Peter Kikkert, August 2021.

are larger vessels to receive people, the cordon will work like a spoked wheel, with rescue ships taking up position at the spokes, and smaller craft—such as community boats—ferrying passengers from the vessel in distress or lifeboats to these receiving craft.[49]

With the expert input of Coast Guard SAR specialists, community responders are sure that they could develop even more potential on-scene roles. If expected to take on these roles, however, community responders would also like plans in place to address the physical and mental toll of responding to an MRO, particularly a mass casualty event. Inuit SAR responders have consistently cited lack of access to mental health supports and critical incident stress management as a key gap that needs to be addressed.[50] Plans for MROs should consider how to provide community responders—both on-scene and shoreside—the mental and physical health supports they require.

Community-based organizations and volunteers would play a leading role in shoreside operations during a mass rescue, which are always complex and demanding, and require extensive coordination between federal, territorial/provincial, and municipal agencies, the JRCC, and cruise/expedition companies.[51] These operations rely on effective local contingency plans developed by territorial/provincial emergency management organizations. TTX participants noted that, in the case of Nunavut, emergency management personnel are stationed in Iqaluit, so much of the responsibility for a shoreside response would fall on local shoulders. Local authorities would need to establish a landing site or casualty reception point in a secure location where rescue craft can efficiently and safely disembark evacuated passengers and crew ashore, emergency services can be provided, and where documentation and accountability procedures can be undertaken. Evacuees may need to be provided local transport, shelter, medical support, food, water, dry clothing, and sanitation services, while individuals may have a wide array of special needs and requirements, such as prescription medication and mobility aids.[52] Working with vessel operators and/or cruise/expedition companies, local authorities must also implement a system that can track passengers from 'ship to shore

---

49   IMRF, *The International Maritime Rescue Federation Mass Rescue Operations Project: The Use of Surface Units* (IMRF, 2019), https://www.international-maritime-rescue.org/Han dlers/Download.ashx?IDMF=d50ee499-a040-42a1-87de-00a343acbf89.

50   See Kikkert *et al.* (n 24).

51   JRCC Trenton (n 39).

52   Button and Gorgol (n 14); IMRF, *The International Maritime Rescue Federation Mass Rescue Operations Project: Maritime / shoreside coordination* (IMRF, 2019), https://www .international-maritime-rescue.org/Handlers/Download.ashx?IDMF=381e2a71-be90 -44d5-8ef2-1f03aaa41170.

to south.' These requirements impose high demands on local resources, need a great deal of human power, and require a whole-of-community approach. While Cambridge Bay might have the ability to meet many of these demands given its size, resources, and pool of potential responders, its health centre and volunteer ambulance services would quickly be overwhelmed if there were substantial injuries or hypothermia cases. Participants from other communities highlighted that they would struggle to transport, shelter, feed, and generally accommodate hundreds or even dozens of evacuees. They would have to get creative. "Local plans have to be strong, because we all won't have the resources of Cambridge Bay. We need to really plan for how to deal with this. Where to put people. How to feed them. How to move them. How to get more community supplies when they are gone. We will try our best."[53]

6 Discussion: Getting Ready

Is the kind of response envisioned by community responders participating in the Kitikmeot SAR Project possible at this time? Certainly, the expansion of the Coast Guard Auxiliary in the Arctic increases its likelihood. The training, community SAR boats, and equipment provided to Auxiliary units would assist in the conduct of an MRO. Likewise, the existing SAR and emergency response skills of Ranger patrols, GSAR teams, volunteer firefighters, and the other first responders discussed in this chapter, could all be used, both on the water and shoreside. Continuing the training and support for these groups is one vital first step in ensuring that they could assist in a mass rescue. Still, more is required. The following represent several options to better prepare for marine MROs in Inuit Nunangat and to ensure that the roles envisioned in this case study can become a reality.

6.1 *Putting the Pieces Together: An Inuit Nunangat MRO Planning Committee*

In their chapter on the challenges of mass rescue operations, Button and Gorgol highlight that "in responding to any MRO event, there is some level of chaos. The goal is to reduce that chaos; one way of doing so is by developing comprehensive and shared MRO plans." Given the complexity of these events and the array of actors involved, effective plans are essential for effective coordination,

---

53   Kugluktuk Ground Search and Rescue and Marine Rescue member, interview with Peter Kikkert, February 2022.

communication, and interaction.[54] Plans should develop roles and responsibilities during a response, document additional resources that could be used
to fill the capability gap, describe how the command, control, and communication network will function, identify places of safety, and establish the requirements of local contingency plans.[55] To ensure effectiveness, it is vital that the
people responsible for implementing the plan are also involved in its crafting.

The International Maritime Rescue Federation presents the MRO planning
process as a "jigsaw puzzle." Each stakeholder has an "important role in the
response, with their own emergency response plans setting policy, as well as
providing specific roles and responsibilities." The MRO planning process must
determine how these stakeholders—each a different piece to the puzzle with
their own plans, procedures, and capabilities—best fit together. "The aim is
not to produce a whole new plan, but to link the existing plans together, and
to do so efficiently, so that there are no gaps and no overlaps—that is, nothing is overlooked, and two organisations are not trying to do the same thing."
Key to this is each stakeholder understanding how they fit into the plan and,
as importantly, feeling ownership over the plan—understanding their tasks
and responsibilities and *accepting* them.[56] A community responder from the
Kitikmeot captured this idea well when he said, "[W]e already feel responsible
for these waters, so give us some responsibility for the plan. If we are going to
be involved, and we will be, work with us to figure out how. Give us some ownership over the planning."[57]

To prepare for mass rescue operations in the region, we recommend
the establishment of an Inuit Nunangat MRO Planning Committee with

---

54   Button and Gorgol (n 14), p. 371.

55   Id., 356–390.

56   IMRF, *The International Maritime Rescue Federation Mass Rescue Operations Project:
      General Planning Guidance* (IMRF, 2019), https://www.international-maritime-rescue.
      org/Handlers/Download.ashx?IDMF=40e7e8ba-d91f-45af-93a6-8d47afb77274; IMRF, *The
      International Maritime Rescue Federation Mass Rescue Operations Project: Complex Incident
      Planning: Ownership of Plans* (IMRF, 2019), https://www.international-maritime-rescue.
      org/Handlers/Download.ashx?IDMF=6e959905-9c6c-4bdc-9b77-88b3aa8b8d28. A place
      of safety is defined in the IAMSAR Manual (n 13) as "a location where rescue operations
      are considered to terminate; where the survivors' safety of life is no longer threatened
      and where their basic human needs (such as food, shelter and medical needs) can be
      met; and, a place from which transportation arrangements can be made for the survivors'
      next or final destination. A place of safety may be on land, or it may be on board a rescue
      unit or other suitable vessel or facility at sea that can serve as a place of safety until the
      survivors are disembarked at their next destination."

57   Kugluktuk Ground Search and Rescue and Marine Rescue member, interview with Peter
      Kikkert, February 2022.

representatives from all government agencies, industry partners, and community-based organizations that might be involved in such an operation.[58] This committee would develop the actions, roles, and responsibilities that community-based groups could take on during a mass rescue and situate them within the broader MRO plan. At the same time, community responders would be able to share their insights to shape and develop the approaches and priorities of government agencies and industry partners.[59] Together, they could identify capability gaps, the means of filling those gaps, and how to best mobilize and coordinate these resources, particularly at the community level. Uniquely, given the resupply challenges for communities in Inuit Nunangat, the planning committee should also consider how to replenish supplies and restore essential services after an evacuation into a community. The planning undertaken by this committee should be a "cyclical and continuing process"—the plan must be a living document rooted in constant improvement.[60]

The establishment of an Inuit Nunangat MRO Planning Committee would reflect two guiding principles of Inuit Qaujimajatuqangit—aajiiqatigiinigniq and piliriqatigiingniq. Piliriqatigiingniq is the concept of equal collaborative relationships or working together for a common purpose, while aajiiqatigiinniq means decision-making through discussion and consensus—building agreement through a fully inclusive and participatory group process.[61] The Planning Committee would bring actors together in the spirit of piliriqatigiingniq to strengthen relationships and pool collective knowledge and resources, which will foster discussion and build consensus on MRO challenges, requirements, and best practices. A continuously improved MRO plan forged through aajiiqatigiinigniq and piliriqatigiingniq would go far to preparing Inuit Nunangat for a marine disaster.

---

58   Such a committee could focus on both marine and aerial mass rescue operations, the latter of which also poses an array of unique and serious challenges.

59   For instance, the committee's work could be used to inform the SAR related procedures contained in Polar Waters Operational Manuals, which are required under the Polar Code, particularly the required content on emergency response coordination and evacuation. See, for instance, International Chamber of Shipping and Oil Companies International Marine Forum, *Guidelines for the Development of a Polar Water Operational Manual* (London: ICS, 2019).

60   IMRF *General Planning Guidance* (n 56), p. 6.

61   "Aajiiqatigiingniq: An Inuit Research Methodology," Aqqiumavvik Society, n.d., https://www.aqqiumavvik.com/aajiiqatigiingniq-research-methodol.

6.2   *Testing the Plan: Inuit Nunangat Training and Exercise Program*

The work done by the Inuit Nunangat MRO Planning Committee must be followed by regular training. The MRO plan "will be useless unless responders know what it is, how they fit into it, and what it expects them to do," concludes the International Maritime Rescue Federation.[62] Community-based groups should be provided with training on how to accomplish the roles outlined for them in the plan, on how to work with strangers, the information required by the JRCC, effective communications, on-scene SAR operations, and how to establish a shoreside landing site and reception centre. This kind of skill-building should be part of the annual training provided to CCGA units and Ranger patrols and can be delivered as required to other community-based organizations. Auxiliary unit leaders and Ranger patrol leadership could also be trained to assume the role of on-scene coordinator and then pass this knowledge down to other team members.

MRO planning and training must be tested and validated through tabletop exercises, functional exercises, which have personnel perform their duties in a simulated operational environment, and full-scale exercises, which are as close to a real operation as possible. Since the inception of Operation Nanook (first an annual event and now the name given to all CAF training activities in the North) in 2007, the CAF has worked with territorial partners to conduct several mass rescue exercises. Likewise, since 2019, CCG Arctic Region's Training and Exercise Program has worked with expedition cruise operators, shipping companies, classification societies, and domestic and international SAR partners, in an effort to identify and navigate the challenges facing MROs in the region. Moving forward, these exercises should be expanded to include more community-based organizations whenever possible and ensure they also focus on shoreside operations.

Community responders in the Kitikmeot SAR Project consistently highlight the need for more exercises that would allow community organizations to practice their horizontal and vertical coordination, collaboration, and communication. Coordination and cooperation between community groups remains informal and often limited at the community-level, and there is confusion about respective missions, roles, responsibilities, and capabilities—even though many community responders serve in multiple groups.[63] Further, while Kitikmeot SAR Project participants understand that they would have to follow the direction of the JRCC, the CAF, or Nunavut Emergency Management during a mass rescue operation, they also think that exercises are required to work

---

62   IMRF *General Planning Guidance* (n 56), p. 6.
63   See Kikkert and Lackenbauer (n 15); Kikkert *et al.* (n 24).

through any possible barriers to cooperation *and* to teach these external agencies to listen to and learn from community responders. Without opportunities for joint exercises, trying to coordinate the various elements of the response in a high-pressure, time-sensitive situation such as an MRO would be stressful and detract from efficiency of effort. Regular exercises between community groups and other governmental agencies can test plans and training, facilitate cooperation and coordination, and improve operational effectiveness.

To facilitate MRO training, the Coast Guard Arctic Region and the CCGA should also consider working together to create a Canadian version of the United States Coast Guard Auxiliary Mass Rescue Operations Specialist (AMROS) program. The program was established to provide for the surge capacity of trained personnel required for a successful MRO. The AMROS Performance Qualification Standard (PQS) provides a roadmap for Auxiliary members who aspire to earn the certification, and includes specialization training in planning, SAR operations, landing site management, and reception.[64] Such an initiative could create a cadre of well-trained and prepared Auxiliarists ready to support MROs throughout Inuit Nunangat.

6.3   *A Holistic Solution: Inuit Nunangat Community Public Safety Officer Program*

The community responders involved in the Kitikmeot SAR Program have highlighted another possible solution to many of the safety challenges facing the communities of Inuit Nunangat: a tailor-made community public safety office (CPSO) program. Modelled off the original Alaska Village Public Safety Officer program launched in 1979, a CPSO program would provide communities with full-time officers responsible for marine safety, fire prevention, emergency medical assistance, SAR, and all-hazards emergency management.

Investing in such a program would not only improve the overall safety and strengthen the resilience of northern communities, it would also help the Government of Canada to prepare for potential marine disasters and mass rescue operations across the region. These officers could work on the local contingency plans required for an effective shoreside response and ensure that they fit with the broader MRO plan developed by the Inuit Nunangat MRO Planning Committee. They could undertake a wide variety of other ongoing activities to help prepare for an MRO: the identification of local resources that

---

64   United States Coast Guard, *Auxiliary Mass Rescue Operations Specialist (AMROS), Performance Qualification Standards,* (United States Coast Guard, 27 June 2017), https://d5srcgauxem.org/wp-content/uploads/2020/02/Master-AMROS-PQS-6-27-2017.pdf.

could be mobilized to close the capability gap, facilitation of community-based MRO training and exercises, and development of lines of communication and coordination between various community groups and external agencies. During an actual mass rescue operation, the CPSO could be the primary point of contact at the community-level, mobilizing and coordinating the shoreside response. While the CPSO's primary purpose would not be responding to mass rescue operations, their skills and capabilities would certainly serve as a force multiplier in the event one should occur.

This initiative would also fit with the commitment to develop new approaches to fund and administer federal policies, programs, services, and initiatives that "support community and individual wellbeing throughout Inuit Nunangat." The new Inuit Nunangat Policy, released in April 2022, highlights how this geographic, cultural, and political region includes more than half of Canada's coastline "and major marine areas, including land fast sea ice, inland waters and offshore areas." Co-managing safety and security programs through a CPSO model would affirm Canada's respect for Inuit rights and co-management, support Inuit self-determination within the context of specific program and policy areas, and promote greater self-reliance throughout Inuit Nunangat.[65]

7 Conclusion

Preparing for marine disasters and mass rescue operations must be a priority for Canada moving forward. Although past marine accidents in Inuit Nunangat have come close to requiring mass rescue operations, favourable conditions and good fortune have prevailed in each case. As vessel traffic increases, however, the risk grows—as does political and public attention to the issue. The Arctic and Northern Policy Framework (ANPF) commits "to increasing Search and Rescue reaction and responsiveness to emergencies for Arctic residents and visitors,"[66] and Inuit have been consistent and clear in their desire for capacity-building in the areas of SAR and emergency management. The Inuit Circumpolar Council, in its 2019 written submission to the Special Senate

---

65   Crown-Indigenous Relations and Northern Affairs Canada (CIRNAC), "Inuit Nunangat Policy," Government of Canada, last modified 21 April 2022, https://www.rcaanc-cirnac. gc.ca/eng/1650556354784/1650556491509.

66   CIRNAC, "Arctic and Northern Policy Framework: Safety, Security, and Defence Chapter," Government of Canada, Government of Canada, last modified 19 September 2019, https:// www.rcaanc-cirnac.gc.ca/eng/1562939617400/1562939658000.

Committee on the Arctic, asserted that "Inuit are always the first to respond to an emergency, and in doing so with limited training and resources they risk their own safety and security." Accordingly, it urged the federal government "to enhance search and rescue and emergency protection infrastructure and training in Inuit communities."[67] The Inuit Tapiriit Kanatami (ITK) partner chapter to the ANPF insists that "Inuit are the stewards of the land, and given appropriate infrastructure, will continue as the principal players and first responders in Canada's Arctic sovereignty and security."[68] These ideas must animate new approaches to mass rescue that more fully integrate and leverage community capacity throughout the region. Our proposals for an Inuit Nunangat MRO Planning Committee, Training and Exercise Program, and Community Public Safety Officer program fit with federal, territorial, and Inuit priorities. These initiatives will support community-based organizations in responding to any marine disasters that occur off their shores. In doing so, they provide one solution to the tyranny of time and distance that makes mass rescue operations so challenging in the Arctic.

Acknowledgements

This work is the result of the Kitikmeot Search and Rescue Project supported by the Marine Environment Observation Prediction and Response Network (MEOPAR), Social Sciences and Humanities Research Council (SSHRC), Mobilizing Insights in Defence and Security Program (MINDS), Irving Shipbuilding Inc., the North American Defence and Security Network (NAADSN), and the Canada Research Chairs program. We are grateful to the members of the community-based search and rescue organizations in Kugluktuk, Cambridge Bay, Gjoa Haven, Taloyoak, and Kugaaruk and to all who participated in the Kitikmeot Roundtable on Search and Rescue (see Kitikmeotsar.ca for a full list).

---

67   Inuit Circumpolar Council Canada (ICC), *Submission to the Special Senate Committee on the Arctic Regarding the Arctic Policy Framework and International Priorities* (ICC, 2019), https://sencanada.ca/content/sen/committee/421/ARCT/Briefs/InuitCircumpolar CouncilCanada_e.pdf.
68   Inuit Tapiriit Kanatami, *Arctic and Northern Policy Framework: Inuit Nunangat* (ITK, 2019), https://www.itk.ca/wp-content/uploads/2019/09/20190925-arctic-and-northern-policy -framework-inuit-nunangat-final-en.pdf.

PART 2

Reimagining the Governance of Shipping in Canadian Arctic Waters

∴

Canada and the Future of Arctic Coastal State Jurisdiction

Kristin Bartenstein

Abstract

This chapter explores how jurisdiction under Article 234 may be used by Arctic coastal States at a time marked by significant change. Warming temperatures reshape the physical and ecological environment of the Arctic, making it more hospitable to shipping, but also more vulnerable to its threats. The Polar Code, adopted as the international response to increasing polar shipping and growing awareness of its detrimental impacts, alters the legal environment by providing the first binding international regulations tailor-made for navigation in polar waters. This chapter sets out to investigate the legal implications of these changes for coastal State regulation under Article 234 with a particular focus on Canada. It starts by tracing Canada's history of regulating shipping in its Arctic waters with the objective to understand how the consequences of this politically fraught endeavour still reverberate today. The chapter then turns to examine the geographical and material scope of jurisdiction under Article 234 against the background of present-day imperatives, before critically assessing Canada's strategy to subject navigation in its Arctic waters to a single set of rules. The chapter closes by summarizing the main conclusions, which may hold lessons for future regulatory action.

Keywords

Arctic shipping – LOSC Article 234 – Arctic coastal State jurisdiction – scope of jurisdiction – Northwest Passage – United Nations Convention on the Law of the Sea

1   Introduction

In recent years, regulatory action has been stepped up significantly to address the strain shipping imposes on polar ecosystems, which already suffer tremendous stress brought on by a warming climate. There is a broad consensus that the risks posed by vessels are best addressed through a global approach, resting upon regulations developed under the auspices of the International Maritime Organization (IMO) and imposed on vessels by their respective flag States.[1] Uniform international standards are perceived as a basic condition for a business sector that is premised on global mobility and a level playing field.[2] The importance of such uniform standards, equal to that of freedom of navigation, is recognized by the general legal framework of the law of the sea and the United Nations Convention on the Law of the Sea (LOSC).[3] Their indispensable role is reflected by Article 94 on the "duties of the flag State."[4] For that same reason, Article 194 on the general obligation to prevent, reduce and control pollution calls for harmonization of State policies,[5] while Article 211 on vessel-source pollution requires flag States to develop international minimum standards to be imposed on their respective vessels.[6] With respect to Arctic shipping, the 2009 Arctic Council AMSA Report echoes the importance of uniformity and calls for the development of international regulatory regimes to address Arctic-specific issues of shipping.[7] After years of negotiation, the entry into force of the Polar Code in 2017 finally ushered in the first international binding regime tailor-made for shipping in polar regions.[8]

In Canadian Arctic waters, navigation has been under specific mandatory rules long before the Polar Code was even envisioned. Driven by a combination of concerns for the environment, vessel safety and—more sweepingly—Canada's "sovereignty"[9] over its Arctic expanse, Canada pioneered by pursuing a coastal State approach to ensure safety of navigation and pollution prevention in its Arctic waters. The decision was prompted by the 1969 crossing of

---

1   For the role of flag States, see Bankes in this volume.

2   See Pauline Pic *et al.*, "The Polar Code and Canada's Regulations on Arctic Navigation: Shipping Companies' Perceptions of the New Legal Environment," *The Polar Journal* 11:1 (2021): 95–117, https://doi.org/10.1080/2154896X.2021.1889838.

3   United Nations Convention on the Law of the Sea, 10 December 1982 (in force 16 November 1994), 1833 *UNTS* 396.

4   Id., Article 94(5).

5   Id., Article 194(1).

6   Id., Article 211(1) and (2).

7   Arctic Council, *Arctic Marine Shipping Assessment 2009 Report*, 6–7 (particularly Recommendation I.C), https://oaarchive.arctic-council.org/bitstream/handle/11374/54/AMSA_2009 _Report_2nd_print.pdf?sequence=1&isAllowed=y.

8   International Code for Ships Operating in Polar Waters (Polar Code), IMO Resolution MSC.385(94) (21 November 2014, effective 1 January 2017); Amendments to the International Convention for the Safety of Life at Sea 1974, IMO Resolution MSC.386(94) (21 November 2014, effective 1 January 2017); Amendments to MARPOL Annexes I, II, IV and V, IMO Resolution MEPC.265(68) (15 May 2015, effective 1 January 2017).

9   See Donald R. Rothwell, "The Canadian-U.S. Northwest Passage Dispute: A Reassessment," *Cornell International Law Journal* 26 (1993): 331, at 337–338.

the US-flagged ice-strengthened oil tanker ss *Manhattan*, sent through the Northwest Passage, as Lackenbauer and Lajeunesse describe in this volume, to determine the feasibility of year-round operations to ship oil from Alaskan extraction sites to refinery sites on the US east coast. In response, Canada enacted the 1970 *Arctic Waters Pollution Prevention Act* (AWPPA),[10] prohibiting any deposit of waste in Arctic waters.[11] This zero-discharge rule is still at the heart of Canada's regulatory regime to prevent vessel-source pollution. In 1977, Canada added NORDREG, a ship reporting scheme combined with vessel traffic services for the Arctic region, applied on a voluntary basis until it became mandatory in 2010.[12]

Eventually, Canada's approach to ensure safety of navigation and pollution prevention in its Arctic waters was internationally validated by the inclusion of Article 234 in the LOSC. Negotiated at the Third United Nations Conference on the Law of the Sea (UNCLOS III) among Canada, the United States and Russia, the provision grants coastal States exceptional jurisdiction over ice-covered waters, enshrining in international law Canada's unilateral, environmentally focused, coastal State-based strategy. At the time, in the absence of specific international standards on Arctic navigation, the purpose of Article 234 was obvious: it allowed coastal States to fill some of the regulatory gaps. However, only Canada and Russia have made use of their jurisdiction. And as Chircop rightly states, since 2017, "the substantive purpose of Article 234 has been addressed by the Polar Code [to a great extent]," conceding "this does not necessarily mean that there is no further purpose for the exercise of Article 234 jurisdiction."[13] As Vincent *et al.* outline in this volume, the Arctic Ocean and its unique ecological features are under increasing stress from warming temperatures, pollution, biodiversity loss and habitat destruction. The additional stress imposed by Arctic shipping therefore calls for continued regulatory action.

For Canada, the international flag State-based approach to regulating Arctic navigation raises the issue of how unilateral coastal State jurisdiction under Article 234 may be used in the future. At stake is not only the technical issue of appropriate standards to address concerns of safety of navigation and environmental protection. Any regulatory action related to international navigation in Canadian Arctic waters always also implies assertion of jurisdiction,

---

10   *Arctic Waters Pollution Prevention Act*, SC 1969–1970, c 47; current version, see RSC, 1985, c A-12 [AWPPA].

11   Id., s 4.

12   For the mandatory version, see *Northern Canada Vessel Traffic Services Zone Regulations*, SOR/2010-127 [NORDREG].

13   Aldo Chircop, "Jurisdiction over Ice-covered Areas and the Polar Code: An Emerging Symbiotic Relationship?," *Journal of International Maritime Law* 22:4 (2016): 275–290, at 290.

a highly sensitive political issue and closely scrutinized since the late 1960s. Focusing its attention on Canada, this chapter sets out to explore the future of coastal State jurisdiction under Article 234. After tracing the complex equilibrium of the current legal state, it successively examines the geographical and the material scope of jurisdiction under Article 234, as well as Canada's "single approach" to regulating shipping in its Arctic waters. The chapter will conclude with some policy suggestions.

2   Shipping in the Canadian Arctic: Tracing Canadian Law-Making

The 1969 SS *Manhattan* crossing of the Northwest Passage made Canada's political leadership and the broader public aware of a twofold risk facing the Canadian Arctic.[14] The hazardous nature of Arctic shipping, due to extremely difficult conditions of navigation, created by sea ice and cold temperatures and compounded by a lack of reliable charting, became common knowledge. The threat posed to the environment had a galvanizing effect at a time when the need for environmental protection started to draw attention beyond scientific circles.[15] Recent incidents, including the oil spill caused by the 1967 grounding of the SS *Torrey Canyon* off the coast of England and, closer to home, the oil spill caused by the 1970 grounding of the SS *Arrow* off the coast of Nova Scotia conjured the striking image of a black tide on white ice cover and fuelled opposition to Arctic shipping.

Furthermore, the refusal by the United States to seek permission for the *Manhattan* crossing made it plain that Canada's view of its Arctic expanse as "national terrain"[16] was not necessarily shared. The reasoning behind the refusal—the fact that the *Manhattan* would not enter Canadian territorial waters, but remain in international waters throughout its voyage—did not prove reassuring enough. Nor did the fact that Canada asserted jurisdiction by granting unasked-for permission, sent the Canadian Coast Guard icebreaker *Sir John A. MacDonald* to escort the *Manhattan* and dispatched a Canadian

---

14   Nicholas C. Howson, "Breaking the Ice: The Canadian-American Dispute over the Arctic's Northwest Passage," *Columbia Journal of Transnational Law* 26:2 (1988): 337–376, at 350.

15   Growing environmental awareness led to the 1972 UN Conference on the Environment held in Stockholm.

16   Expression used in 1958 by the Minister of Northern Affairs and cited in a 1969 policy statement by Prime Minister P.E. Trudeau, see House of Commons, *Debates* (15 May 1969), 8720.

official on board the *Manhattan*.[17] The incident sowed the seeds of what would become the controversy over the legal status of the waters of the Arctic Archipelago, often framed in the politically catchy, but legally misleading phrase of "Canada's Arctic sovereignty."[18]

2.1 *Innovative Coastal State Measures Following the* Manhattan *Crossing*

While the Arctic had long been part of Canadian identity, the *Manhattan* crossing revealed the uncertainties surrounding Canada's jurisdiction over the maritime area. The challenge for Canada was to plot a legal course out of the political conundrum created by the *Manhattan* incident, a course that could both appease domestic concerns and avert international objections. Canada's 1970 response was two-pronged. First, Canada extended the breadth of its territorial sea from three to twelve nautical miles (M),[19] declaring that territorial waters, newly overlapping at several points in the Arctic Archipelago, would make it henceforth impossible to sail through the Northwest Passage without passing through Canadian territorial waters.[20] While the US government criticized Canada for proceeding unilaterally, it did not oppose the extension as such,[21] which followed then developing State practice.[22]

The second, more daring, part of Canada's response was the adoption of the AWPPA. Canada chose to assert jurisdiction over an extensive area, but did so with respect to a narrowly defined subject matter. The AWPPA introduced the concept of 'arctic waters,' taking a broad view of the concerned waters, which included

---

17   Suzanne Lalonde, "Evaluating Canada's Position on the Northwest Passage in Light of Two Possible Sources of International Protection," in *The Limits of Maritime Jurisdiction*, eds., Clive Schofield, Seokwoo Lee and Moon-Sang Kwon (Leiden: Brill Nijhoff, 2014), 575–588, at 577.

18   Franklyn Griffiths, "The Shipping News: Canada's Arctic Sovereignty Not on Thinning Ice," *International Journal* 58:2 (2003): 257–282; Rob Huebert, "The Shipping News Part II: How Canada's Arctic Sovereignty Is on Thinning Ice," *International Journal* 58:3 (2003): 295–308; Donald McRae, "Arctic Sovereignty? What is at Stake?," *Behind the Headlines* 64:1 (2007): 1–23.

19   *Act to amend the Territorial Sea and Fishing Zones Act*, St Can 1969–1970, c 68, s 1.

20   Standing Committee on External Affairs and National Defence, *Minutes of Proceedings and Evidence*, 1069–70, 25:18 ff.

21   Ted L. McDorman, *Salt Water Neighbors: International Ocean Law Relations between the United States and Canada* (Oxford: Oxford University Press, 2009), 63–65.

22   Donald R. Rothwell and Tim Stephens, *The International Law of the Sea*, 2nd ed. (Portland: Hart Publishing, 2016), 69–70; Suzanne Lalonde, "The Northwest Passage," in *Canada and the Maritime Arctic: Boundaries, Shelves, and Waters*, eds., P. Whitney Lackenbauer, Suzanne Lalonde and Elizabeth Riddell-Dixon (Peterborough: NAADSN, 2020), 107, at 113.

waters ... adjacent to the mainland and islands of the Canadian arctic
[sic] within the area enclosed by the sixtieth parallel of north latitude, the
one hundred and forty-first meridian of longitude and a line measured
seaward from the nearest Canadian land a distance of one hundred
nautical miles [except where the presence of Greenland requires a lesser
extent].[23]

Not only did these 'arctic waters' encompass all waters of the Archipelago, they
also formed a belt of up to 100 M in breadth around the Archipelago, extending far beyond the narrow strip of typical coastal waters and Canada's newly
extended territorial sea. Reassuring from a domestic viewpoint, the asserted
jurisdiction was, however, questionable from an international law perspective.
The risk of international opposition was all the more real as Canada's AWPPA
was contemporary with attempts by some coastal States to extend territorial
sovereignty beyond 12 nautical miles.[24] These attempts met with strong resistance and, given their impact on freedom of navigation, never gained enough
traction to become established in law.

     Canada's approach, however, differed in a significant way from these sweep-
ing claims of territorial sovereignty. It was more in line with the restricted
approach that focused on coastal fisheries and eventually led to the concept of
the exclusive economic zone (EEZ).[25] The AWPPA indeed pursued a narrowly
defined objective, that is, the protection against vessel-source pollution. This
"constructive and functional approach,"[26] as McDorman explains, consists in
asserting jurisdiction only to the extent it is "functionally necessary" to achieve
the set goal.[27] The genius of the AWPPA was that it had a geographical scope
broad enough and a 'zero-tolerance' signal firm enough to address immediate,
mainly domestic, concerns that shipping would threaten the Arctic environment, while its narrow pollution prevention focus put potential challengers in
a political and moral bind that held international opposition at bay.

     Although the environmental objective of the AWPPA garnered international
sympathy, Canada's unilateral approach and contribution to creeping jurisdiction nevertheless displeased several States, including the United States.[28] As
a precaution and obviously to prevent formal legal challenges to the AWPPA

23   AWPPA (n 10), s 3(1).
24   See "Jurisdiction Claimed over Territorial Waters and Fishing," ILM 3:3 (1964): 551–552.
25   Rothwell and Stephens (n 22), p. 69.
26   House of Commons, Debates (16 April 1970), 5951.
27   McDorman (n 21), p. 75.
28   Id., at 76–78, citing a Canadian government official mentioning "a drawer full of pro-
      tests." Pointing to consultations Canada was conducting when fleshing out its regulatory

that could have been hard to win,[29] Canada decided to exempt disputes over coastal State jurisdiction from its acceptance of compulsory jurisdiction of the International Court of Justice (ICJ).[30] In 1985, following the conclusion of the LOSC, the exemption was removed,[31] signalling Canada's confidence that its domestic law had not only acquired legitimacy, but also a solid basis in international law thanks to Article 234.[32] Interestingly, it was only in 2010 that Canada's "arctic waters" were extended to reach a maximum of 200 M, in accordance with Article 234.[33]

2.2 Implications of Canada's Claim of a Historic Title over Its Arctic Archipelago

A complicating twist to the legal debate about Canada's coastal State jurisdiction in its Arctic waters is Canada's claim that the waters of the Arctic Archipelago are historic internal waters, arguably derived from the 1880 transfer of the Arctic area from Great Britain to Canada.[34] According to Lajeunesse's account, signs that Canada considered these waters its own can be found throughout the first half of the twentieth century, although a coherent legal policy undergirding the claim was emerging only towards the end of the 1950s. Helped along by the 1951 ICJ *Anglo-Norwegian Fisheries* case,[35] it coalesced around the notion that waters within coastal archipelagos may be considered historic internal waters and enclosed by straight baselines.[36] Pharand traces a

---

regime, McDorman questions the degree to which Canada's measures can be considered unilateral.

29 See Pierre E. Trudeau's remarks on the AWPPA, "Canadian Legislation on Arctic Pollution and Territorial Sea and Fishing Zones: Canadian Prime Minister's Remarks on the Proposed Legislation," *ILM* 9:3 (1970): 600; see also McDorman (n 21), p. 77.

30 Canada, *Declaration Recognizing as Compulsory the Jurisdiction of the Court*, 7 April 1970, 724 *UNTS* 63, at 66 (item 2(d)).

31 Canada, *Declaration Recognizing as Compulsory the Jurisdiction of the International Court of Justice*, 10 September 1985, 1406 *UNTS* 133, at 134.

32 See also Myron H. Nordquist, Satya Nandan and Shabtai Rosenne, *UN Convention on the Law of the Sea, 1982: A Commentary*, vol. IV (Dordrecht: Martinus Nijhoff, 1990): Article 234 (p. 392), at para 234.5(g) (p. 398).

33 *Act to amend the Arctic Waters Pollution Prevention Act*, SC 2009, c 11, s 1.

34 McDorman (n 21), p. 235.

35 *Fisheries Case (United Kingdom v. Norway)*, [1951] ICJ Rep 116.

36 See Adam Lajeunesse, *Lock, Stock, and Icebergs: A History of Canada's Arctic Maritime Sovereignty* (Vancouver: UBC Press, 2016), particularly chapters 1–3. See also conclusions of an internal External Affairs study: Memorandum, "Status of the Waters of the Canadian Arctic Archipelago," March 9, 1959, LAC, RG 25, file 9057-40, reprinted in Adam Lajeunesse, ed., *Documents on Canadian Arctic Maritime Sovereignty: 1950–1988*, DCASS number 13, 2018, 98, https://pubs.aina.ucalgary.ca/dcass/84387.pdf.

first public claim of sovereignty based on historical grounds to a 1969 House of Commons Committee report[37] and the first clear reference to a historic title to a 1973 letter emanating from Foreign Affairs.[38] According to the letter, "Canada ... claims that the waters of the Canadian Arctic Archipelago are internal waters of Canada, on a historical basis, although they have not been declared as such in any treaty or by any legislation."[39] Pre-empting criticism of inconsistency with Canada's functional approach, the letter remarks that exercise of functional jurisdiction does not preclude a "subsequent claim of full sovereignty on historic or other grounds."[40] Lajeunesse explains Canada's subdued public conduct with its anxiousness to avoid open US opposition to the claim, which may have proved irresistible.[41] The functional course steered by Canada since the adoption of the AWPPA, and later reinforced by Article 234, enabled the postponing of a more assertive approach to the status of the waters of the Arctic Archipelago.

Things came, however, to a head in 1985, when the US Coast Guard icebreaker *Polar Sea* was sent through the Northwest Passage. Planned by US and Canadian officials as purely operational, the transit turned into a political crisis when popular perception made it out to be a challenge to Canada's sovereignty[42] and the US government, pressured by its Canadian counterpart, failed to request permission, even asserting that the transit was "an exercise of navigational rights and freedoms not requiring prior notification."[43] Canada did not oppose the passage, which it deemed in compliance with applicable standards. Instead, it again granted unasked-for permission and sent two officers on board the *Polar Sea* to observe the voyage. However, the time had come to assert "Canada's full sovereignty over the waters of the Arctic [A]rchipelago"[44] and the Canadian government decided to do so by drawing baselines around

---

37 Standing Committee on Indian Affairs and Northern Development, *Proceedings*, 1969–70, 1:6.

38 Donat Pharand, *Canada's Arctic Waters in International Law* (Cambridge: University Press, 1988), 111–112.

39 Letter dated 17 December 1973, in Edward G. Lee, "Canadian Practice in International Law during 1973 as Reflected Mainly in Public Correspondence and Statements of the Department of External Affairs," *Canadian Yearbook of International Law* 12 (1974): 272, at 277 ff. (specifically 279).

40 Id., 279.

41 Lajeunesse (n 36), chapters 4–7.

42 Id., 255–261.

43 United States Department of State, Telegram,151842, 17 May 1985, reprinted in Office of Ocean Affairs, *Limits in the Seas No. 112: United States Responses to Excessive National Maritime Claims* (1992), 73, https://www.state.gov/wp-content/uploads/2019/12/LIS-112.pdf.

44 House of Commons, *Debates* (10 September 1985), 6463.

the Archipelago, effective 1 January 1986.[45] They were declaratory only and meant to "define the outer limit of Canada's *historic* internal waters."[46]

Although Canada did not act on that claim, leaving regulation of international navigation in the Archipelago unaltered, the international reaction was noticeable. The US government, considering the Northwest Passage an "international strait" where freedom of navigation applies,[47] ignored the stated purpose of the baselines and responded by reframing them as a means for Canada to "*establish* its claim" of internal water and declaring "that there is no basis in international law to support the Canadian claim."[48] Member States of the European Community essentially endorsed this view.[49] Bilateral US-Canadian attempts to find common ground led to the 1988 "agreement to disagree." In this carefully worded agreement on scientific cooperation in the Arctic, the United States pledges "navigation by U.S. icebreakers within waters claimed by Canada to be internal will be undertaken with the consent of the Government of Canada."[50] The question of the legal status of the Northwest Passage nevertheless remains, with both parties reserving their respective position.[51] In recent years, international opposition to Canada's position on its internal waters seems to have faded, with disapproval being voiced subtly in national Arctic strategies.[52]

---

45   *Territorial Sea Geographical Coordinates (Area 7) Order*, SOR/85–872.

46   House of Commons, *Debates* (n 44), 6463 (emphasis added).

47   For a recent iteration, see White House, *National Strategy for the Arctic Region*, 10 May 2013, 11, https://obamawhitehouse.archives.gov/sites/default/files/docs/nat_arctic _strategy.pdf.

48   James W. Dyer, Acting Assistant Secretary of State for Legislative and Intergovernmental Affairs, Letter dated 26 February 1986, reproduced in United States Department of State (n 43), p. 29 (emphasis added).

49   British High Commission Note No. 90/86 of 9 July 1986, reproduced in United States Department of State (n 43).

50   Agreement on Arctic Cooperation, 11 January 1988 (in force 11 January 1988), CTS 1988/29, cl 3.

51   Id., cl 4.

52   References to "freedom of navigation" appear alongside commitments to respect the law of the sea, which would include respect of historic titles. Among others, see Germany, *Germany's Arctic Policy Guidelines*, August 2019, https://www.auswaertiges -amt.de/blob/2240002/eb0b681be9415118ca87bc8e215c0cf4/arktisleitlinien-data.pdf; China, *China's Arctic Policy*, January 2018, https://english.www.gov.cn/archive/white _paper/2018/01/26/content_281476026660336.htm; France, *Le Grand Défi de l'Arctique: Feuille de Route Nationale sur l'Arctique*, June 2016, https://www.diplomatie.gouv.fr/IMG /pdf/frna_-_vf_-web-ok_cleoddif2.pdf.

2.3   *Canadian Law in the Polar Code Era*

A new era was ushered in when the Polar Code became mandatory in 2017.[53] Regulation of polar navigation now rests mainly on internationally agreed-upon obligations. In a major shift towards flag State-centred responsibility, these are primarily imposed by the flag State on vessels flying its flag.[54] Incidentally, the coastal State may impose them on foreign-flagged vessels navigating in waters under its jurisdiction as "generally accepted international rules and standards."[55] Besides pollution prevention obligations, the Polar Code also prescribes obligations on safety of navigation, extending the functional approach pioneered by Canada in its Arctic waters.

During negotiations, Canada aimed to ensure that the Polar Code would achieve at least the level of protection established by its coastal State regulations.[56] Arguably, this goal was met, as Canada's new 2018 *Arctic Shipping Safety and Pollution Prevention Regulations* (ASSPPR)[57] essentially align domestic standards with the Polar Code. Safety provisions are incorporated by reference[58] and complemented by a few additional requirements.[59] Environmental requirements are directly, albeit selectively, incorporated, preserving the pre-existing level of protection resulting from the AWPPA zero-discharge principle.[60]

---

53   This was accomplished through the amendment of the SOLAS and the MARPOL Conventions: see International Convention for the Safety of Life at Sea Convention, 1 November 1974 (in force 25 May 1980), 1184 *UNTS* 2 [SOLAS], as amended by Resolution MSC.386(94), in *Report of the MSC on its 94th Session*, Annex 7, IMO Doc MSC 94/21/Add.1 (21 November 2014). See also International Convention for the Prevention of Pollution from Ships, 2 November 1973, 1340 *UNTS* 184, as amended by the Protocol of 1978 Relating to the International Convention for the Prevention of Pollution from Ships, 17 February 1978 (both in force 2 October 1983), 1340 *UNTS* 61, as amended by Resolution MEPC.265(68), in *Report of the MEPC on its 66th Session*, Annex 11, IMO Doc MEPC 68/21/Add.1 (15 May 2015).

54   LOSC (n 3), Article 211(2).

55   On the issue of these so-called GAIRS, see Bankes in this volume.

56   Domestic regulation included, besides NORDREG (n 12), in particular the *Arctic Shipping Pollution Prevention Regulations*, CRC, c 353 (repealed) adopted under the AWPPA (n 10).

57   *Arctic Shipping Safety and Pollution Prevention Regulations*, SOR/2017-286 [ASSPPR]. See also Kristin Bartenstein, "Between the Polar Code and Article 234: The Balance in Canada's Arctic Shipping Safety and Pollution Prevention Regulations," *Ocean Development and International Law* 50:4 (2019): 335–362.

58   ASSPPR (n 57), s 6.

59   For example, the requirement of an ice navigator in specific circumstances. Id., s 10.

60   Id., s 12 ff. Discharge restrictions for sewage for example were tightened (Id.,ss 19–20) and some Polar Code allowances were not included in the ASSPPR, see Bartenstein (n 57), p. 344.

The few regulatory departures from Polar Code standards bring attention to another Canadian concern during negotiations. Intent on upholding coastal State jurisdiction under Article 234, Canada sought to ensure that it could not be considered neutralized by the new flag-State regulations of the Polar Code. As a result, a savings clause was included in the new SOLAS chapter on safety provisions,[61] while the general MARPOL savings clause was deemed sufficient regarding the pollution prevention provisions.[62] Although the Polar Code therefore does not stand in the way of unilateral coastal State regulations,[63] it nevertheless has implications for jurisdiction under Article 234, as it provides, in Chircop's words, the "new baseline" for regulation of Arctic shipping.[64] Such guidance may be drawn from the Polar Code's mandatory requirements (Parts I-A and II-A), but also from its additional recommendations (Parts I-B and II-B). Interpretation may further be informed by the more general international outlook on the implications of polar navigation, expressed in the Preamble.

3   Revisiting the Geographical Scope of Article 234

The geographical scope of application of Article 234 has prompted discussion from the outset. Its convoluted wording first raised the question of how the provision fits into the LOSC's general framework of maritime zones. Rising temperatures now prompt concern that receding ice cover might shrink its geographical scope of jurisdiction.

3.1   *Article 234 in the Context of the LOSC's Zonal Framework*
Article 234 provides the coastal State with the authority to adopt and enforce measures related to "pollution from vessels in ice-covered areas *within the limits of the exclusive economic zone*" (emphasis added). Ambiguous and unique in the LOSC, this phrasing may refer to both the EEZ's inner and outer limits or to its outer limits only. While the "ordinary meaning ... given to the terms of

---

61   SOLAS (n 53), Chapter XIV, reg 2, para 5.
62   MARPOL (n 53), Article 9(2). Canada had addressed the meaning of the clause in relation to Article 234 in a statement upon becoming a party to the Convention in 1992, see IMO, *Status of IMO Treaties* (as of 16 August 2022), 133 (Canada, "2. Arctic Waters" b), https://wwwcdn.imo.org/localresources/en/About/Conventions/StatusOfConventions/Status%20-%202021.docx.
63   For details, see Bartenstein (n 57), pp. 351–352.
64   Chircop (n 13), p. 283.

the treaty in their context and in the light of its object and purpose"[65] should generally guide interpretation, the ordinary meaning of the atypical phrasing in Article 234 is all but certain. The EEZ is defined in LOSC Article 55 as "an area beyond and adjacent to the territorial sea" that, according to LOSC Article 57, "shall not extend beyond 200 nautical miles from the baselines." However, none of these provisions clarifies what limits are referred to in Article 234, leading to diverging interpretations.

McRae and Goundrey, followed by Boyle, consider that Article 234 applies to the EEZ only.[66] Franckx and Boone consider that this "narrow or literal interpretation is the most convincing one," arguing that "the geographical extent of Article 234 must be understood as within 12 and 200 [nautical miles], measured from the baseline."[67] This interpretation, which fits neatly into the zonal framework of the LOSC, makes it appealing from a systematic point of view. It does result, however, in Arctic coastal State powers that are broader in the EEZ than in the territorial sea or a strait, not least with respect to enforcement.

Taking the opposite view, Pharand contends that the provision "must have been intended to include the territorial sea."[68] In support, he cites senior Canadian delegate to UNCLOS III, Léonard Legault, who wrote that Article 234 "ratifies Canada's action in adopting the Arctic Waters Pollution Prevention Act in 1970."[69] This is corroborated by declassified US diplomatic cables and other confidential US communications of the time, which clearly envision Article 234 to also apply to the territorial sea.[70] The provision has even been described as applying "from the outer limits of the coastal State's exclusive economic

65   *Vienna Convention on the Law of Treaties*, 23 May 1969 (in force 27 January 1980), 1155 *UNTS* 331, Article 31(1) [VCLT].

66   Donald M. McRae and D. John Goundrey, "Environmental Jurisdiction in Arctic Waters: The Extent of Article 234," *UBC Law Review* 16:2 (1982): 197, at 221. See also Alan E. Boyle, "Marine Pollution Under the Law of the Sea Convention," *American Journal of International Law* 79:2 (1985): 347, at 361–362.

67   Erik Franckx and Laura Boone, "Article 234," in *United Nations Convention on the Law of the Sea: A Commentary*, ed., Alexander Proelss (Munich: C. H. Beck, 2017), 1566, at para 17.

68   Donat Pharand, "The Arctic Waters and the Northwest Passage: A Final Revisit," *Ocean Development & International Law* 38:1–2 (2007): 3, at 47.

69   Léonard Legault, "Protecting the Marine Environment," in *Canada and the New Internationalism*, eds., John Holmes and John Kirton (Toronto: Canadian Institute of International Affairs, 1988), 99, at 107.

70   FM AMEMBASSY OTTAWA TO SECSTATE WASHDC 5404, "Negotiations with Canadians on Environmental Special Area for Arctic and Transit of International Straits," 1975OTTAWA00158, 15 January 1975, ("Negotiations"), 3, https://aad.archives.gov/aad /createpdf?rid=119756&dt=2476&dl=1345; United States Department of State, *Memorandum for the President*, NSC-U/DM-109J, 28 April 1976, 2, https://www.cia.gov/readingroom /docs/CIA-RDP82S00697R000400170026-0.pdf.

zone to that State's coastline."[71] According to Bernard Oxman, US delegate to UNCLOS III and chairman of the English Language Group of the Conference Drafting Committee, Article 234 was "intended to embrace all waters landward of 200 miles, including the territorial sea, internal waters, and straits."[72]

If Article 234 does indeed extend to all waters landward of 200 M, including straits, it may still be questioned whether coastal State powers under Article 234 override the right of transit passage.[73] In other words, in the event that the Northwest Passage is to be considered a strait used for international navigation, would Article 234 still apply? Mostly this is thought to be the case,[74] and for good reason. Canada engaged in UNCLOS III negotiations with the objective to enshrine coastal State jurisdiction for laws such as the AWPPA precisely because Canada's powers over the Northwest Passage were controversial. The United States, pushing for a new straits regime, had their own motives to remove the Northwest Passage from the debate. According to US diplomatic cables of the time, it sought a "quid pro quo"[75] or a "package deal,"[76] that is, Canada's endorsement of the straits regime in return for US support for the "Arctic pollution article, which would apply to the Northwest Passage."[77] As the 1976 US "Memorandum for the President" on the draft provision that became Article 234 explains, "an Arctic strait would be subject to this article and our right of passage, as well as that of others, would be limited by this article."[78]

Interpretation denying the applicability of Article 234 to the Northwest Passage would empty the provision of its intended meaning. It would also

71 Nordquist *et al.* (n 32), para 234.5(d) (p. 397).
72 Martin Tracy Lutz (reporter), "Legal Regimes of the Arctic," *American Society of International Law Proceedings* 82 (1988): 315, 333–334.
73 Michael Byers and Suzanne Lalonde, "Who Controls the Northwest Passage?," *Vanderbilt Journal of Transnational Law* 42:4 (2009): 1133, at 1182, consider the applicability of Article 234 to international straits "unclear."
74 See McRae (n 18), p. 18; Pharand (68), pp. 46–47. Oxman's affirmation (n 72) may also be interpreted in this sense.
75 FM SECSTATE WASHDC TO USDEL SECRETARY IMMEDIATE, "Arctic Pollution Article" 1976STATE108756, 5 May 1976, 2, https://aad.archives.gov/aad/createpdf?rid=263141 &dt=2082&dl=1345. For an earlier cable reporting on US efforts to come to a "package agreement based on US support for liberal vessel-source pollution regime in ice-covered areas in return for Canadian support on unimpeded transit of straits," see "Negotiations" (n 70), p. 2.
76 Donald McRae, "The Negotiation of Article 234," in *Politics of the Northwest Passage*, ed., Franklin Griffiths (Montreal: McGill-Queen's University Press, 1987), 98, at 109.
77 Cable on "Arctic Pollution Article" (n 75), p. 2.
78 *Memorandum for the President* (n 70), p. 4. See also cable on "Arctic Pollution Article" (n 75), p. 2.

be problematic from a drafting point of view. A caveat in Article 233 indeed insulates the straits regime from Part XII sections 5 to 7. By its terms, Article 233 does not extend to Article 234, which forms section 8. This suggests that Article 234 may be applied to straits.[79] Consequently, if the Northwest Passage were to be considered a legal strait, Canada would still have authority under Article 234, limiting the practical relevance of the debate on the status of the Northwest Passage.

All this is not antithetical to Canada considering the Northwest Passage historic internal waters. This position has emerged since the 1950s and crystallized more clearly after the *Manhattan* incident, but as Lajeunesse shows, Canada refrained from openly acting on it. To prevent forceful backlash with potentially irreversible consequences, it steered instead a cautious, functional course in its international dealings.[80] At UNCLOS III this translated into the "package deal," which essentially allowed the two States to agree to disagree on the status of the Northwest Passage.[81] Claiming the waters of the Archipelago as historic internal waters, and delineating them unequivocally through baselines drawn around the Archipelago following the 1985 *Polar Sea* transit, does not prevent Canada from self-restraining and keeping its regulation within the bounds of Article 234.

3.2 *Article 234 in the Context of Receding Sea Ice Cover*

Another question regarding the extent of the geographical scope of Article 234 arises from the provision's reference to ice cover. In recent years, warming temperatures have caused tremendous loss of Arctic sea ice, which decreases in thickness and extent. Regarding the annual minimum extent at the end of the Arctic summer, the loss of sea ice area approaches a staggering 50 percent between 1979 and 2020.[82] Although sea ice attrition affects the entire region, its magnitude varies greatly across Arctic waters.[83] In the Canadian Arctic, some regions already experience a rapid increase in the number of ice-free days, while others are likely to retain thick multiyear ice over the next few decades.[84]

79 See also Nordquist *et al.* (n 32), para 234.1 (p. 393); McRae (n 76), pp. 109–111.
80 Lajeunesse (n 36), p. 178 ff.
81 Id., p. 202 ff.
82 See Lasserre in this volume.
83 Id., in particular Figure 1.
84 Jonathan Andrews, David Babb and David G. Barber, "Climate Change and Sea Ice: Shipping in Hudson Bay, Hudson Strait, and Foxe Basin (1980–2016)," *Elementa: Science of the Anthropocene* 6:19 (2018), https://doi.org/10.1525/elementa.281.

Given the overall trend of continued sea ice loss though,[85] the legal concern is that jurisdiction under Article 234 could simply melt away.

Under the heading 'ice-covered waters,' Article 234 refers to ice cover twice: coastal States are granted jurisdiction regarding "marine pollution from vessels in *ice-covered areas* ... where particularly severe climatic conditions and the *presence of ice covering such areas for most of the year* create obstructions or exceptional hazards to navigation" (emphasis added). Well before global warming became a concern, McRae and Goundrey framed the issue raised by this phrasing as a matter of material scope, focusing on whether coastal State measures are restricted to addressing obstructions and hazards created by the ice cover and severe climatic conditions.[86] This may reflect the general understanding of the time that the geographical scope of the provision was not in doubt.

Although 'ice cover' may in practice refer to a broad range of ice conditions, it is not defined in the LOSC. Its meaning varies depending on context, as illustrated by the various thresholds of ice concentration and ice thickness that are in use for scientific and navigational purposes.[87] Further specification in Article 234 that areas concerned are ice-covered "for most of the year" allows one to infer that the jurisdiction was not intended for regions that experience only seasonal ice cover, such as the North Atlantic, the Baltic Sea, the Bering Sea or the Sea of Okhotsk. It is noteworthy that Canada's regulation of Arctic shipping does not refer to ice cover, but determines the scope of application based on geographic boundaries, such as those of the definition of "arctic waters."[88] There is indeed good reason to think that the reference to ice cover was not intended to be taken in a literal, but rather in a figurative sense or as a general geographical marker.[89]

---

85   Warwick F. Vincent and Derek Mueller, "Witnessing Ice Habitat Collapse in the Arctic," *Science* 370:6520 (27 November 2020): 1031–1032, https://doi.org/10.1126/science.abe4491.

86   McRae and Goundrey (n 66), p. 216 ff. For the discussion on the material scope, see below.

87   NSIDC uses a 15 percent threshold, "meaning that if the data cell has greater than 15 percent ice concentration, the cell is labeled as 'ice-covered'." See National Snow and Ice Data Centre (NSIDC), "Why is Sea Ice Important?," https://nsidc.org/learn/parts-cryosphere /sea-ice/quick-facts-about-sea-ice. For presence of ice to be recorded on Canadian ice charts, its concentration must be at least one tenth. See "Interpreting Ice Charts: Chapter 3," Government of Canada, last modified 7 March 2016, https://www.canada.ca/en /environment-climate-change/services/ice-forecasts-observations/publications /interpreting-charts/chapter-3.html.

88   For the definition, see n 23.

89   Argument first made by Roman Dremliuga, "A Note on the Application of Article 234," *Ocean Development and International Law* 48:2 (2017): 128–135; see also Viatcheslav Gavrilov, Roman Dremliuga and Rustambek Nurimbetov, "Article 234 of the 1982 United Nations Convention on the Law of the Sea and Reduction of Ice Cover in the Arctic Ocean," *Marine*

This finds support in McRae's account of the provision's drafting history. Early references to 'ice-covered waters' were arguably made to contextualize the exceptional authority that was contemplated to allow the coastal State to address the "exceptional hazards to navigation" and the vulnerability of the region brought on by ice.[90] In the same vein, the *Virginia Commentary*—after referring to severe climatic conditions and the presence of ice as if citing criteria—states that it is "the general characteristic of the climate ... that should be borne in mind."[91]

As Kraska underlines, "[o]stensibly applicable to all 'ice-covered areas,' the new article was really only about the Arctic Ocean."[92] This understanding also transpires from the aforementioned US Memorandum for the President. It explains that "[w]hile the Arctic is not specified, the Article will apply only to 'ice-covered' areas ... This will in fact limit the area to the Arctic Ocean," adding that "Antarctica would not ... be included" in its purview.[93] Precisely why it is that the Arctic Ocean is not referred to in Article 234 is not clear, but explicit reference to it would have stood out in a convention applicable to the entire world ocean. A more generic reference to polar waters may have easily derailed negotiations by broadening the issues at stake and by increasing the number of interested States. McRae indeed credits the three-party negotiations and agreement on the terms of the provision for the successful inclusion of Article 234 in the LOSC.[94]

If ice cover was never considered a condition for the application of the 'Arctic exception' or 'Arctic Article,' as the provision is sometimes nicknamed,[95] then there should be no cause for concern that jurisdiction under Article 234 is melting away. Furthermore, despite the increasing likelihood that the Arctic Ocean will become ice-free during summer before mid-century, ice will continue to build up in winter.[96] 'Atlantification' of the Arctic Ocean, which entails

Policy 106 (2019): 103518, https://doi.org/10.1016/j.marpol.2019.103518; Kristin Bartenstein, Roman Dremliuga and Natalia Prisekina, "Regulation of Arctic Shipping in Canada and Russia," *Arctic Review on Law and Politics* 13 (2022): 1–23, https://doi.org/10.23865/arctic.v13.3229.

90   McRae (n 79), pp. 107–110.
91   Nordquist *et al.* (n 32), para 234.5(e) (p. 397).
92   James Kraska, "Governance of Ice-Covered Areas: Rule Construction in the Arctic Ocean," *Ocean Development and International Law* 45:3 (2014): 260, at 266.
93   *Memorandum for the President* (n 70), p. 3.
94   McRae (n 79), pp. 109–110.
95   For the latter, see Nordquist *et al.* (n 32), para 234.1 (p. 393).
96   Dirk Notz and Julienne Stroeve, "The Trajectory Towards a Seasonally Ice-Free Arctic Ocean," *Current Climate Change Reports* 4 (2018): 407–416, https://doi.org/10.1007/s40641-018-0113-2.

sea ice loss in winter, is mostly affecting the Eurasian Arctic.[97] Given long polar winters and the geophysical reality of the Canadian Arctic, ice is likely to remain a defining feature 'for most of the year' in the foreseeable future.

Finally, a teleological argument can be made that decreasing ice should have no bearing on the provision's geographical scope of application. Negotiation of Article 234 was motivated by the recognition that the Arctic environment is exceptionally sensitive and poses exceptional hazards to navigation. Jurisdiction under Article 234 was therefore premised on the acknowledgement that internationally agreed-upon rules and standards for navigation, mostly designed for more temperate ocean areas, may provide insufficient protection and may need to be complemented by unilateral coastal State measures.[98] As argued elsewhere, melting ice does not render the protective purpose of Article 234 obsolete, quite the contrary.[99] The strain it causes makes Arctic ecosystems less resilient to additional stressors, including navigation and vessel-source pollution,[100] and thus preventive measures all the more relevant.

4   Revisiting the Material Scope of Article 234

When Article 234 was negotiated in the 1970s, pollution by oil was by far the most widely known vessel-source threat posed to the Arctic environment. Elicited by the crossing of the SS *Manhattan*, the predominant disaster scenario was a black tide on pristine ice. Yet, Arctic shipping comes with a much more diverse array of threats. As detailed in Vincent *et al.* in this volume, many are invisible and by far not all result from oil pollution; stressors can be chemical, but also physical and biological. Noise pollution,[101] ship strikes,[102] habitat

---

97   Paul Tepes, Peter Nienow and Noel Gourmelen, "Accelerating Ice Mass Loss Across Arctic Russia in Response to Atmospheric Warming, Sea Ice Decline, and Atlantification of the Eurasian Arctic Shelf Seas," *Journal of Geophysical Research: Earth Surface* 126 (2021), e2021JF006068. https://doi.org/10.1029/2021JF006068.

98   See McRae (n 79), pp. 107–110.

99   Bartenstein *et al.* (n 89), p. 348.

100   See Vincent *et al.* in this volume.

101   Protection of the Arctic Marine Environment (PAME), *Underwater Noise in the Arctic: A State of Knowledge Report* (Akureyri: PAME Secretariat, 2019, https://oaarchive.arctic-council.org/bitstream/handle/11374/2394/Underwater%20noise%20report.pdf?sequence=1&isAllowed=y.

102   Donna D.W. Hauser, Kristin L. Laidre and Harry L. Stern, "Vulnerability of Arctic Marine Mammals to Vessel Traffic in the Increasingly Ice-free Northwest Passage and Northern Sea Route," *Proceedings of the National Academy of Sciences* 115:29 (July 2018): 7617–7622; https://doi.org/10.1073/pnas.1803543115.

disruption through icebreaking[103] and introduction of invasive species[104] were all presumably absent from the negotiators' minds. Article 234 provides coastal States with jurisdiction that, even considering its functional approach, seems rather narrow in its focus on "the prevention, reduction and control of marine pollution from vessels." That raises the issue of whether and how Article 234 may help address the broad range of stressors that come with Arctic shipping.

As UNCLOS III president Tommy Koh said, the LOSC is intended to provide a "constitution for the oceans which will stand the test of time."[105] This ambitious goal may be best achieved through an evolutionary approach to interpretation and will inspire the following examination of the kinds of threats a coastal State may address under Article 234. Scrutiny of specific measures as to their compatibility with the obligation spelled out in Article 234 to "have due regard to navigation and the protection and preservation of the marine environment" will, however, be mostly beyond the scope of this chapter.

4.1   Jurisdiction Restricted to Measures Addressing Cold and Ice-Induced Threats?

McRae and Goundrey discuss in detail whether the reference to "severe climatic conditions and the presence of ice" restricts the material scope of Article 234 to measures that address risks of pollution resulting specifically from these Arctic conditions. Tracing the drafting history of Article 234, they note a shift in focus.[106] While early discussions, prompted by Canada, centred on the distinct conditions that make Arctic shipping especially hazardous and warrant particular measures,[107] the region's exceptional ecological vulnerability came into focus at the Conference on the Prevention of Pollution from Ships held in 1973 by the Inter-Governmental Maritime Consultative Organization (IMCO,

---

103   For trends in the so-called Last Ice Area, see Robert Newton et al., "Defining the "Ice Shed" of the Arctic Ocean's Last Ice Area and Its Future Evolution," (2021) 9 Earth's Future, https://doi.org/10.1029/2021EF001988.

104   Conservation of Arctic Flora and Fauna (CAFF) and PAME, Arctic Invasive Alien Species: Strategy and Action Plan 2017 (Akureyri, 2017), https://www.caff.is/strategies-series /415-arctic-invasive-alien-species-strategy-and-action-plan/download. Based on the Strategy, CAFF and PAME collaborate on a project on Marine Invasive Alien Species in Arctic Waters (https://www.pame.is/projects-new/arctic-shipping/pame-shipping-highlights/459 -marine-invasive-alien-species-in-arctic-waters).

105   Tommy T.B. Koh, "A Constitution for the Oceans," adapted from Statements by the President on 6 and 11 December 1982 at the final session of UNCLOS III at Montego Bay, https: //www.un.org/Depts/los/convention_agreements/texts/koh_english.pdf.

106   McRae and Goundrey (n 66), pp. 216–217.

107   Canada, Draft Articles for a Comprehensive Marine Pollution Convention, 9 March 1973, A/ AC.138/SC.III/L.28.

renamed IMO in 1982).[108] At UNCLOS III, this concern translated into the addition of "major harm to or irreversible disturbance of the ecological balance" to the 1975 draft provision.[109] Reference to "ice-covered areas" was added in 1976 to make the provision's "Arctic character" plain.[110] According to McRae and Goundrey, a narrow interpretation of Article 234, providing authority limited to cold and ice-induced threats, does not seem to be supported by the provision's literal reading or its drafting history.[111] A broader interpretation, which would encompass measures warranted by the particular vulnerability of the Arctic ecosystems, would further be in keeping with the contemporary acknowledgment expressed in the Polar Code's Preamble that the impact of ship operations on the environment needs to be minimized.[112]

McRae and Goundrey caution, however, that this broad interpretation of Article 234 may render much of the provision's wording related to climatic conditions and ice cover "unnecessary and essentially repetitive."[113] As emerges from the discussion above, however, the purpose of these references may not be to define the material scope of jurisdiction, but to outline the geographical scope of the jurisdiction under Article 234. This supports the view that coastal States may subject navigation to measures that address the particular vulnerability of the Arctic, whether or not the risk they address is created by the typically Arctic conditions of cold and ice. Accordingly, the main constraint on measures adopted under Article 234 stems from the provision's focus on vessel-source pollution.

4.2   Measures to Respond to Pollution Threats

The word 'pollution' appears twice in Article 234: first, with respect to the goal of coastal State measures, that is, "the prevention, reduction and control of *marine pollution from vessels*"; second, with respect to the geographical scope of jurisdiction, that is, "where ... *pollution of the marine environment* could cause major harm to or irreversible disturbance of the ecological balance" (emphases added). According to the definition in LOSC Article 1(4), "pollution of the marine environment" is

---

108   Greece *et al.*, *Possible alternative text of Article 8*, 18 October 1973, IMCO Doc. MP/CONF /C.1/WP.36.
109   ISNT, A/CONF.62/WP.8/PartIII, Article 20(5).
110   RSNT, A/CONF.62/WP.8/Rev.1/PartIII, Article 43.
111   McRae and Goundrey (n 66), p. 216.
112   Polar Code (n 8), Preamble, first recital.
113   McRae and Goundrey (n 66), p. 217.

the introduction by man, directly or indirectly, of substance or energy into the marine environment, including estuaries, which results or is likely to result in such deleterious effects as harm to living resources and marine life, hazards to human health, hindrance to marine activities, including fishing and other legitimate uses of the sea, impairment of quality for use of sea water and reduction of amenities.

Oil and other chemical substances, but also sewage, food waste and garbage, all addressed by the Polar Code,[114] clearly fall under this definition. Other kinds of chemical, biological and physical stressors, however, raise the issue of the contours of the pollution a coastal State may address.

Black carbon emissions, for example, have an outsize impact in the Arctic, blackening white surfaces and accelerating local melting.[115] Yet, it may seem questionable whether ship exhaust, emitted into the atmosphere, constitutes pollution of the 'marine environment' in the sense of Article 1(4). The broader language of "marine pollution from vessels" in Article 234 suggests, however, that the meaning of pollution is informed both by the emitting medium, that is, the ship and the receiving medium (water column, ice cover and super-jacent atmosphere).[116] As can be drawn from Articles 212 and 222, vessel-source air pollution is in the remit of the LOSC and unilateral coastal State action to tackle black carbon emissions can arguably be considered within the scope of Article 234. This is particularly relevant in the context of slow multilateral standard-setting under Article 212(3): after more than a decade of discussion, the IMO has yet to agree on mandatory measures. That said, Canada, actively engaged in the IMO process by coordinating the Correspondence Group of the IMO Prevention, Preparedness and Response Subcommittee,[117] does not appear to harbour any ambition for unilateral action on the matter.[118]

---

114   Polar Code (n 8), Part II-A.
115   P.K. Quinn *et al.*, *The Impact of Black Carbon on Arctic Climate*, AMAP Technical Report No. 4 (Oslo: Arctic Monitoring and Assessment Programme (AMAP), 2011), in particular 48f, https://www.amap.no/documents/download/977/inline.
116   The same broad understanding also underpins MARPOL (n 53), Article 2, according to which "discharge, in relation to harmful substances or effluents containing such substances, means any release howsoever caused from a ship and includes any escape, disposal, spilling, leaking, pumping, emitting or emptying."
117   See Canada, *Report of the Correspondence Group on Reduction of the Impact on the Arctic of Black Carbon Emissions from International Shipping*, IMO Doc PPR 8/5, 18 December 2020.
118   See also "Joint Statement by Transport Canada and the U.S. Department of Transportation on the Nexus between Transportation and Climate Change," Transport Canada, 25 February 2021, https://www.canada.ca/en/transport-canada/news/2021/02/joint

Alien species introduced in Arctic waters are a biological threat and as such not intuitively perceived as 'pollution,' although they may have a polluting effect. Travelling on ship hulls—as so-called biofouling or hull-fouling—or in ballast water, some of them may thrive well enough in their new environment to become invasive, disturbing or destroying the balance of ecosystems that have little or no defence to hold them in check. While few species have been introduced in the Arctic so far, a warming environment may not only attract more shipping, but could also become more hospitable—and thus more vulnerable—to alien species.[119] The International Convention for the Control and Management of Ships' Ballast Water and Sediments, in force since September 2017, sets forth general minimum standards,[120] which are not designed for the particular needs of Arctic ecosystems. The Polar Code merely recommends that the specific, albeit non-binding guidelines applicable to the Antarctic Treaty area[121] be taken into consideration.[122] As for the issue of invasive species introduced through biofouling, it is only addressed by generally applicable non-binding guidelines, which have been under review for years.[123] The scientific discussion of coating properties in cold temperatures and the risks and benefits of ice abrasion suggests the relevance of Arctic- or polar-specific guidance.[124] Unilateral coastal State action under Article 234 seems defensible, although there may currently be no appetite for it.

Ship-generated noise alters the soundscape of the marine environment with the potential of causing significant harm, in particular to noise-sensitive species. Many Arctic mammals have adapted to life in an ice-covered and therefore comparatively quiet ocean by developing unique sound-depending

---

-statement-by-transport-canada-and-the-us-department-of-transportation-on-the-nexus-between-transportation-and-climate-change.html.

119 Farrah T. Chan et al., "Climate Change Opens New Frontiers for Marine Species in the Arctic: Current Trends and Future Invasion Risks," Global Change Biology 25:1 (2019): 25–38, https://doi.org/10.1111/gcb.14469.

120 International Convention for the Control and Management of Ships' Ballast Water and Sediments, 13 February 2004, IMO Doc BWM/CONF/36 (16 February 2004) (in force 8 September 2017).

121 Guidelines for Ballast Water Exchange in the Antarctic Treaty Area, IMO Resolution MEPC.163(56), IMO Doc MEPC 56/23 (13 July 2007).

122 Polar Code (n 8), Part II-B, at p. 4.

123 Guidelines for the Control and Management of Ships' Biofouling to Minimize the Transfer of Invasive Aquatic Species, IMO Resolution MEPC.207(62), IMO Doc MEPC 62/24/Add.1 (15 July 2011), Annex 26; Sub-Committee on Pollution Prevention and Response, Report to the Maritime Environment Protection Committee, IMO Doc PPR 8/13 (16 April 2021), s 4.

124 Friends of the Earth International (FOEI), Vessel Biofouling and Bioinvasions in Arctic Waters, IMO Doc MEPC 73/INF.24 (17 August 2018).

navigation and communication capabilities. Noise may cause hearing loss, stress and behaviour disruption. According to a 2021 PAME report, the increase in underwater noise in the Arctic is significant and concerning.[125] Interestingly, noise causes pollution within the meaning of the LOSC Article 1(4) definition by the "introduction ... of ... energy." For the moment, IMO instruments do little to address the problem. Non-binding guidelines issued in 2014, considered insufficient, are currently under review.[126] According to the Polar Code, voyage planning and decisions related to route selection and speed can be informed by noise-reducing considerations, but no specific obligation exists.[127] The Polar Water Operational Manual could prove a useful tool to integrate such considerations in the decision-making process, provided its scope is expanded beyond matters of operational capabilities and limitations of ships.[128] As underwater noise in the Arctic is correlated with growing traffic in increasingly ice-free waters, it is among the threats that are not specifically caused by Arctic conditions.[129] Regarding engine and propeller noise in particular, ice cover that prevents shipping activities may even amount to a protective factor. However, if shipping is possible, harm caused by underwater noise is exacerbated by the vulnerability of noise-sensitive Arctic species. Ice-induced noise is notably caused by hull-ice interactions and icebreaking, which may occur even in light ice conditions. Unilateral coastal State measures, including speed limits to reduce acoustic pollution at its source and routeing measures to mitigate its impact, applied where appropriate during critical periods to vulnerable habitats, appears therefore to be covered by Article 234.

4.3   *Measures to Respond to Other Types of Environmental Threats*
Shipping causes disruption in more ways than through pollution by the introduction of substances or energy as envisioned in Article 1(4). For instance, ship strikes, that is, collisions between marine mammals and vessels, are often

---

125   PAME, *Underwater Noise Pollution from Shipping in the Arctic* (PAME, 2021), 8 ff, https://www.pame.is/document-library/pame-reports-new/pame-ministerial-deliverables/2021-12th-arctic-council-ministerial-meeting-reykjavik-iceland/787-underwater-noise-pollution-from-shipping-in-the-arctic/file.

126   Guidelines for the Reduction of Underwater Noise from Commercial Shipping to Address Adverse Impacts on Marine Life, IMO Doc MEPC.1/Circ.833 (7 April 2014); Secretariat, *Outcome of MEPC 76 on the review of MEPC.1/Circ.833*, IMO Doc SDC 8/14 (1 October 2021).

127   Polar Code (n 8), Part I-A, ch 11, 11.3(7) and Part I-B, 12.1, according to which "in the event that marine mammals are encountered, any existing best practices should be considered to minimize unnecessary disturbance."

128   Polar Code (n 8), Part I-A, ch 2 and Part I-B, 3 and Appendix 2.

129   See n 106–113 and accompanying text.

fatal. The risk is highest for mammals that display near-surface behaviour and occupy highly travelled habitats, such as bowhead whales in Lancaster Sound, a gateway to the Northwest Passage.[130] For coastal State measures, such as speed limits and routeing measures, to fall into the scope of Article 234, the ship as such would need to be considered pollution. This was certainly not what negotiators had in mind when drafting Articles 234 and 1(4). Yet, from an ecological point of view, the vessel is an object foreign to the marine environment, harming wildlife that happens to be on its path. An evolutionary, extensive interpretation of Article 234 would be in keeping with the increased awareness of the impact shipping has on the ecology of Arctic waters. However, although a general purpose of Article 234 is to grant coastal States authority for harm reduction, it is uncertain whether the jurisdiction's boundaries can be stretched to encompass the regulation of ship strikes. In waters under Canadian jurisdiction further south, ship routeing measures are currently based on IMO decisions[131] and, in internal waters, on unrestricted jurisdiction.[132] Given this context, it seems unlikely that Article 234 will be invoked—or accepted—as a basis for unilateral regulation of ship strikes.

Equally difficult is the case of icebreaking. Ice provides a habitat for many species, from microorganisms, like algae, all the way up the food chain to marine mammals. Warming temperatures not only melt the icy barrier to navigation, but also a unique ecological niche for ice-dependent species. Icebreaking contributes to the fracturing of ecosystems; it may also disrupt critical migration routes and create death traps for animals and the humans who hunt them.[133] It might even locally speed up melting processes.[134] The only effective way to protect ice habitats against the effects of icebreaking is to prevent icebreaking. Prohibitions could be limited in space and time to balance navigation and protection needs under the due regard clause of Article 234. They could apply to areas identified as particularly valuable habitats or in key periods, including in

---

130   Hauser, Laidre and Stern (n 102), p. 7619.
131   For instance, a seasonal area to be avoided was created by the IMO under SOLAS Chapter V in the Roseway Basin, in Canada's EEZ off of Nova Scotia, to protect the North Atlantic right whale, IMO Doc MSC 83/28/Add.3 Annexe 25 (2 November 2007).
132   In the Gulf of St-Lawrence, Transport Canada has issued seasonal regulation imposing speed limits and areas to be avoided since 2018. See latest Interim Order for the Protection of North Atlantic Right Whales (*Eubalaena glacialis*) in the Gulf of St. Lawrence, 2022, 20 April 2022, 2022-04-30 *Canada Gazette* Part I, Vol. 156, No. 18
133   See Breanna Bishop *et al.*, "How Icebreaking Governance Interacts with Inuit Rights and Livelihoods in Nunavut: A Policy Review," *Marine Policy* 137 (2022): 104957, https://doi.org/10.1016/j.marpol.2022.104957.
134   The effect is comparatively small; see NSIDC, *Are Icebreakers Changing the Climate?*, 17 April 2012, https://nsidc.org/learn/ask-scientist/are-icebreakers-changing-climate.

spring when ice is critical as a breeding or feeding platform or for migration routes and, once broken, may not freeze up again.

Canada's Tuvaijuittuq Marine Protected Area (MPA), located north of Ellesmere Island, provides an interesting case study with respect to icebreaking. The area was granted interim status with the objective to protect part of the Last Ice Area, which retains the thickest and oldest multiyear pack ice in the Arctic.[135] Prohibited is any activity "that disturbs, damages, destroys or removes from the Marine Protected Area any living marine organism or any part of its habitat, or is likely to do so,"[136] which is broad enough to include navigation and icebreaking. However, exceptions apply to national defence and marine scientific research activities,[137] as well as to navigation carried out by a foreign national, ship or State.[138] In clear contradiction to the very purpose of the MPA, icebreaking remains possible, including for the exercise of navigational rights by foreign-flagged vessels. This raises the question of whether Canada could choose to prohibit such icebreaking activities under Article 234.

Icebreaking cannot by any stretch of the imagination be considered 'pollution' and its prohibition would in fact entail prohibition of navigation. It could be argued that prohibition of icebreaking is in keeping with the spirit of Article 234, which was designed to provide Arctic coastal States with the authority to impose reasonable restrictions that help prevent "major harm or irreversible disturbance of the ecological balance." Further support for such a teleological interpretation could be found in the general Article 192 obligation "to protect and preserve the marine environment." However, the exceptions provided by the legal framework of the Tuvaijuittuq MPA suggest that the spirit of Article 234 may have seemed insufficient to support measures that effectively prohibit international navigation. No such jurisdictional restrictions would apply to those waters Canada considers internal waters. However, the result would be a patchwork regime of navigational rights that depend on the vessel's location in the MPA. This is without considering the political risk the claim of full sovereignty entails, a risk that may not be worth taking in an area with no commercial navigation.[139]

---

135   *Order Designating the Tuvaijuittuq Marine Protected Area*, SOR/2019-282.

136   Id., Article 4(1).

137   Id., Article 3.

138   Id., Article 4(2)(a).

139   See Fisheries and Oceans Canada, "Report on the Designation of the Tuvaijuittuq Marine Protected Area," Government of Canada, last modified 25 February 2021, https://www.dfo-mpo.gc.ca/oceans/publications/tuvaijuittuq/designation/index-eng.html.

4.4   *Measures to Respond to Indirect Environmental Threats*

The link between safety measures and pollution prevention is explicitly acknowledged in the Polar Code.[140] Article 234, for its part, acknowledges the "obstruction and exceptional hazards" ice creates. While this lends credit to the argument that coastal State measures may include safety measures,[141] the extent to which this is possible remains uncertain. Although many safety measures may lower the risk of incidents that have the potential to generate pollution, not all of them are directly aimed at "the prevention, reduction and control of marine pollution." A case in point is the measures focusing on lifesaving in case of an accident, including provisions on survival equipment, rescue considerations and firefighting systems. Mitigation of the environmental impact of an accident as a contingent positive side effect may prove insufficient for such measures to fall under Article 234.

By contrast, safety measures designed to reduce the risk of accidents or their environmental fallout can arguably be considered pollution prevention measures under Article 234. Traffic regulation schemes, for instance, are thought to be part of the Article 234 toolbox,[142] as are manning and machinery requirements and hull design and construction standards. The latter were part of Canada's regulatory regime established under the 1970 AWPPA,[143] complementing more conventional measures of pollution prevention, such as restrictions related to the deposit of oil.[144] The whole regime, including the safety measures, has been considered covered by the jurisdiction set forth in Article 234.[145]

5   Revisiting Canada's 'Single Approach' to Regulating Arctic Shipping

Canada subjects navigation in its Arctic waters to several laws and regulations, most prominently the ASSPPR adopted under the AWPPA, but also the *Shipping Safety Control Zones Order*[146] and NORDREG. These regulations follow a 'single approach' in that they set forth a uniform legal regime, which does not distinguish between the various LOSC maritime zones, although these have been

---

140   Polar Code (n 8), Preamble, recital 5.
141   Augustìn Blanco-Bazàn, "Specific Regulations for Shipping and Environmental Protection in the Arctic: The Work of the international Maritime Organization," *International Journal of Marine and Coastal Law* 24:2 (2009): 381, 383.
142   Franckx and Boone (n 67), para 14.
143   RSPPR (n 56), ss 26 and 6, schs V–VII.
144   Id., s 29.
145   Nordquist *et al.* (n 32), para 234.5(g) (p. 397).
146   CRC, c 356.

transposed into Canadian law.[147] Even the zone/date system, which governs access to Shipping Safety Control Zones, differentiates not based on maritime zones, but on vessel capacity and probable ice conditions in a given area at a given time of year.[148]

5.1   *The Single Approach and Article 234*

The single approach dates back to the 1970 AWPPA. The claim that Arctic waters within the Arctic Archipelago are historic waters and under Canada's full sovereignty, which was made explicit only after Canada established its very first shipping regime for the Arctic, had no consequence on that regime. This speaks to Canada's consistently functional approach to regulating navigation with the sole objective of making it safe and protective of the environment. Then Prime Minister Trudeau mapped out the path in 1970 stating that Canada had no intention to prevent navigation altogether and considering it "senseless" "to deny passage to all foreign vessels in the name of Canadian sovereignty."[149] Canada does not display any appetite either for promoting its Arctic waterways as an alternative to established global shipping routes,[150] choosing instead the pragmatic path of adjusting to developing needs through the establishment of low-impact shipping corridors, described by Dawson and Song in this volume.

The single approach may cloud the jurisdictional basis of Canada's Arctic shipping regulations. From the drafting history of Article 234, it is but a small step to conclude that Canada's regulatory regime rests on the authority granted by that provision. Yet, Canada has never said so explicitly until two regulatory reforms in 2010 provided the opportunity to comment on the issue. Regarding the expansion of Canada's Arctic waters to 200 M, the Legislative Summary notes—rather cautiously—that Article 234 "appears to permit [the] proposed extension."[151] As to its newly mandatory vessel traffic services, Canada declared—more assertively—before the IMO that "Article 234 provides a complete legal justification in international law for NORDREG."[152]

The main legal advantage of a single uniform regime is that it provides regulatory coherence that makes application and enforcement relatively

---

147   *Oceans Act*, SC 1996, c 31, in particular ss 4–21.
148   See id.
149   House of Commons, *Debates* (24 October 1969), 39.
150   This is in stark contrast to the Russian approach, see Bartenstein *et al.* (n 89), p. 349.
151   Canada, *Bill-C3: An Act to Amend the Arctic Waters Pollution Prevention Act* (*Legislative Summary*), 13 February 2009, 8, https://lop.parl.ca/staticfiles/PublicWebsite/Home /ResearchPublications/LegislativeSummaries/PDF/40-2/c3-e.pdf.
152   Canada, *Comments on Document MSC 88/11/2*, IMO Doc MSC 88/11/3 (5 October 2010), in particular 5.1 *in fine*.

straightforward.[153] Politically, it also seems easier to contend with challenges related to the extent of coastal State jurisdiction—in particular the material scope of application of Article 234 and its due regard clause—than with challenges related to the claim of full sovereignty. Despite the functional nature of Article 234 and the boundaries it imposes on coastal States, even measures that espouse a more extensive interpretation of the jurisdiction appear to be acceptable.[154] By contrast, measures based on a claim of full sovereignty, even if they are limited to environmental protection, entail the risk that they are challenged as a matter of principle.

The main inconvenience of a single regime based on Article 234 is, of course, that it has to remain within the bounds of the provision's limited jurisdiction. Although Article 234 may provide the jurisdictional basis for Canada's regulations regarding its EEZ and, to some extent, its territorial sea, it seems more accurate to describe the provision as the self-imposed *de facto* ceiling regarding regulations that apply to waters of the Archipelago considered internal waters. Given its claim of full sovereignty and unrestricted jurisdiction, Canada does not need to rely on Article 234, although it may, of course, decide in full sovereignty to regulate navigation in a way that does not exceed its stricter bounds, extending the functional approach to its internal waters.

This entails that Canada may have to contend with the limits of the jurisdiction provided under Article 234. Regulations not related to pollution in the broadest sense may fall outside its material scope and if they have the effect of preventing navigation, they may conflict with its due regard obligation. For instance, prohibition of icebreaking applicable to a sensitive habitat or a vital migration route as part of an area-to-be-avoided within a marine protected area may be difficult to impose based on Article 234.

5.2   *Overcoming the Limitations of Article 234*

One way to deal with the constraints of Article 234 is to push against its boundaries. A broad, evolutionary interpretation, in keeping with present-day knowledge of Arctic ecosystems and the stressors that weigh on them, may help achieve an adequate level of protection. Such an interpretation should take into account, beyond Article 234 itself and its immediate treaty context,

---

153   See also *Whitbread* v. *Walley*, [1990] 3 SCR 1273.
154   While Canada's 2010 decision to make NORDREG mandatory sparked controversy within the IMO (see IMO, *Report of the MSC on its 88th Session*, IMO Doc MSC 88/26 (15 December 2010), para 11.28 ff.), NORDREG has since been effectively applied.

"any relevant rules of international law applicable in the relations between the parties."[155]

The Preamble of the Polar Code in particular may inform the debate on the scope of Article 234. It acknowledges that "coastal communities in the Arctic could be, and that polar ecosystems are, vulnerable to human activities, such as ship operation"[156] and that there is a "relationship between the additional safety measures and the protection of the environment."[157] The unambiguous reaffirmation of the vulnerability of Arctic ecosystems emphasizes what should be the core motivation of any regulation of Arctic shipping. The reference to 'ship operation' in general, for its part, may extend the discussion beyond the narrow issue of vessel-source pollution to the wide range of chemical, physical and biological stressors that come with shipping in the Arctic, as highlighted by Vincent *et al.* in this volume. This and the acknowledgement that safety of navigation has environmental benefits may help make the case for a broad understanding of the material scope of Article 234.

The reference to the vulnerability of coastal communities may reinforce new coastal State approaches to governing the regulation of shipping in waters under their jurisdiction. Canada recently adopted the *United Nations Declaration on the Rights of Indigenous Peoples Act*,[158] committing to go forward by using what Beveridge calls a "decolonizing lens" in this volume. A systematic involvement of Inuit communities in the design and application of Canadian regulations on shipping in Canadian waters of Inuit Nunangat, the Inuit homeland, including with regard to the establishment of low-impact shipping corridors,[159] may not only influence regulatory choices, but also shift our understanding of the "scientific evidence" referred to in Article 234 and required to justify these choices.

Broad, evolutionary interpretation of Article 234 has its limits, however. Regulations intended to apply within the Arctic Archipelago, but difficult to justify under Article 234, may therefore prompt Canada to explore the option of departing from the single approach and relying on the claim of full sovereignty. The ecological risk such regulations are intended to reduce has to be weighed against the political risk this departure entails. The regulation as such could be challenged, but the even greater political risk is that reliance

---

155   VCLT (n 65), Article 31(3)(c).
156   Polar Code (n 8), Preamble, recital 4.
157   Id., recital 5.
158   *United Nations Declaration on the Rights of Indigenous Peoples Act*, SC 2021, ch 14.
159   Related to these corridors, see Dawson and Song, Doelle *et al.* and Lalonde and Bankes, all in this volume.

on full sovereignty is perceived as a departure from the functional approach. This approach—though it was not accepted *de jure* in all respects—has nevertheless enabled Canada to impose regulations that have *de facto* mostly been complied with. A perceived departure from the functional approach may invite enhanced scrutiny of Canadian regulations and even call into question the relative leeway Canada has long enjoyed. Treading the fine line could result in a renewed functional approach, according to which full sovereignty is invoked only if "functionally necessary"[160] to achieve a carefully determined environmental goal. If the ecological risk is significant and well documented, the adoption of protective measures beyond the scope of Article 234 may again put potential challengers in a political and moral bind that leads to *de facto*, if not *de jure*, acceptance of the regulations.

6   Conclusion

This chapter started by tracing the genesis of Canada's legal regime on Arctic shipping, set in motion by the 1969 *Manhattan* crossing. Canada's regulatory choices—and in particular its functional approach centring on pollution prevention—remained essentially unaffected by the claim of full sovereignty over the waters of the Arctic Archipelago on historic grounds, made discreetly in 1973 and openly in 1985, and the disagreement on the merits of that claim, challenged notably by the United States. The inclusion of Article 234 in the LOSC has provided coastal States with exceptional jurisdiction over ice-covered waters and effectively endorsed Canada's functional approach. In 2017, international standard-setting resulted in the entry into force of the Polar Code, which pursues an extended functional approach that aims for pollution prevention and safety of navigation. Canada's new ASSPPR embrace the Polar Code, all while taking advantage in some minor respects of the continued possibility to rely on coastal State jurisdiction under Article 234.

The chapter then turned to the geographical scope of Article 234. Despite uncertainties expressed in the literature as to whether the provision applies to all waters landward of 200 M, Canada's regulation applicable to all Arctic waters seems to be on solid ground. It appears in particular that the Northwest Passage, in the event it is determined to be a strait used for international navigation, can still be subjected to regulations based on Article 234. As for the references to ice cover in Article 234, they are best characterized as a geographical marker, rather

---

160   See McDorman (n 21), p. 75.

than a prerequisite for coastal State jurisdiction. Even the seasonal disappearance of ice during the Arctic summer—an ecological catastrophe waiting to happen—does not seem to entail a shrinking geographical scope of Article 234.

The material scope of Article 234 was examined next. While the provision was arguably fashioned to provide jurisdiction on vessel-source substance pollution, its objective, the awareness that contemporary vessel-caused threats go beyond discharge of substances and the acknowledgement that safety measures may have a protective effect for the environment all contribute to make a compelling case for a broader interpretation of the material scope of Article 234. However, some regulations, although effective from an environmental point of view, may still be difficult to justify under Article 234. Prohibition of icebreaking, which may have the practical effect of preventing navigation altogether, is a prominent example.

Finally, Canada's single approach to regulating Arctic shipping, seemingly based on Article 234, was assessed. Canada has fared well in the past, notably because of the functional course inherent to the single approach, which allowed it to push boundaries and impose regulations all while signalling restraint. Still, Article 234 may prove too limited in scope to address some of the stressors that come with navigation at a time of tremendous environmental change in the Arctic. With respect to shipping within the Arctic Archipelago, reliance on full sovereignty may therefore be worth exploring. Steering a continued, although broadened, functional course may help avoid backlash that calls into question both new and established regulations.

Acknowledgements

This chapter draws on research supported by the Social Sciences and Humanities Research Council. I wish to thank workshop participants, in particular Aldo Chircop and Suzanne Lalonde, for incisive comments on an earlier draft of the chapter.

CHAPTER 11

The Modern Case Law on the Powers and Responsibilities of Flag States: Navigating Canada's Arctic Waters

Nigel Bankes

Abstract

This chapter has two principal goals. First, it assesses the powers and responsibilities of flag States in light of the current jurisprudence, and, second it considers the implications of this case law for flag State powers and responsibilities within an Arctic context, especially in light of the adoption of the Polar Code. The recent case law confirms the plenary and exclusive nature of flag State jurisdiction but it also emphasizes the due diligence obligation of flag States to enforce relevant laws and standards with respect to such matters as the safety of navigation, protection of the environment, or fisheries. These standards include the so-called rules of reference or GAIRS (generally accepted international rules and standards) including the Polar Code.

Keywords

law of the sea – flag State powers – flag State responsibilities – Polar Code – due diligence

1   Introduction

This chapter has two principal goals. First, it assesses the powers and responsibilities of flag States in light of the growing jurisprudence of the International Tribunal for the Law of the Sea and arbitral tribunals established under Annex VII of the United Nations Convention on the Law of the Sea (LOSC) on the interpretation of the relevant provisions of that convention.[1] Second, the chapter considers the implications of this case law for flag State powers and responsibilities within an Arctic context, especially in light of the adoption of the

---

1   United Nations Convention on the Law of the Sea, 10 December 1982 (in force 16 November 1994), 1833 *UNTS* 396 [LOSC].

International Code for Ships Operating in Polar Waters (Polar Code) by the International Maritime Organization (IMO).[2] This volume is largely concerned with Canada's position as an Arctic *coastal* State, but it is also important to consider the rules pertaining to flag States insofar as such rules might impose limits on the powers of a coastal State to prescribe or enforce rules with respect to foreign vessels, while, at the same time, allowing a coastal State to seek the assistance of the flag State in ensuring that its ships observe the lawful rules of the coastal State with respect to navigation and protection of the marine environment.

Much of the literature on flag State jurisdiction emphasizes the plenary and exclusive nature of the flag State's jurisdiction (or power) over vessels flying its flag.[3] While many of the recent decisions canvassed here confirm this interpretation (for example, *M/V 'Norstar'*[4] and *Arctic Sunrise*[5]), other decisions emphasize the due diligence responsibilities of the flag State to enforce relevant laws with respect to such matters as the safety of navigation, protection of the environment, or fisheries. These decisions include the International Tribunal for the Law of the Sea (ITLOS) *Request for an Advisory Opinion Submitted by the Sub-Regional Fisheries Commission* (*SRFC Advisory Opinion*)[6] and the *South China Sea Arbitration* (*The Republic of Philippines* v. *The People's Republic of China*).[7] The laws at issue include both the laws of a coastal State that are opposable against foreign flagged vessels as well as the so-called rules of reference incorporated into the norm structure of the LOSC, either by a general *renvoi* or by reference to the rules adopted by a relevant international organization, most frequently in this context, the IMO.[8] The Polar Code is one such rule of

---

2   International Code for Ships Operating in Polar Waters (Polar Code), IMO Doc MEPC 68/21/Add.1, Annex 10, entered into force 1 January 2017. The consolidated text is available here http://www.imo.org/en/MediaCentre/HotTopics/polar/Documents/POLAR%20CODE%20TEXT%20AS%20ADOPTED.pdf.

3   See, for example, Richard Barnes, "Flag States," in *The Oxford Handbook of the Law of the Sea*, eds., Donald Rothwell, Alex Oude Eflerink, Karen Scott and Tim Stephens (Oxford: Oxford University Press, 2015), 304–324.

4   *M/V 'Norstar'* (*Panama* v. *Italy*), Judgment, 10 April 2019, ITLOS Reports 2018–2019, 10.

5   *Arctic Sunrise Arbitration* (*Netherlands* v. *Russia*), Award, 14 August 2015, Permanent Court of Arbitration (PCA), Case No. 2014-02.

6   *Request for an Advisory Opinion Submitted by the Sub-Regional Fisheries Commission*, Advisory Opinion, 2 April 2015, ITLOS Reports 2015, 4 [*SRFC Advisory Opinion*].

7   *South China Sea Arbitration* (*The Republic of Philippines* v. *The People's Republic of China*), Award, 12 July 2016) PCA, Case No. 2013-19.

8   W Van Reenen, "Rules of Reference in the New Convention on the Law of the Sea in Particular Connection with Pollution of the Sea by Oil from Tankers," *Netherlands Yearbook of International Law* XII (1981): 3–44; Catherine Redgwell, "Mind the Gap in the GAIRS: The Role of Other Instruments in LOSC Regime Implementation in the Offshore Energy Sector," *International Journal of Marine and Coastal Law* 29 (2014): 600–621; and, most recently, Lan Ngoc Nguyen, "Expanding the Environmental Regulatory Scope of UNCLOS Through the Rules of Reference: Potentials and Limits," *Ocean Development & International Law* (ODIL) 52:4 (2021): 419–444.

reference, and it principally falls to flag States to adopt and enforce the terms of the Polar Code. Canada has chosen to implement the Polar Code (with some modifications) through adoption of the *Arctic Shipping Safety and Pollution Prevention Regulations* (ASSPPR).[9] The Regulations apply not only to Canadian flagged vessels navigating in polar waters, but also to foreign vessels navigating in a Canadian Shipping Safety Control Zone. In sum, the Regulations rely on Canada's position as both a flag State and coastal State.

Part I begins with a review of the basic rules with respect to flag State powers, the immunity of foreign flagged vessels, and freedom of navigation before turning to examine the responsibilities and duties of flag States, including those responsibilities arising from the duty of due regard and from any relevant rules of reference.

Part II considers the implications of these rules and the interpretive case law for implementation of the Polar Code and Canada's ASSPPR.

2 Part 1: Flag State Powers, Immunities and Responsibilities

2.1 *The Basic Rules with Respect to Flag State Powers, the Immunity of Foreign Flagged Vessels, and Freedom of Navigation*

It is up to each State to establish the terms and conditions on which it will grant nationality to a ship or different categories of ship.[10] While there must be "a genuine link between the State and ship," the existence of such a link is not a condition precedent to the grant of nationality; rather the requirement of a genuine link supports the need "to secure more effective implementation of the duties of the flag State."[11]

---

9   SOR/2017-286 [ASSPPR]. The regulatory impact assessment statement (RIAS) is available at https://gazette.gc.ca/rp-pr/p1/2017/2017-07-01/html/reg1-eng.html (1 July 2017). For commentary on the regulations, see Kristin Bartenstein, "Between the Polar Code and Article 234: The Balance in Canada's Arctic Shipping Safety and Pollution Preventions Regulations" *ODIL* 50 (2019): 335–362; Kristin Bartenstein and Suzanne Lalonde, "Shipping in the Canadian and Russian Arctic: Domestic Legal Responses to the Polar Code," in *Arctic Shipping: Climate Change, Commercial Traffic and Port Development*, eds., Frédéric Lasserre and Olivier Faury (Routledge, 2019), 137–155 at 140–146.

10   LOSC (n 1), Article 92(1); *M/V 'Saiga' (No 2)* (*Saint Vincent and the Grenadines* v. *Guinea*), Judgment, 1 July 1999, *ITLOS Reports 1999*, 10, para 64 ; *The "Enrica Lexie" Incident* (*Italy* v. *India*), Award, 1 May 2020, PCA Case No. 2015-28, 1022–1025.

11   *M/V 'Saiga' (No 2)* (n 10), para 83; *M/V 'Virginia G' Case* (*Panama* v. *Guinea-Bissau*), Judgment, 14 April 2014, *ITLOS Reports 2014*, 4, paras 111–113, esp para 113:

In the view of the Tribunal, once a ship is registered, the flag State is required, under article 94 of the Convention, to exercise effective jurisdiction and control over that ship in order to ensure that it operates in accordance with generally accepted international regulations, procedures and practices. This is the meaning of "genuine link."

See Barnes (n 3), pp. 308–309.

Article 87 of the LOSC confirms that the high seas are open to all States and that all States may exercise, *inter alia*, the freedom of navigation and other "internationally lawful uses of the sea related to that freedom"[12] such as the right to protest at sea.[13] These freedoms extend to the exclusive economic zone (EEZ) by virtue of Article 58(1).[14] The freedoms are subject to "the obligation of due regard in [their] exercise."[15] In its decision in *MV 'Norstar'*, the ITLOS confirmed the link between the freedom of navigation articulated in Article 87 and the "exclusive jurisdiction" (better expressed as an immunity) of the flag State proclaimed by Article 92.[16] Without such an immunity from the jurisdiction of other States "(f)reedom of navigation would be illusory."[17] The exclusive jurisdiction of the flag State for its ships on the high seas (and in the EEZs of coastal States by virtue of Article 58(2))[18] is paramount except as "expressly provided for in international treaties or in this Convention,"[19] and foreign flagged vessels need only comply with comply with the laws and regulations of the coastal State to the extent that those laws are adopted by the coastal State in accordance with the provisions of the LOSC and other relevant rules of international law.[20]

---

12   *Arctic Sunrise* (n 5), para 226.
13   Id., para 227. But while these freedoms may be extensive, they evidently do not extend to engaging in those activities over which a coastal State has exclusive decision-making and regulatory power (e.g., the construction, operation and use of artificial islands and installations, LOSC (n 1), Article 60). See also *South China Sea Arbitration* (n 7), paras 1031–1038.
14   *MV 'Norstar'* (n 4), paras 214, 220; *Enrica Lexie* (n 10), para 464.
15   *MV 'Norstar'* (n 4), para 214; *Alleged Violations of Sovereign Rights and Maritime Spaces in the Caribbean Sea (Nicaragua v. Colombia)*, Judgment, 21 April 2022, International Court of Justice, para 161.
16   The jural correlative of an immunity is a disability, that is, the absence of power or jurisdiction of another legal actor, in this case, any other State. For the idea of jural correlatives, see Wesley Newcomb Hohfeld, "Some Fundamental Conceptions as Applied in Judicial Reasoning," *Yale Law Journal* 23 (1913):16–59; and for the application of Hohfeld's ideas to the LOSC, see Philip Allott, "Power Sharing in the Law of the Sea" *American Journal of International Law* 77 (1983): 1–30, and for my own views Nigel Bankes "The Nature of Legal Relations between States under the Proposed BBNJ Agreement," in *International Law and Marine Areas beyond National Jurisdiction: Reflections on Justice, Space, Knowledge and Power*, eds., Vito De Lucia, Alex Oude Elferink and Lan Ngoc Nguyen (Leiden/Boston: Brill, 2022), 45–75.
17   *MV 'Norstar'* (n 4), para 216; see also *Enrica Lexie* (n 10), generally paras 463–505, 521–536.
18   *Enrica Lexie* (n 10), para 531; *Arctic Sunrise (Merits)* (n 5), para 231.
19   LOSC (n 1), Article 92(1).
20   Id., LOSC (n 1), Article 58(3); *M/V 'Saiga' (No 2)* (n 10), paras 131–136. In that case, the coastal State (Guinea) breached the LOSC when it purported to apply and enforce its customs laws against the M/V *Saiga* within its EEZ.

The immunity associated with the freedom of navigation will self-evidently be violated by "any physical or material interference" with navigation. The freedom may also be violated by "any act which subjects activities of a foreign ship on the high seas [or a coastal State's EEZ] to the jurisdiction of States other than the flag State."[21] This includes not only "the exercise of [another State's] enforcement jurisdiction on the high seas ... but also the extension of their prescriptive jurisdiction to lawful activities conducted by foreign ships on the high seas."[22] In the case of the MV *Norstar* this latter meant that the application by Italy of its criminal and customs law to the MV *Norstar's* bunkering activities on the high seas constituted a breach of Panama's freedom of navigation.[23]

The Annex VII tribunal in *Enrica Lexie* elaborated on the test for determining whether or not the immunity associated with the freedom of navigation had been violated. It observed that under international law "the exercise of jurisdiction by a State entails an element of prescribing laws, rules or regulations over conduct, or applying or enforcing such laws, rules or regulations over persons or property"[24] and "additionally ... the exercise of jurisdiction over a foreign ship on the high seas, unless justified by the Convention or other international treaties, is generally agreed to constitute a breach of freedom of navigation."[25]

But on the facts of that incident[26] the tribunal concluded that Italy had not discharged the burden on it of establishing that "the Indian Coast Guard,

---

21   MV '*Norstar*' (n 4), para 224. There is a strongly written collective dissent (Judges Cot, Pawlak, Yanai, Hoffmann, Kolodkin, Lijnzaad and Judge *ad hoc* Treves), but the dissent largely turns on what they see as the absence of any nexus between Italy's enforcement activities (carried out by Spain at the behest of Italy in Spanish internal waters) and the activities of the MV *Norstar* on the high seas.

22   Id., para 225.

23   Id. Recall that Italy, like other Mediterranean States, has not proclaimed an EEZ. Recall also that the bunkering activities were to supply luxury yachts based in Italy. High seas freedoms do not extend to include bunkering activities to supply fishing vessels within a coastal State's EEZ. See M/V '*Virginia G*' (n 11), para 223. The MV *Norstar* (n 4) was not engaged in such an activity.

24   *Enrica Lexie* (n 10), para 526; see also para 469, "the interference may take physical or non-physical forms" and para 472, "a breach of freedom of navigation may result from acts including physical or material interference with navigation of a foreign vessel, the threat or use of force against a foreign vessel, or non-physical forms of interference whose effect is that of instilling fear in, or causing hindrance to, the exercise of the freedom of navigation."

25   *Enrica Lexie* (n 10), para 473 (references omitted).

26   The incident began when Italian marines posted on the M/V *Enrica Lexie* perceived a threat of attack from the *St Antony* while navigating through India's EEZ. The marines opened fire on the *St Antony*, an Indian fishing vessel, killing two members of the crew.

'interdicting' and 'escorting' the *Enrica Lexie*, exercised enforcement jurisdiction."[27] Indeed, the evidence showed that the captain of the *Enrica Lexie* voluntarily agreed to the suggestion of the Indian authorities that they proceed to port to clear up what had happened in the incident between the *Enrica Lexie* and the *St Antony*.[28] On the other hand, it was equally clear to the tribunal that the actions of the marines on board the *Enrica Lexie* prevented the *St Antony* (the Indian fishing vessel involved in the incident) from navigating its intended course amounted to a breach of both the freedom of navigation under Article 87(1)(a), and also a breach of the more specific right of navigation articulated in Article 90.[29]

The *Arctic Sunrise* award also offers an example of coastal State interference with the exercise of the freedom of navigation within the EEZ. While the Annex VII tribunal was at pains to examine all possible legal bases that might have been available to Russia to justify the measures that it took within its EEZ in boarding, investigating, inspecting, arresting, seizing and detaining the *Arctic Sunrise* without the consent of the Netherlands as the flag State, the tribunal concluded that none of these possible grounds were available to Russia.[30] Accordingly, the Russian Federation was in breach of Articles 56(2), 58(1), 58(2), 87(1)(a) and 92(1) of the LOSC.[31]

There is no freedom of navigation in either a coastal State's territorial sea or within its internal waters, although there is a right of innocent passage through the territorial sea of a coastal State[32] as well as those internal waters that are enclosed as internal waters as the result of a coastal State establishing drawing straight baselines.[33] Nor, as is illustrated by the award in *Enrica Lexie*, is there

---

Indian coastguard vessels subsequently accompanied the *Enrica Lexie* to an anchorage in Indian territorial waters where the vessel was boarded.

27   Id., para 535.

28   Id., para 480.

29   Id., paras 1037, 1041–1043. Article 87 of the LOSC references freedom of navigation among several other freedoms. Article 90 simply provides in its entirety that "[e]very State, whether coastal or land-locked, has the right to sail ships flying its flag on the high seas."

30   These possible grounds included: right of visit on suspicion of piracy (Article 110); violation of coastal State laws pertaining to installations; terrorist offences; the right of a coastal State to enforce laws pertaining to non-renewable resources; enforcement jurisdiction pertaining to protection of the marine environment; and dangerous manoeuvering.

31   *Arctic Sunrise* (n 5), para 401C and also referencing the proceedings (arrest, detention and judicial proceedings) taken against the captain and crew of the *Arctic Sunrise*.

32   LOSC (n 1), Article 17.

33   Id., Article 8(2). It is important to note that while Canada drew straight baselines around the Arctic Archipelago in 1985, it takes the position that these baselines simply served to define "the outer limits of Canada's historic internal waters." Parliament of Canada, House of Commons Debates, 33rd Parliament, First Session, Vol 5, 10 September 1985 at 6463

the same degree of immunity from the jurisdiction of the coastal State within the coastal State's territorial sea or inland waters. In that case it was clear that at some point India did exercise jurisdiction over the *Enrica Lexie* and its crew, but the tribunal found that this did not happen while the *Enrica Lexie* was within India's EEZ. Thus, there was no interference by India with the freedom of navigation of Italy/*Enrica Lexie*.

Finally, the freedom of navigation on the high seas or within a coastal State's EEZ does not afford a foreign flagged vessel a right to leave the port of a coastal State (which it voluntarily entered) to "gain access to the high seas notwithstanding its detention in the context of legal proceedings against it."[34]

2.2   *The Responsibilities/Duties of the Flag State*
In addition to the above decisions emphasizing freedom of navigation and immunity from the jurisdiction of other States, several decisions and advisory opinions emphasize the responsibilities of the flag State with respect to the provisions of the LOSC dealing with the exploitation of marine living resources and the protection of the marine environment. Some of these decisions also explore the implications of the duty of due regard as applied to the responsibilities of the flag State (explored in more detail in the next section). These decisions dealing with the duties of the flag State are of particular interest to coastal States insofar as a coastal State may be able to use them to engage the flag State in more effective enforcement of valid coastal State rules dealing with marine living resources and environmental protection.

---

per Joe Clarke, Minister for Foreign Affairs. Consequently, Canada takes the view that Article 8(2) is inapplicable insofar as this was not a case of "enclosing waters as internal waters areas which had not previously been considered as such." For the straight baselines order see Territorial Sea Geographical Coordinates (Area 7) Order, SOR/85-872. For more detailed expositions of Canada's position see Suzanne Lalonde, "Increased Traffic through Canadian Arctic Waters: Canada's State of Readiness," *Revue Juridique Thémis* 38 (2004): 49–124 and Bartenstein (n 9), pp. 346–347. See also *Dispute Concerning Coastal State Rights in the Black Sea, Sea of Azov, and Kerch Strait* (*Ukraine* v. *Russian Federation*), Award on Preliminary Objections, 21 February 2020, PCA, Case No. 2017-06 [*Coastal State Rights*] noting that it goes too far to suggest that a dispute pertaining to internal waters could not concern the interpretation or application of the Convention (para 294). Rather, the question must be whether the particular conduct complained of raises questions as to the interpretation or application of the Convention (para 296).

34   *M/V 'Louisa'* (*St Vincent and the Grenadines* v. *Kingdom of Spain*), Judgment, 28 May 2013, *ITLOS Reports 2013*, 4, para 109. ITLOS ultimately concluded that it lacked jurisdiction since the applicant was unable to show the necessary nexus between the facts and any provision of the LOSC.

The first such case is the 2015 ITLOS *SRFC Advisory Opinion.* Three of the four questions put to the ITLOS dealt with the responsibilities of the flag State. Only the fourth question dealt with the responsibilities of the coastal State.

The first question addressed the obligations of the flag State if its flagged vessels are conducting illegal, unreported and unregulated (IUU) fishing activities within the EEZ of another State. The second question addressed the potential liability of the flag State for those activities. And the third question was largely concerned with the responsibility of an international organization, such as the European Union, and its Member States for potential IUU activities of vessels flagged to individual Member States.[35] This chapter focuses on the first two questions since they raise more general issues of flag State responsibility.

With respect to the first question, ITLOS emphasized that while the coastal State may have the primary responsibility for taking the necessary measures to prevent, deter, and eliminate IUU fishing within its EEZ, this does not release other States (i.e., flag States) from their obligations.[36] And, since the LOSC does not expressly address the issue of IUU fishing, the question must be examined "in light of general and specific obligations of flag States under the Convention for the conservation and management of marine living resources."[37] Under the heading of general obligations, the ITLOS listed Articles 91, 92 and 94 as well as Articles 192 and 193 of the LOSC.[38] The tribunal's comments on Article 94 are especially significant.

In general terms Article 94, headed 'Duties of the flag State,' requires the flag State to effectively exercise its jurisdiction and control over ships flying its flag in "administrative, technical and social matters." The subsequent paragraphs of the article give more specific examples of what is required of a flag State in terms of assuming jurisdiction under its domestic law. But, in the view of the ITLOS, these examples are indicative of and not exhaustive of what might be embraced by the term "administrative, technical and social matters."[39] This

---

35   *SRFC Advisory Opinion* (n 6), para 2.

36   Id., paras 106, 108.

37   Id., para 110.

38   Id., para 111.

39   Id., para 117. See also Separate Opinion of Judge Paik, paras 8–10, observing that while Article 94 is perhaps principally concerned with safety at sea, the duties of the flag State are not confined to such matters. He went on to comment on the evolutive character of Article 94 as follows:

>   Over time, however, flag State jurisdiction and control have evolved to cope with new issues, reflecting the changing needs of society and the new demands of the time. In interpreting article 94 of the Convention, it is important to take into account this evolving, open-ended context of the duties of the flag State.

Judge Paik returns to this theme at paras 24–27.

allowed the ITLOS to conclude that "as far as fishing activities are concerned, the flag State ... must adopt the necessary administrative measures to ensure that fishing vessels flying its flag are not involved in activities which will undermine the flag State's responsibilities under the Convention in respect of the conservation and management of marine living resources."[40] Furthermore, and drawing upon the language of Article 94(6), the ITLOS emphasized that should another State observe and report the absence of proper jurisdiction and control, the flag State would be obliged to investigate and, if appropriate, take any action necessary to remedy the situation, and inform the reporting State as to the action taken.[41]

As for Articles 192 and 193, these provisions impose obligations on all States to protect and preserve the marine environment, including the conservation of marine living resources.[42] And for ITLOS this imposes on the flag State "an obligation to ensure compliance by vessels flying its flag with the relevant conservation measures concerning living resources enacted by the coastal State" for its EEZ.[43] However, as the International Court of Justice has observed in its decision on *Alleged Violations of Sovereign Rights*, the obligation to ensure compliance by its flag vessels does not afford a flag State the "jurisdiction to enforce conservation standards on fishing vessels of other States" in the EEZ.[44]

The more specific provisions of Articles 58(3) (due regard) and 62(4) not only supported the conclusion of the ITLOS but also supported the duty of flag States "to take the necessary measures to ensure that their nationals and vessels flying their flag are not engaged in IUU fishing activities."[45] And all of these obligations "to ensure" are due diligence obligations of conduct on the part

---

40   *SRFC Advisory Opinion* (n 6), para 119.
41   Id., paras 116, 118, 119.
42   Id., para 120.
43   Id. The ITLOS explains this in terms of its previous observation (para 102) to the effect that such coastal State laws "constitute an integral element in the protection and preservation of the marine environment." In this somewhat enigmatic passage (para 120) the ITLOS observes as follows:

> One of the goals of the Convention, as stated in its preamble, is to establish "a legal order for the seas and oceans which ... will promote" inter alia "the equitable and efficient utilization of their resources, the conservation of their living resources, and the study, protection and preservation of the marine environment". *Consequently, laws and regulations adopted by the coastal State in conformity with the provisions of the Convention for the purpose of conserving the living resources and protecting and preserving the marine environment within its exclusive economic zone, constitute part of the legal order for the seas and oceans established by the Convention and therefore must be complied with by other States Parties whose ships are engaged in fishing activities within that zone.* (emphasis added)

44   *Alleged Violations of Sovereign Rights* (n 15), para 95.
45   *SRFC Advisory Opinion* (n 6), para 124.

of the flag State.[46] As for the content of the due diligence obligation to effectively exercise jurisdiction and control over its flag vessels, the ITLOS observed that while

> the nature of the laws, regulations and measures that are to be adopted by the flag State is left to be determined by each flag State in accordance with its legal system, the flag State nevertheless has the obligation to include in them enforcement mechanisms to monitor and secure compliance with these laws and regulations. Sanctions applicable to involvement in IUU fishing activities must be sufficient to deter violations and to deprive offenders of the benefits accruing from their IUU fishing activities.[47]

The flag State also has a duty to cooperate with respect to allegations of IUU fishing as it does with respect to the prevention of pollution.[48]

The Annex VII tribunal in the *South China Sea Arbitration* endorsed these observations noting that insofar as Article 62(4) imposes the obligation to observe the laws and regulations of the coastal State,[49] it must follow that "anything less than due diligence by a State in preventing its nationals from unlawfully fishing in the exclusive economic zone of another would fall short of the regard due pursuant to Article 58(3) of the Convention."[50]

The responses to the first question also informed the ITLOS's response to the second question.[51] The responsibility of the flag State would be engaged if it failed to take all necessary and appropriate measures to ensure that vessels flying its flag do not conduct IUU activities, whether as a repeated pattern of

---

46   Id., para 125, and referencing the Seabed Disputes Chamber, *Responsibilities and Obligations of States with Respect to Activities in the Area, Advisory Opinion*, 1 February 2011, *ITLOS Reports 2011*, 10, para 108. For further observations with respect to the nature of due diligence obligations, see Nele Matz-Lück and Erik Van Doorn, "Due Diligence Obligations and the Protection of the Marine Environment," *Observateur des Nations Unies* 42 (2017): 178–195, Barnes (n 3), pp. 323–324, and Nigel Bankes, "Reflections on the Role of Due Diligence in Clarifying State Discretionary Powers in Developing Arctic Natural Resources," *Polar Record* (2020), https://doi.org/10.1017/S0032247419000779.

47   *SRFC Advisory Opinion* (n 6), para 138.

48   Id., para 140 and referencing *MOX Plant* (*Ireland* v. *United Kingdom*), Provisional Measures, Order of 3 December 2001, *ITLOS Reports 2001*, para 82. See also *South China Sea Arbitration* (n 7), para 946, referencing both Article 197 (cooperation on a global or regional basis) and Article 123 (cooperation of States bordering enclosed or semi-enclosed seas).

49   *South China Sea Arbitration* (n 7), para 740.

50   Id., para 744.

51   ITLOS reframed the liability question as a question of State responsibility. *SRFC Advisory Opinion* (n 6), para 145.

behaviour or not.[52] While in some cases it may be difficult to assess whether the flag State has done all that it can, especially with respect to covert activities of its flagged vessels,[53] that was not the case on the facts of the *South China Sea Arbitration*. For in that case the record showed close coordination between Chinese government vessels and Chinese flagged fishing vessels. Indeed, the evidence supported "an inference that China's fishing vessels are not simply escorted and protected, but organized and coordinated by the Government."[54] Certainly, "the officers aboard the Chinese Government vessels in question were fully aware of the actions being taken by Chinese fishermen and were in a position to halt them had they chosen to do so."[55] This constituted a breach of the flag State's obligation of due regard.[56]

The *South China Sea Arbitration* award also elaborated on the obligations of States under Part XII of the LOSC. As the arbitral tribunal noted, these obligations "apply to all States with respect to the marine environment in all maritime areas, both inside the national jurisdiction of States and beyond it."[57] Furthermore it is clear that these provisions can be operationalized without the support of a due regard requirement.

Relying to a significant degree on the obligation under Article 194(5) to protect and preserve fragile ecosystems,[58] the arbitral tribunal concluded that "where a State is aware that vessels flying its flag are engaged in the harvest of species recognized internationally as being threatened with extinction or are inflicting significant damage on rare or fragile ecosystems or the habitat of depleted, threatened, or endangered species, its obligations under the Convention include a duty to adopt rules and measures to prevent such acts and to maintain a level of vigilance in enforcing those rules and measures."[59] The tribunal considered that China was well aware of the activities of its nationals

---

52   Id., para 150. ITLOS confines itself to IUU activities within the EEZ of the SRFC Member States, but in principle these observations are applicable more generally. See also Judge Paik's separate opinion characterizing many of these obligations as obligations of customary international law not just as obligations arising under the LOSC.
53   *South China Sea Arbitration* (n 7), para 754.
54   Id., para 755.
55   Id.
56   Id., para 756.
57   Id., para 940. See also *SRFC Advisory Opinion* (n 6), para 120, and, with respect to the internal waters of a State, *Coastal State Rights* (n 33), para 295.
58   But also informed by the corpus of international environmental law including the Convention on International Trade in Endangered Species of Wild Fauna and Flora, 3 March 1973 (in force 1 July 1975), 993 *UNTS* 243; see also *South China Sea Arbitration* (n 7), para 956.
59   *South China Sea Arbitration* (n 7), para 961.

in harvesting endangered species and inflicting damage on rare or fragile ecosystems and, as such, had breached its obligations as a flag State under Articles
192 and 194(5) of the LOSC.[60] The same was also true of China's construction
activities on various reefs in the Spratly Islands, including dredging activities.[61]
And China was also in breach of its obligation under Article 206 to conduct
an environmental impact assessment with respect to these activities, which
were under its jurisdiction or control, insofar as they might cause substantial
pollution or significant harm to the marine environment.[62]

2.3   The Duty of Due Regard (of the Flag State)

In exercising the freedom of navigation in the high seas, all flag States owe a
duty of due regard for the "interests" of other States exercising their parallel
freedoms, as well as any rights under the Convention with respect to activities
in the Area.[63] A similar rule applies within the EEZ of a coastal State.[64] Presumably, this entails a due diligence obligation on the part of the flag State to
ensure that its vessels observe this duty of due regard.

The majority and dissenting members of the Annex VII tribunal in *Enrica
Lexie* reached very different conclusions as to the content of the due regard
obligation of the flag State (Italy) as it pertained to the exercise of the freedom
of navigation by the *Enrica Lexie* within what was, in that case, India's EEZ.
India took the position in its counterclaim that Italy had violated India's sovereign rights within its EEZ insofar as the *Enrica Lexie* impeded the *St Antony* in
the exercise of its right to fish.[65] The majority rejected that characterization on
the basis that the actions of the marines on board the *Enrica Lexie* "were not
directed at undermining or interfering with India's sovereign rights"[66] but were
instead directed at a perceived act of piracy.[67] More specifically with respect to
the obligation of due regard, the majority observed that Article 58 referentially
applied to the EEZ all of the high seas provisions of the LOSC relating to the
repression of piracy, with the result that the "repression of piracy by States in

---

60   Id., para 964.
61   Id., para 983.
62   Id., para 993.
63   LOSC (n 1), Article 87(2).
64   Id., Article 58(3).
65   *Enrica Lexie* (n 10), para 947.
66   Id., para 953.
67   Id., paras 954, 955, referencing India's obligation "to have due regard to the rights and
        duties of other States and the applicability of Article 110 of the Convention." It is difficult
        to appreciate the relevance of the reference to Article 110 which deals with the right of
        visit of a warship.

the [EEZ] is not only sanctioned by the Convention," but is a "a duty incumbent on all States."[68] For the majority, it followed from this premise that the conduct of the Italian marines on board the *Enrica Lexie* simply could not have been a breach of the duty of due regard.[69] It is difficult to support this reasoning since there is nothing in the text of Article 110 dealing with the duty to cooperate in the repression of piracy (Article 100) that allows a flag State to ignore its due regard obligations.

Both of these conclusions of the majority (no interference with India's sovereign rights—the right to fish of the *St Antony*—and no breach of the duty of due regard) triggered a vigorous joint dissent from Dr PS Rao and Judge Robinson. With respect to the majority's first conclusion, the dissent observed that the intent of the marines should be irrelevant to the question of whether or not there was an interference with India's sovereign rights.[70] And as to the second conclusion, the joint dissenters were of the opinion that Italy must also be in breach of its duty of due regard. Due regard required respect for India's sovereign rights to exploit the fishery resources of its EEZ, and in this case the marines had alternatives to opening fire on the *St Antony* killing two members of its crew.[71] Rao and Robinson put it this way:

> In the instant case, the right for which Italy must have due regard is India's sovereign rights to exploit the living resources (fisheries) in its exclusive economic zone. Italy has a corresponding obligation to respect that right. The conduct of the Marines in firing shots at the "St. Antony", resulting in the death of the two Indian fishermen was a breach of that obligation. This obligation exists notwithstanding that the Marines did not intend to harm India's enjoyment of its right to exploit the living resources in its exclusive economic zone. That is so because a State's international responsibility for wrongful conduct ... is engaged independently of whether it intended to cause harm.

> .... The nature of India's right is such that Italy is not relieved of its obligation to respect and have due regard for that right on the ground that the Marines perceived that there was a threat of a collision and pirate attack.

---

68   Id., para 979.
69   Id., paras 980, 981.
70   *Enrica Lexie* (n 10), Joint Dissenting Opinion, paras 7–9.
71   Id., paras 17–19.

One of the factors identified in the *Chagos Marine Protected Area Arbitration* award for determining the extent of the regard required by the Convention is the "availability of alternative approaches". It was certainly open to the Marines to take some action other than firing at a miniscule vessel, leading to the death of the two Indian fishermen. ... This provides another basis for concluding that the obligation to have due regard to India's rights was breached by Italy.[72]

In this case the dissent seems more persuasive with respect to the content of the due regard obligation of the flag State in these particular factual circumstances.

2.4   *Rules of Reference and Flag State Responsibilities*

Rules of reference incorporating into the LOSC both general and specific norms of international law are found throughout the text of the Convention.[73] While such rules most commonly take the form of a reference to generally accepted international rules and standards (or GAIRS),[74] they may also take the form of a more general *renvoi* to "other rules of international law."[75]

The *South China Sea Arbitration* is an important decision as to how rules of reference may inform and elaborate upon flag State obligations arising under different provisions of the LOSC. One of the Philippines' submissions in this arbitration was that China had breached its obligations under Articles 21 and 94 of the Convention insofar as it operated its enforcement vessels in a manner inconsistent with the provisions of the Convention on the International Regulations for Preventing Collisions at Sea, 1972 (COLREGS).[76] COLREGS entered into force in 1977 and at the time of the arbitration counted 156 contracting parties representing more than 98 per cent of world tonnage.[77]

Both China and Philippines were parties to COLREGS although the Philippines did not join until *after* the events complained of. Nevertheless, the tribunal concluded that the COLREGS was applicable as between the parties as a result of Article 94 of the LOSC. As discussed above, while paragraph 1 of

---

72   Id.

73   See especially van Reenen (n 8).

74   E.g., LOSC (n 1), Article 21(2). It is generally understood that a rule can be generally accepted (a contextual question of fact) even if such a rule could not be considered as a rule of customary law. See, e.g., Nguyen (n 8), pp. 423–424.

75   E.g., LOSC (n 1), Article 2(3), as discussed in *Chagos Marine Protected Area Arbitration* (*Mauritius* v. *United Kingdom*), Award, 18 March 2015, PCA Case No. 2011-03, paras 499–536.

76   20 October 1972 (in force 15 July 1977), 1050 *UNTS* 17.

77   *South China Sea Arbitration* (n 7), para 1081.

Article 94 creates the general obligation for a flag State to exercise effective jurisdiction and control over its vessels, this obligation is further particularized in the subsequent paragraphs. Specifically, paragraph 3 requires flag States to take such measures as are necessary to ensure safety at sea with regard to, *inter alia*, "(c) the use of signals, the maintenance of communications and the prevention of collisions." Further to that, paragraph (5) requires flag States "to conform to generally accepted international regulations, procedures and practices and to take any steps which may be necessary to secure their observance" in giving effect to, *inter alia*, the measures required by paragraph 3(c). Given the status of the COLREGS as a widely adopted multilateral convention concerning maritime safety, this language served to incorporate the COLREGS into the Convention such that a violation of the COLREGS "constitutes a violation of the Convention itself."[78] This important conclusion not only serves to particularize the substantive obligations of the flag State; it also confirms the *jurisdiction* of a Part XV tribunal with respect to the interpretation and application of the COLREGS.[79] Armed with this premise, the tribunal was readily able to conclude that China had repeatedly violated the Rules of the COLREGS and that this was "not suggestive of occasional negligence in failing to adhere to the COLREGS, but rather point to a conscious disregard of what the regulations require."[80]

2.5   *Conclusion to Part I*

This part of the chapter has examined how recent case law has elaborated on flag State powers and the immunity of foreign flagged vessels. It has also examined how the case law has elaborated on flag State responsibilities. These responsibilities include the due diligence obligations of the flag State to have its vessels observe the laws of the coastal State insofar as the applicability of those laws is provided for by the LOSC, as well as due regard obligations and other obligations referentially incorporated into the text of the LOSC by rules of reference. While only one of these decisions, the *Arctic Sunrise* award, is an Arctic case, all of the decisions canvassed here are relevant to the relationship between coastal States and flag States within Arctic waters.

---

78   Id., para 1083.
79   Thus, while the jurisdiction of a Part XV tribunal is prima facie limited to "a dispute concerning the interpretation or application of this Convention" (LOSC (n 1), Article 288(1)), the content of "this Convention" expands through the process of referential incorporation.
80   *South China Sea Arbitration* (n 7), para 1105. It is not entirely clear why the tribunal considers that it needed to rule out mere negligence. All of the instances referenced here involved Chinese State vessels and thus there was no need to assess whether China acted with due diligence to ensure that its non-State flagged vessels adhered to the COLREGS as a pre-condition for China's State responsibility.

Part II of the Chapter considers the implications of these general rules and interpretive case law for the implementation of the Polar Code and Canada's ASSPPR.

3   Part 2: Flag State Powers and Responsibilities and the Polar Code

As discussed elsewhere in this volume,[81] the Polar Code[82] entered into force in January 2017. The Code was developed to "supplement instruments in order to increase the safety of ships' operation and mitigate the impact on the people and environment in the remote, vulnerable and potentially harsh polar waters."[83] The Code takes the form of amendments to the International Convention for the Safety of Life at Sea (SOLAS)[84] and the International Convention for the Prevention of Pollution from Ships (MARPOL).[85] Part I of the Code

---

81   See Bartenstein in this volume.

82   Polar Code (n 2). For background on the Code, see Andrea Scassola, "An International Polar Code of Navigation: Consequences and Opportunities for the Arctic," *Yearbook of Polar Law* 5 (2013): 271–297; David Leary, "The IMO Mandatory International Code of Safety for Ships: Charting a Sustainable Course for Shipping in the Polar Regions," 7 *Yearbook of Polar Law* 7 (2015): 426–447; Øystein Jensen, "The International Code for Ships Operating in Polar Waters: Finalization, Adoption and Law of the Sea Implications," *Arctic Review on Law and Politics* 7 (2016): 60–82; Ted L McDorman, "A Note on the Potential Conflicting Treaty Rights and Obligations between the IMO's Polar Code and Article 234 of the Law of the Sea Convention," in *International Law and Politics of the Arctic Ocean: Essays in Honor of Donat Pharand*, eds., Suzanne Lalonde and Ted L McDorman (Leiden/Boston: Brill Nijhoff, 2015), 141–159; J Ashley Roach, "The Polar Code and Its Adequacy," in *Governance of Arctic Shipping: Balancing Rights and Interests of Arctic States and User States*, eds., Robert C Beckman *et al.* (Brill Nijhoff: Leiden/Boston, 2017) chapter 5; Tore Henriksen, "Coastal State Jurisdiction in Ice-Covered Areas: The Impacts of Climate Change and the Polar Code," in *The Achievements of International Law: Essays in Honour of Robin Churchill*, eds., Jacques Hartmann and Urfan Khaliq (Bloomsbury Publishing, 2021), 175–207.

83   Polar Code (n 2), Preamble, para 1.

84   1 November 1974 (in force 25 May 1980), 1185 UNTS 2; Amendments to the International Convention for the Safety of Life at Sea 1974, IMO Resolution MSC.386(94) (21 November 2014, effective 1 January 2017)

85   2 November 1973 (in force 2 October 1983), 1340 UNTS 184 (as amended); Amendments to MARPOL Annexes I, II, IV and V, IMO Resolution MEPC.265(68) (15 May 2015, effective 1 January 2017). Jensen (n 82), p. 63, describes the options, referring to the advantages offered by IMO's tacit amendment procedures for obtaining speedy entry into force. Jensen (pp. 71–75) also suggests that the provisions of the Code incorporated in SOLAS and MARPOL will also have normative effect as generally accepted international rules and standards (GAIRS) for the purposes of relevant provisions of the LOSC.

prescribes a series of safety measures, and Part II of the Code deals with pollution prevention measures.

This part begins by examining the implications of the Polar Code for flag States and then turns to examine Canada's implementing regulations

3.1 Flag State Responsibilities

As Bartenstein has summarized, "(m)ost of the safety provisions relate to construction, design, manning and equipment."[86] These provisions, along with additional provisions related to voyage planning, represent the minimum standards to be applied by flag States.[87] A flag State owes a due diligence obligation to ensure that these provisions are implemented as part of its domestic law, either through transformation in a dualist State (as noted in the introduction Canada adopted the ASSPPR for this purpose), or through direct application in a monist State (such as Russia).[88] This duty follows from the provisions of Article 94 of the LOSC and the jurisprudence discussed above. Furthermore, since the provisions of the Polar Code have been adopted by the IMO, they must also represent "generally accepted international regulations, procedures and practices." A flag State has a due diligence responsibility to ensure that its domestic measures "conform" to the requirements of the Polar Code.[89] A flag State also has a due diligence obligation "to take any steps which may be necessary to secure" their observance.[90]

Much the same can be said for the mandatory pollution prevention provisions of the Polar Code dealing with the discharge of oil or oily mixtures, noxious liquid substances, sewage, and garbage and associated operational requirements (and, in the case of oil, structural requirements).[91] These provisions must constitute GAIRS, and, as such, Article 211(2) of the LOSC requires flag States to adopt "laws and regulations for the prevention, reduction and control of pollution of the marine environment" from its flagged

---

86 Bartenstein (n 9), p. 337.
87 Id., 340.
88 See Bartenstein and Lalonde (n 9), pp. 146–150.
89 LOSC (n 1), Article 94(5). Bartenstein (n 9), p. 341, however, notes that this view may not be universally shared insofar as the Code's "goal-based approach provides States with a wide discretion as to the requirements they prescribe" and as such "does not ensure the level of uniformity that makes GAIRS acceptable." Bartenstein attributes this position to Tore Henriksen, "Protecting Polar Environments: Coherency in Regulating Arctic Shipping," in *Research Handbook on International Marine Environmental Law*, ed., Rosemary Rayfuse (Cheltenham: Edward Elgar, 2015).
90 LOSC (n 1), Article 94(5); *SRFC Advisory Opinion* (n 6).
91 Polar Code (n 2), Part II-A, Pollution Prevention Measures.

vessels, with at least "the same effect" as those of GAIRS.[92] This is a due diligence obligation, and, as above, must extend to the measures necessary to
secure their observance.[93]

3.2   Canada's ASSPPR

As noted in the introduction, Canada has chosen to implement its responsibilities under the Polar Code through the adoption of the ASSPPR.[94] Part 1 of
the Regulations deals with safety measures and Part 2 deals with pollution prevention measures. Both purport to apply to "Canadian vessels navigating in
polar waters and foreign vessels navigating in a shipping safety control zone."[95]
The Shipping Safety Control Zones divide Canada's Arctic waters as defined
by the *Arctic Waters Pollution Prevention Act*[96] (AWPPA) into "16 subareas in
accordance with usually prevailing ice conditions."[97] Insofar as the Regulations are directed at Canadian vessels operating within polar waters at either
pole, it matters not whether the Regulations go beyond the prescriptions of
the Polar Code.[98] But, to the extent that the Regulations aspire to apply to foreign flagged vessels operating within Canadian Arctic waters, it is important
to interrogate the extent to which they go beyond the Code. To the extent that
they go beyond the Code, they cannot be GAIRS and must be justified under
some other authority of a coastal State under the LOSC.

Bartenstein concludes that three elements of the Regulations go beyond the
safety requirements of the Code, while several aspects of the waste deposit
rules in the Regulations are more stringent than those prescribed by the
Code. The additional safety provisions prescribed by the Regulations relate to
"navigation periods, mandatory message transmission, and the presence on

92   LOSC (n 1), Article 211(2).
93   Id., Article 94(5); *South China Sea Arbitration* (n 7), para 1082.
94   The regulations are adopted pursuant to the *Canada Shipping Act, 2001,* SC 2001, c 26 and
     the *Arctic Waters Pollution Prevention Act,* RSC 1985, c A-12 [AWPPA].
95   ASSPPR (n 9), ss 7, 13. Neither Part applies (s 3) to government vessels and vessels owned
     or operated by a foreign State when they are being used only in government non-
     commercial services.
96   AWPPA (n 94). "Arctic waters means the internal waters of Canada and the waters of the
     territorial sea of Canada and the exclusive economic zone of Canada, within the area
     enclosed by the 60th parallel of north latitude, the 141st meridian of west longitude and
     the outer limit of the exclusive economic zone; however, where the international bound-
     ary between Canada and Greenland is less than 200 nautical miles from the baselines
     of the territorial sea of Canada, the international boundary shall be substituted for that
     outer limit."
97   Bartenstein (n 9), p. 337.
98   Id., 344.

board of an ice-navigator."[99] The increased stringency of the waste deposit rules arises because of the zero-discharge regime of the AWPPA.[100]

The Regulations purport to apply to all of Canada's Arctic waters. These waters include not only the waters within the Arctic Archipelago that Canada regards as its historic internal waters, but also its 12 nautical mile territorial sea and its Arctic EEZ.[101] The LOSC allows a coastal State to prescribe both vessel safety and pollution control rules for vessels exercising a right of innocent passage within its territorial sea,[102] but such laws must not relate to "the design, construction, manning or equipment of foreign ships" unless they are giving effect to GAIRS. Furthermore, such laws may not "impose requirements on foreign ships which have the practical effect of denying or impairing the right of innocent passage."[103] Similarly, within the EEZ, foreign flagged vessels may exercise freedom of navigation[104] and a coastal State may only prescribe additional pollution prevention measures that might affect freedom of navigation with the approval of the IMO.[105]

These restrictions on coastal State authority with respect to the territorial sea and the EEZ lead Bartenstein (writing about the additional safety provisions of the Regulations) to conclude that the navigation rules of the LOSC "do not provide a [legal] basis for the additional non-GAIRS provisions in the ASSPPR."[106] Bartenstein expresses similar reservations with respect to the additional pollution prevention provisions of the Regulations.[107]

In each case these conclusions lead Bartenstein to explore whether the additional requirements of the Regulations can be justified on the basis of Article 234 of the LOSC.[108] This well-known provision authorizes a coastal State to adopt and enforce

---

99   Id., 339 and with a more detailed exposition at 340.
100   Id., 344.
101   See (n 31) re historic internal waters.
102   LOSC (n 1), Article 21(1)(a) and (f).
103   Id., Articles 24(1), 17, 211(4).
104   Id., Articles 58, 87.
105   Id., Articles 56(1)(b)(iii) and (2), 58(2), 211.
106   Bartenstein (n 9), p. 141.
107   Id., 145 noting that, for the territorial sea, the structural requirements for noxious liquid substances represent non-GAIRS construction, design, manning and equipment measures and, with respect to the EEZ, "[s]ince the additional ASSPPR provisions are not GAIRS, their compatibility with the EEZ regime is also not straightforward."
108   On the background to Article 234 of the LOSC, see Donald McRae and DJ Goundrey, "Environmental Jurisdiction in Arctic Waters: The Extent of Article 234," *University of British Columbia Law Review* 16 (1982): 197, at 210–215; Armand de Mestral, "Article 234 of the United Nations Convention on the Law of the Sea: Its Origins and its Future," in Lalonde

non-discriminatory laws and regulations for the prevention, reduction and control of marine pollution from vessels in ice-covered areas within the limits of the exclusive economic zone, where particularly severe climatic conditions and the presence of ice covering such areas for most of the year create obstructions or exceptional hazards to navigation, and pollution of the marine environment could cause major harm to or irreversible disturbance of the ecological balance. Such laws and regulations shall have due regard to navigation and the protection and preservation of the marine environment based on the best available scientific evidence.

While there are some threshold questions as to the applicability of Article 234 (e.g., does it apply to the territorial sea as well as the EEZ),[109] Bartenstein's main conclusion is that Canada can rely on Article 234 to justify both the additional safety and pollution prevention provisions of the Regulations.[110] While Article 234 does not refer to safety-based rules, Bartenstein concludes that safety rules can be justified under Article 234 insofar as the Code itself acknowledges the relationship between the additional safety measures and protection of the environment.[111] Article 234 does require "due regard" for navigation, but, in Bartenstein's view, this must be read in light of the environmental purpose of the article, and thus, even construction, design, manning and equipment measures might be permissible "as long as they do not prevent international navigation."[112]

In summary, Canada, as a flag State, has a due diligence obligation to adopt and enforce the safety and pollution control provisions of the Polar Code with respect to its flag vessels.[113] Canada may elect to adopt more stringent measures with respect to its flag vessels than those contained in the Code. In

---

and McDorman (eds) (n 82), p. 111; Erik Franckx and Laura Boone, "Ice-Covered Areas," in *United Nations Convention on the Law of the Sea: A Commentary*, ed., Alexander Proelss (Munich: Verlag CH Beck , 2017), 1566 at 1571–1573.

109   Bartenstein (n 9), pp. 341–342. On its terms, Article 234 only applies to the EEZ, but it would be odd if the coastal State were to have more extensive powers in its EEZ than in its territorial sea. Bartenstein also notes the argument that Article 234 might be inapplicable to international straits (an issue if the Northwest Passage qualifies as an international strait). For further discussion see Franckx and Boone (n 108), pp. 1576–1577 and Jan Jakub Solski, "The 'Due Regard' of Article 234 of UNCLOS: Lessons from Regulating Innocent Passage in the Territorial Sea" *ODIL* 52(3) (2021): 398–418, at 402–405.

110   Bartenstein (n 9), pp. 342, 345.

111   Id., 342; Polar Code (n 2), Preambular para 5.

112   Bartenstein (n 9), p. 345; Solski (n 109), p. 417, argues in favour of using the jurisdictional balance applicable to the territorial sea under Article 24 of the LOSC "as a yardstick for the test of reasonableness in the exercise of the 'due regard' obligation."

113   LOSC (n 1), Articles 94, 211(2).

its position as a coastal State, Canada may apply more stringent rules within its internal waters as a manifestation of its sovereignty over those waters. With respect to its territorial sea and EEZ, however, the general rule is that the coastal State may not hamper the right of innocent passage or freedom of navigation and is therefore usually only in a position to apply GAIRS rules. As a coastal State, Canada is entitled to insist that foreign flagged vessels comply with the provisions of the Polar Code and its domestic laws implementing the Code. However, to the extent that its domestic laws go beyond the GAIRS provisions of the Code, those incremental requirements would not be opposable against foreign flagged vessels *unless* they could be supported by some other provision of the LOSC. There is good reason to conclude that Canada can rely on Article 234 to support the incremental requirements that it has included in its ASSPPR.

Other flag States have a due diligence obligation to ensure that their vessels comply with the Polar Code as a reflection of GAIRS. They also have a due diligence obligation to have their vessels comply with the requirements of Canada's ASSPPR when navigating in Canada's internal waters. Finally, they have the same due diligence obligation with respect to any incremental requirements of the ASSPPR to the extent that those Regulations are consistent with the LOSC as outlined above, specifically including Article 234. To the extent that they are not consistent with the LOSC, including Article 234, foreign flagged vessels are entitled to immunity from those incremental provisions when navigating in Canada's territorial sea or EEZ to the extent of that inconsistency.[114]

4   Conclusion

Part 1 of this chapter engaged with the recent case law dealing with the powers, immunities and responsibilities of flag States under the terms of the LOSC, including GAIRS, that is to say, the provisions of other instruments that are referentially incorporated within the LOSC's normative framework. This case law has confirmed traditional interpretations of the freedom of navigation and associated immunities, but has also offered an expanded interpretation of those freedoms to include, for example, the right of protest on the high seas and within the EEZ of a coastal State. Perhaps more significant is the way in which the case law has expanded upon the obligations of flag States. While

---

114   *M/V 'Norstar'* (n 4).

the case law has declined to interpret the need for a genuine link between the flag State and a vessel as a precondition for asserting the entitlements of the LOSC, it has expanded upon the due diligence obligations of flag States with respect to the provisions of the LOSC, any relevant GAIRS, as well as the laws of the coastal State to the extent that they are properly opposable against foreign flagged vessels. These provisions include not only provisions concerned with safety and navigation, but also provisions designed to protect the environment.

Part 2 of this chapter addressed the implications of this case law for shipping and navigation in Canada's Arctic, especially in light of the adoption of the Polar Code by the IMO and Canada's implementing regulations. The Polar Code is concerned with both safety measures and pollution control measures. It is an example of a GAIRS and, as such (and as established by Part 1 of this chapter), a flag State has a due diligence obligation to adopt, apply and enforce these new rules with respect to any of its vessels navigating in the waters covered by the Code, including Canada's Arctic waters. Canada as a flag State has implemented the contents of the Code with the adoption of the ASSPPR, but it has also included incremental provisions that it applies not only to its flagged vessels but also to foreign flagged vessels—whether navigating within Canada's internal waters or within its Arctic territorial seas and its Arctic EEZ. The case law surveyed in Part 1 suggests that a foreign flag State and its vessels ordinarily might have a good claim to immunity from the application of these incremental rules on the grounds that they go beyond GAIRS and interfere with the freedom of navigation. However, the literature suggests that such incremental rules might be opposable to foreign flagged vessels on the basis of Article 234. If that is the case, and to the extent to which that is the case, there is no immunity from the application of such rules, and a State of a registry of a foreign flagged vessel has a due diligence obligation to ensure that its vessels observe these incremental requirements.

Acknowledgements

Thanks to Kristin Bartenstein and Aldo Chircop for comments and critical feedback on earlier drafts of this chapter.

CHAPTER 12

The Canadian Policy, Legal and Institutional Framework for the Governance of Arctic Shipping

Aldo Chircop

Abstract

This chapter discusses the fundamental characteristics of the Canadian policy, institutional and legislative framework for the governance of Arctic shipping. Since 1970, the governance of Arctic shipping has evolved into a complex and fragmented system of policy and regulatory instruments servicing Canada's interests as a major trading and coastal State. The institutional framework has become increasingly complex, with the Departments of Transport and Fisheries and Oceans and the Canadian Coast Guard special operating agency playing central roles. While it is unclear whether the designation of low-impact and serviced shipping corridors is likely to increase navigation and shipping in Arctic waters, traditional and centralized maritime administration of shipping will likely not suffice. Uniform rules and standards are important for the facilitation of international maritime trade, but Canada's interests as a coastal State and its responsibilities for this unique region justify high governance standards to ensure environmental protection and equity. In particular, there will be a need to decolonize maritime administration and engage Indigenous peoples in the governance of shipping in their homelands.

Keywords

Arctic shipping – Canada – Canadian Coast Guard – Department of Fisheries and Oceans Canada – governance – International Maritime Organization – Polar Code – maritime regulation – policy – Transport Canada

1 Introduction

With the enactment of the *Arctic Waters Pollution Prevention Act* (AWPPA) in 1970,[1] Canada became the first coastal State to regulate polar shipping

---

1   RSC 1985 c A-12 [AWPPA].

through dedicated standards. At that time, the *Canada Shipping Act* (CSA) provided the framework for the regulation of shipping in all Canadian waters without distinction.[2] At least until 1970, the core of the CSA reflected the *British Merchant Shipping Act* of 1894 and its precursors,[3] essentially imperial legislation advancing the shipping interests and regulatory uniformity needs of a colonial power.[4] The CSA was unwieldy and fragmented because it was amended periodically in a piecemeal manner.[5] Its extensive regulations did not always account for Canada's complex marine regionalism, most especially in Arctic waters. Besides being outmoded and Canada being a modest ship-owning State, the CSA did not fully reflect Canada's maritime profile as a major shipper and coastal State. The Act was more concerned with advancing flag State interests than coastal State concerns. There was little other legislation projecting coastal State interests in shipping, other than protecting the public right of navigation in Canadian waterways and the procedure for restricting it.[6]

Although the AWPPA was novel, Canada stopped short of establishing accompanying polar shipping policy and an institutional framework separate from the national maritime administration, responsibility for which lay with Transport Canada (TC). While the AWPPA constituted a strong assertion of coastal State interests, maritime administration continued to focus on the regulation of safety standards. TC's internal structures operated at national and regional levels, and there was no dedicated public or private body responsible for the administration of Arctic shipping, as was the case of the St. Lawrence Seaway Authority when the seaway opened in 1959.

In the contemporary context, Canada has largely shed off colonial legislation and instead fortified its roles of coastal, port and flag State. Since 1970,

---

2   Until 1970, the *Canada Shipping Act* (CSA) had long provided the framework for regulating shipping through iterations in 1906, 1934, 1956 and 1970: *Canada Shipping Act*, RSC 1906, c 113 (repealed); *Canada Shipping Act*, SC 1934, c 44 (repealed); *Canada Shipping Act*, SC 1956, 4-5 Eliz II (repealed); *Canada Shipping Act*, RSC 197, c S-9 (repealed).

3   *Merchant Shipping Act, 1854*, 17 & 18 Vict c 104 (repealed); *Merchant Shipping Act Amendment Act, 1862*, 25 & 26 Vict c 63; *Merchant Shipping Act, 1894*, 57 & 58 Vict c 60 (repealed).

4   Theodore L. McDorman, "The History of Shipping Law in Canada: The British Dominance," *Dalhousie Law Journal* 7:3 (1982–1983): 620–652; see also Edward C Mayer, *Admiralty Law and Practice in Canada* (Toronto: Carswell, 1916).

5   See David Johansen, "Bill C-14: The Canada Shipping Act, 2001," Law and Government Division, 20 March 2001; Revised 24 May 2001, https://publications.gc.ca/Collection-R /LoPBdP/LS/371/c14-e.htm.

6   *Navigable Waters Protection Act*, RSC 1985, c N-22 (repealed); *Report Addressing Bill C-10, Navigable Waters Protection Act, Ninth Report of the Standing Senate Committee on Energy, the Environment and Natural Resources*, Senate of Canada, June 2009, https://sencanada.ca /content/sen/Committee/402/enrg/rep/rep09jun09-e.pdf. The Act was first enacted in 1882.

maritime legislation has evolved in response to the United Nations Convention on the Law of the Sea (LOSC),[7] major United Nations environmental conferences and multilateral environmental agreements, and instruments of the International Maritime Organization (IMO) concerning pollution, safety, security, and civil liability. The Federal Court was created and became the Admiralty court of Canada in 1971,[8] and the CSA went through further iterations in 1985, 1998 and until the current *Canada Shipping Act, 2001* (CSA 2001).[9] New and reorganized maritime legislation covered a wide range of public and private law topics, including carriage of goods, marine liability, marine insurance, ports and harbours, and salvage. Legislation on environment protection, fisheries and marine conservation grew to encompass shipping. In anticipation of ratification of the LOSC in 2003, the *Oceans Act* reorganized Canada's interests as a coastal State by modernizing maritime zones and jurisdictions, extending the application of domestic law to Canadian waters, and providing a legal framework for the development of ocean policy, management, and planning.[10]

Similarly, the complexity of policy and institutional frameworks increased in response to the liberalization of trade, evolving intergovernmental relations, constitutional recognition of Indigenous rights (including Aboriginal government), environmental concerns, more government to provide services, and demands for inclusive participation in governance. The numerous changes included new or reorganized departmental portfolios for the environment in 1971, fisheries and oceans in 1979, and natural resources in 1994.

Today, federal legislation governing Arctic shipping has largely moved from unilateral rules to the implementation of multilateral international standards in the International Code for Ships Operating in Polar Waters (Polar Code) adopted by the IMO in 2014–2015.[11] In addition to TC's traditional role of national maritime administration, the governance of Arctic shipping involves more institutions at the federal, territorial, Indigenous, industry, and

---

7   Adopted 10 December 1982 (in force 16 November 1994), 1833 *UNTS* 3 [LOSC].

8   *Federal Courts Act*, RSC 1985, c F-7.

9   *Canada Shipping Act*, RSC 1985, c S-9 (repealed); *Canada Shipping Act*, RSC 1985 (3d Supp), c 6 (repealed); *Canada Shipping Act*, SC 1998, c 6 (repealed); *Canada Shipping Act*, SC 2001, c 26 [CSA 2001].

10   SC 1996, c 31.

11   International Code for Ships Operating in Polar Waters (Polar Code), IMO Resolution MSC.385(94) (21 November 2014, effective 1 January 2017); Amendments to the International Convention for the Safety of Life at Sea 1974, IMO Resolution MSC.386(94) (21 November 2014, effective 1 January 2017); Amendments to MARPOL Annexes I, II, IV and V, IMO Resolution MEPC.265(68) (15 May 2015, effective 1 January 2017) [Polar Code].

stakeholder levels. Canadian Arctic policy development also played a role in shaping the governance of shipping in the North.

This chapter undertakes a high-level survey and discussion of the fundamental characteristics of the contemporary Canadian maritime policy, legal and institutional frameworks underpinning the governance of Arctic shipping. It concludes with observations on opportunities for strengthening the governance of shipping with designation of low-impact shipping corridors in Canadian Arctic waters.

2   Policy Framework

Canadian Arctic and national transportation policies inform the policy framework for Arctic shipping. Since 2015, the Trudeau Government's Arctic policy has complemented marine transportation policy by addressing aspects related to polar shipping. The 2016 Joint Arctic Leaders' Statement committed to engaging with Indigenous and Northern communities to develop "a governance model for the Northern Marine Transportation Corridors and Arctic marine shipping, in a way that is environmentally and socially responsible, including respecting modern northern treaties" and improving "coverage of modern hydrography, charting and navigational information in the Arctic."[12] Subsequent policy statements reiterated the commitment to Arctic shipping. In 2017, the Arctic Foreign Policy Statement mentioned shipping as an area of focus in promoting economic and social development.[13] In 2019, the Arctic and Northern Policy Framework (ANPF) aimed to ensure safe and environmentally responsible shipping according to principles that include reconciliation with Indigenous peoples.[14] This includes designation of safe and sustainable

---

12   "United States-Canada Joint Arctic Leaders' Statement," Prime Minister of Canada, 20 December 2016, http://pm.gc.ca/eng/news/2016/12/20/united-states-canada-joint-arctic-leaders-statement.

13   Government of Canada, *Statement on Canada's Arctic Foreign Policy*, 12 May 2017, 12 et seq, https://www.international.gc.ca/world-monde/assets/pdfs/canada_arctic_foreign_policy-eng.pdf.

14   Crown-Indigenous Relations and Northern Affairs Canada (CIRNAC), "Canada's Arctic and Northern Policy Framework," Government of Canada, last modified 22 November 2019, Goal 5.9 and Annex, https://www.rcaanc-cirnac.gc.ca/eng/1560523306861/1560523330587.

navigation corridors with support from the ANPF and the Oceans Protection Plan (OPP).[15]

The *Canada Transportation Act* (CTA) provides the policy backdrop for national transportation for all modes of transport without singling out any region, including the Arctic.[16] The policy goal is overarching, aiming at a "competitive, economic and efficient national transportation system that meets the highest practicable safety and security standards and contributes to a sustainable environment" while optimizing all modes of transportation at the lowest total cost."[17] Accompanying objectives stress competition and market forces as drivers for transportation services while providing a moderating role for regulation and public authority to achieve economic, safety, security, environmental, and social outcomes. The regulator and regulatee are expected to work together to ensure integration in the national transportation system, thus ensuring that industry institutions play important roles in the governance of shipping. The CTA also provides an arbitration framework for disputes on shipping rates between carriers and shippers, including for the resupplying of Arctic communities.[18]

The high-level policy of the CTA creates concern, given the uniqueness of Arctic shipping. The latest review of the CTA recognized this concern and recommended "a new federal policy vision and regulatory regime to strengthen the safety and reliability of marine transport in the Arctic."[19] An ongoing concern is the continuing lack of infrastructure and capacity, such as the lack of preparedness and response capacity for spills.[20] Hence, the CTA review

---

15   CIRNAC, "Arctic and Northern Policy Framework: International Chapter," Government of
      Canada, last modified 22 October 2019, https://www.rcaanc-cirnac.gc.ca/eng/1562867415
      721/1562867459588; Transport Canada, "Oceans Protection Plan," Government of Canada,
      last modified 8 July 2020, https://www.tc.gc.ca/en/initiatives/oceans-protection-plan.
      html.
16   SC 1996, c 10 [CTA].
17   Id., s 5.
18   Id., s 159(1)(c) and (2).
19   Government of Canada, *Canada Transportation Act Review, Pathways: Connecting Can-*
      ada's Transportation System to the World, Volume 1 (2016), 67, http://www.tc.gc.ca/eng
      /ctareview2014/canada-transportation-act-review.html.
20   Office of the Auditor General of Canada, *Report of the Commissioner of the Environment*
      and Sustainable Development to the House of Commons–Fall 2010, Chapter 1: Oil Spills
      from Ships (Ottawa: Minister of Public Works and Government Services Canada, 2010),
      https://publications.gc.ca/collections/collection_2011/bvg-oag/FA1-2-2010-1-eng.pdf;
      Canada, Tanker Safety Expert Panel, *Phase I: A Review of Canada's Ship-source Oil Spill Pre-*
      paredness and Response Regime: Setting the Course for the Future (Ottawa: Tanker Safety
      Panel Secretariat, 2013), https://publications.gc.ca/collections/collection_2013/tc/T29-114
      -2013-eng.pdf; Canada, Tanker Safety Expert Panel, *A Review of Canada's Ship-source Spill*

recommended a policy that would include, among other, stricter regulations for vessel operator experience, consideration of coastal pilotage, compulsory ship reporting for all vessels, and an Arctic-wide governance model for port development.[21] Not all recommendations are practical. For example, stricter standards for vessel operators are potentially inconsistent with IMO standards, which Canada has committed to implementing. On ports, while the *Canada Marine Act* provides for the implementation of marine policies to support port infrastructure development and Canada's trade competitiveness, to date it has had limited implementation in Arctic waters.[22]

Shipping strategies and plans further implement national transportation policy objectives. For example, the National Shipbuilding Strategy[23] is a long-term investment to renew the Royal Canadian Navy and Canadian Coast Guard (CCG) fleets through procurement contracts with Canadian shipyards across the country. While the Strategy is national in scope, it aims to build sovereignty and maritime governance capacity in Arctic waters. The OPP, which at this time plays an important role in the development of governance capacity in Arctic waters, aims to enhance the marine safety system, preserving and restoring marine ecosystems, enhancing accident and pollution prevention and response, and building Indigenous partnerships to enhance safety and environment protection.[24] The OPP also supports the CCG, Canadian Hydrographic Service (CHS) and TC to develop low-impact shipping corridors in Canadian Arctic waters. The initiative is exploring the possibility of a system of routes.[25]

    Preparedness and Response: Setting the Course for the Future, Phase II - Requirements for the Arctic and for Hazardous and Noxious Substances Nationally (Ottawa: Tanker Safety Panel Secretariat, 2014), https://publications.gc.ca/collections/collection_2016/tc/T29-114-2014-eng.pdf.

21   Canada Transportation Act Review (n 19), pp. 66–68.

22   SC 1998, c 10.

23   Public Services and Procurement Canada, "National Shipbuilding Strategy," Government of Canada, last modified 26 July 2022, https://www.tpsgc-pwgsc.gc.ca/app-acq/amd-dp/mer-sea/sncn-nss/index-eng.html.

24   Transport Canada, "Oceans Protection Plan," Government of Canada, last modified 4 August 2022, https://tc.canada.ca/en/campaigns/protecting-our-coasts-oceans-protection-plan.

25   They would consist of: "Main Corridor (Primary): The main traffic highways in the Arctic, which provide a means to enable secondary access to ports"; "Approach Corridor (Secondary): Corridors characterized by medium- to low-density traffic levels, which can provide access to navigational ports to fulfill supply links and the movement of passengers. The three types of vessel to use these traffic corridors are cargo, tanker, and passenger vessels"; "Refuge Corridor (Tertiary): Characterized by medium to low traffic, providing navigational access to places of refuge, including charted anchorage areas located nearest to primary and secondary corridors and furthest away from ports"; "Private

3   Legal Framework

International and Canadian maritime law of general application and polar shipping regulation inform the legal framework.

3.1   *Maritime Legislation of General Application*

In 1970, Canada's maritime legislation consisted of a handful of statutes, chief of which were the AWPPA, CSA and the former *Navigable Waters Protection Act*. At the time, federal law did not address the full scope of shipping matters, and consequently provincial law governed many areas such as carriage of goods by sea, marine insurance, and necessaries (e.g., ship repair, equipment supplies, and provisions). Today, approximately 50 federal maritime, environmental, and other statutes govern the public and private law aspects of shipping generally and Arctic shipping in particular (see Annex 1). The subsidiary legislation also has expanded exponentially. Annex 2 lists the extensive regulations under the CSA 2001 alone, with more accompanying other statutes.

From the 1970s to the 1990s, a series of Supreme Court of Canada decisions emphasized the essentially uniform nature of federal maritime law, thus limiting the application of provincial law to a few maritime issues that fell under provincial powers of property and civil rights and local undertakings.[26] However, in more recent years, the Supreme Court has changed direction on the interface between federal and provincial law on double aspect issues, that is, involving both federal and provincial constitutionally allocated powers. In the spirit of the philosophy of cooperative federalism, in recent years the Supreme Court has been more readily disposed to recognize the complementary role that provincial law could play on shipping and navigation matters.[27]

Interest Corridor (Quaternary): Characterized by geographical extents of low buffered density levels. These corridors provide navigational access to resource development and extraction sites, or other private interests (mining sites, research bases)"; "Projected Corridor (Quinary): Characterized by geographical extents of low buffered density levels, or in the absence of any density analysis or vessel traffic data. These corridors provide navigational access to proposed or potential infrastructure for resource development." René Chénier, Loretta Abado, Olivier Sabourin and Laurent Tardif, "Northern Marine Transportation Corridors: Creation and Analysis of Northern Marine Traffic Routes in Canadian Waters," *Transactions in GIS* (2017): 1085–1097, at 1088.

26   For example, *ITO International Terminal Operators Ltd* v. *Miida Electronics Inc.* (*The Buenos Aires Maru*), [1986] 1 SCR 752, which concerned theft from a warehouse in the port of Montreal and *Ordon Estate* v. *Grail* (1996), 3 SCR 437, which concerned claims for death and personal injury in boating accidents.

27   For example, with respect to occupational health and safety and worker's compensation in the fishing operations in the provinces, *R* v. *Mersey Seafoods Ltd*, 2008 NSCA 67; *Jim*

3.1.1   Functions

The volume of legislation is functionally diverse and demonstrates how far Canada's maritime interests have evolved since Confederation, and most especially since the 1970s. Contemporary maritime legislation enables Canada to assert sovereignty and maintain order and the rule of law in its waters. It regulates navigation safety, environment protection and security of ships and ports, while also facilitating Canada's international trade. Maritime legislation implements Canada's international public law obligations over its ships and provides for extraterritorial jurisdiction, including over Canadian ships in Antarctic waters. The regulated standards include construction, design, equipment, and crewing (CDME), and operational standards for the safety of life at sea, load lines, collision avoidance, and operational vessel-source pollution prevention.

At the private law level, maritime legislation implements rules and model clauses set out in private maritime law conventions Canada is party to, thereby providing the framework for maritime transactions. The numerous topics include civil liability for oil pollution damage, limitation of liability, and salvage model rules for the provision of commercial assistance to ships and minimization of environmental damage. The civil liability and limitation of liability instruments establish rules for compensation for oil pollution from ships, including in Arctic waters.

Uniformity of domestic maritime rules and standards has long been a central aspiration of Canadian maritime law. The purpose is to ensure the consistent implementation of Canada's treaty obligations and to enable the application of the same safety standards to all navigable waters.[28] At times, uniformity has been elusive and in some private law areas controversy continues to reign over the application of provincial law to transactions that federal law historically governed.[29] In other areas, the diversity of marine regionalism provides a compelling argument for regulatory diversity to ensure relevance for local concerns. The Arctic and its unique treatment in the AWPPA and its regulations are a case in point because of the unique environmental and navigational conditions and hazards. In addition, and on a smaller and local scale,

---

  Pattison Enterprises v. *British Columbia (Workers' Compensation Board)*, 2011 BCCA 35; *Marine Services International Ltd* v. *Ryan Estate*, [2013] SCJ 44. More recently, *Desgagnés Transport Inc* v. *Wärtsilä Canada Inc*, 2019 SCC 58, permitted the application of Quebec law, instead of federal non-statutory maritime law, to the sale of marine engine parts.

28 *Whitbread* v. *Walley*, [1990] 3 SCR 1273.

29 For example, with respect to the contract of supply of necessaries, such as equipment, where Quebec law was recently held to apply. *Desgagnés Transport* (n 27).

the conservation of sensitive marine areas, ecosystems and species requires higher standards than the norm for ship operations.

3.1.1.1   *Safety*

The CSA 2001 and its regulations enable Canada to exercise its rights and responsibilities as a flag State and its coastal State right to regulate shipping in Canadian waters in accordance with international law. The Act sets out regulatory, enforcement and institutional responsibilities and procedures. As the principal instrument regulating safety, the CSA 2001 regulates CDME standards, marine documents, and ship operations, including the rules and standards in international maritime conventions and subsidiary instruments referentially incorporated by the Act.[30] It also sets out the Canadian Register of Ships, regulatory framework for vessel traffic services and navigation aids, and makes provision for search and rescue. Regulations under the Act address safety and operational competency of small vessels and pleasure craft traffic in Canadian Arctic waters, which often raise safety and search and rescue challenges, most especially in remote areas.[31] As will be discussed below, the CSA 2001 also serves as an umbrella for polar shipping safety regulation. The CSA 2001 does not address all maritime safety matters, and separate legislation regulates other aspects such as the safe loading and movement of cargo in containers,[32] dangerous goods transportation,[33] and carriage of nuclear substances.[34]

The CSA 2001 establishes a system of offences and enforcement procedures, as well as procedures for the investigation of the causes of incidents, accidents, and casualties to prevent their recurrence, conducted by the Transportation Safety Board of Canada (TSB), which is established by separate legislation.[35] The TSB has conducted several investigations concerning occurrences in Arctic waters, including instances of grounding of passenger vessels.[36]

---

30   CSA 2001 (n 9), Schedule 1 instruments for which TC is responsible and Schedule 2 instruments for which DFO is responsible.

31   *Small Vessel Regulations*, SOR/2010-91; *Competency of Operators of Pleasure Craft Regulations*, SOR/99-53.

32   *Safe Containers Convention Act*, RSC 1985, c S-1.

33   *Transportation of Dangerous Goods Act*, 1992, SC 1992, c 34; *Transportation of Dangerous Goods Regulations*, SOR/2001-286.

34   *Nuclear Safety and Control Act*, SC 1997, c 9.

35   *Canadian Transportation Accident Investigation and Safety Board Act*, SC 1989, c 3.

36   Transportation Safety Board of Canada (TSB), *Marine Investigation Report M96H0016, Grounding - Passenger vessel "Hanseatic", Simpson Strait, Northwest Territories* (Gatineau: TSB, 29 August 1996), https://www.tsb.gc.ca/eng/rapports-reports/marine/1996/m96h 0016/m96h0016.pdf; TSB, *Marine Investigation Report M10H0006, Grounding Passenger vessel Clipper Adventurer, Coronation Gulf, Nunavut* (Gatineau: TSB, 27 August 2010),

3.1.1.2   *Marine Environment Protection and Damage/Loss Compensation*
Maritime and environmental statutes and regulations govern the environmental impacts of shipping in all Canadian waters. A first layer consists of
maritime statutes implementing international conventions. The CSA 2001
implements the International Convention for the Prevention of Pollution
from Ships (MARPOL),[37] ballast waters management convention,[38] and anti-
fouling systems convention[39] and establishes an enforcement system based on
public welfare offences.[40] The *Wrecked, Abandoned and Hazardous Vessels Act*
(WAHVA) implements the International Convention on Salvage[41] and further
regulates ships to prevent them from becoming wrecks and abandonment of
substandard ships in ports.[42]

A second legislative layer regulates waste discharges harmful to sensitive
environments, species, and resources. The *Canadian Environmental Protection
Act* and regulations under it implement international rules on dumping at sea,
defined to also include Arctic waters, and prohibit discharges using ships as
platforms and the dumping of ships without permits.[43] The *Fisheries Act* and
Migratory Birds Convention Act further prohibit the discharge of substances
that are harmful respectively to fisheries habitats and areas frequented by
migratory birds.[44] The establishment of marine protected areas under various

https://www.bst-tsb.gc.ca/eng/rapports-reports/marine/2010/m10h0006/m10h0006.
html; TSB, *Marine Transportation Safety Investigation Report M18C0225, Grounding Passenger vessel Akademik Ioffe, Astronomical Society Islands, Nunavut* (Gatineau: TSB, 24
August 2018), https://www.tsb.gc.ca/eng/rapports-reports/marine/2018/m18c0225/m18c
0225.html.

37   International Convention for the Prevention of Pollution from Ships, 2 November 1973,
1340 UNTS 184 as amended by Protocol of 1978 Relating to the International Convention for the Prevention of Pollution from Ships of 1973, 17 February 1978 (both in force 2
October 1983), 1340 UNTS 61 [MARPOL].

38   International Convention for the Control and Management of Ships' Ballast Water and
Sediments, 13 February 2004 (in force 8 September 2017), IMO Doc BWM/CONF/36 (16
February 2004).

39   International Convention on the Control of Harmful Anti-fouling Systems, 5 October 2001
(in force 17 September 2008), Can TS 2010 No 15.

40   Public welfare offences are offences subject to strict liability but entailing the defence of
due diligence. *R v. Glenshiel Towing Co*, [2000] BCTC 665 (SC).

41   International Convention on Salvage, 28 April 1989 (in force 14 July 1996), 1953 UNTS 165.

42   *Wrecked, Abandoned or Hazardous Vessels Act*, SC 2019, c 1 [WAHVA].

43   *Canadian Environmental Protection Act, 1999*, SC 1999, c 33, ss 122(2), 123; *Disposal at Sea
Regulations*, SOR/2001-275. The instruments implement the London Convention and
Protocol to the Convention on the Prevention of Marine Pollution by Dumping Wastes
and Other Matter, 1972, 8 November 1996 (in force 24 March 2006), Can TS 2006 No 5.

44   *Fisheries Act*, RSC 1985, c F-14, s 36; *Migratory Birds Convention Act, 1994*, SC 1994, c 22, s 5.1.

federal statutes may include conditions or restrictions for shipping routes and activities, including offences for infringements.[45] However, regulations for National Marine Conservation Areas restricting or prohibiting marine navigation or maritime safety activities otherwise regulated by the CSA 2001 and AWPPA require the recommendation of the Minister of Environment and Climate Change (as the Minister responsible for the Parks Canada Agency) and the Minister of Transport.[46] Such regulations prevail over other regulations.[47] The *Species at Risk Act* is a further major statute providing protection of marine species listed in the schedules and critical habitats in internal waters and the territorial sea and applies to violations by persons on board ships.[48]

Similarly, the *Canadian Navigable Waters Act* regulates obstructions in navigable waters, requiring that major works in navigable waters must not interfere with navigation.[49] For the purpose of such works, the Act defines navigable waters in the Arctic Ocean as "[a]ll waters from the outer limit of the territorial sea up to the higher high water mean tide water level and includes all connecting waters up to an elevation intersecting with that level."[50] Antarctic waters are also protected, and Canadian ships require prior permission to sail those waters and must comply with waste discharge rules.[51]

A third layer concerns a civil liability system for compensation of environmental damage, economic loss and response efforts for spills based on international conventional regimes that Canada has implemented through the *Marine Liability Act*.[52] The three principal regimes—concerning accidental spills of cargo oil, bunker fuel, and hazardous and noxious substances—provide compensation based on limited liability.[53] In the event of a large spill in Canadian Arctic waters, these regimes will establish international compensation funds

---

45   *Oceans Act* (n 10), s 39.2 empowers an enforcement officer to direct the movements of or detain a ship in Canadian waters and the EEZ when they have reasonable doubt an offence will be committed in those waters. *Canada National Marine Conservation Areas Act*, SC 2002, c 18, s 17; *Canada Wildlife Act*, RSC 1985, c W-9, s 4, re power of Minister and s 11(2) and 11.7(2) re the power of a wildlife officer to inspect a conveyance, which may include waterborne craft and move a vessel into port and unload its contents.

46   *National Marine Conservation Areas Act* (n 45), s 16(3).

47   Including regulations made under the AWPPA, CNWA, CSA 2001, *Fisheries Act*, the *Coastal Fisheries Protection Act*, and WAHVA to the extent of any conflict between them. Id., s 16(5).

48   SC 2002, c 29.

49   RSC 1985, c N-22, s 4.1.

50   Id., sch, Part 1.

51   *Antarctic Environmental Protection Act*, SC 2003, c 20, ss 9, 17, 18.

52   SC 2001, c 6 [MLA].

53   Id., Part 6 and schs 6, 7, 8.

administered through a claims process in the Federal Court. The domestic Ship-source Oil Pollution Fund (SOPF), also established by the Act, further complements the judicial process as a domestic fund empowered to compensate claims on an administrative basis.[54] While to date there has not been a spill in Arctic waters large enough to engage the full range of compensation regimes, the SOPF has compensated CCG response claims in Arctic waters.[55] Differently from the international regimes, the SOPF's liability is unlimited.[56]

A fourth and general layer consists of national goals and standards for sustainable development, decarbonization and environmental impact assessment. Federal sustainable development legislation requires, among other, coordination across all the federal government and in compliance with Canada's international obligations.[57] Canada's commitment to net-zero greenhouse gas (GHG) emissions by 2050 in pursuit of its Paris Agreement obligations affects all economic activities,[58] although IMO energy efficiency regulations do not apply to domestic shipping unless expressly extended at the domestic level.[59] Port activities and destination and logistics shipping in Canadian Arctic waters constitute activities captured by Canada's national GHG policy. Similarly, it is arguable that environmental assessment legislation is pertinent to shipping because the *Impact Assessment Act* addresses activities that could affect habitats and species in internal waters, territorial sea, the exclusive economic zone (EEZ) and on the continental shelf.[60] Designated projects under the Act include activities in National Marine Conservation Areas.[61] Environmental assessments include those conducted by port authorities.[62] The concentration of shipping in designated low-impact shipping corridors in Arctic

---

54   Id., Part 7.

55   In the 2020–2021 reporting year, the Ship-source Oil Pollution Fund (SOPF) had two open files: *Akademik Ioffe* passenger and scientific research vessel grounding in Kugaruuk, Nunavut, in 2019, and *Investigator*, a barge grounding in Toker Point, Northwest Territories in 2016. SOPF, *The Administrator's Annual Report 2020–2021* (Ottawa: SOPF, 2021), 58, https://sopf.gc.ca/wp-content/uploads/pdf/annual%20reports/2020-2021-SOPF-Annual -Report-EN.pdf. In 2010, a claim for CDN$468,801.72 concerning the *Clipper Adventure* passenger vessel in Coronation Gulf, Nunavut, was closed. SOPF, *The Administrator's 30th Annual Report 2018–2019* (Ottawa: SOPF, 2019), 49, https://sopf.gc.ca/wp-content /uploads/pdf/annual%20reports/RapportAnnuelSOPF_2018-2019-ENG.pdf.

56   MLA (n 52), s 93.1. In the event the SOPF cannot meet its liabilities, the Minister of Finance is empowered to direct that the overage is charged to the Consolidated Revenue Fund.

57   *Federal Sustainable Development Act*, SC 2008, c 33, s 3.

58   *Canadian Net-Zero Emissions Accountability Act*, SC 2021, c 22, ss 4, 6.

59   MARPOL (n 37), Annex VI, reg 19.

60   SC 2019, c 28, s 7.

61   *Designated Classes of Projects Order*, SOR/2019-323, s 12.1.

62   *Canada Port Authority Environmental Assessment Regulations*, SOR/99-318.

waters arguably has the potential to produce such impacts (see chapter by Doelle *et al.* in this volume).

3.1.1.3   *Ship Reporting and Security*

Maritime security in Arctic waters emerged as a concern with the AWPPA and the establishment of the ship reporting system under the *Northern Canada Vessel Traffic Services Zone Regulations* (NORDREG) in 1977, initially based on voluntary compliance.[63] In 2010, reporting became mandatory. There have been instances of vessels not complying with NORDREG mandatory reporting requirements and navigating without an active automatic identification system.[64] Domain awareness requires that NORDREG is able to track vessel movements and issue clearances.

In addition to NORDREG, and while not applying to naval vessels and facilities, the *Marine Transportation Security Act* (MTSA) aims to ensure the security of the marine transportation system, including ships and marine facilities,[65] thus providing a security backdrop for Arctic shipping. Among other, regulations under the Act implement the IMO's International Ship and Port Facility Security Code and set out a security regime for ships, cargoes, bunkers, and port facilities.[66] The Minister of Transport is empowered to prohibit entry into Canadian waters and direct the movement of vessels.[67] Security offences against shipping and navigation are also criminal offences.[68]

3.1.1.4   *Seafarers and Maritime Training*

Federal labour law applies to most aspects of Arctic shipping. The *Canada Labour Code*[69] and *Maritime Occupational Health and Safety Regulations*[70] implement the International Labour Organization's Maritime Labour

---

63   SOR/2010-127 [NORDREG]. *The Coast Guard in Canada's Arctic: Interim Report, Standing Committee on Fisheries and Oceans, Fourth Report* (Senate of Canada, June 2008), 31, https://sencanada.ca/content/sen/committee/392/fish/rep/rep04jun08-e.pdf. Ships are report to Coast Guard Marine Communications and Traffic Services (MCTS) system. The CCG informs TC, and the latter determines the permitting of entry.

64   For instance, the passage of the *Kiwi Roa*. "New Zealander Sails Through Arctic on Custom Yacht in Violation of COVID-19 Restrictions," CBC News, 26 August 2020, https://www.cbc.ca/news/canada/north/new-zealand-yacht-cambridge-bay-nunavut-1.5698347.

65   SC 1994, c 40, s 4 [MTSA].

66   *Marine Transportation Security Regulations*, SOR/2004-144 [MTSR].

67   MTSA (n 65), s 16.

68   For example, piracy and hijacking. *Criminal Code*, RSC 1985, c C-46, ss 75, 78.

69   RSC 1985, c L-2.

70   SOR/2010-120.

Convention, 2006.[71] The Convention sets out fundamental seafarer human and labour rights and occupational health and safety standards for seafarers. The regulations apply to both commercial and government-owned Canadian vessels, but not to CCG vessels. The CSA 2001 regulates occupations on board ships, training requirements, and certification, as well as occupational health and safety matters not covered by the *Canada Labour Code*, such as accommodation for crew, workspaces, fire safety, and medical examinations.[72] Regulations under the CSA 2001 implement the International Convention on Standards for Training, Certification and Watchkeeping for Seafarers (STCW) and accompanying code.[73] The IMO amended these instruments after adopting the Polar Code to regulate polar seafaring standards.[74] In addition to standards for seafarers, the regulations provide for the certification of supervisors of oil transfer operations in Arctic waters.[75]

In the event of injury or death, seafarers and their dependents benefit from a worker compensation scheme set out in the *Merchant Seamen Compensation Act*.[76] Differently, provincial and territorial safety regulations and worker compensation schemes apply to personnel based in the provinces and territories and injured while working at sea, such as wildlife harvesters.[77] Seafarers and other maritime workers covered by provincial and territorial schemes do not enjoy rights of action under the *Marine Liability Act*.[78]

3.1.1.5   *Maritime Public Health*

In addition to the public health concerns over the release of aquatic organisms or pathogens in ballast waters or toxic substances from anti-fouling systems regulated under the CSA 2001, ships may be vectors of other public

---

71   Adopted 23 February 2006 (in force 20 August 2013), Can TS 2013 No 16.

72   CSA 2001 (n 9), s 100(l).

73   *Marine Personnel Regulations*, SOR/2007-115.

74   Amendments to the International Convention on Standards of Training, Certification and Watchkeeping for Seafarers (STCW) 1978, as amended, Resolution MSC.416(97) (25 November 2016, effective 1 July 2018); Amendments to Part A of the Seafarers' Training, Certification and Watchkeeping (STCW) Code, Resolution MSC.417(97) (25 November 2016, effective 1 July 2018). See STCW Code s B-V/g: "Guidance regarding training of masters and officers for ships operating in polar waters."

75   *Marine Personnel Regulations* (n 73), s 162.

76   RSC 1985, c M-6.

77   *Mersey* and *Pattison* (n 26). See Workers Safety and Compensation Commission concerning Legislation on workers' compensation and workplace health and safety in the Northwest Territories and Nunavut, https://www.wscc.nt.ca/about-wscc/policy-and-legislation /legislation#WorkersCompensation.

78   *Ryan Estate* (n 27).

health risks. In such instances, the *Quarantine Act*, which is legislation of general application, empowers the Public Health Agency of Canada to take measures to control infectious outbreaks and communicable deceases on board ships, such as the COVID-19 outbreaks in the cruise ship industry.[79] Where a crew member or passenger dies or is taken ill, regulations under the *Quarantine Act* require the master to notify the quarantine officer under the Act at least 24 hours before port arrival.[80] This reporting requirement applies to ships in Canadian Arctic waters in addition to NORDREG reporting requirements.

3.1.1.6 *Transportation of Goods and Passengers*

Public and private law govern the transportation of goods and passengers in Canadian Arctic waters. We have seen the public law regulation of the safety aspects of ships carrying goods and passengers, safe containers and dangerous goods, and the security aspects of cargo handling and certain dangerous goods.

Domestic shipping in Arctic waters, defined as shipping whose ports of departure and destination are in Canada, remains reserved exclusively for Canadian ships.[81]

The *Marine Liability Act*, whose provisions prevail over the AWPPA in cases of inconsistency,[82] provides the private law framework for the commercial carriage of goods and passengers in Canadian Arctic waters. It implements the international carriage of goods and passengers' regimes Canada is party to and provides the framework for maritime contracting based on model clauses. Canada is currently party to the Hague-Visby Rules regime setting out the relationship between carriers and shippers and a limited liability regime for carriers,[83] and complemented by legislation on bills of lading.[84] The Rules apply to carriage in Arctic waters.[85]

---

79 *Quarantine Act*, SC 2005, c 20. See "Canada's Cruise Ship Instructional Reference Tool," Transport Canada, last modified 17 February 2022, https://tc.canada.ca/en/initiatives/covid-19-measures-updates-guidance-issued-transport-canada/canada-s-cruise-ship-instructional-reference-tool; Transport Canada, "Measures to Support Safe Cruise Travel in Canada," Ship Safety Bulletin No. 18/2021 (modified 18 February 2022), https://tc.canada.ca/en/marine-transportation/marine-safety/ship-safety-bulletins/measures-support-safe-cruise-travel-canada-ssb-no-18-2021-modified-february-18-2022.
80 *Quarantine Regulations*, CRC c 1368, s 12(1).
81 *Coasting Trade Act*, SC 1992, c 31, s 3.
82 MLA (n 52), s 141.
83 Protocol to amend the International Convention for the Unification of Certain Rules of Law Relating to Bills of Lading, 1924, 23 February 1968 (in force 14 February 1984), 1412 UNTS 121; MLA (n 52), s 43(1) and sch 3.
84 *Bills of Lading Act*, RSC 1985, c B-5.
85 MLA (n 52), s 43(2).

The carriage of passengers, such as on cruise ships and ferries, is regulated by the Athens Convention Relating to the Carriage of Passengers and their Luggage by Sea, 1974[86] as amended by subsequent protocols, and as implemented through referential incorporation in the *Marine Liability Act*.[87] The carriage of passengers is similarly subject to a limited liability regime and applies in Arctic waters except for adventure tourism.[88] Providers of adventure tourism services potentially benefit from general limitation of liability elsewhere in the Act.[89]

3.1.1.7   *Services to Shipping*

The full range of services normally available for safe navigation in Canadian waters is limited in Arctic waters. When services are available, they are governed by federal statutory law and the maritime common law. For example, the *Pilotage Act* established pilotage authorities in Canada's marine regions,[90] but not in Arctic waters. This might come across as puzzling, because the purpose of pilotage is to enable ships to navigate safely in areas prone to navigation hazards and for masters to benefit from the pilot's local knowledge of navigational conditions and regulations. While pilotage may be mandatory or recommended, mandatory pilotage is widespread in major ports and only recommended in Arctic waters and there are only isolated cases of pilotage in those waters related to resource development.[91] A recent review of the *Pilotage Act* noted that, while the adoption of the Polar Code and use of ice navigators might mitigate the need for pilotage in the short term in Arctic waters, there is potential for pilotage in conjunction with the low-impact shipping corridors in the long term.[92] An earlier legislative review noted the related issue of a shortage of ice pilots.[93]

Federal law does not regulate towage and pushing, except for the operational aspects covered by the collision avoidance regulations.[94] Model clauses usually govern the contract, and they speak to the rights and responsibilities

---

86   Adopted 13 December 1974 (in force 28 April 1987), 1463 *UNTS* 20.

87   MLA (n 52), s 37(1) and sch 2.

88   Id., ss 37(2), 37.1.

89   Id., s 26(1) and sch 1 providing for limitation under the Convention on Limitation of Liability for Maritime Claims, 1976, as amended.

90   RSC 1985, c P-14.

91   In addition, the Port of Churchill is serviced by the Great Lakes Pilotage Authority. Transport Canada, *2018 Pilotage Act Review* (Transport Canada, 2018), 96, https://tc.canada.ca/sites/default/files/migrated/17308_tc_pilotage_act_review_v8_final.pdf.

92   Id., VIII.

93   Canada Transportation Act Review (n 19), p. 60.

94   *Collision Regulations*, CRC c 1416.

of the tug and tow, the distribution of risk, liability, and insurance. Unlike the case of Atlantic and Pacific towage operations, there are no model clauses dedicated to towage in Canadian Arctic waters and therefore towage in the region tends to involve other model clauses.[95]

The WAHVA, complemented by the maritime common law, provides the legal framework for the very limited salvage capacity in Canadian Arctic waters.[96] In Arctic waters, CCG ships assist vessels in difficulty in addition to providing search and rescue, but they do not have the capabilities and know-how of commercial salvage providers. However, the experience of the *Clipper Adventurer*, a small passenger vessel that grounded on a shoal in Coronation Gulf, Nunavut, in 2010, appears to have set an important precedent. The vessel did not carry on board the latest information for safe navigation in Canadian Arctic waters and the CCG provided assistance to free the vessel. Subsequently the owners sued the Crown, alleging that CCG and CHS did not properly notify shipowners of the shoal. An action by the Crown to recover costs followed. Efforts at mediation failed and the owners' case in the Federal Court failed in trial and on appeal and leave to appeal to the Supreme Court of Canada was dismissed.[97] While the circumstances of the case were unusual, it appears the Crown is able to charge for the assistance it provides, particularly when the predicament of the vessel results from lack of seaworthiness or negligence. The eventual enactment of the WAHVA made provision for Canadian government tugs or vessels equipped with a salvage plant to provide and claim salvage.[98]

3.1.1.8 *Marine Insurance*
The federal *Marine Insurance Act* governs this maritime contract in Canada.[99] Originally modelled on the UK *Marine Insurance Act of 1906*, the Act operates instead of provincial marine insurance legislation and provides model clauses for the insurance contract.[100] The CSA 2001 requires ships to operate with marine insurance, and ships engaged in the carriage of oil, hazardous and noxious substances and passengers must carry dedicated cover, usually obtained

---

95 For example, TOWCON and TOWHIRE model clauses. "Contracts and Clauses," BIMCO, https://www.bimco.org/contracts-and-clauses.
96 WAHVA (n 42).
97 *Adventurer Owner Ltd* v. *Canada*, 2017 FC 105; *Adventurer Owner Ltd* v. *Canada*, 2018 FCA 34.
98 WAHVA (n 42), s 51.
99 SC 1993, c 22.
100 *Zavarovalna Skupnost (Insurance Community Triglav Ltd.)* v. *Terrasses Jewellers Inc.*, [1983] 1 SCR 283.

from Mutual Protection and Indemnity Associations.[101] There are relatively few marine insurers providing cover for Arctic shipping, mostly because of the risks involved and the insufficient actuarial basis to quantify the risk and thereby enable the establishment of premiums.[102]

3.1.1.9   *Ports and Harbours*

There are very few ports in Canadian Arctic waters and hence the *Canada Marine Act* has little role to play currently. The Port of Churchill in Manitoba is located in the Hudson Bay below the 60th parallel but falls within Arctic waters as defined for the purposes of NORDREG.[103] Other than Churchill, there is no other public port or port run by a port corporation under the Act in Arctic waters.[104]

Separately from ports governed by the *Canada Marine Act*, the *Fishing and Recreational Harbours Act* and regulations govern small crafts harbours,[105] for which the Department of Fisheries and the Canadian Coast Guard (DFO) are responsible. The regulations apply to scheduled harbours, which in Arctic waters include designated harbours in Nunavut and the Northwest Territories.[106] The Minister of Fisheries and Oceans controls and administers selected harbours with respect to their use, management, maintenance, and collection of charges for use. Commercial vessels operating in the Yukon and Northwest Territories enjoy an exemption from berthage charges.[107]

---

101   CSA 2001 (n 9), s 167(1)(b)(i); MLA (n 52), ss 55, sch 5 and annex, sch 8 and annex.
102   Mark Rosanes, "Marine Insurers Tackle Uncharted Arctic Risks," *Insurance Business Canada*, 29 October 2020, https://www.insurancebusinessmag.com/ca/news/marine /marine-insurers-tackle-uncharted-arctic-risks-237574.aspx. When provided, the insurance premium tends to have a high mark up, as much as 40 percent.
103   NORDREG (n 63), s 2.
104   *Public Ports and Public Port Facilities Regulations*, SOR/2001-154, sch 1. A privately owned port, Churchill is a public port of regional significance. It is important for grain and other exports and supplying northern communities. TC oversees the port to ensure compliance with environmental and navigable waters regulations. Churchill is now under Indigenous ownership and closed until 2023 pending replacement of the railway line.
105   *Fishing and Recreational Harbours Act*, RSC 1985, c F-24; *Fishing and Recreational Harbours Regulations*, SOR/78-767.
106   Northwest Territories: Hay River, Moraine Bay and Simpson Islands; Nunavut: Pangnirtung. Several other provincial harbours in the Hudson Bay are also included in the regulations. *Fishing and Recreational Harbours Regulations* (n 105), sch I.
107   Id., s 26.

3.1.2   *Arctic Shipping Regulation*

Arctic shipping involves additional risks to those usually faced by ships trading in other regions, and hence justifies specialized CDME and operational standards. Canada regulates Arctic shipping by virtue of the sovereignty it claims over historic internal waters under general international law, sovereignty over the territorial sea, and the special jurisdiction over ice-covered areas permitted by Article 234 of the LOSC.[108] The following discussion does not deal with the legal basis for the exercise of jurisdiction over Arctic waters in the law of the sea, but rather with the domestic law that nourishes that jurisdiction and enables Canada to act as a coastal and flag State. The core statutes concerned are the AWPPA and CSA 2001. The AWPPA did not replace maritime legislation of general application, but rather added specialized regulations to Arctic shipping. Regulations under the CSA 2001 further complement AWPPA rules and standards.

The AWPPA was motivated by coastal State concerns over sovereignty, protection of the unique Arctic marine environment, maritime safety in the harsh navigation conditions, lack of infrastructure, and the inherent rights of Indigenous peoples.[109] The definition of Arctic waters includes all waters north of 60 degrees North up to the limits of the EEZ and within the 141st meridian of west longitude claimed as the maritime boundary with the United States and the maritime boundary with Greenland.[110]

The AWPPA established a strict pollution prevention regime and framework for the designation of Shipping Safety Control Zones (SSCZs), which regulations established in turn.[111] The SSCZs enable ships to operate in the zones according to their polar class and the Arctic Ice Regime Shipping System (AIRSS) for the assessment of risk. Regulations address CDME standards, fuel carried on board, cargo, onboard supplies, required navigation information, and pilot and ice navigator requirements, including icebreaking assistance, for all ship classes to enable them to navigate during periods of the year or when ice conditions permit.[112] The Governor in Council has the discretion to exempt foreign government owned ships from the requirements of the Act

---

108   *Oceans Act* (n 10), ss 7, 11, 12, 14; LOSC (n 7), Article 234.
109   AWPPA (n 1), preamble.
110   Id., s 2. Arctic waters extended to the outer limits of the EEZ in 2009. Bill C-3 amending the AWPPA to extend the definition of Canadian Arctic waters from 100 to 200 nautical miles was introduced in the House of Commons by the Minister of Transport, Infrastructure and Communities. Legislative Summary of Bill C-3: An Act to amend the Arctic Waters Pollution Prevention Act, 40th Parliament, 2nd Session (2009).
111   *Shipping Safety Control Zones Order*, CRC c 356.
112   Id., s 12(1).

although compliance with the regulated standards is expected.[113] The Act sets out enforcement powers of pollution prevention officers, including boarding and issuing orders to ships to report, directing their movements and requiring assistance in containing waste,[114] and a range of offenses committed by persons and ships.[115] Prior to 2017, the regulations under the AWPPA set out unilateral standards, because mandatory international polar shipping standards did not exist until the adoption of the Polar Code.

In 2017, the *Arctic Shipping Safety and Pollution Prevention Regulations* (ASSPPR) implemented the Polar Code and amendments to the International Convention for the Safety of Life at Sea (SOLAS)[116] and MARPOL under the authority of both the AWPPA and CSA 2001.[117] The new regulations referentially incorporated much of the mandatory and voluntary provisions of the Polar Code with some adjustments to account for transitional arrangements for Canadian ships and to ensure strict compliance with the AWPPA's zero discharge regime.[118] As a flag State, Canada extended the application of the new standards to its ships in polar waters without change. Ships operating in polar waters are required to carry a Polar Ship Certificate certifying compliance with the Polar Code and all Canadian ships must have a low temperature notation.[119] As a coastal State, Canada incorporated the Polar Code's Part I safety rules to SOLAS ships of 500 gross tonnage and more, other than fishing vessels and pleasure craft.[120] Existing ships may continue to use the regime for navigation in Canadian Arctic waters based on a zone-date system, SSCZs, and AIRSS.[121] The new Polar Operational Limit Assessment Risk Indexing System (POLARIS) set out in the Polar Code will apply to new ships and will eventually replace AIRSS.[122] An onboard ice navigator is required for vessels using AIRSS and non-SOLAS ships, such as fishing vessels.[123] New STCW rules govern the training

---

113   Id., s 12(2).
114   Id., s 15.
115   Id., s 18.
116   International Convention for the Safety of Life at Sea, 1 November 1974 (in force 25 May 1980), 1184 *UNTS* 2 [SOLAS].
117   *Arctic Shipping Safety and Pollution Prevention Regulations*, SOR/2017-286 [ASSPPR].
118   Drummond Fraser, "A Change in the Ice Regime: Polar Code Implementation in Canada," in *Governance of Arctic Shipping: Rethinking Risk, Human Impacts and Regulation*, eds., Aldo Chircop, Floris Goerlandt, Claudio Aporta and Ronald Pelot (Cham: Springer, 2020), 285–300, at 294.
119   Polar Code (n 11), Part IA, reg 1.3.1; ASSPPR (n 117), s 11.
120   ASSPPR (n 117), s 6.
121   Id., s 8(2).
122   Id.
123   Id., s 10.

and competence of the master and officers, as discussed above. The pollution prevention rules concerning oil, hazardous and noxious substances carried in bulk, sewage and garbage apply to all ships, including non-SOLAS ships, and the AWPPA zero discharge rule holds, even though Part II of the Polar Code appears to permit the release of trace amounts of oil in clean ballast.[124]

As noted above, Canada's ship reporting system in Arctic waters is set out in NORDREG. The system covers the SSCZs and includes an area larger than the definition of Arctic waters under the AWPPA.[125] NORDREG's reporting requirements include reporting to the Iqaluit MCTS Centre the following:

- sailing plan when about to enter the NORDREG zone;
- daily position report after a vessel has entered;
- additional position report when another ship is in difficulty, there is an obstruction to navigation, a navigation aid is not functioning, ice and weather conditions are hazardous; or there is a pollutant in the water;
- final report before a vessel exits the zone; and
- deviation reports indicating changes from the sailing plan.[126]

The reporting requirements apply to vessels of 300 gross tonnage or more, vessels engaged in towing or pushing another vessel when the aggregate tonnage is 500 gross tonnage or more, and vessels that carry pollutants or dangerous cargo or towing vessels carrying such cargoes.[127]

4   Institutional Framework

The institutional framework consists of TC, DFO, their agencies, and other bodies for which their respective ministers are responsible for the performance of core roles, and other departments playing supportive roles or providing specific services.

---

124   Fraser (n 118), p. 294 et seq.
125   The other areas include: Ungava Bay, Hudson Bay and Kugmallit Bay that are not in a Shipping Safety Control Zone; James Bay; the waters of the Koksoak River from Ungava Bay to Kuujjuaq; the waters of Feuilles Bay from Ungava Bay to Tasiujaq; the waters of Chesterfield Inlet and Baker Lake; and the waters of the Moose River from James Bay to Moosonee. NORDREG (n 63), s 2.
126   Fisheries and Oceans Canada and Canadian Coast Guard, *Radio Aids to Marine Navigation 2022* (Ottawa: Government of Canada, 2022), 3–5 et seq, https://www.ccg-gcc.gc.ca /publications/mcts-sctm/ramn-arnm/docs/ramn-arnm-2022-eng.pdf.
127   NORDREG (n 63), s 3.

4.1   *Transport Canada*

Established by the *Department of Transport Act*,[128] TC is the national maritime administration of Canada. The concept of national maritime administration entails responsibility for the administration of international maritime conventions adopted by the IMO. As such, TC is the national focal point for shipping in Canada and the organization that represents Canada's international shipping interests in the IMO. In addition to the Minister of Transport's powers under the constitutive act, several statutes expressly allocate powers to TC that are pertinent to Arctic shipping. Although the AWPPA leaves regulatory authority to the Governor in Council and does not expressly mention the Minister of Transport, TC also oversees this statute.

TC has five major administrative regions, and the Prairie and Northern Region includes the Arctic shipping division.[129] Its regulatory functions include interpretation and application of legislation applicable to polar shipping and interfacing with the IMO and the International Association of Classification Societies with respect to polar shipping standards. The division also represents Canada on the Arctic Council's Protection of the Arctic Marine Environment Working Group and co-chairs the Arctic Shipping Best Practices Forum. Further, it provides advice on polar CDME and operational standards in Canadian Arctic waters.[130]

The Minister of Transport has extensive express regulatory and executive authority over most of the CSA 2001 and regulations. The CSA 2001 tasks marine safety inspectors and recognized organizations with inspection functions to ensure compliance with rules and standards. TC administers marine documents, including for Polar Code purposes. Operating within TC, the Marine Technical Review Board considers requests for exemptions from marine documents or alternative requirements for Canadian ships or persons. TC enjoys wide-ranging enforcement powers such as ship inspections, issuing of clearances, investigations, detention, and sale of ships, including foreign ships contravening international rules and standards. The Minister of Transport is also empowered to enforce vessel-source pollution offences and for directing the movements of ships.

The growth of Arctic shipping has led to an increase in stakeholder industry organizations and interested non-governmental environmental and other organizations. Separately, Indigenous organizations represent Indigenous

---

128   RSC 1985, c T-18, s 3.
129   The other regions are Atlantic, Ontario, Quebec and Pacific.
130   Transport Canada, "Arctic Shipping," Government of Canada, last modified 19 August 2010, https://tc.canada.ca/en/marine-transportation/arctic-shipping/arctic-shipping.

peoples as rightsholders in their Arctic homelands. These organizations participate in meetings of Arctic Council working groups discussing shipping, and TC and CCG consultative processes (see chapter by Beveridge in this volume).

For its part, TC convenes the Canadian Marine Advisory Council (CMAC), a structured forum for interested parties to engage, participate and contribute to policy and regulatory initiatives operating at the national and regional levels.[131] CMAC mirrors TC's five regions, and consultations with stakeholders of Arctic shipping occur through the Prairies and Northern Region CMAC. Separately, TC also engages with Indigenous organizations directly as part of the Crown's fiduciary duty to consult on matters affecting Indigenous rights. Together with CCG, such consultations with Indigenous communities include the initiative to designate low-impact shipping corridors (see chapter by Dawson and Song in this volume).

4.2   Department of Fisheries and Oceans

While TC is the national maritime administration, DFO plays multiple roles in maritime governance in accordance with its constitutive instrument and the *Oceans Act*.[132] It operates through seven administrative regions, one of which is dedicated to the Arctic.[133] The DFO and CCG regions within the Arctic include the Yukon North Slope, Northwest Territories, Nunavut, Nunavik, Nunatsiavut, Hudson Bay, and James Bay encompassing the entirety of Inuit Nunangat.[134]

The *Oceans Act* tasks DFO with leadership in developing a national ocean strategy and integrated management plans in collaboration with other ministers, federal boards and agencies, provincial and territorial governments, affected Aboriginal organizations, coastal communities and other persons and bodies, which by implication includes navigation and shipping as an ocean use.[135] The Beaufort Sea Large Ocean Management Area is currently the only

---

131   Canadian Marine Advisory Council, "Terms of Reference," Government of Canada, last modified 14 January 2010, https://tc.canada.ca/en/marine-transportation/marine-safety /terms-reference.

132   *Department of Fisheries and Oceans Act*, RSC 1985, c F-15.

133   The others are Newfoundland and Labrador, Maritimes, Gulf, Quebec, Ontario and Prairie, and Pacific.

134   "Fisheries and Oceans Canada and Canadian Coast Guard Confirm New Regions' Boundaries to Improve Services to the Arctic," Government of Canada, DFO News Release, 5 March 2021, https://www.canada.ca/en/fisheries-oceans/news/2021/03/fisheries-and -oceans-canada-and-canadian-coast-guard-confirm-new-regions-boundaries-to -improve-services-to-the-arctic.html.

135   *Oceans Act* (n 10), ss 29, 31; Fisheries and Oceans Canada, *Canada's Oceans Strategy: Our Oceans, Our Future* (Ottawa: DFO, 2002), https://waves-vagues.dfo-mpo.gc.ca /Library/264678.pdf.

integrated management plan in Arctic waters and the economic and ecosystem goals include shipping.[136] The Act also enables the Governor in Council, on the recommendation of the DFO Minister, to designate marine protected areas (MPAs), three of which are in Arctic waters.[137] Navigation in MPAs is permissible as long as it complies with the AWPPA and CSA 2001 or when authorized.[138]

DFO contributes more directly to governance of shipping through the CCG and CHS. Under the CSA 2001, the DFO Minister is responsible for oil handling facilities and response organizations certified by the CCG and oversees enforcement by pollution prevention officers.[139] The CCG operates under the authority of the *Oceans Act* and CSA 2001 and the Arctic is one of its four operational regions.[140] The CCG is responsible for aids to navigation, waterways management and maintenance of navigable channels, search and rescue, pollution response, ice-breaking and ice management services, marine communications, vessel traffic management, and responding to wrecked, abandoned and hazardous vessels.[141]

In Arctic waters, the CCG plays a critical role in establishing and managing navigation aids, providing icebreaking services, responding to calls for assistance and providing search and rescue. Although there are no vessel traffic services in Arctic waters at this time, there are marine safety advisory procedures in danger areas in the Mackenzie River area in the Western Arctic.[142]

---

136   Beaufort Sea Partnership, *Integrated Ocean Management Plan for the Beaufort Sea: 2009 and Beyond* (Inuvik: Beaufort Sea Planning Office, 2009), 4 and tables 3, 10, 14, http:// www.beaufortseapartnership.ca/wp-content/uploads/2015/04/integrated-ocean -management-plan-for-the-beaufort-sea-2009-and-beyond.pdf.

137   *Oceans Act* (n 10), s 35. Designated Arctic MPAs: Tarium Niryutait (2010), Anguniaqvia Niqiqyuam (2016), and Tuvaijuittuq (2019). See Fisheries and Oceans Canada, "Marine Protected Areas across Canada," Government of Canada, last modified 3 March 2020, https://www.dfo-mpo.gc.ca/oceans/mpa-zpm/index-eng.html.

138   *Anguniaqvia niqiqyuam Marine Protected Areas Regulations*, SOR/2016-280, s 3. In the case of Tarium Niryutait, permissible shipping includes "any movement or other activity of a ship, submarine or aircraft if the movement or other activity is carried out for the purpose of: (i) public safety, law enforcement or national security or for the exercise of Canadian sovereignty and the ship, submarine or aircraft is owned or operated by or on behalf of Her Majesty in right of Canada or by a foreign military force acting in cooperation with, or under the command or control of, the Canadian Forces, or an emergency response under the direction, command or control of the Canadian Coast Guard." *Tarium Niryutait Marine Protected Areas Regulations*, SOR/2010-190, s 7(j).

139   CSA 2001 (n 9), ss 167, 174.

140   The other three operational areas are Central, Atlantic, Central and Western.

141   *Oceans Act* (n 10), s 41; CSA 2001 (n 9), Part 5; *Vessel Traffic Services Zones Regulations*, SOR/89-98, s 2: "marine traffic regulator" is defined as a person designated by the CCG Commissioner under CSA 2001, s 562.18(2).

142   *Radio Aids to Marine Navigations* (n 126), pp. 3–10.

Hence, the CCG will play a crucial role in the management of low-impact shipping corridors. Unsurprisingly, aspects of its mandate (e.g., vessel traffic services) potentially overlap with TC's, in part because until 1995 the CCG was part of TC. A memorandum of agreement between TC and DFO promotes coordination and manages the potential overlap.[143]

Operating under the DFO constitutive statute, the CHS also plays a critical role in maritime safety in Arctic waters by surveying Arctic waters and creating and maintaining navigation charts.[144] The CCG and CHS are essential partners to TC in the development of low-impact shipping corridors in Arctic waters.

4.3   *Other Departments and Agencies*

Other departments contribute to Arctic shipping. For example, Environment and Climate Change Canada issues timely meteorological and ice forecasts through the Meteorological Service of Canada[145] and the Canadian Ice Service within it.[146] Established under the *National Defence Act*,[147] the Department of National Defence provides a supporting role in the governance of shipping, for example, by undertaking maritime and aeronautical search and rescue in coordination with the CCG and providing a platform for Royal Canadian Mounted Police policing action. Global Affairs Canada is responsible for maintaining and advancing Canada's foreign policy and Canadian interests on the legal status of Arctic waters.[148]

5   Discussion

Canada is a major trading nation and aspires for uniformity in maritime law and policy. However, it has vital local interests that should weigh on its domestic and international maritime policies. The policy directions set out in the CTA

---

143   Memorandum of Understanding between: Transport Canada and Fisheries & Oceans Respecting Marine Transportation Safety and Environment Protection (April 1996), https://tc.canada.ca/en/marine-transportation/marine-safety/memorandum-understanding -tc-dfo.

144   *Department of Fisheries and Oceans Act* (n 132), s 4.

145   Environment and Climate Change Canada (ECCC), "Meteorological Service Standards," Government of Canada, last modified 15 November 2021, https://www.canada.ca/en /environment-climate-change/services/meteorological-service-standards.html.

146   ECCC, "Canadian Ice Service," Government of Canada, last modified 11 March 2022, https: //www.canada.ca/en/environment-climate-change/services/ice-forecasts-observations /about-ice-service.html.

147   RSC 1985, c N-5.

148   *Department of Foreign Affairs, Trade and Development Act*, SC 2013, c 33, s 174.

do not necessarily align with the needs of Arctic shipping in all respects. The commercial policy in the Act serves the needs of Canada as a trading nation, but there is little in the Act, except for hortatory references to the environment and sustainability, that speaks to the unique interests of its marine regions, let alone the Arctic. The shipping policy imperatives in the North, while also entailing trade considerations, trigger fundamental coastal State interests, including the protection of the unique environment and homeland of Indigenous peoples. The kinds of shipping issues that arise in the North are not limited to the supplying of Northern communities, but extend also to the protection of their homeland and the economy and culture it nurtures. Shipping is both a major intervention in the region and a platform for economic development that could potentially transform the region.

Hence, the demand for equitable participation in the governance of Arctic shipping is central to marine transportation in the region, but Canada's trade-driven national transportation policy does not address it. Perhaps the reason for this is the underlying rationale for national and international uniformity. Arctic shipping interests are a complex mixture of local, national and global concerns, and local concerns are the principal drivers for Northern communities. Canada's interests in national and global trade tend to overwhelm sub-national regional concerns. There needs to be a balance between global, national and local shipping policy concerns. The recent review of the CTA argued that the measures recommended "will also serve to demonstrate that Canada is exerting control and sovereignty over its waters, consistent with meeting the safety and security challenges in Canada's Arctic" but did not consider Indigenous engagement and participation in decision-making as a means to ensure policy relevance in the region.

The legal framework for shipping in Canada is unwieldy, complex and fragmented. Understanding the regulation of shipping in Arctic waters requires an appreciation of maritime law, as informed by international maritime conventions to which Canada is party or which it embraces without being a party, as well as dedicated polar shipping regulation. Unlike in civil law jurisdictions, Canadian maritime law is not consolidated into a code.

Historically, much of Canada's general maritime regulation first reflected British imperial shipping interests and subsequently Canadian trade interests as supported by the international conventions. Multilateralism and the aspiration of regulatory uniformity underpinned Canadian maritime law. The regulation of Arctic shipping bucked that general trend and between 1970 and 2017 was primarily unilateral. The Polar Code marked a major shift from unilateralism to multilateralism in polar shipping regulation in Canada, resulting in alignment with general maritime law. However, this does not mean that

Canada might not resort to unilateral action if the Polar Code fails to provide sufficient protection of the Arctic marine environment from international shipping. Canada's declaration on acceding to MARPOL, saving clauses in MARPOL and SOLAS and Article 234 of the LOSC, enable Canada also to act unilaterally to protect its Arctic shipping regulation.[149]

The AWPPA stopped short of defining the 'Northwest Passage'. Perhaps definition of the passage was unnecessary at the time of adoption because the Act covered all Canadian Arctic waters. The need for a definition of routes in Canadian Arctic waters might arise in connection with the initiative to designate low-impact shipping corridors. The adoption of routeing measures, such as deep water and coastal routes, traffic separation schemes in straits, and areas to be avoided coinciding with MPAs, will need to occur through regulations. The focus of certain services along the route, such as pilotage, will similarly necessitate legislative support, perhaps even the creation of an Arctic pilotage authority analogous to sister organizations in the other marine regions.

Low-impact shipping corridors provide a unique opportunity for Canada to pursue an integrated approach to policy, regulatory and institutional measures focused to support the corridors. With this in mind, good sense suggests legislative definition of the corridors and establishment of vessel traffic services. The CSA 2001 and regulations provide for the establishment of vessel traffic services zones within Canadian waters or in SSCZs prescribed under the AWPPA.[150] Given that the corridors will include multiple routes, not just Northwest Passage transit routes, a legal definition of the Northwest Passage *per se* might not be necessary. However, legal definition of the various corridors currently under consideration, including transit routes and related vessel traffic regulations, will likely be needed.[151]

The institutional framework for Arctic shipping needs strengthening to reflect the needs of modern governance rather than simply maritime administration, especially in view of impending designation of low-impact shipping

---

149   Canada's accession to MARPOL was "without prejudice to such Canadian laws and regulations as are now or may in the future be established in respect of Arctic waters within or adjacent to Canada." IMO, *Status of IMO Treaties* (7 April 2020), http://www.imo.org/en /About/Conventions/StatusOfConventions/Pages/Default.aspx (accessed 11 June 2020), 131. SOLAS provides that nothing in it "shall prejudice the rights or obligations of States under international law." SOLAS (n 116), chap XIV, reg 2. MARPOL (n 37), Article 16 is similar. LOSC (n 7), Article 234 enables Canada to exercise legislative and enforcement jurisdiction on international shipping in its EEZ in the Arctic.

150   CSA 2001 (n 9), s 136(1); *Vessel Traffic Services Zones Regulations* (n 141). At this time, no areas of Arctic waters are designated as traffic services zones under the regulations.

151   Chénier *et al.* (n 25).

corridors. The national maritime administration model works well for the management of Canada's interface with the IMO and the international maritime conventions, but it falls short when demands for equitable participation are considered. Mere consultation of rightsholders and stakeholders entrenches a hierarchical national maritime administration rather than opening it up to more equitable participation and genuine partnerships. The low-impact shipping corridors in Inuit and other Indigenous homelands are more than mere transportation concerns because they affect a range of economic, environmental, and cultural needs and interests. A more inclusive approach to the governance of Arctic shipping would be an institutional framework similar to the St. Lawrence Seaway. Moreover, it is time for TC to diversify the composition of the national delegation to the IMO, which traditionally included only federal government and industry actors, to reflect other actors, such as Indigenous and non-governmental environmental organizations. While the Inuit Circumpolar Council's recent attainment of consultative status at the IMO is an important development, the Canadian delegation to the IMO could include Indigenous delegates and possibly other representatives to better reflect Canada's interests in navigation and shipping.

6   Conclusion

Perhaps the most pointed characteristics of the governance of Arctic shipping in Canada surveyed in this chapter are the lack of policy coherency, regulatory fragmentation, and insufficient institutional framework. While it is unclear whether the designation of low-impact and serviced shipping corridors is likely to increase navigation and shipping in Arctic waters, it is becoming clear that traditional and centralized maritime administration of shipping will not suffice. Uniformity of rules and standards are important for the facilitation of international maritime trade, but Canada's interests as a coastal State and its responsibilities for this unique region justify higher governance standards than the general norm to ensure efficient and environment protection while also advancing equity. In particular, there will be need to decolonize the system in favour of more in-depth engagement of Indigenous peoples in the governance of shipping in their homelands.

ANNEX 1: Federal legislation applicable to Arctic shipping

Subject matter	Statute	Public	Private
Transportation policy	Canada Marine Act	•	
	Canada Transportation Act	•	
	Oceans Act	•	
Jurisdiction over ships	Federal Courts Act	•	•
	Oceans Act	•	
Maritime safety	Canada Shipping Act, 2001	•	
	Canadian Transportation Accident Investigation and Safety Board Act	•	
	Nuclear Safety and Control Act	•	
	Safe Containers Convention Act	•	
	Transportation of Dangerous Goods Act	•	
Environment protection	Arctic Waters Pollution Prevention Act	•	
	Canada Shipping Act, 2001	•	
	Canada Wildlife Act	•	
	Canadian Environment Protection Act	•	
	Canadian Navigable Waters Act	•	
	Canadian Net-Zero Emissions Accountability Act	•	
	Federal Sustainable Development Act	•	
	Fisheries Act	•	
	Marine Liability Act	•	
	Migratory Birds Convention Act	•	
	National Marine Conservation Areas Act	•	
	Oceans Act	•	
	Species at Risk Act	•	
	Wrecked, Abandoned and Hazardous Vessels Act	•	
Maritime security	Criminal Code	•	
	Marine Transportation Security Act	•	
Necessaries	Federal Courts Act	•	•
	Marine Liability Act	•	•
Carriage of goods and passengers	Bills of Lading Act		•
	Canada Transportation Act	•	
	Coasting Trade Act	•	
	Marine Liability Act	•	•
	Marine Transportation Security Act	•	

Subject matter	Statute	Public	Private
	Safe Containers Convention Act	•	
	Transportation of Dangerous Goods Act	•	
Pilotage, salvage	*Pilotage Act*	•	
	Wrecked, Abandoned and Hazardous Vessels Act	•	•
Recreational boating	*Canada Shipping Act, 2001*	•	
	Marine Liability Act	•	•
	Provincial safe boating legislation	•	
Marine insurance	*Marine Insurance Act*		•
Maritime workers	*Canada Shipping Act, 2001*	•	
	Canada Labour Code	•	
	Merchant Seamen Compensation Act	•	
	Provincial occupational health and safety legislation	•	
Maritime public health	*Canada Shipping Act, 2001*	•	
	Quarantine Act	•	
Ports, harbours, and seaway	*Canada Marine Act*	•	
	Customs Act	•	
	Fishing and Recreations Harbours Act	•	
Liability	*Marine Liability Act*		•
	Provincial worker compensation legislation	•	

ANNEX 2: Regulations under the *Canada Shipping Act,* 2001

Administrative Monetary Penalties and Notices (CSA 2001) Regulations (SOR/2008-97)

Arctic Shipping Safety and Pollution Prevention Regulations (SOR/2017-286)

Ballast Water Regulations (SOR/2021-120)

Board of Steamship Inspection Scale of Fees (CRC c 1405)

Cargo, Fumigation and Tackle Regulations (SOR/2007-128)

Certain Areas Covered with Water Proclaimed Public Harbours (SI/80-8)

Collision Regulations (CRC c 1416)

Competency of Operators of Pleasure Craft Regulations (SOR/99-53)

Crew Accommodation Regulations (CRC c 1418)

Cross-border Movement of Hazardous Waste and Hazardous Recyclable Material Regulations (SOR/2021-25)

Eastern Canada Vessel Traffic Services Zone Regulations (SOR/89-99)

Environmental Response Regulations (SOR/2019-252)

Fire and Boat Drills Regulations (SOR/2010-83)

Fishing Vessel Safety Regulations (CRC c 1486)

Government Ships from the Application of the Canada Shipping Act, Regulations Excluding Certain (SOR/2000-71)

Home-Trade, Inland and Minor Waters Voyages Regulations (CRC c 1430)

Hull Construction Regulations (CRC c 1431)

Large Fishing Vessel Inspection Regulations (CRC c 1435)

Life Saving Equipment Regulations (CRC c 1436)

Load Line Regulations (SOR/2007-99)

Long-Range Identification and Tracking of Vessels Regulations (SOR/2010-227)

Marine Machinery Regulations (SOR/90-264)

Marine Personnel Regulations (SOR/2007-115)

Marine Safety Fees Regulations (SOR/2021-59)

Minor Waters Order (CRC c 1448)

Navigation Safety Regulations, 2020 (SOR/2020-216)

Northern Canada Vessel Traffic Services Zone Regulations (SOR/2010-127)

Private Buoy Regulations (SOR/99-335)

Response Organizations Regulations (SOR/95-405)

Sable Island Regulations (CRC c 1465)

Safe Working Practices Regulations (CRC c 1467)

Safety Management Regulations (SOR/98-348)

Ship Radio Inspection Fees Regulations (CRC c 1472)

Shipping Casualties Reporting Regulations (SOR/85-514)

Ships' Elevator Regulations (CRC c 1482)

Small Vessel Regulations (SOR/2010-91)

Special-purpose Vessels Regulations (SOR/2008-121)
Steering Appliances and Equipment Regulations (SOR/83-810)
Tackle Regulations (CRC c 1494)
Towboat Crew Accommodation Regulations (CRC c 1498)
Vessel Clearance Regulations (SOR/2007-125)
Vessel Detention Orders Review Regulations (SOR/2007-127)
Vessel Fire Safety Regulations (SOR/2017-14)
Vessel Operation Restriction Regulations (SOR/2008-120)
Vessel Pollution and Dangerous Chemicals Regulations (SOR/2012-69)
Vessel Registration and Tonnage Regulations (SOR/2007-126)
Vessel Safety Certificates Regulations (SOR/2021-135)
Vessel Traffic Services Zones Regulations (SOR/89-98)
Vessels Registry Fees Tariff (SOR/2002-172)

CHAPTER 13

Goal-Based Standards, Meta-regulation and Tripartism in Arctic Shipping: What Prospects in Canadian Waters?

Phillip A. Buhler

Abstract

This chapter looks at alternative forms of regulation of Arctic shipping. Traditional prescriptive regulatory concepts have many problems. These include, *inter alia*, a lack of flexibility in a technologically vibrant environment, a rigid and minimalist response by regulatees and a reactive approach by regulators, economic inefficiency, imbalanced expertise, barriers to open markets, problems with transparency and accountability, and regulator capture. An alternative approach would be meta-regulation, which is essentially modified self-regulation monitored by regulators. Another concept, utilized by the International Maritime Organization (IMO), is goal-based standards, wherein regulators set basic end-goals and allow regulatees to develop rules that are designed to reach those goals. While most Canadian rules governing Arctic shipping are still prescriptive in nature, the adoption of numerous IMO conventions gives some prospect for the development of a more goal-based or flexible regulatory system. Input and consideration of the interests of impacted Indigenous communities is another key concern. The concept of tripartism, in which "third party" interests are included in the regulatory development process, has the advantage of adding a further knowledge base and of making the interests of impacted communities part of a more flexible and inclusive regulatory system.

Keywords

prescriptive regulation – polar – Inuit – marine – deregulation – Arctic shipping

1   Introduction and Overview

The polar waters of the Arctic region have witnessed an unprecedented growth
in commercial shipping over the last several decades.[1] The steady decline in
the extent of multiyear sea ice has culminated in virtually ice-free passage
through the Northern Sea Route (over Siberia) and parts of the Northwest
Passage in the Canadian Archipelago for short periods in the late summer
navigation season in recent years. As a result, the volume of traffic in terms
of the number of distinct vessels transiting Arctic waters, as well as the number of transits made by single vessels, has multiplied substantially since 2010.[2]
Regulation of this traffic in the territorial waters, contiguous zone and exclusive economic zone (EEZ) of individual States and the high seas is governed
by national laws and aspects of certain international conventions otherwise
applicable to worldwide commercial vessel traffic generally. However, the
unique geographic, oceanographic and climatological conditions encountered
in the polar region beg for unique regulatory schemes tailored for this environment. Further, many Arctic hazards are little known or understood except
by a handful of regional operators and more than 90 percent of the Arctic

---

1   The terms 'polar' and 'Arctic' are used throughout this and other chapters of this work. They
     can be but are not necessarily referencing the same area or waters, depending upon the con-
     text and the document referenced. A primary distinction of course is that 'polar' can refer to
     waters in both the Arctic and Antarctic regions, as the Polar Code itself is to apply in both,
     whereas 'Arctic' is limited to lands and waters above the Arctic Circle at roughly 66 degrees,
     30 minutes north latitude, often generally termed the area around the North Pole. Even the
     definition of the northern Polar region in the Polar Code includes a map which for purposes
     of application of the Code provisions dips into waters south of the Arctic Circle in some
     locales, where 'polar' climate conditions exist. Statutes and conventions often contain a defi-
     nition where needed. This chapter addresses solely the Canadian Arctic and where specific
     legislation or international convention does not define terms, the term 'Arctic' will be used as
     it is applied in specific laws and to Canadian waters above the Arctic Circle plus other waters
     included in the Polar Code definition, while 'polar,' where not a term of art in specific laws,
     will be used for waters where polar climatological conditions exist. In addressing general
     conditions in these waters the two terms are used interchangeably.
2   The number of vessels increased by 25 percent between 2013 and 2019, and fuel consump-
     tion (and commensurate environmental impact) increased 82 percent between 2016 and
     2019. Frederic Lasserre, *Canadian Arctic Marine Transportation Issues, Opportunities and
     Challenges*, School of Public Policy Publications SPP Research Paper 15:6 (Calgary: University
     of Calgary, February 2022), 3; Protection of the Arctic Marine Environment Working Group
     (PAME), *Summary Report, 4th Meeting of the Arctic Shipping Best Practice Information Forum,
     24–25 November 2020* (Arctic Council, 2021), 4. See also the chapter by Frederic Lasserre in
     this work, *supra,* and that by Jackie Dawson and Gloria Song, *infra.*

region remains uncharted.[3] Commercial navigation in this new environment thus presents unique regulatory problems.

Given the unique issues faced by vessels and their crews operating in the polar environment, it is clear that at least some aspects of the regulations must be developed beyond the regulatory regimes in place for vessels operating in the rest of the world. The three principal subjects for such vessel regulation are safety for crew and passengers, protection of the marine environment, and governance of qualifications and standards for personnel operating commercial vessels.[4]

In the territorial sea and EEZ of Canada, as in most developed maritime nations, regulation of commercial traffic is governed by both national laws (and in some cases supplemented by state or provincial laws) as well as international conventions. The latter are often referentially incorporated into national law, added as annexes or through enactment, in whole or part. Such is the case in Canada.[5] This chapter includes a very brief review of current applicable international conventions and regulations as well as Canadian federal statutory and regulatory law governing commercial shipping in its Arctic waters and all waters subject to Canadian jurisdiction.

The nature of regulation is at the core of this chapter. As modern States began to develop regulations governing a myriad of subjects, the general approach was prescriptive in nature. That means that domestic legislation and most aspects of international conventions set forth detailed affirmative requirements for regulatees to follow. This approach has been termed 'classical prescriptive' or 'command and control regulation.'[6]

Commencing in the late 1970s political leaders, jurists, legal theoreticians and economists, among others, began to promote a movement to deregulation. The concept of 'deregulation' is not a particular method of regulation or

---

3 Melody Schreiber, "How Ordinary Ship Traffic Could Help Map the Uncharted Arctic Ocean Seafloor," *ArcticToday*, 16 October 2018, https://www.arctictoday.com/ordinary-shipping -help-map-uncharted-arctic-ocean-seafloor.

4 Governed primarily by the International Convention for the Safety of Life at Sea, 1 November 1974 (in force 25 May 1980), 1184 *UNTS* 2 [SOLAS]; International Convention for the Prevention of Pollution from Ships, 2 November 1973, 1340 *UNTS* 184 as amended by Protocol of 1978 Relating to the International Convention for the Prevention of Pollution from Ships of 1973, 17 February 1978 (both in force 2 October 1983), 1340 *UNTS* 61 [MARPOL]; International Convention on Standards of training, Certification and Watchkeeping for Seafarers, 7 July 1978 (in force 28 April 1984), 1361 *UNTS* 2 [STCW].

5 See in particular the numerous international maritime conventions incorporated into Canadian law in the *Marine Liability Act*, SC 2001, c 6.

6 There are several works discussing this concept, see particularly, Malcolm K. Sparrow, *The Regulatory Craft* (Washington: Brookings Institution Press, 2000); Robert Baldwin, Martin Cave and Martin Lodge, *Understanding Regulation* (Oxford: Oxford University Press, 2012).

theory. As used here and in the literature cited, it is simply describing the general movement away from highly prescriptive, command and control forms of regulation to something allowing more flexibility and autonomy, that is, pure self-regulation, meta-regulation or something else, as will be discussed in more detail below. Many problems were identified with traditional prescriptive regulation, and the reaction was generally towards an effort to reduce or even eliminate what were seen to be overly burdensome regulations on many industries. Among political leaders, those most often associated with the push for deregulation in the English-speaking world were President Ronald Reagan and Prime Minister Margaret Thatcher. Such political leaders and many jurists and academics were looking for alternatives to the prescriptive regulatory State/method, either from a firm belief in the most flexible alternatives, or to head off what they worried would be too extreme a move away from prescriptive regulation towards complete self-regulation.[7] Since the financial crisis of 2008, and perhaps reinforced by more recent events related to the COVID-19 pandemic, there has been a reversal by many governments of the move to deregulation back towards more strict regulation, or perhaps better said, an expansion of prescriptive regulations and heavier State involvement in many industries. *The Economist* recently labelled this "the new interventionism."[8]

For regulation of commercial vessels, especially in the unique polar conditions, a return to strict prescriptive concepts for many subjects is likely unsatisfactory. Much more flexibility in regulation is probably necessary, especially allowing reliance upon the greater knowledge and experience of the companies and individuals working in the Arctic and subject to such regulation. Participation in the development of regulations should include not only vessel owners and operators, and the industries relying upon their services, but also inhabitants of the Arctic region who are increasingly reliant upon commercial vessels for their supply and services, stand to benefit from the growth of resource development, and are impacted by the increased vessel traffic. Many of these local inhabitants are Indigenous peoples with a long history of living and working in the Arctic environment, and thus offer a potential wealth of knowledge and experience to contribute to development of regulations. The search for alternatives to strict command and control regulation should apply well beyond the Arctic region to vessel operations worldwide, and the use of these concepts in the new polar environment may serve as a model for future vessel regulation elsewhere.

---

7   See, e.g., Ian Ayres and John Braithwaite, *Responsive Regulation: Transcending the Deregulation Debate* (Oxford: Oxford University Press, 1992).

8   Jan Piotrowski, "Special Report: The New Interventionism," *The Economist*, 15 January 2022. See also editorial in the same issue: "Beware the Bossy State", at 9.

This chapter will summarize the principal problems identified with prescriptive or command and control regulation. Not all of those who see problems with prescriptive regulation, however, are in favour of complete deregulation (or self-regulation). A number of alternatives somewhere between strict command and control regulation and complete deregulation ('no rules') have been developed in the last decades. One concept that may find application in the maritime environment, particularly for Arctic shipping, is that of 'meta-regulation,' which this chapter will focus on in more detail.

A concept that could be a part of meta-regulation, tripartism, is considered, as it has to date not appeared in the context of maritime regulation internationally, much less in Canada. Tripartism may have a particularly important application for regulation of Canadian Arctic shipping because it takes into account the interests of communities most impacted by shipping, namely, the Indigenous communities that make up more than half of the total population living in the Canadian Arctic.[9] Only by involving those Indigenous communities can regulators and the regulated industries develop a proper balance of interests benefiting all concerned. Commercial shipping would obtain the input of experience and knowledge of local inhabitants (Indigenous and otherwise) with lifelong experience in the Arctic environment, and communities both dependent upon Arctic shipping economically and impacted by the positive aspects of increased transport and communication and the negative environmental effects would have a voice in the development of regulations.

2   Problems with Traditional Prescriptive Regulation[10]

To understand the importance of exploring an alternative mode of regulation to that which has been applied almost uniformly over the last century, one must identify the most salient problems stemming from classical prescriptive or command and control regulation (CPR). The problems identified are particularly relevant when discussing the unique circumstances of Arctic shipping.

A lack of flexibility in a technologically vibrant environment has been highlighted as one of the principal concerns with CPR.[11] This prompts Sparrow to

---

9   See "Canada," Arctic Council, https://arctic-council.org/about/states/canada.

10   Most of the research and sources for this section were assembled and are part of an unpublished paper written by this author in partial fulfillment of the requirements for a PhD. Phillip A. Buhler, *A Spectral Change in Theory Between Prescriptive and Self-Regulation: A Literature Review Focused on Non-Prescriptive Concepts* (submitted to the Schulich School of Law, Dalhousie University, Canada, 2019), 3–15.

11   Sparrow (n 6), pp. 22–23.

call for "regulatory versatility."[12] Sparrow believes that the promotion of dynamic mechanisms to enhance regulatory craftsmanship and innovation are a vital necessity.[13] Particularly noteworthy in industries that are rapidly moving forward with technology is the fact, as critics note, that CPR can prevent experimentation and reduce the ability of a business to keep up with the pace of new technology.[14] Heavily prescriptive regulations produce unnecessarily complex and inflexible rules that prevent the regulatees from taking flexible approaches to quickly respond to ever changing environments.[15] Critics argue that the CPR approach has evolved to such an extent that it produces "a counterproductive regulatory overload" and even prevents potential new entrants into a field because they cannot break through this regulatory barrier.[16] In the unique environment of Arctic shipping, vessel operators need to have the flexibility to develop new design and construction technologies and operating criteria in response to new geophysical and environmental conditions that they discover as their vessels move deeper into uncharted waters.

Another problem with CPR has been termed the "check the box" response of regulatees.[17] The burden of rules has created what some term "rule following automatons,"[18] with regulatees adopting "checklist style approaches to compliance," which reduces further incentives for innovative behaviour in favour of a behaviour protecting the regulatee from myriad violations by only strictly complying with the regulatory environment.[19] In other words, regulatees are discouraged from going "beyond minimum standards."[20] For a maritime industry that should have every encouragement to pursue innovative strategies to address the unique environment it will be facing, this result is disturbing.

Another problem with CPR is the economic inefficiency of strict rules, strongly encouraging a cost-benefit analysis for both regulatees and regulators, particularly where the latter lack the resources to pursue and enforce extensive

12   Id., 27.
13   Id., 89.
14   Christopher Decker, *Goals-Based and Rules-Based Approaches to Regulation*, BEIS Research Paper No. 8 (London: Department for Business, Energy and Industrial Strategy, 2018), 21.
15   Baldwin, Cave and Lodge (n 6), p. 108; Cass R. Sunstein, "Problems with Rules," *California Law Review* 83:4 (1995): 953, at 955.
16   Neil Gunningham and Darren Sinclair, "Instruments for Environmental Protection," in *Smart Regulation: Designing Environmental Policy*, eds., Neil Gunningham and Peter Grabosky (Oxford: Clarendon Press, 1998), 46.
17   Decker (n 14), p. 10.
18   Id., 11.
19   Id., 21.
20   Gunningham and Sinclair (n 16), p. 45.

strict regulations.[21] This lack of resources can even cause regulators to take an unreasonably strict legalistic approach to enforcement and produce unnecessarily complex and inflexible rules that are overbroad and strangle enterprise and competition.[22] The cost-benefit analysis of burdensome regulations has been a center point of many studies.[23] The financial burden on both regulators and regulatees is widely acknowledged. This writer in his years representing shipowners and operators with regulatory problems has often heard from both industry and regulators that they do not have the resources to respond adequately to some regulatory demands or to enforce many of the regulations under their writ. In the Arctic, where the expertise of regulators can be particularly limited, the cost of developing and enforcing detailed regulations on every possible issue of concern could be prohibitive.

Another key problem is the imbalance of expertise between regulators and regulatees. In Canada as elsewhere, some regulators would readily admit that they have little to no knowledge of vessel operating conditions in Arctic waters, and only vessel operators with long experience in polar waters would know how to respond to many issues. This 'knowledge gap' can exist even for regulators (and operators) with extensive experience with vessels in non-polar waters, since extreme temperatures, sea ice conditions, long periods of darkness and vast areas of uncharted waters are just some of the issues not normally encountered in many other areas of navigable waters. Many regulators even lack the expertise to know what to ask in order to develop regulations.[24] Command and control regulation "requires regulators to have comprehensive and accurate knowledge of the workings and capacity of industry."[25] In the unique Arctic environment, it is difficult for national government regulators to have acquired comprehensive knowledge in all areas of concern.[26] Because of this, "regulators are likely to find themselves at a significant information disadvantage compared to the industries that they oversee."[27] With this problem,

---

21   Sparrow (n 6), p. 12.
22   Baldwin, Cove and Lodge (n 6), p. 108; Gunningham and Sinclair (n 16), p. 45.
23   Anthony Ogus, *Regulation: Legal Forum and Economic Theory* (Oxford: Clarendon Press, 1994).
24   Baldwin, Cove and Lodge (n 6), pp. 29–30, 39.
25   Gunningham and Sinclair (n 16), p. 44.
26   Perhaps only those who have either worked in private industry or served in specialized government agencies such as the Canadian Coast Guard would be able to glean the knowledge necessary for this environment.
27   Cary Coglianese and Evan Mendelson, "Meta-Regulation and Self-Regulation," in *The Oxford Handbook of Regulation*, eds., Robert Baldwin, Martin Cave and Martin Lodge (Oxford: Oxford University Press, 2010), 153.

the idea of bringing in the special knowledge of Indigenous persons and other Arctic residents who have lived and worked in the environment suggests a way to fill the knowledge gap.

Highly prescriptive regulation can also be a barrier to open markets and interoperability. As various international agreements in recent years have sought to promote open markets and interoperability between nations and their economies, an effort must be made to avoid disruption.[28] The importance of encouraging foreign shipping to call at Canadian ports, and in future facilitating international commerce transiting the Arctic regions, makes this issue as important as any for seeking an alternative to heavily prescriptive regulation.

Transparency and accountability are other problems identified with traditional prescriptive regulation. With every prescriptive regulation, questions have been raised about both the accountability of the regulators and their transparency, particularly in an international setting.[29] This issue is likely to come to the fore due to the emotionally and politically charged nature of the developing Arctic, particularly environmental impacts and the interests of Indigenous peoples. Many global interest groups, and the public at large, already have a stake in how the polar regions will be governed in the coming decades.[30]

Closely related to the problem of transparency and accountability is the concern for capture and corruption. Regulator 'capture' can occur when the relationship between a regulator and regulatee becomes so close that it results in the pursuit of the regulated enterprise's own interest rather than that of the public.[31] Command and control regulation can be subject to political manipulation and capture by interest groups with great power and influence, which can be detrimental to the policies themselves and those who the policies are designed to protect.[32] In fact, "regulators themselves may succumb to self-interested behaviour, variously being captured by the very industries

28   J. Penny, A. Eaton, P.G. Bishop and P.G. Bloomfield, "The Practicalities of Goal-Based Safety Regulation," in *Aspects of Safety Management*, eds., Felix Redmill and Tom Anderson (London: Springer, 2001), 35–48, at 38.
29   Baldwin, Cove and Lodge (n 6), pp. 338–340.
30   See in particular the participation at the International Maritime Organization (IMO) of environmental groups as observers, and their submissions relative to various environmental conventions. The participation of both environmental and Indigenous advocacy groups in the development of Canadian domestic legislation is commonly reported.
31   Baldwin, Cove and Lodge (n 6), p. 107; Ayres and Braithwaite (n 7), pp. 71–73.
32   Gunningham and Sinclair (n 16), p. 46.

they purport to regulate or engaging in rent seeking, whereby the regulatory bureaucracy seeks to extend its own interests at the expense of the public."[33]

Prescriptive regulation can also become 'reactive regulation.' Arguably a variation on the check the box regulatory approach, reactive regulation means that the process of development becomes so regimented that it has no flexibility to seek avoidance of a problem, but rather will cause the creation of regulations only after a problem occurs, rather than encouraging pre-emptive or anticipatory rules. Regulators may merely respond to events as they occur,[34] as is in the case of some major International Maritime Organization (IMO) conventions, which were drafted and accepted only in response to major maritime catastrophes. The most well-known examples include the International Convention for Safety of Life at Sea (SOLAS), in response to the sinking of RMS *Titanic*, subsequently amended and supplemented in response to later vessel losses, and the International Convention for the Prevention of Pollution from Ships, drafted in response to the *Torrey Canyon* oil spill in the English Channel in 1968, amended in part after the *Amoco Cadiz* oil spill in 1978.

These enumerated problems make it clear that in a dynamic and still not fully understood environment like the Arctic, an alternative to traditional strict prescriptive or command and control regulation must be found. That alternative may likely be in the approach of meta-regulation.

3   Defining Meta-regulation[35]

To understand meta-regulation, one has to begin near the self-regulation end of a spectrum of regulatory concepts that runs from, at one end, classical prescriptive regulation or CPR all the way to the concept of self-regulation. Non-regulation is a step beyond this spectrum, the complete lack of any regulation, which is essentially theoretical, except perhaps to some who promote 'deregulation.' The rather simple idea of self-regulation, wherein regulatee industries take over their own governance, is still a rare concept in practice, if not in theory. Pure self-regulation has been addressed by, among others, John Braithwaite and Ian Ayers in their seminal work *Responsive Regulation*[36] and

---

33   Id.
34   Sparrow (n 6), pp. 181–184.
35   Part of the research and formulation of this section was developed by this author for his unpublished paper (n 10).
36   Ayres and Braithwaite (n 7).

Neil Gunningham, and Cary Coglianese and Evan Mendelson in their essays in
Baldwin's *Oxford Handbook of Regulation*.[37]

In fact, one of the best approaches to understanding meta-regulation is to
understand the distinction between meta and self-regulation as set forth by
Gunningham, and Coglianese and Mendelson. Gunningham describes meta-
regulation as an "enforcement model which, like smart regulation, also seeks to
identify a 'surrogate regulator' and to minimize the hands-on enforcement role
of the state," which is "far more than passive compliance monitoring – actively
challenging the enterprise to demonstrate that its systems work in practice."[38]
Coglianese and Mendelson, in a separate essay, view self-regulation as "unconstrained freedom," the opposite of conventional prescriptive regulation in the
regulatory pyramid they developed.[39] Meta-regulation, by contrast, includes
"the state's oversight of self-regulatory arrangements," and also includes the
concept of "regulating the regulators" and, more broadly, any kind of regulatory monitoring by entities other than the regulatees themselves.[40] In the maritime realm, this would include non-governmental regulator surrogates such
as classification societies (addressed *infra*).

Coglianese and Mendelson illustrate their distinction by creating a
"regulatory pyramid", with four levels of regulatory discretion. "Unconstrained
freedom" (no regulation) is the widest, on the bottom, then rising in order
self-regulation, meta-regulation and "conventional regulation" on the narrow
top.[41] This pyramid gives far more emphasis to what should be considered just
one end of a long spectrum, as there are a host of regulatory variants apart
from CPR that leave more control with regulators and less autonomy with
regulatees. For instance, goal-based standards (discussed *infra*) leave the establishment of goals or guidelines with the regulator, thus do not go quite as far
as pure self-regulation, and other concepts such as standards-based or princi-
ples-based regulation again leave the establishment of some requirements and
parameters with regulators.[42] Clearly, meta-regulation is the last stop before
pure self-regulation.

At its core, meta-regulation sets guidance for regulatees which otherwise
are encouraged to govern themselves. In old English law, the term 'meta' was

---

37 Neil Gunningham, "Enforcement and Compliance Strategies," in Baldwin *et al.* (eds.,)
    (n 27); Coglianese and Mendelson (n 27).
38 Gunningham (n 37), p. 135.
39 Coglianese and Mendelson (n 27), p. 152.
40 Id., 147–148.
41 Id., 152.
42 Sunstein (n 15), pp. 964–965.

used to denote landmarks or boundary lines,[43] providing a logical moderate interpretation of meta-regulation as a form of boundary or guidance to a self-governing regulatee. Some legal authorities argue that meta-regulation is something less than what has been termed outcome-based regulation or performance standards, distinguishing this from regulatory commands firmly setting out a means or ends.[44] As Coglianese and Mendelson summarize, "meta-regulation focuses very much on outside regulators but also incorporates the insight from self-regulation that targets themselves can be sources of their own constraint."[45] They go on to explain that "meta-regulation seeks to address some of the drawbacks of a purely self-regulatory approach ... self-regulation almost always stems from meta-regulation in a very broad sense."[46]

Ayers and Braithwaite use the term "enforced self-regulation," defined as a method whereby regulatees write the rules which are then ratified by the public and can be publicly enforced (see the discussion of the concept of tripartism *infra*).[47] They view meta-regulation as "private rules publicly enforced" or "enforced self-regulation," which is different from the concept of "co-regulation."[48] They consider the advantages of meta-regulation as follows: (1) rules are tailored to match the company; (2) rules can be adjusted more quickly to changing business environments; (3) the flexibility of meta-regulation fosters regulatory innovation; (4) rules can be made by the company with more knowledge and its resources are more comprehensive; (5) companies are more committed to rules they write themselves, and cannot turn over the responsibility to governments; (6) the concept reduces the volume of rules required, with only one, company drafted rulebook; (7) the business bears the cost of enforcing its own regulations; (8) the regulatee can catch more offenders with internal expert audits; (9) offenders are disciplined in a larger proportion of cases; (10) it is easier for prosecutors to get convictions; and (11) meta-regulation follows the compliance path of least corporate resistance since the corporation made the rules.[49]

Other authors seem to view the application of meta-regulation as a concept following on a natural development among regulatees, which for a host of self-beneficial reasons are seeking ways to better govern themselves. Julia Black posits that

---

43   Henry Campbell Black, *Black's Law Dictionary* (5th Ed., West Publishing Co., 1979), "Meta".
44   Coglianese and Mendelson (n 27), p. 150.
45   Id.
46   Id., 161.
47   Ayres and Braithwaite (n 7), p. 6.
48   Id., 101.
49   Id., 110–115.

governments do not ... have a monopoly on regulation and that regulation is occurring within and between other social actors, for example large organizations, collective associations, technical committees, professions, etc., all without the government's involvement or indeed formal approval: there is "regulation in many rooms."[50]

Writing in 2001, Black recognizes that third parties have been playing a role in regulation and notes that "the regulation of self-regulation is the new challenge" in the era of "post-regulatory regulation of self-regulation."[51] Black's concept is simply that regulation should not be "state-centered," and since governments often have insufficient knowledge and "inappropriate and unsophisticated" methods to approach regulation, it is necessary for the businesses to be as self-regulatory as possible.[52] Black focuses on the "asymmetry (of knowledge) between regulator and regulated," since governments cannot know as much about a business as the business itself, and "no single actor has all the knowledge required to solve complex, diverse, and dynamic problems, and no single actor has the overview necessary to employ all the instruments needed to make regulation effective."[53] These observations and one potential solution will be addressed below under the discussion on tripartism.

The proponents of meta-regulation or controlled self-regulation address most of the problems identified by those who initially sought alternatives to strict prescriptive regulation in the era of deregulation. One other important concept for meta-regulation as it can be applied in the maritime world, and to Arctic shipping in particular, is addressed by Cristie Ford who places emphasis on the need for 'learning' and regulatory learning resources in meta-regulation.[54] Ford considers that meta-regulation, as a version of process-oriented regulation, "inhabits an even more indeterminate space" than other forms of "enforced self-regulation."[55] Therefore, in her view meta-regulation

> focuses on learning, rather than knowing. That is, it focuses on determining whether the systems and controls being used are designed to both

50   Julia Black, "Decentering Regulation: Understanding the Role of Regulation and Self-Regulation in a Post-Regulatory World," *Current Legal Problems* 54 (2001): 103.

51   Id., 104–105.

52   Id., 106.

53   Id., 107.

54   Cristie Ford, "Macro and Micro Level Effects on Responsive Financial Regulation," *University of British Columbia Law Review* 44 (2011): 589–626.

55   Id., 590, 592.

generate and respond to ongoing learning, thereby improving outcomes as measured by reference to a high-level set of principles.[56]

Sharon Gilad believes that meta-regulation "directly confronts what the regulator does not know and tries to build learning systems to work with it."[57] Ford, Braithwaite[58] and others put emphasis on "embedding learning paradigms and building systematic learning processes into regulatory architecture."[59] Ford and Affolder posit that "meta-regulation and new governance envision learning both at the regulator level, and at the regulatee level, and an energetic feedback loop between them."[60] In developing regulations for Arctic shipping, the importance of learning, sharing and cooperation in the development of regulations is paramount, considering the many environmental and technological unknowns.

It must also be noted that in the wake of the financial crisis of 2008 and the ensuing severe introspection concerning the application of meta-regulation in the financial industry, not all criticism of regulation has focused upon the shortcomings of regulators. Some authorities, while acknowledging the strengths inherent in meta-regulation, have also identified the "incompetence or ineptitude of the regulated firms" and note the shortcomings that have only been exacerbated by the "regulatory inertia of regulators," holding that even meta-regulation "can lead to regulatory capture."[61] This has been noted as an issue with classification societies, which can become beholden to the vessel owners they purport to monitor and regulate, or to 'flag of convenience' States, which themselves can be lax with enforcement of major maritime conventions such as SOLAS in order to attract vessel owner registrants.[62] This problem of

---

56   Id., 592; referring also to Sharon Gilad, "It Runs in the Family: Meta-Regulation and Its Siblings," *Regulation and Governance* 4 (2010): 485, at 486.

57   Gilad (n 56), p. 486; Ford (n 54), p. 592.

58   Ford refers to Braithwaite's more recent writings than those otherwise cited in this chapter.

59   Cristie Ford and Natasha Affolder, "Preface: Responsive Regulation in Context, Circa 2011," *University of British Columbia Law Review* 44 (2011): 463, at 466. This is the introductory essay to a volume devoted to responsive regulation.

60   Id., 466.

61   Folarin Akinbami, "Is Meta-Regulation All It's Cracked Up to Be? The Case of UK Financial Regulation," *Journal of Banking Regulation* 14 (2013): 16, at 20.

62   See Hristos Karahalios, *The Management of Maritime Regulations* (London: Routledge Taylor & Francis Group, 2015), 22; Craig H. Allen, "Revisiting the Thames Formula: The Evolving Role of the International Maritime Organization and Its Member States in Implementing the 1982 Law of the Sea Convention" (2009) 10 *San Diego Law Journal* 10 (2009): 265, at 322. See also the chapter by Bankes in this volume.

flag State control (or lax control) and reliance upon third party 'surrogates,' in turn stems from the fact that the IMO "has no enforcement powers and does not directly monitor the performance of its member states."[63] This spotlights a distinction between regulation under the auspices of the IMO and that of national governments. This problem also dovetails into the discussion above about learning and shared learning processes between regulators and regulatees in order to address the limitations of knowledge in the polar regions. Another critic in the post-financial crisis era, taking a cynical view of efforts at deregulation, from an openly anti-capitalist approach, has argued that "meta-regulatory structures are as much about regulating regulation as they are about regulating non-regulation – that is, defining areas where regulation is permissible or, to use familiar language, efficient, as well as areas where it is not."[64]

The concept of meta-regulation does not mean the same thing to all people, nor are the benefits, or detriments, to the concept agreed upon by all authorities. At most, meta-regulation, as it is generally understood across industries, means some variable of encouraging regulatees to both make the rules for themselves and self-enforce, while preserving a given amount of oversight by government regulators and, increasingly, with oversight or at least input by impacted third parties.

4   The Current Nature of Maritime Regulation in Canadian Arctic Waters

The regulation of commercial vessel traffic in Canadian waters, including the Arctic, involves national legislation[65] and regulations promulgated pursuant to national law and international law and conventions. Canada's legal regime for the Arctic is noteworthy in the global arena for being one of the most comprehensive and also one of the earliest to adopt regulation specifically to Arctic waters. It is therefore not surprising that much of the current Canadian Arctic regulatory regime is prescriptive in nature, perhaps in part because its foundations were developed prior to the trend towards deregulatory or self-regulatory concepts. This raises concern about how feasible it would be

---

63   Karahalios (n 62), p. 19.

64   Mohsen al Attar, "Reframing the 'Universality' of International Law in a Globalizing World," *McGill Law Journal* 59:1 (2013): 95, at 106.

65   Some Canadian legislation addresses maritime traffic in all waters and all vessels under Canadian jurisdiction, some is directed exclusively to the Arctic.

to shift the regime towards alternatives such as meta-regulation. A brief over-view of some aspects of regulation in the Arctic follows; consult chapters by Bartenstein and Chircop for a complete review of Canadian legislation and regulation.

The most comprehensive statute governing shipping in Canada is the *Canada Shipping Act, 2001* (CSA 2001).[66] The CSA 2001 is one of the bases for regulations promulgated concerning construction, design, equipment and operations of vessels in Canadian waters, and/or governing vessels registered in Canada. However, the Act contains no specific provisions governing Arctic waters. Provisions address, *inter alia*, maritime personnel (Part III), vessel safety (Part IV), including aspects of construction of vessels, vessel traffic services or zones (Part V), response to incidents, accidents and casualties (Part VI), and pollution prevention and response under the Department of Transport and the Department of Fisheries and Oceans (Parts VIII and IX). These sections of the CSA 2001 mandate specific actions to be followed by parties governed under the statute and are of a traditional prescriptive nature.

Canada became the first Arctic nation to adopt comprehensive domestic legislation, before any international conventions addressed the Arctic, directed exclusively to pollution prevention in Arctic waters.[67] The *Arctic Waters Pollution Prevention Act* (AWPPA)[68] was enacted in its original form in 1970.[69] The current version of the AWPPA contains provisions governing waste disposal in Arctic waters, recovery of costs and penalties, control over construction of industrial works in Arctic waters, detailed regulation of Shipping Safety Control Zones and regulation of vessel traffic in Arctic waters, with both civil and criminal penalties available. The language of the AWPPA, again, is prescriptive.

Based upon the AWPPA and the CSA 2001, several comprehensive regulations directed exclusively to Arctic waters have been promulgated and are the most comprehensive and innovative of any regulatory regime created by any Arctic nation to govern shipping prior to the International Code for Ships Operating in Polar Waters (the Polar Code).[70] The *Arctic Shipping Safety and Pollution*

---

66 SC 2001, c 26 [CSA 2001].

67 See the chapter by Bartenstein in this volume.

68 RSC 1985, c A-12 [AWPPA].

69 RSC 1970, c 2. This legislation has been amended consistently, notably in 1985, 1992, 2002, 2009, 2014 and 2019.

70 International Code for Ships Operating in Polar Waters (Polar Code), IMO Resolution MSC.385(94) (21 November 2014, effective 1 January 2017); Amendments to the International Convention for the Safety of Life at Sea 1974, IMO Resolution MSC.386(94) (21 November 2014, effective 1 January 2017); Amendments to MARPOL Annexes I, II, IV and V, IMO Resolution MEPC.265(68) (15 May 2015, effective 1 January 2017); Amendments

Prevention Regulations (ASSPPR)[71] contain a comprehensive system governing most aspects of vessel operations in the Arctic. First and foremost, the ASSPPR incorporate by reference the requirements of the new SOLAS Chapter XIV. The ASSPPR contains provisions mandating the terms and conditions for the use of an ice navigator, vessels operating in low air temperatures and a separate Part II governing pollution prevention measures, which adopt the Polar Code changes to MARPOL and detailed prescriptive regulations for waste disposal, prevention of oil pollution, control of pollution by noxious liquid substances in bulk, and vessel sewage and garbage disposal.

The control of vessel traffic in Arctic waters is also the subject of further regulations promulgated under the AWPPA.[72] Even prior to the Polar Code additions to SOLAS and MARPOL, Canada had already established the NORDREG system through the *Northern Canada Vessel Traffic Services Zone Regulations*.[73]

Interestingly, there is one piece of maritime legislation, predating most of the enumerated regulations and some of the statutory provisions and conventions, which takes a different tack to what has been summarized above. The *Marine Transportation Security Act* (MTSA)[74] includes a section governing the development of security rules for vessels and marine facilities that potentially allows industry to create their own procedures and rules to best achieve the goals of transportation security contemplated in the Act. Section 7 of the MTSA provides that "the Minister may formulate measures respecting the security of marine transportation, including measures containing provisions that may be included in the regulations," and may also "require or authorize the operator of a vessel or marine facility to carry out the security measures, and the measures may apply instead of or in addition to any provision of the regulations."[75] Further, under a section entitled "Security Rules," the regulation provides that "(t)he purpose of this section is to allow operators of vessels and marine facilities to formulate and operate under security rules as an alternative to security measures required or authorized by the Minister."[76] In addition, "[t]he operator

---

  to the International Convention on Standards of Training, Certification and Watchkeeping for Seafarers (STCW) 1978, as amended, Resolution MSC.416(97) (25 November 2016, effective 1 July 2018); Amendments to Part A of the Seafarers' Training, Certification and Watchkeeping (STCW) Code, Resolution MSC.417(97) (25 November 2016, effective 1 July 2018) [Polar Code].

71 SOR/2017-286. These regulations were promulgated following the Polar Code.

72 *Shipping Safety Control Zones Order*, CRC c 356.

73 SOR 2010-127.

74 SC 1994, c 40.

75 Id., ss 7(1) and (2).

76 Id., s 10(1).

of a vessel or marine facility may formulate rules respecting any matter relating to the security of the vessel or facility and the operator may submit the rules to the Minister for approval."[77] It appears that these short provisions in the MTSA may be one of the few, if not the only, provisions in current Canadian maritime legislation (the MTSA is the statutory implementation of the International Ship and Port Security Code) that unequivocally defer, in whole or in part, to a regulatee (operator of a vessel or marine facility) the discretion to develop their own rules, subject only to the approval of the regulator. This is classic meta-regulation.

5   Potential Path towards Meta-Regulation in the Canadian Arctic: The IMO and Goal-based Standards

The preceding review of Canadian statutes and regulations promulgated for regulation of Arctic shipping, and for that matter shipping in Canadian waters generally, does not evince significant adoption of what is understood to be meta-regulation, and certainly no preference for self-regulation. Apart from some of the academic writings cited earlier in this chapter, there seems to be no significant judicial or academic discussion on meta-regulation in Canada. Is there any prospect that Canadian legislators or regulators would consider some sort of meta-regulatory formula for at least some of the aspects of regulation governing Arctic waters? Indeed, is there a reasonable avenue open through existing laws that could lead eventually to a move in this direction?

Some encouragement may be found through Canada's adoption of numerous international maritime conventions and acceptance of international norms reflected therein. Canada is a signatory to five fundamental international maritime conventions which have become universal and are to be considered traditional maritime regulatory documents. These are the International Convention on Load Lines,[78] the Convention on International Regulations for Preventing Collisions at Sea,[79] SOLAS,[80] the International Convention for the Prevention of Pollution from Ships 1973/1978 (MARPOL),[81] and the International Convention on Standards of Training, Certification and Watchkeeping

---

77   Id., s 10(2).
78   5 April, 1966 (in force 21 July 1968), 640 *UNTS* 133.
79   20 October 1972 (in force 15 July 1977), 1050 *UNTS* 16.
80   SOLAS (n 4).
81   MARPOL (n 4).

for Seafarers (STCW).[82] SOLAS, MARPOL and STCW were amended to include provisions of the Polar Code and otherwise (in the case of STCW).[83] These amendments brought the first adoption by tacit acceptance in Canada of an international instrument containing provisions that are both prescriptive and of a non-mandatory level of 'guidance.' Indeed, Canada's openness to a host of maritime conventions indicates perhaps some consideration for alternative approaches to regulation of maritime commerce. This is most notable in comparison with Canada's southern neighbour, the United States, which as of this writing has still failed to ratify a number of the modern conventions, including the United Nations Convention on the Law of the Sea.[84]

Canada is a party to most significant maritime conventions in force. Therefore, one can reasonably hope that Canada will likewise follow on the general consensus of the IMO with regard to the approach to future maritime regulation. The IMO introduced an alternative to traditional prescriptive regulation for at least a limited aspect of maritime regulation when it gave consideration and eventually adopted the concept of goal-based standards (GBS). In 2002, the concept was formally introduced to the IMO by two ship-owning and flag States, Greece and the Bahamas, in the Marine Safety Committee (MSC) and the IMO Council when they proposed the use of GBS to regulate vessel construction standards.[85] The IMO has since outlined the basic concept of GBS as (1) broad and overarching standards that vessels are required to meet, (2) a level of achievement of the standards as required by the IMO or government authorities and their designated agents, (3) "clear, demonstrable, verifiable, long-standing, implementable and achievable" standards, and (4) rules specific and not subject to "differing interpretations," with (5) these principles "to

---

82   STCW (n 4).

83   Polar Code (n 70). See STCW Code s B-V/g: 'Guidance regarding training of masters and officers for ships operating in polar waters'.

84   The author has been involved with maritime organizations in the United States that continue to make efforts to obtain US Senate ratification of the United Nations Convention on the Law of the Sea (LOSC), 10 December 1982 (in force 16 November 1994), 1833 *UNTS* 3. There is no logical explanation for why the LOSC has not been formally adopted by the United States, a signatory thereto, considering that interests in all quarters, from the US Coast Guard and US Navy to private vessel owners and operators, even cargo interests and labour groups are supportive of its ratification.

85   Greece, *Bulk Carrier Safety: Building of Robust Ships*, IMO Doc MSC 76/5/10 (27 September 2002); Bahamas and Greece, *Consideration of the Strategy and Policy of the Organization Including the Report of the Working Group: IMO Strategic Plan*, IMO Doc C 89/12/1 (8 October 2002).

be applicable to all goal-based standards developed by IMO."[86] Early on in the discussion of the use of GBS, the IMO set out five basic principles: (1) GBS standards to represent "the top tiers of the framework, against which the ship safety should be verified," (2) "goals are not intended to set prescriptive requirements or to give specific solutions," (3) goals are to ensure that a "properly operated and maintained ship remains safe," (4) goals are to be achieved by compliance with technical standards or alternative solutions, and (5) requirements of national organizations or administrations must demonstrate compliance with GBS.[87] The IMO went on to include GBS in its strategic plan for the period of 2004–2010.[88] Finally, in 2010 the IMO formally adopted the International Goal-Based Ship Construction Standards for Bulk Carriers and Oil Tankers.[89]

The work of the IMO on GBS went on hand-in-hand with work on the related concept of formal safety assessment (FSA),[90] including the establishment of a joint MSC/Marine Environment Protection Committee (MEPC) working group on FSA.[91] The use of FSA added another layer of evaluation to set standards for GBS. In brief, at the IMO, GBS "in general are considered to be rules for rules," with separate SOLAS requirements in order to meet functional requirements.[92] Even though GBS has been adopted by the IMO for vessel construction standards, and may potentially be utilized for other regulatory fields, it has been criticized, particularly in the run up to its adoption. Some have argued that GBS is based upon a risk analysis that threatens to cover over many safety issues that would then remain unaddressed.[93] In other words, some appear concerned that setting overarching goals will cause some safety problems to be ignored or overlooked. This school of thought basically does not trust industry at the national level to adequately create or enforce sufficient regulations, unlike an overarching government bureaucracy under CPR. In the end, the IMO

---

86   "IMO Goal-based Standards," IMO, https://www.imo.org/en/OurWork/Safety/Pages/Goal-BasedStandards.aspx.

87   The Bahamas, Greece and IACS, *Goal-Based New Ship Construction Standards*, IMO Doc MSC 78/6/2 (5 February 2004), para 5.

88   Strategic Plan for the Organization (for the Six-year Period 2004 to 2010), IMO Resolution A.944(23), 25 November 2003.

89   MSC 87/287 (20 May 2010).

90   Guidelines for Formal Safety Assessment (FSA) for Use in the IMO Rule-making Process, IMO Docs MSC/Circ.1023, MEPC/Circ.392 (5 April 2002).

91   "Goal-Based Standards Take Shape at IMO's Maritime Safety Committee," *Oil Spill Intelligence Report* 28:23 (2 June 2005): 1.

92   Mikael Huss, "Status at IMO: Where Are We Heading with Goal-Based Standards?," Presentation to SAFEDOR mid-term conference, Brussels, May 2007, https://mhuss.se/documents.html.

93   Panos Zachariadis, "Goal-Based Standards: Aim, Progress and Latest Developments," *Naftika Chronika* (May 2009): 42.

did adopt the Generic Guidelines for Developing IMO Goal-based Standards in 2010, which were amended in 2015 and again in July 2019.[94]

Goal-based standards are probably not pure meta-regulation as conceived by those formulating the concept. However, GBS is certainly far removed from detailed prescriptive regulations as traditionally understood, and as illustrated by some of Canada's current Arctic regulations, including part of the detailed ASSPPR. Establishing a set of parameters or 'goals' is a significant step away from detailed and unalterable bullet point regulations. As earlier considered, the most plausible development of meta-regulation is a system whereby the regulatees develop their own rules subject to review and approval by the regulators who keep certain goals in mind. This is a further step away from prescriptive regulation than found with GBS. GBS arguably confines the regulatees to developing their rules and procedures within pre-defined strictures of the goals set by the regulator. For maritime operations in the Arctic, reaching a system of meta-regulation would mean that the vessel operators and others would also define the goals they wish to reach as well as the procedures and rules to get there. These would all be subject to final approval or overview by the regulator, but it would be hoped that the regulator would not in the first instance put any restrictions upon the regulatees as to either goals or methods, subject to final approval.

One must be reminded, however, that even in the IMO the concept of GBS has so far been restricted formally to the rather narrow arena of vessel construction. Most certainly vessel construction is critical for both vessel safety (SOLAS) and the prevention of marine pollution (MARPOL, etc.). Therefore, the application of GBS arguably reaches further and broader in the maritime regulatory field than one would first consider. In addition, the Polar Code,[95] containing both mandatory provisions and 'guidance,' is arguably partially grounded in the concept of GBS. Part I-A of the Polar Code contains the mandatory safety provisions (as amendments to SOLAS), while Part I-B is entitled "Additional guidance regarding the provisions of the Introduction and Part I-A". Canada and perhaps some other nations have, or will, adopt the provisions of Part I-B as additional mandatory (prescriptive) elements under their domestic laws. Others will utilize them merely as helpful guidelines. The same goes with Part II-A (mandatory environmental provisions) and Part II-B (additional guidance), the latter also adopted in Canada as mandatory provisions. The Polar Code non-mandatory sections, however, do not quite rise to formal GBS, as they are merely recommendations, not formally-set goals. This means that Canada has converted Sections I-B and II-B of the Polar Code into strong

---

94   IMO Doc MSC.1/Circ.1394/rev.1 (12 June 2015); IMO Doc MSC.1/Circ.1394/rev.2 (8 July 2019).
95   Polar Code (n 70).

prescriptive requirements, moving away from using them as a goal-setting parameter. In sum, the formal reach of GBS beyond vessel construction standards has not been adopted yet in international conventions or arguably in Canadian legislation, and maritime nations may not yet be on the verge of a significant shift to meta-regulation.

6   **Putting the Third Leg on the Stool: Could the Application of the Doctrine of Tripartism Protect the Interests of Impacted Communities and Also Provide Critical Expertise for Regulators and Regulatees?**

The concept of tripartism was developed by Ayres and Braithwaite in the early 1990s, and set forth in detail in their foundational book *Responsive Regulation*.[96] According to the concept of tripartism, regulatory development and application should not be merely an exercise between regulators (government) and regulatees (industries and firms), but should include third party entities such as non-governmental organizations (NGOs), public interest groups, industry associations and even outside experts.[97] Ayers and Braithwaite focused particularly on the risk of agency capture or the 'defection' of both regulators (movement to punitive enforcement) and regulatees (law evasion and 'gaming the system') from their ideal of the cooperative pyramid.[98] The concern was that regulators and regulatees can become too close, particularly when regulation moves to some sort of cooperative model, and this concern is often expressed by consumers and public interest groups.[99] Put another way, a good goal in theory is cooperation of regulators and regulatees for the benefit of all, including the affected 'public' and non-parties. In practice such cooperation can evolve into capture, defection, evasion and other negative outcomes if the parties do not act with all good intention. Thus, affected interests may need to be involved at some level to oversee the relationship, although even then these third parties cannot be given such power as to interfere with the rightful autonomy of the regulatees. That preserved 'autonomy' is needed to allow the regulatees to properly and efficiently function, as explained above in this chapter.

---

96   Ayres and Braithwaite (n 7). Tripartism is explained in great detail in Chapter III of this work, pp. 54–100.

97   Id., 54–98. A summary of tripartism is also contained in this author's unpublished paper (n 10), pp. 23–24.

98   Ayres and Braithwaite (n 7), pp. 54–55.

99   Id., 56.

Ayers and Braithwaite's proposed solution of tripartism is to bring in concerned third parties who would be provided with all information available to the regulator, and perhaps even invited to participate in negotiations between regulators and regulatees, allowing them to monitor the results of regulations and have standing to sue the regulator if it fails in its duties.[100] This assumes that participating third parties will be provided with information sufficient to monitor the outcomes in a non-prescriptive regulatory system, such as meta-regulation, where rules promulgated by the regulatee are approved by the regulator.[101] Of note, the problem with expertise is not necessarily addressed, and the details of determining the suitability of a third party participant would have to be carefully considered.

In developing the concept of tripartism, Ayers and Braithwaite recognized that even this model has its potential problems. They identified the problem of the "zealous public interest group", and the related issue of fourth party "capture" of public interest groups (mainly political).[102] This plausible scenario would mean that regulatee interests with enough power and political muscle could seek control of the supposedly independent third party interests and direct them for their own benefit, in essence using them as a type of Trojan Horse to in turn capture the regulator, the very scenario that tripartism is designed to prevent. Ayers and Braithwaite posited one solution to this potential problem, the concept of "empowerment theory" wherein any regulatory system utilizing tripartism would have to work out a "communitarian tripartism" where a balance could be reached between the three interest centers to help offset any improper actions by a single actor.[103]

Tripartism has great promise as a method to design future regulatory systems in the Arctic. Given the relatively limited number of actors on all sides, a regulatory system utilizing meta-regulation in conjunction with tripartism is feasible. Canadian regulators in the Arctic, facing limits to resources as well as knowledge, must look to the participation of regulatees to address the myriad unique issues in that environment. The number of vessels entering or transiting the Canadian Arctic, as well as the expected growth in facilities, is still rather limited, and involves a relatively small number of discreet players, although it is growing significantly. These industries certainly have the most knowledge about the conditions in which they operate, as well as the equipment and personnel involved. Further, the third parties impacted by Arctic shipping are easy to identify.

---

100   Id., 57.
101   See id., 71–74.
102   Id., 75–76.
103   Id., 81–86.

The human population of the Canadian Arctic is small, but roughly half of that population is made up of persons living in Indigenous Inuit communities. Inuit have inhabited this region for about a millennium, and have passed down their knowledge and experience from generation to generation. Non-Inuit who live and make their livelihoods in the Canadian Arctic likewise are assumed to have gained the knowledge necessary to survive in this environment. It is plausible that these inhabitants have in many respects a similar knowledge of the environment in which they live and work as do the regulated industries which operate there. Furthermore, the inhabitants of the Canadian Arctic rely upon shipping to provide essential goods and services to their communities and as a primary source of communication with the rest of Canada and the world. Inuit in particular are directly impacted by Arctic shipping, not only positively but also negatively in the event of increased air and water pollution and disturbance or dislocation of wildlife upon which they rely for subsistence and cultural purposes. These closely intertwined dependencies are more magnified in the Arctic than in many other areas of the world, since there are few if any alternatives to the services provided by shipping in this remote area.

Given the above, a regulatory system utilizing the concept of tripartism to bring in Arctic communities, particularly the Inuit, is critical to any successful, and respectful, regulation of shipping as the area opens up more every year. It is submitted that neither regulators nor regulatees can adequately develop rules and procedures for Arctic operations without the input of knowledge from Inuit and other long-time Arctic residents, the 'learning' element in meta-regulation described above. Any such requirement should also comport with Canadian law and policy encouraging consultation, respect and coordination with Indigenous communities when developing laws and regulations that impact them.

How can tripartism be incorporated into maritime regulation in the Canadian Arctic? As with proposals to move towards non-prescriptive regulation discussed above, guidance may be found with the IMO. Non-State party actors play an important role in the development of IMO instruments. While full membership in the IMO is restricted to sovereign States, the IMO has also accepted a great number of non-State parties in a consultative status.

Rule 2 of the Rules and Guidelines for Consultative Status of Non-Governmental International Organizations with the International Maritime Organization[104] sets out the "purposes of consultative status" that include

---

104   IMO Resolution A.1144(31) (4 December 2019) [Consultative Status Rules]. The text of the rules was originally adopted on 13 April 1961, and amended several times, including the addition of guidelines in 2012, with the most recent amendments made in 2019. See also

"to enable IMO to obtain information or expert advice" from organizations "representing large groups whose activities have an important and direct bearing on the work of the IMO to express their points of view to it." Rule 3 likewise sets out that to be granted consultative status an NGO must be able to "contribute new expertise to IMO." The purposes behind admitting NGOs to consultative or observer status at the IMO in many ways match precisely the purposes given by the developers of the concept of tripartism for including interested third parties in the regulatory milieu.

The type of non-State actors with consultative status at the IMO are in two broad categories: (1) inter-governmental organizations (including some other UN agencies) and (2) NGOs covering a vast array of organizations representing everything from shipping industry interests to maritime labor and technical organizations to environmental protection groups to trade organizations. It is the latter category to which we must look. As of 2014 there were some 77 NGOs with consultative (observer) status at the IMO,[105] and as of this writing in August 2022, there were 85 international non-governmental organizations with consultative status and 66 intergovernmental organizations with observer status.[106] NGOs "lobby and participate, without the right of voting, in the IMO conferences as non-governmental organizations."[107]

The IMO has admitted to provisional consultative status, for the first time, an organization representing the interests of Inuit in Canada and neighbouring States after a long application process. The Inuit Circumpolar Council (ICC) is an organization representing the interests of Indigenous Arctic communities in Canada, the United States, Greenland (Denmark) and Russia.[108] At the Extraordinary Session of the IMO Council (CES 34), held in November 2021, the ICC's application to obtain consultative status at the IMO was granted on a provisional basis.[109]

Kenneth R. Simmons, *The International Maritime Organization* (London: Simmons & Hill Publishing Ltd, 1994), appendix 5, at 220, 226.

105   Md Saiful Karim, *Prevention of Pollution of the Marine Environment from Vessels* (Cham: Springer, 2015), 20.

106   "Member States, IGOs and NGOs," IMO, https://www.imo.org/en/About/Membership/Pages/Default.aspx.

107   Hristos Karihalios, *The Management of Maritime Regulations* (London: Rutledge, Taylor & Frances Group, 2015), 29.

108   See generally the Inuit Circumpolar Council website https://www.inuitcircumpolar.com/.

109   "IMO Council, Extraordinary Session (CES 34), 8–12/22 November 2021," IMO Media Centre, https://www.imo.org/en/MediaCentre/MeetingSummaries/Pages/Council,-Extraordinary-Session-(CES-34).aspx; Ellis Quinn, "Int'l Inuit Org Receives Provisional Consultative Status on the International Maritime Organization," *Eye on the Arctic*, 11 November 2021, https://rcinet.ca/eye-on-the-arctic/2021/11/11; ICC, "Inuit Voices to be Heard at IMO on Critical

The potential impact and influence of the ICC on IMO regulatory formation is illustrated in submissions made on behalf of the ICC prior to its acceptance as a consultative party. In support of a ban on heavy fuel oil (HFO) in the Arctic (with some qualifications), and under IMO procedures, the ICC's position was presented to the MEPC Subcommittee on Pollution Prevention and Response (PRP) at its December 2019 meeting through a submission with other consultative parties.[110] Now that the ICC is a consultative member, it can be expected to present its own submissions to IMO committees.

Observation of the importance of the ICC participation at the IMO, and its impact upon future policies and regulations, may give some guidance as to how Canada can advance participation by these impacted communities as it approaches new methods for Arctic shipping meta-regulation. Under the IMO's Consultative Status Rules, Rule 7 sets forth the "privileges conferred by consultative status," which include the right to receive provisional and meeting documents, the right to submit documents for items on IMO committee agendas, the right to have an observer at plenary meetings of the Assembly and, upon invitation, at meetings of committees, and the right to receive texts of resolutions adopted by the Assembly and various committees.[111]

An example of potential movement in Canada to a form of tripartism is seen in the development of low-impact shipping corridors in Arctic waters. This is being created in close consultation and cooperation with Inuit communities, especially with the authorities in Nunavut, where the most important corridors are located. See the chapters in this volume by Dawson and Song, and Lalonde and Bankes.

The extent of 'authority' that a third-party participant is granted in regulatory processes must remain to be carefully considered, perhaps on a case-by-case basis. No assumption should be made that the 'third leg of the stool' must be as strong as the other two (government regulators and regulatee industries). The nature of the proposed regulations, extent of coverage and public policy considerations must be analyzed in each case. The design of a tripartism system requires further extensive study. It is symptomatic of the emerging nature of this concept, even after some thirty years since it was first proposed, that very little detail of the mechanics of such a system have been worked out. Maritime regulation, particularly in the Arctic, could be one its first major test grounds.

Shipping Issues," Press Release, 9 November 2021, https://www.inuitcircumpolar.com /news/inuit-voices-to-be-heard-at-imo-on-critical-shipping-issues/. The ICC's provisional status is to be reviewed in no more than two years.

110   World Wildlife Fund, the Pacific Environment Group and the Friends of the Earth International, "Development of Measures to Reduce Risks of Use and Carriage of heavy Fuel Oil as Fuel by Ships in Arctic Waters," IMO Doc PPR 7/14/1 (12 December 2019).

111   Consultative Status Rules (n 104).

7   Conclusion

Despite little history of the use of meta-regulation or GBS for maritime governance in Canada, and a so-far limited use globally, necessity is likely the driver
to promote a shift from classic prescriptive regulation in the years ahead.
The many problems encountered with prescriptive regulation are if anything
magnified in the Arctic. The polar regions present the most challenging environment on Earth for the operation of any vessel, and the rapid evolution of
technology to deal with the high risks must not be fettered by any unnecessarily complex and binding regulations and bureaucratic delays. Regulatees must
be encouraged to make the maximum effort to study risks and innovate with
solutions beyond what they may be required to do. This applies equally to regulators who must think outside the box, and be willing to give latitude to maritime operators to do the same. Regulators in the Arctic have limited resources,
both assets and personnel, not to mention budgetary limits common to most
governments, and must husband these limited resources. Regulatees also have
limits, but their operations in the Arctic give them an advantage of knowledge and situated assets. A better system to foster sharing of these assets and
encouraging their most cost-effective use is of benefit to all interested parties
and would be best realized through a system based upon meta-regulation.

Many persons with knowledge and experience in the Arctic would agree
that vessel owners and operators, other Arctic industry players, and certainly
members of Arctic communities, have far more expertise and experience operating in the region. No thorough regulatory system for Arctic shipping can be
developed without the participation of these parties, and everything must be
done to seek their cooperation, and indeed their lead, in future developments.
Qualifications can be put in place to ensure transparency and accountability,
and avoid regulatory capture, particularly if a third participating group is permitted to give their input and review proposed rules and procedures through
the application of some form and extent of tripartism. The freedom provided
to regulatees to develop their own rules subject to oversight by regulators and
third parties should not only eliminate most of these concerns, but should
strongly encourage all involved to approach regulation of Arctic shipping in a
proactive rather than reactive way, hopefully avoiding major incidents rather
than responding to them and hashing out yet more rules in their wake. What is
needed is recognition of common ground and interests and a basic trust that
everyone involved really has the same ultimate goals.

Modernizing the Governance of Passenger Vessel Operations in the Canadian Arctic

Meagan Greentree

Abstract

The uncoordinated governance of passenger vessel operations in the Canadian Arctic has produced an unnecessarily complex permitting system. This chapter utilizes process mapping, an international jurisdictional scan, and a multidisciplinary literature review to re-evaluate Canada's Arctic passenger vessel governance and permit requirements. It expands on previous research findings through the inclusion of macro-level constraints, including the complexity and dynamism of the external environment, the rapid pace of technological change within the international shipping sector, and the impetus for a re-delegation of tasks between organizations within the existing governance arrangement. The findings suggest that the permitting system cannot be effectively streamlined via a temporary horizontal coordination mechanism, as more systemic reforms are required to coordinate Canada's Arctic passenger vessel governance. While critics may argue that the current volume of polar passenger vessel traffic does not warrant the costs of creating a new alternative service delivery agency, this chapter recommends that an 'Arctic Passenger Vessel Coordination Entity' be established under Transport Canada's portfolio to foster the horizontal integration of services between departments, the vertical integration of services across governments, and a more efficient passenger vessel permit system in the Canadian Arctic.

Keywords

Arctic cruise tourism – passenger vessel – Northwest Passage – polar tourism – interagency coordination

1 Introduction

Climate change has opened the door for trans-Arctic shipping to become a viable transport option for commercial activities. The Arctic Ocean's historically impenetrable ice has thinned considerably in the last century, and global climate model simulations indicate that the sea ice will retreat at an exponential pace in the coming decades.[1] However, the disappearance of ice has already had a measurable impact on the volume of shipping in the Canadian Arctic (see Lasserre in this volume for trends in Arctic shipping traffic). Between 1990 and 2015, the volume of vessel traffic tripled, with much of that growth occurring in the previous decade.[2] Despite the expanded vessel activity, the Northwest Passage is unlikely to become a viable commercial route to transport cargo route anytime in the foreseeable future.[3] However, an alluring history, rich Indigenous cultural heritage and ruggedly beautiful landscape make the Northwest Passage a marketable region for cruise ship and adventure expedition tourism.

Over the last four decades, Canada's Arctic cruise tourism industry has developed at an inconsistent pace, marked by brief periods of dramatic growth amongst a general trend of stagnation. In 1984, the Swedish-owned *Lindblad Explorer* became the first passenger ship to traverse the Northwest Passage.[4] The industry's development looked promising at the turn of the twenty-first century, when tourist-carrying ships began to arrive in the region regularly and in greater numbers.[5] Between 2005 and 2006, the average number of passenger vessel voyages in the Canadian Arctic doubled, from 11 to 22.[6] However, despite an upward trend of passenger vessel traffic in recent years, the sector's

---

1   Ge Peng *et al.*, "What Do Global Climate Models Tell Us about Future Arctic Sea Ice Coverage Changes?," *Climate* 8:1 (2020): 15, https://doi.org/10.3390/cli8010015.

2   Michael Meredith *et al.*, "Polar Regions," in *IPCC Special Report on the Ocean and Cryosphere in a Changing Climate*, eds., H.-O. Pörtner *et al.* (Cambridge, UK and New York, NY: Cambridge University Press, 2019), 203–320, at 205–206, https://www.ipcc.ch/site/assets/uploads/sites/3/2019/11/07_SROCC_Ch03_FINAL.pdf.

3   Forecasts suggest that the Northwest Passage will be the last region in the circumpolar Arctic to contain multiyear ice. Hazardous ice conditions, along with the Passage's variable depth restrictions, will pose significant navigational challenges for many years to come. See Willy Østreng *et al.*, "The Northeast, Northwest and Transpolar Passages in Comparison," in *Shipping in Arctic Waters A Comparison of the Northeast, Northwest and Trans Polar Passages*, eds., Willy Østreng *et al.* (Berlin: Springer, 2013), 299–353, https://doi.org/10.1007/978-3-642-16790-4.

4   "First Passenger Ship Navigates Northwest Passage," *United Press International Archives*, 12 September 1984, https://www.upi.com/Archives/1984/09/12/First-passenger-ship-navigates-Northwest-Passage/8564463809600/.

5   Emma Stewart *et al.*, "Sea Ice in Canada's Arctic: Implications for Cruise Tourism," *Arctic* 60:4 (2007): 370–380.

6   Emma Stewart, Jackie Dawson and Margaret Johnston, "Risks and Opportunities Associated with Change in the Cruise Tourism Sector: Community Perspectives from Arctic Canada," *Polar Journal* 5:2 (2015): 409.

growth has remained relatively stagnant; averaging 21 voyages annually for a three-year period between 2017 and 2019 cruise seasons (see Lasserre in this volume for trends in Arctic shipping traffic).[7] Moreover, Canada possesses a miniscule share of the polar cruise tourism market relative to other circumpolar destinations, and the literature suggests that Canada's convoluted passenger vessel regulatory regime and permit system is at least partially to blame for the sector's stagnation.[8] Thus, this chapter attempts to answer a simple question for a complex public management problem: how can the Government of Canada streamline the permit system to improve the governance of passenger vessel operations in the Canadian Arctic?

This study contributes to the existing body of literature regarding the governance of Arctic cruise operations in the Canadian Arctic by demonstrating that Canada's permitting process is not the root of the problem; rather, it is a symptom of irreconcilable fractures amongst the multijurisdictional administrative bodies responsible for the management of cruise vessel activity in the Canadian Arctic. This chapter expands on previous research findings through the inclusion of relevant macro-level considerations, such as the complexity and dynamism of the external regulatory environment, the rapid pace of technological change within the global shipping industry and the impetus for a re-allocation of responsibilities within Canada's Arctic passenger vessel governance model.

While critics may argue that the current volume of Arctic vessel traffic does not warrant the costs of creating a new alternative service delivery (ASD) agency, this chapter recommends that an 'Arctic Passenger Vessel Coordination Entity' be established under Transport Canada's portfolio.[9] The proposed ASD agency would improve passenger vessel services by bringing together cross-sectoral and multijurisdictional organizations to provide more seamless service delivery through a horizontal integration of services between departments, and a vertical integration of services across governments. The addition of a new liaison agency within Canada's Arctic passenger vessel governance structure would help to build the capacity of its stakeholders and foster more

---

7   See Table 5.1 in chapter by Lasserre in this volume.

8   Frédéric Lasserre and Pierre-Louis Têtu, "The Cruise Tourism Industry in the Canadian Arctic: Analysis of Activities and Perceptions of Cruise Ship Operators," *Polar Record* 51:1 (2015): 24–38, at 28, https://doi.org/10.1017/S0032247413000508.

9   An alternative service delivery (ASD) agency provides public services via an organizational arrangement outside the traditional departmental structure. See "Assessing Alternative Service Delivery Arrangements," Office of the Auditor General of Canada, accessed 12 May 2022, https://www.oag-bvg.gc.ca/internet/English/meth_gde_e_10195.html.

efficient co-management of Arctic passenger vessels for the economic, social and cultural benefit of northern communities.

To lay out this argument, the chapter is divided into five sections. The first section combines a literature review with relevant background information to describe what was previously known about the problematic permit system, and recent measures the federal government has undertaken to streamline requirements. The second section provides a brief overview of the jurisdictional division of responsibilities within Canada's Arctic passenger vessel governance process and identifies several critical factors that increase its requirements for effective interagency coordination. Section three conducts an evaluation of the processes, service results and consequences of the permit system, which demonstrates that the existing governance model is devoid of rational mechanisms to coordinate its activities. The fourth section considers the options and constraints to address the described interagency coordination deficits and identifies the requirement for the establishment of a permanent multijurisdictional intra- and interagency coordination mechanism. The final section of the chapter recommends the establishment of an 'Arctic Passenger Vessel Coordination Entity' within Transport Canada's portfolio and describes how this new ASD agency could modernize the governance of passenger vessels in the Canadian Arctic.

2   Literature Review and Background

There is a small body of academic literature pertaining to the governance of cruise tourism in the Canadian Arctic. Academics have broadly utilized a qualitative methodology to assess various stakeholders' attitudes towards Arctic cruise tourism management. Multiple studies have documented the attitudes of local northern residents, polar cruise vessel firms and operators, and the various federal authorities responsible for passenger vessel operations.[10] The early literature is instrumental to contextualize the issues identified in this chapter.

---

10   Stewart, Dawson and Johnston (n 6), pp. 403–427; Emma Stewart, Jackie Dawson and
        Dianne Draper, "Cruise Tourism and Residents in Arctic Canada: Development of a
        Resident Attitude Typology," *Journal of Hospitality and Tourism Management* 18:1 (2011):
        95–106; Jackie Dawson, Margaret Johnston and Emma Stewart, "The Unintended Conse-
        quences of Regulatory Complexity: The Case of Cruise Tourism in Arctic Canada," *Marine
        Policy* 76 (2017): 71–78; Lasserre and Têtu (n 8), pp. 24–38; Adrianne Johnston, Marga-
        ret Johnston, Jackie Dawson and Emma Stewart, "Challenges of Arctic Cruise Tourism
        Development in Canada: Perspectives of Federal Government Stakeholders," *Journal of
        Maritime Law and Commerce* 43:3 (2012): 335–347.

Canada's permit system has triggered a growing chorus of complaints from the cruise tourism industry, northern residents and academics alike. Many have criticized the permit system for its undue complexity. Polar cruise operators have described the system as "a nightmare," "a mess," "a maze," and "laughable."[11] In 2014, the Association of Arctic Expedition Cruise Operators (AECO) stated in a media release that "Canada's cruise requirements are out of control."[12] Several academics have concluded that Canada's polar cruise tourism industry has suffered due to the significant transaction costs imposed by the existing permitting system.[13] Northern residents have also suggested that the underdeveloped Arctic cruise industry, writ large, reflects more systemic governance issues. As one local resident commented, "there isn't any one single agency taking the lead and there isn't any one agency willing to be the coordinating agency."[14] A diverse array of stakeholders appears to agree that the governance of Arctic passenger vessels requires reform.

The federal government has made several unsuccessful attempts to clarify and streamline the permit process. In 2014, the former Environment Minister Leona Aglukkaq, the Member of Parliament for Nunavut, responded to her constituents' longstanding frustrations with the inefficient permit system by initiating a multi-agency working group to streamline permit requirements.[15] Nothing material came of this group because it was quietly shutdown following a change of government in the 2015 federal election.[16] However, the fact that a Nunavut Minister attempted to overhaul a transport-related permit system—despite the system's meagre relevance to Environment and Climate Change Canada—may give credence to residents' arguments regarding the system's absence of leadership.[17]

---

11   Dawson *et al.* (n 10), p. 75.
12   The Association of Arctic Expedition Cruise Operators (AECO) is an international association for expedition cruise operators operating in the Arctic that provides its voluntary membership with guidelines to promote passenger safety, environmental protection, and positive relationships with Indigenous populations. See AECO website at https://www.aeco.no/.
13   Lasserre and Têtu (n 8), p. 69; Dawson *et al.* (n 10), pp. 71–78.
14   Stewart *et al.* (n 6), p. 421.
15   Dawson *et al.* (n 10), pp. 72–73.
16   Id., 73.
17   Per section 4(1) of the *Department of the Environment Act* (RSC 1985, c E-10), the mandate of Environment and Climate Change Canada includes "the preservation and enhancement of the quality of the natural environment, including water, air and soil quality; renewable resources, including migratory birds and other non-domestic flora and fauna; water; meteorology; the enforcement of any rules or regulations ... and; the coordination

Following the collapse of the interagency working group, Transport Canada published a revised edition of the Guidelines for Passenger Vessels Operating in the Canadian Arctic, a guidance document intended to assist vessel operators to navigate the permit system.[18] Initially published in 2005, the Guidelines had collected dust for twelve years before their long-overdue revisions in 2017.[19] While the updated document offers new insights into passenger vessel requirements, the complexity that has defined the permit system in recent decades remains unchanged owing to systemic deficits in the Arctic passenger vessel governance structure.

3   The Governance of Arctic Passenger Vessel Operations

Governance of Canada's Arctic passenger vessel operations is complex. This chapter conceptualizes Canada's Arctic passenger vessel governance as the overarching multijurisdictional framework of structures, systems and relationships—consisting of federal, territorial and local governments, co-managed regulatory boards, and Indigenous and community organizations—which contribute various functional capacities to directly influence or control polar cruise tourism operations.[20] Over 55 federal, territorial, Indigenous and local governance bodies are responsible for managing various aspects of passenger vessel operations in the Canadian Arctic.[21] These governance bodies interact within a complex domestic legislative regime, which includes 25 federal acts, 14 territorial acts and two comprehensive land claim agreements.[22] The

---

    of the policies and programs of the Government of Canada respecting the preservation and enhancement of the quality of the natural environment."

18   The term 'vessel operators' is used figuratively in this chapter to capture both operators and designated vessel representatives. See Transport Canada, *Guidelines for Passenger Vessels Operating in the Canadian Arctic*, TP 13670E (Ottawa: Government of Canada, 2017), https://tc.canada.ca/sites/default/files/migrated/tp13670e.pdf.

19   Transport Canada, *Guidelines for Passenger Vessels Operating in the Canadian Arctic*, TP 13670 (Ottawa: Government of Canada, 2005).

20   Governance is not the exclusive purview of governments; industry associations like AECO certainly share a role in influencing their member's behaviour. However, this chapter excludes industry stakeholders from its conceptualization of governance owing to its focus on a government/community-enabled permit regime.

21   This number is based on a count of organizations' contact information attached as an appendix to Transport Canada's revised Guidelines. However, the number of authorities involved in Arctic passenger vessel approvals exceeds 55 because the contact information for the numerous hamlets and hunter and trapper organizations are not included in the source material. Transport Canada 2017 (n 18), pp. 40–42.

22   Id., 38–39.

overarching legislative regime includes a broad array of multijurisdictional regulatory frameworks that intersect with cruise tourism activities, including national shipping and navigation, environmental protection, marine resources (e.g., fisheries), national and territorial parks and heritage sites, wildlife management, cultural resources and tourism-related service sector businesses.

Passenger vessel governance resides under federal authority. Broadly speaking, the federal government designs the national shipping and navigation policy framework, harmonizes national regulations in accordance with international safety and environmental standards, and provides services to promote an efficient domestic shipping sector, protect the marine environment and enhance maritime safety and security. The federal division of responsibilities over Arctic shipping is fractured across many departments and agencies (see Chircop, this volume, for a detailed overview of Canada's intuitional framework for Arctic shipping). Transport Canada is for all intents and purposes the lead maritime administrator within the federal cadre; however, the Department of Fisheries and Oceans (DFO) and its special operating agency, the Canadian Coast Guard (CCG), play a significant role in marine policy development, regulatory enforcement and service delivery.[23] A variety of other federal actors provide marine-related regulatory or service functions that directly interface with Arctic passenger vessels, including the Canada Border Services Agency (CBSA), Royal Canadian Mounted Police (RCMP), Canadian Armed Forces (CAF), Environment and Climate Change Canada (ECCC), the Public Health Agency of Canada (PHAC), Global Affairs Canada (GAC) and Immigration, Refugees and Citizenship Canada.[24] Despite the centralization of maritime administrative functions under federal authority, Canada's institutional compartmentalization of marine-related regulatory authorities and services signals a structural basis for piecemeal shipping services to polar passenger vessels.

The federal government further contributes to the tourism-related domains of passenger vessels. Several departments manage and maintain national tourist attractions, heritage and cultural resources. Parks Canada (PC) operates coastal national parks and national historic sites in the Canadian Arctic, which offer shore access, and serve as popular attractions for cruise-based passengers.[25] The Canadian Wildlife Service (CWS), a branch of ECCC, manages

---

23   See "Institutional Framework" in chapter by Chircop in this volume.
24   Passenger vessels engage with each of these actors throughout pre-voyage planning activities. Transport Canada 2017 (n 18), pp. III, 40.
25   Emma Stewart *et al.*· "Cruise Tourism in a Warming Arctic: Implications for Northern National Parks," Paper presented at Canadian Parks for Tomorrow: 40th Anniversary Conference, Calgary, AB, 8–11 May 2008.

and maintains national wildlife areas and migratory bird sanctuaries, including the Bylot Island Bird Sanctuary in Nunavut, which it co-manages with the Asungasungaat Area Co-Management Committee of Pond Inlet.[26] Several federal departments collaborate with the territorial governments to manage wildlife. Working in conjunction with the CBSA, the CWS administers and coordinates the Convention on International Trade in Endangered Species of Wild Fauna and Flora (CITES) in relation to the international community, and DFO manages the transportation of marine mammal wildlife products between jurisdictions.[27] The collaborative management of the international and domestic export of wildlife products intersects with popular recreational tourist activities, such as fishing and hunting, as well as Indigenous arts and crafts souvenirs, including hides, carved walrus and narwhal tusks, wolf-lined parkas and whale bone carvings.[28]

Canada's Arctic passenger vessel governance is highly decentralized. Within their respective jurisdictions, the territorial governments are responsible for developing the regulatory framework for tourism and tourism-related service sectors, including business licensing (e.g., extraterritorial corporations and crew labour), environmental protection and wildlife management.[29] The territories also manage and maintain territorial parks, heritage sites and cultural resources, with the view to ensuring that passenger vessel activity does not cause adverse socio-cultural impacts to northern residents.[30] The waterways in the Northwest Passage are subject to two comprehensive land claims agreements, which have established formal co-managed regulatory boards and Regional Inuit Organizations (RIO).[31] While the conditions of these agreements vary, the resultant governance bodies generally participate in the governance of passenger vessels through land use planning, environmental screening, water licensing and wildlife management.[32] Northern communities contribute directly to the management of passenger vessel operations by authorizing

---

26   Id., 4, 33–36, 43.

27   Environment and Climate Change Canada, "Trade in Protected Species: Roles and Responsibilities in Canada," Government of Canada, last modified 4 July 2017, https://www.canada.ca/en/environment-climate-change/services/convention-international-trade-endangered-species/roles-responsibilities.html.

28   Department of Environment, "Wildlife Export," Government of Nunavut, accessed 2 May 2022, https://gov.nu.ca/sites/default/files/export_brochure_4_eng.pdf; Transport Canada 2017 (n 18), pp. 35–36.

29   Transport Canada 2017 (n 18), p. 38.

30   Id., 5.

31   Id., 56.

32   Id., 11.

vessel visits and providing local tourism services, including cultural performances and community coordination/logistics support.[33] Hunter and trapper organizations manage local wildlife, and authorize vessel visits, with the view to mitigating the risks of disruption to residents' traditional activities.[34]

Canada's Arctic passenger vessel governance structure possesses several unique characteristics that increase the requirement for effective interagency coordination. Namely, a significant quantity number of (co-)governance bodies, splintered across multiple levels of government, are responsible for managing complex, overlapping and interrelated regulatory regimes. Nonetheless, the permit system offers ample evidence that Canada's Arctic passenger vessel governance is largely devoid of formal mechanisms to coordinate its activities.

4　The Passenger Vessel Permit System

Before analyzing the passenger vessel permit system, a general disclaimer that specifies the scope of this analysis is required. The 'passenger vessel permit system' refers to the variety of federal, territorial and local government, Indigenous and community organization, and regulatory body permits, certificates, licences approvals and permission requirements, processes or procedures that may be required to conduct a passenger vessel voyage in the Canadian Arctic. This section does not evaluate the necessity of Canada's robust domestic regulatory regime that governs passenger vessel operations. Shipping operations in the Northwest Passage are as hazardous as the marine ecosystem is fragile, so the robust management of polar passenger vessels is accepted at face value as both reasonable and justified. Comprehensive land claim and self-government agreements in the Canadian Arctic add another layer of regulatory complexity, which rightfully increase the challenges of conducting commercial activities in the region. In sum, this section does not evaluate the merits of the passenger vessel permit system, but instead evaluates the *implementation* of the overarching permit requirements.

A condensed outline of Canada's Arctic passenger vessel permitting process and authorities, as described in Transport Canada's revised Guidelines, are detailed in Figure 14.1. The Guidelines include recommended timelines for

---

33　Nunavut, Department of Economic Development and Transportation, *Annual Tourism Report 2018–2019*, Report no. 209-5(2) (Government of Nunavut, October 2019), 4, https://assembly.nu.ca/sites/default/files/TD-209-5(2)-EN-2018-2019-Annual-Report-Tourism.pdf.

34　Transport Canada 2017 (n 18), p. 7.

operators to acquire authorizations or submit required permitting or licensing applications at specified intervals in the pre-trip planning stage. The conservative nature of these timelines reflect the many interdependent organizational requirements interwoven throughout the permitting process (interdependencies are denoted with a * in Figure 14.1), and the Guidelines are intended to mitigate the downstream impacts of permitting and authorization delays.[35] Several of Transport Canada's recommended timelines are expressed as an interval range; where applicable, these recommendations have been organized and depicted in Figure 14.1 using the most conservative timeline.[36] Additionally, the source material for Figure 14.1 is incomplete, so numerous organizational requirements have been excluded from the process map.[37]

4.1   *Evaluating the Process*

The most glaring issue with the permitting process is the length of time required to obtain all required permits and authorizations. As detailed in Transport Canada's Guidelines, it may take vessel operators two years to obtain all required permits and approvals to conduct a voyage in the Canadian Arctic. Operators are instructed to initiate consultations with representatives from each Nunavut hamlet they hope to visit a minimum of 18 to 24 months before their intended voyage departure, which may include additional written permissions from hunter and trapper organizations.[38] This is a critical first step in the

---

35   Considering that multijurisdictional permit requirements must be pursued concurrently, permit interdependencies are relevant to note because they represent risk to the vessel operator. For example, if the operator is delayed in acquiring one interdependent requirement, such as written approval from applicable hunter and trapper organizations, then it may risk delaying territorial permits further down the permitting process chain. Furthermore, acquired federal and/or territorial permits are considered invalid until the cruise proposal is approved by the Nunavut Planning Commission and Nunavut Impact Review Board. Transport Canada 2017 (n 18), pp. 12, 48.

36   For example, the Guidelines recommend that vessel operators contact Parks Canada 6–8 months prior to intended departure to complete applicable permit and entry requirements. Id., 4.

37   The Government of Yukon did not participate in the Guideline's revision, and in the absence of publicly available information for vessel operators, Yukon's requirements are missing from Figure 14.1. Additionally, the Guidelines do not include recommended timelines to contact each authority. For example, vessel operators are instructed to provide the Canadian Forces with an itinerary, but the timeline to do so is not provided. Organizations with unspecified requirements are omitted from Figure 14.1. Transport Canada 2017 (n 18), pp. iii, 30.

38   Id., 5–7, 11–14, 16, 48.

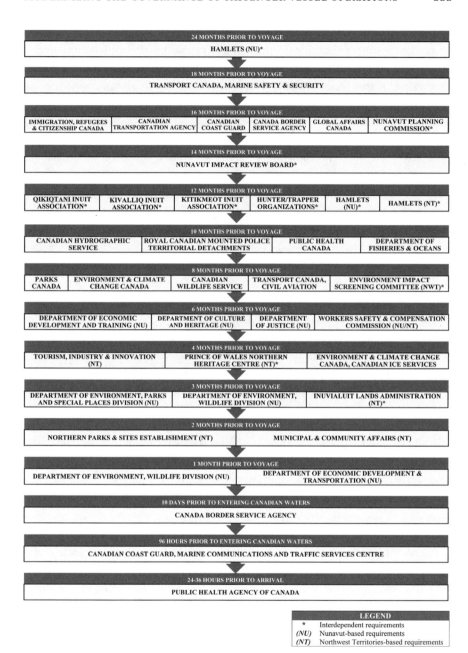

FIGURE 14.1   Condensed outline of passenger vessel permit process

FIGURE COMPILED BY THE AUTHOR WITH DATA PROVIDED BY CANADA'S *GUIDELINES FOR PASSENGER VESSELS OPERATING IN THE CANADIAN ARCTIC*, TRANSPORT CANADA, REPORT NO. 13670E (OTTAWA: GOVERNMENT OF CANADA, 2017): 1–67.

process, because proof of community consultation and approvals are required before the Nunavut Planning Commission (NPC) will evaluate an application.[39]

The logistics of obtaining community permissions represents an immediate kink in the process chain. Transport Canada's Guidelines recommend that operators call communities, rather than email, due to the "technological limitations" within the communities.[40] However, the logistics of contacting the community via telephone can also prove problematic. As one operator lamented, "I called [a community] every day for a month and finally got through and then still got yelled at when we showed up."[41] This experience may reflect a common human resource capacity issue in many remote northern communities. Residents have suggested that there is a high rate of turnover in community tourism positions owing to the seasonal nature of the job, which can make it difficult for operators to form sustainable relations with the communities.[42] Transport Canada recommends that operators physically visit the communities to overcome this hurdle.[43] This suggestion also proves impractical owing to the absence of transportation infrastructure along Canada's Arctic coastline, which makes visiting these communities prohibitively expensive and time consuming.[44] If vessel operators manage to successfully acquire all local permissions, they must still jump through a myriad of regulatory hoops until the date of their departure.

Permit and vessel reporting requirements vary, so the next challenge an operator encounters is to identify which acts, regulations and permit requirements are applicable to their vessel and voyage itinerary. Most federal and territorial permits pertaining to safety, environmental protection and commercial activities (e.g., business licenses) are mandatory for all passenger vessel operations, regardless of the destination or activities conducted. However, many permits and/or permissions, particularly local requirements, are dependent on the intended vessel route or voyage length. Additionally, entrance requirements for national and territorial parks, national wildlife areas and migratory bird conservatories vary based on the location of tourist activities and/or the number of visitors in attendance.[45] To successfully navigate the permit system, the vessel operator must possess an intimate understanding of a litany of

39   Id., 6, 16.
40   Id., 5.
41   Dawson *et al.* (n 10), p. 75.
42   Stewart, Dawson and Johnston (n 10), p. 418.
43   Transport Canada 2017 (n 18), p. 9.
44   No communities in Nunavut are connected via an all-weather road. Consequently, flights into remote airstrips are often the only viable option to travel to a community.
45   Transport Canada 2017 (n 18), p. 8.

multijurisdictional legislation, regulations and policies to identify their voyage requirements.

Vessel operators must also identify each responsible authority to identify and fulfil all applicable requirements, but this task may also prove challenging. Aside from several tourism-related permit applications offered on the territorial government websites, and regulatory board applications, few other permits or license applications are digitized or located online.[46] Consequently, operators must initiate contact with each organization to acquire its respective documentation or permit applications. In a previous research study, operators have described the experience of spending hours making phone calls, often being re-directed from one department, agency, or individual to the next, owing to the system-wide confusion that permeates each organization's siloed activities.[47] Transport Canada endeavoured to solve this problem by attaching a three-page list of contact information as an appendix item within its Guidelines.[48] The contact information for the various local representatives are notably absent from this list, however, suggesting that operators must still conduct detective work to identify all applicable authorities.

Variances between community and Indigenous organization requirements contribute to uncertainties in the passenger vessel permitting process. In Nunavut, RIOs utilize the standardized NPC application template, however the RIO's respective Community Lands and Resources Committees have established different translation requirements for various sections of the application.[49] Consequently, operators must translate different portions of the NPC application into Inuktitut to satisfy each RIO's requirements.[50] The RIOs application processing timelines and service delivery standards also vary considerably. For example, the Qikiqtani Inuit Association often processes an application within two to four weeks, while the Kivalliq Inuit Association's processing time averages five to six months.[51]

Redundancies are interwoven throughout the permitting process and undue administrative burdens flourish in the absence of interagency coordination.

---

46   Environment Yukon, "Welcome to Environmental eLicensing," Government of Yukon, accessed 1 December 2021, https://env.eservices.gov.yk.ca/pub/Signin.aspx; Department of Economic Development and Transportation, "Documents – Tourism," Government of Nunavut, accessed 27 December 2021, https://gov.nu.ca/edt/documents-tourism; "Nunavut Planning Commission," accessed 1 September 2022, https://www.nunavut.ca/.

47   Dawson *et al.* (n 10), p. 75.

48   Transport Canada 2017 (n 18), pp. 40–42.

49   Id., 7.

50   Id.

51   Id.

For example, vessel operators need to submit an itinerary and applicable vessel information to Transport Canada's Safety and Security Branch a minimum of 12 to 18 months prior to their intended voyage departure.[52] Transport Canada does not share this information with any of its federal counterparts. Instead, the vessel operator must re-submit the same information to almost a dozen different departments on staggered occasions throughout the permitting process, including the CCG, CBSA, GAC, CAF, PHAC, ECCC, and RCMP.[53] Aside from the federal authorities, operators must also re-submit their itineraries to various territorial departments and community organizations.[54]

Canada's Arctic passenger vessel governance is further afflicted by intra-agency coordination failures. Some federal departments do not share vessel or voyage information between their own branches. For example, rather than submit an itinerary to a single point of contact within the RCMP, the vessel operator must contact each territorial RCMP detachment to discuss their voyage. This suggests the department duplicates its own efforts by obliging vessel operators to answer to the same lines of inquiry over and over again.[55]

Unnecessary administrative burdens emerge between governments owing to an overlap of jurisdictional responsibilities. For example, DFO regulates Canada's fish stocks through fishing regulations and licenses, while various territorial departments manage non-residential fishing activities via sport fishing and angling permits.[56] Regulatory requirements for the export of game and wildlife also transcend jurisdictions, resulting in redundant requirements. A federal CITES permit is required for all parts of endangered or threated species taken out of Canada (e.g., polar bears and narwhale); however, additional territorial certification and Wildlife Export Permits, as well as federal Marine Mammal Transportation Licenses, may be required to remove wildlife products from territorial jurisdiction.[57] Multijurisdictional firearms permit requirements are also repetitive. Vessel operators must register any firearms carried on board with the RCMP.[58] However, operators must also obtain a National Park Firearm Permit from Parks Canada, as well as Park Firearms

---

52   Id., 1.
53   Id., 1–6, 35, 44.
54   Id., 6, 16, 30, 42, 45, 47.
55   Id., 3, 33.
56   Id., 36, 49–50.
57   Id., 49; "Wildlife Export" (n 28), pp. 1–2.
58   Arctic tour guides and vessel operators frequently carry firearms for protection in the event of a polar bear encounter. See "Polar Bear," Guidelines, Association of Arctic Expedition Cruise Operators, accessed 26 December 2021, https://www.aeco.no/guidelines/polarbear/.

Permits from the territorial governments.[59] To be clear, the co-administration of the marine environment, wildlife and firearm safety is not in itself redundant. However, the absence of integrated service delivery options for federal and territorial permit applications represents an avoidable administration burden, because the requirements for each jurisdiction's fishing, wildlife export and firearms permits are likely similar. Harmonized permit requirements and enhanced information sharing between governments would help to reduce unnecessary transaction costs to vessel operators.

4.2   *Evaluating the Service Results*

A jurisdictional scan was conducted to contextualize the administrative burden placed on Canadian polar cruise operators, relative to the more streamlined permitting of Russia and Svalbard (Norway). However, some caution is due before comparisons are made between cruise tourism permitting systems owing to fundamental differences between each nation's systems of government and Indigenous-state relations. Norway is a unitary state. The Norwegian Archipelago of Svalbard has a uniquely centralized administrative system, and its single incorporated community, Longyearbyen, has limited local authority.[60] Moreover, Svalbard is not home to any Indigenous communities.[61] Alternatively, Russia is a constitutional federation of semi-autonomous republics, yet it broadly functions as a unitary state.[62] Russia's twenty-six northern Indigenous communities are largely excluded from economic development planning, and the Northern Sea Route Administration (NSRA) does not consider the cultural impacts of passenger vessel operations on Russia's northern Indigenous populations.[63] Bearing in mind that Canada's power-sharing arrangements

---

59   Transport Canada 2017 (n 18), pp. 43–45.

60   Svalbard's administrative system is in accordance with the Svalbard Treaty. Treaty between Norway, The United States of America, Denmark, France, Italy, Japan, the Netherlands, Great Britain and Ireland and the British overseas Dominions and Sweden concerning the Archipelago of Spitsbergen (Svalbard Treaty), 9 February 1920, in force 14 August 1925, 2 *LNTS* 8–19.

61   Kathrine Nitter, "Svalbard's Arctic Heritage is Threatened by Climate Change," Norwegian University of Science and Technology, 3 February 2022, https://phys.org/news /2022-02-svalbard-arctic-heritage-threatened-climate.html.

62   Martin Russel, *Russia's Constitutional Structure: Federal in Form, Unitary in Function*, European Parliamentary Research Service, Report no. 569035 (Brussels: EPRS, 20 October 2015), https://policycommons.net/artifacts/1335821/russias-constitutional-structure/1942565/.

63   In 2013, Russia established the Northern Sea Route Administration (NSRA) as a federal institution to organize navigation in the water area of the Northern Sea Route. Since its establishment, the NSRA has been tasked with improving national service delivery (including streamlining permit requirements) and ensuring Russia's maritime governance is harmonized with international law. See Albert Buixadé Farré *et al.*, "Commercial

with northern Aboriginal communities are unique to Canada, and federalist regimes increase the complexities of implementing single-window service delivery, there are significant limitations when comparing permit systems. While Canada's requirements will inevitably be more cumbersome, this should not dissuade efforts to streamline a system that is brimming with gross inefficiencies.

A comparison of each jurisdiction's stated permit process time benchmarks, service delivery interfaces, and application requirements can be found in Table 14.1. As previously indicated, Transport Canada advises vessel operators to initiate pre-authorization requirements 18 to 24 months (or 78 to 104 weeks) in advance of their planned departure. In comparison, Svalbard (Norway) completes the cruise operator permit process within eight weeks.[64] Alternatively, Russia's NSRA is mandated to issue a permit decision within 12 working days from the date an application is received, although an analysis of the NSRA's performance for the 2019 shipping season suggests the Administration often processes permit applications far quicker than their mandated service delivery standard.[65]

From an international competitiveness perspective, Canada's circumpolar cruise tourism requirements are costly and labour intensive. Canada's permit requirements vary considerably depending on the vessel and voyage itinerary, so it is difficult to estimate the average administrative burden placed on polar cruise tourism operators. However, in a previous research study, one operator lamented the need to submit over 3,000 emails and 603 documents to obtain all required pre-authorizations and permits for the 2016 cruise season.[66] Another operator reported the need to hire either a full-time employee for a six-month period or a part-time employee year-round to acquire all necessary permits within a given season.[67] While anecdotal, this suggests that it costs

---

Arctic Shipping through the Northeast Passage: Routes, Resources, Governance, Technology, and Infrastructure," *Polar Geography* 37:4 (2014): 308; Østreng *et al.* (n 3), p. 21.

64 "Notification of Travel Plans for Tour Operators in Svalbard," Sysselmesteren på Svalbard, accessed 13 November 2021, https://skjema.no/sysselmesteren/Turoperator.

65 Analysis of the 2019 shipping season data reveals that NSRA's average permit processing time, measured from the date the application was accepted for consideration to the date a permit decision was issued, was 0.6 days. See Russian Federation's Decree No. 1487 *Rules of Navigation in the Water Area of the Northern Sea Route* (passed 18 September 2020), http://www.nsra.ru/files/fileslist/137-en5894-2020-11-19_rules.pdf; 'Permissions for Navigation in the Water Area of the Northern Sea Route', Northern Sea Route Administration, accessed 20 December 2021, http://www.nsra.ru/en/rassmotrenie_zayavleniy/razresheniya.html?year=2019.

66 Dawson *et al.* (n 10), p. 74.

67 Id., 75.

TABLE 14.1   Comparison of Canada, Russia and Svalbard passenger vessel permitting

	Canada	Russia	Svalbard (Norway)
Processing time	78–104 weeks	< 2 weeks	8 weeks
Quantity of interface(s)	27 windows - minimum[a]	Single window[b]	Single window
Category of interface(s)	Phone and/or email Operators are also encouraged to physically visit remote communities to initiate consultations	Online	Online
Operator requirements	Submit 3000+ emails, 603 supporting documents (*single operator's experience*)[c]	Submit a 2-page application electronically; attach international safety certificates and, if applicable, a copy of the icebreaking service contract within the electronic application form	Submit a 2-page application and a tour operator notification form electronically; attach international safety certificates within the electronic application form

a Based on an analysis of the permit inventory included in Transport Canada's revised Guidelines (Appendix 11), a cruise operator must contact a minimum of 27 organizations to obtain all mandatory permits and approvals; this assumes that the voyage is based exclusively in Nunavut, only includes one community stop-over, and one National Park visit. Source: Transport Canada 2017 (n 18), pp. 40–50.

b While an application to transit the Northern Sea Route is submitted electronically to a single authority (the NSRA), vessel operators must negotiate icebreaking and pilotage agreements with a third party (generally the State Corporation 'Rosatom'). However, only select vessel classes are mandated to acquire icebreaking and pilotage services. Source: Russian Federation Decree No. 1487 *Rules of Navigation in the Water Area of the Northern Sea Route* (passed 18 September 2020), 2–4, 12–13, http://www.nsra.ru/files/fileslist/137-en5894-2020-11-19_rules.pdf.

c Dawson *et al.* (n 10), p. 74.

FIGURES COMPILED BY THE AUTHOR WITH DATA EXTRAPOLATED FROM OFFICIAL GUIDANCE DOCUMENTS AND VESSEL APPLICATIONS OF TRANSPORT CANADA, NORTHERN SEA ROUTE ADMINISTRATION, AND GOVERNOR OF SVALBARD

some cruise tourism firms roughly 960 hours of labour to navigate Canada's permit system annually, never mind the costs of the actual permit fees. In comparison, both Russia and Svalbard's permit systems are offered through an online single-window service delivery model. To conduct a polar cruise in Russia, operators submit a two-paged online application.[68] To visit Svalbard, operators submit a vessel questionnaire and travel notification electronically via an online application.[69]

4.3   *Evaluating the Consequences*

Canada's burdensome permit requirements likely curtail the potential economic, social and cultural benefits northern communities derive from cruise tourism. The literature suggests that the northern cruise tourism sector stagnated due (in part) to the significant transaction costs imposed by the permit system.[70] Regulatory impediments to the sector's development likely have broader economic development implications because tourism can act as an engine of economic development, contributing to most service-sector businesses, including food and beverage, hospitality, outdoor adventure, transportation services and retail. The revenues communities receive from cruise tourism also funds social development. For example, the Government of Nunavut estimated that operators spent a little over CDN\$677,000 in direct fees to access community services during the 2019 cruise season; a figure which excludes passenger spending and underestimates other economic benefits, such as the salaries of Inuit culturalists employed by cruise tourism companies.[71] Communities reinvest much of these revenues directly into their local economies, generating social benefits such as employment and skills development opportunities.[72] Beyond providing economic and social development opportunities, tourism contributes to the region's cultural economy by providing new markets for Indigenous performers, artists and guides to earn a livable wage from their traditional skill sets.[73] Consequently, cruise tourism

---

68   "Application for Admission and Enclosure to Application to Navigate in the Northern Sea Route Area," Northern Sea Route Administration, accessed 15 November 2021, http://www.nsra.ru/en/rassmotrenie_zayavleniy/zayavlenie/f83.html.

69   "Vessel Questionnaire," Notification, Insurance and Reporting Obligations, Governor of Svalbard, accessed 26 December 2021, https://www.sysselmesteren.no/en/forms/vessel-questionnaire; "Notification of Travel Plans" (n 64).

70   Lasserre and Têtu (n 8), p. 69; Dawson *et al.* (n 10), pp. 71–78.

71   Nunavut (n 33), p. 29.

72   "Communities Aim to Make Most of Cruise Ship Visits," *Nunavut News*, 15 July 2019, https://www.nunavutnews.com/nunavut-news/communities-aim-to-make-most-of-cruise-ship-visits/.

73   While estimates vary, according to a 2017 report commissioned by Indigenous and Northern Affairs Canada, 26 percent of the Inuit population aged 15 years and older are engaged in the production of visual arts and crafts, and a further 8 percent report deriving a part-time income from their art. Despite the high concentration of artists in remote northern

can support the preservation and promotion of Inuit culture by providing economic incentives for Indigenous youth to acquire traditional skills and cultural competencies. In sum, failure to reduce the transaction costs of the passenger vessel permit system may represent a lost opportunity to buttress the region's economic development, social welfare and cultural continuity.

Promoting increased vessel traffic in the Canadian Arctic is not without risks. Northern residents have raised a variety of concerns related to the potential negative impact of cruise vessels on the environment due to vessel pollution and garbage/sewage dumping, disruptions to wildlife and traditional Inuit hunting activities, and risks to public health and safety via passenger-introduced drugs, alcohol and infectious disease.[74] Nunavut residents have also voiced frustrations that cruise visits provide too few financial benefits to communities.[75] To wit, it is conceivable that some northern residents may appreciate Canada's existing permit system as an administrative barrier which limits the number of vessel operators and cruise-based tourists visiting their communities. However, this chapter posits that the complexity of the permit system may unintentionally increase the risks associated with passenger vessel operations.

Complex regulatory regimes increase the risk of regulatory non-compliance.[76] The complexity of existing passenger vessel permitting requirements may increase the risk of non-compliance when operators unintentionally fail to complete requirements—due to lack of awareness or comprehension of the requirements—or they intentionally choose not to owing to the costs of compliance.[77] The risk of non-compliance may be more acute in the Canadian Arctic owing to

communities, local artists often live below the poverty line, owing to the lack of opportunities to get their product to market. See Crown-Indigenous Relations and Northern Affairs Canada, "Impact of the Inuit Arts Economy," Government of Canada, last modified 12 July 2017, https://www.rcaanc-cirnac.gc.ca/eng/1499360279403/1534786167549; Lee Huskey, Ilmo Mäenpää, and Alexander Pelyasov, "Economic Systems," in *Arctic Human Development Report: Regional Processes and Global Linkages*, eds., Joan Nymand Larsen and Gail Fondahl (Copenhagen: Nordisk Ministerråd, 2014), 151–183, at 168, https://doi.org/10.6027/TN2014-567.

74   Emma Stewart *et al.* (n 10), pp. 95–106.

75   Jane George, "Canada's Arctic Communities Unprepared for Cruise Ship Visits: Researchers," *Nunatsiaq News*, 1 September 2011, https://nunatsiaq.com/stories/article/65674canadas_arctic_communities_unprepared_for_cruise_ship_visits/.

76   Organisation for Economic Co-operation and Development (OECD), *Reducing the Risk of Policy Failure: Challenges for Regulatory Compliance* (Paris: OECD, 2000), 11–17, https://www.oecd.org/gov/regulatory-policy/1910833.pdf.

77   Id., 12; Gary Becker, "Crime and Punishment: An Economic Approach," *Economic Analysis of the Law: Selected Readings*, ed., Donald A. Wittman (Oxford: Blackwell Publishing Ltd, 2008); Jon G Sutinen and K Kuperan, "A Socio-Economic Theory of Regulatory Compliance," *International Journal of Social Economics* 26:1/2/3 (1999): 174–193.

the region's constrained enforcement capabilities.[78] Intuitively, the impacts of non-compliance would likely be concentrated locally. For example, if operators modified their intended routing or voyage itinerary without prior authorization from local authorities, then there is increased risk of the vessel disrupting wild-life, traditional marine-based activities, or the safety of Inuit hunters. This is not to suggest that Canada's polar passenger vessel operators are flippant towards local requirements. On the contrary, operators have a strong incentive to respect local authorities to ensure communities remain receptive to their future business activities. However, as the region continues to become more accessible to new cruise tourism firms and operators, it will become increasingly important to pro-mote compliance with passenger vessel requirements by ensuring that permit-ting procedures are comprehensible and that guidance documents are accurate.

5   Options and Constraints

While it is evident that a multijurisdictional, intra- and interagency coordina-tion mechanism is required to harmonize requirements and streamline service delivery, the appropriate scope of the coordination mechanism is less obvious. Academics and politicians alike have suggested that the establishment of a temporary interagency working group is all that is needed to streamline the permitting process.[79] This suggestion ignores several criteria which ought to be factored into this public management problem, which includes the dynamic and complex external environment, the impending requirement to integrate information and communications technology (ICT) into national maritime service delivery, and the impetus for a re-allocation of responsibilities within the existing governance network. While the establishment of a temporary interagency working group may improve the symptoms of the problem (e.g., administrative redundancies), any improvements born from the working group's efforts would likely be short-lived, as a temporary coordination mea-sure will neglect to address the underlying systemic issues.

Canada's Arctic passenger vessel (co-)governance bodies require a permanent coordination mechanism because they operate within a complex external environment. The adoption of a broad variety of policy frameworks and initiatives that intersect with the cruise tourism sector have downstream governance implications. For example, recent additions to the national marine policy framework, through initiatives like the Oceans Protection Plan and the Northern Low-Impact Shipping Corridors Initiative, may have operational

---

78   OECD (n 76), pp. 11–17.
79   Dawson *et al.* (n 10), p. 78.

implications for passenger vessel operators (see Dawson, this volume, for a detailed overview of the Northern Low-Impact Shipping Corridors Initiative).[80] The Canadian government's collective efforts to advance reconciliation can also have downstream implications for polar passenger vessel operations. For example, Nunavut's devolution process will transition in legislative limbo for the foreseeable future, and there are multiple outstanding northern settlement agreements still in negotiation, such as the 2016 Agreement in Principle in northern Manitoba, which broadly applies to a seven million acre footprint that borders the Hudson Bay coastline and Nunavut land border.[81] In the absence of an overarching permanent framework to coordinate their activities, Canada's Arctic cruise tourism governance organizations will continue to react to the plethora of complex external forces within their respective silos.

Canada's Arctic passenger vessel (co-)governance bodies operate in an external environment that is as dynamic as it is complex. The highly globalized nature of the shipping industry contributes to much of this dynamism. The previous decades have been characterized by growing international efforts to harmonize the governance of national shipping operations to improve the efficiency of global trade and transport activities.[82] As a result, International Maritime Organization (IMO) conventions and continuous international shipping harmonization activities now drive many national marine regulatory regimes.[83] A brief glance at the Canadian Gazette reveals there have been several maritime regulatory overhauls and legislative amendments influenced by international conventions in recent years, including the safety and pollution prevention regulatory amendments following the implementation of the Polar

80   The Oceans Protection Plan initiative endeavours to conserve 30 percent of Canada's marine and coastal areas by 2030. Department of Fisheries and Oceans, "Canada's Oceans: Protecting and Conserving Marine and Coastal Areas," Government of Canada, accessed 18 November 2021, https://www.dfo-mpo.gc.ca/oceans/conservation/plan/MCT-OCM-eng.html.

81   Crown-Indigenous Relations and Northern Affairs, "Canada, Nunavut and Nunavut Tunngavik Inc. Reach a Significant Milestone towards Devolution in Nunavut with Signing of an Agreement-in-Principle," News Release, 15 August 2019, https://www.canada.ca/en/crown-indigenous-relations-northern-affairs/news/2019/08/canada-nunavut-and-nunavut-tunngavik-inc-reach-a-significant-milestone-towards-devolution-in-nunavut-with-signing-of-an-agreement-in-principle.html; Manitoba Indigenous Reconciliation and Northern Affairs, "Inuit South of 60° Settlement Efforts," presentation to Hudson's Bay Regional Roundtable, 30 March 2017, accessed 16 May 2022, https://estatedocbox.com/Buying_and_Selling_Homes/103680137-Inuit-south-of-60-settlement-efforts.html.

82   Michael Roe, "Shipping, Policy and Multi-Level Governance," *Maritime Economics & Logistics* 9:1 (2007): 84–87.

83   Michael Roe, "Multi-Level and Polycentric Governance: Effective Policymaking for Shipping," *Maritime Policy and Management* 36:1 (2009): 39–41.

Code.[84] Within such a dynamic external environment, interagency coordination should be conceptualized as an ongoing process, rather than a fixed state that can be achieved through temporary collaboration.

The dynamic and complex external environment underpins the challenge Transport Canada has encountered in developing accurate guidelines to assist vessel operators navigate the passenger vessel permit system. Transport Canada's revised Guidelines cautioned operators about the document's accuracy, warning that permit and permission requirements "can change frequently."[85] In fact, the Guidelines were out-of-date almost as soon as they were published, owing to an array of shifting stakeholder requirements. When the Guidelines were published in 2017, the Nunavut Land Use Plan had not yet been established, nor had the Qikiqtani Inuit Association's land use fee structure, nor had the Inuvialuit Regional Corporation's multiyear cruise ship management plan and community consultation requirements been published.[86] Presently, Parks Canada is overhauling the National Marine Conservation Areas (NMCA) policy framework.[87] Based on the public consultation documents, the pending NMCA reforms will likely intersect with Arctic passenger vessel operations through the establishment of a new NMCA maritime zoning framework, which includes new entrance requirements and fees.[88] In other words, a whole new slew of permits, fees, pre-authorizations and other requirements are already absent from Transport Canada's recently revised Guidelines. Without addressing the institutional factors which have shaped the existing permit system, Canada's Arctic passenger vessel governance system will be chronically plagued by redundancies and unharmonized requirements.

84   Transport Canada, "Canadian Marine Advisory Council (CMAC) Engagement Opportunity: Marine Safety and Security Regulations," Government of Canada, last modified 25 October 2021, https://tc.canada.ca/en/marine/canadian-marine-advisory-council-cmac-engagement-opportunity-marine-safety-security-regulations.

85   Transport Canada 2017 (n 18), p. 5.

86   Id., 6; Eilís Quinn, "Inuit Association in Canada's Eastern Arctic to Levy Fees on Tourism Operators," *Eye on the Arctic*, 15 October 2019, https://www.rcinet.ca/eye-on-the-arctic/2019/10/15/inuit-association-canada-arctic-to-levy-fees-on-tourism-operators-nunavut-cruises/; Inuvialuit Regional Corporation (IRC), *Inuvialuit Settlement Region Cruise Ship Management Plan 2022–2025* (IRC, 2022), https://irc.inuvialuit.com/sites/default/files/ISR_Cruise_Ship_Management_Plan.pdf.

87   Parks Canada, "Protecting Canada's Marine Heritage: Proposed Policy and Regulations for Canada's National Marine Conservation Areas – Discussion Paper, May 2019," Government of Canada, last modified 25 August 2020, https://www.pc.gc.ca/amnc-nmca/~/~/link.aspx?_id=3A4F49BAFA6B4D8B90CEFABDE86AB48C&_z=z.

88   Id.

The rapid pace of technological advancements in the global shipping indus-try also supports the establishment of a permanent (interagency) coordination mechanism. Over the previous decades, new technologies have revolutionized both global shipping operations, as well as the provision of national shipping services. Many jurisdictions have already incorporated ICT into national marine sector service delivery, facilitating the implementation of single-window ser-vices.[89] For example, the Swedish Maritime Administration embedded ICT to establish an electronic single-window system for the provision of all national shipping services, including icebreaking, hydrographic surveying, pilotage, navigational aids, search and rescue, maritime training and ship inspections.[90]

The body of scholarship pertaining to 'best practices' for interagency ICT implementation is unanimous; organizations require standardized technol-ogy infrastructure, data requirements, processes and information channels before they can effectively adopt ICT.[91] However, Canada's Arctic passenger vessel governance embodies several of the major organizational impediments to successful ICT adoption, including structural fragmentation, poor commu-nication between functional departments and meagre relationships between key internal stakeholders.[92] Consequently, if we accept the common wisdom that large organizational networks require a high degree of continuous coor-dination to competently respond within complex external environments, and that a high degree of interagency alignment must occur before Canada's Arctic passenger vessel governance system is capable of integrating ICT into its service delivery, then the establishment of a permanent coordination mechanism becomes a necessary stepping stone before Canada can establish a single-window permit system for polar passenger vessel operations.

---

89   Mikael Lind, "Do Maritime Authorities Have a Role in Digitalization of Shipping?," *Trans. Info*, 14 April 2021, https://trans.info/de/do-maritime-authorities-have-a-role-in-digitali zation-of-shipping-231825.

90   Id.

91   United Nations, Economic and Social Commission for Asia and the Pacific (ESCAP), *Guide-lines on Establishing and Strengthening National Coordination Mechanisms for Trade and Transport Facilitation in the ESCAP Region* (Bangkok: UN ESCAP, 2012), 24–25, https:// www.unescap.org/sites/default/files/0%20-%20Full%20Report_12.pdf; Leslie Alexander Pal, *Beyond Policy Analysis: Public Issue Management in Turbulent Times* (Toronto: Nelson Education, 2014), 165, 251; S. Sharma and J. Gupta, "Transforming to E-Government: A Framework," paper presented at 2nd European Conference on e-Government, Public Sector Times (2002), 383–390.

92   G. Aichholzer and R. Schmutzer, "Organizational Challenges to the Development of Electronic Government," *Proceedings 11th International Workshop on Database and Expert Systems Applications* (London: IEEE Computer Society, 2000), 379–383.

Finally, a permanent coordination mechanism is better suited to address the fact that there are simply too many organizations which share too few management responsibilities within Canada's Arctic passenger vessel governance system. To address the issue, there will likely need to be a re-delegation of tasks between organizations over certain processes. For example, rather than compel cruise companies through the rigmarole of re-submitting their itineraries to numerous departments, a single authority could be charged with receiving this information and distributing it internally, further placing the onus on the respective (co-)governance bodies to contact the operators, should they require additional information. The presence of strong political will, as manifested by instituting a legal basis for a permanent coordination mechanism, would help to facilitate the system wide re-organization of tasks needed for streamlined service delivery.[93]

6   Recommendation

Following on the above discussion, it is recommended that a federal 'Arctic Passenger Vessel Coordination Entity' be established within the Department of Transport portfolio. The specific organizational form or structure for this proposed ASD agency is outside the scope of this research, and would require further study. However, its purpose would be to serve as a client-centric umbrella organization, which could better coordinate the delivery of Arctic passenger vessel services between departments and across governments. To be clear, it is not recommended that this entity replace the existing regulatory authorities within the existing governance structure. Rather, that it be responsible for supplementing the client service delivery functions that have been chronically neglected under the existing Arctic passenger vessel governance framework.

The mandate for the Arctic Passenger Vessel Coordination Entity would be to promote an efficient, sustainable and safe Arctic cruise vessel tourism sector in support of Indigenous culture and local economies. The institution's responsibilities would include the integration and ongoing harmonization of policies, permit procedures and administrative requirements. Furthermore, this entity could be responsible for the development of accurate information instruments (i.e., vessel operator guidelines) by virtue of its service functions. The service functions would include acting as an internal information and communication channel, whereby all policy, regulatory and service delivery changes within the Arctic passenger vessel governance network would be funnelled. Other internal information channel functions could include coordinating with

---

93   UN ESCAP (n 91), pp. 20–22.

stakeholders to capture and monitor traffic vessel data, which would allow for enhanced evidence-based Arctic passenger vessel policy development.[94] The entity could also provide a client service delivery function by assisting operators navigate the permitting requirements, at least as an interim measure until the Arctic passenger vessel co-governance bodies are adequately synchronised to integrate ICT into the entity's service delivery.

Most importantly, this new entity could foster collaborative partnerships to build capacity across the spectrum of stakeholders—including federal, territorial and local government departments, Inuit and community organizations, regulatory boards and private operators—to strengthen the economic and cultural management dimensions of Canada's Arctic passenger vessel governance system. For example, this entity could improve cultural management functions by partnering with local stakeholders and offering a platform for Inuit to host cultural awareness training seminars for vessel operators. These seminars could replace Transport Canada's current cultural management practice, which is the distribution of a single-page document to inform vessel operators of respectful cultural behaviour when visiting Nunavut.[95] By providing a tangible platform for stakeholder collaboration, this entity could help foster relationships between cruise operators and communities, which would create a more sustainable relation-building framework than the current ad hoc practice.[96] In short, an Arctic Passenger Vessel Coordination Entity

---

94   Cruise tourism data in the Canadian Arctic is collected independently by Parks Canada (park entrance counts), the Canadian Coast Guard (NORDREG traffic monitoring), and the territorial governments. No organization amalgamates or distributes this information into a useful public data set that would benefit all stakeholders. Instead, data remains within organizational silos. See "Revised Passenger Numbers for the Canadian Arctic," Of Penguins and Polar Bears, last modified 29 May 2020, https://ofpenguinsandpolarbears .ca/revised-passenger-numbers-canadian-arctic/.

95   Transport Canada 2017 (n 18), p. 15.

96   Some passenger vessel (co-)governance bodies are attempting to bridge the coordination gap between government, industry and communities. In 2019, the Government of Nunavut signed two memorandums of understanding with AECO and the Indigenous Tourism Association of Canada (ITAC) to enhance public-private sector cooperation to grow cruise ship tourism in the territory. While such cross-sectoral coordination efforts are encouraging, the strategic development capacity of territorial, Indigenous and community governments are often limited by significant human and financial resource constraints. For example, Nunavut's Economic Development Minister, David Akeeagok, was unable to respond to inquiries at Nunavut's legislature on how his department was preparing for the return of the 2021/2022 cruise season, because the division responsible for cruise ships was not "fully staffed." This circumstance is not an outlier; Nunavut's annual Public Service Report (2021/22) reported a 30 percent vacancy rate across Nunavut's public service. To wit, it appears unlikely that Canada's Arctic passenger vessel governance coordination gaps can be adequately addressed without the participation and resource capacity

would serve as an all-encompassing liaison agency, which would promote capacity-building for all Arctic passenger vessel stakeholders.

A likely criticism against the establishment of a new coordination institution is that the current volume of passenger vessel traffic in the Canadian Arctic does not warrant the costs of creating a new agency. However, Canada has a long tradition of establishing transport ASD mechanisms as policy instruments for nation-building.[97] The department's portfolio includes several ASD organizations, including the Canadian Port Authorities and the St. Lawrence Seaway Management Corporation.[98] The prevailing theory behind the establishment of these ASD agencies was to create more flexible and responsive organizational models, outside the traditional department structure, which could better cater to the needs of cross-sectoral and multi-jurisdictional users— including shipping interests, marine agencies, and provincial and federal jurisdictions—to serve as enhanced instruments for economic and regional development.[99] Furthermore, the exorbitant inefficiencies produced by the existing governance model are not without cost. Recall that one operator reportedly submitted over 3,000 emails and 603 documents to obtain all permit requirements in 2016, and that many of these information exchanges were redundant. Multiply the enormous bureaucratic effort on the receiving end of those submissions by roughly 21 annual voyages, and it raises serious doubts whether the substantial human and financial resources expended through the current governance system are more cost-effective than the establishment of a small coordination agency.

The final argument in favour of establishing a new ASD mechanism to address Canada's Arctic cruise shipping governance problem, is that such an entity could

of the federal government. See Courtney Edgar, "Nunavut Government Strikes New Tourism Partnerships," *Arctic Today* 22 April 2019, https://www.arctictoday.com/nun avut-government-strikes-new-tourism-partnerships/; Jane George, "Pond Inlet MLA Asks How Community Can Seek Benefits From Cruise Ship Traffic," CBC, 14 June 2022, https://www.cbc.ca/news/canada/north/cruis-ship-traffic-pond-inlet-nunavut-tourism -1.6487168; Government of Nunavut, *Public Service Annual Report 2021–2021* (Department of Human Resources, 2021), 10–11, https://www.gov.nu.ca/human-resources/documents /2020-21-public-service-annual-report.

97   Eric Mintz, Livianna Tossutti and Christopher Dunn, *Canada's Politics: Democracy, Diversity and Good Governance* (Toronto: Pearson, 2014), 486–490.

98   Transport Canada, "The Transport Canada Portfolio," Government of Canada, last modified 21 June 2019, https://tc.canada.ca/en/corporate-services/transport-canada-portfolio; Gregory J. Inwood, *Understanding Canadian Public Administration: An Introduction to Theory and Practice* (Toronto: Pearson, 2012), 140–141.

99   Transport Canada, "Canadian Port Authorities," Government of Canada, last modified 7 October 2020, https://tc.canada.ca/en/corporate-services/policies/canadian-port-author ities; "SLSMC Management," St. Lawrence Seaway Management Corporation, accessed 21 April 2022, https://greatlakes-seaway.com/en/about-us/slsmc-management/.

be designed through any number of innovative organizational arrangements to mitigate the political risks associated with its establishment. For example, there is a risk that the public would object to the cost of establishing the organization. However, the organization's instituting legislation could allow for delegated financial authority, such as the capacity to charge service fees to recoup some of the costs of its operations. Alternatively, if designed as an intergovernmental agency, the institution's operating budget could be supplemented through a cost-sharing initiative between federal, territorial and Indigenous governments.

There is also a risk that internal stakeholders, including the northern land claim and Inuit (co-)governance bodies, would not be amenable to the establishment of a centralized federal entity that meddles with their affairs. However, the Arctic Passenger Vessel Coordination Entity (as envisioned in this chapter) would not replace the legitimate resource management and environmental stewardship mandates of the northern land claim administrations, corporations, RIOs, or regulatory boards. Instead, it would serve as a beneficial resource for these entities by sharing information to support their functional management capacities and promoting awareness amongst industry of regional/local requirements. Moreover, the Arctic Passenger Vessel Coordination Entity could be designed to facilitate reconciliation through the inclusion of legislative provisions that included Inuit representatives within its governance structure. Arguably, designing the Entity's governance structure to include representatives from each jurisdiction may help to mitigate potential resistance from internal stakeholders and foster future cooperation between the various departments and authorities.

From the federal perspective, there may be an open policy window to support an enhanced role for Inuit over the management Arctic shipping operations. Per Article 10 of the Tallurutiup Imanga NMCA Inuit Impact and Benefit Agreement (IIBA), Transport Canada has a mandate to "develop a Joint Arctic Maritime Management initiative in partnership with Inuit and other partners across Inuit Nunangat, including relevant federal departments, territorial governments and Inuit organizations to explore management of marine navigation matters within the Arctic" and to enhance communication with northern communities on marine vessel movements and navigation more broadly.[100] While Article 10 of the IIBA is only applicable within the Tallurutiup Imanga NMCA, it would be logically consistent for the federal government to

---

100   In 2017, the Governments of Canada and Nunavut and the Qikiqtani Inuit Association (QIA) entered negotiations for an Inuit Impact and Benefit Agreement (IIBA) to support the establishment of the new Tallurutiup Imanga National Marine Conservation Area (NMCA) as is required by the Nunavut Land Claims Agreement. The IIBA was signed by all parties in August 2019. Article 10 of the IIBA deals with marine navigation. See Parks Canada, "Tallurutiup Imanga National Marine Conservation Area Inuit Impact and Benefit Agreement, Article 10: Marine Navigation," Government of Canada, last modified 10 January

extend the principles of this agreement to other Inuit partners, should those partners wish to participate in a similar arrangement.

7   Conclusion

Climate change is placing growing demands on Arctic States to command effective governance over polar shipping operations. Despite this, Canada's Arctic passenger vessel governance framework suffers from systemic coordination failures. An evaluation of the permit system reveals an unduly complex, inefficient and costly abomination of administrative burden. Failure to streamline permitting requirements and improve client service delivery functions will limit the economic viability of the Arctic cruise tourism industry, increase the risk of non-compliance with permitting requirements, and squander the nation's opportunity to support northern communities in their economic, social and cultural development.

It is recommended that an Arctic Passenger Vessel Coordination Entity be established under Transport Canada's portfolio. The establishment of a permanent intra- and interagency multi-jurisdictional coordination mechanism is a necessary instrument to address the unique features of the Canada's Arctic passenger vessel governance system, including its monumental quantity of multijurisdictional co-governance bodies, diverse array of interrelated regulatory functions, dynamic and complex external operating environment, and an impending requirement to incorporate ICT into national maritime service delivery. The Arctic Passenger Vessel Coordination Entity would promote horizontal integration of services between departments and, by virtue of its policy and service functions, and foster a vertical integration of services across governments. As a client-centric umbrella agency, an Arctic Passenger Vessel Coordination Entity would build on the capacity of government, community and industry stakeholders, improve the coordinated management of cruise tourism in the Canadian Arctic, and promote the economic and social development of a region that is long overdue for nation-building.

2020, https://www.pc.gc.ca/en/amnc-nmca/cnamnc-cnnmca/tallurutiup-imanga/entente -agreement#article-10.

CHAPTER 15

Governing Canadian Arctic Shipping through Low-impact Shipping Corridors

Jackie Dawson and Gloria Song

Abstract

The concept of low-impact shipping corridors was developed by the Government of Canada in the early 2000s to support core maritime shipping routes throughout Arctic Canada, where marine traffic can be encouraged to travel and where infrastructure and service investments can be prioritized. Given the region's vast geographic scope, historically minimal amount of shipping activity, and relative remoteness, a targeted approach to investing in navigational supports and services through the corridors approach, versus the use of formal routing measures, was identified as ideal. Low-impact shipping corridors have garnered substantial traction over the past decade and are regularly viewed as a promising governing framework that can adaptively support growing Arctic shipping. Although the concept is relatively new and additional considerations are still needed as climate change and reductions in sea ice continue to facilitate increases in Arctic shipping activities across Canada, the corridors framework is well positioned to underpin effective governance and management measures for shipping sector growth. In this chapter, we discuss how shipping activities have evolved both temporally and spatially in Arctic Canada, outline how the corridors were established, including through identification and consideration of culturally significant marine areas, identify strengths and weaknesses of the corridors concept, and provide a critical discussion of how low-impact shipping corridors support self-determined and sustainable oceans governance.

Keywords

Arctic – shipping corridors – co-governance – Inuit knowledge – Indigenous knowledge – climate change

1   Introduction

Indigenous peoples, including Inuit whose rights and culture are legally
enshrined in the region through several settled land claim agreements collectively encompassing Inuit Nunangat (i.e., Inuit homeland in Arctic Canada)
(Figure 15.1), have for centuries utilized Canadian Arctic waters in support
of subsistence and trade. Early European settlers later used these waterways
to engage in whaling activities and have for years aspired to engage in formal international maritime trade via the Arctic. The most famous of these
aspirations involved the race to discover the Northwest Passage, a route
connecting the Atlantic and Pacific oceans through Arctic Canada.[1] During
what is often referred to as the heroic age of Arctic exploration, the ill-fated
Franklin expedition failed in its attempt to discover and traverse the complete
Northwest Passage, leaving behind a collection of mysteries, cultural heritage,
and folklore of a time now long past.

What is not long past since these historic days of exploration, however, is
the continued and unrelenting global desire to exploit the Northwest Passage
in support of trade, tourism, transportation, and other prosperous economic
activities.[2] Until relatively recently, the reality of regular shipping through the
Northwest Passage, and throughout Arctic Canada in general, was commonly

---

1   Larissa Pizzolato *et al.*, *Climate Change Adaptation Assessment for Transportation in Arctic
    Waters* (CATAW) *Scoping Study: Summary Report*, Report prepared for Transport Canada
    (Ottawa: Transport Canada, 2013), 3, https://www.arcticcorridors.ca/?acr_download=%2Fwp
    -content%2Fuploads%2F2018%2F09%2FCATAW_Transport_Canada_DAWSON
    .pdf&v=1644502523620.
2   Id.; Stephen E.L. Howell *et al.*, "Recent Changes in the Exchange of Sea Ice between the
    Arctic Ocean and the Canadian Arctic Archipelago," *Journal of Geophysical Research: Oceans*
    118 (2013): 1– 13, doi: 10.1002/jgrc.20265; Stephen E.L. Howell and Mike Brady, "The dynamic
    Response of Sea Ice to Warming in the Canadian Arctic Archipelago," *Geophysical Research
    Letters* 46:22 (2019): 13119–13125, https://doi.org/10.1029/2019GL085116; Luke Copland, Jackie
    Dawson and Alison Cook, *Impacts of Climate Change on Navigational Choke Points for Ships
    Operating in the Canadian Arctic*, Report prepared for Transport Canada (Ottawa: University
    of Ottawa, 2021), 51; Stephen E.L. Howell and J.J. Yackel, "A Vessel Transit Assessment of Sea
    Ice Variability in the Western Arctic, 1969–2002: Implications for Ship Navigation," *Cana-
    dian Journal of Remote Sensing* 30:2 (2004): 205–215; Po-Hsing Tseng and Kevin Cullinane,
    "Key Criteria Influencing the Choice of Arctic Shipping: A Fuzzy Analytic Hierarchy Process
    Model," *Maritime Policy and Management* 54:4 (2018): 422–438; Jackie Dawson, Luke Cop-
    land, Alison Cook, Jean Holloway, and Will Kochtitzky, *Analysis of Ice Navigational Risks by
    Level of Ice Strengthening among Vessels in the Canadian Arctic* (1990–2019), Report prepared
    for Transport Canada (Ottawa: University of Ottawa, 2021), https://www.arcticcorridors
    .ca/?acr_download=%2Fwp-content%2Fuploads%2F2021%2F10%2FTC-Risk-Threshold
    -Draft-Report_Final_Mar31_2021.pdf&v=1644672569519.

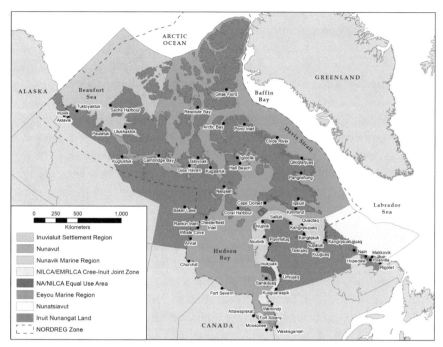

FIGURE 15.1   Map of marine regions in Arctic Canada. Legend: EMRLCA–EEYOU Marine
Region Land Claims Agreement; NA- Nunavut Agreement; NILCA–Nunavik
Inuit Land Claims Agreement
COURTESY OF ENVIRONMENT, SOCIETY & POLICY GROUP, UNIVERSITY
OF OTTAWA

considered ill-advised and in large part was outright dangerous, considering
the presence of extensive and thick multiyear sea ice that limited reliable passage even among ice-strengthened vessels. However, in more recent years, a
changing climate combined with technological innovations in ship design
have interfaced with this continued global fascination for Arctic trade, leading to a relatively rapid increase in shipping activity throughout Arctic Canada and along the Northwest Passage. With this evolution comes an urgent
need for effective governance in support of sector development and regional
sustainability. The low-impact shipping corridors represents a framework
that, if established and implemented effectively, could provide this important
foundation for safe and sustainable shipping and reconciliation, considering
the federal government's commitment to ensuring a distinction-based and
self-determined approach to governance in Canada's Arctic.[3] This chapter will

---

3   "Inuit Nunangat Policy," Government of Canada, last modified 21 April 2022, https://www
.rcaanc-cirnac.gc.ca/eng/1650556354784/1650556491509.

explore the low-impact shipping corridors as part of the governing framework for a self-determined and sustainable Canadian Arctic.

2   The Evolution of Shipping Activities in Canadian Arctic Waters

Many different types of marine vessels operate in the Canadian Arctic, each with distinct characteristics and cargo (Table 15.1). Over the past ten years, there has been a 150 percent increase in the number of unique ships in Arctic Canada—meaning there are an increasing number of 'new entrants' who lack localized expertise on the unique navigational challenges in the region.[4] There has also been 300 percent increase in total voyages undertaken in the region, with the largest proportion of voyage increases attributed to cargo ships (community re-supply and servicing of mines), government vessels (military, search and rescue, and research), fishing vessels (small-scale commercial and non-commercial) and pleasure craft (commercial and personal yachts) (Figure 15.2 – left panel).[5] In addition to the observed increases in the total number of unique vessels and the total number of voyages undertaken by these vessels, each of these vessels are now, on average, traveling further per voyage in terms of total kilometres traveled, than ever witnessed before. For example, the total number of kilometres travelled by all ships in Artic Canada has increased by over 75 percent in the past six years alone. These observations are underpinned by the fact that the characteristic season length of a shipping season in Arctic Canada has been increasing beyond the typical months of July, August and September, to include months earlier in the fall and later in the spring. This season length extension is largely attributable to climate change, although other broad factors such as globalization, commodity prices, demographics, and societal trends are certainly also at play.[6]

---

4   Pizzolato *et al.* 2013 (n 1), p. 15; Copland *et al.* 2021 (n 2), p. 49; Jackie Dawson, Louie Porta, Seyi Okuribido-Malcolm, M. deHann and Olivia Mussels, *Proceedings of the Northern Marine Transportation Corridors Workshop, December 8, 2015, Vancouver* (Ottawa: University of Ottawa, 2016), 1, https://www.arcticcorridors.ca/?acr_download=%2Fwp-content%2Fuploads %2F2021%2F01%2FNMTC_Workshop_Proceedings.pdf&v=1644502523620; Larissa Pizzolato, Stephen E.L. Howell, Jackie Dawson, Frédéric Laliberté and Luke Copland, "The Influence of Declining Sea Ice on Shipping Activity in the Canadian Arctic," *Geophysical Research Letters* 43:23 (2016): 12146–12154, https://doi.org/10.1002/2016GL071489.

5   Dawson *et al.* 2021 (n 2).

6   Terry D. Prowse *et al.*, "Implications of Climate Change for Economic Development in Northern Canada: Energy, Resource, and Transportation Sectors," *AMBIO* 38:5 (2009): 272–281; Council of Canadian Academies, *Commercial Marine Shipping Accidents: Understanding the Risks in Canada, Workshop Report* (Ottawa: Council of Canadian Academies, 2016), https: //cca-reports.ca/wp-content/uploads/2018/10/cca_marine_shipping_risks_en_fullreport.

TABLE 15.1   Main vessel types (AMSA class) found in the NORDREG zone

Classification	Description	Examples
Government vessels and icebreakers	– Designed to move and navigate in ice-covered waters – Must have a strengthened hull, an ice-clearing shape, and the power to push through ice	– Icebreakers (private, research, government) – Research vessels
Container ships	– Cargo ships that carry their load in truck-size containers	– Cargo transport
General cargo	– Carries various types and forms of cargo	– Community resupply – Roll on/roll off cargo
Bulk carriers	– Bulk carriage of materials	– Timber, oil, ore – Automobile carriers
Tanker ships	– Bulk carriage of liquids or compressed gas	– Oil, natural gas, chemical tankers
Passenger ships	– Ships that carry paying passengers	– Cruise ships – Ferries
Pleasure craft	– Recreational vessels that do not carry passengers for remuneration	– Motor yachts – Sail boats – Row boats
Tug / Barge	– Tug: designed for towing or pushing – Barge: non-propelled vessel for carriage of bulk or mixed cargo	– Used for resupply – Bulk cargo transport
Fishing vessels	– Used in commercial fishing activity	– Small fishing boats – Trawlers – Fish processing boats
Oil and gas exploration vessels	– Designed for the exploration and extraction of natural gas and oil	– Seismic, hydrographic, oceanic survey vessels – Offshore resupply – Portable oil platform

SOURCE: AFTER ARCTIC COUNCIL, *ARCTIC MARINE SHIPPING ASSESSMENT* (2009) [AMSA], HTTPS://WWW.PAME.IS/PROJECTS/ARCTIC-MARINE-SHIPPING/AMSA; DAWSON *ET AL.* 2016 (N 4)

pdf; Jackie Dawson *et al.*, *Climate Change Adaptation Strategies and Policy Options for Arctic Shipping*, Report prepared for Transport Canada (Ottawa, 2017).

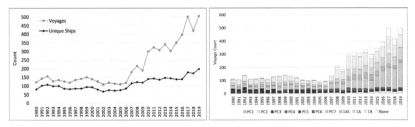

FIGURE 15.2   Total annual voyage counts and unique ship counts in the Canadian
            Arctic between 1990 and 2019 (left). Total number of ship voyages for
            vessels with different levels of ice strengthening (i.e., by ice class (PC)).
            PC1 ships are highly strengthened, PC7 have medium strengthening, and
            1B have little strengthening (right)
            COURTESY OF ENVIRONMENT, SOCIETY & POLICY GROUP,
            UNIVERSITY OF OTTAWA

The Canadian Arctic is warming at three times the rate of the global average,[7] and between 1979 and 2010, sea ice declined by 1.3 percent per decade,[8] resulting in massive losses of thick multiyear ice and corresponding increases of thin, first year ice with significant variability from year-to-year.[9] Recent trends in sea ice show substantial reductions in the central Arctic and Canadian Arctic Archipelago, including the Northwest Passage,[10] with expectations that

7   Mark C. Serreze and Julienne Stroeve, "Arctic Sea Ice Trends, Variability and Implications for
     Seasonal Ice Forecasting," *Philosophical Transactions of the Royal Society A* 373 (2015), https://
     doi.org/10.1098/rsta.2014.0159; R. Kwok, "Arctic Sea Ice Thickness, Volume, and Multiyear Ice
     Coverage: Losses and Coupled Variability (1958–2018)," *Environmental Research Letters* 13
     (2018), doi: 10.1088/1748-9326/aae3ec; Emma J. Stewart, Stephen E. L. Howell, Dianne Draper,
     John J. Yackel and Adrienne Tivy, "Sea Ice in Canada's Arctic: Implications for Cruise Tourism,"
     Arctic 60:4 (2007): 370–380; Tessa Sou and Gregory Flato, "Sea Ice in the Canadian Arctic
     Archipelago: Modeling the Past (1950–2004) and the Future (2041–60)," *Journal of Climate*
     22:8 (2009): 2181–2198, doi: 10.1175/2008JCLI2335.1; Stephen E.L. Howell, A. Tivy, J.J. Yackel and
     R.K. Scharien, "Application of a SeaWinds/ QuikSCAT Sea Ice Melt Algorithm for Assessing
     Melt Dynamics in the Canadian Arctic Archipelago," *Journal of Geophysical Research: Oceans*
     111:C07025 (2006): doi:10.1029/2005JC003193; Emmanuel Guy, "Evaluating the Viability of
     Commercial Shipping in the Northwest Passage," *Journal of Ocean Technology* 1:1 (2006): 9–18;
     Adrienne Tivy *et al.*, "Trends and Variability in Summer Sea Ice Cover in the Canadian Arctic
     Based on the Canadian Ice Service Digital Archive," *Journal of Geophysical Research: Oceans*
     116:C3(2011), doi:10.1029/2011JC007248; Josefino C. Comiso, "Large Decadal Decline of Arctic
     Multiyear Ice Cover," *Journal of Climate* 25 (2012): 1176–1193, doi: 10.1175/JCLI-D-11-00113.1; D.J.
     Cavalieri and C.L. Parkinson, "Arctic Sea Ice Variability and Trends, 1979–2010," *The Cryo-
     sphere* 6 (2012): 881–889, https://doi.org/10.5194/tc-6-881-2012.
8   Cavalieri and Parkinson (n 7).
9   Id.; Howell *et al.* 2013 (n 2); Howell and Brady (n 2).
10   Pizzolato *et al.* 2016 (n 4); V.C. Khon, I.I. Mokhov, I. M. Latif, V.A. Semenov and W. Park,
     "Perspectives of Northern Sea Route and Northwest Passage in the Twenty-first Century,"

the Northwest Passage will be increasingly ice-free in the next few decades.[11] Warmer temperatures appear to be increasing sea ice mobility, as the removal of first year ice allows larger amounts of thick older (multiyear) ice from the north to migrate into the area.[12] Loose ice can move rapidly, pushed by high winds and storms, transforming an area that was previously navigable open water to a non-navigable area clogged with ice, all within hours.[13] This congestion of ice can result in choke points along typical shipping corridors. The impacts of these highly variable sea ice conditions from year-to-year, including increased ice mobility, present significant operational and navigational challenges, leaving marine vessels without ice strengthening particularly vulnerable.[14] Risks include ships colliding with ice causing damage, becoming stuck in the sea ice, or other issues related to a lack of experience in navigating hazardous ice conditions.[15] These risks to vessels are higher than in years past and may continue to increase as sea ice dynamics in the Arctic change under the warming

---

    Climatic Change 100:3–4 (2009): 757–768, doi:10.1007/s10584-009-9683-2; Adrienne Tivy *et al.* 2011 (n 7).

11   Sou and Flato (n 7); Scott R. Stephenson, Laurence C. Smith and John A. Agnew, "Divergent Long-Term Trajectories of Human Access to the Arctic," *Nature Climate Change* 1 (2011) 156–160; Laurence C. Smith and Scott R. Stephenson, "New Trans-Arctic Shipping Routes Navigable by Mid-Century," *Proceedings of the National Academy of Sciences of the United States of America* 110:13 (2013): E1191–E1195, https://doi.org/10.1073/pnas.1214212110; F. Laliberté, S.E.K. Howell and P.J. Kushner, "Regional Variability of a Projected Sea Ice-free Arctic During the Summer Months," *Geophysical Research Letters* 43:1 (2016): 256–263, doi: 10.1002/2015GL066855.

12   Howell *et al.* 2013 (n 2).

13   Copland *et al.* 2021 (n 2), p. 51.

14   Tseng and Cullinane (n 2), p. 35; Howell and Yackel (n 2); Dawson *et al.* 2021 (n 2), p. 35; Copland *et al.* 2021 (n 2), pp. 7, 42.

15   P. Kujala *et al.*, "Review of Risk-based Design for Ice-class Ships," *Marine Structures* 63 (2019): 181–195, https://doi.org/10.1016/j.marstruc.2018.09.008. See, for example, incidents of pleasure craft sinking in Chris Mooney, "Even Small Boats Are Tackling the Fabled Northwest Passage. The Ice Doesn't Always Cooperate," *The Washington Post*, 9 August 2017, https://www.washingtonpost.com/news/energy-environment/wp/2017/08/09/we-wanted-to-be-early-northwest-passage-adventurers-held-back-by-lingering-ice/; "Coast Guard Rescues 2 Passengers of Sinking Sailboat Stranded on Ice Floe," CBC News North, 29 August 2018, https://www.cbc.ca/news/canada/north/coast-guard-sail-boat-rescue-1.4804102; Katie Toth, "Fog, Ice and a Sinking Sailboat Involved in 16th Arctic-based Emergency of the Year," CBC News North, 5 September 2018, https://www.cbc.ca/news/canada/north/arctic-rescue-coast-guard-1.4810420; Government of Canada, "Canadian Coast Guard 2018 Arctic Operations Coming to an End," Canadian Coast Guard News Release, 19 November 2018, https://www.canada.ca/en/canadian-coast-guard/news/2018/11/canadian-coast-guard-2018-arctic-operations-coming-to-an-end.html.

conditions of climate change,[16] with weather becoming more unpredictable and an increased number of hazardous multiyear ice floes.[17]

The risks associated with sea ice change are only enhanced when considering the distribution of ice strengthened vessels that operate in Arctic Canada. Over the past decade the number of highly ice strengthened vessels (i.e., Polar Class 1, 2, 3) has decreased whereas the number of vessels with little to no ice strengthening (i.e., Polar Class 7 and 1B) have increased dramatically (Figure 15.2 – right panel).[18] Climate models project a seasonally ice-free Arctic Ocean within the next 30 years that will make key corridors more accessible even to non-ice strengthened vessels in summer months by mid-century and to moderately ice-strengthened vessels for 10–12 months a year by late century. This is significant to consider in the context of Canada's limited capability to provide icebreaking services in the Canadian Arctic (see further Choi in this volume). This situation is only exasperated by the limited infrastructure and emergency response capabilities in the region, including a lack of critical search and rescue services, in the Canadian Arctic (see further Kikkert, Pedersen and Lackenbauer this volume).[19] Recent research funded by Transport Canada has revealed that despite implementation of the Polar Code and clear operational guidelines for navigating in ice-infested waters, a number of vessels have still been found to be operating in elevated and high-risk ice areas, especially among non-ice strengthened vessels.[20]

The changing patterns and trends associated with shipping activities in Arctic Canada outlined here highlight the urgency of establishing effective governance frameworks for both managing and supporting shipping sector developments through Arctic Canada. The low-impact shipping corridors, if implemented effectively, could provide the backbone of what would be a revolutionary and visionary framework for supporting safe, sustainable and self-determined shipping in Arctic Canada.

---

16   Dawson et al. 2021 (n 2), p. 1.
17   Cecilie Mauritzen and Erik Kolstad, "The Arctic Ocean: An Ocean in Transition" in Marine Transport in the High North, eds., John Grue and Roy H. Gabrielson (Oslo: The Norwegian Academy of Science and Letters, 2011), 25–36; Larissa Pizzolato et al., "Changing Sea Ice Conditions and Marine Transportation Activity in Canadian Arctic Waters Between 1990 and 2012," Climatic Change 123:2 (2014): 161–173; Copland et al. 2021 (n 2), p. 49.
18   Dawson et al. 2021 (n 2), pp. 21, 50; Pizzolato et al. 2014 (n 17); Jackie Dawson et al., "Temporal and Spatial Patterns of Ship Traffic in the Canadian Arctic from 1990 to 2015," Arctic 71:1(2018): 15–26, https://doi.org/10.14430/arctic4698; Luke Copland et al., "Changes in Shipping Navigability in the Canadian Arctic Between 1972 and 2016," Facets 6:1 (2021), https://doi.org/10.1139/facets-2020-0096.
19   Copland et al. 2021 (n 2), pp. 49, 53; Dawson et al. 2021 (n 2), pp. 35–36.
20   Dawson et al. 2021 (n 2).

3   Development of Low-impact Shipping Corridors

As a management response to changing Arctic shipping activity and related levels of shipping risks in Canada, the Government of Canada began developing low-impact shipping corridors. These corridors are federally designated shipping routes representing the safest passage for sea vessels.[21] The corridors are not mandatory, and voluntary compliance with these low-impact shipping corridors is encouraged by providing enhanced levels of infrastructure, navigational support, and emergency response services within these shipping corridors, motivating vessel operators to use these routes in order to reduce the risk to their crew and vessel.[22] Existing regulatory frameworks still apply, such as the reporting requirement of certain classes of vessels in the Northern Canada Vessel Traffic Services Zone (see further Chircop in this volume who elaborates on the NORDREG reporting requirements; chapters by Bankes, Bartenstein and Buhler further outline the general governance framework relating to Arctic shipping).[23] However, recognizing that the regulatory framework alone is not sufficient for ensuring safe marine transportation,[24] an innovative aspect of the low-impact shipping corridors is that a softer approach is being employed by using incentivization, rather than relying on a 'hard' governance strategy that enforces mandatory compliance with established shipping routes.[25] This voluntary approach represents, to some extent, a departure from classical prescriptive regulation that characterizes the Canadian legal regime for Arctic shipping, as described by Buhler in this volume. This approach could also potentially have implications for marine insurance as well, with respect

---

21   Dawson *et al.* 2017 (n 6), pp. 9, 113; Dawson *et al.* 2021 (n 2), p. 1; Louie Porta, Erin Abou-Abssi, Jackie Dawson, and Olivia Mussells, "Shipping Corridors as a Framework for Advancing Marine Law and Policy in the Canadian Arctic," *Ocean and Coastal Law Journal* 22:1 (2017): 63–84, at 65; Transport Canada, "Government of Canada introduces new measures to protect the marine environment and coastal communities in Canada's Arctic," News Release, Government of Canada, 27 August 2017, https://www.canada.ca /en/transport-canada/news/2017/08/government_of_canadaintroducesnewmeasuresto protectthemarineenvir.html.

22   Porta *et al.* 2017 (n 21), p. 78; Dawson *et al.* 2017 (n 6), p. 105; Canadian Coast Guard (n 21).

23   Transport Canada, *Arctic Ice Regime Shipping System (AIRSS) Standards*, 2nd ed. (TP 12259E, January 2018), https://tc.canada.ca/sites/default/files/migrated/tp12259e.pdf; Porta *et al.* 2017 (n 21), p. 71.

24   For example, Vincent, Lovejoy and Bartenstein (this volume) note that the establishment of marine protected areas as conservation zones has not always been successful in limiting ship traffic, and are not necessarily always designed to do so.

25   Porta *et al.* 2017 (n 21), p. 73; Dawson *et al.* 2016 (n 4), p. 2.

to warranties for the seaworthiness of sea vessels and the identification of regions to be covered by insurance policies. This, in turn, may further incentivize vessel operators to use the low-impact shipping corridors. The low-impact shipping corridors approach therefore also represents a planning framework, providing geographical guidance for future infrastructure investments to be prioritized within the Canadian Arctic.[26]

Preliminary versions of the low-impact shipping corridors were developed by the Canadian Coast Guard and the Canadian Hydrographic Service in consultation with commercial master mariners and Canadian Coast Guard commanding officers, based on available information on ocean depth and historic shipping traffic over a period of three years (Figure 15.3).[27] However, it soon became apparent that decisions on the location and management of these low-impact shipping corridors needed to be informed by a wider range of input through additional research and consultation.[28] Such decisions should be based on considerations beyond existing traffic patterns and limited data from vessels that carry automatic identification system instrumentation.[29] In particular, it was recognized that there was a need to further consider ecologically sensitive sites that could be impacted by future marine traffic, taking into account that those areas may change depending on the time of year and due to climate change.[30]

Inuit and northern residents also highlighted that the location and management of low-impact shipping corridors should consider culturally sensitive marine areas, informed by the concerns and knowledge of Inuit and northern residents who live in and use these areas and whose way of life may be impacted by shipping traffic.[31] Lajeunnesse and Lackenbauer (this volume) observe how, for decades, Inuit have raised concerns about the impacts of

26 Dawson *et al.* 2016 (n 4), p. 2; Porta *et al.* 2017 (n 21), p. 68; Transport Canada 2017 (n 21); Canadian Coast Guard (n 21).
27 Dawson *et al.* 2016 (n 4), p. 2; Rene Chénier, Loretta Abado, Olivier Sabourin and Laurent Tardif, "Northern Marine Transportation Corridors: Creation and Analysis of Northern Marine Traffic Routes in Canadian Waters," *Transactions in* GIS 21:6 (2017): 1085–1097, doi:10.1111/tgis.12295; Jackie Dawson *et al.*, *Tourism Vessels and Low Impact Shipping Corridors in Arctic Canada: Trends, Risks, Community Perspectives and Management Strategies* (Ottawa: University of Ottawa, 2021), 7, doi: 10.20381/d3dd-yk49.
28 Dawson *et al.* 2017 (n 6), p. 107; Dawson *et al.* 2016 (n 4), pp. 3–4.
29 Porta *et al.* 2017 (n 21), p. 67; Dawson *et al.* 2016 (n 4), p. 4.
30 Porta *et al.* 2017 (n 21), p. 78; Dawson *et al.* 2017 (n 6), pp. 106, 111.
31 Dawson *et al.* 2016 (n 4), p. 4; Porta *et al.* 2017 (n 21), pp. 73, 78; Natalie Ann Carter, Jackie Dawson, Natasha Simonee, Shirley Tagalik and Gita Ljubicic, "Lessons Learned through

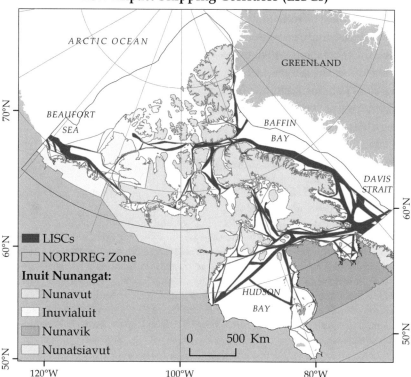

Low Impact Shipping Corridors (LISCs)

FIGURE 15.3   Low-impact shipping corridors in Arctic Canada
COURTESY OF ENVIRONMENT, SOCIETY & POLICY GROUP,
UNIVERSITY OF OTTAWA

Arctic shipping on their communities and way of life. Many communities in the Canadian Arctic rely on sea ice and the marine ecosystem for their sustenance and livelihoods,[32] as marine wildlife serves as a crucial source of clothing

Research Partnership and Capacity Enhancement in Inuit Nunangat," *Arctic* 72:4 (2019): 381–403, https://doi.org/10.14430/arctic69507 at 384.

32   Claudio Aporta, "The Trail as Home: Inuit and Their Pan-Arctic Network of Routes, "*Human Ecology* 37:2 (2009): 131–146, https://doi.org/10.1007/s10745-009-9213-x; Gita J. Laidler *et al.*, "Travelling and Hunting in a Changing Arctic: Assessing Inuit Vulnerability to Sea Ice Change in Igloolik, Nunavut," *Climatic Change* 94:3–4 (2009): 363–397, https://doi.org/10.1007/s10584-008-9512-z; Igor Krupnik, Claudio Aporta, Shari Gearheard, Gita J. Laidler, and Lene Kielsen Holm, eds., *SIKU: Knowing Our Ice: Documenting Inuit Sea-Ice Knowledge and Use* (Dordrecht: Springer, 2010); Shari Fox Gearheard *et al.*, eds.,

and food that is fundamental to community members' health, well-being and identity.[33] As emerges from the discussions with community members during the research project described in the next section, local use of sea ice areas for hunting and traveling and other community practices—and the impacts that increased ship traffic has and may have on these areas—should be considered when developing the low-impact shipping corridors.[34]

Indigenous peoples, including Inuit, have noted that, historically, the knowledge of Indigenous peoples have often been excluded from decision-making affecting their homelands.[35] It has been noted that by working with Inuit

The Meaning of Ice: People and Sea Ice in Three Arctic Communities (Hanover, NH: International Polar Institute Press, 2013).

33   Matilde Tomaselli *et al.*, "Iqaluktutiaq Voices: Local Perspectives about the Importance of Muskoxen, Contemporary and Traditional Use and Practices," *Arctic* 71:1 (2018): 1–14, https://doi.org/10.14430/arctic4697; John Bennett and Susan Rowley, eds., *Uqalurait: An Oral History of Nunavut* (Montreal: McGill-Queen's University Press, 2004); Ashlee Consolo Willox *et al.*, "From This Place and of This Place: Climate Change, Sense of Place, and Health in Nunatsiavut, Canada," *Social Science and Medicine* 75:3 (2012): 538–547, https://doi.org/10.1016/j.socscimed.2012.03.043; Agata Durkalec, Chris Furgal, Mark W. Skinner, and Tom Sheldon, "Climate Change Influences on Environment as a Determinant of Indigenous Health: Relationships to Place, Sea Ice, and Health in an Inuit Community," *Social Science and Medicine* 136–137 (2015): 17–26, https://doi.org/10.1016/j.socscimed.2015.04.026.

34   Dawson *et al.* 2016 (n 4), p. 6; Pew Charitable Trusts, *The Integrated Arctic Corridors Framework: Planning for Responsible Shipping in Canada's Arctic Waters* (Washington, DC: The Pew Charitable Trusts, 2016), https://www.pewtrusts.org/~/media/assets/2016/04/the-integrated-arctic-corridors-framework.pdf; Natalie Ann Carter, Jackie Dawson, Jenna Joyce and Annika Ogilvie, *Arctic Corridors and Northern Voices: Governing Marine Transportation in the Canadian Arctic (Arviat, Nunavut Community Report)* (Ottawa: University of Ottawa, 2017), https://doi.org/10.20381/RUOR36924; Natalie Ann Carter, Jackie Dawson, Jenna Joyce and Annika Ogilvie, *Arctic Corridors and Northern Voices: Governing Marine Transportation in the Canadian Arctic (Gjoa Haven, Nunavut Community Report)* (Ottawa: University of Ottawa, 2017), https://doi.org/10.20381/RUOR36911; Natalie Ann Carter *et al.*, *Arctic Corridors and Northern Voices: Governing Marine Transportation in the Canadian Arctic (Pond Inlet, Nunavut Community Report)* (Ottawa: University of Ottawa, 2018), https://doi.org/10.20381/RUOR37271; Natalie Carter *et al.*, *Arctic Corridors and Northern Voices: Governing Marine Transportation in the Canadian Arctic (Cambridge Bay, Nunavut Community Report)* (Ottawa: University of Ottawa, 2018), https://doi.org/10.20381/RUOR37325; Chénier *et al.* (n 27); Jackie Dawson *et al.*, "Infusing Local Knowledge and Community Perspectives into the Low Impact Shipping Corridors: An Adaptation to Increased Shipping Activity and Climate Change in Arctic Canada," *Environmental Science and Policy* 105 (2020): 19–36, https://doi.org/10.1016/j.envsci.2019.11.013; Environment, Society and Policy Group (ESPG), *Arctic Corridors Research for Policy on Shipping Governance in Arctic Canada* (Ottawa: ESPG, University of Ottawa, 2019), http://www.arcticcorridors.ca.

35   Shari Gearheard and Jamal Shirley, "Challenges in Community-Research Relationships: Learning from Natural Science in Nunavut," *Arctic* 60:1 (2007): 62–74, https://doi.org/10.14430/arctic266; Northern Governance Policy Research Conference (NGPRC),

communities, decision-makers as well as researchers can not only benefit from their knowledge of the local region, but also contribute towards respecting Indigenous rights, complying with relevant provisions of land claim agreements and other constitutional rights (see further chapter by Bankes and Lalonde in this volume) to support Inuit empowerment and self-determination.[36] As a response to this historical exclusion, the Government of Canada has committed to the inclusion of Indigenous rights holders' perspectives in federal decision-making as part of its efforts towards reconciliation.[37] These efforts towards reconciliation include meaningfully engaging with and directly involving Inuit communities, and considering Inuit and local knowledge within policy, management, and legal development discussions about Arctic shipping, including in the establishment and governance of the corridors.[38]

In general, it has become clear that there is a need for a coordinated approach to developing and strategically managing the low-impact shipping corridors in the Canadian Arctic—and ensuring marine safety and environmental protection—through strategic collaborations amongst federal, Indigenous, provincial, territorial, academic and other non-governmental partners, particularly given the complex nature of the various regulatory

---

NGPRC *Draft Recommendations. Recommendations from the* NGPRC, *3–5 November 2009* (Yellowknife, Northwest Territories, 2009); Deborah McGregor, Walter Bayha and Deborah Simmons, "Our Responsibility to Keep the Land Alive: Voices of Northern Indigenous Researchers," *Pimatisiwin: A Journal of Aboriginal and Indigenous Community Health* 8:1 (2010): 101–123; Inuit Tapiriit Kanatami (ITK), *National Inuit Strategy on Research* (Ottawa: ITK, 2018), https://www.itk.ca/wp-content/uploads/2018/04/ITK_NISR-Report_English _low_res.pdf.

36   Dawson *et al.* 2016 (n 4), p. 8; ITK 2018 (n 35), p. 76.

37   *United Nations Declaration on the Rights of Indigenous Peoples Act,* SC 2021, c 14; Crown-Indigenous Relations and Northern Affairs Canada, "Canada's Arctic and Northern Policy Framework," Government of Canada, last modified, 18 November 2019, https://www .rcaanc-cirnac.gc.ca/eng/1560523306861/1560523330587; "Principles Respecting the Government of Canada's Relationship with Indigenous Peoples," Government of Canada, last modified 1 August 2021, https://www.justice.gc.ca/eng/csj-sjc/principles-principes.html; Advisory Panel on Federal Support for Fundamental Science, *Investing in Canada's Future: Strengthening the Foundations of Canadian Research* (2017), http://www.sciencereview .ca/eic/site/059.nsf/vwapj/ScienceReview_April2017-rv.pdf/$file/ScienceReview _April2017-rv.pdf.

38   Dawson *et al.* 2016 (n 4), p. 6; Porta *et al.* (n 21), p. 74. For more discussions on the importance of including Indigenous perspectives, see also Nicolien van Luijk *et al.*, "At the Front Lines of Increased Shipping and Climate Change: Inuit Perspectives on Canadian Arctic Sovereignty and Security," *Arctic Yearbook* (2021), https://arcticyearbook.com/arctic-yearbook /2021/2021-scholarly-papers/379-at-the-front-lines-of-increased-shipping-and-climate -change-inuit-perspectives-on-canadian-arctic-sovereignty-and-security.

regimes governing Arctic shipping at different levels.[39] In direct response to this need, the Arctic Corridors and Northern Voices Project was developed as a partnership among the Environment, Society and Policy Group at the University of Ottawa, the Canadian Coast Guard, Transport Canada, the Canadian Hydrographic Service, Inuit organizations, and fourteen communities across Arctic Canada.

4   Identifying Culturally Significant Marine Areas for the Low-impact Shipping Corridors Framework

The Arctic Corridors and Northern Voices (ACNV)[40] (www.arcticcorridors.ca) project began in 2015 with the goal of documenting and spatially mapping Inuit knowledge about shipping impacts on culturally significant marine areas (CSMAs) for the purpose of infusing new, local, and Inuit knowledge into the low-impact shipping corridors framework. At that time, the corridors framework had already considered historic ship traffic density, existing infrastructure, as well as ecologically and biologically significant areas, but thus far had neglected to include cultural components of marine use due to a lack of available information.[41] The ACNV project, established out of the University of Ottawa and in consultation with the Canadian Coast Guard, was instrumental in filling in this information gap by implementing a community-based research partnership approach with a co-leadership model[42] that involved a collaboration among southern-based university researchers, regional and national decision-makers, and northern-based Inuit and northern community

39   Dawson *et al.* 2016 (n 4), pp. 8–9; David L. VanderZwaag *et al.*, *Governance of Arctic Marine Shipping* (Halifax: Marine & Environmental Law Institute, 2008); Porta *et al.* (n 21), pp. 65–66.
40   In May 2021, the ACNV project received the Governor General's Innovation Award, in recognition for the project's collaborative approach. Given the success of this project, the community-based partnership model of the ACNV project may serve as a useful model for ensuring all relevant data is available—including the knowledge and perspectives of Inuit and northern communities—for informing policy and decisions in other areas of marine activity management and planning.
41   Carter *et al.*, *Arviat, Nunavut Community Report* (n 34); Carter *et al.*, *Gjoa Haven, Nunavut Community Report* (n 34); Carter *et al.*, *Pond Inlet, Nunavut Community Report* (n 34); Carter *et al.*, *Cambridge Bay, Nunavut Community Report* (n 34); Dawson *et al.* 2020 (n 34).
42   For full details of the methods used in this project, see Jackson Dawson *et al.*, "Arctic Corridors and Northern Voices Project: Methods for Community-based Participatory Mapping for Low Impact Shipping Corridors in Arctic Canada," *MethodsX* 7 (2020): 101064, https://doi.org/10.1016/j.mex.2020.101064.

members. As of 2022, fourteen communities across Inuit Nunangat have been involved in the project (note that work in six additional communities is ongoing), including Aklavik, Inuvik, Paulatuk, Sachs Harbour, Tuktoyaktuk, Ulukhaktok, Arviat, Iqaluktuuttiaq (Cambridge Bay), Salliq (Coral Harbour), Uqsuqtuuq (Gjoa Haven), Iqaluit, Mittimatalik (Pond Inlet), Qausuittuq (Resolute) and Salluit.

The ACNV project involved 59 Inuit and northern youth and over 150 expert knowledge holders who worked together using well-established marine spatial planning techniques in order to identify a series of CSMAs (Figure 15.4).[43] CSMAs are marine areas that hold cultural importance to nearby communities, organized by season (i.e., including open water and non-open water season) (Figure 15.5). Aggregately, the CSMAs can be used to guide placement of the corridors officially through federal government processes, and can also be

FIGURE 15.4   ACNV community mapping workshop
COURTESY OF ENVIRONMENT, SOCIETY & POLICY GROUP,
UNIVERSITY OF OTTAWA

---

43   The results of the ACNV can be found on the project website: https://www.arcticcorridors
.ca/reports/.

used to support ship operators in voluntarily considering different culturally significant areas at different times of the year.[44]

To fully understand the extent to which CSMAs and corridors are in conflict and the extent to which existing corridors as identified by the Government of Canada overlap with and may impact CSMAs, a spatial analysis was conducted as part of this project. Figure 15.6 provides an outline of ecologically and biologically significant areas (EBSAs) and CSMAs (left), including the extent to which these identified areas overlap, and EBSAs, CSMAs and low-impact shipping corridors (right), again displaying the extent to which these areas overlap. The analysis shows that 62 percent of the CSMAs identified by Inuit communities overlap with government identified EBSAs. This means that the remainder of these areas that do not overlap with EBSAs are not officially protected within federal regulations or within any official mechanisms. Should the Government of Canada formally adopt the CSMAs, this could change, but for now 38 percent of marine areas identified by Inuit as culturally significant are not officially recognized. When considering the extent to which CSMAs fall within or outside of the low-impact shipping corridors, we find that only 28 percent are within the corridors and 72 percent lay outside of the corridors. The areas where there is overlap between CSMAs and the low-impact shipping corridors (approximately 107,072 kilometres) occur within regions that may be difficult for ships to avoid, including through Hudson Strait, the western end of Lancaster Sound, and around Victoria Island.

5   Strengths and Weaknesses of Low-impact Shipping Corridors

Another part of the ACNV project involved using a policy Delphi methodology through an iterative three-part survey to engage with rights holders, stakeholders, and other experts in Inuit Nunangat about their knowledge and perspectives about the management and governance of the low-impact shipping corridors. This involved a collaborative design process for the survey questions, involving external reviewers affiliated with federal, territorial, and regional governments, Inuit organizations, institutions of public government, shipping and cruise ship industry, universities and non-governmental organizations. This process produced a number of insights relevant to the

---

44   Dawson *et al.* 2020 (n 34).

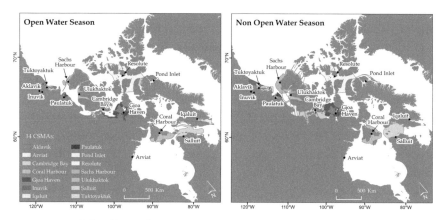

FIGURE 15.5   Culturally significant marine areas
COURTESY OF ENVIRONMENT, SOCIETY & POLICY GROUP,
UNIVERSITY OF OTTAWA

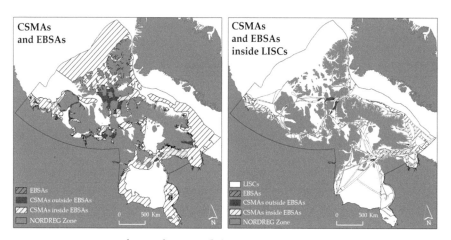

FIGURE 15.6   CSMAs and EBSAs locations (left) and CSMAs and EBSAs inside identified low-
impact shipping corridors (right)
COURTESY OF ENVIRONMENT, SOCIETY & POLICY GROUP,
UNIVERSITY OF OTTAWA

strategic management of the low-impact shipping corridors. In particular, strengths and weaknesses of the low-impact shipping corridors approach were identified by participants, divided by categories based on the government of Canada's stated goals for the corridors, as summarized in Table 15.2.

Many of the results of the Arctic Corridors and Northern Voices project reinforce, and shed new insights on, considerations that have been explored elsewhere with respect to Arctic shipping. The chapter in this

volume by Vincent, Lovejoy, and Bartenstein note a number of threats to
marine wildlife related to increased Arctic shipping, many of which were
also noted by knowledge holders during this project, demonstrating how
such threats can impact Inuit and northern communities who depend on
marine wildlife. Some of these concerns have been expressed by Inuit in past
decades, as noted in this volume's chapter by Lajeunesse and Lackenbauer.
These concerns are highlighted again by Monica Ell-Kanayuk in her conversation with Aporta (this volume), including concerns about pollution, emergency response capabilities, and the disturbance of marine wildlife from
ship noise.

Lajeunesse and Lackenbauer (this volume) also describe how the prospect
of Arctic shipping helped catalyze discussions of Inuit self-government in the
past, highlighting the intricate historical link between Arctic shipping and Inuit
self-determination. Knowledge holders in this project raised concerns about
their lack of knowledge and lack of control over shipping activities affecting
their sense of sovereignty, reinforcing the points made by Ell-Kanayuk (this
volume) in explicitly connecting Inuit self-determination with Arctic shipping issues and highlighting the need for Inuit participation in Arctic shipping
management. These corridors should therefore be managed in a manner that
is sustainable, effective, in compliance with relevant land claim agreements
and Indigenous rights (as outlined by Bankes and Lalonde in this volume), and

TABLE 15.2   Summary of identified strengths and weaknesses of the low-impact shipping corridors
framework

Enhanced marine navigation safety	Strengths	Voluntary nature of the corridors enables vessel operator to be responsive to changing environmental conditions and avoid hazards by transiting outside the corridors whe needed.
		Helps to concentrate (improved) communication and navigational support, including charting, required to fost safer shipping in the region, thus strengthening Canada's position as a global northern stakeholder.
		Increases navigational safety for vessels to use (at their discretion) when voyage-planning and operating in Canadian Arctic waters. Also supports pre-season preparation and quicker response to incidents.
		Simple, graphical way of providing guidance for ships on where they should go, and (Arctic community-identified) areas of concern to bypass.

TABLE 15.2   Summary of identified strengths and weaknesses of the low-impact shipping corridors framework (*Cont.*)

	Weaknesses	Compliance among ship operators may be a challenge as corridors are voluntary. Finding innovative approaches to compliance/conformity monitoring and communication with vessels will be critical to success.
		Cruise operators may actively avoid these corridors. The corridors framework does little to address the safety concerns raised by cruise ship traffic.
		Keeping corridors up to date, making the corridors dynamic (temporally), collecting and integrating data, as well as communicating changes and anomalous events could be challenging.
		A comprehensive monitoring system is required. Simply drawing lines on a map/chart indicating boundaries is not enough; without a strong AIS-based monitoring and surveillance system, as a waterways system the corridors will not be effective. A public-private partnership is needed, like the Marine Exchange of Alaska where industry, the United States Coast Guard, and the State of Alaska are partners in an effective ship-tracking system.
		Concentrating most of the 21st century charting in the corridors will lead to potential marine accidents/disasters. With a voluntary system, vessels will venture outside the corridors. Charting the corridors must be only the first step in a larger charting plan. A development plan for additional charting, outside of the corridors, is missing.
		The focus (physical size and placement) of the corridors is too narrow. They do not allow flexibility for normal navigation in ice-free conditions as well as in ice-covered conditions and may also cause congestion and detract from tourism experiences. This may increasingly be an issue due to climate changes and as historic shipping season dates change.
		The circumstances under which vessels may deviate from the corridors are not clearly laid out.

TABLE 15.2   Summary of identified strengths and weaknesses of the low-impact shipping corridors
framework (*Cont.*)

Minimizing ecological and cultural impacts	**Strengths**	Provides a foundation for measures to reduce the negative impact of vessel operations in the Arctic. Values and utilizes Inuit and other Indigenous knowledge to identify local concerns and support decisions about corridor location and management. Will support solutions to northern food insecurity by mitigating negative impacts on wildlife and harvesting areas Could be used as a tool for adaptive management of wildlife and the marine environment.
	Weaknesses	Although corridors are important, understanding wider spread effects of shipping traffic beyond the corridors needs to be part of the conversation, with the ability to alter corridors if required. Corridors currently pass through protected areas and regions identified as culturally and ecologically significant If Canada is to have effective corridors system in Arctic waters, many will pass through culturally and ecologically significant areas; this cannot be avoided unless Canada closes these waters to all traffic. Inuit and local knowledge are not sufficiently documented to enable strategic planning in remote areas.
Guiding investment	**Strengths**	Provides an opportunity to harmonize economic development, Indigenous community priorities, and environmental protection. Provides a comprehensive framework for regional development and infrastructure investment. Helps to focus deployment of limited federal resources for service delivery, search and rescue (SAR) including monitoring and emergency response (to spills, groundings etc.).
	Weaknesses	Significant resources (capital, infrastructure, and human will be required to provide the needed extensive coverage Harmonizing economic development, Indigenous community priorities, and environmental protection is neither possible nor feasible with the corridor approach. All of these are driven by multiple external factors, not navigation rules and regulations.

LE 15.2 Summary of identified strengths and weaknesses of the low-impact shipping corridors framework (*cont.*)

		The corridors framework will not be a primary driver of regional development and infrastructure investment. Corridors placement resulting in vessel re-routing may impact existing economic activity such as commercial fishing or community re-supply.
laborative nagement	Strengths	Sets a vision and provides one platform i.e. a national governance structure, for management of Arctic shipping, taking into account social, Indigenous, environmental, and logistical considerations, and supports responsive, adaptive planning and refinement to respond to rights holder and stakeholder priorities.
		Provides a framework under which Inuit and Government of Canada can try new models for shared operations including, potentially, shared authority for monitoring and reporting.
		Provides an opportunity to try innovative approaches and establish Canada as a world leader in circumpolar marine policy.
	Weaknesses	The complexity of the operating environment may make governance a challenge. The regulatory complexity of the region may not be addressed by the corridors approach.
		The process for developing corridors has lacked transparency and has not always included all stakeholders and rights holders appropriately. This may delay implementation and generate opposition and a lack of compliance.
		The ongoing development of navigable corridors may lack input from ship operators due to budgetary constraints and failure to effectively communicate.
		Interregional coordination may be a challenge.

informed by all relevant considerations, including impacts on environmentally and culturally sensitive areas.[45]

---

45   Porta *et al.* (n 21), p. 68.

The insights from the Arctic Corridors and Northern Voices project could provide useful guidance in governing the low-impact shipping corridors and Arctic shipping in general. Carter *et al.* 2022 identified two main principles that should be used to guide the implementation of low-impact shipping corridors management strategies:

1. The low impact shipping corridors should be managed in a manner that is **responsive** and **inclusive**. This involves, among other things:
    – including Inuit in all stages of decision-making;
    – prioritizing Inuit communities' perspectives;
    – giving equal consideration to Indigenous knowledge and western scientific methods;
    – meeting the needs of Inuit, allowing Inuit communities to benefit; and
    – providing essential services to ships and their crews.
2. The low impact shipping corridors should be managed in a **dynamic** manner, by:
    – incorporating not only federal government-sourced feedback, but also feedback from Indigenous communities;
    – addressing seasonal activities and informational needs, such as harvesting by Inuit, changing ice and weather conditions, and the presence or absence of wildlife;
    – communicating real-time information to ship crews and affected communities; and
    – enabling current and emerging priorities to be integrated into the low impact shipping corridors framework.[46]

Some of the strengths of the corridor's framework identified by Carter *et al.* 2022 (see Table 15.2) are related to the role of Inuit and other Indigenous knowledge holders in supporting decisions about the location and management of low-impact shipping corridors. Inversely, one identified weakness was that the process for developing corridors has not always included all rights holders and stakeholders appropriately. As such, this relates to the first guiding principle for implementing low-impact shipping corridors management strategies in a manner that is inclusive, including involving Inuit in all stages of decision-making, prioritizing Inuit community perspectives and needs, and integrating Indigenous knowledge. Developing and managing the low-impact shipping corridors framework therefore requires not only considering the knowledge and concerns of those living in these very regions (such as Inuit

---

46   Natalie A. Carter, Jackie Dawson, and Annika Stensland, *Opportunities and Strategies for Effective Management of Low Impact Arctic Shipping Corridors* (Ottawa: University of Ottawa, 2022), doi: 10.20381/epj4-fz32 (emphasis in original) [Carter *et al.* 2022].

and northern communities), but collaboratively working with them to ensure that their perspectives are included in decisions and policies that are developed with respect to the land, ice and waters where they live, a theme that has also been highlighted in chapters in this volume by Ell-Kanayuk and Aporta, and Beveridge.

The community-based partnership approach of the ACNV project described in this chapter may serve as a useful practical model for how to operationalize such a collaborative and inclusive approach to managing Arctic shipping. As was done in the ACNV project, community partners can provide an integral role to help produce fulsome, informative, inclusive and accurate results to inform the development of the low-impact shipping corridors, by considering the needs of the community, leveraging local ties to maximize the engagement of the community, and providing invaluable locally-relevant guidance and logistical support.

Besides managing the low-impact shipping corridors in a responsive and inclusive manner, the results from the project suggest that this management should done in a dynamic manner, as captured in the second principle above. There is further substantial work to be done. The governance framework for Arctic shipping must be able to adapt effectively on an ongoing basis to account for the dynamic conditions of the Canadian Arctic due to climate change and increasing international interest in the region, as well to respond to changes in shipping traffic trends and the dynamic needs of communities and vessels.[47]

One of the weaknesses of the low-impact shipping corridors is that the complexity of the operating environment of Arctic shipping may make governance a challenge, as the corridors approach may not full address the regulatory complexities involved. Although the low-impact shipping corridors will be a useful management approach for governing many of the marine vessels that are traveling and will travel through the Canadian Arctic, further governance options will need to be explored for other types of marine vessels, such as tourism passenger ships and pleasure craft, which are known to travel through routes outside of these low-impact shipping corridors— including through ecologically or biologically significant marine areas and culturally significant marine areas—for tourism experiences, a concern noted when assessing the weaknesses of the corridors framework.[48] As these Arctic

47   Dawson *et al.*, 2016 (n 4), p. 9.
48   Dawson *et al.*, 2021 (n 4), p. 23; Jackie Dawson, Emma J. Stewart, Harvey Lemelin and Daniel Scott, "The Carbon Cost of Polar Bear Viewing in Churchill, Canada," *Journal of Sustainable Tourism* 18:3 (2010): 319–336, doi:10.1080/09669580903215147; Jackie Dawson *et al.*, "Ethical Considerations of Last Chance Tourism," *Journal of Ecotourism* 10:3 (2011): 205–262, doi:10.1080/14724049.2011.617449; Jackie Dawson, M.E. Johnston and E.J. Stewart, "Governance of Arctic Expedition Cruise Ships in a Time of Rapid Environmental

shipping management systems are further developed, it will be beneficial to continue to employing collaborative and inclusive approaches.

Acknowledgements

The authors gratefully acknowledge funding for chapter activities from the Canada Research Chairs program, Transport Canada's Northern Transportation and Adaptation Initiative and other funders and supports of the Arctic Corridors and Northern Voices project (various funders listed at www.arcticcorridors .ca). The authors also acknowledge the large number of important researchers involved in the Arctic Corridors research project including Dr. Natalie Carter (among many others) who was the community research lead and guided mapping exercises to establish culturally significant marine areas. The views expressed in this chapter reflect the personal perspectives of the authors, and do not represent the views of their employers, the Government of Canada, or the Department of Justice Canada.

---

and Economic Change," *Ocean & Coastal Management* 89(2014): 88–99, https://doi .org/10.1016/j.ocecoaman.2013.12.005.; Harvey Lemelin *et al.*, "Last Chance Tourism: The Doom, the Gloom and the Boom of Visiting Destinations," *Current Issues in Tourism* 13:5 (2010): 477–493, doi: 10.1080/13683500903406367; Adrianne Johnston, Margaret E. Johnston, Jackie Dawson and Emma Stewart, "Challenges of Arctic Cruise Tourism Development in Canada: Perspectives of Federal Government Stakeholders," *Journal of Maritime Law and Commerce* 43:3 (2012): 335–347.

The New Federal *Impact Assessment Act* and Arctic Shipping: Opportunities for Improved Governance

Meinhard Doelle, David V. Wright, A. John Sinclair, and Simon Dueck

Abstract

This chapter explores opportunities to improve the governance of shipping and related activities in the Canadian Arctic waters through the application of the federal *Impact Assessment Act* (IAA). It considers a range of activities potentially associated with shipping in the Arctic and their key associated impacts, such as vessels used in fishing and aquaculture, supply vessels for northern communities and industries, shipping related to the transportation of resources extracted in the Canadian Arctic, shipping related to energy projects, tourism related shipping, and the Arctic as a shipping route for global trade. The chapter then considers the role each of four distinct assessment processes under the IAA could make to the governance of shipping. Given the prevalence of other assessment processes in the Canadian Arctic, the chapter then considers how the IAA's processes will interact with existing assessment processes beyond the IAA, such as those at territorial and Indigenous levels of government.

Keywords

impact assessment – environmental assessment – co-management – Arctic – shipping – Canada – federal

1   Introduction

This chapter explores opportunities to improve the governance of shipping and related activities in Canadian Arctic waters through the application of the federal *Impact Assessment Act* (IAA).[1] Arctic waters, for the purposes of this chapter, will consist of the waters within the NORDREG Zone, including the portion

---

1   *Impact Assessment Act*, SC 2019, c 28, s 1 [IAA].

of Hudson Bay below 60.[2] When the IAA was passed in 2019, it represented a significant departure from past approaches to federal impact assessments. Most notable for purposes of this chapter is that the scope of the assessment changed fundamentally from assessments focused primarily on biophysical impacts to considering a broad range of biophysical, social, health, cultural and economic impacts and benefits of proposed activities.[3]

The chapter considers a range of activities potentially associated with shipping in the Arctic, such as vessels used in fishing and aquaculture, supply vessels for northern communities and industries, shipping related to the transportation of resources extracted in the Canadian Arctic, shipping related to energy projects, tourism and other passenger related shipping, and the Arctic as a shipping route for global trade. The chapter considers the role that each of four distinct assessment processes under the IAA could make to the governance of shipping. Given the prevalence of other assessment processes in the Canadian Arctic, the chapter then considers how the IAA's processes will interact with assessment processes beyond the IAA, such as those at territorial and Indigenous levels.

The first two processes under the IAA with potential implications for shipping in the Arctic are project level assessments. One is the assessment process for designated projects, which includes any project listed in a regulation under the IAA and associated activities.[4] The chapter explores which of the projects currently listed may have relevance to Arctic shipping, and whether other activities with shipping implications could be considered for addition to the designated project list or ad hoc designation by the Minister of the Environment (the Minister). We also offer an overview of the assessment process requirements for designated projects. The other project level process relates to the assessment requirements for projects on federal lands.[5]

The two other processes in the IAA deal with higher tier assessments rather than with individual projects. One of these offers opportunities for sectoral or other strategic assessments to inform project level assessment decisions. Examples include a strategic assessment of particularly pressing issues such as potential shipping routes, a strategic assessment of shipping in the Canadian Arctic more broadly, or of a particular type of activity or industry sector, such as fishing, mining, or energy production. The other higher tier process provides for regional assessment. Regional assessment could be developed at a range

2 *Northern Canada Vessel Traffic Services Zone Regulations*, SOR/2010-127, s 2 [NORDREG].

3 Meinhard Doelle and A. John Sinclair, eds., *Impact Assessment in Transition: A Critical Review of the Canadian Impact Assessment Act* (Toronto: Irwin Law, 2021), 58.

4 *Physical Activities Regulations*, SOR/2019-285. There are opportunities to include broader issues in project assessments. For example, an assessment of a marine terminal could consider shipping routes as part of the assessment of the marine terminal.

5 IAA (n 1), ss 81–91.

of possible scales, from the whole Arctic region to specific areas such as the Beaufort Sea or Hudson Bay, all the way to a small area of particular focus.[6]

1.1 *Activities with Implications for Arctic Shipping*

Dawson *et al.* suggest that the Arctic may be the region most dependent on the marine transportation industry in Canada.[7] In considering the application of the IAA to shipping activities in the Canadian Arctic, there is potentially a huge range of human activities that can influence shipping in Canadian Arctic waters. This section offers a high-level overview of some of the key activities that either are taking place in the Canadian Arctic, or that can be anticipated to be proposed in the foreseeable future, that could be subject to assessment processes. These activities are considered broadly in two categories, land-based activities that have implications for Arctic shipping, and ocean-based activities.

Starting with land-based activities, marine terminals and associated infra-structure are an obvious category of activity to consider. Marine terminals in national parks of any size, and marine terminals outside national parks for vessels over 25,000 DWT are included as designated projects under the IAA. Port developments can be critical to ensure adequate infrastructure to respond to emergencies, including environmental emergencies such as spills of cargo and fuel from ships. Port developments can include a range of elements, from emergency and spill response to inland transportation infrastructure to sup-port the port, storage facilities such as tank farms and fuel supply to measures to improve access to a port in harsh winter conditions, and places of refuge for ships in need of assistance. Of course, port infrastructure can also lead to an increase in ship traffic, on the basis of 'if you build it, they will come.' Port developments may be proposed for a particular purpose, such as improved safety and emergency response, or improved supply of existing communities, but may affect shipping in many other ways, such as an increase in tourism, transit of commercial vessels through the area, or other commercial activity enabled by improved port facilities. Currently there are multiple proposals for ports in the Canadian Arctic, most notably in Tuktoyaktuk, Northwest Territo-ries[8] (NWT) and in Qikiqtarjuaq and Chesterfield Inlet, Nunavut.[9]

---

6   Id., ss 92–103.

7   Jackie Dawson *et al.*, "Temporal and Spatial Patterns of Ship Traffic in the Canadian Arctic from 1990 to 2015," *Arctic* 71:1 (2018): 15–26, https://doi.org/10.14430/arctic4698.

8   David Thurton, "Deep Water Port in Tuktoyaktuk Could Bring Business to N.W.T.," *CBC*, 2 December 2014, https://www.cbc.ca/news/canada/north/deep-water-port-in-tuktoyaktuk -could-bring-business-to-n-w-t-1.2857238.

9   The Canadian Press, "Feds Announce Long-Awaited Deepwater Port for Qikiqtarjuaq, Nunavut," *CBC*, 4 August 2021, https://www.cbc.ca/news/canada/north/qikiqtarjuaq-port -announcement-1.6129497; Patricia Lightfoot, "Chesterfield Inlet Mayor Pitches Deep-Sea

Marine terminals and associated port developments are of course not the only land-based activity with the potential to affect shipping in the Canadian Arctic. Increased settlement in Arctic communities and a range of commercial activities can also lead to an increase in Arctic shipping patterns. Another example would be tourism in the form of cruise ships. In 2016, history was made when the *Crystal Serenity*, carrying a complement of around 1000 passengers and 600 crew, completed a voyage through the Northwest Passage. This was the first ever attempt by a cruise ship to complete this voyage, and one that has been repeated since by Crystal Cruises. The first bulk carrier completed a voyage through the passage in 2013.[10]

Among other land-based activities with clear connection to shipping are mining, oil and gas exploration and other resource extraction industries. A recent example is the assessment of the expansion of Baffinland's Mary River Mine, which was expected to cause a significant increase in shipping in the region.[11] Such industrial activities also tend to lead to an influx of workers, who in turn will depend in part on supply vessels for the provision of food and other essentials. The activities themselves will require supplies that may have an impact on shipping patterns. Finally, these industries ultimately extract resources that will be required to be shipped to markets, usually outside the Arctic region.[12] Other land-based activities with implications for shipping are Arctic settlements in need of supplies ranging from fuel to building materials and food.

In addition to land-based activities, there are a number of ocean-based activities that can be expected to have implications for Arctic shipping patterns.

Port to Ease Effects of Increased Shipping," *Nunatsiaq News*, 11 February 2020, https://nunatsiaq.com/stories/article/chesterfield-inlet-mayor-pitches-deep-sea-port-to-ease-effects-of-increased-shipping/; Simione Sammurtok, "Deep-Sea Port Harbour – Chesterfield Inlet, Nunavut" (Tabled Document, Chesterfield Inlet NU, 2018), https://assembly.nu.ca/sites/default/files/TD-10-5(1)-EN-Correspondence-from-the-Municipality-of-Chestefield-Inlet-Marine-Infrastructure.pdf.

10   WWF Canada, *Arctic Shipping, Avoiding Catastrophe: Managing the Risks of More Marine Traffic in Canada's Arctic Waters* (Toronto: World Wildlife Fund Canada, 2014). See also Nicole Mortillaro, "Crystal Serenity's Journey Through Northwest Passage Draws Excitement, Climate Change Fears," *Global News*, 29 August 2016, https://globalnews.ca/news/2908883/crystal-serenitys-journey-through-northwest-passage-draws-excitement-climate-change-fears/; Ben Weber, "Northerners Consider New Cruise Ship Rules After Crystal Serenity's Voyage," *The Canadian Press*, 18 September 2016, https://www.cbc.ca/news/canada/north/new-rules-for-arctic-cruises-1.3767846.

11   Julien Gignac, "Massive Increase in Nunavut Mine Shipping Traffic Puts Narwhals at Risk," *The Narwhal*, 19 February 2021, https://thenarwhal.ca/massive-increase-in-nunavut-mine-shipping-traffic-puts-narwhals-at-risk-study/.

12   Dawson *et al.* (n 7), pp. 15–26.

Some are existing activities. Given the fundamental changes underway in Arctic waters as a result of climate change, many new activities that are currently not feasible can be expected in the foreseeable future. Among ocean-based activities that have implications for Arctic shipping are trans-Arctic shipping routes, fishing, aquaculture, offshore renewable energy production, offshore oil and gas exploration, seabed mining, marine scientific research and the creation and management of marine and land-based protected areas.

Some of these activities, such as offshore aquaculture or offshore renewable energy exploration, may be a long way off or may never become technically or economically feasible. Other activities, such as offshore oil and gas development, are currently subject to a moratorium, and may never again be approved in the Canadian Arctic region in light of concerns about local environmental impacts and global efforts to decarbonize. However, if they are proposed, their approval would have considerable implications for Arctic shipping and assessment. Other activities, such as trans-Arctic shipping, tourism, fishing, marine scientific research and marine protection are already taking place or under active consideration in the Canadian Arctic, and can be expected to continue and increase in the future.

The question of the federal role in dealing with this range of activities in the Canadian Arctic is less of a constitutional issue than it is a question of the evolving relationship between the federal government and the relevant territorial and Indigenous governments and Indigenous organizations in the region. Nevertheless, the constitutional division of powers between the federal and provincial levels of government have clearly been influential in the development of these relationships, as has section 35 of the Constitution with respect to Indigenous communities and organizations.[13] Ultimately, there are many issues that arise from these activities for which the federal government has responsibility. Most directly, in light of the focus of this chapter, the federal government has responsibility for navigation and shipping, as well as jurisdiction over many of the potential biophysical impacts of shipping and related activities, such as marine pollution, and the protection and management of aquatic, endangered and migratory species to name a few.[14] Of course, other elements such as occupational health and safety and workers' compensation,

---

13   Of course, the *United Nations Declaration on the Rights of Indigenous Peoples Act*, SC 2021, c 14, will have significant implications, particularly the commitment to review federal legislation to ensure consistency with United Nations Declaration on the Rights of Indigenous Peoples (UNDRIP).

14   Anna Johnston, "Federal Jurisdiction and the *Impact Assessment Act*: Trojan Horse or Rational Ecological Accounting?", in Doelle and Sinclair, eds. (n 3), pp. 97–118.

are under provincial jurisdiction. Ultimately, courts have applied the double aspect principle and cooperative federalism to deal with this complex picture of overlapping jurisdiction.

The potential for environmental degradation of the Arctic marine and coastal ecosystems due to shipping is well known.[15] Environmental concerns in the Arctic region are heightened as a result of the extreme fragility of the ecosystems found there. The species that make the Arctic marine environment their home are highly specialized to the cold temperatures and ice covered oceans, meaning that the ability of Arctic ecosystems to evolve and adapt to changes is low.[16] In the context of climate change, the Arctic's vulnerability to oil pollution and invasive species impacts is compounded by ongoing changes to environmental conditions resulting from changes to the climate system.[17]

The reality of maritime shipping is that some degree of pollution and consequent environmental degradation is inevitable as ships spill and leak oil as part of regular operations, and even where zero discharge rules exist such as under the *Arctic Waters Pollution Prevention Act*, monitoring and enforcement of this is challenging.[18] Ultimately, the pollution risk from shipping increases with the amount of vessel traffic in a given area.[19] There are several important factors that make the Arctic especially vulnerable to damages from oil spills, including vulnerable species, highly specialized ecosystems, extreme remoteness, and difficult conditions for cleanup efforts.[20] Oil contains elements that are toxic to many forms of animal and plant life meaning that oil in the environment, either through large discharge events or prolonged leaks, can have

---

15   Layla Hughes *et al.*, "Framework for the Development of Nunavut Community Oil Spill Response Plans: A Report to WWF Canada" (2017), retrieved from http://awsassets.wwf .ca/downloads/170405__oilspillresponsecapacitynunavut_web.pdf?_ga=1.192463919.464 88933.1485191209.; Sarah Gulas *et al.*, "Declining Arctic Ocean Oil and Gas Developments: Opportunities to Improve Governance and Environmental Pollution Control," *Marine Policy* 75 (2017): 53–61, https://doi.org/10.1016/j.marpol.2016.10.014; J. Fredrik Lindgren *et al.*, "Discharges to the Sea," in *Shipping and the Environment: Improving Environmental Performance in Marine Transportation*, eds., Karin Andersson *et al.* (Berlin, Heidelberg: Springer-Verlag, 2016), 125–168, at 131, https://doi.org/10.1007/978-3-662-49045-7. See also Vincent, Lovejoy and Bartenstein in this volume.

16   Gulas *et al.* (n 15), pp. 53–61, at 55.

17   WWF Canada (n 10).

18   Lindgren *et al.* (n 15), pp. 125–168, at 131.

19   Jerome Marty *et al.*, "Evaluation of the Risk of Oil Spills in Canadian Arctic Waters," June 2016, AMOP Conference.

20   Jeremy Wilkinson *et al.*, "Oil Spill Response Capabilities and Technologies for Ice-covered Arctic Marine Waters: A Review of Recent Developments and Established Practices," *Ambio* 46:3 (2017): 423–441, https://doi.org/10.1007/s13280-017-0958-y.

anything from acute to long-term effects on aquatic life and the function of ecosystems.[21] These factors suggest that an oil spill poses a significant and serious risk to the Arctic marine environment and the people who live in the region.[22]

Lindgren *et al.* found that 34 percent of global hydrocarbon pollution in marine regions resulted from shipping. Broken down further, only 9.8 percent of global discharges to the sea are the result of accidental spills from events such as groundings, collisions or explosions that release enormous amounts of oil.[23] The remaining 24 percent of shipping related discharges to the sea, representing the largest source of oil discharged to the sea from human activity, result from operational discharges from routine operations. Routine operations, like discharges of bilge water, cleaning of tanks and bunkering, are responsible for the majority of small oil spills, and small continuous leaks are common on older ships. Small leaks can come from propeller shaft bearings, for example.[24] Rules in the Arctic are more stringent than elsewhere, so the contribution of operational discharges in the region would be expected to be well below the global average, but this has not been tested.[25]

Projections of expected increase in trans-Arctic shipping and significantly longer shipping seasons are common place.[26] Receding summer sea ice, while it represents one of the most dramatic depictions of climate change on the

---

21   Lindgren *et al.* (n 15), pp. 125–168, at 140–141.
22   Dawson *et al.* (n 7), pp. 15–26.
23   Lindgren *et al.* (n 15), pp. 125–168.
24   Id., 125.
25   The impact of icebreaking is among the many shipping related impact that warrants consideration in assessments of shipping activities in the Arctic. Icebreaking is expected, for example, to contribute to Arctic ice loss that, in turn, can exacerbate the climate change effects by reducing ice albedo. See Adolf K.Y. Ng *et al.*, "Implications of Climate Change for Shipping: Opening the Arctic Seas," *WIREs Climate Change* (2018). See also Jackie Dawson *et al.*, "Infusing Inuit and Local Knowledge into the Low Impact Shipping Corridors: An Adaptation to Increased Shipping Activity and Climate Change in Arctic Canada," *Environmental Science and Policy* 105 (2020): 19–36, https://reader.elsevier.com/reader/sd/pii/S1462901119309451?token=EC2EF6421923CBC84F7762CD86CA8BD5BE633C57B9FA02017908381116928563A3EE349155856DCBE46E0FC06E8613CB&originRegion=us-east-1&originCreation=20220526161948.
26   Alun Anderson, "The Great Melt: The Coming Transformation of the Arctic," *World Policy Journal* 26:4 (2009): 53–64, https://doi.org/10.1162/wopj.2010.26.4.53; Dimitrios Theocharis *et al.*, "Arctic Shipping: A Systematic Literature Review of Comparative Studies," *Journal of Transport Geography* 69 (2018): 112–128, https://doi.org/10.1016/j.jtrangeo.2018.04.010; Shengda Zhu *et al.*, "The Environmental Costs and Economic Implications of Container Shipping on the Northern Sea Route," *Maritime Policy and Management* 45:4 (2018): 456–477, https://doi.org/10.1080/03088839.2018.1443228.

globe, at the same time has some in the shipping industry excited about the prospect of shorter shipping paths connecting Europe and China through the Arctic.[27]

2   Assessment Processes under the IAA

This section introduces four distinct assessment processes under the IAA that have the potential relevance for shipping related activities in the Canadian Arctic. We first introduce the standard project level assessment process for projects designated for assessment. We then consider separate project level assessment requirements in the IAA for projects on federal lands and projects outside Canada that are funded or otherwise supported by the federal government. This is followed by an overview of strategic and regional assessments, two processes included in the IAA that allow for assessment to go beyond individual projects to consider a broader range of issues and activities.

2.1   *Assessment of Designated Projects*
Projects can be designated for assessment either through a physical activity list in regulations or through ministerial discretion. This assessment process is most commonly initiated for projects on the physical activity list. The physical activity list regulation essentially creates a presumption that an impact assessment is required, but the Impact Assessment Agency of Canada (the Agency), which is the federal agency tasked with administering the IAA regime, has the ultimate power to determine, during the planning phase of the assessment, whether an assessment ultimately has to be carried out. For projects not on the list, the presumption is that no assessment is required. However, the Minister has the power to require an assessment either in response to a request to designate a project or on the Minister's own initiative.[28] The request can be made by anyone.

It is of course difficult to predict with certainty which of the activities designated under the IAA, if proposed in the Arctic region, would involve significant shipping activity. Our aim here is to highlight some of the types of activities that could be involved, not to offer a definitive list. Some, such as aquaculture

---

27   See Lasserre in this volume.
28   IAA (n 1), s 9. The power to designate is fairly broad, however, the expectation is that assessments that go beyond individual activities will be assessed under the processes for strategic or regional assessments rather than under the designated project assessment process.

facilities, are only triggered if they are proposed in a national park or protected area. Others trigger the IAA regardless of where they are proposed. Activities listed include a broad range of energy projects, from fossil fuel-based energy to nuclear and renewable energy, including related infrastructure such as pipelines and transmission lines. Also included are a range of mining activities, and transportation infrastructure such as roads, railways, airports, and marine terminals.[29]

The process for conducting an impact assessment for designated projects consists of a number of phases, including the planning phase, the assessment and review phase, the decision-making phase and the post approval follow-up phase (Figure 16.1). The process is outlined in detail in the growing literature on the new IAA, so a brief overview will suffice for purposes of this chapter.[30]

The planning phase is one of the innovations of the IAA. Its aim is twofold, to determine whether an assessment is needed, and, assuming one is needed,

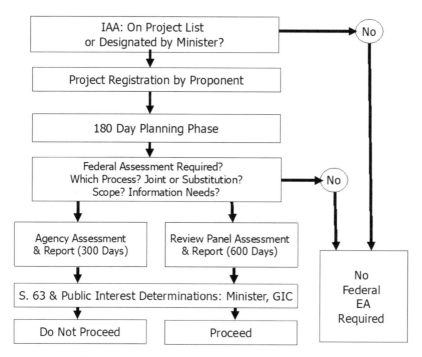

FIGURE 16.1 Overview of IAA process for designated projects

29 *Physical Activities Regulations*, SOR/2019-285.
30 See Meinhard Doelle and A. John Sinclair, "The New IAA in Canada: From Revolutionary Thoughts to Reality" *Environmental Impact Assessment Review* 79 (2019): 106292, https://doi.org/10.1016/j.eiar.2019.106292.

to plan the details of the assessment, including through consultations with potentially affected Indigenous communities, other jurisdictions with impact assessment requirements (including Indigenous organizations), and the public. A key outcome of the planning process is the release of Tailored Impact Statement Guidelines (TISG) to offer direction to project proponents on the content of the Impact Statement it has to prepare to initiate the assessment phase of the process. The planning phase is limited to 180 days, leaving limited time for the planning phase to fulfill other important planning roles, such as the identification of information needs from government actors, and the design of an effective public participation plan.[31]

Ultimately, the Agency, which leads the planning phase, has to plan an assessment that considers the factors set out in section 22 of the Act. Factors listed in section 22 include both positive and negative effects of the proposed project, and cover a broad range of biophysical, social, economic, health and cultural effects of the proposed project, including mitigation measures, cumulative effects, alternatives, accidents, impacts on Indigenous communities and the rights of Indigenous peoples. Included in the factors is also the requirement to take into account project-specific and regional assessments conducted by an Indigenous governing body.[32] The assessment has to inform a number of key determinations that need to be made under section 63 of the Act as part of the ultimate public interest determination, including the extent to which the project contributes to sustainability, the impact it will have on rights and interests of Indigenous communities, the impact it will have on Canada's ability to meet its climate commitments and environmental obligations, and the significance of adverse effects of the project that are within federal jurisdiction.[33]

Following the conclusion of the planning phase, the proponent has up to three years to prepare its impact statement and initiate the assessment phase. In the meantime, the Minister has to decide whether the assessment is to be carried out by way of an Agency led process or by an independent review panel. With some exceptions, the Agency led assessment has to be carried out within 300 days of the commencement of the assessment phase, and the assessment by a review panel has to be carried out within 600 days, subject to time stoppages and extensions available under the Act. The substantive requirements of the assessment are similar, as are the decisions the assessments will inform. The key legislative differences between the processes are the timelines and

31   Id., 57–59.
32   IAA (n 1), s 22(1)(q) and (r), respectively.
33   Id.

the entity responsible for carrying out the assessment and filing the assessment report. Special rules apply to assessments carried out when the Canadian Energy Regulator, the Canada Nuclear Safety Commission, or the Offshore Petroleum Boards are involved as regulators of the proposed project. In practice, the nature and level of public engagement is likely to differ significantly depending on the process option chosen.[34]

At the conclusion of the assessment phase, a final report is prepared by the Agency or the review panel and submitted to the Minister or Cabinet for a project decision. The report has to inform the key determinations noted above that must be made under section 63 of the Act, and ultimately the report informs the public interest determination and the terms and conditions under which a proposed project may be approved. One of the terms and conditions of approval will be the implementation of a follow-up program designed during the course of the assessment.[35]

2.2   *Assessment of Projects on Federal Lands*

There are two categories of projects that require some form of assessment even if they are not designated for assessment under the process described in the previous section. We refer to these as federal projects because these are projects that are either proposed by or substantially supported by the federal government that may require assessment under the IAA. One category of federal projects involves projects on federal lands. This is the category of projects most relevant to this chapter.[36] There are a number of fundamental differences between the assessment requirements for designated projects and those for projects on federal lands. We highlight the key differences in this section.[37]

At the start, these requirements apply to projects on federal land, so it is important to consider the definition of federal land, and what it means in an Arctic context. Federal land includes all land owned by the federal government, including any offshore area that is not part of a province (or territory), including Canada's internal waters, territorial sea, the continental shelf and the exclusive economic zone. Also included under federal lands are lands that are set aside for bands under the *Indian Act*, which would primarily have relevance in areas of the Arctic within provincial boundaries, notably the Hudson

---

34   Doelle and Sinclair eds. 2021 (n 3), p. 61.

35   Id., 67.

36   The other category not relevant here involves projects outside Canada that are supported in some way by the federal government, usually in the form of federal funding.

37   See Jamie Kneen, "Impact Assessment for Projects on Federal Lands and Outside Canada: The "Federal Projects" Process," in Doelle and Sinclair eds. (n 3), pp. 388–411.

Bay area. Specifically excluded from the definition are lands that are under the administration and control of one of the three territorial governments, which, in the case of Nunavut, includes the offshore. No reference is made in the definition to lands that are subject to comprehensive land claims agreements or self-government agreements with Indigenous peoples. In the Canadian Arctic this leaves a complex mosaic, with some marine waters, particularly in the Western Arctic, and potentially some national parks and land set aside under the *Indian Act* considered federal land, and the remainder, particularly lands administered by the three territories, considered non-federal.[38]

The trigger for projects on federal lands is similar to the trigger under the *Canadian Environmental Assessment Act, 2012* (CEAA 2012). At the core is a definition of project that is quite broad for activities carried out in relation to a physical work. For such activities proposed on federal land, the assumption is that the requirements in sections 81–91 of the Act apply, unless the project is excluded in some way. For other activities not related to a physical work, the assessment requirements in this part only apply if the activity is designated by the Minister.[39]

The scope of an assessment under this part is similar to CEAA 2012 in the sense that environmental effects are limited to biophysical impacts and their socioeconomic consequences, plus impacts on Indigenous peoples. The process requirements are minimal. There is a requirement to post a notice before making a project determination, and a requirement to post a notice of the determination made. There is no requirement to consider public input, but when input is sought, a notice has to be posted inviting such input.[40]

In short, the process is largely discretionary and in the hands of the federal project decision-maker. There are no legislative process requirements beyond notice, there is no guaranteed public participation, no participant funding, and no legislated role for Indigenous communities, though the duty to consult of course remains, as does the government's commitment to the United Nations Declaration on the Rights of Indigenous Peoples (UNDRIP). Having said this, some federal decision-makers to whom these provisions apply have their own established assessment processes, as they had similar assessment responsibilities under CEAA 2012.[41]

The project decision involves two steps, also based on the decision-making process in CEAA 2012. First, the federal authority in charge of the federal

---

38   IAA (n 1), s 2.
39   See id., ss 81–91.
40   See id., ss 84, 86, 89.
41   Kneen (n 37), p. 390.

decision that triggered the assessment determines whether the project is likely to cause significant adverse environmental effects. In case of a determination that the project is likely to cause significant adverse environmental effects, Cabinet then determines whether these effects are justified in the circumstances. In case of a conclusion that the project is not likely to cause significant adverse effects, the final decision is made by the federal authority without having to go to Cabinet.[42]

2.3   *Regional and Strategic Assessments*

The IAA has separate provisions for the conduct of regional and strategic assessments. The Act does not include definitions of regional or strategic assessments, and the line between them is not clearly drawn in the Act or guidance to date, so we deal with them together in this section.[43]

Regional assessments are not defined; however, the Act does offer some indication of the types of assessments contemplated. As a starting point, the Act suggests that there are three categories of regional assessments. One category would be assessments of regions that are entirely on federal lands. A second category would be assessments of regions that are completely outside federal lands. A third category are assessments of regions that are partly on and partly outside federal lands.[44]

Ultimately, regional assessments can be carried out in each of the three categories identified, so they are not determinative of whether a federal regional assessment will be carried out. Having said this, it seems clear that the categories are motivated by the recognition that carrying out a regional assessment on federal lands will be less complex than one in the other two categories. In practical terms, it seems likely that regional assessments in categories two and three are more likely to be carried out if the other jurisdictions are willing to cooperate in the conduct of a regional assessment. In the Canadian Arctic, this means cooperation with either a territorial government, co-management boards, or an Indigenous organization under a land claims agreement.[45]

Strategic assessments are also not defined in the Act. Again, there are some indications of what types of assessment are contemplated. The Act specifically identifies the possibility of conducting a strategic assessment of proposed or

---

42   Id.

43   See IAA (n 1), ss 92–103.

44   See discussion of the definition of federal lands in the previous subsection.

45   At present there are no self-government agreements finalized across Nunavut, the North Slope, or the Inuvialuit Settlement Region/NWT. In light of the Arctic focus of the book, we are not discussing Nunavik or Nunatsiavut in this chapter.

existing federal policies, plans and programs that are relevant to the conduct of assessments. Section 95 makes it clear, however, that a strategic assessment can be carried out with respect to any issue that is relevant to an assessment of a designated project or class of designated projects. Not expressly included are issues that are relevant to the assessment of federal projects under sections 81–91 of the IAA.[46]

3   The IAA and Other Assessment Regimes in the Canadian Arctic

There are several assessment regimes in the Canadian Arctic other than the IAA. They exist under territorial legislation and land claims agreements, and they typically have significant, if not primary, roles to play in impact assessment in the Arctic. For the most part, these regimes are based on a co-management model, whereby the assessment regime is a requirement under a land claims agreement and the reviewing body is composed of individuals appointed by the Indigenous treaty party and the federal and territorial governments, respectively. However, in most situations the responsible federal minister is the final decision-maker.[47] Beyond these formal assessment regimes, there are various ways in which strategic or regional assessment could be undertaken; examples of these are discussed further below.

3.1   Project-Level Assessment in the Western Arctic: Inuvialuit Settlement Region, Yukon, and Northwest Territories
In most of the Western Arctic, project-specific assessment is governed by the Inuvialuit Final Agreement[48] (IFA) and the *Impact Assessment Act*.[49] Unlike in the Nunavut context discussed below, the IAA can indeed apply in the

---

46   IAA (n 1), s 95. These provisions are new to the federal assessment process, so while there are examples of strategic and regional assessments carried out elsewhere, there is not enough experience to draw on federally to predict how these discretionary provisions will be exercised.

47   See Daniel W. Dylan, "The Complicated Intersection of Politics, Administrative and Constitutional Law in Nunavut's Environmental Impacts Assessment Regime," *University of New Brunswick Law Journal* 68 (2019): 202–231.

48   Indian and Northern Affairs Canada, *The Western Arctic Claim: The Inuvialuit Final Agreement* (1984) [IFA], https://yukon.ca/sites/yukon.ca/files/eco/eco-ar-western_arctic _claim_inuvialuit_final-agreement.pdf.

49   Crown-Indigenous Relations and Northern Affairs Canada, "Environmental Assessments in Canada's North," Government of Canada, last modified 19 December 2018, https: //www.rcaanc-cirnac.gc.ca/eng/1466431262580/1547478287247#Northwest_Territories _inuvialuit.

Inuvialuit Settlement Region, which includes much of the Beaufort Sea (see Figure 16.2).[50] However, the IAA would only be triggered according to its own terms described above in this chapter (i.e., a project listed in the regulations or specific designation by the Minister). Where a proposed project triggers the IAA, the assessment may be integrated with the IFA regime to provide a single assessment process that meets all applicable requirements.[51] Alternatively, the IAA provides for the IFA regime to be substituted for the IAA process with approval of the federal Minister.[52] As noted above, the IAA also requires that the IAA process takes into account findings from any parallel Indigenous-led assessment.[53]

Aside from the Mackenzie Gas Project,[54] which proceeded by Joint Review Panel and did not have a shipping component, there are no examples of the legislated federal impact assessment regime being deployed in the Inuvialuit Settlement Region (i.e., not under the IAA or its predecessors). However, there are at least two proposals in the very early stages that could change this situation, both of which would have significant shipping dimensions. One is focused on developing natural gas fields in the offshore, as well as associated pipelines and two offshore liquefaction and tanker loading platforms far off Tuktoyaktuk.[55] The other is a long-standing proposal to

---

50   IFA (n 48), Article 11(32). See also Crown-Indigenous Relations and Northern Affairs Canada (n 49); Figure 16.2.

51   See, e.g., Canada Energy Regulator, "ARCHIVED – Agreement for an Environmental Impact Review of the Mackenzie Gas Project," last modified 29 September 2020, https://www .cer-rec.gc.ca/en/about/acts-regulations/other-acts/cooperative-agreements/archive /agreement-environmental-impact-review-mackenzie-gas-project.html.

52   See generally Government of Canada, "Territorial Environmental Assessment Processes," last modified 25 May 2021, https://www.northernstrategy.gc.ca/eng/1619440955879/16194 40977808?wbdisable=true.

53   IAA (n 1), s 22(1)(q); see also David V. Wright, "Interest Versus Indigenous Confidence: Indigenous Engagement, Consultation, and 'Consideration' in the Impact Assessment Act" (23 July 2020), https://ssrn.com/abstract=3692839; Sarah Morales, "Indigenous-led Assessment Processes as a Way Forward," *Centre for International Governance Innovation: Environmental Challenges on Indigenous Lands Series*, 4 July 2019, https://www.cigionline.org /articles/Indigenous-led-assessment-processes-way-forward (providing a succinct description and discussion of Indigenous-led assessment, including examples).

54   Mackenzie Valley Review Board, "Mackenzie Gas Project – EIR0405-001," https://reviewboard .ca/registry/eir0405-001.

55   Jimmy Thomson, "N.W.T. Gov't Exploring LNG Project Off Canadian Arctic Coast," *CBC*, 10 November 2020, https://www.cbc.ca/news/canada/north/nwt-lng-offshore-arctic-request -proposal-oil-1.5795317.

develop a deep water port at Tuktoyaktuk.⁵⁶ Subject to the federal Minister
of the Environment exercising ministerial discretion and a screening decision under the IAA, these projects would attract application of the IAA by
virtue of new marine terminals and expansion of existing marine terminals
being on the IAA project list.⁵⁷ They would also attract application of the IFA
regime, and, in practical terms, these assessments would likely be integrated.
It is foreseeable that the Inuvialuit would take a leadership role, considering the relatively broad jurisdiction provided to an "Indigenous Governing
Body" under the IAA, and given that Inuvialuit have expressed a preference
to not have the IAA apply in the Inuvialuit Settlement Region at all.⁵⁸ What
this means, however, is that the broad-based assessment regime of the IAA,
including its broad scope of factors, would have to be part of such an integrated assessment, which could make it more comprehensive than if it were
only under the IFA.

In the Yukon, similar to the Nunavut context discussed below, the *Yukon
Environmental and Socio-economic Assessment Act* (YESAA) explicitly states
that the *Impact Assessment Act* does not apply in the Yukon.⁵⁹ As such, for
land-based (but potentially shipping related) projects in the North Slope of
the Yukon (see Figure 16.2) there would be interrelated processes between the
IFA regime and an assessment under YESAA. The North Slope is given special
explicit treatment in YESAA,⁶⁰ which in basic terms creates a crosswalk to
the IFA regime. For example, section 90(2) requires that the reviewing body
under YESAA also takes into consideration "the need to protect the rights of
the Inuvialuit" under the IFA, and "may take into consideration any matter
that it considers relevant."⁶¹ However, it is the IFA regime that takes over the
process in contexts where the Inuvialuit Screening Committee refers to the

56   David Thurton, "Deep Water Port in Tuktoyaktuk Could Bring Business to N.W.T," *CBC*, 2
      December 2014, https://www.cbc.ca/news/canada/north/deep-water-port-in-tuktoyaktuk
      -could-bring-business-to-n-w-t-1.2857238.
57   *Physical Activities Regulations*, SOR/2019-285, ss 52, 53.
58   See Duane Ningaqsiq Smith and John Lucas, "Re: Brief to the Standing Committee on
      Environment and Sustainable Development regarding Bill C-69 An Act to enact the
      Impact Assessment Act and the Canadian Energy Regulator Act, to amend the Navigation
      Protection Act and to make consequential amendments to other Acts" (Letter to Standing
      Committee on Environment and Sustainable Development, Our Commons Commit-
      tee Brief, Ottawa, 6 April 2018), https://www.ourcommons.ca/Content/Committee/421
      /ENVI/Brief/BR9837758/br-external/InuvialuitRegionalCorporation-e.pdf.
59   *Yukon Environmental and Social-Economic Assessment Act*, SC 2003, c 7, s 6 [YESAA].
60   Id., ss 90–91.
61   Id., s 90(2).

project to the Inuvialuit Environmental Impact Review Board.[62] In practical terms, a project with land- and marine-based activities and shipping dimensions would likely be of a magnitude that it would be referred to the Inuvialuit Environmental Impact Review Board, and thus the IFA process would take over. On a related and similar point, it should also be noted that, in contrast to the application of YESAA, on the NWT side of the territorial border the *Mackenzie Valley Resource Management Act* (MVRMA) does not apply in the Inuvialuit Settlement Region.[63]

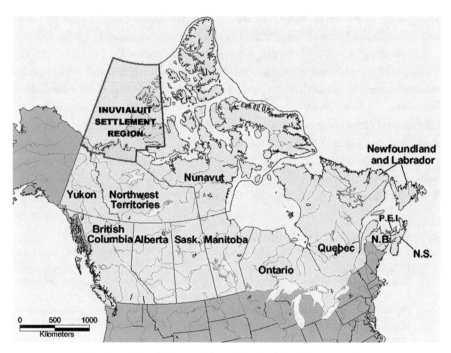

FIGURE 16.2   Map identifying the boundaries of the Inuvialuit Settlement Region
SOURCE: IFA JOINT SECRETARIAT

62   This is by virtue of YESAA, id., s 91(2) which states, "[w]here a project located on the Yukon North Slope is referred to the Review Board by the Screening Committee... the provisions of this Part relating to assessments and decision documents cease to apply in respect of the project" (note that this "Part" is referring to YESAA "Part 2 – Assessment Process and Decision Documents").
63   *Mackenzie Valley Resource Management Act*, SC 1998, c 25, ss 2, 6.

3.2   Project-level Assessment in the Eastern Arctic: Nunavut[64]

The process for project-specific assessment in Nunavut is set out in Article 12 of the Nunavut Land Claims Agreement (Nunavut Agreement),[65] which provides a comprehensive impact assessment regime that takes into account ecosystemic and socioeconomic impacts of proposed projects.[66] The Nunavut Impact Review Board (NIRB) is responsible for implementation of impact assessment (IA) in Nunavut, as detailed in Article 12.[67] Since coming into force in 2015, the *Nunavut Planning and Project Assessment Act*[68] (NuPPAA) provides additional detail and structure for IA in the Nunavut context for both IA and land use planning.[69] NuPPAA is explicit in stating that the *Impact Assessment Act* does not apply in the Nunavut Settlement Area and the Outer Land Fast Ice Zone.[70]

However, if a NIRB screening decision[71] determines that a review of the proposed project is required, the responsible minister[72] has discretion under section 94(1) to refer the project to a "federal environmental assessment panel" or a "joint panel."[73] Such discretionary referral is constrained by specific parameters such as a project involving a matter of national interest, a project being carried out partly outside the designated area, and consultation with the territorial minister and NIRB. The national interest dimension is additionally constrained through subsection 94(2) which stipulates that the Minister may only refer the project to a federal panel on the national interest

---

64   See also Lalonde and Bankes in this volume.
65   Agreement between the Inuit of the Nunavut Settlement Area and Her Majesty the Queen in Right of Canada (25 May 1993), Article 12, http://www.tunngavik.com/documents/publications/1993-00-00-Nunavut-Land-Claims-Agreement-English.pdf [Nunavut Agreement].
66   Id., Article 12.2.2. See generally Crown-Indigenous Relations and Northern Affairs Canada, "Nunavut's Regulatory Regime," Government of Canada, last modified 19 December 2018, https://www.rcaanc-cirnac.gc.ca/eng/1466431262580/1547478287247#Nunavut_regulatory_regime.
67   Nunavut Agreement (n 65), Article 12.2.
68   *Nunavut Planning and Project Assessment Act*, SC 2013, c 14, s 2 [NuPPAAA].
69   Crown-Indigenous Relations and Northern Affairs Canada, "Nunavut Planning and Project Assessment Act (NuPPAAA) – Highlights," Government of Canada, accessed 1 June 2022, https://www.rcaanc-cirnac.gc.ca/eng/1436379471116/1547483079595.
70   IAA (n 1), s 7. Note that these areas are both explicitly defined in Articles 3 and 16 of the Nunavut Agreement (n 65), respectively.
71   Pursuant to the process set out in NuPPAA (n 68), ss 86–98.
72   The definition of responsible minister is set out in section 73(1) as follows: (a) the federal minister or the territorial minister, as the case may be, who has the jurisdictional responsibility for authorizing a project to proceed; or (b) the Minister of Northern Affairs, if there is no federal minister or territorial minister who has the responsibility referred to in paragraph (a).
73   NuPPAA (n 68), s 94(1). The details of a Federal Environmental Assessment Panel and associated process are explicitly set out in sections 115–133. In such a situation, it is the federal Minister of the Environment who is responsible for the federal environmental assessment panel process.

basis "on an exceptional basis".[74] Further, NuPPAA is explicit in stating that NIRB must be the review body "if the only activity relating to a project to be carried out outside the designated area is the transportation of persons or goods" (i.e., shipping), "unless that Minister determines that the transportation of persons or goods is a significant element of the project and that it is more appropriate for the review to be conducted by a federal environmental assessment panel or a joint panel."[75] In short, relevant NuPPAA provisions steer project-specific IAs toward being conducted by NIRB, not a federal panel, and even where a federal panel is the reviewing body, that review would not be conducted under the IAA as the IAA is explicitly ousted from application in Nunavut.

Nevertheless, though it has yet to happen in practice, the IAA may still be relevant in a few ways. First, if a project is to be carried out partly outside the Nunavut Settlement Area and beyond the Outer Land Fast Ice Zone, and the transportation of goods is a significant element of the project that warrants a federal review, then presumably the IAA could apply. While the regime offers a very narrow pathway to this process, this could be the case in federal waters in Baffin Bay and Davis Strait, which would be very relevant from an Arctic shipping perspective.[76] Second, notwithstanding the IAA not applying in Nunavut, if a project is in fact referred to the federal Minister of the Environment for a "federal environmental assessment panel" to conduct the review, presumably that federal panel would be structured in the likeness of review panels under the IAA, even though all aspects of this process option are explicitly laid out in NuPPAA, and NuPPAA would be the governing statute.[77] Those provisions include, for example, rules pertaining to panel composition, scoping, consultation, public and Indigenous participation, factors to consider, traditional and community knowledge, final determinations, and approval conditions.[78] Third, NIRB has broad powers to consider a range of factors, including "any other matter within the Board's jurisdiction that, in its opinion, should be considered,"[79] meaning that NIRB could take into account factors set out in the IAA but not explicitly set out in NuPPAA, such as climate change and sustainability considerations.[80] Finally, there is potential for projects on federal

74   Id., s 94(2).
75   Id., s 94(3).
76   For the general context about these waters see Oceans North, "Baffin Bay & Davis Strait," https://www.oceansnorth.org/en/where-we-work/baffin-bay-davis-strait/.
77   NuPPAA (n 68), ss 115–133.
78   Id.
79   Id., s 103(1)(p).
80   IAA (n 1), ss 22(1)(i), 22(1)(h).

land as defined in the IAA to trigger the federal Act. However, the process requirements are so minimal and the scope so narrow that they would most likely be met without a separate federal process.[81]

There is an additional, and perhaps practically most important, basis for the incorporation of IAA considerations into NIRB led assessments. This comes from the responsible Minister's ability to find that a NIRB report is deficient "with respect to issues relating to the ecosystemic and socio-economic impacts of the project,"[82] and to then require the NIRB to conduct further review, including holding a public hearing, on issues identified by the Minister. In cases where the responsible minister is the federal Minister, as was the case for the Mary River Project discussed below, it is reasonable to expect that the federal Minister would require consideration of issues set out in the IAA, such as climate change and sustainability.

An example in the Nunavut context of a project-specific review with shipping dimensions is the Mary River Project. This large iron ore mining project was approved in 2012[83] after a lengthy, comprehensive review by NIRB under Nunavut Agreement Article 12.[84] The project, situated in northern Baffin Island near the community of Pond Inlet, includes exploration, construction, operation, closure, and reclamation of an open-pit mine and associated infrastructure for extraction, transportation and shipment of iron ore (including ports).[85] From a shipping perspective, the ore is transported to Europe via a shipping route through Eclipse Sound, Pond Inlet and Baffin Bay.[86] The project

---

81   See discussion above on projects on federal lands.

82   NuPPAA (n 68), s 104(3).

83   See Nunavut Impact Review Board (NIRB), *Project Certificate [No.:005]*, 28 December 2012, https://www.nirb.ca/portal/dms/script/dms_download.php?fileid=290662&applicationid =123910&sessionid=mg6cmd2pc9g12pvoqnp642ql43.

84   Note that this project predated NuPPAA. Prior to NuPPAA there was an amendment to the Nunavut Agreement to explicitly clarify that CEAA "and any successor legislation replacing that Act" did not apply in the Nunavut context. See Nunavut Tunngavik, "Article 12.12.7–Canadian Environmental Assessment Act," https://nlca.tunngavik.com/?page_id =1475. For context and analysis of the Nunavut regime in the early days after the Nunavut Agreement was finalized, see Michael J Hardin and John Donihee, eds., *Mineral Exploration and Mine Development in Nunavut: Working with the New Regulator Regime* (Canadian Institute for Resources Law, 1997).

85   See NIRB Project Certificate [NO.: 005] (n 83), p. 4.

86   Canadian Science Advisory Secretariat Science Response, *Science Review of the Phase 2 Addendum to the Final Environmental Impact Statement for the Baffinland Mary River Project*, Fisheries and Oceans Canada, April 2019, https://waves-vagues.dfo-mpo.gc.ca /Library/40783844.pdf.

was assessed entirely by NIRB, not by a federal environmental assessment panel or a joint panel.[87]

In the time since the Mary River project was approved, the proponent has made several amendments,[88] and then sought approval for "Phase 2."[89] The second phase proposed an increase in extraction to a total of 12 millon tonnes per annum road and rail haulage, infrastructure development at the Milne Port, and increased marine shipping.[90] Similar to the initial process, NIRB led the Phase 2 assessment. There was no federal panel, though federal departments provided input to the process and seemed to play an influential role, which is not surprising given their capacity and expertise.[91] The IAA has not been applied to date (nor was CEAA 2012), and it is unlikely to be applied going forward. Despite Phase 2 being a very large mining project, it was not determined to be a project of national significance under NuPPAA and it was not otherwise referred to the relevant federal minister to establish a federal panel. This is presumably owing to the above-described explicit ousting of the IAA and the very narrow pathway for any triggering of the IAA regime in the Nunavut context. Ultimately, NIRB recommended that the Phase 2 not be allowed to proceed, finding that the proposal "cannot proceed in a manner that will protect and promote the existing and future well-being of residents and communities of the Nunavut Settlement Area, and Canada in general, and would not be protective of the ecosystemic integrity of the Nunavut Settlement Area."[92] That NIRB recommendation was accepted by the responsible ministers in a final decision released in November 2022, meaning that Phase 2 is not permitted to proceed at this time due to unacceptable impacts.[93]

3.3   *Strategic and Regional Environmental Assessments in the Canadian Arctic*

A strategic environmental assessment or regional environmental assessment of shipping in the Canadian Arctic would not be the first assessment in the

---

87   Id., p. 2.

88   See Project Certificate No. 005, Amendment 003, "Schedule of Amendments to the Nunavut Impact Review Board's Mary River Project Certificate," 18 June 2020.

89   NIRB File No.: 08MN053; NWB File No.: 2AM-MRY1325 (Amendment No. 2).

90   Canadian Science Advisory Secretariat (n 86), pp. 2–3.

91   See, e.g., id., 38.

92   See NIRB, "Highlights Document for the Board's Reconsideration Report and Recommendations for Baffinland's Phase 2 Development Proposal," NIRB File No. 08MN053, May 2022, p. 1, https://www.nirb.ca/portal/dms/script/dms_download.php?fileid=339559& applicationid=124701.

93   Honourable Dan Vandal, Member of Parliament and Minister of Northern Affairs, Letter to Chairperson of the Nunavut Impact Review Board, 16 November 2022, https://www .nirb.ca/portal/dms/script/dms_download.php?fileid=342156&applicationid=124701& sessionid=tbgvg6qmij3fliur3ocud84is4.

region to go beyond the project-specific level. The discussion below presents two recent examples, one from the Western Arctic and one from the Eastern Arctic. Both serve as informative examples; however, both resemble relatively narrow approaches to these types of assessments, thus leaving room and potential need for further assessments under the IAA or otherwise.

The Beaufort Regional Environmental Assessment (BREA) was a four-year process focused on a specific sector in a specific region, namely, offshore oil and gas development in the Beaufort Sea.[94] Its purpose was to generate a basis for "a more efficient and effective environmental assessment regime through the development of regional information to address issues that are likely to recur in individual project-level environmental assessments."[95] BREA did not take place under a specific statute. Rather, the process was launched by the federal government in 2010, led by the then Department of Aboriginal Affairs and Northern Development Canada (AANDC), and was carried out in partnership with the Inuvialuit, industry, government, regulators, and researchers.[96] At a practical level, the process included six working groups focused on nine research areas, none of which were directly focused on shipping.[97] Key BREA findings were released in 2016.[98]

A subsequent phase of the process began in 2016, led by the Inuvialuit Regional Corporation, the Inuvialuit Game Council and Crown-Indigenous Relations and Northern Affairs Canada in the form of the Beaufort Region Strategic Environmental Assessment (BRSEA).[99] BRSEA built on BREA as a "proactive planning tool in which hypothetical future industrial development scenarios are assessed to provide an understanding of the mechanisms

94   Beaufort Regional Environmental Assessment (BREA), "Key Findings: Research and Working Group Results," March 2016, https://www.beaufortrea.ca/wp-content/uploads /2018/06/NCR-10615510-v1-BREA_FINAL_REPORT.pdf.

95   Id., xi.

96   Id., xi, 157; see generally Government of Canada, "Backgrounder: Beaufort Regional Environmental Assessment (BREA)," last modified 27 February 2012, https://www.canada.ca /en/news/archive/2012/02/backgrounder-beaufort-regional-environmental-assessment -brea.html.

97   Id. The nine research areas: baseline fish information; coastal and marine birds; bird, fish, and marine mammal information; worst-case environmental design limits for ice; sea ice types and extreme ice features; coupled ocean-ice-atmosphere modeling and forecasting; offshore geohazards and coastal processes; web-based geospatial analysis tool; community priorities. The six working groups: Cumulative Effects Working Group; Climate Change Working Group; Social, Cultural, and Economic Indicators Working Group; Oil Spill Preparedness and Response Working Group; Waste Management Working Group; Information Management Working Group.

98   BREA (n 94), p. 150.

99   Beaufort Regional Strategic Environmental Assessment, "About," accessed 31 May 2022, https://rsea.inuvialuit.com/.

through which adverse and positive effects could occur, the potential out-comes (e.g., adverse effects and positive benefits), and applicable management approaches, as well as important information gaps and research needs."[100] As such, it too was focused on a single sector in a single region.

Following the federal government's announcement of a moratorium on oil and gas development in the Canadian Arctic,[101] the NIRB led a strategic environmental assessment focused on potential oil and gas activities in Baffin Bay and Davis Strait.[102] This matter was formally referred to the NIRB by then Indigenous and Northern Affairs Canada pursuant to section 12.2.4 of the Nunavut Agreement,[103] and NIRB issued a final report in July 2019.[104] The purpose was to develop "an improved understanding of potential types of oil and gas related development activities that could one day be proposed within the Canadian waters of Baffin Bay and Davis Strait outside of the Nunavut Settlement Area (NSA), along with their associated adverse effects, benefits, and management strategies."[105] Ultimately, NIRB issued a number of detailed recommendations, including that the federal government extend the five-year moratorium.[106]

100   KAVIK-Stantec Inc. "Beaufort Region Strategic Environmental Assessment: Data Synthesis and Assessment Report," 31 July 2020, https://rsea.inuvialuit.com/docs/NCR10615510 -v1-BREA_FINAL_REPORT.PDF; Beaufort Regional Environmental Assessment website, https://www.beaufortrea.ca/.

101   Marco Vigliotti "Trudeau Government Expands Moratorium on Oil and Gas Work in Arctic Waters," *iPolitics*, 8 August 2019, https://ipolitics.ca/2019/08/08/trudeau-government -expands-moratorium-on-oil-and-gas-work-in-arctic-waters/.

102   NIRB, "Final Scope List for the NIRB's Strategic Environmental Assessment in Baffin Bay and Davis Strait," NIRB File No. 17SN034, 9 March 2018, https://www.nirb.ca/publications /strategic%20environmental%20assessment/180309-17SN034-Final%20Scope%20List -OPAE.pdf.

103   Crown-Indigenous Relations and Northern Affairs Canada, "Arctic Regional Environmental Studies: Beaufort Regional Strategic Environmental Assessment," Government of Canada, accessed 31 May 2022, https://www.rcaanc-cirnac.gc.ca/eng/1492023135343/1538 588674968#chp1.

104   NIRB, "Final Report for the Strategic Environmental Assessment in Baffin Bay and Davis Strait: Volume 1: SEA Summary Report," July 2019, https://www.nirb.ca/publications /Strategic%20Environmental%20Assessment/first%20row-first%20file%20 -190731-17SN034-Final%20SEA%20Report-Volume%201-OPAE.pdf.

105   Id., iii.; see also, NIRB "Strategic Environmental Assessment in Baffin Bay & Davis Strait," Presentation, Arctic Oil & Gas Symposium, Calgary, Alberta, 20 March 2018, https://www .nirb.ca/publications/presentations/180321-NIRB%20Presentation%20Arctic%20 Oil%20and%20Gas%20Symposium-OEDE.pdf.

106   Elaine Anselmi, "Extend Offshore Oil and Gas Moratorium, Says Nunavut Review Board," *Nunatsiaq News,* 2 August 2019, https://nunatsiaq.com/stories/article/extend-offshore-oil -and-gas-moratorium-says-nunavut-review-board/.

This SEA was not focused on any particular project, but it did include types of oil and gas projects that could be proposed. In this way, this SEA was an approach that included elements of regional assessment (i.e., focus on Baffin Bay and Davis Straight) and sector-specific strategic assessment (i.e., oil and gas). Its focus was narrow, as it did not consider a broad range of activities beyond oil and gas. However, viewed in relation to shipping in Canada's Arctic, it offers a potentially useful model as it is foreseeable that a future strategic assessment could be sector specific (i.e., shipping and associated on-land infrastructure) in a specific geographic region (Canada's Arctic, or sub-regions).

It should also be noted that the Nunavut Agreement and NuPPAA include a comprehensive land-use planning regime that plays a role analogous to regional assessment. This takes the form of a conformity assessment whereby a proposed project must proceed through a threshold step to determine whether the proposal conforms with the relevant land-use plan. In practical terms, a project proponent must submit a proposal to the Nunavut Planning Commission, and the Commission then determines whether the project conforms to the requirements of any approved land use plans.[107] If it does, then it can proceed to the project-specific process described above.[108] At the time of writing, a draft Nunavut wide land-use plan had been released by the Nunavut Planning Commission,[109] which does include content on marine shipping.[110]

4   Discussion

In this section, we consider the potential for the four assessment processes under the IAA to be part of the governance and decision-making process for considering the impact of shipping on ecological and social systems in the Arctic. We first reflect on the role of the designated project process, and then proceed to projects on federal land, followed by strategic and regional assessments.

---

107   NIRB, "Projects Requiring Assessment," accessed 1 June 2022, https://www.nirb.ca/content/projects-requiring-assessment.
108   Id.
109   Nunavut Planning Commission, *Draft Nunavut Land Use Plan Draft*, July 2021, https://www.nunavut.ca/land-use-plans/draft-nunavut-land-use-plan.
110   Id., 42, and tables 4 and 5.

4.1   *The Designated Project Assessment Process*

The designated project process, if it were to be applied in the Western Arctic, would offer the opportunity to consider the full range of implications of shipping in the Arctic associated with any project assessed. The assessment would include benefits and negative impacts, and would assess a broad range of biophysical, economic, social, cultural, and health impacts. The Act specifically requires consideration of gender-based analysis, impacts on Indigenous peoples, and impacts on climate commitments and environmental obligations, among others. The public interest determination to be made at the end of the process is informed by determinations on the contribution of the project on sustainability among other elements. In short, when the process is triggered, it provides every opportunity to broadly consider the shipping element of any proposed new project. As noted in the above discussion about the Nunavut context, by virtue of final decisions resting with a federal minister, the factors in the IAA may also influence assessments even where the IAA is not formally triggered.

As discussed above, the application of the designated project assessment process in the Arctic is limited by the physical activities list and the interplay with territorial and co-management assessment processes. The list does not include a number of activities that may become viable in the longer term, such as aquaculture outside national parks and offshore renewable energy projects other than tidal energy. More immediately, thresholds for listed mining, transportation and energy related activities will exclude smaller projects. Of course, the ministerial discretion to designate projects not listed does provide an opportunity to fill this gap, as does the possibility of amending the list.[111]

More fundamentally, the application of the designated project assessment process is limited through the interplay between the IAA and the territorial assessment processes discussed above. In the Western Arctic, other than the Yukon North Slope, the IAA, including its designated project process, generally does apply. However, its application is of course shaped by the exercise of harmonization powers that include potentially not requiring a federal assessment even for listed projects, and opportunities for substitution, delegation and joint assessments. In the Eastern Arctic, the default is that the IAA does not apply. As discussed above, there may be opportunities for federal assessments in certain circumstances, particularly panel reviews, but past practice would suggest that these opportunities will be limited. There are also opportunities in the case of the NuPPAA for the responsible minister to consider issues set out in the IAA, such as climate change, impacts on Indigenous communities

---

111   IAA (n 1), s 9.

and gender-based analysis plus (GBA+), if they feel there are deficiencies in the environmental impact statements related to these issues.

4.2 *The Federal Projects Assessment Process*

As outlined above, there are very few process requirements for so-called federal projects, which for purposes of this chapter is about projects on federal land. Federal land does not include land under the administration of one of the three territorial governments. This will exclude many land-based projects in the Arctic from the IAA's assessment requirement for projects on federal lands. This is consistent with the exclusion of the application of the IAA in the Yukon and Nunavut.

Where projects are proposed on federal lands in the Arctic, the assessment requirement under sections 81 to 91 would apply to impose some minimal process obligations along with a requirement to make a determination whether the proposed project is likely to cause significant adverse biophysical effects, and, if so, whether such effects are justified in the circumstances. Ultimately, these provisions may serve as a safeguard in case a project on federal lands is not subject to a territorial or Indigenous assessment process, but it is unlikely to add any meaningful process requirements.

It is important to note that while the potential for project level assessments under the IAA to play a significant role in the assessment of shipping related projects is relatively limited, this does not mean the federal government has relinquished its decision-making responsibility. This is apparent from the requirements for projects on federal lands, but is also inherent in the relationship between territorial, co-management, and federal processes outlined in section 4 of the Act. The bottom line is that the federal government still makes project decisions. If the new IAA is the new standard for how federal decisions about major projects are to be made to ensure they are in the public interest, it would be reasonable to expect that federal decision-makers would consider some—if not most—of the same questions set out in section 63 of the IAA when deciding whether to exercise their powers, duties and functions with respect to proposed projects assessed under a territorial or Indigenous assessment process in the Arctic. Thus, while the IAA may strictly speaking not apply to many of the projects, it could still serve as a standard for federal decision-making by considering whether projects make a net contribution to sustainability, and contribute to Canada's climate commitments and environmental obligations, for example.[112]

---

112   For discussion of the IAA as a potential basis for reform of northern assessment regimes, see David V. Wright, "Bill C-88 Elimination of the MVRMA 'Superboard': Small Step or Start

THE NEW FEDERAL IMPACT ASSESSMENT ACT AND ARCTIC SHIPPING

As with the IAA itself, what is currently missing is meaningful guidance on how such determinations would be made by federal decision-makers, and what the public interest means in an Arctic-specific context with primarily Indigenous populations. Put another way, in the present context there is a need for the federal government, territorial governments, and Indigenous organizations and governments to take stock of the different regimes and clarify how to improve integration and harmonization of the different regimes. This could take the form of a strategic assessment of policies and programs, further discussed below. Given Canada's "full support" [113] for the UNDRIP [114] and new federal UNDRIP implementation legislation,[115] it is reasonable to expect that next steps also ought to be consistent with and guided by the objectives and provisions of the Declaration.

4.3   The Strategic and Regional Assessment Processes

It is with respect to strategic and regional assessments that the most promising opportunities for the application of the IAA arise. Given the discretionary nature of the IAA provisions for regional and strategic assessments, it matters less whether these provisions have formal application in a given part of the Canadian Arctic. In that regard, the limits imposed on the application of the IAA in the Yukon and Nunavut would extend to sections 92–103 of the IAA. In other parts of the Arctic, the provisions for strategic and regional assessments would seem applicable, including with respect to any ocean-based activities in Arctic waters.

However, perhaps the more important consideration is that similar to the project level assessment provisions of the IAA, there is potential for strategic and regional assessments carried out under the IAA to serve as role models for similar assessments in the Arctic region. The examples discussed above illustrate the appetite for higher tier assessments in the region, even if the processes themselves were far from perfect.

---

of Big Leaps in Modern Treaty Implementation," November 2019 Northern Public Affairs (Modern Treaties Implementation Research Project).

113   Carolyn Bennett, Minister of Indigenous and Northern Affairs Canada, "Announcement of Canada's Support for the United Nations Declaration of Indigenous Peoples" (Speech delivered at the 15th Session of the United Nations Permanent Forum on Indigenous Issues, New York, 10 May 2016), https://www.canada.ca/en/indigenous-northern-affairs /news/2016/05/speech-delivered-at-the-united-nations-permanent-forum-on-indigenous -issues-new-york-may-10-.html.

114   United Nations Declaration on the Rights of Indigenous Peoples, UN Doc A/RES/61/295 (13 September 2007) [UNDRIP].

115   *United Nations Declaration on the Rights of Indigenous Peoples Act* (n 13).

There is certainly significant potential for well-designed and executed regional assessments, either under the IAA or outside the parameters of the Act, to contribute to sustainable Arctic shipping. Regional assessment would be particularly helpful in this regard if they were done at a manageable scale, and included all existing and potential human activities, and included a range of reasonable future development scenarios that allowed participants to see the interaction among these activities, where they complement each other, where they conflict with each other, and how they individually and collectively affect the health and resilience of ecosystems. Such regional assessments would hold the promise of building some level of agreement on the ideal mix of human activities to serve the social, cultural and economic needs of Arctic communities while ensuring the health and resilience of the natural systems they depend upon. They would consider both the impacts and benefits of various shipping related activities and position decisions-makers better to consider whether specific shipping activities should be allowed, at what scale and under what circumstances.

There is similarly potential for strategic assessments to contribute to a better understanding of where, how, and under what conditions shipping can maximize its contribution to sustainability in the Canadian Arctic. While the distinction between regional and strategic assessments under the IAA is not clear, a key difference appears to be that strategic assessments are not regionally focused, and their mandate is more constrained than regional assessments. Still, the strategic assessment process offers opportunities to consider specific industry sectors and their potential to make a net contribution to sustainability in the Canadian Arctic, while minimizing negative impacts on natural systems and local communities. Among the issues that could be addressed in strategic assessments are a range of operational impacts, such as vessel source pollution, invasive species, underwater noise, icebreaking, conflict with Indigenous peoples land use, water pollution from operational fuel, and air and land pollution in the form of emissions and black carbon. Another set of challenges includes impacts related to accidents, which would include the consideration of appropriate spill responses, and potentially the ban of certain vessels or cargo from sensitive areas.

Two shipping related issues that are currently under consideration, that seem to us particularly important for inclusion in a strategic assessment on Arctic shipping, would be the establishment of low-impact shipping corridors and deep water ports. As Porta *et al.* note, questions about northern marine destination/transportation routes have persisted nearly four decades.[116] The

---

116   Louie Porta *et al.*, "Shipping Corridors as a Framework for Advancing Marine Law and Policy and the Canadian Arctic," *Ocean and Coastal Law Journal* 22:1 (2017): 63–84.

Northern Marine Transportation Corridors Initiative, now called the Northern Low-Impact Shipping Corridors Initiative, "seeks to minimize potential effects of shipping on wildlife, respect culturally and ecologically sensitive areas, enhance marine navigation safety, and guide investments in the North."[117] Levitt defines these corridors as "dynamic shipping routes throughout Canada's North where the necessary infrastructure, marine navigational support, and emergency response services could be provided to ensure safer marine navigation, while respecting the sensitive northern environment and its ecological and cultural significance."[118] Dawson *et al.* outline the work of the Arctic Corridors and Northern Voices Project that is working to compile local and Indigenous knowledge from Arctic communities to help fill gaps in knowledge.[119] The use of any established corridors is currently voluntary and a strategic assessment could help to encourage needed regulatory and policy initiatives to formally establish appropriate corridors. As important, the location of destination ports is a question very much in play, with some communities having now expressed interest in establishing deep water ports. An SEA aimed at considering existing and needed port infrastructure would certainly help to bring clarity to where ports should be located from a pan-Arctic perspective.

As a general observation, it is clear that there has been experience with higher tier assessments in the Arctic, however, the process has tended to be ad hoc, and the scope has tended to be narrow, as seen for example in the sector-specific BREA example discussed above. A more systematic and comprehensive approach to regional and strategic assessments has significant potential, and the provisions in the IAA have the potential to assist with efforts to move in this direction. However, it is important to note that much work remains at the federal level to realize the potential of regional and strategic assessments.[120]

More generally, it may be time to revisit how the new federal IAA interacts with other assessment processes in the Arctic region. The federal government

---

117   Fisheries and Oceans Canada, "Northern Low-Impact Shipping Corridors," Government of Canada, accessed 1 June 2022, https://www.dfo-mpo.gc.ca/about-notre-sujet/engagement /2021/shipping-corridors-navigation-eng.html.

118   Michael Levitt, Chair, *Nation-Building at Home, Vigilance Beyond: Preparing for the Coming Decades in the Arctic*, Report of the Standing Committee on Foreign Affairs and International Development, April 2019, 42nd Parliament, 1st Session, 68. Retrieved from House of Commons, http://www.ourcommons.ca/Content/Committee/421/FAAE/Reports/RP10411277 /faaerp24/faaerp24-e.pdf.

119   Dawson *et al.* 2020 (n 25). See also Dawson and Song in this volume.

120   Jason MacLean, Bram Noble and Jill Blakley, "Strategic and Regional Environmental Assessments," in Doelle and Sinclair, eds. (n 3), 372–387, at 381.

indicated in 2016 that in addition to reviewing CEAA 2012, it would also review the northern assessment regimes. That was never done. With the IAA now in place, and the complexity of the assessment regime explored in this chapter, this review is more important than ever.

Another assessment process with potential implications for the Arctic region on the horizon is the environmental assessment system currently being negotiated as part of the emerging Marine Biodiversity of Areas Beyond National Jurisdiction (BBNJ) regime under the United Nations Convention on the Law of the Sea. Negotiations were delayed by the COVID pandemic, but have now resumed. The environmental assessment regime is being designed for areas beyond national jurisdiction, but two issues currently under negotiation have potential implications for Canadian Arctic waters. One is the impact of projects in Canadian waters on the high seas. The other is the impact of activities on the high seas on Canadian waters. It remains to be seen to what extent these contentious issues will come within the scope of the BBNJ environmental assessment regime.[121]

Another international dimension relates to the impact of activities in Canada on other coastal States in the Arctic region. For example, in the Mary River Project, the assessment of the expansion of the mine had to consider transboundary impacts in accordance with the UNECE Convention on Environmental Impact Assessment in a Transboundary Context (Espoo Convention), particularly impacts of the project on Greenland. Denmark was identified as an affected party under the Convention and a report outlining potential impacts on Greenland was prepared as part of the assessment.[122]

5   Conclusion

This chapter highlights the relevant features and attributes of four assessment processes under the IAA. The IAA is far from perfect but has much to offer at the levels of project assessments and higher tier assessments for undertakings related to shipping in the Arctic. Ultimately, any attempts to apply the IAA in the shipping context will have to be sensitive to the complex territorial and

---

121   See, for example, Meinhard Doelle and Gunnar Sander, "Next Generation Environmental Assessment in the Emerging High Seas Regime? An Evaluation of the State of the Negotiations," *International Journal of Marine and Coastal Law* 35:3 (2020): 498–532, https://ssrn.com/abstract=3479657.

122   NIRB, "Espoo Report Phase 2 Proposal – Mary River Project, Baffinland Iron Mines Corporation, Mary River Project," NIRB File No. 08MN053.

co-management assessment regimes that exist in the region, particularly given that the bases for those regimes are in constitutionally protected land claims agreements. Having said this, there is good reason to resist the temptation to just not apply the IAA in the Arctic. The IAA is reasonably well suited to the task of cooperative impact assessments given the broad statutory bases for cooperation and harmonization. This is particularly important with respect to other assessment processes that may be led by other jurisdictions in the Canadian Arctic, in particular Indigenous organizations, and includes a broad range of impact considerations beyond biophysical. In today's context of reconciliation, attempts to renew nation-to-nation relationships, and government commitments to the implementation of UNDRIP, the deployment of impact assessments in the Arctic region ought to be approached as an opportunity to build trust and relationships toward a shared interest of long-term sustainability and prosperity.

With the continued recession of multiyear ice and the advent of longer shipping seasons there is no doubt about the potential for development in Canada's Arctic region—development that will rely largely on shipping for the delivery and movement of goods. It is also clear that there has been little consideration of potential shipping impacts in IAs completed for projects that involve shipping. In fact, the inclusion of shipping impacts into IA processes is uncommon, at least in a global context, even though many of the procedural and analytic tools used in IA could be of use when managing shipping practices, impacts and risks.[123] It is also clear that the Canadian Coast Guard and local communities have very limited capacity to respond to ship-based spills.[124] As a result, many local people have expressed their concerns about the potential for spills and accidents due to increased shipping, as well as the effects of shipping on marine mammals.[125]

It is in response to this, that the IAA provides an opportunity to consider the impacts of shipping through each of the four assessment processes under the Act. As outlined above, there are critical decisions that need to be made regarding shipping in the Arctic that are particularly well suited for joint strategic or

123   Karin Andersson *et al.*, "Methods and Tools for Environmental Assessment," in Andersson *et al.*, eds. (n 15), 265–293 https://doi.org/10.1007/978-3-662-49045-7. Impact assessments carried out by the NIRB in Canada have commonly included shipping-related impacts.

124   Elise DeCola, Sierra Fletcher and Layla Hughes, *Framework for the Development of Nunavut Community Oil Spill Response Plans: Report to WWF-Canada* (March 2017); see also, Layla Hughes, *Background Information for Community Oil Spill Response Planning in Pond Inlet, Resolute, Grise Fiord, and Arctic Bay: Report to WWF-Canada* (March 2017), both at http://awsassets.wwf.ca/downloads/170405__oilspillresponseframeworknunavut_web.pdf.

125   Dawson (n 7), p. 33.

regional assessments involving federal, territorial, Indigenous, and co-management assessment regimes. There are also important opportunities at the project level through federal lands provisions under the IAA and the involvement of
federal ministers in project level decisions in the Arctic. This decision-making
role provides discretion for the consideration of areas of impact of particular
concern to the federal government and as required under the IAA.[126]

As such, there is the potential to improve governance for shipping in the
Canadian Arctic through the application of the IAA at the project, regional
and strategic levels, including through enhanced integration and harmonization between the IAA and other assessment regimes. This is especially so since
the IAA identifies specific impacts that require consideration that territorial
and co-management assessments currently do not, such as GBA+ and climate
change, and that capacity for assessing impacts related to these is being built
at the federal level. IA in the Arctic as it applies to shipping and related developments is going to require effort from all governments, local and Indigenous
communities, and every research institution active in the Arctic given how
rapidly change is actually occurring and the effects of such change on natural
and human systems. In the present context, there is great potential for IA in
general, and the IAA in particular, to become a well-utilized tool of governance
and decision-making in the Arctic.[127]

---

126   And it should be noted that the IAA will be implemented in an administrative law con-
      text that involves closer scrutiny of administrative decision-making and associated jus-
      tification given the standard of review set out in *Canada (Minister of Citizenship and
      Immigration)* v. *Vavilov*, 2019 SCC 65. See Shaun Fluker, "*Vavilov* and the Judicial Review of
      Natural Resources, Energy and Environmental Decisions in Canada," Canadian Institute
      of Resources Law No 123 (2020), https://cirl.ca/sites/default/files/Resources/Resources123
      .pdf. See also Nigel Bankes, "The Discipline of *Vavilov*? Judicial Review in the Absence of
      Reasons" (*ABlawg*, 12 May 2020), https://ablawg.ca/2020/05/12/the-discipline-of-vavilov
      -judicial-reason-in-the-absence-of-reasons/.
127   Andersson *et al.* (n 123), pp. 265–293.

Indigenous Self-determination and the Regulation of Navigation and Shipping in Canadian Arctic Waters

Suzanne Lalonde and Nigel Bankes

Abstract

Rapidly shrinking sea ice and changing socioeconomic factors have encouraged an increase in Arctic shipping traffic. This reality is testing Canada's marine safety and security regime and creating profound challenges for northern Indigenous communities that rely on the marine environment for their food, transport and way of life. This chapter explores the legal and policy opportunities available to Inuit communities in the Canadian Arctic, under both international and domestic law, to achieve self-determination with respect to navigation and shipping activities in the Arctic.

Keywords

Indigenous peoples – self-determination – human rights – constitutional law and principles – Nunavut Agreement – Arctic – navigation – shipping

1 Introduction

Rapidly shrinking sea ice and changing socioeconomic factors have encouraged an increase in Arctic shipping traffic. According to the lead researcher of the Arctic Corridors and Northern Voices project, "the total kilometers travelled by ships in Inuit Nunangat has more than tripled since 1990 and most of this increase has occurred in Nunavut waters."[1] This reality is testing Canada's

---

1 Jackie Dawson *et al.*, *Development and Management of Low-Impact Shipping Corridors in Nunavut: Workshop Discussion Paper* (Ottawa: University of Ottawa, 2019), 4. The territory of Nunavut encompasses most of the Canadian Arctic archipelago and covers 157,077 km² of water. "Nunavut," *The Canadian Encyclopedia*, https://www.thecanadianencyclopedia.ca/en/article/nunavut.

marine safety and security regime and creating profound challenges for northern Indigenous communities that rely on the marine environment for their food, transport and way of life.[2] "Inuit are a marine people; ... the sea is integral to the Inuit way of life."[3]

This chapter explores the legal and policy opportunities available to Inuit communities in the Canadian Arctic to achieve self-determination with respect to navigation and shipping activities in the Arctic. The chapter first canvasses the opportunities available under international law and then considers domestic law. The first section of Part 1 identifies the principal international law instruments which comprise a specially tailored Indigenous human rights regime and briefly considers their legal status and scope of application. The second section focuses on four of the most important rights that afford Indigenous peoples a say in the management of marine spaces and highlights some examples of Indigenous agency in the Canadian and international contexts.

Within domestic law and under Part 2, the chapter first examines Canada's constitutional order both as a matter of text and as a matter of constitutional principles. The second section examines how the terms of the Nunavut Agreement create opportunities for Indigenous communities to assert their influence over navigation and shipping within their seascapes. The commentary focuses on how the planning and project review processes established under the Nunavut Agreement, including commitments made by proponents in the course of those reviews (e.g., speed restrictions, vessel capabilities and flag status), can enhance the influence and effective participation of Indigenous communities with respect to navigation and shipping matters.

2   Part 1: International Law

The first part of this chapter considers international human rights norms that guarantee Indigenous communities a right to participate in and influence the governance of navigational activities in Canada's Arctic waters.[4] The first

---

2   Network of Centres of Excellence of Canada, "Inuit Guide Research on Low Impact Corridors," 10 July 2017, https://www.nce-rce.gc.ca/Research-Recherche/Stories-Articles /2017/lowImpact-faibleImpact_eng.asp.

3   Inuit Circumpolar Council (ICC), *The Sea Ice Never Stops: Circumpolar Inuit Reflections on Sea Ice Use and Shipping in Inuit Nunaat*, December 2014, pp. ii–iii, https://www.inuitcir cumpolar.com/project/the-sea-ice-never-stops-circumpolar-inuit-reflections-on-sea-ice -use-and-shipping-in-inuit-nunaat/.

4   Endalew Lijalem Enyew, "International Human Rights Law and the Rights of Indigenous Peoples in Relation to Marine Space and Resources," in *The Rights of Indigenous Peoples in*

section broaches two preliminary matters of vital importance: the status of the principal international instruments and their scope of application. The second section then briefly considers four fundamental rights guaranteed to Indigenous peoples under international law as they relate to the marine environment: the right to self-determination; the right of ownership and possession of traditional territories; the right to culture; and the right to consultation and free, prior and informed consent.

2.1   *Preliminary Issues of Status and Scope*

> Inuit are a marine people. Our culture and way of life is inextricably linked to the ocean. The marine environment is central to our identity, the way that we perceive the world, and the way that we think of ourselves.[5]

It is this collective spiritual relationship between Indigenous peoples and their natural environment, explains Wiessner, which separates Indigenous peoples from other groups or minorities, and created a need for a special legal regime.[6] "To accommodate indigenous peoples' aspirations ... traditional human rights concepts had to be adjusted and redefined."[7]

2.1.1   The Status of International Human Rights Instruments

Human rights specifically tailored to Indigenous peoples are recognized in international customary law and also in general and Indigenous-specific human rights instruments. Among the most important general international legal texts are the United Nations Charter,[8] the International Convention on the Elimination of All Forms of Racial Discrimination (CERD Convention),[9] the International Covenant on Civil and Political Rights (ICCPR)[10] and the International Covenant on Economic, Social and Cultural Rights (ICESCR).[11]

Marine Areas, eds., Stephen Allen, Nigel Bankes and Øyvind Ravna (New York: Hart, 2019), 45–68. The authors wish to acknowledge the important contribution made by Dr. Enyew's groundbreaking study.

5   Natan Obed, "Foreword," in *Nilliajut 2 – Inuit Perspectives on the NWP, Shipping and Marine Issues*, ed., Inuit Tapirit Kanatami (ITK) (Ottawa: ITK, 2017), 4.

6   Siegfried Wiessner, "The Cultural Rights of Indigenous Peoples: Achievements and Continuing Challenges," *The European Journal of International Law* 22:1 (2011): 121, at 129.

7   Id., 122.

8   Charter of the United Nations, 26 June 1945 (in force 24 October 1945), 1 *UNTS* XVI.

9   21 December 1965 (in force 4 January 1969), 660 *UNTS* 195 [CERD Convention].

10   16 December 1966 (in force 23 March 1976), 999 *UNTS* 171 [ICCPR].

11   16 December 1966 (in force 3 January 1976), 993 *UNTS* 3 [ICESCR]. Among regional instruments of a general nature, there are the European Convention on Human Rights,

Canada is a party to all four treaties[12] and is therefore legally bound to respect them in good faith.[13]

The Convention concerning Indigenous and Tribal Peoples in Independent Countries (ILO Convention 169),[14] adopted by the International Labour Organization (ILO) in 1989, is the most important legally-binding international instrument exclusively dedicated to the rights of Indigenous and tribal peoples. Described as an "unprecedented and visionary instrument,"[15] the Convention ensures Indigenous peoples' control over their "legal status, internal structures, and environment" and guarantees their rights to ownership and possession "of the total environment they occupy or use."[16] Unfortunately, the Convention has to date only been ratified by 24 countries, and Canada does not feature among its parties.

The Swedish Supreme Court recently assessed the impact of ILO Convention 169 in the context of a case on the rights of the Girjas reindeer herding community.[17] Though Sweden is also not a party to the Convention, the Court referred to Article 8(1)[18] and declared that it reflected a *general principle of international law*.[19] Thus in applying Swedish law, due regard had to be taken of the Sami people's customs and customary law.

Nearly 15 years before the Girjas decision, Chief Justice A.O. Conteh of the Belize Supreme Court had already declared: "Treaty obligations aside, it is my considered view that both customary international law and general international law would require that Belize respect the rights of its indigenous people

---

4   November 1950 (in force 3 September 1953), 213 *UNTS* 2; the American Convention on Human Rights, 22 November 1969 (in force 18 July 1978), 1144 *UNTS* 143; and the African Charter on Human and Peoples' Rights, 27 June 1981 (in force 21 October 1986), OAU Doc CAB/LEG/67/3 rev. 5, 21 *ILM* 58 (1982).

12   Canada is a founding member of the United Nations. It adhered to the CERD Convention in 1970 and to the ICCPR in 1976, and ratified the ICESCR in 1976.

13   Vienna Convention on the Law of Treaties, 23 May 1969 (in force 27 January 1980), 1155 *UNTS* 331 [VCLT], Article 26.

14   27 June 1989 (in force 5 September 1991), 1650 *UNTS* 383 [ILO Convention 169].

15   Peter Bille Larsen and Jérémie Gilbert, "Indigenous Rights and ILO Convention 169: Learning from the Past and Challenging the Future," *The International Journal of Human Rights* 24:2–3 (2020): 83, at 83.

16   Weissner (n 6), pp. 134–135.

17   Swedish Supreme Court Case No. T 853-18, decided 23 January 2020.

18   Article 8(1) states: "In applying national laws and regulations to the [Indigenous] peoples concerned, due regard shall be had to their customs or customary law." ILO Convention 169 (n 14).

19   Christina Allard and Malin Brännström, "Girgas Reindeer Herding Community v. Sweden: Analysing the Merits of the Girjas case," *Arctic Review on Law and Politics* 12 (2021): 56, at 64, referring to paragraph 130 in the decision. Emphasis in the original.

to their lands and resources."[20] These judicial findings on the legal status of the core principles defined in ILO Convention 169 are of real import when assessing the governance regime in Canadian Arctic waters.

While recognizing the vital role of ILO Convention 169 for the advancement of Indigenous rights, Wiessner asserts that "[t]he most comprehensive effort to safeguard indigenous peoples' cultures"[21] was the adoption of the UN Declaration on the Rights of Indigenous Peoples (UNDRIP) on 13 September 2007.[22] Noting that the Declaration was adopted by 143 affirmative votes with only four votes against and eleven abstentions, Wiessner emphasizes that all of the opposing States (Australia, Canada,[23] New Zealand and the United States) have since reversed their position and endorsed the Declaration, "making its support virtually universal."[24] Coulter concurs, declaring that the Declaration testifies to a "nearly world-wide consensus among nations that indigenous peoples … have a right to maintain their cultures, societies, customs, and languages, and have a right to self-governance."[25]

Although the Declaration is a non-binding instrument, many of the rights proclaimed in the Declaration are binding as rules of customary international law.[26] In his 2008 report, UN Special Rapporteur S. James Anaya noted how the UNDRIP embodied "to some extent general principles of international law" and that insofar as they connected with a pattern of consistent international and State practice, "some aspects of the provisions of the Declaration can also be considered as a reflection of norms of customary international law."[27]

---

20   *Aurelio Cal* v. *Attorney General of Belize*, 18 October 2007, Sup Ct of Belize, Judgment, para 1.27, www.elaw.org/node/1620.

21   Wiessner (n 6), p. 129.

22   UN Doc A/RES/61/295 (13 September 2007) [UNDRIP].

23   On 21 June 2021, the *United Nations Declaration on the Rights of Indigenous Peoples Act* (UNDRIPA), SC 2021, c 14, received Royal Assent and came into force [UNDRIPA].

24   Wiessner (n 6), p. 129.

25   Robert T. Coulter, "The U.N. Declaration on the Rights of Indigenous Peoples: A Historic Change in International Law," *Idaho Law Review* 45 (2009): 539, at 543.

26   Coulter cites as examples of binding customary rules Articles 1 and 2, concerning discrimination against Indigenous individuals; Article 5 concerning political participation; and Article 26 concerning land and resource rights. He refers in support to *The Case of the Mayagna (Sumo) Awas Tingni Community* v. *Nicaragua*, Judgment of 31 August 2001, reprinted in *Arizona Journal of International & Comparative Law* 19 (2002): 395, at 438.

27   S. James Anaya, *Report of the Special Rapporteur on the situation of human rights and fundamental freedoms of indigenous people*, UN Doc A/HRC/9/9 (11 August 2008), para 41. See also S. James Anaya and Siegfried Wiessner, "The UN Declaration on the Rights of Indigenous Peoples: Towards Re-empowerment", *Jurist*, 3 October 2007.

Canadian courts take direct judicial notice of customary international law, a rule most recently confirmed in *Nevsun Resources Ltd.* v. *Araya*.[28]

Furthermore, the Declaration is an official statement by most member countries of the United Nations of the legal rights afforded Indigenous peoples under international law. The Declaration thus has "considerable political and moral force,"[29] such that "no country can ultimately escape its obligation to respect these rights, regardless of whether or not they are formally binding."[30] This was also the conclusion of the ILA Committee on the Rights of Indigenous Peoples in its final 2012 report.[31] The preamble to Canada's implementation act recognizes that the UNDRIP is "a source for the interpretation of Canadian law."[32] The very purpose of the federal act, as British Columbia's Supreme Court recently emphasized, was "to affirm the Declaration as a universal international human rights instrument with application in Canadian law."[33]

2.1.2   The Scope of International Human Rights Instruments

The spatial scope of application of a treaty is determined by the parties themselves. For example, Article 2(1) of the ICCPR stipulates that "[e]ach State Party ... undertakes to respect and to ensure to all individuals within *its territory and subject to its jurisdiction* the rights recognized in the ... Covenant."[34] With respect to treaties that do not contain a territorial scope clause, like the CERD Convention, the ICESCR or ILO Convention 169, Article 29 of the Vienna Convention on the Law of Treaties (VCLT) provides as a general rule that "unless a different intention appears from the treaty or is otherwise established, a treaty is binding upon each party in respect of its *entire territory*."[35]

The territory of a coastal State includes its internal waters and territorial sea. Consequently, human rights instruments apply within these maritime zones in the same manner as on land. A more sensitive issue is whether human rights norms apply within maritime zones beyond a State's territorial limits. Enyew argues that the concept of jurisdiction has a broad meaning and includes

---

28   2020 SCC 5, para 90.
29   Coulter (n 25), p. 546.
30   Id., 552.
31   Second Conclusion, International Law Association Committee on the Rights of Indigenous Peoples, "Final Report", presented at the 75th Biennial Meeting in Sofia, Bulgaria, 28 August 2012, p. 29. Footnote in original omitted.
32   UNDRIPA (n 23).
33   *Saik'uz First Nation* v. *Rio Tinto Alcan Inc.*, 2022 BCSC 15, para 206, (CanLII), https://canlii.ca/t/jlnn6.
34   ICCPR (n 10). Emphasis added.
35   VCLT (n 13). Emphasis added.

the exercise of authority or effective control over an area (e.g., the exclusive economic zone) or persons.[36] This interpretation is supported by the Human Rights Committee's (HRC) analysis of the scope of the ICCPR: "a State party must respect and ensure the rights laid down in the Covenant to anyone within the power or effective control of that State party, even if not situated within the territory of the State Party."[37] It also accords with the International Court of Justice's (ICJ) finding in its 2004 Advisory Opinion that "the ICCPR is applicable in respect of acts done by a State in the exercise of its jurisdiction outside its own territory."[38]

While the HRC and the ICJ were commenting specifically on the ICCPR, there is a growing consensus that human rights law applies within a State's territory and to persons over whom a State has control or responsibility. As Enyew underlines, this view is consistent with the universal character of human rights, "whereby all states are bound 'to promote universal respect for, and observance of, human rights and freedoms'."[39] Thus Canada is duty bound to respect the human rights of Indigenous peoples within its territory or under its jurisdiction.

2.2   *International Human Rights Law*

It is beyond the scope of this chapter to provide a comprehensive analysis of all the rights and guarantees conferred upon Indigenous peoples under international law. The next section therefore focuses on some of the more important rights that guarantee Indigenous peoples a say in the management of marine spaces.

2.2.1   The Right to Ownership and Possession of Traditional Territories

Article 14(1) of ILO Convention 169 asserts that the "rights of ownership and possession of the peoples concerned over the lands which they traditionally occupy shall be recognised."[40] The same paragraph also provides that measures must be taken in appropriate cases to safeguard the rights of the peoples

---

36   Enyew (n 4), p. 47.

37   Human Rights Committee (HRC), *General Comment No. 31 (80) – The Nature of the General Legal Obligation Imposed on State Parties to the Covenant*, UN Doc CCPR/C/21/Rev.1/Add. 13 (26 May 2004), para 10.

38   *Legal Consequences of the Construction of a Wall in the Occupied Palestinian Territory*, Advisory Opinion, *ICJ Reports 2004*, 136, para 111.

39   Enyew (n 4), p. 47, citing the language of Article 1(3) of the UN Charter, recital 4 in the preamble to both the ICCPR and ICESCR, and recital 2 in the preamble to the European Convention on Human Rights.

40   ILO Convention 169 (n 14).

concerned to use land not exclusively occupied by them, but to which they have traditionally had access for their subsistence and traditional activities. Article 15 further mandates that the rights of Indigenous peoples to the natural resources of their lands must also be specially safeguarded.[41] These resource rights are defined as including the right to participate in "the use, management and conservation of these resources." Article 16(1), for its part, declares that "the peoples concerned shall not be removed from the lands which they occupy" save in very limited, exceptional circumstances.[42]

A vital question is whether the rights defined in Articles 14, 15 and 16 by reference to Indigenous "lands" include marine spaces. An affirmative answer is provided, in part, by Article 13(2) which offers a broad definition of the key concept of 'land': "The use of the term lands in Articles 15 and 16 shall include the concept of *territories*, which covers the *total environment of the areas* which the peoples concerned occupy or otherwise use."[43] It is regrettable, however, that the principal right, as defined in Article 14, is not explicitly captured by the comprehensive definition provided in Article 13(2).

The ILO Secretariat's guide to Convention 169, in the section devoted to the land rights provisions, begins with a discussion of the "concept of land": "[t]he concept of land usually embraces *the whole territory* [Indigenous peoples] use, including forests, rivers, mountains and *sea*, the surface as well as the sub-surface."[44] The guide also emphasizes that "the concept of land encompasses the land which a community or people uses and cares for *as a whole*."[45] This all-encompassing understanding of the concept of land, according to the Secretariat, underpins *all* of the Convention's provisions.

This broader interpretation is reinforced by the UNDRIP with its explicit recognition under Article 25 that Indigenous peoples have the right "to maintain and strengthen their distinctive spiritual relationship with their traditionally owned or otherwise occupied and used *land, territories, waters and coastal seas and other resources*."[46] The rights that flow from this special relationship are fleshed out under Article 26: "Indigenous peoples have the right to the lands, territories and resources which they have traditionally owned, occupied or otherwise used or acquired." Paragraph 2 of Article 26

---

41   Id.

42   Id. See Part II of ILO Convention 169 entitled "Land" which covers Articles 13–19 and establishes several other land-related rights.

43   Id. Emphasis added.

44   International Labour Office, *ILO Convention on Indigenous and Tribal Peoples, 1989 (No 169): A Manual* (Geneva: ILO, 2003), 29. Emphasis added.

45   Id., 30. Emphasis added.

46   UNDRIP (n 22), Article 25. Emphasis added.

specifies that this right includes the "right to own, use, develop and control the land, territories and resources that they possess by reason of traditional ownership or other traditional occupation or use, as well as those which they have otherwise acquired." The last paragraph obliges States to give legal recognition and protection to these lands, territories and resources.

Enyew spells out the importance of this broad concept of traditional Indigenous 'lands':

> [T]he meaning of 'land' when applied to Indigenous peoples covers the marine space, where Indigenous peoples occupy or use as part of their traditional territories, or traditionally had access to satisfy their subsistence needs or to conduct their spiritual, customary or traditional activities. These marine areas may include internal waters (such as foreshores and fjords), archipelagic waters, the territorial sea and the EEZ to the extent that Indigenous peoples have traditionally used them. The actual extent of Indigenous peoples' occupation or traditional use determines the areal extent of 'land' or territory out in the sea.[47]

Referencing practice at the international and domestic levels, the ILA Committee on the Rights of Indigenous Peoples concluded in their 2012 Final Report that "indigenous peoples' land rights – grounded on the special, in many cases spiritual, relationship of indigenous communities with their traditional territories typically considered their *motherland* – have attained the status of customary international law."[48] This finding echoed an earlier assertion by Anaya and Wiessner that "indigenous peoples have a right under customary international law to 'demarcation, ownership, development, control and use of the lands they have traditionally owned or otherwise occupied and used'."[49] Thus, Indigenous communities in the Canadian Arctic have recognized legal rights of ownership and possession in all marine areas they have traditionally occupied or used.

2.2.2   The Right to Self-determination

The right to self-determination, a collective right of peoples, has the highest normative value in international law as a peremptory norm or *jus cogens*.[50]

---

47   Enyew, (n 4), p. 58. See also Victor Prescott and Stephen Davis, "Aboriginal Claims to Seas in Australia," *International Journal of Marine and Coastal Law* 17 (2002): 1, at 15.

48   ILA Committee on the Rights of Indigenous Peoples (n 31), p. 23.

49   Anaya and Wiessner (n 27).

50   There is an enormous literature on self-determination, including with respect to Indigenous peoples. For a small sample, see S. James Anaya, *Indigenous Peoples in International Law*, 2nd ed. (Oxford: University Press, 2004); James Youngblood Henderson, *Indigenous*

It is recognised in various global and regional human rights instruments[51] and in recent decades, treaty-monitoring bodies and human rights courts have accepted Indigenous peoples as 'peoples' entitled to the right of self-determination.[52] This determination has been incontrovertibly confirmed in Article 3 of the UNDRIP:

> Indigenous peoples have the right to self-determination. By virtue of that right they freely determine their political status and freely pursue their economic, social and cultural development.

As a companion to this "historic and much sought after advance,"[53] Article 4 establishes the right to self-government:

> Indigenous peoples, in exercising their right to self-determination, have the right to autonomy or self-government in matters relating to their internal and local affairs, as well as ways and means for financing their autonomous functions.

Enyew in his study emphasizes the economic dimension of the right of self-determination, which is of critical importance in the context of this chapter.[54] He refers to common Article 1(2) of the ICCPR and ICESCR which provide that "[a]ll peoples may, for their own ends, freely dispose of their natural wealth and resources... In no case may a people be deprived of its own means of subsistence." Referencing the practice of treaty-monitoring bodies (e.g., the Human Rights Committee and the Committee on Economic Social and Cultural Rights), Enyew asserts that these bodies "clearly recognise the right of Indigenous peoples to freely dispose of their natural resources 'for their own ends', including to fulfil their means of subsistence, as their inherent right."[55]

Diplomacy and the Rights of Peoples (Vancouver: UBC Press, 2008); Karen Knop, *Diversity and Self-Determination in International Law* (Cambridge: Cambridge University Press, 2002); and Sharon Helen Venne, *Our Elders Understand Our Rights* (Penticton, BC: Theytus Books, 1999).

51   See for example Article 1 of the ICCPR (n 10) and the ICESCR (n 11) and Articles 2021 of the African Charter on Human and Peoples' Rights (n 11).

52   For example, the Committee on Economic, Social and Cultural Rights, United Nations Economic and Social Council, *Concluding Observations on the Fourth Periodic Report of Chile*, UN Doc E/C.12/CHL/CO/4 (7 July 2015), para 8.

53   Coulter (n 25), p. 548.

54   Enyew (n 4), pp. 49–50.

55   Id., 50. In his comprehensive canvassing of international human rights law, Enyew also analyses the "right to marine space and resources as a proprietary right." In the interest of

In this way, the general right of economic self-determination has been adapted to reflect Indigenous peoples' symbiotic relationship with their traditional lands and resources.

While none of the instruments cited define the term 'natural resources,' Enyew,[56] Fitzmaurice[57] and Woker[58] argue that the term is broad and its ordinary meaning must extend to marine areas and marine living resources. Thus, the right of economic self-determination entitles Indigenous peoples to occupy or use certain traditional maritime territories to harvest marine mammals to satisfy their subsistence needs. This right also necessarily entitles Indigenous peoples to actively participate in decisions relating to the conservation and management of marine resources.[59]

The right of Indigenous self-determination is explicitly acknowledged in recent federal marine governance initiatives. For example, one of the four priority areas for Canada's ambitious Oceans Protection Plan (OPP) announced in November 2016 was to strengthen partnerships and launch co-management practices with Indigenous communities. An important project under the OPP has been the Northern Low-Impact Shipping Corridors Initiative,[60] which seeks to minimize the impacts of shipping in Canadian Arctic waters through the creation of voluntary, incentive-based shipping routes that will guide future decision-making and enhance safe navigation that respects local communities, wildlife and the environment. Inuit perspectives and knowledge have been integrated in the designation of the corridors and any applicable measures (e.g., maximum speeds, seasonal restrictions) and mechanisms to allow for the effective participation of local communities in the monitoring and management of the corridors are currently being explored.[61]

One of us (Bankes) has also highlighted that in the exercise of their right to self-determination, Canada's northern Indigenous peoples have also developed their own agenda "to meet their own values and needs rather than simply

---

space, this chapter does not discuss Indigenous proprietary rights. Readers are referred to pages 56–65 in Enyew's excellent study.

56   Id.

57   Malgosia Fitzmaurice, "Indigenous Peoples in Marine Areas – Whaling and Sealing," in Allen, Bankes and Ravna, eds. (n 4), pp. 45–68.

58   Hilde Woker, "The Rights of Indigenous Peoples to Harvest Marine Mammals in the Arctic," Master thesis, The Arctic University of Norway (2015), https://munin.uit.no/handle/10037/8468.

59   Nigel Bankes, "Arctic Ocean Management and Indigenous Peoples: Recent Legal Developments," *The Yearbook of Polar Law* XI (2019): 81, at 88–91.

60   The initiative is co-led by the Canadian Coast Guard, Transport Canada and the Canadian Hydrographic Service. See Dawson and Song in this volume.

61   Dawson (n 1), p. 4.

responding to the policies and programs of the State."[62] He cites as an important example, the establishment of the Pikialasorsuaq Commission by the Inuit Circumpolar Council (ICC) in 2016, tasked with consulting Inuit in Canada and Greenland on the best way to safeguard and monitor the waters between Ellesmere Island and Greenland. Known to Greenlandic Inuit as Pikialasorsuaq and to Canadian Inuit as Sarvarjuaq (the Great Upwelling),[63] the polynya is one of the most productive marine areas north of the Arctic Circle and is an area of special interest to Inuit.[64] The first of three recommendations formulated by the Commission is to establish an Inuit Management Authority (IMA) for the Pikialasorsuaq. The IMA would have the authority to oversee monitoring and research and "promote the conservation of living resources within and adjacent to the Pikialasorsuaq, and the related wellbeing of communities that depend on these resources."[65]

2.2.3   The Right to Culture

The right to culture is a widely recognised human right incorporated in various instruments. Article 27 of the ICCPR provides that persons belonging to minorities "shall not be denied the right, in community with the other members of their group, to enjoy their own culture." Enyew confirms that these and other provisions in general regional human rights instruments have been evolutively interpreted and applied by their respective treaty-monitoring bodies and human rights courts to recognise and protect the cultures of Indigenous peoples.[66]

The HRC has emphasized that Article 27 of the ICCPR guarantees the material manifestations of Indigenous culture:

---

62   Bankes (n 59), p. 118.
63   Pikialasorsuaq Commission, "People of the Ice Bridge: The Future of Pikialasorsuaq," Report, November 2017, http://pikialasorsuaq.org/en/Resources/Reports.
64   "This polynya provides food security for regional communities and it remains an enduring cultural and spiritual cornerstone linking Inuit across borders to each other and their shared history." Id., A-9. The polynya is also known as the North Water Polynya. See also Fisheries and Oceans Canada, *Identification of Ecological Significance, Knowledge Gaps and Stressors for the North Water and Adjacent Areas*, Canadian Science Advisory Secretariat, Science Advisory Report 2021/052 (December 2021).
65   Pikialasorsuaq Commission (n 63), p. A-20. See Bankes (n 59), p. 118 where he explains that while the Pikialasorsuaq proposal "is still very much at the proposal and discussion stage," there are "some signs that at least some elements of the proposal are gaining traction." For further evidence of this progress, see Pikialasorsuaq Leaders Statement, Ottawa, 4 April 2019, https://pm.gc.ca/en/news/backgrounders/2019/04/04/pikialasorsuaq-leaders-statement.
66   Enyew (n 4), p. 51. See footnote 40 for specific examples.

Culture manifests itself in many forms, including a particular way of life associated with *the use of land resources, especially in the case of Indigenous peoples.* That right may include such *traditional activities as fishing or hunting* and the right to live in reserves protected by law.[67]

The protection of the right to culture under Article 27 extends not only to traditional practices but also to those that have adapted to modern technologies.[68] In *Apirana Mahuika*, the HRC observed:

> The right to enjoy one's culture cannot be determined *in abstracto* but has to be placed in context. In particular, Article 27 does not only protect traditional means of livelihood of minorities, but allows also for the adaptation of those means to the modern way of life and ensuing technology.[69]

In line with this broad interpretation of culture, the Norwegian Supreme Court recently ruled that the Sami people are a minority within the meaning of Article 27, "and that reindeer husbandry is a form of protected cultural practice."[70]

ILO Convention 169 also recognizes the special connection between Indigenous peoples and their traditional territories, and the importance of this connection for the survival and development of their culture. Article 13, for example, obligates States to "respect the special importance for the cultures and spiritual values of the peoples concerned of their relationship with the lands and territories, or both as applicable, which they occupy or otherwise use, and in particular the collective aspects of this relationship."[71]

The UNDRIP also recognises the right to culture of Indigenous peoples in all its manifestations, including the "right to maintain, control, protect and develop their cultural heritage, traditional knowledge and traditional cultural expression."[72] The Declaration also protects in various articles, Indigenous peoples' right to natural resources as an integral part of their culture:

---

67   HRC, *General Comment No. 23 (50)*, UN Doc CCPR/C/21/Rev.1/Add.5 (1994), para 7. Emphasis added.

68   Enyew (n 4), p. 54.

69   HRC, *Apirana Mahuika et al. v. New Zealand*, Communication No 547/1993, 27 October 2000, UN Doc CCPR/C/70/D/547/1993 (16 November 2000), para 9.4.

70   Supreme Court of Norway, HR-2021-1975-S, Judgment, 11 October 2021, para 101, unofficial English text: https://www.domstol.no/globalassets/upload/hret/decisions-in-english-translation/hr-2021-1975-s.pdf.

71   See also ILO Convention 169 (n 14), Article 23(1).

72   UNDRIP (n 22), Articles 15, 31.

Indigenous peoples have the right to maintain and strengthen their distinctive spiritual relationship with their traditionally owned or otherwise occupied and used lands, territories, waters and coastal seas *and other resources* and to uphold their responsibilities to future generations in this regard.[73]

Beveridge argues that this broad interpretation of culture is beginning to have an impact upon the international regulatory framework governing Arctic shipping.[74] She cites as an example the "Methodology to Analyse Impacts of a Ban on the Use and Carriage of Heavy Fuel Oil as Fuel by Ships in Arctic Waters" developed by the Prevention, Preparedness and Response Subcommittee of the International Maritime Organization (IMO) and its recommendation that the "subsistence culture and lifestyle of Arctic indigenous and local communities" be taken into consideration when evaluating the potential impacts of banning the use of heavy fuel oil by ships in the Arctic.[75] The Methodology interprets 'subsistence' not only as a monetary matter or one of food security, but also acknowledges that "subsistence activities are integrated more broadly in a cultural sense as an aspect of the underpinnings of social cohesion, language, public health and identity."[76]

International law provides special safeguards against interference with the right to culture of Indigenous peoples. Those safeguards were considered by Norway's Supreme Court in its recent decision on whether wind power developments had 'denied' the Sami their right to enjoy their culture as guaranteed by Article 27 of the ICCPR. The Court made a critical determination, finding that an interference that does not constitute a total denial may nevertheless violate the right to cultural enjoyment.[77] Referring to the ruling of the HRC in *Ángela Poma Poma* v. *Peru*,[78] the Norwegian Supreme Court defined the test as whether "a substantive negative impact" results from a given measure. "The term 'substantive' in this context means 'considerable' or 'significant'."[79]

---

73   Id., Article 25. Emphasis added. See also UNDRIP Articles 11, 12, 15, 31.

74   Leah Beveridge, "Chapter 7 – Inuit Nunangat and the Northwest Passage" in *Governance of Arctic Shipping*, eds., A. Chircop *et al.* (Cham: Springer, 2020) EBOOK, 137–149, at 141.

75   IMO, *Report to the Marine Environment Protection Committee*, IMO Doc PPR 6/20/Add. 1 (26 March 2019), Annex 16: Draft Methodology to Analyse Impacts of a Ban on the Use and Carriage of Heavy Fuel Oil as Fuel by Ships in Arctic Waters, Annex: Details of Step Four of the Impact Assessment Methodology, para 13.

76   Id., para 14.

77   Supreme Court of Norway (n 70), para 111.

78   *Ángela Poma Poma* v. *Peru*, HRC, Communication No 1457/ 2006, 27 March 2009, UN Doc CCPR/C/95/D/1457/2006 (24 April 2009).

79   Supreme Court of Norway (n 70), para 118.

Norway's Supreme Court also ruled that there is no margin of appreciation granted under Article 27 and that it does not allow for a proportionality assessment balancing other interests of society against the minority's or Indigenous people's interests. "This is a natural consequence of the reason for the provision, as the protection of the minority population would be ineffective, if the majority population were to be able to limit it based on its legitimate needs."[80] In support of this conclusion, the Court again referred to the HRC in *Ángela Poma Poma* and its ruling that "economic development may not undermine the rights protected by Article 27."[81]

Finally, the Norwegian Supreme Court also declared that while the consequences of a given measure largely dictate whether the rights in Article 27 have been violated, "it is also essential whether the minority has been consulted in the process."[82]

> It appears from the Human Rights Committee's decision and the mentioned [Norwegian] Supreme Court judgments that whether and to which extent the minority has been consulted cannot be decisive. This is rather an aspect to be included in the assessment of whether the right to cultural enjoyment has been violated ... If the consequences of the interference are sufficiently serious, consultation does not prevent violation. On the other hand, it is not an absolute requirement under the Convention that the minority's participation has contributed to the decision, although that, too, may be essential in the overall assessment.[83]

As discussed below, the right to consultation is an essential procedural right under international law in its own right, independently of the provisions on the right to culture.

2.2.4   The Right to Consultation and Free, Prior and Informed Consent

Tauli-Corpuz, UN Special Rapporteur on the rights of Indigenous Peoples has described the right to be consulted (and the correlative duty to consult) as essential safeguards of the substantive human rights afforded Indigenous

---

80   Id., para 129.
81   Id., para 126, referring to para 7.4 in the *Ángela Poma Poma* ruling. The Norwegian Supreme Court does acknowledge that a balancing of rights might be needed where the rights in Article 27 conflict with other "basic rights." Id., para 130.
82   Id., para 120.
83   Id., para 121.

peoples under international legal sources and instruments.[84] Article 6(1)(a) of ILO Convention 169 stipulates that governments "shall consult the [Indigenous] peoples concerned, through appropriate procedures and in particular through their representative institutions, whenever consideration is being given to legislative or administrative measures which may affect them directly."[85] Paragraph 2 of the same article commands that such consultations "shall be undertaken, in good faith and in a form appropriate to the circumstances, with the objective of achieving agreement or consent to the proposed measures." Similarly, Article 19 of the UNDRIP obliges States to "consult and cooperate in good faith with the indigenous peoples concerned through their own representative institutions in order to obtain their free, prior and informed consent before adopting and implementing legislative or administrative measures that may affect them." Tauli-Corpuz has stressed that State obligations to consult Indigenous peoples also derive from universal and regional instruments of general application and the interpretative jurisprudence of supervisory mechanisms under these instruments.[86] These instruments include, for instance, the ICCPR and the CERD Convention.

These provisions, Enyew emphasizes, are general and apply to a wide range of matters.

> In the present context, this might require consultation before the adoption of any fishery conservation and management measures having a negative impact on Indigenous communities, such as prohibition of fishing and hunting, processes to determine quotas, restrictions on fishing and hunting methods, or the establishment of MPAs within traditional fishing grounds.[87]

More specifically, Article 15(2) of ILO Convention 169 and Article 32(2) of the UNDRIP require consultation in the context of resource exploitation projects on the traditional lands and territories of Indigenous peoples. Both Enyew and Tauli-Corpuz insist that this obligation requires that coastal States consult the affected communities *before* the approval of any project affecting their traditionally used marine areas, particularly with respect to projects involving "the

---

84   Victoria Tauli-Corpuz, "Consultation and Consent: Principles, Experiences and Challenges," *International Colloquium on the Free, Prior, and Informed Consultation: International and Regional Standards and Experiences* (Mexico City, 8 November 2016), 4.

85   ILO Convention 169 (n 14), Article 6(1)(a). See also Articles 7, 15, 16.

86   Tauli-Corpuz (n 84), p. 2.

87   Enyew (n 4), p. 65.

development, utilization or exploitation of ... resources,"[88] and involve them in impact assessment studies.[89] Enyew's assessment of what this duty entails, in concrete terms, bears repeating:

> *Good faith* requires that coastal states must be open to hear, and be influenced by, the views of the coastal Indigenous communities concerned, and be prepared to abandon or modify the proposed measure or marine-related project in a manner that minimises its potential impacts. Consultation undertaken solely as a symbolic gesture or to provide information without follow-up action does not constitute good faith consultation.[90]

The duty to consult does not apply solely in a domestic context and appears to have been recognized in some important Arctic regional mechanisms. For example, the Arctic Council, while clearly intended to represent the interests of the eight Arctic States, also boasts a unique feature in having granted Permanent Participant status to six Indigenous peoples' organizations, including the ICC.[91] Permanent Participants have full consultation rights and sit at the table alongside member State delegations at ministerial, working group and task force meetings. Though they do not formally vote, it has become standard practice among the Arctic States to refrain from adopting any decision, recommendation or programme in the face of opposition from them.

In 2009, the ICC adopted "A Circumpolar Inuit Declaration on Sovereignty in the Arctic" which demanded the inclusion of Inuit as active partners in all national and international deliberations on Arctic matters.[92] This demand was further fleshed out in the 2014 Kitigaaryuit Declaration, which advocates for, among other rights, the "inclusion of Inuit representatives on all councils, committees,

88   UNDRIP (n 22), Article 32(2).
89   ILO Convention 169 (n 14), Article 7. See Enyew (n 4), p. 66; Tauli-Corpuz (n 84), p. 5.
90   The author refers to the ILO Committee of Experts on the Application of Conventions and Recommendations (CEACR), General Observation on the Right of Indigenous and Tribal Peoples to Consultation (Observation 2010/81), 8–9. Enyew (n 4), p. 66. Emphasis in original. See the similar discussion in the *Clyde River* case (n 116) below.
91   The status of Permanent Participant is open to Arctic organizations of Indigenous peoples with a majority of Arctic Indigenous constituency representing either "a single Indigenous people resident in more than one Arctic State" or "more than one Arctic Indigenous people resident in a single Arctic State." "Permanent Participants," Arctic Council, https://arctic-council.org/index.php/en/about-us/permanent-participants.
92   ICC, "A Circumpolar Inuit Declaration on Sovereignty in the Arctic," 28 April 2009, para 3.6, http://inuit.org/about-icc/icc-declarations/sovereignty-declaration-2009/.

and commissions formed to address Arctic fishing issues."[93] In response to those calls, some Arctic States included representatives from Indigenous organizations in their delegations for the negotiation of a fisheries agreement for the Central Arctic Ocean.[94] As Schatz underlines, their participation resulted in the incorporation of novel provisions concerning the interests and knowledge of Indigenous communities.[95] The preamble to the Agreement, for instance, recalls the UNDRIP and recognizes "the interests of Arctic residents, including Arctic indigenous peoples, in the long-term conservation and sustainable use of living marine resources and in healthy marine ecosystems in the Arctic Ocean" and underlines "the importance of involving them and their communities."[96]

The call articulated at paragraph 18 of the Kitigaaryuit Declaration for Inuit leadership "to assert Inuit rights and responsibilities in relation to Inuit waters, seas and passages used from time immemorial" and to do so through active participation in the work of the IMO and other relevant bodies, seems also to have resonated. On the 8 November 2021, the ICC became the first Indigenous organization to receive provisional consultative status at the IMO. As articulated in the IMO's rules and guidelines, consultative status serves two fundamental purposes: (1) to enable the IMO to obtain information and expert advice from organizations with special knowledge; and (2) to enable such organizations to express their point of view.[97] The IMO's Sub-Committee on Ship Design and Construction recently acknowledged the need for Inuit involvement in reviewing its existing Guidelines for Reducing Underwater Noise Caused by Commercial Shipping and in formulating recommendations for future action.[98]

Procedural rights guaranteed under international law may go beyond good faith consultation and may require, in the domestic context, that States

---

93   ICC, "Kitigaaryuit Declaration," 24 July 2014, para 20, http://www.inuitcircumpolar.com
      /uploads/3/0/5/4/30542564/img-724172331.pdf.

94   Canada, Denmark and the United States included Indigenous representatives in their
      delegations.

95   Valentin Schatz, "The Incorporation of Indigenous and Local Knowledge into Central Arctic Ocean Fisheries Management," *Arctic Review on Law and Politics* 10 (2019): 130, at 134.

96   Agreement to Prevent Unregulated High Seas Fisheries in the Central Arctic Ocean,
      adopted 3 October 2018, in force 25 June 2021, https://www.dfo-mpo.gc.ca/international
      /agreement-accord-eng.htm.

97   IMO, External Relations Office, *Rules and Guidelines for Consultative Status of Non-governmental Organizations with the International Maritime Organization* (London: IMO, 2019),
      https://wwwcdn.imo.org/localresources/en/About/Membership/Documents/RULES
      %20AND%20GUIDELINES%20FOR%20CONSULTATIVE%20STATUS%20-%20December
      %202019.pdf.

98   Ellis Quinn, "Inuit Knowledge to Play Role in IMO Guidelines Review for Reducing Underwater Noise," *Eye on the Arctic*, 25 January 2022, https://www.rcinet.ca/eye-on-the-arctic
      /2022/01/25/inuit-knowledge-to-play-role-in-imo-guideline-review-for-reducing
      -underwater-noise/.

obtain the free, prior and informed consent (FPIC) of an affected Indigenous community. The UNDRIP and ILO 169 identify two situations where FPIC is expressly required: (1) where a project involves the storage or disposal of hazardous materials in the territories of the Indigenous peoples;[99] and (2) where a project requires the forcible removal of Indigenous peoples from their territories.[100] The concept of territory in this context, as discussed above, clearly encompasses traditionally used marine areas and traditional fishing grounds.

In other situations, explains Enyew, the question of whether FPIC is required will depend "on the nature of the proposed measure and the extent of its impact"[101] and will be assessed on a case-by-case basis. The Expert Mechanism on the Rights of Indigenous Peoples, created to provide expertise and advice to the UN Human Rights Council, has had occasion to consider the critical question of FPIC. It concluded in 2011 that the consent of Indigenous peoples is mandatory with respect to "matters of fundamental importance for their rights, survival, dignity and well-being."[102] The Inter-American Court of Human Rights (IACtHR) and the HRC have similarly adopted "a major impact"[103] and "substantial interference" [104] test to determine whether a State has a duty to obtain the FPIC of the Indigenous peoples concerned.[105] As Enyew concludes, the rights to consultation and FPIC

> serve as important procedural safeguards against all measures, including resource development projects, which involve the re-allocation of rights to access, control or use of the marine space and the associated resources away from the traditional user coastal Indigenous communities.[106]

---

99   UNDRIP (n 22), Article 29(2).
100   Id., Article 10; ILO Convention 169 (n 14), Article 16.
101   Enyew (n 4), p. 66.
102   United Nations, Human Rights Council, *Final Report on the Study of Indigenous Peoples and the Right to Participate in Decision-making, Report of the Expert Mechanism on the Rights of Indigenous Peoples*, UN Doc A/HRC/18/42 (17 August 2011), Annex: Expert Mechanism Advice No. 2(2011): Indigenous Peoples and the Right to Participate in Decision-Making, para 22.
103   *Saramaka People* v. *Suriname*, Case No. 172 (IACtHR, 28 November 2007), paras 134, 137.
104   *Ángela Poma Poma* (n 78), paras 7.2, 7.3.
105   For a general discussion of FPIC, see Leena Heinämäki, "Global Context – Arctic Importance: Free, Prior and Informed Consent, a New Paradigm in International Law Related to Indigenous Peoples," in *Indigenous Peoples' Governance of Land and Protected Territories in the Arctic*, eds., Thora Martina Herrmann and Thibault Martin (Cham: Springer, 2016), 209–240.
106   Enyew (n 4), p. 67.

3   Part 2: Domestic Law

Part 2 of this chapter examines the tools available to Indigenous communities under domestic law to influence and participate in the regulation of navigation and shipping in Canada's Arctic waters. We begin by considering constitutional law issues and then consider the terms of the Nunavut Agreement as an example of a modern claims agreement that applies within Canada's Arctic waters.

3.1   *Constitutional Law*
Canada's constitutional order recognizes the rights of Indigenous communities both as a matter of text and as a matter of constitutional principles.

3.1.1   Constitutional Text
Canada's constitution was amended in 1982 to recognize Indigenous rights. As subsequently amended in 1983 to recognize the ongoing nature of land claims negotiations, section 35 now provides:

(1)   The existing aboriginal and treaty rights of the aboriginal peoples of Canada are hereby recognized and affirmed.
(2)   In this Act, *'aboriginal peoples of Canada'* includes the Indian, Inuit and Métis peoples of Canada.
(3)   For greater certainty, in subsection (1) *'treaty rights'* includes rights that now exist by way of land claims agreements or may be so acquired.
(4)   Notwithstanding any other provision of this Act, the aboriginal and treaty rights referred to in subsection (1) are guaranteed equally to male and female persons.

For present purposes, the principal significance of section 35 is that it provides constitutional protection to the terms of modern land claims agreements, including those land claims agreements with relevance to Canada's Arctic waters, principally the Inuvialuit Final Agreement (1984), the Nunavut Land Claims Agreement (1993), the Nunavik Inuit Land Claims Agreement (2006) and the Labrador Inuit Land Claims Agreement (2005).[107] As a result, government action that is inconsistent with such agreements, or that fails to

---

107   These agreements (organized by province and territory) can be accessed at Crown-Indigenous Relations and Northern Affairs Canada, "Final Agreements and Related Implementation Matters," Government of Canada, last modified 18 June 2018, https://www.rcaanc-cirnac.gc.ca/eng/1100100030583/1529420498350. A fifth agreement, the Eeyou Marine Region Land Claims Agreement (2011) is also relevant insofar as it includes areas of interest to both the Crees of Eeyou Istchee and Nunavik Inuit.

fulfill government's obligations under those agreements, will be sanctioned as unconstitutional.[108] These agreements serve to particularize the obligations of other orders of government, and establish co-management or co-jurisdictional arrangements, but they do not represent a complete code as to the legal relationship between the Crown and the particular Indigenous community. This means that general constitutional obligations, including the duty to consult and accommodate, may still operate where the land claims agreement is silent.[109]

3.1.2   Constitutional Principles

In the *Quebec Secession Reference*,[110] the Supreme Court of Canada identified four foundational constitutional principles that were relevant to the issue at hand (self-determination of the people of Quebec) including respect for (or protection of) minority rights as "an independent principle underlying our constitutional order."[111] The Court recognized that the inclusion of section 35 in the *Constitution Act* of 1982 was consistent with a "long tradition" of respect for minorities.[112]

The Supreme Court has also recognized that "the Crown's assertion of sovereignty over an Aboriginal people and *de facto* control of land and resources that were formerly in the control of that people" engages the honour of the Crown which in turn supports the Crown's duty to consult and accommodate.[113] The duty to consult and accommodate is engaged in the context of treaty rights when the Crown "contemplates conduct that might adversely affect" those treaty rights.[114] A serious limitation on the duty to consult and

---

108   See, for example, *First Nation of Nacho Nyak Dun* v. *Yukon*, 2017 SCC 58 (CanLII), [2017] 2 SCR 576; *Nunavut Tunngavik Inc.* v. *Canada (Minister of Fisheries and Oceans)*, 1998 CanLII 9080 (FCA), [1998] 4 FC 405. While that constitutional protection may not be absolute, it does require that other orders of government (federal, provincial or territorial) have the onus of justifying any infringement: *R.* v. *Sparrow*, 1990 CanLII 104 (SCC), [1990] 1 SCR 1075; *Grassy Narrows First Nation* v. *Ontario (Natural Resources)*, 2014 SCC 48 (CanLII), [2014] 2 SCR 447; *Campbell et al.* v. *AG BC/AG Cda & Nisga'a Nation et al.*, 2000 BCSC 1123 (CanLII); *Chief Mountain* v. *Canada (A.G.)*, 2012 BCCA 69 (CanLII).

109   *Beckman* v. *Little Salmon/Carmacks First Nation*, 2010 SCC 53 (CanLII), [2010] 3 SCR 103.

110   *Reference re Secession of Quebec*, 1998 CanLII 793 (SCC), [1998] 2 SCR 217.

111   Id., para 80.

112   Id., para 81.

113   *Haida Nation* v. *British Columbia (Minister of Forests)*, 2004 SCC 73 (CanLII), [2004] 3 SCR 511 [32]. For a more detailed review of the case on the Crown's duty to consult and accommodate, see Nigel Bankes, "The Duty to Consult in Canada post-Haida Nation," *Arctic Review on Law and Politics* 11 (2020): 256.

114   *Haida Nation* (n 113), para 35, with respect to Aboriginal rights, but with respect to treaty rights, see *Mikisew Cree First Nation* v. *Canada (Minister of Canadian Heritage)*, 2005 SCC 69 (CanLII), [2005] 3 SCR 388.

accommodate in the present context is that the parliamentary process does not engage the duty to consult and accommodate.[115]

While it is not possible to point to any decided case dealing with the duty to consult and accommodate in the context of navigation and shipping in Canadian Arctic waters, there is one important decision that engages with the duty to consult and accommodate in the context of marine seismic operations. In *Clyde River (Hamlet)* v. *Petroleum GeoServices Inc.*,[116] the Supreme Court of Canada concluded that the National Energy Board (NEB) had breached the Crown's constitutional obligations to the Indigenous community of Clyde River when the Board failed to adequately consult and accommodate the community before issuing an authorization to PGS to engage in seismic testing activities in Baffin Bay and Davis Strait, "adjacent to the area where the Inuit have treaty rights to harvest marine mammals."[117]

The court summarized its conclusions as follows:

> The consultation process here was, in view of the Inuit's established treaty rights and the risk posed by the proposed testing to those rights, significantly flawed. Had the appellants had the resources to submit their own scientific evidence, and the opportunity to test the evidence of the proponents, the result of the environmental assessment could have been very different. Nor were the Inuit given meaningful responses to their questions regarding the impact of the testing on marine life. While the NEB considered potential impacts of the project on marine mammals and on Inuit traditional resource use, its report does not acknowledge, or even mention, the Inuit treaty rights to harvest wildlife in the Nunavut Settlement Area, or that deep consultation was required.[118]

---

115   *Mikisew Cree First Nation* v. *Canada (Governor General in Council)*, 2018 SCC 40 (CanLII), [2018] 2 SCR 765. On the face of it, this is inconsistent with Article 19 of the UNDRIP, and see UNDRIPA (n 23).

116   *Clyde River (Hamlet)* v. *Petroleum GeoServices Inc.*, 2017 SCC 40. For more detailed commentary, see Nigel Bankes, "Clarifying the Parameters of the Crown's Duty to Consult and Accommodate in the Context of Decision-making by Energy Tribunals," *Journal of Energy and Natural Resources Law* 36 (2017): 163. See also *Qikiqtani Inuit Assn.* v. *Canada (Minister of Natural Resources)*, 2010 NUCJ 12.

117   *Clyde River* (n 116), para 7.

118   Id., para 51.

The duties associated with the honour of the Crown include the duty of diligent implementation of treaty promises[119] and the duty to implement treaties in a manner that gives effect to their purpose.[120]

3.2 How Do the Terms of Modern Land Claims Agreements Address Navigation and Shipping Issues in Canada's Arctic Waters?

Modern land claims agreements are not homogenous. They are complex and detailed and while the more general provisions follow a common template, this is not the case for many of the more detailed provisions. Our commentary focuses on the Nunavut Agreement on the grounds that this agreement embraces by far the largest part of Canada's Arctic waters.[121]

The Nunavut Agreement principally applies to the Nunavut Settlement Area (NSA) as defined in Article 3 of the Agreement, including an area surrounding the Belcher Islands in the south east of Hudson Bay.[122] Article 3 of the Nunavut Agreement indicates that the NSA "includes all those lands, water and marine areas" within the prescribed metes and bounds description of the NSA. 'Marine areas' are defined as "that part of Canada's internal waters or territorial sea, whether open or ice-covered" lying with the NSA.[123] Inuit also enjoy constitutionally protected harvesting and management rights in marine areas beyond the NSA, in particular within a zone known as the Outer Land Fast Ice Zone.[124]

Article 15 of the Nunavut Agreement, entitled "Marine Areas", comprises five parts. Part 1 articulates a set of principles that inform the article.[125] Part 2 is perhaps the most important for present purposes insofar as it specifies those articles of the Agreement that apply to marine areas. These are listed as: Articles 5 (wildlife), 6 (wildlife compensation), 8 (parks), 9 (conservation

119   *Yahey* v. *British Columbia*, 2021 BCSC 1287 (CanLII), esp para 1724 et seq.; *Restoule* v. *Canada (Attorney General)*, 2021 ONCA 779 (CanLII).

120   *Makivik Corporation* v. *Canada (Attorney General)*, 2021 FCA 184 (CanLII), paras 111–112, 136, 146, 158.

121   Agreement between the Inuit of the Nunavut Settlement Area and Her Majesty the Queen in Right of Canada (25 May 1993), http://www.tunngavik.com/documents/publications /1993-00-00-Nunavut-Land-Claims-Agreement-English.pdf [Nunavut Agreement]. See also the chapter by Doelle *et al.* in this volume. Interestingly, the Nunatsiavut (Labrador) Agreement contains specific provisions related to marine shipping (Parts 6.5 and 6.6) as part of a chapter on ocean management.

122   This is the area referenced as 'Area B' in Article 3 and as depicted in greater detail in Schedule 3–1 of the Nunavut Agreement.

123   Nunavut Agreement (n 121), Article 1.1.1.

124   Id., Articles 15, 16. Land fast ice is ice that is attached to land; the floe edge is biologically productive and is a favoured hunting zone. Rick Riewe, "Inuit Use of the Sea Ice," *Arctic and Alpine Research* 23 (1991): 3.

125   These principles include the principle (Article 15.1.1(c)) that "Canada's sovereignty over the waters of the arctic archipelago is supported by Inuit use and occupancy."

areas), 11 (land use planning), 12 (development impact), 23 (Inuit employment within government), 24 (government contracts), 25 (resource royalty sharing), 27 (natural resource development), 33 (archaeology) and 34 (ethnographic objects and archival materials). Even if this list were exhaustive (which it cannot be[126]) it is evident from the breadth of the topics covered that the parties intended that the Agreement would have much to say about the planning for, and management of, marine spaces within the NSA.

Part 3 of Article 15 is principally concerned with wildlife management and harvesting in marine areas beyond the NSA facilitated by appropriate institutional structures.[127] Allocation of commercial fisheries licences in these adjacent areas is to be informed by the principles of adjacency and economic dependence of communities in the NSA on marine resources.[128] The Federal Court of Appeal considers that these provisions must inform and constrain the exercise of the otherwise highly discretionary powers of the Minister of Fisheries and Oceans to grant fishing licences under the terms of the *Fisheries Act*[129] and regulations.[130]

Part 4 of Article 15 contemplates that each of the Nunavut Impact Review Board (NIRB), the Nunavut Water Board, the Nunavut Planning Commission (NPC) and the Nunavut Wildlife Management Board might severally, or jointly as a Nunavut Marine Council (NMC), "advise and make recommendations to other government agencies regarding the marine areas, and Government shall consider such advice and recommendations in making decisions which affect marine areas."[131] It may be inferred that the honour of the Crown would require Government (depending on the context) to offer reasoned responses to such advice and recommendations.[132] The NMC has not been particularly active, but in recent years it has offered advice and recommendations with respect to such matters as marine noise,[133] and draft MARPOL (International Convention

---

126   The list cannot be exhaustive. For example, these provisions only make sense when read in light of the definitions of Article 1, the general provisions of Article 2 and the definition of the Nunavut Settlement Area in Article 3.

127   Nunavut Agreement (n 121), Article 15.3.1.

128   Id., Article 15.3.7.

129   *Fisheries Act*, RSC 1985, c F-14, s 7.

130   *Nunavut Tunngavik Inc.* v. *Canada* (*Minister of Fisheries and Oceans*), 1998 CanLII 9080 (FCA), [1998] 4 FC 405; for commentary, see Nigel Bankes, "Implementing the Fisheries Provisions of the Nunavut Claim: Re-Capturing the Resource?," *Journal of Environmental Law and Policy* 12 (2003): 141.

131   Nunavut Agreement (n 121), Article 15.4.1. For the NMC's website see https://www.nunavutmarinecouncil.com/.

132   See, for example, *Makivik Corporation* v. *Canada* (*Attorney General*), 2021 FCA 184.

133   Letter to Marine Planning and Conservation Directorate, Fisheries and Oceans Canada, 12 January 2021, https://www.nunavutmarinecouncil.com/dms/publishing/download.aspx?fileid=193.

for the Prevention of Pollution from Ships) amendments prohibiting the use and carriage for use as fuel of heavy fuel oil by ships in Arctic waters.[134] Subject to budgetary constraints, the Council could take a more proactive role.

Finally, Part 5 contains a savings clause indicating that Article 15 must be "interpreted in a manner consistent with Canada's sovereignty, sovereign rights and jurisdiction, and with Canada's international obligations."[135] The same idea is repeated in Article 16 dealing with Inuit harvesting rights in the Outer Land Fast Ice Zone.[136]

3.2.1 The Land Use Planning and Development Impact Provisions of the Nunavut Agreement

We now turn to examine the land use planning and impact assessment provisions of the Nunavut Agreement. In our view, it is these provisions, Articles 11 and 12 of the Nunavut Agreement, that are most likely to afford Inuit a measure of influence and control over navigation and shipping in Canadian Arctic waters. Both Articles "apply" to the marine areas of the NSA.[137] Section 12.12.2 is even more specific insofar as it provides that Article 12 shall apply to "both land and marine areas within the Nunavut Settlement Area and to the Outer Land Fast Ice Zone" and that "[s]hipping associated with project proposals" in the NSA "shall be subject to this Article" except for "normal community resupply or individual ship movements not associated with project proposals."[138] Similarly, section 11.1.4 makes it clear that the land use planning provisions apply to marine areas within the NSA and the Outer Land Fast Ice Zone.

While the impact review provisions of Article 12 are triggered by project proposals,[139] the land use planning provisions are not so contingent and seek to establish "planning policies, priorities and objectives regarding the conservation, development, management and use of land" (and, by virtue of section

---

134   Letter to Hon Marc Garneau, Minister of Transport, and Hon Bernadette Jordan, Minister of Fisheries, Oceans and the Coast Guard, 6 May, 2020, https://www.nunavutmarinecouncil .com/dms/publishing/download.aspx?fileid=96.

135   Nunavut Agreement (n 121), Article 15.5.1.

136   Id., Article 16.1.1.

137   Id., Article 15.2.2 and discussed above. The provisions of the Agreement are further operationalized by the terms of the *Nunavut Planning and Project Assessment Act*, SC 2013, c 14 [NPPAA].

138   Normal community resupply is defined in Article 12.1.1.

139   This is a defined term, see Article 1.1 as amended (2015). The definition is broad enough to include cruise boats intending to visit Nunavut communities and other sites. See, for example, NIRB, Screening Decision Report, File # 16TN039, re "MS Crystal Serenity – Crystal Cruises LLC Northwest Passage 2017", 9 June 2017.

11.1.4, marine areas in the NSA) and "to prepare land use plans which guide and direct resource use and development" in the NSA.[140] As such, the Nunavut land use planning process has the potential to establish relevant ground rules not only for destination-based shipping in Canadian Arctic waters, but also for shipping transiting Canadian Arctic waters (to the extent permitted by the United Nations Convention on the Law of the Sea and discussed elsewhere in this volume).[141] While the planning provisions set the ground rules within which development may occur, they also inform the project review provisions insofar as (and subject to some exceptions)[142] a project cannot proceed through the project review process unless the NPC has determined that a project proposal is in conformity with an applicable land use plan.[143]

In what follows we will use the example of the Mary River iron ore project to discuss an example of non-conformity under the terms of one of the existing land use plans and show how the draft Nunavut land use plan might have an impact on navigation and shipping issues. The Mary River expansion project also shows how navigation and shipping issues might lead the NIRB to reject a project. There are currently two approved land use plans: the North Baffin Regional Land Use Plan (North Baffin Plan) and the Keewatin Regional Land Use Plan. The NPC has been working to develop a new Nunavut-wide land use plan since approximately 2007. Once adopted and approved, that plan will replace the two regional plans.[144]

3.2.2   The North Baffin Plan and the Mary River Iron Ore Mine
Baffinland's Mary River iron ore project was approved for conformity by the NPC and by NIRB in 2012.[145] The project is located on northern Baffin Island

---

140   Nunavut Agreement (n 121), Article 11.2.2.
141   See chapters by Bartenstein and Bankes in this volume. See also Nunavut Planning Commission, Leading the Way Through Land Use Planning, Nunavut Land Use Plan, Draft, July 2021 [Nunavut Draft Plan], 10:
       The Plan should be interpreted and applied in a way that respects Canada's international rights and obligations, including those under the 1982 United Nations Convention on the Law of the Sea, customary international law and any other binding international instrument.
142   Nunavut Agreement (n 121), Article 11.5.11.
143   Id., Articles 11.4.4(k) and 11.5.10 as amended (2015). For additional discussion see Daniel Dylan, "The Complicated Intersection of Politics, Administrative and Constitutional Law in Nunavut's Environmental Impacts Assessment Regime" *University of New Brunswick Law Journal* 68 (2017): 202.
144   Nunavut Draft Plan (n 141).
145   The plan was approved in 2010. The approved plan is available on the NPC's website. For further commentary see Dylan (n 143), pp. 215–225.

with possible marine access to the south at Steensby Inlet and to the north at Milne Inlet, Eclispe Sound and Pond Inlet. The project was originally approved to use the Steensby Inlet port with year-round shipping. In 2014, the NPC and NIRB approved a second phase of the project (the early revenue phase) to add shipping from Milne Inlet, but only during the open water season.

Baffinland subsequently proposed a Phase II of the project to include shipping from Milne Inlet for ten months of the year with associated icebreaking activities. The NPC concluded that the project as proposed was not in conformity with the North Baffin Plan.[146] This was the first negative conformity decision of the NPC under either of the two approved plans.[147] The NPC reached its conclusion largely on the basis that the regular icebreaking activities required by Phase II would interfere with community access and travel routes to areas that were essential for hunting, fishing and trapping and which the Plan sought to protect. While the proponent subsequently secured a ministerial exemption for Phase II as originally formulated,[148] the point for present purposes is simply that the terms of approved land use plans, even those that operate at a high level of generality (which is certainly the case for the provisions of the North Baffin Plan that were invoked in this case) may make the shipping and navigational aspects of proposed projects non-conforming uses. Such projects will not be able to proceed absent a plan amendment or a ministerial exemption.[149] And, insofar as the principal purpose of planning in the NSA is to protect and promote the existing and future well being of residents of Nunavut, such plans do afford a means to further the choices and values of Nunavumiut.

Baffinland subsequently revised its Phase II project on several occasions leading to further screening by the NPC before the Phase II project was ultimately referred to NIRB for its assessment in May 2018. In May 2022, NIRB, for reasons discussed below, ultimately recommended against Phase II.[150]

3.2.3   Nunavut Land Use Plan (Draft July 2021)
In July 2021 the NPC released the proposed land use plan for the entire NSA preparatory to public hearings on the draft.[151] The draft plan is all encompassing

---

146   NPC, Conformity Determination, Mary River Project Phase II, 8 April 2015.
147   Id., para 39.
148   See Nunavut Agreement (n 121), Article 11.5.11.
149   The availability of a ministerial exemption also confirms a significant limitation on Inuit influence over land and sea use decision-making.
150   NIRB, Reconsideration Report and Recommendations for Baffinland's Phase 2 Development Proposal, May 2022, NIRB File No. 08MN053.
151   The Nunavut Draft Plan (n 141), along with related documents, is available online https://www.nunavut.ca/land-use-plans/draft-nunavut-land-use-plan. The NPC currently anticipates

in the sense that it proposes to apply one of three land use designations to all areas covered by the plan.[152] The three designations are: (1) limited use (year-round prohibitions of one or more types of land use), (2) conditional use (use permitted but subject to seasonal prohibitions[153] or setback requirements), or (3) mixed use (all uses are considered to conform to the plan).[154]

It is not possible within the compass of this chapter to provide an exhaustive account of the proposed land use plan, but we can give some examples of how the requirements of the plan may have an impact on shipping and navigation. These include:

- Conditional use measures to protect known caribou sea ice crossings.[155]
- Measures to protect walrus terrestrial haul outs as limited use areas, including an obligation on vessels of different sizes to remain at prescribed distances from a walrus haul out.[156]
- Conditional use measures to protect whale (beluga) calving areas.[157]
- Measures to protect the North Water (Sarvarjuaq) Polynya as a conditional use area.[158]

While the plan recognizes the need for seasonal restrictions or set back requirements for navigation, it also recognizes the importance of marine shipping to the current and future development of Nunavut, and, in particular, the "heavy lift capacity of marine transport" for the resources sector.[159] Furthermore, most if not all of the more specific restrictions do not apply to vessels engaged in community resupply or emergency response.[160]

---

holding public hearings on the Plan as required by Article 11.5.4 of the Nunavut Agreement in March 2022 (see https://www.nunavut.ca/news/2021/notice-reopening-record-and-next-steps-2021-draft-nunavut-land-use-plan-0).

152   Draft Land Use Plan (n 141), s 1.4.5.

153   Seasonal prohibitions are expressed in terms of six Inuit seasonal cycles. Id., s 1.4.6.

154   Id., s 1.4.5.3.

155   Draft Land Use Plan, s 2.2.5–1, no icebreaking activities in certain channels at prescribed times of the year.

156   Id., s 2.4–2; see also s 2.4–3 applying to project-related activities and s 4.11–9 providing more extensive protection (to protect community interests) for one specific site at Walrus Island.

157   Id., s 2.5.1–2 no operation of vessels by project proponents in the calving areas adjacent to Southampton Island and Clearwater Fjord during the Aujaq season.

158   Id., s 2.8.2–1 provides "except as required for safe navigation, no person is to conduct ice-breaking activities during Ukiaq, Ukiuq, Upingaksaaq and Upingaaq (December 1 to July 31)." See above (text to notes 62–65) for discussion of the international significance of Sarvarjuaq/Pikialasorsuaq.

159   Id., s 5.3.2.

160   See, for example, Draft Land Use Plan, s 2.4–5.

3.2.4   Development Impact Review

As noted above, the NIRB provisions are triggered by the existence of a project proposal which is defined in terms of a physical work or a physical activity.[161] As such, the definition includes not only physical projects such as a mine, but also marine-based activities such as marine science projects[162] and ship-based tourism activities.[163] Any such project must be in conformity with the terms of an applicable plan. For example, if the draft land use plan were to be approved as it stands, it would follow that a marine science project that involved a vessel transit in a limited or conditional use area in conflict with the types of restrictions described above would not be a conforming use.

In common with other impact assessment authorities, the NIRB will routinely examine the impact of activities directly related to the particular project that is the subject of an application. Hence, in the case of an application for the approval of a new mine such as Baffinland's Mary River iron ore project, the Board examines the impact of the marine transportation activities associated with the mine, including those activities associated with construction, fuel supply for the mine and the shipment of the produced ore. Such considerations may factor into whether or not the NIRB is prepared to recommend that the project should proceed or not,[164] but may also result in the imposition of terms or conditions to help achieve the objective of Article 12, namely, "to protect and promote the existing and future well-being of the residents and communities of the [NSA], and to protect the ecosystemic integrity of the [NSA]."[165]

This affords intervenors in project applications the opportunity to explore with the proponent and the Board the types of undertakings that a proponent is prepared to make, and the terms and conditions the Board might impose in relation to the marine shipping aspects of a project. While the proponent may not own or charter the ships that will provide services to the project, the proponent will typically own and control the marine terminal and thus will be in a position to determine the types and age of vessels that may be accepted for docking,[166] and impose terms and conditions on vessels as part of that process.

---

161   Nunavut Agreement (n 121), Article 11, as amended (2015).
162   For example, see the NIRB website https://www.nirb.ca/ under public registry, project type and select 'marine based activities' category.
163   See note 139 re MV *Crystal Serenity*.
164   Nunavut Agreement (n 121), Article 12.5.6.
165   Id., Article 12.2.5.
166   For example, in both the initial and reconsideration proceedings related to the TransMountain Expansion (TMX) project before the National Energy Board (NEB), TMX made commitments to use tankers of particular age classes (National Energy Board,

For example, the NIRB project certificate for the original Baffinland's Mary River project included a condition that "the Proponent shall require project vessels to maintain a route to the south of Mill Island to prevent disturbance to walrus and walrus habitat on the northern shore of Mill Island."[167] A further condition deals with scheduling of vessels, vessel speed and vessel routing (and not just in the immediate vicinity of the marine terminal).[168] Other conditions relate to such matters as shipboard observers[169] and ship noise.[170]

While proponents may argue that project vessels should only be subject to international standards established by the IMO and domestic laws of general application, and not more stringent standards that may impose increased costs, reduce the number of vessels available to provide project services, and affect the competitiveness of the project,[171] there is at least some, albeit limited, practice that suggests that the provision of marine terminal services provides both the leverage and the opportunity to impose terms and conditions (and/or accept proponent undertakings) to address community concerns.[172] However, this will be subject to the consideration that the proposed terms and conditions

Application for the Trans Mountain Expansion Project: Reconsideration of aspects of its OH-001-2014 Report as directed by Order in Council P.C. 2018–1177, MH-052-2018 (NEB, February 2019), 390, 395, 397, https://docs2.cer-rec.gc.ca/ll-eng/llisapi.dll/fetch/2000/90464/90552/548311/956726/2392873/3614457/3751789/3754555/A98021-1_NEB_-_NEB_Reconsideration_Report_-_Reconsideration_-_Trans_Mountain_Expansion_-_MH-052-2018_-_A6S2D8.pdf?nodeid=3754859&vernum=-2). The Board formalized this and related commitments by imposing condition 134, which requires TMX to file with the Board and update a "Vessel Acceptance Standard and Westridge Marine Terminal Regulations and Operations Guide." In addition to 156 conditions, the NEB also made 16 recommendations to address issues that went beyond its jurisdiction over the pipeline proponent. Some of these recommendations related to navigational issues. In the Order in Council directing the NEB to issue a project certificate, the Government of Canada undertook to implement those recommendations (P.C. 2019-820, 18 June 2019).

167   NIRB, Project Certificate-005, 28 December 2012, Term and Condition No 104.
168   Id., Term and Condition No 105 contemplates that the project proponent might be responsible for requiring a number of things: project vessels to change the frequency and timing (including periodic suspensions) of shipping during winter months, when interactions with marine mammals are likely to be the most problematic; reduce shipping speeds where ship–marine mammal interactions are most likely; and identify alternate shipping routes through Hudson Strait for use when conflicts between the proposed routes and marine mammals could arise.
169   Id., Terms and Conditions Nos 106–108.
170   Id., Terms and Conditions Nos 109–112.
171   One can see this debate reflected throughout chapter 14 (Project related increased shipping activities) of the NEB's TMX Reconsideration Report (n 166). In addition, the Board was sensitive to the concern that tankers should not assume all the responsibility for responding to the cumulative impacts of increased shipping from a number of different sources.
172   See the NEB's TMX reconsideration decision (n 166).

may also need to respond to commercial realities and the availability of vessels that can meet the terms and conditions.[173]

In the end, NIRB recommended rejection of the Phase II expansion project. It did so on a number of grounds, including the potential for the expansion to have significant and lasting adverse effects on marine mammals and fish, and that this in turn would have significant adverse socioeconomic effects on Inuit harvesting, culture, land use and food security.[174] Under section 106 of the *Nunavut Planning and Project Assessment Act*, the Minister must, within 150 days of the receipt of a negative report, either accept the report or reject it "if, in the opinion of the responsible Minister, the project is in the national or regional interest."[175] After taking additional time, the Minister ultimately decided to accept NIRB's decision.[176]

4   Conclusion

What emerges from our brief canvass of international law is that human rights instruments (both general and specific) afford Indigenous peoples rights of ownership and possession over the lands, territories and resources they have traditionally owned, occupied or otherwise used. Critically, these fundamental rights—which are an integral part of the right to self-determination and the right to culture of Indigenous peoples and which trigger the right to consultation and FPIC—are now recognized as customary norms. As such, Canada has a legal obligation to respect and protect those rights, including in its Arctic waters. Indeed the second preambular paragraph of the federal implementation act recognizes that "the rights and principles affirmed in the Declaration constitute the *minimum standards* for the survival, dignity and well-being of the Indigenous

---

173   For example, in its decision on Phase II, NIRB (n 150), pp. 194–195 and 208, ultimately rejected submissions that would have required the proponent to immediately eliminate the use of heavy fuel oil in all vessels using the Milne Port. This would have exceeded current regulatory requirements, which do not impose a ban until 2025. NIRB seems to have accepted Baffinland's submissions (p. 194) to the effect that an immediate ban would have affected its ability to source vessels.

174   Id., IX, XII, 177–185 (detailing potential effects on marine mammals, acoustic disturbance, ballast water and invasive species), 195–196 (covering shipping and marine spill response capacity).

175   NPPAA (n 137).

176   Statement by the Minister of Northern Affairs regarding the Federal Government's Decision on Baffinland's Mary River Mine Phase 2 Development Project Proposal, 16 November 2022, https://www.canada.ca/en/crown-indigenous-relations-northern-affairs/news/2022/11/statement-by-the-minister-of-northern-affairs-regarding-the-federal-governments-decision-on-baffinlands-mary-river-mine-phase-2-development-project.html.

peoples of the world, and *must be implemented in Canada.*"[177] This is a strong commitment. The territorial and resource rights proclaimed in the UNDRIP are very broad in scope and include, for example, the right to "own, use, *develop and control*" the land, territories and resources that Indigenous peoples possess by reason of traditional ownership or other traditional occupation or use.[178]

With the coming into force of the *United Nations Declaration on the Rights of Indigenous Peoples Act* in June of 2021, one would therefore expect that Indigenous human rights norms will henceforth have a greater impact in Canadian judicial decisions. For while Canadian courts have progressively become more receptive to international law, this practice has not been reflected in cases dealing with Indigenous rights. The Supreme Court's decision in the 2018 *Mikisew Cree First Nation* case,[179] for instance, contrasts unfavourably with the more recent decisions of its Swedish[180] and Norwegian[181] counterparts. In reaching its conclusion in that case, that the duty to consult Indigenous peoples does not apply to the law-making process, a determination of great import for Indigenous communities, the Supreme Court of Canada did not refer to the UNDRIP or any other international human rights instrument.[182]

Our investigation into examples of Indigenous agency has revealed a modest trend in favour of meaningful and active Indigenous involvement in Arctic regional governance mechanisms. While Permanent Participant status at the Arctic Council has been an important vehicle for Indigenous self-determination since 1996, other key institutions and processes are only slowly responding to the legal imperative of consulting with and involving the region's Indigenous peoples. The participation of Indigenous representatives on State delegations tasked with negotiating the new Central Arctic Ocean Fisheries Agreement and the granting of provisional consultative status to the ICC by the IMO are positive steps forward. However, it is perhaps time for other agencies or bodies with important mandates and responsibilities for the Arctic marine environment to follow suit.

The Northwest Atlantic Fisheries Organization (NAFO) and the North East Atlantic Fisheries Commission (NEAFC), the most important sub-Arctic regional fisheries management organizations (RFMOs), could be interesting candidates. The two RFMOs are tasked with ensuring the long-term

---

177   UNDRIPA (n 23).

178   UNDRIP (n 22), Article 26(2). Emphasis added.

179   *Mikisew Cree First Nation* (n 115).

180   Swedish Supreme Court (n 17).

181   Supreme Court of Norway (n 70).

182   See Nigel Bankes, "The Duty to Consult and the Legislative Process: But What About Reconciliation?," ABlawg, 21 December 2016, http://ablawg.ca/wp-content/uploads /2016/12/Blog_NB_Courtoreille_MCFN_FCA.pdf.

conservation and optimum utilisation of the fishery resources in their respective areas (which stretch into the Arctic), as well as providing sustainable economic, environmental and social benefits. To this end, the two organizations have the power to adopt management measures for various fish stocks (e.g., quotas) and control/enforcement mechanisms (e.g., vessel inspections). Both organizations can also adopt measures to protect other parts of the marine ecosystem from potential negative impacts of fisheries. As Schatz notes, neither the NAFO Convention nor the NEAFC Convention contains provisions mandating the incorporation of Arctic Indigenous knowledge.[183] Nor are Indigenous organizations or communities afforded a formal status or role.

It is of course possible to include Indigenous voices and knowledge in the work and decision making process of NAFO, NEAFC and other relevant bodies by integrating Indigenous representatives within State delegations. Canada is a contracting party to NAFO and a 'cooperating non-contracting party' to NEAFC. However, whatever form Indigenous involvement takes, Enyew's *mise en garde* bears repeating: Good faith consultation only occurs if States are open to hear, and *be influenced by*, the views of the coastal Indigenous communities concerned.[184] Furthermore, the focus cannot solely be on securing a right of participation for Indigenous peoples and communities in different fora. There must be an equal emphasis on the correlative duty of governments to support and adequately resource their involvement.

Over time the domestic implementation of UNDRIP should secure a greater convergence between domestic law and international law. Within the domestic legal system, the duty to consult and accommodate offers the principal opportunity for Indigenous communities to engage with government initiatives and decisions relating to navigation and shipping but only if, as the *Clyde River* decision demonstrates, that consultation is meaningful. Beyond that, the terms of modern land claims agreements also provide opportunities for influence and engagement where those agreements cover marine areas. Absent specific provisions dealing with navigation and shipping, the most important provisions of those agreements are likely to be the land and marine use planning provisions and impact assessment provisions of such agreements. Our analysis of the practice under the Nunavut Agreement shows how these provisions can be used to address at least some community concerns. But this practice also points up the weaknesses of these provisions to the extent that ministerial overrides may undercut the planning provisions of the agreement or to the extent that the impact review board proves reluctant to make full use of its powers to add terms and conditions.

---

183   Schatz (n 95), p. 130.
184   Enyew (n 4), p. 66.

CHAPTER 18

Conclusion

Aldo Chircop and Kristin Bartenstein

Abstract

This concluding chapter reflects issues and directions for the governance of shipping in Canadian Arctic waters at a time of unprecedented change drawing on the themes discussed throughout the book, in particular the interface between shipping, Indigenous rights and environment protection. The Arctic is a unique ecoregion that is subject to mixed adverse and beneficial impacts due to the consequences of climate change, most especially because of enhanced mobility enabled by shipping. Most importantly, the Canadian Arctic is Inuit Nunangat, the homeland of Inuit, and calls for development that places the interests of its inhabitants at the centre. The potential risks and benefits of increasing industrialization and other economic activities must be subject to socially and environmentally responsible governance. At this time, the governance of shipping in Canadian Arctic waters is fragmented and needs to be strengthened in view of the designation of low-impact shipping corridors. Future maritime governance demands strengthening and concertation of State powers and measures with respect to clear policy directions, modernized coordinated regulation, coordinated institutional framework, effective management measures, proper funding of initiatives and capacity-building.

Keywords

Arctic ecoregion – capacity-building – Inuit Nunangat – Indigenous rights – institutional framework – jurisdiction – management measures – maritime governance – maritime regulation – policy – shipping – social and environmental licence – UNDRIP

1   Introduction

In this book we reflected on the governance of shipping in Canadian Arctic waters at a time of unprecedented change. We undertook this task from the perspectives of several disciplines and fields, including defence and strategic studies, geography, history, international relations, law (Canadian and international), oceanography, political science, public policy, and cultural anthropology. Our focus has been on the role policy plays and possible future directions for the governance of Arctic shipping. Each chapter has drawn its own conclusions and this closing chapter provides cumulative and integrative insights into the complexity and prospects of maritime governance in Canadian Arctic waters.

2   The Arctic as Homeland: Inuit Nunangat

The Arctic has long been a homeland for Indigenous peoples. Over millennia, Inuit Nunaat encompassed wide swaths of the Arctic regions of Canada, Denmark (Kalaallit Nunaat/Greenland), Russian Federation (Chukotka) and United States (Alaska). In Canada, Inuit are organized in groups across Inuit Nunangat.[1] There are also Cree, Dene, Gwich'in, Innu and Métis communities. Inuit and other Indigenous communities have been involved in the development of land claims agreements, known as modern treaties, in the region since the 1970s.[2] As pointed out by Ell-Kanayuk and Aporta, Inuit are a land, sea and ice people with a unique maritime culture. They have long considered land, landfast ice, sea ice and marine waters as a continuity. The Western legal bifurcation of the legal status of land and water and the international law of the sea idea that the land dominates the sea are alien and colonial concepts to Inuit.

Hence, Inuit Indigenous rights to lands, territories and resources must be understood to comprehend the entirety of the spaces used since time immemorial for subsistence, mobility, settlement, and cultural practices. Shipping impacts on Inuit uses of ice and marine areas. Hence, public authorities and commercial and recreational users should respect Indigenous rights enshrined in the United Nations Declaration on the Rights of Indigenous Peoples (UNDRIP),[3] such as the right to self-determination, the principle that their free,

---

1   Inuit groups include: Iglulingmiut (Iglulik Inuit), Inuinnait (Copper Inuit), Inuvialuit (Western Arctic Inuit or Mackenzie Delta Inuit), Kivallirmiut (Caribou Inuit), Labradormiut (Labrador Inuit), Nunavimmiut (Nunavik Inuit or Ungava Inuit), Nunatsiarmiut (Baffin Island Inuit), Netsilingmiut (Netsilik Inuit) and Qikirtamiut (Sanikiluaq Inuit).
2   These include: James Bay and Northern Quebec Agreement, 1975; Inuvialuit Final Agreement, 1984; the Umbrella Final Agreement for Yukon, 1990 (Yukon First Nations); Gwich'in Comprehensive Land Claim Agreement, 1992; Nunavut Agreement, 1993; Sahtu Dene, 1993; Métis Comprehensive Land Claim Agreement, 1993; Tlicho Land Claims and Self-government agreement, 2003; Labrador Inuit Land Claims Agreement, 2005; and Nunavik Inuit Land Claim Agreement, 2006.
3   UN Doc A/RES/61/295 (13 September 2007).

prior, and informed consent must be obtained before a major development activity proceeds, cultural and education rights, and the protection of the environment to enable them to enjoy their rights.

3   A Unique Ecoregion Subject to Mixed Impacts from Shipping

The Arctic is a unique ecoregion, characterized by ecosystems and species adapted to extreme temperatures and light cycles, and dominant ice conditions. As Vincent *et al.* observed, it is a vital component of planetary systems, acting as a critical contributor to global climate, weather, and ocean water circulation. At the same time, it is disproportionally affected by global environmental and anthropogenic stressors that are amplified in the region. The Arctic is experiencing the highest warming rate on the planet, affecting not only the regional environment and its inhabitants and economies, but also planetary well-being. These biogeophysical and anthropogenic characteristics justify treating the Arctic as a matter of both regional and global concern.

The Canadian Arctic is an underdeveloped economic region, with communications, infrastructure, education, employment, energy, health, and transportation standards well behind the rest of the country. Canada's Arctic and Northern Policy Framework acknowledges these gaps and highlights economic development as a major concern for Indigenous peoples in the North.[4] Lajeunesse and Lackenbauer noted that the region has a terrestrial mining history, characterized by boom-and-bust cycles, which have not dented underdevelopment. Geographical remoteness ensures that shipping will remain an agent of economic development, both by providing a platform and transport for a range of economic activities, and because of the needs to support shipping itself.

Shipping produces mixed biological, chemical, physical, economic, and cultural impacts on the region. Some forms of shipping, such as northern logistics cabotage, are beneficial for Arctic communities because they facilitate mobility, supplies to communities and food security. Canadian cabotage policy and law have long supported domestic shipping through incentives, such as exclusivity of carriage and exemption from certain fees, including icebreaking, and should continue to do so. Government vessels providing navigational safety services and research platforms, constitute vital infrastructure to promote maritime safety, pollution response, search and rescue,

---

4   Crown-Indigenous Relations and Northern Affairs Canada, "Canada's Arctic and Northern Policy Framework," Government of Canada, last modified 22 November 2019, Goal 5.9 and Annex, https://www.rcaanc-cirnac.gc.ca/eng/1560523306861/1560523330587.

hydrographic surveying, and strengthen the science behind climate and ocean change. Privately owned commercial vessels play a critical role in supporting natural resource development and exporting minerals. Lasserre observed that at this time there is minimal commercial transit shipping in Canadian Arctic waters to service distant markets, because of the costs involved, advantages of established routes and lack of interest in the shipping industry, although this could conceivably change if Arctic hubs emerge. However, according to Choi, current Canadian Coast Guard icebreaking capability in Arctic waters is barely meeting current needs, suggesting that future growth will necessitate enhancing the capacity to deliver this vital service.

Shipping also produces negative impacts with the potential of significantly increasing pressure on the region's sensitive ecosystems and species. These include multiple harmful impacts such as atmospheric emissions from the use of hydrocarbon-derived fuels, operational pollution such as garbage, sewage, and 'clean' ballast (albeit with low oil content), surface and underwater noise, and potential disruption of animal and human ice routes. The burning of heavy fuel oil produces black carbon, an accelerator of sea ice loss and a climate forcer. Shipping also increases the risk of environmental and safety emergencies through serious spills and the need to provide timely search and rescue in a remote region having little such capacity. Coastal communities are expected to be first responders, adding risk and stress to their lives and livelihoods. Fortunately for northern Canadians, the federal Ship-source Oil Pollution Fund, which is now subject to unlimited liability, extends assistance to pollution damage claims in Arctic waters.

Some forms of cruise shipping and recreational boating do not leave beneficial economic impacts in the region. In some cases, cruise ships have been known to provide minimal if any opportunity for Inuit communities to benefit from their presence. Ell-Kanayuk gave some examples in her interview with Aporta. Inuit artwork and products from locally hunted exotic species might not be bought by tourists from countries that ban the import of products from such species. Tourists on shore visits may easily outnumber the remote communities they visit and might buy goods that are in limited supply to those communities.

Cruise ships also raise other safety concerns because of the large numbers of passengers and crew on board. A few such ships have grounded in Canadian Arctic waters and usually because the owners and masters on board assumed unnecessary risks, such as not notifying authorities on entering the Northern Canada Vessel Traffic Services Zone (NORDREG)[5] before entering Arctic waters

---

5 *Northern Canada Vessel Traffic Services Zone Regulations*, SOR/2010-127.

and not communicating or changing their passage plans, potentially risking delayed search and rescue (if needed), failing to carry on board all the requisite charts and notices to shipping for safe navigation, navigating in uncharted or not fully chartered waters to provide passengers on board unique experiences, and even proceeding at unsafe speeds. In the *Clipper Adventurer* case, the operator did not comply with the vessel's own safety management system, did not evaluate the passage plan, failed to provide its crew with safeguards such as a serviceable forward-looking sonar, and ensuring that navigational warnings were obtained.[6] Indeed, Canadian authorities billed the owners of that grounded ship for the provision of services to free it and thereby established an important policy precedent on the internalization of costs of the operation of negligent vessels.

The future development trajectory of Arctic shipping remains uncertain and unpredictable, although traffic has been increasing, as noted by Lasserre, Dawson and Song. For shipping to really become an agent of socioeconomic change in the region, Canadian Arctic waters cannot simply be promoted as a new navigation route to service external markets. Without critical infrastructure such as improved cartography, navigation aids, pilotage, ports, towage and salvage support, search and rescue, and pollution emergency response, the environmental risks are likely to outweigh benefits from increased shipping. The promotion of shipping must bring benefits at reasonable cost to Indigenous communities.

4   The Need to Rethink Arctic Maritime Governance

The Arctic is not a last frontier to be conquered. In the nineteenth century, the exploration for a new trade route through the Northwest Passage motivated many failed expeditions. The search for a new navigation route between the Atlantic and Pacific, until Roald Amundsen finally succeeded in navigating the Northwest Passage in 1906, was energized by romantic and imperial notions of 'discovery.' European sea power, industrialization and maritime trade underscored interests in the new navigation route. They ignored long-established Indigenous settlements, vibrant cultures, and their governance systems. The narrative of discovery continues to some extent today in the pursuit of new Arctic trade routes, perhaps with even greater cogency because of a combination of dramatic and progressive sea ice loss and technological development to overcome what is left. Economists might even argue that trade routes are international public goods, to be enjoyed by all and for everybody's benefit.

---

6   *Adventurer Owner Ltd* v. *Canada*, 2017 FC 105, 2018 FCA 34.

There is genuine concern that increased access to and industrialization of the region could yet again push to the side Indigenous interests and concerns. Maritime trade routes are intermediaries between markets; they facilitate the interests of distant actors. Arctic trade routes, much like superhighways, could reduce sailing distances and time for voyages linking North American, northern European, and Asian continents. However, the potential danger of such developments is that the unique region and its Indigenous peoples serve external interests in an inequitable manner. Some would argue that new and shorter trade routes mean shorter distances entailing lower greenhouse gas emissions. This is a self-serving argument because the reduced emissions of non-regional polluters extend the range of their polluting emissions to a different region. They also externalize substantial risks to the region and its peoples.

Even Canada, in claiming to protect the region's unique environment through ground-breaking regulation, focused its efforts on setting standards for vessel-source pollution prevention purposes, rather than the Arctic as a human space. In 1970, the *Arctic Waters Pollution Prevention Act* (AWPPA) mentioned Indigenous interests only once, and in the preamble.[7] That narrative was continued in the negotiation of Article 234 of the United Nations Convention on the Law of the Sea, 1982 (LOSC),[8] which concerned the power and limits of exceptional coastal State jurisdiction over international shipping in ice-covered areas, as explained by Bartenstein. Article 234 says nothing on the rights and interests of historic Indigenous users of the region, unlike other provisions in the Convention that provide a measure of protection to traditional or habitual fishing rights of States. This narrow narrative carried through as recently as during the development of the International Code of Safety for Ships Operating in Polar Waters (Polar Code)[9] at the International Maritime Organization (IMO), where ten years of negotiations did not include discussion of Indigenous rights and interests impacted by shipping in the region. The trade and shipping narrative has not included the conception of the Arctic as Inuit Nunaat (and Inuit Nunangat in Canada), at least not until today in Canada.

As an Arctic coastal State, Canada has special responsibilities to safeguard its Arctic region's uniqueness, protect its territorial integrity and sovereignty,

---

7   RSC 1985, c A-12.
8   Adopted 10 December 1982 (in force 16 November 1994), 1833 *UNTS* 3.
9   International Code for Ships Operating in Polar Waters (Polar Code), IMO Resolution MSC.385(94) (21 November 2014, effective 1 January 2017); Amendments to the International Convention for the Safety of Life at Sea 1974, IMO Resolution MSC.386(94) (21 November 2014, effective 1 January 2017); Amendments to MARPOL Annexes I, II, IV and V, IMO Resolution MEPC.265(68) (15 May 2015, effective 1 January 2017).

and ensure the well-being of its Indigenous peoples. The geographical scope of these responsibilities is extensive. However, Canada's responsibilities for the region are not limited to the polar space itself and must be exercised in regional and global fora making decisions that affect Inuit Nunangat.

Today, it is no longer appropriate, sensible, or even ethical, to discuss maritime governance in Canadian Arctic waters in a purely trade and shipping narrative. The federal government's efforts to engage Indigenous communities and their knowledge in the process of designation of low-impact shipping corridors is laudable, but also carries certain consequences for maritime governance. Facilitation of Indigenous participation in governance should not be pursued in a paternalistic manner. There must be decolonization and genuine partnership on a nation-to-nation basis, in the spirit of reconciliation and guided by the UNDRIP, as echoed by Beveridge. The structures and processes of maritime governance need to change to reflect this imperative.

Canadian shipowners are aware of this changing context and are responding accordingly. However, the developments in Canadian Arctic waters may not be understood or appreciated by international regulators, other States and shippers who may simply regard navigation in polar waters as a public good, entailing mobility rights buttressed and protected by uniform rules adopted at the global level. The trade and shipping narrative has obscured the reality of the region as a human space, where Indigenous peoples have had homelands since time immemorial. They have used the land, waters and ice for subsistence, mobility, community building and cultural development. They are entitled to the advancement of their interests through direct and meaningful participation in the governance of Arctic navigation and shipping. It is incumbent on Canada to sensitize the international community to the uniqueness of this human and environmental space, and the necessary corollary uniqueness of its governance. The Inuit Circumpolar Council's recent attainment of provisional consultative status at the IMO provides an enhanced opportunity to raise awareness and educate States and the industry and thereby ensure that continued regime-building in the region is cognizant and respectful of Indigenous rights as much as maritime regulation's concern with maritime safety, security, labour rights and environment protection.

5   Towards Socially and Environmentally Responsible Governance

What could policy directions for socially and environmentally responsible governance of Arctic shipping look like and how would they differ from those extant today? At the outset, there is a need to reconsider values and principles underpinning policy goals. The traditional administration of shipping in Canada has been implicitly guided by certain values. The purpose of maritime trade is to generate wealth, to move it in a safe manner while minimizing pollution of the marine environment and maintaining public order at sea to ensure security and unimpeded mobility. Moreover, sovereignty as a value has also guided Canada in regulating shipping. Indeed, the regulation of shipping through the AWPPA was to a great extent an exercise of sovereignty in the region and a message to outsiders.

In the contemporary context of shipping governance in Canadian Arctic waters, there are additional values that play important roles. They should be seen as complementary, rather than competing *inter se*. Justice and equity underscore the process of reconciliation in the north as elsewhere in Canada. Canada's commitment to implement UNDRIP constitutes an undertaking to pursue these values and to redress historic harm. Corollary values accompany justice and equity, and they include rights of self-determination and cultural identity. To Canadians living outside the region, the Arctic is part of the national identity; but to Inuit, the Arctic is an integral part of their lived cultural identity. The process of reconciliation demands that Canada should do what is just and right for the region's peoples and the environment. Rectitude entails social responsibility as an intrinsic value that should guide the federal government's fiduciary duty towards Inuit and responsibilities in the governance of shipping. The pursuit of values necessarily entails respect for Inuit Nunangat, the Inuit homeland, and rights Inuit have long had, but that have not been necessarily recognized and respected. Modern treaties in the Arctic region and Indigenous policies, such as the Inuit Nunangat Policy,[10] should inform federal shipping policy. It is possible for Canada to pursue wealth and the other core values traditionally guiding shipping in the region, including environment protection, while recognizing, respecting, and acting on the rights, interests, and developmental needs of the region's Indigenous peoples.

Decision support systems are also important. IMO and Canadian maritime legislation tend to be evidence-based, but also the product of extensive lobbying, mostly by industry lobbies. Buhler discussed regulatory capture of maritime regulators by industry regulatees as a potential concern. There is a need for an inclusive approach to the governance of shipping that necessitates diversity of knowledge in decision support systems, as discussed by Dawson and Song. In addition to industry-generated and scientific knowledge,

---

10   Inuit Nunanganut Atuagaq (Inuit Nunangat Policy), Prime Minister of Canada (21 April 2022), https://pm.gc.ca/en/news/news-releases/2022/04/21/inuit-crown-partnership-committee-endorses-historic-inuit-nunangat.

consideration of other ways of knowing, in particular traditional ecological and user knowledge, is essential. In the Arctic context, Aporta and others have argued that Inuit ontologies should be an integral component of decision support systems for sustainable shipping.[11]

The enactment of the *United Nations Declaration on the Rights of Indigenous Peoples Act* (UNDRIPA) indicates how Canada intends to honour its general international law obligations towards Indigenous peoples, as evidenced by UNDRIP, and to implement UNDRIP by setting out a framework for a federal legislative review.[12] Applied to the navigation and shipping field, the Act provides an opportunity for the undertaking of a systematic regulatory audit of some fifty statutes and numerous sets of subsidiary regulations. Core public and private law statutes will need to be studied to determine how, for example, Indigenous marine territories, resources, and uses are protected from shipping through area-based management tools under the *Canada Shipping Act, 2001*,[13] and in the case of damage or loss, how Indigenous interests would be compensated under the *Marine Liability Act*.[14] More specifically in the Arctic region, and as argued by Beveridge, Inuit interests and concerns would need to be better reflected in the AWPPA beyond the preamble.

As a matter of policy, the UNDRIPA legislative audit of Canadian maritime law should be accompanied by a parallel and interrelated review of the institutional aspects of the governance of shipping discussed by Chircop. Canada has international legal obligations under the IMO conventions, and Transport Canada acts as the national maritime administration and first point of contact for the domestication of IMO rules and standards. It is already guided by cooperative federalism, reconciliation, and fiduciary duties towards Indigenous peoples; however, the notion of 'administration' is outdated and ought to be replaced by 'governance.' This is more than a terminological change because governance implies inclusion, transparency, and accountability. A governance approach should also make room for bottom-up approaches, enabling rights holders and stakeholders to propose regulatory and policy changes.

---

11   Claudio Aporta, Breanna Bishop, Olivia Choi, and Weishan Wang, "Knowledge and Data: An Exploration of the Use of Inuit Knowledge in Decision Support Systems in Marine Management," *Governance of Arctic Shipping: Rethinking Risk, Human Impacts and Regulation*, eds., Aldo Chircop, Floris Goerlandt, Claudio Aporta and Ronald Pelot (Cham: Springer Polar Sciences, 2020), 159–169, https://doi.org/10.1007/978-3-030-44975-9_8.
12   SC 2021, c 14.
13   SC 2001, c 26.
14   SC 2001, c 6.

Now that Canada has embraced UNDRIP and committed to its domestic implementation, it should also consider assuming a leadership role in its further promotion and implementation at the global level. As an Arctic coastal and flag State with extensive experience in regulating polar shipping, Canada has the credentials and is well-positioned to advance Indigenous rights in the governance of polar shipping at the IMO. Global shipping interests need to be cognizant of the footprint they impose on Indigenous lands, territories, and resources. Industry is not used to doing this because their global logistical operations miss what could be characterized as matters of mere local concern. However, as argued by Lalonde and Bankes, shipping in Inuit Nunangat must respect Indigenous self-determination, consider the impacts produced by vessel operations and how adverse impacts can be prevented or mitigated.

Canada needs to engage with major flag States and the largest ship registers. Canada's own fleet is small and the cabotage fleet is clearly within easy jurisdiction and control. However, the increasing presence of foreign flags exercising international navigation rights in Arctic waters constraints Canada's ability to exercise unfettered jurisdiction and control, most especially in the territorial sea and exclusive economic zone (EEZ). As Bankes argues, flag States have a fundamental due diligence duty to exercise effective jurisdiction and control over their ships. It is in Canada's interest to engage the cooperation of flag States whose ships navigate Arctic waters to sensitize them to the need for socially and environmentally responsible shipping. For Canada to play a leadership role in the IMO in scaling-up polar shipping standards, it will need the cooperation of the major flag States, including open registers. In turn, flag States have to ensure their ships comply with domestic regulation based on IMO rules and standards.

6   Concerting the Use of Governance Powers and Measures

Several contributors to this book observed that the various aspects of the Canadian governance of shipping are not necessarily consistent or coordinated or maintained over time. Lajeunesse and Lackenbauer noted that Canadian Arctic policy has waxed and waned, with high points usually driven by hortatory sovereignty claims, invocations of environmental uniqueness, and aspirations for northern development. However, policy has not always produced tangible results, as was the case of the unfulfilled longstanding promise of northern development to respond to Indigenous communities' frequent lack of even the most basic of human needs, including appropriate shelter and food security.

6.1   *Policy Criteria*

While Canada has policies for the Arctic and national transportation, it does not appear to have a dedicated policy for Arctic shipping. A policy for shipping in the Canadian Arctic context should ideally state the principles guiding it, clear goals to be pursued, institutional leadership and the resources allocated to achieve intended outcomes over a specified timeline. An Arctic shipping policy must have a transparent and inclusive structure and process and a metric to determine when goals are achieved. Policy goals cannot simply be about the usual maritime regulatory outcomes, such as trade facilitation. Shipping must produce benefits for the region, for example, with respect to maritime infrastructure development and improved well-being for communities in the region while maintaining environmental values. The complexity of the shipping industry and Arctic context justify an integrated approach. Writing in 1980, Underdal explained integration as an effort to unify various elements around a conception, and implying comprehensiveness at the input stage of a policy, aggregation during the processing of inputs, and consistency among the outputs intended to be achieved.[15]

Comprehensiveness includes, at a minimum, temporal dimension of a policy in its long-term perspective, space in terms of the geographical scope, actors in terms of the reference group in the policy's issue area, and issues as interdependent concerns to be addressed by the policy framework.[16] An Arctic shipping policy would need to consider the climate change context and the point at which science suggests ice cover in Canadian Arctic waters will reduce to such an extent as to permit commercial transit shipping. While at this time the industry is not expressing interest in commercial transit shipping, as suggested by Lasserre, this could change by mid-century, at which point Canadian Arctic waters must have viable infrastructure in place. The geographical scope is the spatial extent of low-impact shipping corridors and consequential routeing areas for different sub-regions. The actors are public authorities, industry and commercial interests, Indigenous organizations, and civil society and scientific institutions concerned about the future of the region. As the chapters in this book have demonstrated, the issues are many and interrelated. Along with the traditional shipping concerns of safety, environmental impact, security and trade facilitation, the status of Inuit Nunangat as Inuit homeland and the imperative of reconciliation should play a central role.

---

15   Arild Underdal, "Integrated Marine Policy: What? Why? How?" (1980) *Marine Policy* 4(3):159–169, at 159.
16   Id., 160.

Aggregation demands that 'big picture' policy alternatives are considered to determine cost-benefit outcomes. International rules and standards adopted by the IMO play a central role. However, in the Canadian Arctic context, the big picture cannot simply continue to be the traditional regulatory concerns in the interests of maritime trade, but must also consider the human and cultural context against the backdrop of historic injustices and at a time of fundamental environmental change. Arctic shipping produces economic, environmental, and socio-cultural costs given that the Canadian Arctic is a homeland for the Inuit people. Meaningful inclusion of Indigenous interests will enable legitimacy.

Consistency entails the pursuit of harmony within the policy.[17] There must be consistency among the various policy goals advanced by the different federal, territorial, and Indigenous organizations and the implementing actions for specific issue areas. The coordinated approach to the designation of low-impact shipping corridors—involving Transport Canada, Canadian Coast Guard and Canadian Hydrographic Service—is a good example of collaboration. However, the trio should be expanded to reflect comprehensiveness of approach and aggregation of other actors, for example by involving other relevant departments (e.g., Environment and Climate Change Canada) and Indigenous organizations such as the Inuit Circumpolar Council (Canada), Inuit Tapiriit Kanatami, Qikiqtani Inuit Association and governments established by land claims agreements, among others. From a law of the sea and maritime law perspective, consistency suggests that Canada also acts in compliance with its own domestic constitutional requirements and international legal obligations. The pursuit of uniformity entails support for IMO regional polar shipping rules, which Canada in fact applies. But even on this point, the principle of uniformity must be reconciled with other concerns. Underdal suggests that consistency does not necessarily mean equal treatment,[18] and indeed in the Canadian Arctic context there will be need to prioritize Indigenous interests and environmental considerations over trade with respect to issues which the Polar Code does not address, or does not do so sufficiently, for example, with respect to non-SOLAS ships such as fishing and recreational vessels.

An Arctic shipping policy should be a dynamic rather than a static commitment to act. It should be updated and calibrated to achieve policy goals on a periodic basis. It should give direction for problem solving and prescription of specific measures to be undertaken, such as regulatory and institutional aspects, management, capacity-building, and resources. Its impact must then

---

17   Id., 161–162.
18   Id., 162.

be evaluated periodically to determine what goals are achieved over time and if any adjustments to goals and measures are needed.

6.2   *Maritime Jurisdiction and Regulation*

Maritime regulatory measures tend to serve both international and domestic policy goals. At a minimum, domestic regulation implements international standards and rules adopted under conventions to which Canada is a party, and when Canada is not a party, that it at least supports in principle or in part. Clearly, Canada's decision to become a party is in itself a policy decision and commitment to multilateralism and uniformity of rules and standards, of which the Polar Code is a good example. In addition to commitment to international regulation, Canada may also regulate in pursuit of policy goals that are not readily addressed in international instruments, but which address important local concerns. In the Arctic shipping context, there is an opportunity for Canada to develop and apply standards for gaps in the Polar Code, such as standards for non-SOLAS vessels, grey water, underwater noise, and icebreaking. It can do this with respect to shipping activities in its internal waters where most of the concerns reside, and for areas beyond it would need to consider additional concerns related to jurisdiction. As observed by Bartenstein, the LOSC Article 234 power enables Canada to scale-up standards for pollution prevention. Using its sovereignty over internal waters and the territorial sea and functional jurisdiction over the EEZ, Canada has the jurisdiction necessary to address Indigenous and environmental concerns in shipping regulation.

Whatever regulatory measures might be needed for Arctic shipping, it is important to ensure that proposed regulatory change is driven by compelling need and evidenced through inclusive decision support systems drawing on science and Indigenous knowledge. It would be helpful for initiatives to be launched in consultation with affected ocean users and adopted in a manner which makes them clear and operationally achievable, consistent across waters subject to different extents of jurisdiction (e.g., internal waters, territorial sea, EEZ).

As Chircop and Greentree demonstrated, Canadian maritime law is complex and fragmented and at times subject to federal-provincial jurisdictional conflicts, giving rise to occasional unpredictability, making compliance potentially difficult and costly. Hence, an Arctic shipping policy should consider a regulatory strategy that combines clarity, efficiency, predictability, and effectiveness. The policy should also consider the industry's self-regulatory power discussed by Buhler, which plays an important role in populating Polar Code goals with technical rules and standards.

6.3 *Institutional Framework*

Federal institutions, while having the powers and resources necessary for effective governance, do not always coordinate efficiently and consult on their initiatives. For example, the original Northern Marine Transportation Corridors initiative necessitated a policy rethink and was eventually relaunched as the Northern Low-Impact Shipping Corridors Initiative characterized by consultations with Indigenous communities and stakeholders. A lesson to be drawn from Dawson and Song is that an inclusive governance approach is better and more likely to find legitimacy in the eyes of those affected than simply a top-down federal administrative approach.

An Arctic shipping policy would need to address the institutional framework to deliver on policy goals. It should identify the federal institutions playing lead roles, as well as the roles of other federal and relevant provincial and territorial institutions whose mandates overlap with the policy's goals. The criterion of aggregation in the integrated approach suggests that all relevant institutional actors are actively engaged in policy implementation, and for this purpose, some form of an inter-governmental and inter-departmental consultative body would be necessary to provide structure and process to that engagement. As indicated above, Indigenous organizations and industry and non-industry stakeholders would also have to be involved in meaningful ways. The current model of the Canadian Marine Advisory Council (North), while helpful as a clearing house of information, is likely insufficient because stakeholders are engaged infrequently and receive policy and regulatory updates rather than being actively engaged in discussing and proposing policy directions.

In addition to identifying the roles for leading, steering, and monitoring, an Arctic shipping policy should provide for institution-building. For example, it is possible that designation of low-impact shipping corridors might need to be accompanied by a dedicated institutional framework for their management, possibly similar to the St. Lawrence Seaway model, which includes a directing body composed of representatives of regulators and stakeholders. Also, given the lack of up-to-date navigation charts and local navigational concerns, an Arctic pilotage authority operating with regulatory power like similar authorities in other parts of the country might well be needed.

6.4 *Management Measures*

The governance of Arctic shipping will need to be supported by maritime domain awareness and area-based management. As Charron and Snider argued, maritime domain awareness needs and capabilities in Canadian Arctic waters need to be significantly enhanced and integrated. Actively managed low-impact shipping corridors and MPAs are important area-based management measures to strengthen maritime domain awareness.

An Arctic shipping policy should give direction to area-based management efforts, drawing on the broader legal framework. The *Oceans Act* provides a framework for the designation of large offshore management areas, such as the Beaufort Sea Initiative, local area integrated management plans, and MPAs.[19] MPAs may also be designated under the *National Marine Conservation Areas Act*[20] and as marine wildlife areas under the *Canada Wildlife Act*.[21] Additionally, maritime legislation provides management tools that can be and have been successfully used for effective area-based management, such as routeing and reporting measures. These have been effectively used in the NORDREG zone where the regulations provide for a mandatory ship reporting system for ships entering, navigating, and exiting Canadian Arctic waters, an important domain awareness tool. Transport Canada's recent initiative of proactive vessel management programs for different regions is another good example of how a policy direction can be supported with management measures. Indeed, the notion of dynamic low-impact shipping corridors in Arctic waters, which means shipping routes are modified in real time in response to ice, weather, and other conditions, are also under discussion and can be supported in a similar manner as vessel traffic management generally.

The management of shipping can also be enhanced in other ways. Greentree identified possible management elements that could be improved, for example, with respect to the permitting of cruise ship activities where duplication and redundancy of permitting procedures are an issue. Doelle *et al.* further suggested exploring the employment of impact assessments in Arctic shipping. The shipping industry is not new to risk assessment, and indeed the business models and regulatory approaches tend to be underlain by risk governance considerations. However, given the recent enactment of the *Impact Assessment Act*[22] and the developing low-impact shipping corridors, it is useful to consider how impact assessment of the corridor system can be undertaken.

6.5   *Resources and Capacity-Building*

An Arctic shipping policy would need to be properly resourced for the long term. It must ensure that the federal departments concerned are truly pooling and using common resources to achieve common policy goals. The needs include massive capital investments for physical infrastructure, such as a system of regional ports, fleet maintenance and renewal, establishing standing

---

19   SC 1996, c 31.

20   SC 2002, c 18.

21   RSC 1985, c W-9.

22   SC 2019, c 28, s 1.

search and rescue and pollution response capacities, and ongoing provision of other services such as salvage and towage. Human resource development will also be needed. The funding may well have to be a mixture of public and private. It would be unwise for Canada to levy fees for transit alone, as this might unnecessarily provoke neighbouring and other maritime States. However, fees may be justified for services that are legitimate safety requirements, such as icebreaking and pilotage to support transit shipping.

While shipping industry and other stakeholders are usually well-resourced, knowledgeable, and connected participants, and able to undertake effective lobbying and participate meaningfully in consultation processes, Indigenous communities do not fare as well. Significant concerns for Indigenous communities are lack of transparent information and frequent lack of capacity to advance concerns about shipping and to participate effectively in consultation processes. Capacity-building for effective participation is called for, and Kikkert *et al.* demonstrated how this could be pursued in the context of search and rescue.

7   Concluding Thought

As we conclude this book, we leave the reader with the thought that the need to review the governance of shipping in Arctic waters in the light of reconciliation, low-impact shipping corridors and the mandated maritime legislative review to facilitate implementation of UNDRIP provides Canada with a testbed for exploring novel approaches for managing the interface between shipping and Indigenous rights. Given the profound environmental change underway in the region and the consequential scientific, economic, and social uncertainties, Canada is well advised to embrace precaution as it rethinks the governance of Arctic shipping.

Index

Agreement on Cooperation on Aeronautical
    and Maritime Search and Rescue   144
Agreement on Cooperation on Marine Oil
    Pollution Preparedness and Response
    in the Arctic   144
air surveillance   142, 151, 152–153, 155, 193
Akademik Ioffe   134, 167, 185, 188, 276*n*55
alien species. *See* invasive species
anthropogenic noise   51, 55–56, 233–234,
    424, 430
Arctic Coast Guard Forum   143–144
Arctic Council   144
    Arctic Best Practices Forum   286
    Arctic Marine Shipping Assessment
        113–114, 214
    Permanent Participants   114, 423, 438
    Protection of the Arctic Marine
        Environment working group
        (PAME)   128, 286
Arctic environment protection *See* marine
    environmental protection
Arctic fisheries   30, 32, 75, 85, 95, 98, 379,
    419, 422, 423–424, 430, 433
Arctic infrastructure. *See* Canada, shipping
    (Arctic); ports and harbours
Arctic Ocean   12, 37–38
    acidification   47–48
    ambient noise   41
    anthropogenic noise   51, 233–234, 430
    chemical pollution   49–50
    circulation   45
    contaminants   31, 46–47
    environmental effects of shipping   12,
        23–24, 28–31, 48–56, 74–75, 95, 115–116,
        229–237, 341, 366–368, 380–381,
        405, 443
    ice cover   2, 12, 28, 37–38, 41–44, 45, 51,
        79–80, 170, 226, 228–229, 235, 323–324,
        352–353, 356–358, 380, 381
    marine ecosystems   39–48
        amplification of warming   42
        climate change effects   41–48, 442
    plastic litter   47
Arctic security (defence)   13, 62–67, 126–129,
    137–143, 152–153, 155–156, 209, 277,
    312–313

Arctic Security Forces Roundtable   149
Arctic Security Working Group   128, 155,
    156
continental security   64–67, 140–141,
    148–150, 154, 155
Marine Security Operation Centres   128,
    151–152, 153
Arctic shipping   12, 98–99, 216–217
    accidents/groundings   132–134, 155, 167,
        183–184, 188, 273, 276*n*55, 281, 444
    alien (invasive) species   31, 38, 52–53,
        54, 229–230, 233, 380, 402
    and climate change   28, 38–39, 51,
        78–80, 226, 229, 235, 323–324, 352–353,
        356–358, 380, 381–382
    emissions control/standards   54–55, 232,
        276, 445
    environmental effects   12, 23–24, 28–31,
        48–56, 74–75, 95, 115–116, 229–237, 341,
        366–368, 380–381, 405, 436, 443
    globalization   91–92, 99
    heavy fuel oil regulation   54–55, 95–96,
        116, 118, 122, 321
    impact assessment processes   375–382,
        389–391, 393, 394–395, 398–406,
        435–437, 454
    maritime safety   13, 74–75, 128–137,
        143–145, 214, 222–223, 237, 240, 260–
        261, 270, 272–275, 280–282, 283–285,
        286, 288–289, 443–444
    occupational health and safety   146–147,
        277–278
    resource extraction support   56, 67–72,
        75, 76, 81–85, 86–87, 89–90,
        163–164, 354–355, 378–379, 389, 394–
        395, 396, 399, 400, 404, 432–433,
        435–436, 437
    traffic/shipping corridors   13, 16,
        22, 57, 77, 78–79, 97, 143, 156, 238,
        240, 268–269, 270, 276–277, 280,
        289, 291, 321, 353–354, 359–374,
        402–403, 417, 444–445, 446, 453,
        454, 455
    traffic volume   78–79, 81–92, 99, 128–129,
        162, 164, 185, 270*n*25, 298, 324–325,
        354–356, 407, 444–445

Arctic shipping (*Cont.*)
    trans-Arctic shipping 381–382
    transshipment hubs 93–95, 99, 443
    See also Canada, shipping (Arctic);
        cruise ships; icebreaking; low-impact
        shipping corridors; Northern Sea
        Route; Northwest Passage; passenger
        vessels; shipping
Arctic Shipping Corporate Pledge 97–98
Arctic soundscape 41
area-based management measures 448,
    453–454
    See also low-impact shipping corridors;
        marine protected areas
areas beyond national jurisdiction 404
Association of Arctic Expedition Cruise
    Operators (AECO) 327, 328n20,
    336n58, 347n96
Athens Convention Relating to the Carriage
    of Passengers and their Luggage by
    Sea 280
atmospheric emissions. *See* shipping emissions
automatic identification system 129, 131,
    147–148, 369
    See also vessel traffic services/information
        systems

Baffin Bay 397–398
    Pikialasorsuaq/Sarvarjuaq (North Water
        Polynya) 118n112, 418, 434
ballast water 50, 52–53, 54, 138n36, 233, 274,
    278, 283, 285, 443
Beaufort Sea 38, 287–288, 389
    Beaufort Region Strategic Environmental
        Assessment 396–397
    Beaufort Regional Environmental
        Assessment 396
Belize 410–411
black carbon. *See* shipping emissions

Canada (Arctic)
    Arctic (northern) policy 3, 13, 102–110,
        156, 268–269, 450
        Arctic and Northern Policy
            Framework 209, 268–269, 442
        Arctic Foreign Policy Statement 268
    marine environmental protection 10–11,
        74–75, 95–97, 272, 218, 231–237,
        259–262, 274–277, 283–285, 311–312,
        316, 445

emissions control 54–55, 276
    North American Emission Control
        Area 54–55
    impact assessment 276–277,
        375–382, 389–391, 393, 394–395,
        398–406, 454
    oil spill response and
        preparedness 75, 269, 380–381,
        405, 454–455
    vessel-source pollution 49–50,
        74–75, 215, 218, 222, 232, 261–262,
        274, 284–285, 445
marine living resources
    management 30, 32, 137, 140, 274,
        379, 417, 428, 430–431, 433, 434,
        436n168, 437
marine tourism 15–16, 28–29, 82, 280,
    324, 329–331, 340–342, 346, 369, 373,
    378, 443
maritime security 13, 62–67, 126–129,
    137–143, 149, 152–153, 155–156, 209, 277,
    312–313
    continental security 64–67, 140–141,
        148–150
    Marine Security Operation
        Centres 128, 151–152, 153
    maritime domain awareness 151–153,
        155, 277, 453–454
maritime zones 5–6, 217, 237–238,
    240–241, 267, 404
    Arctic Archipelago 217–218, 240,
        248n33, 298
    historic title 219–221, 261
    "arctic waters" 5–6, 79n1, 217–219,
        227, 260n96, 261, 274, 275, 283, 285
    continental shelf 276
    exclusive economic zone 218,
        223–225, 261, 263, 264, 276, 299,
        449, 452
    (historic) internal waters 5, 73,
        219–221, 226, 236, 248n33, 263, 264,
        275, 276, 283, 385, 412, 415, 429, 452
    'single approach' 237–241
    straight baselines 248n33
    straits used for international
        navigation 220–221, 225–226, 241,
        262n109, 291
    territorial sea 217–218, 224, 261, 263,
        264, 275, 276, 299, 449, 452
offshore renewable energy 399

Canada (Arctic) (*Cont.*)
    resource (non-living) development   34,
        67–72, 378–379, 442
        minerals   30–31, 56, 442
            Mary River/Baffinland Iron
                Mine   56, 71, 84, 86–87, 163–
                164, 378, 394–395, 404, 432–433,
                435–436, 437
            oil and gas   67–72, 76, 379, 389,
                396–397
    See also Canada, shipping (Arctic);
        Northwest Passage
Canada, Indigenous peoples. *See* Indigenous
    peoples; Inuit
Canada, shipping (Arctic)   2–4, 11–17, 38,
        77, 91–92, 98–99, 216–217, 237–242,
        265–271, 279, 280, 289–292, 298–299,
        352–358, 442–449
    accidents/groundings   132–134, 155, 167,
        183–184, 188, 273, 276*n*55, 281, 444
    community sealift/resupply   2, 12, 13, 14,
        32, 59, 62, 74, 83, 85, 90, 108, 128–129,
        134, 161–162, 165–166, 354–355, 378, 431,
        434, 442
    defence/strategic/sovereignty related
        62–67, 69–70, 73, 74–75, 105, 126–128,
        130*t*7.1, 140–142, 148–150, 152–155–156,
        161, 166–167, 214–217, 220, 236, 238,
        240–241, 242, 263, 270, 283, 290, 447
    globalization   91–92
    historic commercial use   58–62, 352, 442
    icebreaking   14, 69–70, 73–74, 75, 89–90,
        157–170, 172–181, 442, 443
    infrastructure/services   34, 35, 190–191,
        202–210, 269–270, 280–282, 283,
        298–299, 303–304, 325–326, 334,
        347–348, 358, 370, 377–378, 442–444,
        451, 453, 454–455
        passenger vessel permitting   325–328,
            331–350, 454
    marine insurance   281–282, 359–360
    marine terminals   376*n*4, 377, 383, 390,
        435, 436–437
    maritime/navigation safety   13, 74–75,
        128–137, 143–145, 214, 222–223, 237,
        240, 260–261, 270, 272–275, 280–282,
        283–285, 286, 288–289, 443–444
    National Shipbuilding Strategy   14,
        159–160, 170–176, 270

    Arctic and Offshore Patrol Ships
        (AOPS) (*Harry DeWolf*-class
        vessel)   148, 153–154, 160, 177–181
        polar icebreaker construction   159–
            160, 170–176
    Northern Marine Transportation
        Corridors Initiative (NMTC)   268, 453
    occupational health and safety   146–147,
        277–278
    Oceans Protection Plan   120–122, 131, 192,
        269, 270, 342, 417
        Arctic Engagement Hub   121
    pilotage   280, 291, 453
    ports and harbours   147, 270, 274, 276,
        282, 377, 389–390, 403
    public health   278–279
    resource (land-based) development
        support   56, 67–72, 75, 76, 81–84, 86–
            87, 90, 163–164, 354–355, 378, 394–395,
            400, 404, 432–433, 435–436, 437
    resource (offshore) development
        support   70–71, 72, 355, 379, 389, 396,
            399
    search and rescue resources   14, 131–132,
        142, 143, 154, 156, 167, 183–186, 188–196,
        204–210, 289, 358, 434
        Joint Rescue Coordination
            Centres   132, 142, 179, 183–184, 188,
            194–195, 196–197, 198, 201, 202, 207
        scenario case study   189–190, 196–204
    shipping activities and patterns   60,
        63, 65–66, 68–72, 74–75, 77, 89–90,
        162–167, 442, 449
        cruise ships   28–29, 30, 82, 132, 139,
            145, 167, 187–188, 324–325, 369, 378,
            443–444
        traffic volume   78–79, 81–84,
            85–87, 89–90, 99, 128–129, 162, 164,
            185, 270*n*25, 298, 324–325, 354–356
    Shipping Safety Control Zones   237–238,
        245, 260, 283, 284, 285, 291, 311
    transshipment hubs   93–95, 99, 443
    vessel traffic services/reporting   2, 73,
        79*n*1, 138–139, 147, 215, 238, 269–270,
        273, 277, 279, 285, 288, 289, 291, 311, 359,
        371, 454
        MCTS (Canadian Coast
            Guard)   138*n*36, 139*n*37, 277*n*63,
            285, 333*f*14.1

Canada, shipping (Arctic) (*Cont.*)
  surveillance systems 129, 131, 147–148,
   369
  See also Arctic shipping; Canada (Arctic);
   Canada, shipping governance,
   institutional framework; Canada,
   shipping governance, legal framework;
   low-impact shipping corridors;
   Northwest Passage
Canada, shipping governance, institutional
  framework 285–292, 342–346, 448,
  451, 453–454
  Arctic Security Working Group 128, 155, 156
  Canadian Armed Forces 127–128, 137,
   140–142, 148–151, 152, 194–195, 329, 336
   Arctic exercises 128, 148, 154–155, 156,
    193, 207
   GIUK-Norway Gap 150
   Rangers 144, 148, 184, 186, 192–193,
    197–200
   Royal Canadian Navy 66, 128, 141, 148,
    149–150, 171, 178–179
  Canadian Border Services Agency
   127, 138, 152, 329, 330, 333*f*14.1, 336
   Private Vessel Remote Clearance 139
  Canadian Transportation Agency 163,
   333*f*14.1
  Crown-Indigenous Relations and
   Northern Affairs Canada 396, 397
  Department of Fisheries and Oceans
   (DFO) 48, 127, 137, 152, 282, 287–289,
   311, 329, 330, 333*f*14.1
   Canadian Hydrographic Service 127,
    270, 281, 288, 289, 333*f*14.1, 360
  Department of National Defence 31,
   151–152, 289
  Environment and Climate Change
   Canada 289, 329, 333*f*14.1, 336, 451
   Canadian Ice Service 127, 164, 289,
    333*f*14.1
   Canadian Wildlife Service 329–330,
    333*f*14.1
   Minister of the Environment 376,
    382, 384, 385, 386, 389, 390, 392–391,
    393, 394
  Global Affairs Canada 289, 329, 333*f*14.1,
   336
  Immigration, Refugees and Citizenship
   Canada 138, 329, 333*f*14.1

  Impact Assessment Agency of
   Canada 382, 384, 385
  Parks Canada 142, 194, 275, 329, 332*n*36,
   336, 344, 347*n*94
  Public Health Agency of Canada 279,
   329, 333*f*14.1, 336
  Royal Canadian Mounted Police 107,
   108, 127, 137, 138, 152, 194, 289, 329,
   333*f*14.1, 336
  Transport Canada 120–122, 127,
   136–138, 152, 266, 270, 286–287, 292, 311,
   333*f*14.1, 336, 448
   Arctic Ice Regime Shipping
    System 136, 283, 284
   Canadian Marine Advisory
    Council 287, 453
   Marine Security Operation Centres
    (MSOCs) 128, 151–152, 153
   National Aeronautical Surveillance
    Program 140
   passenger vessel management 328,
    329, 331–332, 335–336, 338
   alternative service delivery
    agency 325–326, 346–350
   Guidelines for Passenger Vessels
    Operating in the Canadian
    Arctic 139–140, 328, 331–334,
    335, 344
  Transportation Safety Board 183, 273
  See also Canada, shipping (Arctic);
   Canadian Coast Guard
Canada, shipping governance, legal
  framework 2–7, 8, 10–17, 73, 113,
  116–119, 120–137, 214–216, 237–242,
  265–268, 269–285, 289–296, 299, 304,
  359–360, 379–380, 444–452
  Admiralty court 267
  and Article 234 14–15, 215–216, 219, 220,
   223, 224, 225–226, 236, 237, 238–239,
   240–242, 261–262, 263, 291
  Canadian Constitution 110–111, 426–429
   Charter of Rights and Freedoms 110
  coastal State jurisdiction 14–15, 214–216,
   217–219, 222–223, 224, 232, 236,
   237–242, 245, 260–264, 266, 273, 283,
   292, 445–446, 449
  enforcement 130, 136–140, 145–148, 224,
   238–239, 245, 273, 277, 283–284, 286,
   303, 341–342

Canada, shipping governance, legal
framework (*Cont.*)
flag State jurisdiction   15, 95–96, 138, 147,
215, 222–223, 245, 259, 260–264, 266,
273, 283, 284, 449
heavy fuel oil regulation   54–55, 95–96,
118, 122
Indigenous peoples participation   3,
8–9, 12, 13, 16, 21–24, 31–36, 75–76,
100–102, 114, 116–119, 120–125, 131, 133,
153, 206, 240, 292, 286–287, 292, 300,
301, 303–304, 319–321, 328, 330–331,
337–338, 349, 353–354, 360–374, 379,
408–409, 417–418, 424, 429– 439,
444–451, 453, 455
international legal regime   95–96,
116–119, 215–216, 223, 232, 236, 237,
238–241, 259, 262–263, 274, 276,
277–278, 279–280, 284, 291, 343–344,
449, 452
Polar Code implementation   3, 6–7,
14–15, 96, 97, 135, 138–139, 214–216,
222–223, 245, 260–264, 267, 278,
284–285, 290–291, 311–312, 314,
316–317, 452
and Indigenous peoples   116,
123–124, 445, 451
liability and compensation
civil (environmental damage)
275–276
Ship-source Oil Pollution Fund   276,
443
transportation of goods and
passengers   279–280
workers/seafarers   278
maritime administration   15, 129, 266,
267, 273, 286, 291–292, 448
maritime legislation (federal)   265–268,
293–296, 310–313
Arctic Waters Pollution Prevention Act
(AWPPA)   5, 7, 73, 113, 123–124, 125,
135, 138, 215, 217–219, 222, 237, 238,
260, 265–266, 275, 279, 283–285,
286, 288, 291, 311, 445, 448
*Arctic Shipping Safety and Pollution
Prevention Regulations*
(ASSPPR)   123–124, 137, 222,
237, 245, 259, 260–264, 284–285,
311–312, 381

enforcement powers   137, 147,
273, 284
Shipping Safety Control Zones
Order   237, 283, 285
zero discharge rule   215, 218,
222, 261, 284–285, 380
Canada Labour Code   277–278
Canada Marine Act   270, 282
Canada Shipping Act   266, 267,
275n45, 287–288
Canada Shipping Act, 2001 (CSA
2001)   123, 135, 138, 147, 267, 271,
273, 274, 275, 278, 281, 295–296,
283–285, 286, 288, 311, 448
*Administrative Monetary Penalties
and Notices* (CSA 2001)
Regulations   137
Marine Personnel Regulations
146–147
*Northern Canada Vessel Traffic
Services Zone Regulations*
(NORDREG)   2, 6–7, 73, 139,
147, 215, 237, 238, 277, 279, 282,
285, 312, 359, 443–444, 454
Canada Transportation Act   269–270,
289–290
Canada Wildlife Act   275n45, 454
*Canadian Environmental Assessment
Act, 2012*   386–387, 394n85, 395,
403–404
*Canadian Environmental Protection
Act*   274
Canadian Navigable Waters Act   275
Fisheries Act   140, 274, 430
*Fishing and Recreational Harbours
Act*   282
Impact Assessment Act   16, 276,
375–377, 404–406
and Arctic shipping   375–382,
389–391, 393, 394–395, 398–406,
454
and Indigenous peoples/governing
bodies   384, 386, 387, 388–398,
399, 400–401, 403, 404–406
and other Arctic assessment
regimes   388–398, 403–405
assessment processes   382–388
designated projects   376,
382–385, 399–400

Canada, shipping governance, legal
    framework (*Cont.*)
        federal projects   376, 385–387,
            400–401
        strategic and regional   376–
            377, 387–388, 401–404
        federal lands   376, 385–386, 387,
            400, 406
        Indian Act   386
        *Mackenzie Valley Resource
            Management Act*   391
        Marine Insurance Act   281
        Marine Liability Act   278, 279–280,
            448
        *Marine Transportation Security
            Act*   277, 312–313
        *Maritime Occupational Health and
            Safety Regulations*   277–278
        *Merchant Seamen Compensation
            Act*   278
        Migratory Birds Convention Act   274
        *National Marine Conservation Areas
            Act*   275n45, 454
        *Nunavut Planning and Project
            Assessment Act*   392–395, 398,
            399–400, 431n137, 437
        Oceans Act   5, 267, 287, 288, 454
        Pilotage Act   280
        Quarantine Act   279
        *Security of Canada Information
            Disclosure Act*   152n72
        Species at Risk Act   275
        *United Nations Declaration on the
            Rights of Indigenous Peoples
            Act*   3, 13, 112, 240, 379n13, 401, 412,
            437, 439, 448, 455
        *Wrecked, Abandoned or Hazardous
            Vessels Act*   123, 137, 274, 281
        *Yukon Environmental and Socio-
            economic Assessment Act*
            390–391
    nature of maritime regulation in Arctic
        waters   299, 300–301, 310–313, 314,
            322
        goal-based standards   316–317
        meta-regulation   310–311, 313, 316,
            321, 322
        prescriptive   310–314, 316, 359–360
        tripartism   318–322

    passenger vessels   15–16, 139–140, 273,
        279–280, 281, 324–325
        governance framework   325–326,
            328–331, 342–350
        permit system   325–328, 331–350, 454
    POLARIS   284
    policy development criteria   450–452
    port State measures   138, 147
    private law   272
    Proactive Vessel Management   121–122
    provincial/territorial law   271, 330,
        336–337, 379–380, 386, 400, 401
    seafarers and maritime training   277–278
    ship reporting requirements   2, 73, 139,
        147, 215, 277, 279, 285, 443–444, 454
    'single approach'/uniformity   237–241,
        272–273, 292, 451, 452
    social and environmental
        responsibility   446–449
    sovereignty assertion   73, 74–75, 214–217,
        272, 447
    surveying/charts   133–135, 289, 298–299,
        369
    towage   280–281
    transportation of goods and
        passengers   279–280
    See also Canada, shipping (Arctic)
Canadian Coast Guard (CCG)   66, 121, 127,
        132, 135, 137–138, 142, 143, 152, 153, 270,
        278, 281, 282, 288–289, 329, 333f14.1,
        336, 347n94, 360
    Arctic Corridors and Northern Voices
        project   364–374
    Auxiliary and Inshore Rescue Boat
        program   131–132
    CCG Auxiliary   185–186, 191–192, 201–202,
        204, 207, 208
    icebreaking   14, 122, 159–167, 180–181,
        288, 443
        fleet   73–74, 89–90, 158, 168–170,
            176–181
            Icebreaker Requirements   167
            National Shipbuilding Strategy
                159–160, 170–176
        science missions   169
        search and rescue missions   166, 179,
            183–184, 188
            mass rescue operation tabletop
                exercise   191–196, 200–204

Canadian Coast Guard (CCG) (*Cont.*)
    scenario case study   189–190,
        196–204
  Marine Communications and Traffic
      Services (MCTS)   138*n*36, 139*n*37,
      277*n*63, 285, 333*f*14.1
  northern resupply   165–166
  See also Canada, shipping governance,
      institutional framework
capacity-building   34, 35, 190–191, 202–210,
    270, 303–304, 325–326, 334, 347–348,
    451, 454–455
Cape Town Agreement to Enhance Fishing
    Safety 2012   135
carbon dioxide (CO_2). *See* shipping emissions
central Arctic Ocean   356, 424
China (People's Republic of)   141, 149–150,
    252–254
Civil Air Search and Rescue Association   144,
    186, 193
classification societies   309
climate change
  and Indigenous peoples   1–2, 28, 33,
      48, 51
  and the Arctic   37–39, 41–48, 53–54, 356,
      380, 442
    sea ice coverage   2, 12, 28, 37–38,
        41–44, 45, 51, 78–80, 170, 226,
        228–229, 235, 323–324, 352–353,
        356–358, 380, 381
Clipper Adventurer   133, 134, 183–184, 188,
    276*n*55, 281, 444
coastal communities   6–9, 117, 118, 120, 240,
    287, 443
coastal State jurisdiction   14–15, 138, 147,
    214–216, 217–219, 222–223, 224, 231, 232,
    233, 234, 236, 237–242, 245, 260–264,
    266, 273, 283, 292
  safety measures and protection of the
      environment   215–216, 218, 222, 236,
      238, 239, 240, 241, 260–264
  ship design and construction
      standards   237, 261, 262, 272, 273
  territorial/geographical scope
      412–413
commercial shipping. *See* Arctic shipping
construction, design, equipment and crewing
    (manning) measures. *See* ship design
    and construction

Convention on Environmental Impact
    Assessment in a Transboundary
    Context   404
Convention on International Trade in
    Endangered Species of Wild Fauna
    and Flora (CITES)   253*n*58, 330, 336
COVID-19 pandemic   82, 85, 132, 279,
    300, 404
cruise ships   28–29, 30, 82, 132, 139, 145, 185,
    324–325, 340–342, 346, 347*n*94, 369,
    378, 443–444
  groundings   133, 134, 167, 183–185, 188,
      273*n*36, 276*n*55, 281, 444
  international legal regime   280
  national legal regime   279, 280, 378
    permit systems   325–328, 331–350,
        454
  See also Arctic shipping; passenger
      vessels; tourism
culturally significant marine areas   360–362,
    364–367, 370, 373

Davis Strait   397–398
decision support systems. *See* shipping,
    governance
Denmark   144, 154, 155, 177–178, 404

ecologically and biologically significant
    areas   366–367, 370, 373
emergency prevention, preparedness, and
    response. *See* maritime safety; oil
    spills, preparedness and response
    capacity; search and rescue,
    preparedness and response planning
emission control areas. *See* shipping
    emissions
endangered species   253–254, 275, 336
environmental impact assessment. *See*
    impact assessment, environmental
exclusive economic zone
  international legal regime   223–225,
      246, 247, 249, 250, 251, 254–255, 261,
      263, 415
  national legal regime   218, 223–225, 261,
      263, 264, 276, 299, 449, 452

fishing vessels   81t5.1, 82, 83, 128–129, 140,
    146, 164, 247*n*23, 284, 354–355, 376, 451
  safety standards   135

flag State   15, 244
    case law   243–244, 246–257, 264
    international legal regime   15, 214, 215,
        222–223, 243–246, 248, 250–254,
        256–257, 259–260, 264, 449
        basic rules   245–249
        coastal State duties   250, 252–254
        due diligence obligation   244, 251–
            252, 254, 259–260, 263–264, 449
        duty of due regard   246, 249, 251–253,
            254–256
        enforcement jurisdiction   246–254, 310
        flag of convenience   309–310
        freedom of navigation   246–249
        genuine link   245, 264
        immunity of foreign flagged
            vessels   246–249, 263, 264
        responsibilities/duties   249–257,
            259–260
        rules of reference   244–245, 246–249,
            256–257
    national legal regime   15, 95–96, 138, 147,
        215, 222–223, 244–245, 260–264, 266,
        273, 283, 284, 449
    See also shipping
formal safety assessment   315
France   155
freedom of navigation   218, 220–221,
    246–249, 254, 261, 263

generally accepted international rules and
    standards (GAIRS). See international
    law
governance. See Arctic shipping, governance;
    Canada, shipping governance,
    institutional framework; Canada,
    shipping governance, legal framework;
    shipping, governance

Hague-Visby Rules   279
heavy fuel oil   29, 31, 54–55, 95–96, 116, 118,
    122, 321, 420, 430–431
high seas   246, 247, 249, 254, 263, 404, 424
Hudson Bay   8, 287, 343, 376
hydrocarbons. See offshore oil and gas

icebreakers   14, 69–70, 71, 73–74, 89–90,
    148n63, 149, 157–159, 161, 167, 168–170,
    176–181

National Shipbuilding Strategy (Canada)
    159–160, 170–176
icebreaking   14, 51, 75–76, 89–90, 122,
    160–163, 165, 177–180, 235–236, 239,
    288, 381n25, 442, 443
    See also Arctic shipping; navigation
ice navigation and piloting   136, 156,
    260–261, 280, 283, 284, 291, 453
illegal, unreported and unregulated (IUU)
    fishing   140, 250–253
impact assessment
    activities associated with Arctic
        shipping   375–382, 389–391, 393,
        394–395, 398–406, 435–437
    assessment processes   382–388
        designated projects   382–385,
            399–400
            planning phase   383–384
        federal projects   385–387, 400–401
        regional   376–377, 387, 398
        regional environmental   396–397
        strategic   376, 387–388
        strategic environmental   396–398
    environmental impacts   276–277, 384,
        386–387
    environmental/climate obligations   400,
        406
    gender-based analysis plus   399–400, 406
    regulatory regimes
        international   404
        national   16, 276, 375–377, 382–390,
            393–394, 395, 396, 398–406
        other regimes   388–398
            Nunavut   386, 392–395, 397–398,
                400, 401, 431–432, 435–437
            Mary River/Baffinland Iron
                Mine   56, 71, 84,
                86–87,163–164, 378,
                394–395, 404, 432–433,
                435–436, 437
    sustainability contribution   384, 393,
        394, 399, 400, 402, 405, 406
    See also marine environmental protection
incident data analysis. See search and rescue
Indigenous peoples
    and climate change   1–2, 28, 33, 48, 51
    capacity-building   34, 35, 190–191,
        202–210, 270, 303–304, 325–326,
        334, 347–348, 451, 454–455

Indigenous peoples (*Cont.*)
  governance (federal)   10, 11, 13, 22
    case law   410–411, 412, 427–429, 438
    domestic law   408, 426–438, 413
      constitutional rights   13, 110–112,
        426–429
      duty to consult/
        accommodate   120, 287, 386,
        421–422, 423, 427–429, 438, 439
      impact assessments   379–380,
        384, 431–432
      Indigenous Guardians
        Program   133, 186, 194
      Inuit Nunangat Policy   3, 12,
        119–120, 125, 209, 447
      land claims and self-
        government   76, 110–111, 330,
        352, 368, 386, 387n45, 426–427,
        429–439, 441
  international human rights law   3, 13,
    22, 110–112, 116–117, 125, 379n13, 386,
    401, 408–425, 428n115, 437–438, 439,
    441–442, 446, 447, 448, 455
    free, prior and informed consent   112,
      114, 409, 422, 424–425, 437, 441–442
    right to consultation   409, 421–425,
      437
      duty to consult   421–425
    right to culture/traditional
      activities   409, 411, 418–421,
      437, 447
    right to ownership and possession of
      traditional territories   409, 410,
      413–415, 437–438
      marine spaces   414–415, 417,
        420, 425
    right to self-determination   112, 125,
      409, 410, 415–418, 437, 441, 447
    right to self-government   411, 416, 437
  participation in Arctic regional
    governance   114, 423, 438–439
  participation in Arctic shipping
    governance   3, 8–9, 12, 13, 16, 21–24,
      31–36, 75–76, 100–102, 114, 116–119, 120–
      125, 131, 133, 153, 206, 240, 292, 286–287,
      292, 300, 301, 303–304, 319–321, 328,
      330–331, 337–338, 349, 353–354,
      360–374, 379, 408–409, 417–418, 424,
      429–439, 444–451, 453, 455

marine living resources
  management   30, 32, 140, 423–424,
    430, 434, 438–439
  reconciliation   9–10, 101, 112, 121, 343, 363,
    405, 446, 447, 450–451, 455
  decolonization   101, 124–125, 446
  National Inquiry into Missing and
    Murdered Indigenous Women and
    Girls   101, 108–110
  Royal Commission on Aboriginal
    Peoples   101, 106–107, 108
  Truth and Reconciliation
    Commission   13, 103
  sea ice and land conceptions/use   6–8,
    12, 22–36, 48, 51n66, 75–76, 360–362,
    409, 446
  See also Inuit; traditional knowledge
innocent passage   248, 261, 263
Inter-American Court of Human Rights
  425
internal waters   5, 73, 219–221, 226, 236,
  248n33, 263, 264, 275, 276, 283, 385, 412,
  415, 429, 452
International Convention for the
  Control and Management of Ships'
  Ballast Water and Sediments   52,
  233, 274
International Convention for the
  Prevention of Pollution from Ships
  (MARPOL)   53, 54, 114–115, 223, 274,
  284, 291, 311
  heavy fuel oil   54, 430–431
  shipping emissions   53–54
    North American Emission Control
      Area   54–55
International Convention for the Safety of
  Life at Sea (SOLAS)   52, 54, 57,
  223, 291
  Chapter XIV (Safety Measures for Ships
    Operating in Polar Waters)   114–115,
    312
International Convention on Salvage   274
International Convention on Standards
  of Training, Certification and
  Watchkeeping for Seafarers
  (STCW)   136, 146–147, 278,
  313–314
International Convention on the Control of
  Harmful Anti-fouling Systems   274

International Convention on the Elimination
    of All Forms of Racial Discrimination
    (CERD) 409, 410*n*12, 412, 422
International Court of Justice (ICJ)
    2004 Advisory Opinion 413
    Alleged Violations of Sovereign Rights 251
    Anglo-Norwegian Fisheries 219
International Covenant on Civil and Political
        Rights 409, 410*n*12, 412–413, 416,
        418–419, 420, 422
    Human Rights Committee 413, 416,
        418–419, 420, 421
        Ángela Poma Poma 420–421, 425
        Apirana Mahuika 419
International Covenant on Economic, Social
        and Cultural Rights 409, 410*n*12, 412,
        413*n*39, 416
international human rights law 3, 13, 22,
        111–112, 116–117, 125, 240, 379*n*13, 386,
        401, 409–425, 428*n*115, 437–438, 439,
        441–442, 446, 447, 448, 455
International Labour Organization 277–
        278, 410, 423*n*90
    Convention 169 410–411, 412, 413–414,
        419, 422–423, 425
international law
    customary 111, 112, 253*n*52, 256*n*74,
        410–412, 415, 437
    generally accepted international rules and
        standards (GAIRS) 229, 256, 259–264
    territorial scope 412–413
International Law Association, Committee
        on the Rights of Indigenous
        Peoples 412, 415
International Maritime Organization 186,
        213–214, 286, 310, 343–344
    and Indigenous peoples 116–117, 122,
        292, 319–321, 424, 449
    Inuit Circumpolar Council 12, 21–22,
        32–33, 117, 118, 320–321, 424, 446
    consultative status 319–321
    emissions control 55, 95–96, 232
    energy efficiency 276
    goal-based standards 314–317
    Guidelines for Consultative Status
        319–320, 321
    Guidelines for the Reduction of
        Underwater Noise 55–56, 234, 424
    Guidelines for Voyage Planning 117

    Guidelines on Passenger Ships in Remote
        Areas 117
    heavy fuel oil regulation 55, 321, 420
    International Ship and Port Facility
        Security Code 277, 313
    See also Polar Code
International Regulations for Preventing
        Collisions at Sea (COLREGS) 256–
        257
international straits. *See* straits used for
        international navigation
International Tribunal for the Law of the
        Sea 243
    M/V Norstar 244, 246–247
    M/V 'Saiga' (No 2) 246*n*20
    M/V 'Virginia G' 245*n*11, 247*n*23
    SRFC Advisory Opinion 244, 250–251,
        252*n*51, 253*n*52
Inuit 203, 340–341, 408
    and search and rescue operations 203,
        209–210
        community-based operations 184–
            186, 188–210
    conceptualization/worldview 6–8, 12,
        22–36, 75–76, 117–118, 409, 441
    culturally significant marine areas
        360–362, 364–367
    economic development 28–29, 30–31,
        34–36, 75, 415–418, 423–424, 447
    Hunters and Trappers Organizations 29,
        122, 331, 332, 333*f*14.1
    international participation 12, 21–22,
        32–33, 117, 118, 320–321, 423–424, 446
    Inuit-Crown relationship 100–110, 116,
        117, 118–125, 209, 267, 286–287, 292, 371,
        426–427, 428, 430–431, 439
    decolonization 101, 292
    duty to consult (and
        accommodate) 120, 287, 386,
        421–422, 423, 427–429, 438, 439
    High Arctic relocations 105–108, 110
    Inuit-Crown Partnership
        Committee 119
    Inuit Marine Monitoring Program
        (IMMP) 131, 133, 194
    Inuit Nunangat Policy 3, 13, 119–120,
        125, 209, 447
    residential schools 102–105, 110
    tuberculosis epidemic 108–110

Inuit (*Cont.*)
    Inuit Guardians and Marine
        Monitors   194
    Inuit Impact and Benefit
        Agreement   349–350
    Regional Inuit Organizations   330,
        335, 349
    shipping governance participation   12,
        13, 16, 22–24, 31–33, 34–36, 100–102, 116,
        117–118, 120–125, 133, 206, 292, 319–321,
        330–331, 362–364, 371–374, 408, 424,
        430–431, 439, 446
    See also Indigenous peoples; Nunavut;
        traditional knowledge
Inuit Circumpolar Council (ICC)   12, 21–22,
    32–33, 76, 111, 116, 117–118, 320–321, 424,
    446, 451
    Pikialasorsuaq Commission   118, 418
Inuit Nunaat   7, 22, 117, 124, 441, 445
Inuit Nunangat   1–2, 6–9, 31, 33, 109, 110–111,
    119n117, 185, 441
    Arctic Corridors and Northern Voices
        project   364–374
    culturally significant marine
        areas   360–362, 364–367
    community public safety officer
        208–209
    Inuit Nunangat Policy   3, 13, 119–120, 125,
        209, 447
    marine rescue operations planning and
        training   204–210
Inuit Tapiriit Kanatami   7–8, 75,
    128–129, 451
Inuvialuit Settlement Region   7–8, 110–111,
    333f14.1, 388–391
    Inuvialuit Environmental Impact
        Board   390–391
    Inuvialuit Final Agreement   388–391, 426
    Inuvialuit Regional Corporation   119n117,
        344, 396
invasive species   31, 38, 52–53, 54, 229–230,
    233, 380, 402

knowledge   35, 280, 300, 303–304, 308, 310,
    318–319, 322, 447–448, 455
    and risk management   200–201
    See also traditional knowledge

large offshore management areas   287–288,
    454

liability and compensation
    civil (environmental damage)   272,
        275–276
    transportation of goods and
        passengers   279–280
    worker compensation   278
low-impact shipping corridors   13, 16, 22,
    57, 97, 143, 156, 238, 240, 268–269, 270,
    276–277, 280, 289, 291, 321, 353–354,
    359–374, 402–403, 417, 446, 453, 454
    implementation management
        strategies   372–374, 450
    Inuit participation   360–374, 430–431
    Arctic Corridors and Northern Voices
        project   364–374, 403
    Northern Low-Impact Shipping Corridors
        Initiative (formerly NMTC)   22,
        342–343, 403, 417
    See also Arctic shipping; area-based
        management measures; Canada,
        shipping (Arctic); navigation

marine insurance   281–282, 359
marine mammals   116, 336, 405, 417, 437
    and underwater noise   41, 51, 55–56, 74,
        233–234, 430
    harvesting (Inuit)   107, 118, 370, 372, 417,
        428, 429, 430, 431, 437
    vessel strikes   52, 57n94, 234–235, 436n168
    See also narwhals; polar bears; walrus;
        whales
marine environmental protection   10–11, 12,
    23, 272, 380–381
    regulatory measures   54–55, 95–97, 218,
        231–237, 253–254 , 259–262, 274–277,
        283–285, 309, 311–312, 316, 445
    vessel-source pollution   49–50, 74–75,
        215, 218, 222, 232, 261–262, 274, 284–285
    See also impact assessment; oil spills
marine protected areas   56, 236, 274–275,
    288, 422, 454
    culturally significant marine areas
        360–362, 364–367, 370, 373
    National Marine Conservation
        Areas   194, 275, 276, 344, 349n100
    Tallurutiup Imanga Inuit Impact and
        Benefit Agreement   349–350
    Tuvaijuittuq MPA   56, 236
    See also area-based management
        measures

marine terminals. *See* ports and harbours

Maritime Labour Convention 2006   277–278

maritime occupational health and safety. *See* occupational health and safety

maritime safety   13, 74–75, 129–137, 143–145, 214, 222–223, 237, 240, 260–261, 270, 272–275, 280–282, 283–285, 286, 288–289, 443–444

    See also navigation; ship design and construction

maritime search and rescue activities. *See* search and rescue

maritime security   13, 62–67, 126–129, 137–140, 152–153, 155–156, 277, 312–313

    Marine Security Operation Centres   128, 151–152, 153

monitoring (vessels)   31, 128, 131, 133, 138, 140, 147–148, 166, 193, 194, 252, 369, 371, 380, 417, 418

narwhals   24, 43, 44, 46, 51, 52, 336

    See also marine mammals

navigation   60, 69

    accidents/groundings   74–75, 132–134, 155, 167, 183–184, 188, 273, 276*n*55, 281, 444

    and climate change   2, 13, 38, 78, 80, 229, 356–358

    and Indigenous peoples   16, 408, 417, 426, 428, 431, 432, 434, 439, 444, 446

    and land use plans   434

    legal regimes   2–3, 6, 15, 135, 138, 140, 145, 215–216, 222–223, 228, 229, 231, 235–236, 256–257, 288, 379, 408, 426, 428, 431, 439, 448, 449

        freedom of navigation   218, 220–221, 246–249, 254, 261, 263

    safety   2, 6, 11, 22, 67, 74–75, 97, 103, 127, 131, 133–136, 143, 146–147, 164, 216, 222, 223, 229, 260–261, 275, 368–369, 403, 444, 453

        ice navigators   136, 156, 260–261, 280, 283, 284

    NAVWARNS (Canadian Coast Guard)   135*n*27

    See also icebreaking; low-impact shipping corridors; maritime safety; shipping

nitrogen oxides (NO$_x$). *See* shipping emissions

non-governmental organizations   35, 97–98, 115–116, 118, 286, 292, 306, 317, 319–320, 363–364, 366

North American Aerospace Defense Command   140–141, 148

North American Emission Control Area   54–55

North Atlantic Fisheries Organization   438–439

North Atlantic Treaty Organization   130*t*7.1, 140, 141, 150

North-East Atlantic Fisheries Commission   438–439

Northern Sea Route   13, 38, 52, 80, 81, 83*t*5.2, 84–85, 88–93, 337–340

    transshipment hubs   93–95

    See also Arctic shipping; Russian Federation

Northwest Passage   11, 12, 38, 51, 52, 57, 80, 85–87, 89–90, 92, 128–129, 144, 215, 324, 330, 352–353, 356–357, 444

    historic commercial use   58–62, 352

    legal status   220–221, 225–226, 291

    Polar Sea transit   220–221

    resource (land-based) development support   67–72, 81–84, 86–87, 90

    SS *Manhattan* transit   69–70, 73, 74–75, 214–215, 216–217

    strategic role   62–67

    transshipment hubs   93–94

    See also Arctic shipping; Canada (Arctic); Canada, shipping (Arctic)

Northwest Territories   282, 333*f*14.1, 377

Norway   154, 337–340, 419, 420–421, 438

Nunatsiavut   7–9, 110–111, 119*n*117, 134*n*24, 155, 287, 429*n*121

Nunavik   7–8, 110, 155, 287, 420

Nunavut   7–8, 110–111, 155, 166, 183–184, 282, 333*f*14.1, 340, 341, 343, 377, 392–395

    impact assessment   386, 392–395, 397–398, 400, 401

        Nunavut Impact Review Board   332*n*35, 333*f*14.1, 392–395, 397–398, 405*n*124, 430, 432–433, 435–437

    Kitikmeot SAR Project   190–196, 207–208

    land-use planning regime   398, 431–432, 439

        North Baffin Land Use Plan   432–433

        Nunavut Land Use Plan   344, 398, 432, 433–434

        Nunavut Planning Commission   332*n*35, 333*f*14.1, 334, 335, 398, 430, 432–433

Nunavut (*Cont.*)
   marine living resources
      management   30, 32, 140, 428, 430,
         433, 434, 436n168, 437
   Nunavut Agreement (Land Claims)   110,
      349n100, 392, 394, 397, 398, 408, 426,
      429–432, 439
   Nunavut Emergency Management   184,
      192, 194–195, 198, 207
   Nunavut Marine Council   430–431
   Nunavut Planning and Project Assessment
      Act   392–395, 398, 399–400,
      431n137, 437
   See also Inuit
Nunavut Settlement Area   392, 393, 395, 397,
      428, 429–432, 433, 435
   'marine areas'   429–432
   Outer Land Fast Ice Zone   392, 393,
      429, 431
Nunavut Tunngavik   119n117, 122
   Inuit Marine Monitoring Program   131

occupational health and safety   146–147,
      277–278
   See also seafarers
offshore oil and gas   67, 68, 70–72, 76, 379,
      389, 396–397
oil spills   49–50, 74–75, 380–381
   preparedness and response
      capacity   269, 405, 454–455
   See also marine environmental protection

participatory approach. *See* Indigenous
      peoples, participation in shipping
      governance; Inuit, participation in
      shipping governance
passenger vessels   15–16, 139–140, 273,
      279–280, 281, 324–325, 355
   governance framework   325–326,
      328–331, 342–350
   management framework   328, 329,
      331–332, 335–336, 338
      alternative service delivery
         agency   325–326, 346–350
      Guidelines for Passenger Vessels
         Operating in the Canadian
         Arctic   139–140, 328, 331–334,
         335, 344
      permit system   325–328, 331–350, 454

   See also Arctic shipping; cruise ships;
      tourism
Permanent Court of Arbitration:
   Arctic Sunrise   244, 246, 248, 257
   Coastal State Rights   248n33
   Enrica Lexie   247–249, 254–256
   South China Sea Arbitration   244,
      252–254, 256–257
pilotage   280, 291, 453
pleasure craft. *See* recreational vessels
polar bears   29, 43, 47, 336
   See also marine mammals
Polar Class rating   2, 84, 148, 149, 154, 283,
      356f15.2, 358
Polar Code   2–3, 54, 95, 113, 115–117, 314
   and coastal State jurisdiction   214, 215,
      222–223, 234, 237, 240, 241
   and goal-based standards   316–317
   and Indigenous peoples   114–117, 123–124,
      445, 451
   alien species   233
   domestic implementation   3, 6–7, 14–15,
      96, 97, 135, 138–139, 214–216, 222–223,
      245, 260–264, 267, 278, 284–285,
      290–291, 311–312, 314, 316–317, 452
   flag State jurisdiction/responsibilities   15,
      222–223, 244–245, 259–260
   non-SOLAS vessels   129, 284, 285, 451,
      452
   Polar Operational Limit Assessment Risk
      Indexing System (POLARIS)   284
   Polar Ship Certificate   138, 284
   pollution prevention measures   232, 233,
      234, 237
   safety measures   129, 144–145, 237
      Polar Waters Operations Manual   145,
         234
   seafaring standards and
      certifications   278, 284–285
   See also International Maritime
      Organization
port State control   136, 138, 147
ports and harbours   147, 270, 274, 276, 282,
      377, 389–390, 403
   marine terminals   376n4, 377, 383, 390,
      435, 436–437
   transshipment hubs   93–95, 99, 443
precautionary approach   10, 17, 54, 455
public health   278–279

Qikiqtani Inuit Association 194, 335, 344, 349*n*100, 451

recreational vessels 82, 89, 128–129, 130, 139, 146, 273, 284, 354–355, 443, 451
   See also tourism
risk management 29–30, 136, 137–139, 145, 283
Russian Federation 90–91, 95–99, 127, 141, 149, 150, 215, 248, 259, 337–340
   icebreakers 90, 158, 167, 169–170
   See also Northern Sea Route

salvage operations 274, 281, 444, 455
sea ice 40, 51, 93
   and ambient noise 41
   and anthropogenic noise 234
   and Article 234 226–229, 234, 236
   and climate change 2, 12, 28, 37–38, 41–44, 45, 51, 79–80, 170, 226, 228–229, 235, 323–324, 352–353, 356–358, 380, 381
   and heavy fuel oil 55
   and icebreaking 235–236, 381*n*25
   and Indigenous peoples
      conceptualization and contextualization 23–24, 28, 33, 75–76
      traditional uses and practices 6–8, 23–24, 31, 48, 51*n*66, 360–362, 446
seafarers 135, 136, 139, 145, 146–147, 277–278, 299, 372, 443
   See also occupational health and safety
search and rescue 128, 156, 358, 278, 279, 443–444
   incident analysis 132, 183–186, 200–204
   incident statistics 132, 167
   preparedness and response planning 14, 131–133, 142, 143–145, 154, 184–196, 203–210, 270, 289, 434, 454–455
      Joint Rescue Coordination Centres 132, 142, 179, 183–184, 188, 194–195, 196–197, 198, 201, 202, 207
      mass rescue operations 14, 183–190
         community-based operations 184–186, 188–210
         definition 186, 189
         Kitikmeot SAR Project 190–196
      scenario case study 189–190, 196–204

search and rescue regions 142, 183–184, 194–195
   voyage planning 139–140, 144–145
ship design and construction 71, 72, 75, 76, 160, 161, 176–178, 237, 259, 261, 262, 272, 273, 283, 286, 302, 316
   goal-based standards 314–315, 316–317
   ice-class 2, 84, 148, 149, 154, 283, 356*f*15.2, 358
   See also maritime safety
ship routeing measures 13, 16, 22, 57, 77, 78–79, 97, 143, 156, 235, 237–238, 240, 268–269, 270, 276–277, 280, 289, 291, 321, 353–354, 359–374, 402–403, 417, 446, 453, 454
shipping
   environmental impacts 12, 23–24, 28–31, 48–53, 229–230, 232, 276–277, 341, 436, 443
      atmospheric emissions 50, 55, 95, 232
      heavy fuel oil 29, 31, 54–55, 95–96, 116
      icebreaking 235–236
      introduction of invasive species 31, 38, 52–53, 54, 229–230, 233, 380, 402
      marine mammal strikes 52, 57*n*94, 229, 234–235, 436*n*168
      noise 51, 55–56, 229, 233–234, 368, 424, 430
      oil spills 49–50, 74–75, 116, 380–381, 405
   governance 10–17
      decision support systems 304–305, 317–318, 360–368, 372–373, 438–439, 447–448, 452
      enforcement 130, 136–140, 145–148, 224, 238–239, 245, 273, 277, 283–284, 286, 302–303, 341–342
      information and communications technology 340, 342, 345, 347
      Indigenous peoples participation 3, 8–9, 12, 13, 16, 21–24, 31–36, 75–76, 100–102, 114, 116–119, 120–125, 131, 133, 153, 206, 240, 292, 286–287, 292, 300, 301, 303–304, 319–321, 328, 330–331, 337–338, 349, 353–354, 360–374, 379, 408–409, 417–418, 424, 429–439, 444–451, 453, 455

shipping
  governance (*Cont.*)
    international legal regime   2–3,
      95–96, 52–56, 116–119, 213–216, 223,
      231–237, 238–241, 259, 262–263, 274,
      276, 277–278, 279–280, 284, 291,
      343–344, 449, 452
      Polar Code implementation   3,
        6–7, 14–15, 96, 97, 116, 123–124,
        135, 138–139, 214–216, 222–223,
        245, 260–264, 267, 278, 284–285,
        290–291, 311–312, 314, 316–317,
        445, 451, 452
    land use plans   434
    nature (forms) of regulation   299,
      300–301, 302, 305, 310–322
      deregulation   299–301, 310
      goal-based standards   15, 306,
        314–317
      meta-regulation (modified self-
        regulation)   15, 300, 301,
        305–310, 312–313, 316, 318,
        321, 322
      prescriptive (command and
        control)   300–305, 310, 311, 312,
        314, 316, 359–360
      'regulator capture'   304–305,
        317–318
      self-regulation   300, 301, 305–306,
        307, 308, 313, 452
      tripartism   15, 301, 317–322
      transparency/accountability   304–
        305, 322, 371, 448, 450, 455
    See also Arctic shipping; flag State;
      navigation
shipping emissions   445
  emission control areas   54–55
  emissions
    black carbon   50, 55, 95, 232
    nitrogen oxides (NO_x)   50
    particulate matter (PM)   50
    sulphur oxides (SO_x)   50
  international regulatory regime   232
  national regulatory regime   276
sovereign rights   254–255, 431
sovereignty   11, 31, 61–62, 64, 73, 105, 166–167,
  214, 219–221, 240–241, 283, 447, 452
ss *Manhattan*   69–70, 73, 74–75, 214–215,
  216–217

St. Lawrence Seaway Authority   266, 292,
  348, 453
straits used for international
  navigation   220–221, 225–226, 241,
  262n109, 291
sulphur oxides (SO_x). *See* shipping emissions
Supreme Court of Canada   271, 427–428, 438
sustainable development   10, 22, 29–30, 35–
  36, 268–269, 276, 290, 346, 353–354,
  368, 384, 393, 394, 399, 400, 402, 405,
  406, 424, 448
Sweden   410

territorial sea   73, 217–218, 224–225, 239,
  248–249, 261, 262, 263, 264, 275, 276,
  415, 449, 452
tourism   28–29, 89, 114, 134, 329–331,
  340–342, 346, 369, 373, 378, 443–444
  adventure   197, 280, 324
  See also cruise ships; passenger vessels;
    recreational vessels
traditional knowledge   23–25, 35, 100–101,
  120, 144, 189, 190–191, 192, 200–201, 206,
  207, 300, 301, 303–304, 360, 362–368,
  372–373, 417, 438–439, 446, 447–448,
  452
  See also Indigenous peoples; Inuit;
    knowledge
transit passage   225
transparency/accountability   304–305, 322,
  371, 448, 450, 455
transportation of goods and
  passengers   279–280

underwater noise. *See* Arctic, ambient noise;
  anthropogenic noise; shipping,
  environmental impacts, noise
United Kingdom   149, 176–177
United Nations Charter   409, 413n39
United Nations Convention on the Law of the
  Sea   256
  Article 234   14–15, 215, 291
    and coastal State jurisdiction   215–
      216, 219, 231, 232, 233, 234, 236,
      237–242, 261–263, 264
    and Indigenous peoples 240, 445
    and Polar Code   215, 223, 237, 240
    geographical scope   223–229, 238,
      261–262

United Nations Convention on the Law of the
    Sea (*Cont.*)
    'ice-cover'   227–229
    material scope   231–237, 261–262
    duty of due regard   255, 262
    environmental impact assessment   254
    exclusive economic zone   224, 261
    flag State   214, 245–246, 248, 250–254,
        256–257, 259–260, 264
    marine environmental protection   254,
        259–260, 261–262
    marine living resources   250–252
    pollution control   214, 231–237
    territorial sea   262n112
United Nations Declaration on the Rights of
    Indigenous Peoples (UNDRIP)   22,
    111–112, 116–117, 386, 401, 411–412, 414–
    416, 419–420, 422–423, 425, 428n115,
    437–438, 441–442, 446, 447
    national implementation   3, 13, 112, 240,
        379n13, 401, 412, 437, 439, 448, 455
United Nations Framework Convention
    on Climate Change, Paris
    Agreement   276
United Nations Human Rights
    Council   425
United Nations Sustainable Development
    Goals   10

United States   73, 118–119, 144, 158, 208, 218,
    224–225
    Arctic continental security   64–67,
        140–141, 148–150, 154, 155
    Polar Sea transit   220–221
    ss *Manhattan* voyage   69–70, 73, 74–75,
        214–215, 216–217

vessel traffic services/information
    systems   2, 73, 79n1, 138–139, 147, 215,
    238, 269–270, 273, 277, 279, 285, 288,
    289, 291, 311, 359, 371, 454
    MCTS (Canadian Coast Guard)   138n36,
        139n37, 277n63, 285, 333f14.1
    See also automatic identification system
Vienna Convention on the Law of
    Treaties   223–224, 239–240, 412

walrus   23, 27, 28, 29, 330, 434, 436
    See also marine mammals
whales   41, 46, 49, 52, 57n94, 235, 330, 434
    harvesting (Inuit)   118
    whaling (commercial)   59, 60–62, 105
    See also marine mammals
wrecks   274

yachts. *See* recreational vessels
Yukon   282, 332n37, 390, 401